Business STATISTICS using Excel®

A FIRST COURSE FOR SOUTH AFRICAN STUDENTS

Business STATISTICS using Excel®

A FIRST COURSE FOR SOUTH AFRICAN STUDENTS

Glyn Davis | Branko Pecar | Leonard Santana

OXFORD
UNIVERSITY PRESS

Oxford University Press is a department of the University of Oxford.
It furthers the University's objective of excellence in research, scholarship,
and education by publishing worldwide. Oxford is a registered trade mark of
Oxford University Press in the UK and in certain other countries.

Published in South Africa by
Oxford University Press Southern Africa (Pty) Limited

Vasco Boulevard, Goodwood, N1 City, Cape Town, South Africa, 7460
P O Box 12119, N1 City, Cape Town, South Africa, 7463

Business Statistics using Excel was originally published in English in 2010 by
Oxford University Press, Great Clarendon Street, Oxford, OX2 6DP, United Kingdom
with the ISBN 978 0 19 955689 2. This adapted edition is published by arrangement.
Oxford University Press Southern Africa (Pty) Limited is solely
responsible for this adaptation from the original work.

First published 2014

Business Statistics using Excel: A first course for South African Students

ISBN 978 0 19 904409 2

Second impression 2015

Typeset in Utopia 9.5pt on 12pt
Printed on [insert paper quality e.g. acid-free paper]

Acknowledgements
Publisher: Penny Lane
Project manager: Marguerite Lithgow
Subject specialist copy editor: Connie Skelton
Copy editors: Allison Lamb, Alpa Somaiya
Proof readers: Connie Skelton, Nadine Botha
Designer: Design Studio
Typesetter: Barbara Hirsch
DTP typesetter: Merrick James

Printed and bound by: Mega Digital (Pty) Ltd

All Excel screenshots used with permission from Microsoft
Cover photo: Gallo Images

CONTENTS

PREFACE

Aims of the book

It has long been recognised that the development of modular undergraduate programmes coupled with a dramatic increase in student numbers has led to a reconsideration of teaching practices. This statement is particularly true in the teaching of statistics and in response a more supportive learning process has been developed. A classic approach to teaching statistics, unless one is teaching a class of future professional statisticians, can be difficult and is often met with very little enthusiasm by the majority of students. A more supportive learning process based on method application rather than method derivation is clearly needed. The authors thought that by relying on some commonly available tools, Microsoft Excel in particular, such an approach is possible.

To this effect, a new programme relying on the integration of workbook-based open-learning materials with information-technology tools has been adopted. The current learning and assessment structure may be defined as:

- To help students 'bridge the gap' between school and university
- To enable a student to be confident in handling numerical data
- To enable students to appreciate the role of statistics as a business decision-making tool
- To provide a student with the knowledge to use Excel to solve a range of statistical problems.

This book is aimed at students who require a general introduction to business statistics that would normally form a foundation level business school module. The learning material in this book requires minimal input from a lecturer and can be used as a self-instruction guide.

The growing importance of spreadsheets in business is emphasised throughout the text by the use of the Excel spreadsheet. The use of software in statistics modules is more or less mandatory at both diploma and degree level and the emphasis within the text is on the use of Excel to undertake the required calculations. The practical application of all techniques and methods discussed in this textbook are implemented using Microsoft Excel 2010, and in the case of smaller examples, pen and paper.

How to use the book effectively

The sequence of chapters has been arranged so that there is a progressive accumulation of knowledge. Each chapter guides students step-by-step through the theoretical and spreadsheet skills required. Chapters also contain exercises that give students the chance to check their progress.

Hints on using the book

- Be patient and work slowly a nd methodically, especially in the early stages when progress may be slow.
- Do not omit or 'jump around' between chapters; each chapter builds upon knowledge and skills previously gained. You may also find that the Excel applications that you develop require earlier ones in order to work.
- Try not to compare your progress with others too much. Fastest is not always best!
- Don't try to achieve too much in one session. Time for rest and reflection is important.
- Mistakes are part of learning. Do not worry about them. The more you repeat something, the fewer mistakes you will make.
- Make time to complete the exercises, especially if you are learning on your own. They are your best guide to your progress.
- The visual walkthroughs have been developed to explore using Excel to solve a particular statistical problem. If you are not sure about the Excel solution then use the visual walkthrough as a reminder.

AUTHORS

Glyn Davis

MPhil (Teesside), MSc (CNAA), BSc (Hons) (Leeds), PGCE (Hull), SFHEA

Glyn Davis is a Principal Lecturer at the School of Social Science, Business and Law at Teesside University, Middlesbrough, in the United Kingdom, where he teaches courses in e-business and data analysis. He is currently the subject group leader for Business Management and Marketing, and a Teesside University Teaching Fellow. Glyn has received the grant of Senior Fellow of the Higher Education Academy (Great Britain), in recognition of his learning and teaching leadership within Teesside University. He publishes research related to teaching quantitative methods and business statistics.

Branko Pecar

PhD (Zagreb)

Branko Pecar is Vice President of Educational Services for the Final Controls group of companies in Emerson Process Management. He has held senior positions within Emerson, across the globe, including Europe, North America, the Middle East and Africa. Branko remains a Visiting Fellow at the University of Gloucestershire, in the United Kingdom where, as a Senior Lecturer, he lectured in quantitative methods and information technology-related subjects. Branko publishes research on quantitative methods and related information technology fields.

Leonard Santana

PhD (Statistics) (North-West)

Leonard Santana is a Senior Lecturer in the School of Computer Science, Statistics and Mathematics, at the Potchefstroom campus of North-West University, South Africa, where he teaches courses on Linear Models, Nonparametric Statistics, and Categorical Data Analysis. He has served on the Executive Committee of the South African Statistical Association, and, in 2013, was appointed Managing Editor of the South African Statistical Journal. Leonard publishes research within his areas of expertise, which include computational statistics, nonparametric statistics, and bioinformatics.

HOW TO USE THIS BOOK

Improve the probability of your success!
We understand that as a business student your skill set differs from that of an accounting student. Although statistics may not have the reputation of being the most 'animated' of subjects, it has been brought to life with a bespoke online learning package from OUP, designed with you in mind.

We all know that practice makes perfect, so you cannot go wrong with your very own numerical skills workbook. Featuring over 180 examples and 40 exercises to equip you with the skills you need to study the topics, the textbook goes on to successfully apply your learning in the world of business.

You do not have to know it all immediately; because for every statistical procedure featured, there is a visual walkthrough with author commentary. Take advantage of this unique resource now and make sure that when it matters, you will know your histogram from your box plot.

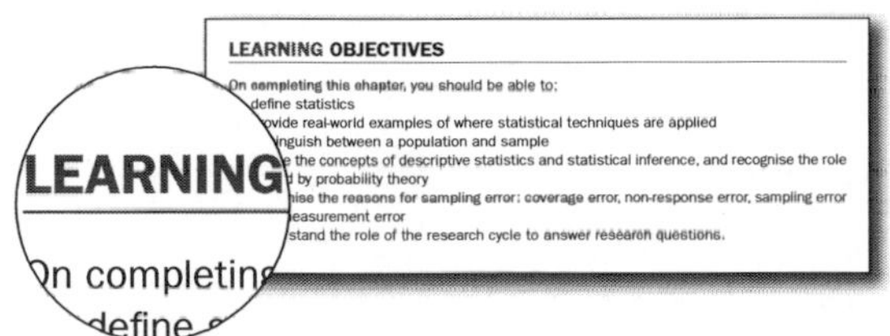

Learning objectives

Each chapter identifies the key learning objectives that you will be able to achieve after completing the unit. They also serve as helpful recaps of the important concepts when revising.

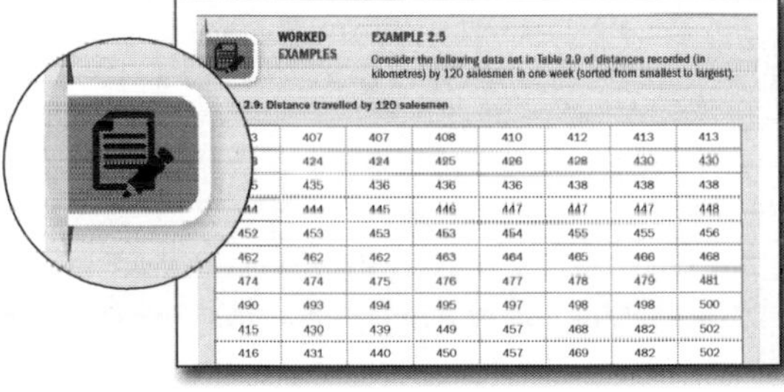

Worked examples

Detailed worked examples run throughout each chapter to show you how theory relates to practice. The authors break concepts down into clear step-by-step phrases, which are often accompanied by a series of Excel screenshots to enable you to assess your progress.

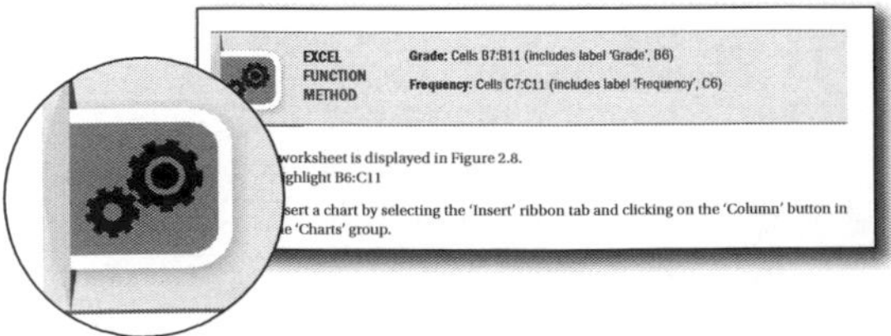

Step-by-step Excel guidance

Excel screenshots are fully integrated throughout the text, and regular boxes showing Excel formula functions and solutions provide you with clear step-by-step guidance on how to solve the statistical problems posed.

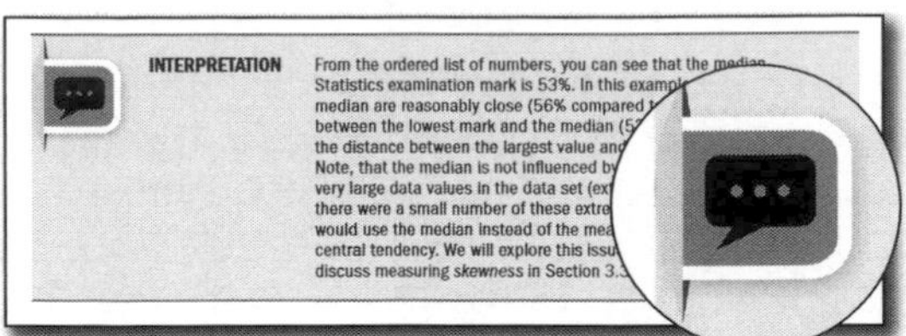

Interpretation boxes

Interpretation boxes appear throughout the chapters, providing you with further explanations to aid your understanding of the concepts being discussed.

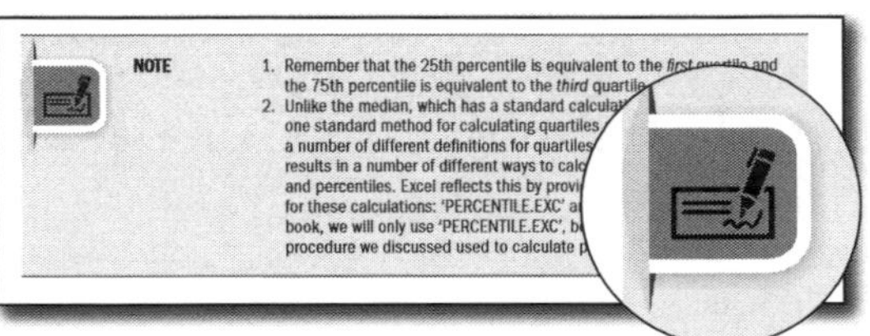

Note boxes

The note boxes, featured throughout each chapter, present additional information such as important points to remember, areas where extra care should be taken, or to point out certain exceptions to the rules.

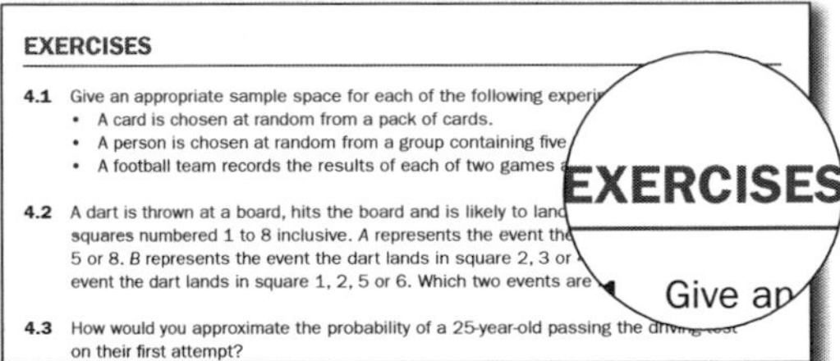

Exercises

You are regularly given the chance to test your knowledge and understanding of the topics covered using exercises provided at the end of each chapter. You can then monitor your progress by checking the answers at the back of the textbook.

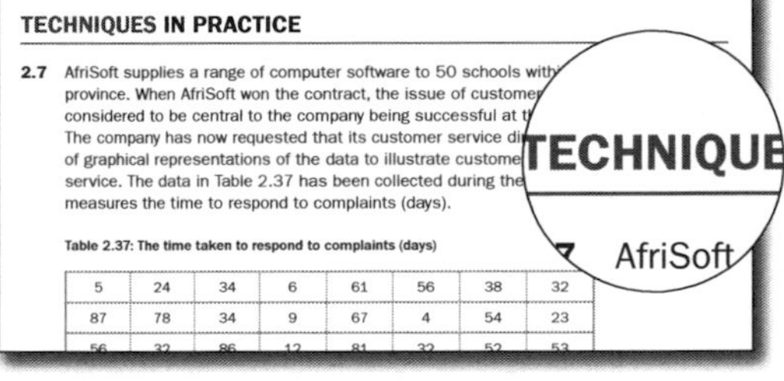

Techniques in practice

Techniques in practice exercises appear at the end of many chapters and reinforce learning by presenting questions to test the knowledge and skills covered in that chapter. You can use these to check your understanding of a topic before moving on to the next chapter.

SUMMARY

In this chapter, we introduced the important statistical concept of sampling and e
that will be useful for constructing estimators in the next chapter. We have sho
Limit Theorem is a very important theorem that allows us to apply a range
We showed how the Central Limit Theorem can eliminate the need to
distribution by examining all possible samples that might be drawn from a p
Limit Theorem allows us to determine the sampling distribution by using
and variance values, or estimates of these, obtained from a sample.
From the Central Limit Theorem, we know that the sampling distribution
by the normal distribution.
Using the sampling distribution of the sample mean, we can answer quest
the probabilities related to the potential values of the sample mean. We will im
probability concepts in a practical way in the next few chapters. These concepts form
for constructing and calculating confidence intervals and hypothesis tests for the population mean.

SUMMARY

In this chapter,

will be

Summary

Each chapter ends with an overview of the techniques covered, an ideal tool for you to check your understanding of the key areas in this topic.

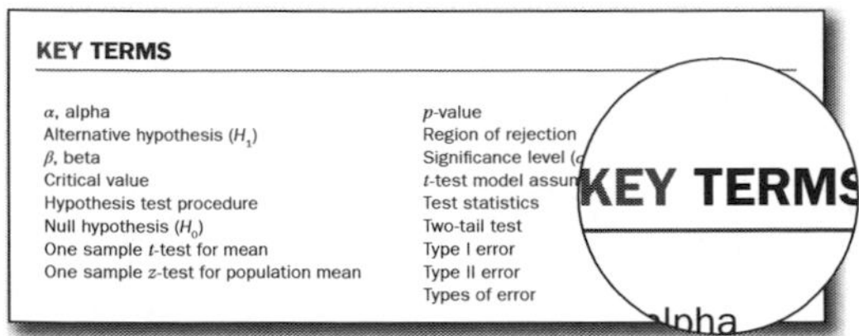

Key terms

Key terms are listed at the end of each chapter as a quick reference tool.

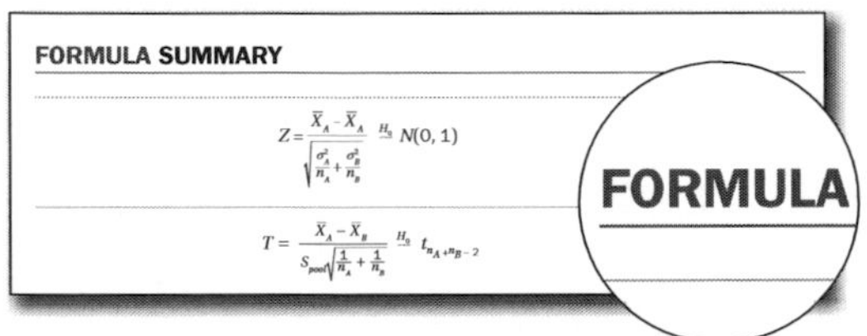

Formula summary

The formula summary gives all the formulae used in a chapter. This provides a quick reference before tackling the exercises at the end of the chapter.

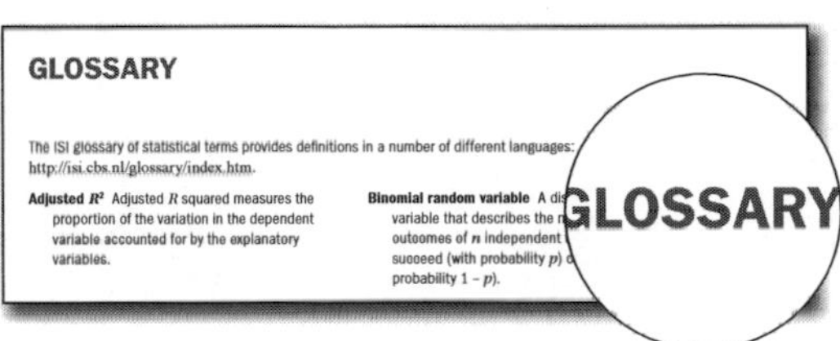

Glossary

The glossary provides a list of common statistical terms that you will come across in your studies along with their definitions.

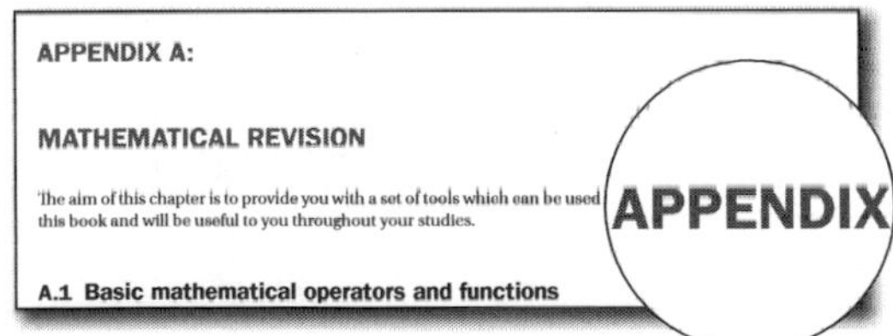

Appendices

Appendix A provides a list of some essential mathematics skills that will be used in a statistics course and how to enter them in Excel. Appendix B provides a very basic beginner's guide to Excel for students who have not used the program before. Appendix C provides normal distribution tables while Appendix D provides the table for the Wilcoxon signed-rank test.

CHAPTER 1

INTRODUCTION TO STATISTICS

CHAPTER CONTENTS

OVERVIEW

This chapter gives you a brief look at some basic definitions and concepts that you will require throughout the textbook. Specifically, we will explore the definition of 'statistics', along with the related concepts of 'descriptive statistics', 'statistical inference' and 'probability theory'. The chapter then introduces the research cycle in order to relate all these concepts to one another and set a framework for the entire text.

LEARNING OBJECTIVES

On completing this chapter, you should be able to:

- define statistics
- provide real-world examples of where statistical techniques are applied
- distinguish between a population and sample
- define the concepts of descriptive statistics and statistical inference, and recognise the role played by probability theory
- recognise the reasons for sampling error: coverage error, non-response error, sampling error and measurement error
- understand the role of the research cycle to answer research questions.

1.1 Introduction

The focus of this book is on the practical application of statistical techniques and, to a lesser degree, the basic theory that underpins these techniques. However, in this book, we keep the theory component relatively simple, as you only need it to help you understand these techniques. The true purpose then, is not to provide you with a thorough understanding of the statistical concepts and theory being presented, but rather a practical understanding of *how* you can apply these concepts to real-world problems and how they can help you in decision-making processes in business (and elsewhere). Wherever possible, we have used South African examples to illustrate the concepts being discussed.

The practical application of all techniques and methods discussed in this text are implemented using Microsoft Excel 2010 and, in the case of smaller examples, pen and paper. In practice, statisticians seldom (if ever) perform numerical calculations using pen and paper, but we have presented them here anyway to ensure that you are aware of the underlying calculations that occur within software packages such as Excel. Once you have mastered the concepts, you will be very glad to know that the pen-and-paper method of calculation is never actually used anywhere outside of a classroom, and that larger data sets can easily be processed using computer software.

It is said that terminology and subject-specific jargon is mostly used by professionals to confuse the uninitiated and to make themselves seem more clever. So, to ensure that you are not too confused during the course of this text, this first introductory chapter focuses on some basic terminology and concepts that will crop up throughout the textbook.

One question that often hounds students is 'What is statistics?' A common misconception is that the field of statistics is *only* concerned with recording and tabulating numerical values (such as those values seen in sports, for example, a cricketer's batting statistics or the ball possession statistics that you see during televised football matches). This view, while not entirely incorrect, is a little myopic, since the field of statistics covers so much more. We can equate the subject of statistics to subjects like zoology, the study of animals, or botany, the study of plants, since we can describe statistics as the *study of **data***. This definition includes all aspects related to data, such as collection, tabulation, analysis, and so on. The following definitions perhaps express the idea more clearly.

Data Data are the values recorded or collected from a specific source on a topic of interest.

Data set A data set is a collection of data.

Statistics The subject of statistics (the study of data) is the collected set of methods related to obtaining, organising, summarising, presenting, analysing, interpreting and drawing conclusions from data.

Ultimately, statistics is concerned with attempting to draw meaning or information from data. Each of the concepts given above in the definition of statistics assists in achieving this goal.

Note that we can also use the word 'statistics' to refer to summarising measures calculated from data. Take care not to confuse the concept of 'the subject of statistics' with statistics calculated from data.

1.1.1 Which fields make use of statistics?

Another question that often gets asked is 'Which fields make use of statistics?' Fortunately, the answer to this is quite easy: 'Every field that collects data!' This means that no matter what seemingly unrelated field of work you imagine, if the work involves creating or collecting data, then statistics will typically be involved in some way. Modern business or research undertakings usually generate vast amounts of data. These data are collected with the expectation that it will be analysed to produce information that we can use to make informed decisions or conclusions. Statistics is then simply the tool we use to extract the necessary information from the data.

Examples of fields that use statistical techniques include:

- medicine
- economics
- agriculture
- market research
- industry.

1.1.2 Populations and samples

Two of the most important concepts in statistics are the notions of '**population**' and '**sample**'. These two concepts are defined below.

Population The complete set of objects (possessing one or more common characteristic, such as height, age, sales, income, and so on) that are considered in a study.

Sample A portion or subset of a population under study derived from sample data.

Population size The number of items in the population or population size, denoted by N.

Sample size The number of items in a sample or sample size, denoted by n.

Here are some examples of populations and samples:

- Population: All men aged between 21 and 27 living in the Western Cape ($N = 465\ 789$).
  Sample: 50 randomly selected men from the Western Cape aged between 21 and 27 ($n = 50$).
- Population: The set of all people in Mpumalanga suffering from tuberculosis ($N \approx 120\ 000$).
  Sample: The 1 500 individuals from Mpumalanga with tuberculosis that are selected to take part in a drug trial ($n = 1\ 500$).
- Population: A study is conducted to determine the mean weight of all adult female African elephants living in the Kruger National Park ($N = 4\ 821$).
  Sample: A small set of Kruger National Park adult female African elephants used in the study ($n = 20$).

We usually collect sample data using survey instruments, but they can also be collected by observation, archival record or other method. What is important to realise is that no matter what method you use to collect the data values, the purpose is to determine how much and how well you can use the data set to generalise the findings from the sample to the population.

An entire set of measurements drawn from a population or sample is often difficult to interpret and work with, and so we usually summarise aspects of the population or sample using **summarising measures**.

Population parameter A summarising measure of a specific aspect of an entire population.

Sample statistic A summarising measure of a specific aspect of a sample.

We discuss examples of these summarising measures in Chapter 3, and include things such as the mean and the standard deviation.

Before drawing a sample from a population, we must first determine the actual unit that must be drawn from the population. To do this, divide the population into parts (called **sampling units**). Sampling units are the basic units drawn from a population and from which individual measurements are made. A sampling unit can be a single item from the population or a group of items that naturally group together and produce a single measurement. These units subdivide the whole population in such a way that the units do not overlap, i.e. every individual item in the population belongs to one, and only one, unit. For example, in sampling the supermarket spending habits of people living in a town, the unit could be an individual, a family or a group of individuals living in a particular neighbourhood.

Developing a total list of sampling units (a **sampling frame**) is often a major practical problem. The sampling frame is a list that contains the population list of sampling units that you would like to measure. For example, a market research firm gains permission to access university administration records to create a sample. If the sampling unit is a single registered student, then the list of registered students can be seen as the *sampling frame* for a survey of the student body at a university. Practical realities can sometimes cause certain sections of a population to be under-represented. In these cases, we have what is known as *sampling frame bias.* For example, in the past, telephone directories were often used as sampling frames, but tended to under-represent the poor (who had fewer or no phones) and the wealthy (who had unlisted numbers).

Sampling unit The basic unit drawn from a population from which a measurement is made. It can be an individual item from the population or a group of items that naturally group together and produce a single measurement.

Sampling frame The list of all sampling units in the population from which a sample is drawn.

The device used to obtain measurement values from a sampling unit is called the **measurement instrument**. Typical examples of measurement instruments used to obtain values from sampling units include:

- a scale used to measure the mass of a newborn baby (measured in kg)
- an IQ questionnaire form used to measure the IQ of a student (measured as a number between 0 and 200)
- a barometer used to measure air pressure (measured in kPa)
- an online survey used to measure a user's preference for an advertised product (measured as a score between 1 and 5).

A study in which an entire population is observed is called a **census**. Most statistical analyses aim to collect knowledge about population parameters derived from the population. However, as we discuss shortly, these parameters cannot always be observed because they require complete knowledge of the entire population, or a census, which is not always easy to obtain.

Measuring instrument Any device capable of obtaining measurement values from a sampling unit.

Census Studies that collect data from the entire population.

Problems with a census

Typically, in studies that involve data collection, it is difficult (or impossible) to observe a complete population, and so it is usually more practical and convenient to work with a sample of that population. Some reasons why a census cannot be obtained stem from practical considerations such as:

- being unable to access every single item in the population, whether this is due to items being too numerous, or just hard to gain access to (for example, collecting information on the length of ants for the entire population of ants in a country)

- prohibitive costs associated with recording values for each item in the population. For example, in conducting a medical study into the health of individuals for which a very expensive medical test needs to be conducted on each individual. The cost of the medical procedure may mean that only a few individuals can be tested because of the budget for the study
- when a population item must be damaged or even destroyed in order to obtain a measurement, and so collecting information for all items in the population might be impractical if it means that all the items in that population will be destroyed (for example, a car tyre manufacturer who wants to determine the average melting temperature of the tyres in stock).

1.1.3 Statistical inference

We can solve the census problems described above by working with a subset of the population rather than the entire population (i.e. a sample). Unfortunately, the information contained in a sample clearly does not contain all of the information within the entire population. However, if you choose the sample using appropriate methods so that it is representative of the population, then you can use **statistical inference** and **probability theory** to make various conclusions about the population from which the sample was obtained.

Statistical inference The generalisation of results from a sample to the population from which the sample was drawn. The uncertainty of the result is typically expressed in terms of probability using *probability theory.*

Probability theory A branch of mathematics that deals with uncertainty and probability.

The goal of statistical inference is to say something meaningful about a population, or a population parameter, based only on the small amount of information provided by the sample.

For example, suppose you are interested in determining the population mean weight of adult female African elephants in the Kruger National Park using only a sample of 20 randomly selected female elephants in the park. You can use the mean weight of the 20 elephants in the sample to estimate the population mean weight. However, this sample value will not be exactly the same as the true (unknown) population mean weight. Probability theory can be employed to attach a level of certainty to the estimate. For example, if the sample mean weight is found to be 4 235 kg, then we might be able to determine, using probability theory, that the true population mean weight lies somewhere between 3 185 kg and 5 285 kg with 95% certainty.

Note that whenever you apply statistical inference, the population that you are going to sample should coincide with the population that you want information about. This population is called the **target population**. However, sometimes for reasons of practicality or convenience, the **actual sampled population** is more restricted than the target population and the two can be substantially different. In cases like this, you need to take care when reporting results from statistical inference, because the generalisation from the sample will always apply to the actual sampled population and not necessarily to the intended target population.

For example, if your target population is the entire population of men aged between 21 and 27 living in the Western Cape, but you only obtained information from men aged between 21 and 27 living in Cape Town, then we could argue that your actual population is the population of men aged between 21 and 27 living in Cape Town, rather than those living in the Western Cape. This sample is not representative of the entire target population, and you should be wary of any inference about the target population made from the sample.

Target population The population that you are interested in studying.

Actual sampled population The population from which items were obtained. This population is possibly more restricted than the target population. When conclusions are made, they must always refer to the population from which the sample was obtained. Ideally, the target population and the population sampled are the same, but this is not always the case.

1.1.4 Types of sample error

In this book, we deal with sampling from populations using probability sampling methods; a prerequisite for the application of most statistical inference. If we base our decisions on a sample rather than the whole population, by definition we are going to make some errors, since the sample does not contain perfect information about the population. The concept of sampling implies that we will also have to deal with a number of errors, including sampling error, coverage error, measurement error and non-response error.

- **Sampling error** is the calculated statistical imprecision due to surveying a random sample instead of the entire population. The margin of error provides an estimate of how much the sample results may differ due to chance when compared to what would have been found if the entire population were considered. This type of error is inherent in all samples.
- **Coverage error** is associated with being unable to contact portions of the population. Telephone surveys usually exclude people who do not have access to a landline telephone in their homes. It also excludes people who are not at home or unavailable for a number of reasons, for example, they are at work, on holiday, or unavailable at the time that the telephone calls are made.
- **Measurement error** is error or bias that occurs when surveys do not focus on what they were intended to measure. This type of error results from flaws in the measuring instrument, for example, the question wording, question order, interviewer error, timing and question response options. This is the most common type of error in the polling industry.
- **Non-response error** results from being unable to interview people who would be eligible to take part in the survey. Many households now have answering machines and caller identification that prevent easy contact, or people may simply not want to respond to calls. Non-response bias is the difference in responses between those people who complete the survey and those who refuse to. While we cannot calculate the error itself, we can calculate response rates in a number of ways.

Sampling error When a sample cannot convey the same amount of information as the entire population. It is inherent in all samples.

Coverage error The inability to access all portions of the population.

Measurement error The error made by the measuring instrument itself, i.e. the instrument's inability to measure the true value of the sampling unit.

Non-response error The error incurred when respondents do not complete forms or reply to surveys.

1.1.5 The research cycle

We now discuss the way in which most research is carried out by defining the so-called *research cycle.*

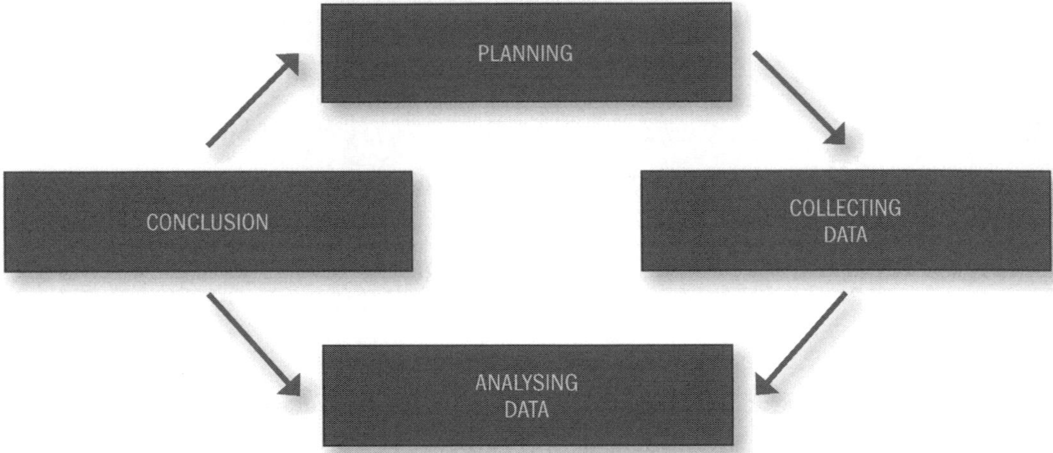

Figure 1.1: The research cycle

We describe the process by which research is conducted as a circular process, in which the final step feeds back into the first step, resulting in a continuous cycle. The four main phases of the research cycle are the *planning* phase, *data collection* phase, *data analysis* phase and *conclusion.* Under each phase, there are multiple factors that need to be considered.

Planning phase

As with any enterprise, planning the research is very important. In terms of research that requires statistical analysis, the most important factor in the planning phase is the *research question.* The research question will typically relate to some unknown population quantity or population parameter. In answering the research question, the researcher can then attempt to determine:

- the target population
- the method of data collection that will produce the most representative sample of the target population
- the appropriate sample size
- the appropriateness of the measurement instrument used to measure aspects of the sample units in the study
- the type of data that will be obtained
- the analyses that will be used to analyse the data.

Data collection phase

The data collection phase involves obtaining data using the method that was agreed on in the planning phase. The collection procedure should produce a representative sample of the target population. We discuss the various methods of drawing samples from a population in Chapter 8.

Once you have obtained the sampling units, you need to obtain their measurements using the measurement instrument defined in the planning phase. Take care to ensure that the measurement instrument is accurate to avoid any instances of measurement error. The measurement data are then captured (in an Excel spreadsheet, for example) and edited so that they can be used in the analysis phase.

Data analysis phase

Data obtained and edited in the collection phase are then analysed in the analysis phase so that the relevant information can be extracted. Broadly speaking, analysing the data entails two basic components: descriptive statistics and statistical inference. Descriptive statistics (discussed in Chapters 2 and 3) are used to summarise sample data with numerical statistics, using tables and/or graphs in order to gain an intuitive perspective on the data and to 'eyeball' any pertinent characteristics that may be present. Statistical inference, with the help of probability theory, attempts to generalise descriptive statistics to the population of interest (target population).

Conclusion phase

Once you have completed the statistical inference, you can now attempt to answer the research question developed in the planning phase. If your study was correctly planned, the data were appropriately obtained and were representative of the target population, and the analysis conducted was appropriate for the problem, then your conclusions should be trustworthy and meaningful for the research question posed.

Finally, the result of the research question invariably leads to new research questions and a new research cycle begins.

SUMMARY

In this chapter, we briefly discussed the various definitions used in statistics and how these concepts relate to the way in which statistics is conducted in practice. The concepts defined in this chapter form the basis for future chapters in which we discuss these aspects in more detail by using numerical examples and exercises.

KEY TERMS

Actual population sampled
Census
Coverage error
Data
Data set
Measurement error
Measuring instrument
Non-response error
Population
Population parameter
Population size, N
Probability theory
Sample
Sample size, n
Sample statistic
Sampling error
Sampling frame
Sampling unit
Statistical inference
Statistics
Target population

CHAPTER 2

FREQUENCY TABLES AND GRAPHICAL REPRESENTATIONS OF DATA

CHAPTER CONTENTS

OVERVIEW

This chapter looks at methods to summarise data using tables and charts.

We will begin by considering the distinction between variables and the data that they generate. The distinction between 'qualitative' and 'quantitative' variables, and 'discrete' and 'continuous' data will also be discussed.

Methods that can be used to represent quantitative data will be discussed using:

- tables (through the use of frequency tables)
- graphs (through the use of histograms and frequency polygons).

Finally, we discuss the representation of qualitative or categorical data in:

- tables (through the use of frequency tables)
- graphs (through the use of bar charts and pie charts).

LEARNING OBJECTIVES

On completing this chapter, you should be able to:

- understand the different types of variables and data that can be used to represent a specific measurement
- present data in table form
- present data in a variety of graphical forms
- construct frequency distributions from raw data
- distinguish between discrete and continuous data
- understand what frequency polygons are
- solve problems that involve frequency tables, histograms, bar charts and frequency polygons using Microsoft Excel.

2.1 Introduction

These days, we often see various types of data or information displayed as tables and graphs. Newspapers, magazines and television all use these methods to convey information in a way that is easy to understand. The purpose of these methods of displaying data is to summarise large sets of raw data so that we can easily see the 'behaviour' of the data.

This chapter and Chapter 3 introduce a variety of techniques that we can use to present data in an easy to understand way.

In this chapter, we look at using tables and graphical methods to represent raw data.

2.2 Different types of variables and data

In this section, we briefly discuss different types of **variables** and distinguish them from different types of data. The variables we discuss each produce a particular type of data, which in turn is associated with its own tables and graphical representations. Therefore, it is important that you can identify the type of variable (and resulting data) being dealt with, so that you then know the correct tables and graphical representations to use.

2.2.1 Types of variables and their measurement scales

The data we collect in a study comes from the subjects in the study. However, the data collected is not about the subject as a whole, but rather about a characteristic of that subject. Typically, subjects have a number of characteristics, but we are usually only interested in one or two of these characteristics. This measured characteristic, or attribute, is called a **variable** and its value will be different for different subjects in the study. For example, if you are involved in a study that measures the height of 1 000 people, then the variable is 'height', as the value of this will be different for each subject. Other possible variables that could have been considered for these subjects include 'age', 'weight' and 'shoe size'.

Variable A measurable characteristic of a subject that can take on any of a specified set of values. Variables are typically denoted using symbols.

We can broadly classify variables as being either *qualitative* or *quantitative* in nature:

- **Qualitative variables** (sometimes called **categorical variables**) are used to measure qualitative, descriptive or categorical characteristics of subjects. Examples of qualitative variables include 'name of cell phone service provider of a cell phone owner' (with categorical values such as 'MTN', 'Cell C' or 'Vodacom') and 'marital status of employee' (with values such as, 'married', 'single', 'divorced' and 'widowed').

Qualitative or categorical variable A variable is qualitative or categorical if the value cannot be described meaningfully using numbers.

- **Quantitative variables** are used to measure quantitative characteristics of subjects, i.e. the size of the characteristics can be measured numerically. Examples of quantitative variables include 'amount of platinum mined per day' (measured in metric tonnes), 'amount of time a customer spends in a supermarket queue' (measured in minutes), and 'annual profit recorded by a fast-food restaurant' (measured in rands).

Quantitative variable A variable that measures a quantitative characteristic, the magnitude of which can be expressed numerically.

We can further sub-divide these two classes of variables into the following scales:

- **Nominal-scaled variable:** We often use numerical values as a way to distinguish between the possible values of these variables, but numerical values for these variables are not always necessary, since we can also use labels. For example, if a group of business students were asked to name their favourite brands of coffee, then the variable would be qualitative since the possible values for 'coffee brand' have no numerical or quantitative interpretation. *Nominal* measurement involves assigning items to groups or categories. No quantitative information is conveyed and no ordering of the items is implied. 'Football club allegiance', 'gender', 'degree type' and 'courses studied' are all examples of nominal scales. Qualitative variables are almost always measured on a nominal scale. Variables measured on a nominal scale are often referred to as qualitative or categorical variables.

Nominal-scaled variable A set of data is said to be nominal if the values can be assigned a label rather than a number.

- **Ordinal-scaled variable:** Measurements with ordinal scales are ordered, in the sense that higher numbers represent higher values. However, the intervals between the numbers are not necessarily equal or have any meaningful interpretation attached to them. For example, on a five-point rating scale measuring student satisfaction, the difference between a rating of 1 ('very poor') and a rating of 2 ('poor') may not represent the same difference as the difference between a rating of 4 ('good') and a rating of 5 ('very good'). The lowest point on the rating scale in the example was arbitrarily chosen to be 1 and this scale does not have a 'true' zero point. The only conclusion you can make is that one value is better (or worse) than another, but it is not possible to state that one value is twice as good (or as bad) as another. Both qualitative and quantitative variables can be measured on an ordinal scale.

Ordinal-scaled variable A set of data is said to be ordinal if the values can be ranked.

- **Interval-scaled variable:** For variables measured on interval measurement scales, we can interpret the *difference* between the measurements from two different subjects. For example, if you were measuring the variable 'student stress' on an interval scale, then the difference between a score of 5 and a score of 6 is the same as the difference between a score of 9 and a score of 10. In other words, one unit on the scale represents the same magnitude of the characteristic being measured across the whole range of the scale. However, interval scales do not have a 'true' zero point, and therefore it is not possible to make statements about *how many times higher* one score is than another. Note that a variable has no 'true' zero point if the potential units that could be used to measure it do not have a *common* zero value. The variable 'temperature' is an example of this, since 0 °C, 0 °F and 0 K do not coincide at the same value, meaning that the zero value depends on the unit being used to measure the variable. For the stress measurement example, it would not be correct to say that a person with a score of 6 was twice as anxious as a person with a score of 3, because the zero point of the score used to measure stress from person to person is arbitrary. Only quantitative variables can be measured on an interval scale.

Interval-scaled variable An interval scale is a scale of measurement where the distance between any two adjacent units of measurement (or 'intervals') is the same, but the zero point is arbitrary.

- **Ratio-scaled variable:** Ratio scales have the properties of both ordinal- and interval-scaled variables (i.e. the order of the values and the interval between the values can be logically interpreted), but they also possess the 'ratio' property. This means that when we divide one measured value by another, the result has a logical interpretation. This is because the scale has a true zero point unlike the interval scale for which the ratio cannot be logically interpreted. For example, the variable 'weight' is measured on a ratio scale because it has a true zero (i.e. the interpretation of zero is the same no matter whether we measure weight in grams, kilograms, pounds, tonnes, and so on) and so we can interpret a measurement of 100 g as being twice as much as 50 g. Only quantitative variables can be measured on an interval scale. Interval and ratio measurements are sometimes also called **continuous variables**.

Continuous variable A set of data is said to be continuous if the values belong to a continuous interval of real values.

Ratio-scaled variable Ratio data are continuous data where both differences and ratios are interpretable and have a natural zero.

Table 2.1 below summarises the different measurement scales with examples.

Table 2.1: A summary of the measurement scales and their characteristics

SCALE	RECOGNISING A MEASUREMENT SCALE	EXAMPLE VARIABLES
Nominal-scaled data	Data values typically represent descriptions or classifications. Data values have arbitrary labels (could be encoded numerically, with alphabet characters or names). The order of the values has no logical interpretation.	The variable 'gender' with possible values 'f' and 'm'. The variable 'country' with possible values encoded as 1 = 'SA', 2 = 'USA', 3 = 'UK' and 4 = 'Australia'. The variable 'car colour' with possible values 'red', 'blue', 'green', 'white' and 'black'.
Ordinal-scaled data	Data values form an ordered list. Typically, a numerical code is used to show the order, but the difference between these values can be arbitrarily large or small. Differences between values are not important and cannot be logically interpreted.	The variable 'customer satisfaction' using the following four-point scale: 1 = not satisfied', 2 = 'slightly satisfied', 3 = 'satisfied' and 4 = 'very satisfied'. The variable 'political alignment' with possible values of 6 = 'far left', 3 = 'left', 0 = 'mid', 4 = 'right' and 8 = 'far right' (only the order is important and not the difference between numerical values). The variable 'university position' with possible values of 1 = 'junior lecturer', 2 = 'lecturer', 3 = 'senior lecturer' and 4 = 'professor'.

SCALE	RECOGNISING A MEASUREMENT SCALE	EXAMPLE VARIABLES
Interval-scaled data	Data values are ordered and have a continuous scale, but have no natural zero. Differences between measured values make sense, but ratios do not.	The variable 'daily temperature', if measured in °C, takes on a continuum of values between –40 °C and +50 °C (for example). Note that we can interpret the temperature difference between 10 °C and 20 °C as a 10 °C increase, but we cannot say that it is twice as hot. In °F, these temperatures are 50 °F and 68 °F, which is not twice the temperature. The variable 'date', measured as the number of days that have passed since 1 January 1960 (note that the choice of the start or zero point is arbitrary).
Ratio-scaled data	Data values are ordered, have a continuous scale and a have natural or true zero. The order of values, differences between values and ratios of values have a logical interpretation.	The variable 'length of fish', if measured in centimetres, takes on a continuum of values between 0 cm and 100 cm (for example) The variable 'weight of a truck's load', if measured in metric tonnes, takes on a continuum of values between 0 tonnes and 15 tonnes (for example).

2.2.2 Types of data

Data obtained from variables can exist in two forms: **discrete data** and **continuous data**. Discrete data occur as integers (or whole numbers), for example, 1, 2, 3, 4, 5, 6, ... Continuous data occur as continuous numbers with any level of accuracy, for example, for the variable 'the amount of diesel used by a fleet of delivery vehicles (litres)' the values could be 1 454.3 ℓ, 1 454.34 ℓ, 1 454.342 ℓ, and so on.

It is important to note that whether a data value is discrete or continuous depends not upon how it is appears when collected, but how it occurs in reality. Therefore, height, distance and age are all examples of continuous data even though we can also represent them as whole numbers when we collect the data (theoretically, they can all be expressed as numbers with multiple decimal places).

Typically, continuous data are generated by quantitative variables and discrete data by qualitative or quantitative variables.

For example, consider the variable 'number of children in a family'. This variable can only have the values of 0, 1, 2, 3, and so on. This variable produces discrete data as the data can only be whole numbers. However, what scale is this variable measured on? If we consider the three qualities that we use to identify the measurement scale of a variable, i.e. 'order', 'interval' and 'ratio', we find that this variable possesses all three. The variable is thus a quantitative, ratio-scaled variable that produces discrete data.

Once again, please note that it is very important that you understand the type of data that you have, since the type of graph or summary statistic you calculate will depend on the type of data.

2.3 Frequency tables

Raw data, which is the unprocessed data we obtain in the data collection phase, is often difficult to interpret because there are usually too many values to easily distinguish any patterns in the data. The solution is to summarise the data by creating tables that report how often certain sections of the data appear in the data set. We do this by drawing up a **frequency table**.

Raw data Unprocessed or ungrouped data that are obtained from variables associated with the units in the study.

Presenting raw data in a table can make even the most comprehensive collection of data more readily understandable. Apart from taking up less room, a table allows us to locate figures more quickly, makes it easy to compare different classes and may reveal patterns that we might otherwise not see.

Tables come in a variety of formats, and range from simple tables that contain frequencies of categories to frequency tables for continuous data that contain groupings of values (or classes). Tables allow us to summarise data sets in a form that allows us to access important information.

2.3.1 What is a frequency table and what does it look like?

Tables differ depending on whether the variable is qualitative (categorical) or quantitative. Further, if the data are from quantitative variables, then there is the further distinction of continuous and discrete data.

The simplest type of frequency table is one that is based on categorical data. It shows the frequency of occurrence of categories (observed from a variable). Microsoft Excel provides a number of ways of constructing these tables using raw data.

Each frequency table contains a number of elements.

- The **classes** or **class intervals** of a frequency table represent the possible data values that the variable can assume. In the case of categorical variables, the classes are simply the unique data values or categories that the variable can assume. In the case of quantitative variables (discrete or continuous), the classes represent intervals of values. These intervals partition the entire observed range of values in such a way that each observation in the data set must fall into *exactly one* of these intervals. We will discuss the construction of these class intervals in the next section. The total number of classes is k.
- The **class midpoint** represents the middle value of a class interval. This component of a frequency table only applies when we use class intervals and not when the classes are simply categories (i.e. the class midpoint only applies when we use quantitative data in a table with class intervals). You will learn more about class midpoints in Chapter 3, when we calculate summarising measures from tables. The class midpoints are denoted by m_j where $j = 1, 2, ..., k$.

- The **frequencies** (or 'the count') represent the number of times that observations fall within a specified class. Each observation must fall into exactly one class. Hence, the sum of these frequencies is equal to the **total sample size,** n. When the frequencies are expressed as a percentage of the total sample size (i.e. $\frac{\text{frequency}}{\text{sample size}} \times 100$), then these are called the **percentage frequencies**. Note that the percentage frequencies will add up to 100%. The class frequencies (or percentage frequencies) are denoted by f_j (or p_j) where $j = 1, 2, ..., k$.
- The total number of observations is denoted by $n = \sum_{j=1}^{k} f_j$

Not all tables exhibit all of these elements, as this depends on the type of variable and data. Table 2.2 shows the general form of a frequency table.

Table 2.2: General form of a frequency table

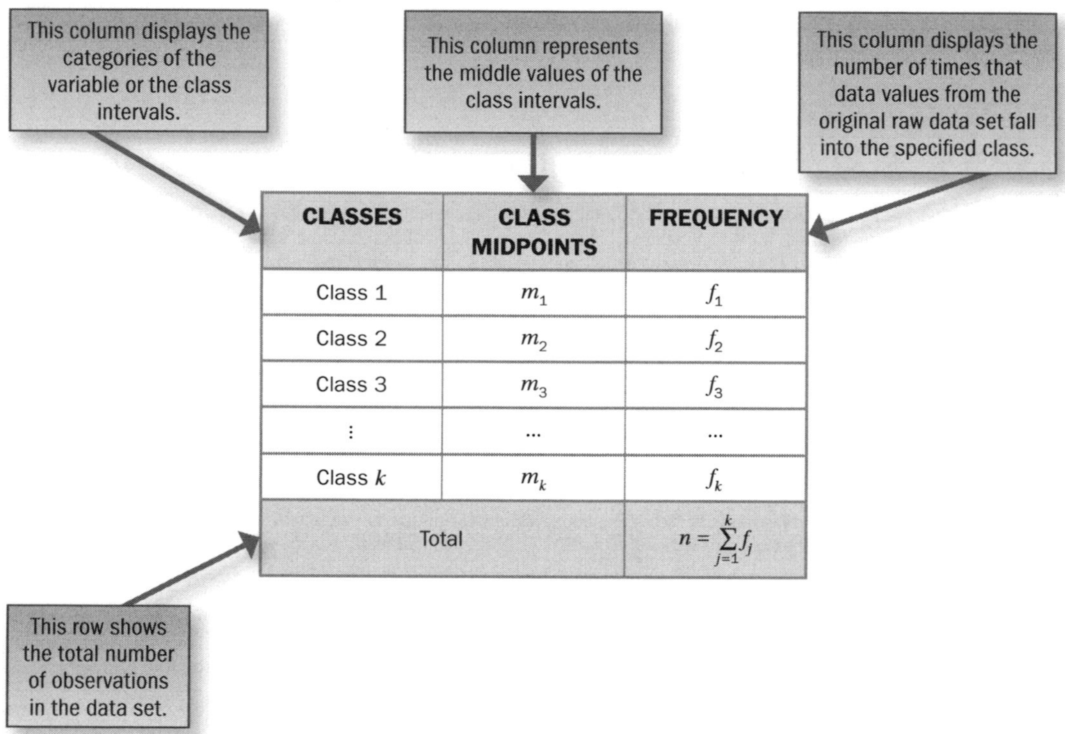

CLASSES	CLASS MIDPOINTS	FREQUENCY
Class 1	m_1	f_1
Class 2	m_2	f_2
Class 3	m_3	f_3
⋮	…	…
Class k	m_k	f_k
Total		$n = \sum_{j=1}^{k} f_j$

WORKED EXAMPLES

EXAMPLE 2.1

Table 2.3 shows an example of a frequency table constructed from categorical data. The data used to construct this table were the homework grades of 30 students. The grades were A, B, C, D or E. In this case, the number of classes is $k = 5$.

Table 2.3: A frequency distribution table for the categorical data 'grade received for homework assignment'

This column displays all the possible data values (categories) for the variable 'grade received for homework assignment'. Note that since the data are categorical, these 'classes' are not intervals, but the categories themselves.

This column displays the number of times each of the grades was obtained by the 30 students. It is clear that C is the most common grade because it occurs most frequently.

CLASS ('GRADE RECEIVED FOR HOMEWORK ASSIGNMENT')	FREQUENCY ('THE NUMBER OF STUDENTS WITH EACH GRADE')
A	3
B	5
C	12
D	7
E	3
Total	30

The total number of observations in the data set is 30.

We can use this frequency table to answer questions such as the following:

- 'How many students received a distinction for the assignment?' and 'What proportion of students received a distinction for the assignment?' We can answer these two questions by simply noting that only 3 of the 30 students received a distinction (i.e. an A grade). The total is thus 3 and the proportion is $\frac{3}{30} = 0.1$.
- 'What is the most common grade?' The grade with the highest frequency (i.e. the grade that appears most often) is, according to the table, the C grade.

WORKED EXAMPLES

EXAMPLE 2.2

Table 2.4 shows an example of a frequency table constructed from continuous data. The data were the total sales registered by 15 till points operated by cashiers working in a large supermarket. In this case, the number of classes is $k = 5$.

Table 2.4: A grouped frequency distribution table for the continuous data 'total sales'

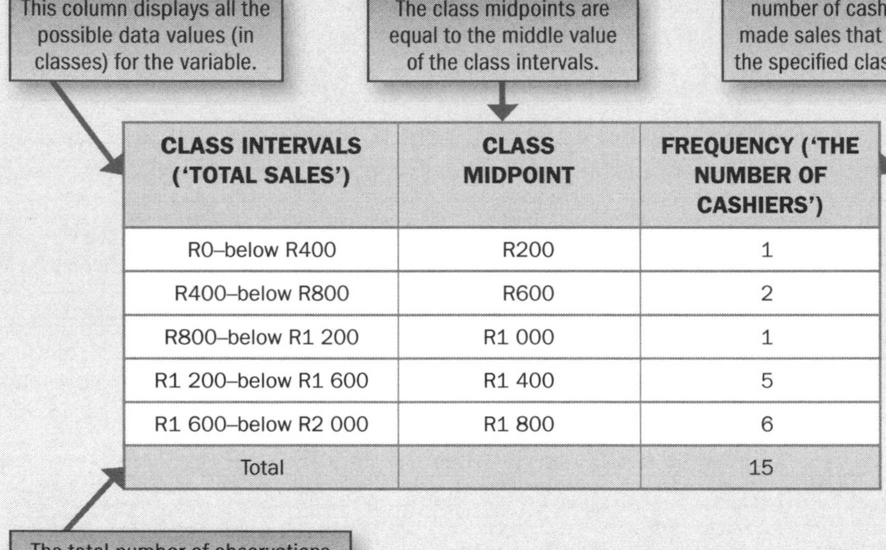

CLASS INTERVALS ('TOTAL SALES')	CLASS MIDPOINT	FREQUENCY ('THE NUMBER OF CASHIERS')
R0–below R400	R200	1
R400–below R800	R600	2
R800–below R1 200	R1 000	1
R1 200–below R1 600	R1 400	5
R1 600–below R2 000	R1 800	6
Total		15

We can use this frequency table to answer questions such as the following:

- 'How many cashiers made R1 200 or more in total sales?' We can find the answer to this question by looking at the sum of frequencies for the last two classes, as these classes represent total sales greater than or equal to R1 200, i.e. 5 + 6 = 11 cashiers.
- 'Are any till points underperforming?' This question is perhaps somewhat subjective, but it is clear from the previous answer that the majority of till points made sales greater than or equal to R1 200, so the four till points that made less than R1 200 could be underperforming. We cannot tell what the reasons for this underperformance are from the table, but the table has at least helped to identify the source of a potential problem.

The above examples are relatively simple, but we can increase the complexity of a frequency table (and also increase the amount of useful information it will provide) by subdividing the table according to some grouping or by simultaneously representing multiple variables in a single table. We briefly discuss these tables, sometimes called **contingency tables** or **cross-tabulation tables**, here, but they are discussed more fully in Chapter 14.

Categories can sometimes be subdivided and tables can be constructed to convey this subdivided information together with the frequency of occurrence within the subcategories.

WORKED EXAMPLES

EXAMPLE 2.3

A newspaper distribution company records the number of monthly sales of *The Star* newspaper from all the places that they deliver to in the North-West province. Table 2.5 shows the categorical frequency table that is obtained for the first six months of the year.

Table 2.5: Half-yearly sales of *The Star* newspaper

MONTH	NUMBER OF SALES (FREQUENCY)
January	20 261
February	21 242
March	23 653
April	23 544
May	20 563
June	19 542
Total	128 805

The sales figures appear to show that the sales of the newspaper increase from March to April, but this increase does not appear to be very significant compared to the other sales amount.

However, the delivery personnel have reported that the stores in certain towns in the province complain that the company delivers too many papers during the school holidays (January and June), and other towns complain that they receive too few papers during the other months.

The company then constructs Table 2.6 to show the sales in each of the towns.

Table 2.6: Half-yearly sales of *The Star* newspaper sub-divided by town

	TOWN				TOTAL
MONTH	POTCHEFSTROOM	KLERKSDORP	MAFIKENG	RUSTENBURG	
January	1 375	5 895	4 645	8 346	20 261
February	3 567	5 845	6 506	5 324	21 242
March	3 847	6 115	6 235	7 456	23 653
April	3 467	6 748	7 084	6 245	23 544
May	2 896	5 254	5 724	6 689	20 563
June	447	6 624	4 021	8 450	19 542
Total	15 599	36 481	34 215	42 510	128 805

In this contingency table, we can see that the sales in Potchefstroom and Mafikeng decline significantly in the school holiday months, but Klerksdorp and Rustenburg see increases in those months.

The newspaper distribution company can use this information to target individual towns to ensure that they receive the correct number of newspapers in the future.

2.3.2 Creating a frequency table for quantitative data (continuous and discrete)

When constructing a frequency table for continuous data, we need to set up class intervals in order to group the values into classes. Naturally, the number of classes will affect the size of each of the class intervals, and vice versa, as each class is one part of the whole observed range.

How easy the table is to read depends on choosing the right number and width of classes; too many classes and the information is not much better than raw data, whereas too few classes drastically reduces the amount of meaningful information that we can glean from the table.

The following is a list of the steps involved in constructing a frequency table from a set of raw *continuous* data.

Step 1: Determine the sample size, n.

Step 2: Determine the difference between the largest observed value in the data set (x_{max}) and the smallest observed value in the data set (x_{min}). The difference $x_{max} - x_{min}$ is the **range** of the data. Note that it is easier to work with 'round' numbers when constructing a frequency table, but the values of x_{max} and x_{min} are often decimals. To overcome this, we often replace x_{min} with the largest 'round' number smaller than x_{min} and we replace x_{max} with the smallest 'round' number larger than x_{max}. We then calculate the (approximate) range from these two new round numbers.

Step 3: Determine the number of classes, k, for the table. It is sometimes difficult to decide how many classes there should be, as there are no 'rules' as such. Usually, we choose the number of classes that conveys an appropriate amount of information. A rule of thumb is Sturges's rule, which states that the number of classes is:

$$k = 1 + \frac{\log(n)}{\log(2)}$$

We then round off the result to the nearest integer value. However, this rule can sometimes force you to use too few classes (especially for sample sizes smaller than 50). In general, we use between 5 and 12 classes to ensure that we have an 'aesthetically pleasing' table.

Step 4: The width of each class, or *class width* (CW), is calculated as:

$$CW = \frac{x_{max} - x_{min}}{k}$$

Again, we prefer to work with round numbers, and so we round off this value. Class widths are easier to handle if they are in multiples of 2, 5 or 10 units.

Step 5: Next, we determine the class limits for each class. We can do this in one of two ways:

- Calculate or choose the number of classes, k (using the guidelines in the steps above). From this value, calculate the appropriate class width, CW. Then, starting with the smallest chosen value, x_{min}, add the value CW to obtain the first class, i.e. the first class will be x_{min} to $(x_{min} + CW)$. Each subsequent class is then created by adding the class width to the upper boundary of the previous class. For example, suppose that for a raw data set we choose $k = 4$, $x_{min} = 10$ and $x_{max} = 34$. Using these values, we find that $CW = 6$. The $k = 4$ classes that we construct will then be [10; 16), [16; 22), [22; 28) and [28; 34). (Note: The square brackets represent 'inclusion' and the round brackets represent 'exclusion', i.e. the class [10; 16) represents all the values starting with and including 10, up to, but excluding, 16.)

- Alternatively, you may decide that the class width must equal a specific value. In this case, you will determine the class width, *CW*, and then reverse the equation for *CW* to get a value for *k*:

$$k = \frac{x_{max} - x_{min}}{CW}$$

Then, carry on with the procedure as above, i.e. start with the smallest chosen value, x_{min}, add the value *CW* to obtain the first class, and so on, so that each subsequent class is created by adding the class width to the upper boundary of the previous class. For example, suppose we choose $CW = 25$, $x_{min} = 150$ and $x_{max} = 275$. The number of classes would then be $k = 5$ and the classes would be [150; 175), [175; 200), [200; 225), [225; 250) and [250; 275).

NOTE

A NOTE ON THE EXCEL IMPLEMENTATION AND THE [AND) BRACKETS

The class limits calculated in the above discussion are the extreme bounds of a class and, in a frequency distribution, are called the **stated** limits. However, for practical situations it is usually very difficult to define these limits so precisely in Excel and we have to use appropriate approximations for these limits instead.

For example, suppose that we want to create a frequency table for the following data:

150 175 195 215 271 272

Using a class width of 25, we might get [200; 225) as one of the class intervals for the table.

The expression [200; 225) represents the values starting at 200 (i.e. the square bracket indicates that the value 200 is *included* in the interval) and ending at the value just below 225 (the round bracket indicates that the value 225 is *excluded* from the interval). This means that the interval contains all values from 200 up to, but not including, 225.

However, in Excel, we replace the lower and upper limits of the interval with a slightly smaller value, for example, 199.9 for the lower limit (to ensure that 200 is *included*) and 224.9 for the upper limit (to ensure that 225 is *excluded*). Therefore, in Excel, the interval would be 'between 199.9 and 224.9'. These will be called the **practical** limits.

Step 6: The class midpoints for each class interval are equal to the average of the lower and upper stated class limits, i.e. the class midpoint for the jth class is:

$$m_j = \frac{UCB_j + LCB_j}{2}$$

UCB_i and LCB_j are the upper class and lower class bounds of the jth class.

Step 7: Finally, using the practical limits, we can determine the frequencies for each class by tallying the observations from the raw data set that fall within the class limits.

In the following examples, there are relatively few cases, but we have used them to illustrate how a frequency table can be constructed for continuous data.

WORKED EXAMPLES

EXAMPLE 2.4

Consider the following data set in Table 2.7 of the mass of 20 teenagers (sorted from smallest to largest).

Table 2.7: The mass of 20 teenagers measured in kilograms

41.49	48.22	61.63	65.03	79.99
81.71	81.75	83.52	87.59	89.77
93.29	94.10	104.67	105.60	108.36
117.12	119.79	128.50	132.82	139.96

Using the seven steps given above, we can construct the frequency table.

Step 1: The sample size is $n = 20$.

Step 2: The smallest observed value is 41.49, but we will select $x_{\text{min}} = 40$. The largest observed value is 139.96, but we will select $x_{\text{max}} = 140$. The range is then $140 - 40 = 100$.

Step 3: Using the rule of Sturges, the number of classes that will be used is:

$$k = 1 + \frac{\log(20)}{\log(2)} \approx 5$$

Step 4: The class width is calculated as $CW = \frac{\text{range}}{k} = \frac{100}{5} = 20$.

Step 5: The classes for the table are then [40; 60), [60; 80), [80; 100), [100; 120) and [120; 140).

Step 6: The class midpoint are the average of the lower and upper class limits, for example, $\frac{(40 + 60)}{2} = 50$. The midpoints are then 50, 70, 90, 110, and 130.

Step 7: The frequencies are then tallied for each class and given in Table 2.8.

Table 2.8: Mass of teenagers

MASS OF TEENAGERS	CLASS MIDPOINT	TALLY	FREQUENCY
[40; 60)	50	||	2
[60; 80)	70	|||	3
[80; 100)	90	~~||||~~ ||	7
[100; 120)	110	~~||||~~	5
[120; 140)	130	|||	3
Total			$\sum_{j=1}^{5} f_j = 20$

WORKED EXAMPLES

EXAMPLE 2.5

Consider the following data set in Table 2.9 of distances recorded (in kilometres) by 120 salesmen in one week (sorted from smallest to largest).

Table 2.9: Distance travelled by 120 salesmen

403	407	407	408	410	412	413	413
423	424	424	425	426	428	430	430
435	435	436	436	436	438	438	438
444	444	445	446	447	447	447	448
452	453	453	453	454	455	455	456
462	462	462	463	464	465	466	468
474	474	475	476	477	478	479	481
490	493	494	495	497	498	498	500
415	430	439	449	457	468	482	502
416	431	440	450	457	469	482	502
418	432	440	450	458	470	483	505
419	432	441	451	459	471	485	508
420	433	442	451	459	471	486	509
421	433	442	451	460	472	488	511
421	434	443	452	460	473	489	515

Construct a table with class widths equal to 20.

These data convey little in terms of information, so using the steps listed above, we get the following.

Step 1: The sample size is $n = 120$.

Step 2: The smallest observed value is 403, but we will select $x_{min} = 400$. The largest observed value is 515, but we will select $x_{max} = 520$. The range is then $520 - 400 = 120$.

Step 3: The instruction states that the class width must be 20.
The number of classes is $k = \frac{(x_{max} - x_{min})}{CW} = \frac{120}{20} = 6$

Step 4: The class width is given as 20.

Step 5: The classes for the table are then [400; 420), [420; 440), [440; 460), [460; 480), [480; 500) and [500; 520). For practical purposes, these limits could be stated in Excel as 'from 399.5 to 419.5', 'from 419.5 to 439.5', 'from 439.5 to 459.5', 'from 459.5 to 479.5', 'from 479.5 to 499.5' and 'from 499.5 to 519.5'.

Step 6: The class midpoints are the average of the upper and lower class interval limits, for example, $\frac{(400 + 420)}{2} = 410$. The midpoints are thus 410, 430, 450, 470, 490 and 510.

Step 7: The frequencies are then tallied using the limits for each class and are given in the Table 2.10

Table 2.10: Grouped frequency table for Example 2.5

DISTANCE TRAVELLED	CLASS MIDPOINTS	TALLY	FREQUENCY (F)
[400; 420)	410	~~||||~~ ~~||||~~ ||	12
[420; 440)	430	~~||||~~ ~~||||~~ ~~||||~~ ~~||||~~ ~~||||~~ ||	27
[440; 460)	450	~~||||~~ ~~||||~~ ~~||||~~ ~~||||~~ ~~||||~~ ~~||||~~ ||||	34
[460; 480)	470	~~||||~~ ~~||||~~ ~~||||~~ ~~||||~~ ||||	24
[480; 500)	490	~~||||~~ ~~||||~~ ~~||||~~	15
[500; 520)	510	~~||||~~ |||	8
Total			$\sum_{j=1}^{6} f_j = 120$

We can convert this frequency table into a **percentage frequency table** by dividing the frequency values by the sample size $n = 120$ and then multiplying by 100. Table 2.11 is the resulting table.

Table 2.11: Percentage frequency table for Example 2.5

DISTANCE TRAVELLED	CLASS MIDPOINTS	PERCENTAGE FREQUENCY (p)
[400; 420)	410	10.00%
[420; 440)	430	22.50%
[440; 460)	450	28.33%
[460; 480)	470	20.00%
[480; 500)	490	12.50%
[500; 520)	510	6.67%
Total		$\sum_{j=1}^{6} p_j = 100\%$

2.3.3 Creating a frequency table using Excel

We obtain the Excel spreadsheet solution for Example 2.5 using the following steps.

Step 1: Input data into cells A5:H19.

	A	B	C	D	E	F	G	H	I
1	Histogram								
2									
3	Distances recorded by 120 salesmen								
4									
5	403	407	407	408	410	412	413	413	
6	423	424	424	425	426	428	430	430	
7	435	435	436	436	436	438	438	438	
8	444	444	445	446	447	447	447	448	
9	452	453	453	453	454	455	455	456	
10	462	462	462	463	464	465	466	468	
11	474	474	475	476	477	478	479	481	
12	490	493	494	495	497	498	498	500	
13	415	430	439	449	457	468	482	502	
14	416	431	440	450	457	469	482	502	
15	418	432	440	450	458	470	483	505	
16	419	432	441	451	459	471	485	508	
17	420	433	442	451	459	471	486	509	
18	421	433	442	451	460	472	488	511	
19	421	434	443	452	460	473	489	515	

Figure 2.1: Excel spreadsheet displaying the data from Example 2.5

Step 2: Use Analysis ToolPak in Excel. We can construct frequency tables from raw data in Excel by using a special macro called Analysis ToolPak (see Appendix B.3.11 for instructions on how to install the Analysis ToolPak). However, before we can use this add-in, we have to input the lower and upper class bounds into Excel. Excel calls this the bin range. In this example, we will create the bin range by using upper and lower limits that, in a practical sense, are identical to the stated limits. The bin values are the practical lower and upper limits. Table 2.12 shows the bin range calculated from these group values.

Table 2.12: Class and bin range

DISTANCE TRAVELLED	PRACTICAL LIMITS: *LCB – UCB*	CLASS WIDTH	BIN RANGE
			399.5
[400; 420)	399.5–419.5	20	419.5
[420; 440)	419.5–439.5	20	439.5
[440; 460)	439.5–459.5	20	459.5
[460; 480)	459.5–479.5	20	479.5
[480; 500)	479.5–499.5	20	499.5
[500; 520)	499.5–519.5	20	519.5

You can see that the class widths are all equal and the corresponding bin range is 399.5, 419.5, …, 519.5. We can now use Excel to calculate the grouped frequency distribution.

Bin range: Cells C24:C30 (with the label in cell C23).

	A	B	C	D	E	F	G	H
1								
2	**Histogram**							
3								
4	**Distances recorded by 120 salesmen**							
5								
6	403	407	407	408	410	412	413	413
7	423	424	424	425	426	428	430	430
8	435	435	436	436	436	438	438	438
9	444	444	445	446	447	447	447	448
10	452	453	453	453	454	455	455	456
11	462	462	462	463	464	465	466	468
12	474	474	475	476	477	478	479	481
13	490	493	494	495	497	498	498	500
14	415	430	439	449	457	468	482	502
15	416	431	440	450	457	469	482	502
16	418	432	440	450	458	470	483	505
17	419	432	441	451	459	471	485	508
18	420	433	442	451	459	471	486	509
19	421	433	442	451	460	472	488	511
20	421	434	443	452	460	473	489	515
21								
22								
23			**Bin Range**					
24			399.5					
25			419.5					
26			439.5					
27			459.5					
28			479.5					
29			499.5					
30			519.5					
31								

Figure 2.2: Excel spreadsheet displaying the data and bin range for Example 2.5

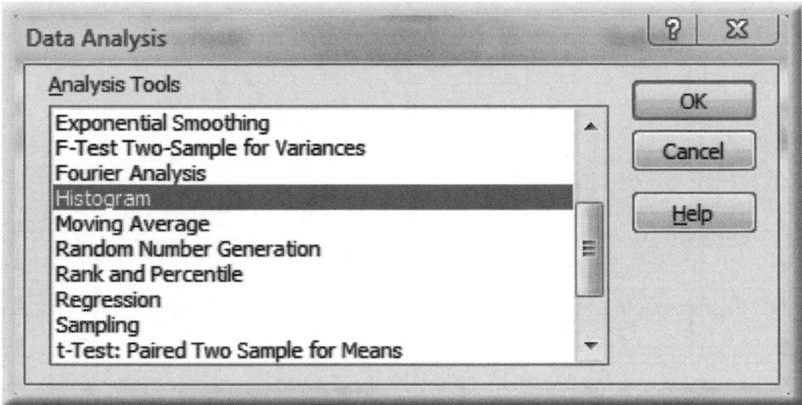

Figure 2.3: The 'Data analysis' add-in tool window

Now create the histogram:

- Select the 'Data' ribbon tab.
- Click on the 'Data Analysis' button in the 'Analysis' group.
- Click on 'Histogram' (see Figure 2.3).
- Click OK.

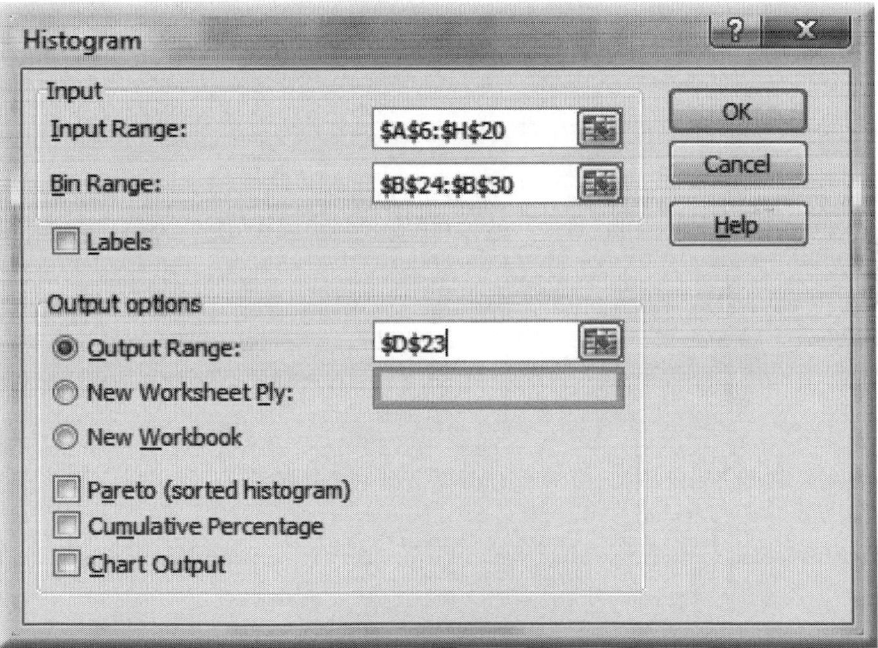

Figure 2.4: The histogram window of the data analysis add-in

In the 'Histogram' window that appears (see Figure 2.4), do the following:

- Input the data range: Cells A6:H20
- Input the bin range: Cells B24:B30
- Choose the location of the output range: Cell D23
- Click OK

Excel will now print out the grouped frequency table (bin range and frequency of occurrence) as presented in cells D23–E31.

	A	B	C	D	E	F	G	H
1								
2	**Histogram**							
3								
4	**Distances travelled by 120 salesmen**							
5								
6	403	407	407	408	410	412	413	413
7	423	424	424	425	426	428	430	430
8	435	435	436	436	436	438	438	438
9	444	444	445	446	447	447	447	448
10	452	453	453	453	454	455	455	456
11	462	462	462	463	464	465	466	468
12	474	474	475	476	477	478	479	481
13	490	493	494	495	497	498	498	500
14	415	430	439	449	457	468	482	502
15	416	431	440	450	459	469	482	502
16	418	432	440	450	458	470	483	505
17	419	432	441	451	459	471	485	508
18	420	433	442	451	459	471	486	509
19	421	433	442	451	460	472	488	511
20	421	434	443	452	460	473	489	515
21								
22								
23		**Bin Range**		Bin	Frequency			
24		399.5		399.5	0			
25		419.5		419.5	12			
26		439.5		439.5	27			
27		459.5		459.5	34			
28		479.5		479.5	24			
29		499.5		499.5	15			
30		519.5		519.5	8			
31				More	0			

Figure 2.5: Excel spreadsheet displaying the generated frequency table for Example 2.5

Table 2.13 shows the resulting frequency table.

Table 2.13: Bin and frequency values.

BIN RANGE	FREQUENCY
399.5	0
419.5	12
439.5	27
459.5	34
479.5	24
499.5	15
519.5	8
More	0

We can now create the frequency table from this table.

Table 2.14: Frequency table

BIN RANGE	FREQUENCY	DISTANCE TRAVELLED
419.5	12	[400; 420)
439.5	27	[420; 440)
459.5	34	[440; 460)
479.5	24	[460; 480)
499.5	15	[480; 500)
519.5	8	[500; 520)

2.3.4 Creating a frequency distribution for discrete or categorical data

When data are categorical in nature, or quantitative with very few levels, we can create a table that uses all the unique values of the variable as the classes. These tables are called *frequency distributions* of the data.

We construct these frequency tables from a data set by following these basic steps.

Step 1: Determine the number of unique values for the variable. The number of unique values is k.

Step 2: Sort the unique values and place them in the first column of the frequency distribution table.

Step 3: Create the frequency column by counting the number of times each of the unique values in the first column occur in the raw data set.

Example 2.6 illustrates the construction of a frequency distribution for a data set of discrete data.

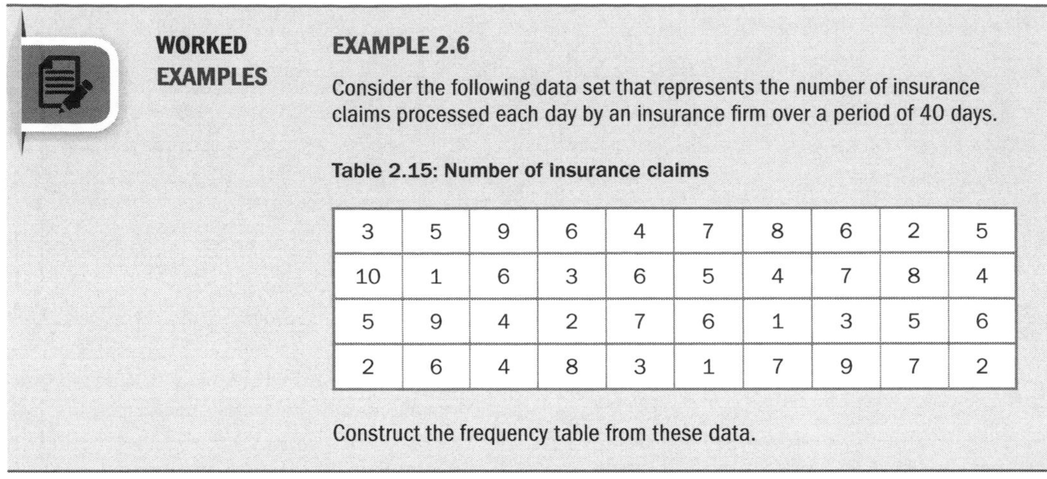

WORKED EXAMPLES

EXAMPLE 2.6

Consider the following data set that represents the number of insurance claims processed each day by an insurance firm over a period of 40 days.

Table 2.15: Number of insurance claims

3	5	9	6	4	7	8	6	2	5
10	1	6	3	6	5	4	7	8	4
5	9	4	2	7	6	1	3	5	6
2	6	4	8	3	1	7	9	7	2

Construct the frequency table from these data.

Using the three steps described above, we obtain the frequency table in Table 2.16.

Table 2.16: Frequency table of number of insurance claims

<table>
<tr><th>SCORE</th><th>TALLY</th><th>FREQUENCY (f)</th></tr>
<tr><td>1</td><td>|||</td><td>3</td></tr>
<tr><td>2</td><td>||||</td><td>4</td></tr>
<tr><td>3</td><td>||||</td><td>4</td></tr>
<tr><td>4</td><td>𝍸</td><td>5</td></tr>
<tr><td>5</td><td>𝍸</td><td>5</td></tr>
<tr><td>6</td><td>𝍸 ||</td><td>7</td></tr>
<tr><td>7</td><td>𝍸</td><td>5</td></tr>
<tr><td>8</td><td>|||</td><td>3</td></tr>
<tr><td>9</td><td>|||</td><td>3</td></tr>
<tr><td>10</td><td>|</td><td>1</td></tr>
<tr><td>Total</td><td></td><td>$\sum_{j=1}^{10} f_j = 40$</td></tr>
</table>

We can create frequency distributions in Excel using the same procedure that we used above to create the frequency tables in the previous section. The bin range will simply be equal to the unique values of the data sets.

Table 2.16 shows the frequency distribution constructed from the data. We tally the items in the same way as before, except that now there are no intervals and the unique data values are simply counted and tabulated.

We can use the frequency distribution to show on how many days the company only processed one claim, on how many days it processed only two claims, and so on. A useful tip for constructing these tables is by creating a *tally chart*. Write down the range of values from the lowest (1) to the highest (10) and then go through the data set recording each score in the table with a tally mark. It is useful to cross out figures in the data set as you go through them to prevent double counting.

2.3.5 Principles of table construction

To summarise the above information, the following is a list of good principles to follow when constructing tables:

- Aim for simplicity.
- Include a comprehensive and explanatory title.
- State the source of the original data.
- Clearly state the units.
- The headings of the columns and rows should be unambiguous.
- Avoid double counting.
- Show totals where appropriate.
- Compute and show percentages and ratios where appropriate.
- Use your imagination and common sense.

2.4 Cumulative frequency tables

A **cumulative frequency table** is similar to a standard frequency table, except that the class intervals do not have bounds. For example, the classes in a frequency table typically have the form [50; 70), meaning that the class covers the values between 50 (inclusive) and 70 (exclusive). The corresponding cumulative frequency table only uses the upper bound of each class. In other words, the classes in a cumulative frequency table are characterised by upper bounds, for example, <70 (this cumulative frequency class upper bound means that it covers all values that are less than 70). Note, however, that when the data are discrete in nature, we use the notation ≤ and not <.

Cumulative frequency table The cumulative frequency for a value x, is the total number of observed values that are less than x. For discrete data, it is the number of values less than or equal to x.

The fact that the classes in a cumulative frequency table are constructed from the class upper bounds of a standard frequency table means that they can only be constructed for quantitative data.

We use the term 'cumulative frequency' because each subsequent class overlaps all the previous classes, and so the frequency values in each row represent the *accumulated* frequency of all items with values less than the upper bound of that class. This means that the frequency associated with each subsequent class is greater than or equal to the frequency of the previous class. Cumulative frequencies will never decrease from one class to the next.

The general form of a cumulative frequency table is outlined in Table 2.17.

Table 2.17: The general form of the cumulative frequency table

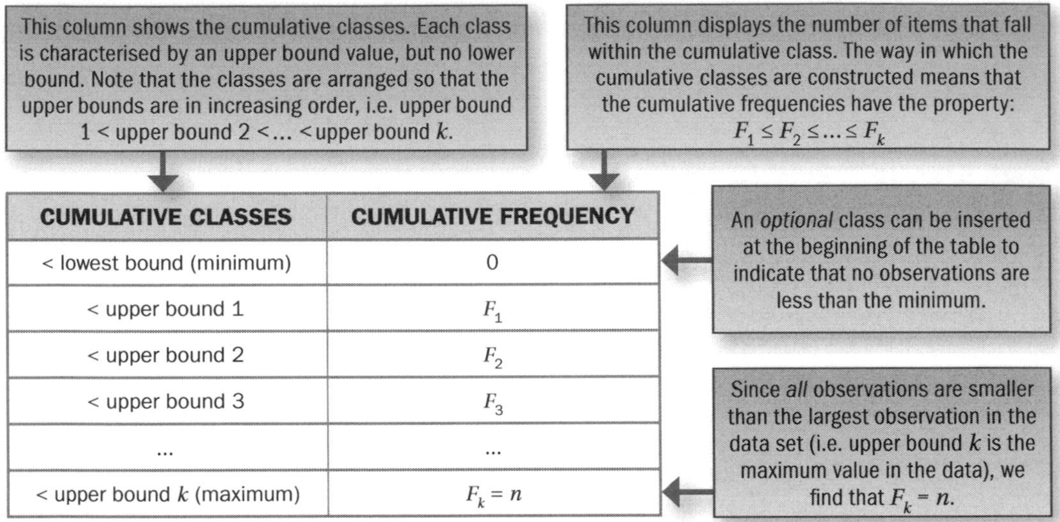

CUMULATIVE CLASSES	CUMULATIVE FREQUENCY
< lowest bound (minimum)	0
< upper bound 1	F_1
< upper bound 2	F_2
< upper bound 3	F_3
...	...
< upper bound *k* (maximum)	$F_k = n$

A basic cumulative frequency table (shown in Table 2.17) consists of the following elements:

- The cumulative classes of the cumulative frequency table (defined by class upper bounds) represent the upper bounds of the classes created in the standard frequency table. Each cumulative class is defined by a class upper bound, which has no lower limit. Hence, in cumulative frequency tables, the classes overlap one another (as opposed to the standard frequency table in which all the classes are mutually exclusive).
- The cumulative frequencies (or 'the accumulated count') represent the number of times observations fall within a specific cumulative class. However, since the classes in a cumulative frequency table overlap, it is possible for a particular observation to appear in a number of these classes. We use the notation F_j to denote the cumulative frequency that corresponds to the jth cumulative class where $j = 1, 2, ..., k$. Note that F_k is equal to the total number of observations in the sample, n.

You need to be able to construct these cumulative frequency tables from standard frequency tables. In the next section, we consider two types of cumulative frequency tables: tables constructed from discrete data and tables constructed from continuous data.

2.4.1 Cumulative frequency tables for discrete data

It is relatively simple to construct the cumulative frequency for a frequency table created from discrete data. To construct the table, follow these steps.

Step 1: First identify the unique values in the data set, sort them from smallest to largest, and then create a new set of classes that have the form '≤ unique value' (note that for discrete data, we use ≤ and not <).

Step 2: Determine the cumulative frequencies by counting how many observations are less than or equal to the upper bound value for each class.

Step 3: An initial class is sometimes also introduced to indicate that there are no values smaller than the smallest value.

These steps are illustrated in Example 2.7.

WORKED EXAMPLES

EXAMPLE 2.7

In n = 10 randomly selected households, the variable 'number of children in a household' is measured. The data are shown in Table 2.18.

Table 2.18: Raw data: Number of children in 10 households

3	1	2	1	0	0	0	1	3	1

The frequency table for these data is given in Table 2.19.

Table 2.19: Frequency table of the number of children in a household

NUMBER OF CHILDREN	FREQUENCIES (f_i)
0	3
1	4
2	1
3	2

Construct the cumulative frequency table from these data.

To create the cumulative frequency table from this frequency table, follow these steps.

Step 1: Create the new set of cumulative classes by first identifying and sorting all the unique values in the data (i.e. 0, 1, 2 and 3) and then simply placing a ≤ symbol in front of all the unique values, i.e. ≤ 0, ≤ 1, ≤ 2 and ≤ 3.

Step 2: For each class, determine how many observations are less than or equal to the specified cumulative class upper bound. For example, for the class ≤ 2 there are 8 observations less than or equal to 2.

Step 3: An extra class is also introduced at the beginning of the table to indicate that no observations are *strictly less* than 0 (this is optional). The cumulative frequency table is given in Table 2.20.

Table 2.20: Cumulative frequency table of the number of children in a household

NUMBER OF CHILDREN	CUMULATIVE FREQUENCIES (F_i)
< 0	0
≤ 0	3
≤ 1	7
≤ 2	8
≤ 3	10

2.4.2 Cumulative frequency tables for continuous data

When constructing a cumulative frequency table for continuous data, it is easier to first construct the standard frequency table (using the rules discussed earlier). The steps involved in this construction are the following.

Step 1: Obtain or create the standard frequency table from the data (see Section 2.3).

Step 2: From the standard frequency table, create the cumulative classes for the cumulative frequency table by extracting the upper bound of each class in the standard frequency table and placing a < symbol in front to indicate that the new cumulative class covers all values strictly less than the upper bound of the specified frequency table class.

Step 3: For each class specified in this way, determine the cumulative frequencies by counting how many observations are less than the upper bound value for each class.

Step 4: Optionally, you can place an additional class at the beginning, which is used to indicate that no observations are smaller than the *lower bound* of the first class in the standard frequency table. The cumulative frequency associated with this initial cumulative class is always zero.

These steps are illustrated in Example 2.8.

WORKED EXAMPLES

EXAMPLE 2.8

The 'weekly expenses' collected from a small business over a n = 12-week period are summarised in Table 2.21.

Table 2.21: Frequency table of the weekly expenses of a small business over a 12-week period

CLASS INTERVAL	CLASS MIDPOINT	FREQUENCIES (f_i)
[600; 800)	700	$f_1 = 1$
[800; 1 000)	900	$f_2 = 7$
[1 000; 1 200)	1 100	$f_3 = 3$
[1 200; 1 400)	1 300	$f_4 = 1$

Construct the cumulative frequency table from these data.

The steps to create the cumulative frequency table are the following.

Step 1: The frequency table is given in Table 2.21.

Step 2: The cumulative frequency table's classes are constructed by first extracting the upper bound of each class in Table 2.21 and then placing a < symbol in front, i.e. < 800, < 1 000, < 1 200 and < 1 400.

Step 3: Count how many observations fall within each cumulative class. Note that if the data are already arranged in a frequency table, then this task is relatively simple.

- The first cumulative class frequency is equal to the first standard class frequency, i.e. $F_1 = f_1 = 1$.
- The second cumulative class frequency is equal to the sum of the first and second standard class frequencies, i.e. $F_2 = f_1 + f_2 = 1 + 7 = 8$.
- The third cumulative frequency, F_3, is then the sum of all previous standard frequencies, i.e. $F_3 = f_1 + f_2 + f_3 = 1 + 7 + 3 = 11$.
- The final cumulative frequency is equal to the sum of all the frequencies in the standard frequency table, i.e. $F_4 = f_1 + f_2 + f_3 + f_4 = 1 + 7 + 3 + 1 = 12$. Note that since this is the last cumulative class, this cumulative frequency is equal to the sample size, $n = 12$.

Step 4: You can place an additional class at the beginning of the table, which is constructed from the lower bound of the first class, i.e. < 600. By definition, no observations are strictly less than the lower bound of the first class.

The cumulative frequency table is given in Table 2.22.

Table 2.22: Cumulative frequency table of the weekly expenses of a small business over a 12-week period

CLASS INTERVAL	CUMULATIVE FREQUENCIES (F_i)
< 600	0
< 800	$F_1 = 1$
< 1 000	$F_2 = 8$
< 1 200	$F_3 = 11$
< 1 400	$F_4 = 12$

2.5 Graphical representation of data

The next stage of analysis (after you have tabulated the data) is to graph the data. In this section, we will explore bar charts, pie charts, histograms and frequency polygons. The type of graph you choose to use will depend on the type of variable you are dealing with within your data set, for example, category (or nominal), ordinal or interval (or ratio) data.

Table 2.23: Data type and corresponding graph type

DATA TYPE	WHICH GRAPH TO USE?
Category or nominal	Bar chart, pie chart
Ordinal	Bar chart, pie chart
Interval or ratio	Histogram, frequency polygon

2.5.1 Bar charts

Graph and *chart* are terms that are often used to refer to any form of graphical display. *Categorical* data are represented largely by bar and pie charts. *Bar charts* are very useful for providing a simple pictorial representation of frequency tables for single or multiple sets of data on one graph. We use bar charts for categorical data where each category is represented by a vertical (or horizontal) bar. The frequency is represented by the height of the bar. All the bars are of equal width and the distance between each bar is constant.

It is important that the axes (x- and y-) are labelled and the chart has an appropriate title. You should also clearly state on the chart what each bar represents

Example 2.9 illustrates the bar chart for the data in Example 2.1.

WORKED EXAMPLES

EXAMPLE 2.9

The categorical data in Example 2.1 represents the homework grades of 30 students. We can use Excel to create a bar chart to represent this data set. For each category, draw a vertical bar, so that the vertical height of the bar represents the number of students in that category (or frequency). The width of each bar, and distance between each bar, should be equal.

Each bar represents the number of students who received a specific grade. From the bar chart, you can easily see the differences of frequency between the five grade categories (A, B, C, D and E). Figure 2.6 represents the bar chart for the homework grades of the students.

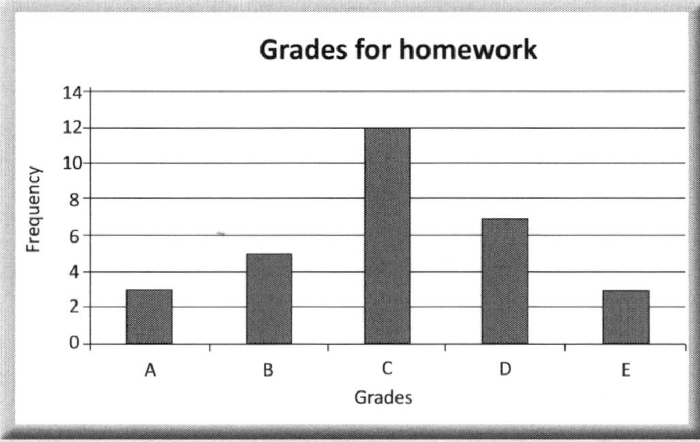

Figure 2.6: The bar chart for the data in Example 2.1

It is much easier to find information from a bar chart than it is from a frequency table. In Example 2.9, the height of the column labelled C clearly shows that it was the grade that was received the most often by the students, and that A and E were received the least frequent.

Next, we consider graphically representing a contingency or cross-tabulation table. In these cases, we use the frequencies of each column to construct a bar chart and then place these bar charts side-by-side in the plotting area. These bar charts are called **multiple bar charts**.

The bar chart in Example 2.10 is constructed from the contingency table in Example 2.3, i.e. the newspaper sales in four towns over a period of six months.

WORKED EXAMPLES

EXAMPLE 2.10

We use a multiple bar chart when we want to compare each component over time but the totals are of little importance.

We have used the contingency table data in Example 2.3 to construct Figure 2.7.

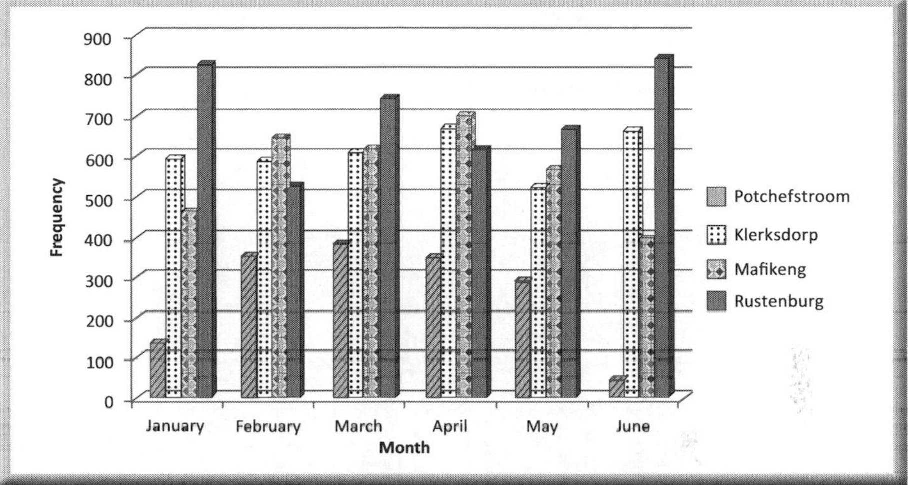

Figure 2.7: The multiple bar chart of the contingency table data in Example 2.3

This multiple bar chart represents the newspaper sales over six months for four different towns in the North-West Province. You can see that the newspaper sales for Potchefstroom and Mafikeng decrease during the school holiday months.

2.5.2 Excel Chart Wizard solution

We can also use the Excel Chart Wizard to draw a bar chart.

Step 1: Input the data series: The data in Example 2.1 consists of two columns of data. The first column represents the possible grades that students could obtain for a homework assignment and the second column represents the number of students that obtained these grades (also called *frequency of occurrence*). We can use Excel to create a bar chart for these data by placing the data in Excel as follows.

	A	B	C	D	E
1	VISUAL DISPLAYS				
2					
3		**Bar chart: Grades for homework**			
4					
5					
6		Grade	Frequency		
7		A	3		
8		B	5		
9		C	12		
10		D	7		
11		E	3		
12					
13					
14					
15					

Figure 2.8: Excel spreadsheet of frequencies for the homework grades of students

EXCEL FUNCTION METHOD

Grade: Cells B7:B11 (includes label 'Grade', B6)

Frequency: Cells C7:C11 (includes label 'Frequency', C6)

The Excel worksheet is displayed in Figure 2.8.

Step 2: Highlight cells B6:C11.

Step 3: Insert a chart by selecting the 'Insert' ribbon tab and clicking on the 'Column' button in the 'Charts' group.

Chart manipulation: Chart type

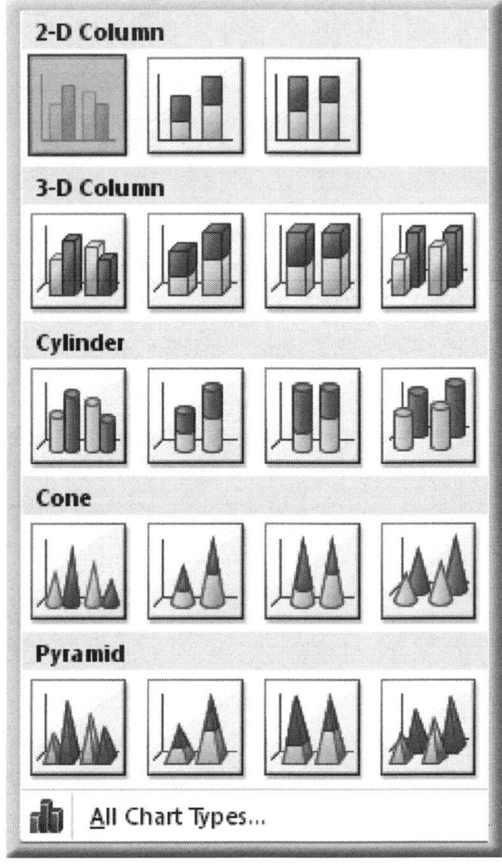

Figure 2.9 The column plot options in Excel

Choose your chart type by clicking on the type of chart you wish to create.

For this example, choose the 'Clustered column' chart (i.e. the chart type in the top left-hand corner as shown in Figure 2.9). This will automatically generate a chart in the active sheet.

Chart manipulation: Chart labels

Once you have created the chart, you will notice that a few new ribbon tabs have appeared when the chart is the active (selected) component in the spreadsheet. These are the 'Chart tools', and they allow you to change the design, layout and format of the selected chart. To add labels to the graph, select the 'Layout' ribbon tab and use the buttons in the 'Labels' group.

Figure 2.10: Adding labels to graphs in Excel

For example, to label the horizontal axis, click on the 'Axis Titles' button in the 'Labels' group. Select 'Primary Horizontal Axis Title', and then select 'Title Below Axis'. Once selected, a default title will appear in the graph, which you can freely edit by clicking on the axis label itself.

You then follow similar steps to label the vertical axis label and add the chart title.

Change the chart title to 'Grades for homework', change the horizontal axis label to 'Grades' and change the vertical axis label to 'Frequency'.

Chart manipulation: Chart location

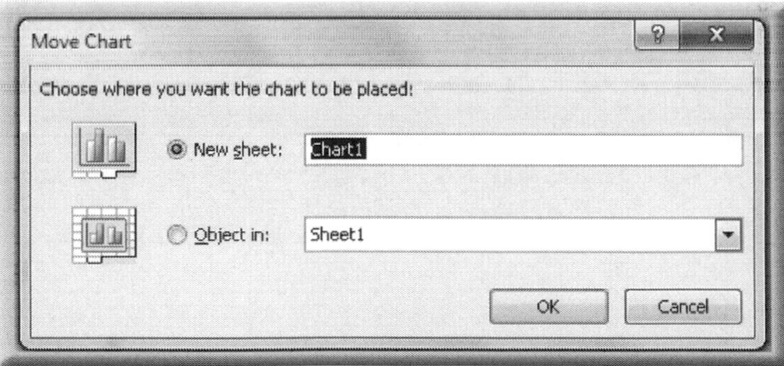

Figure 2.11: Moving a chart in Excel

Move the chart to a new sheet by selecting the 'Design' ribbon tab and clicking on the 'Move Chart' button in the 'Location' group. Select 'New sheet' and click on 'OK'. This will place the bar chart in the location you specified. Your bar chart should look like the chart in Figure 2.12.

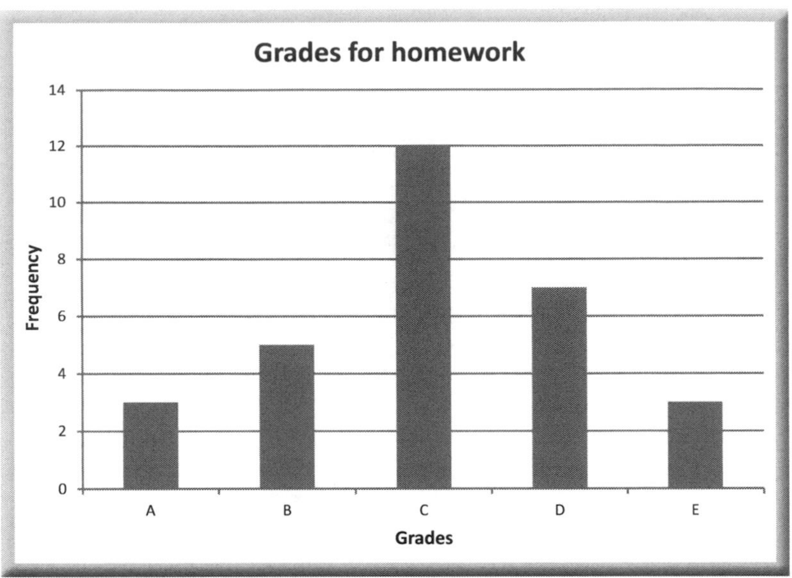

Figure 2.12: The bar chart of the categorical data from Example 2.1

2.5.3 Pie charts

In a pie chart, the classes and associated frequencies are represented by a sector of a circle. Each sector of the circle represents a category and the area of a sector represents the frequency or number of objects within that category. Pie charts are particularly useful in showing relative proportions (or percentage frequencies), but their effectiveness tends to diminish for more than eight categories.

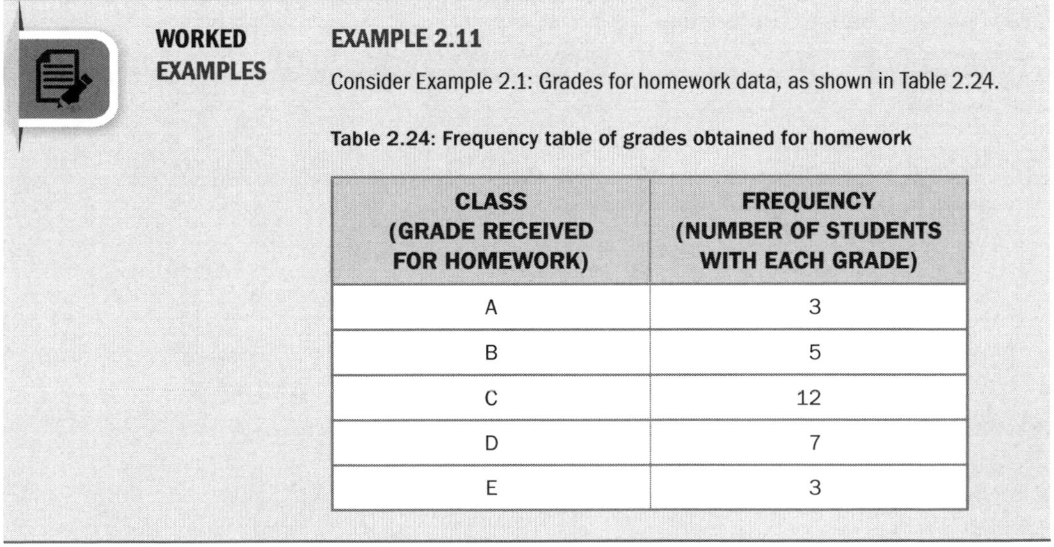

WORKED EXAMPLES

EXAMPLE 2.11

Consider Example 2.1: Grades for homework data, as shown in Table 2.24.

Table 2.24: Frequency table of grades obtained for homework

CLASS (GRADE RECEIVED FOR HOMEWORK)	FREQUENCY (NUMBER OF STUDENTS WITH EACH GRADE)
A	3
B	5
C	12
D	7
E	3

We can represent these data using a pie chart, as in Figure 2.13.

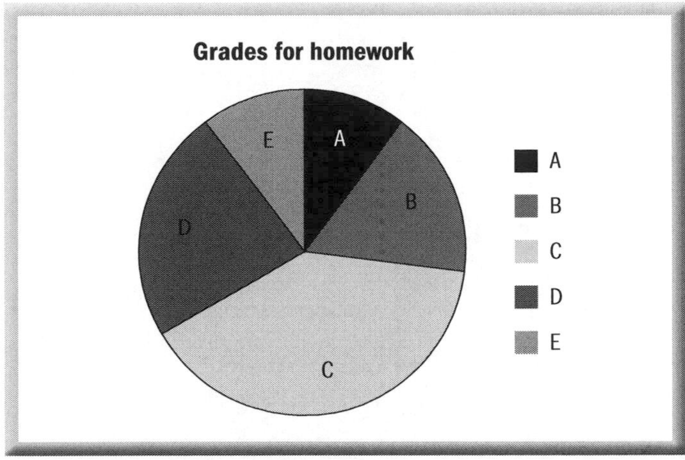

Figure 2.13: The pie chart of the categorical 'grades' data of Example 2.1

From Figure 2.13, you can see that each sector of the circle represents the proportion of students in the data set that obtained each grade.

NOTE

MANUAL SOLUTION

We have provided a set of instructions here if you would like to calculate the angle of each slice in the circle that represents each grade category. From the table, you can calculate that

the total number of students = 3 + 5 + 12 + 7 + 3 = 30.

Given that 360° represents the total number of degrees in a circle, we can calculate how many degrees each student would represent. In this example, we have 360° – 30 students. Therefore, each student is represented by $\frac{360}{30}$ degrees. Based on this, we can now calculate each angle for each of the five homework grades (see Table 2.25).

Table 2.25: The angles of the sectors of a pie chart

GRADE	FREQUENCY	ANGLE CALCULATION (degrees)	ANGLE
A	3	$\frac{360}{30} \times 3$	36°
B	5	$\frac{360}{30} \times 5$	60°
C	12	$\frac{360}{30} \times 12$	144°
D	7	$\frac{360}{30} \times 7$	84°
E	3	$\frac{360}{30} \times 3$	36°
Total	30		360°

The size of each sector depends on the angle at the centre of the circle, which in turn depends on the number in the category that the sector represents. Before drawing a pie chart, you should always check that the angles you have calculated add up to 360°. You can construct a pie chart on a percentage basis, or you can use the actual figures.

2.5.4 Excel spreadsheet solution

You can use Excel to draw a pie chart. We have used the data from Example 2.1 to illustrate this.

Step 1 and **Step 2** are identical to the first two steps of the Excel solution in Section 2.5.2.

Step 3: Insert a chart by selecting the 'Insert' ribbon tab and clicking on the 'Pie' button in the 'Charts' group.

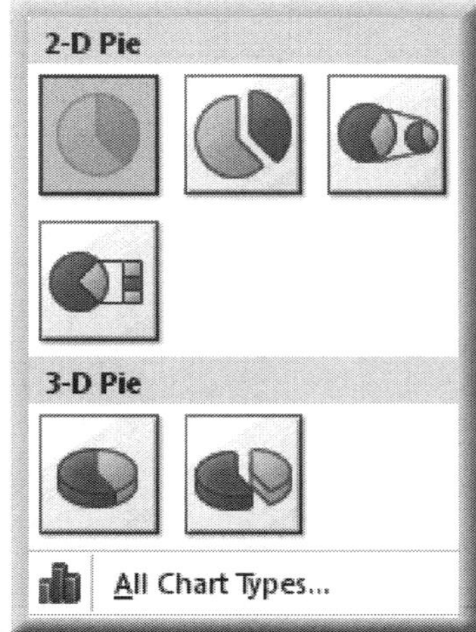

Figure 2.14: The pie chart options in Excel

Chart manipulation: Chart type

Choose the desired pie chart type from those available by clicking on the appropriate button. This will automatically create the chart in the active sheet.

Charts manipulation: Chart labels

Once you have created the chart, you will notice that a few new ribbon tabs will appear when the chart is the active component (selected) in the spreadsheet. These are the 'Chart tools' and allow you to change the design, layout and format of the selected chart. To add labels to the graph, select the 'Layout' ribbon tab and use the buttons in the 'Labels' group.

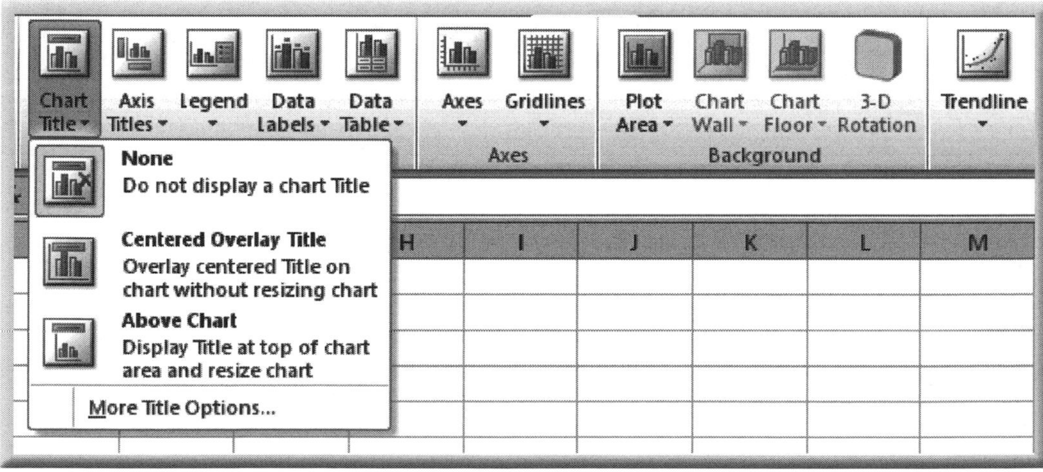

Figure 2.15: Placing a title on a chart in Excel

For example, to add a title to a chart, click on the 'Chart Title' button in the 'Labels' group and then select 'Above Chart'. The chart title will appear above the chart and you can edit it by clicking on the title and typing in 'Grades for homework'.

Chart manipulation: Chart location

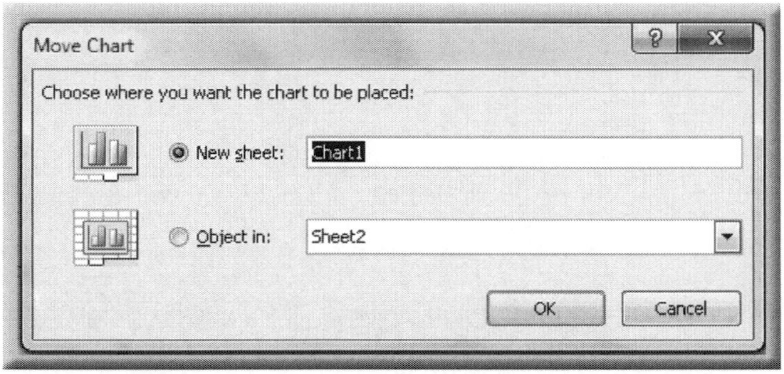

Figure 2.16: Moving a chart in Excel

Move the chart to a new sheet by selecting the 'Design' ribbon tab and clicking on the 'Move Chart' button in the 'Location' group. Select 'New Sheet' and click on 'OK'. The chart will be placed in the desired location. The result of these steps is shown in Figure 2.13 (page 43).

2.5.5 Histograms

We have already discussed displaying category-level data with tables and bar charts. One point to remember when displaying any type of data, is that the aim is to summarise information clearly and in such a way that the information is not distorted or lost. The method we use to graph a frequency table (or distribution) is to construct a **histogram**. Although a histogram looks like a bar chart, they are different and should not be confused with each other.

Histogram A way of summarising data that are measured on an interval scale (either discrete or continuous).

Frequency polygon A a graph that is made by joining the centre of the top of the columns of a frequency histogram.

Histograms are constructed according to the following principles:

- The horizontal axis (x-axis) is a continuous scale (meaning there are *no gaps* between the bars).
- Each class is represented by a vertical rectangle, the base of which extends from one true limit to the next.
- The area of the rectangle is proportional to the frequency of the class.

It is important to note that we can use either frequencies or percentage frequencies to construct a histogram. The shape of the histogram will be exactly the same no matter which frequency type we chose to graph.

We demonstrate how to construct a histogram using the data from Example 2.5.

2.5.6 Excel spreadsheet solution

WORKED EXAMPLES

EXAMPLE 2.12

The data in Example 2.5 represents the recorded distances travelled by 120 salesmen in one week. These data are summarised in Table 2.26.

Table 2.26: Frequency table of the distances travelled by 120 salesmen

DISTANCE TRAVELLED	FREQUENCY (f)
[400; 420)	12
[420; 440)	27
[440; 460)	34
[460; 480)	24
[480; 500)	15
[500; 520)	8
Total	$\sum_{j=1}^{6} f_j = 120$

Use Excel to construct the histogram of these data.

Figure 2.17 represents the histogram for the recorded distances travelled by the 120 salesmen.

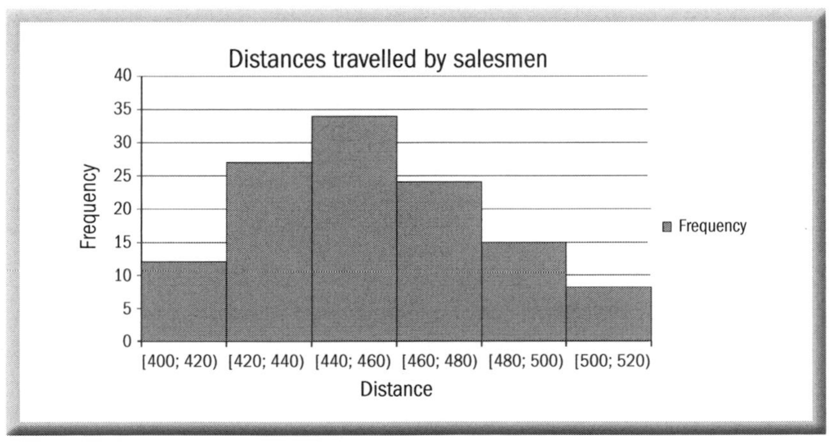

Figure 2.17: Histogram of the distances travelled by 120 salesmen (Example 2.5 data)

Step 1 and **Step 2** are identical to the first two steps in Section 2.5.4.

Step 3: Create a column that contains the correct upper and lower limits for each of the classes (as shown in Figure 2.18). You create this column using the stated limits as determined originally. Input the data series as shown in Figure 2.18.

	A	B	C	D
86				
87		Distance	Frequency	
88		[400; 420)	12	
89		[420; 440)	27	
90		[440; 460)	34	
91		[460; 480)	24	
92		[480; 500)	15	
93		[500; 520)	8	
94				

Figure 2.18: The frequency table constructed in Excel

EXCEL FUNCTION METHOD

Distance travelled: Cells B87:B93 (includes data label)

Frequency: Cells C87:C93 (includes data label)

Step 4: Highlight the cells B87:C93.
Create a bar chart of the data in the table by selecting the 'Insert' ribbon tab and clicking on the 'Column' button in the 'Charts' group. Figure 2.19 shows the column plots that you can choose from it. Select the first (top left-hand) 2-D bar chart.

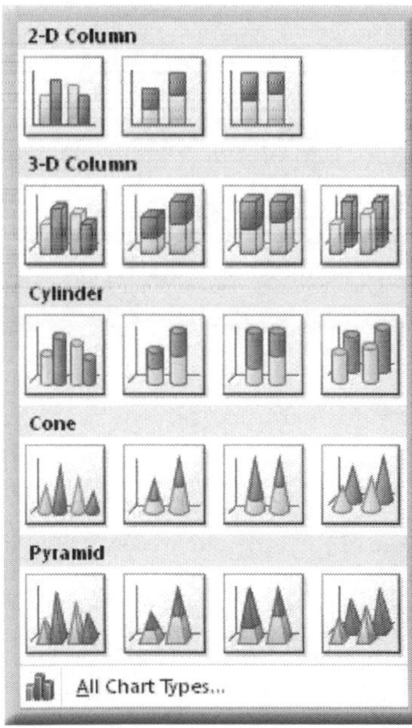

Figure 2.19: The column chart options in Excel

Chart manipulation: Chart titles and labels

Once you have created the bar chart, you can add or remove labels as described before. Ensure that the chart is the active item in the sheet (by clicking on it) and then select the 'Layout' ribbon tab. Use the buttons in the 'Labels' group to alter the titles and labels.

Change the chart title (by selecting the 'Chart Title' button) to 'Distance travelled by salesmen' and the two axes labels (by selecting 'Axis Titles') to 'Frequency' and 'Distance'.

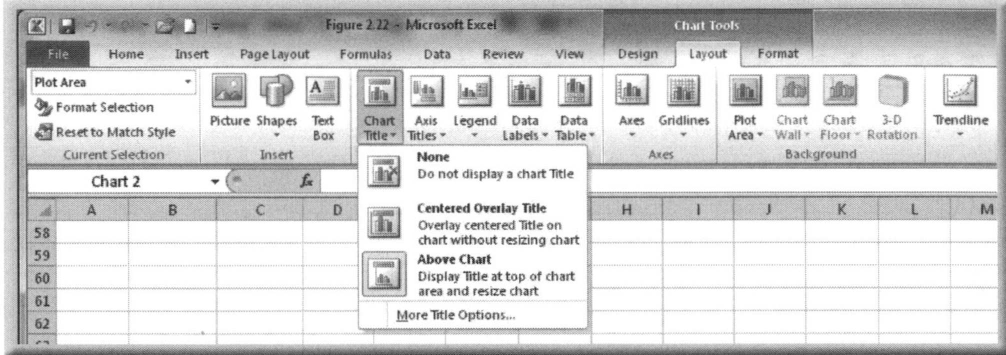

Figure 2.20: The 'Layout' ribbon tab buttons in Excel

Chart manipulation: Chart location

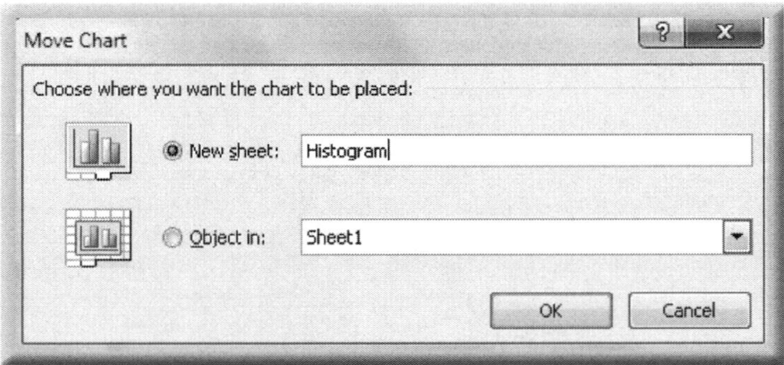

Figure 2.21: Moving a chart in Excel

Once you have created the bar chart, move it to a new sheet by first selecting it, then choosing the 'Design' ribbon tab, and then clicking on the 'Move Chart' button.

Specify where you want to move the bar chart (in this case it will be to a new chart sheet named 'Histogram') and click 'OK' (Figure 2.21).

Figure 2.22 shows the resulting bar chart. Unfortunately, since there are large gaps between the bars of the chart, this cannot strictly be called a histogram.

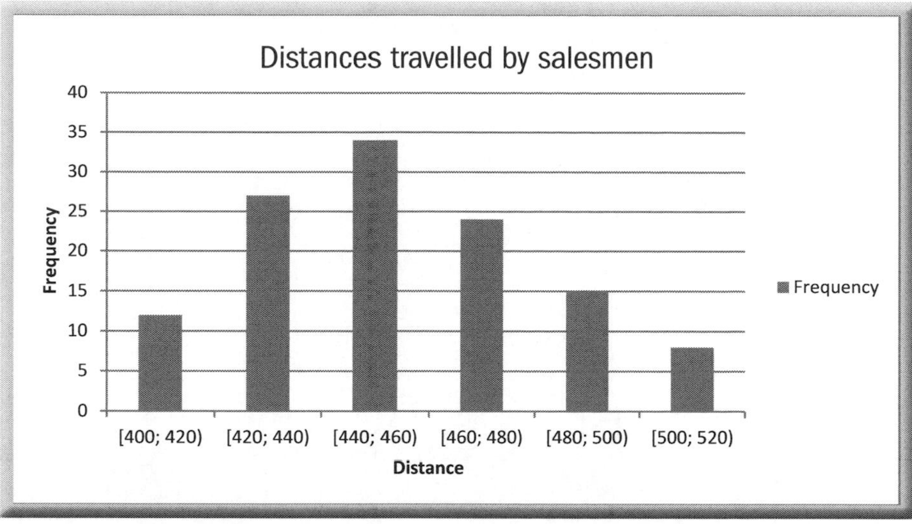

Figure 2.22: The bar chart version of the distances travelled by salesmen, which still needs to be converted into a histogram

Step 5: Transform the bar chart to a histogram.

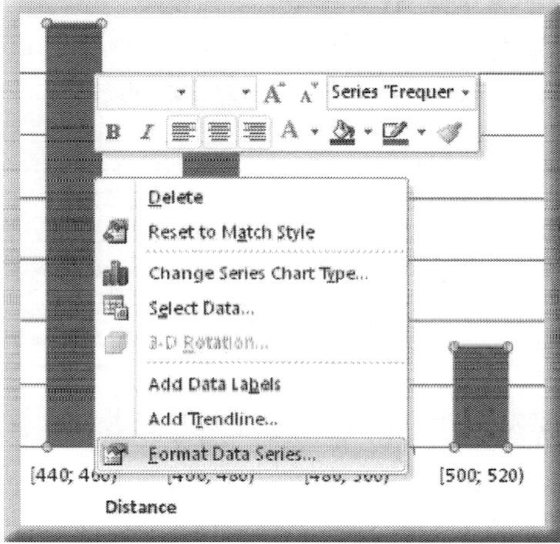

Figure 2.23: Accessing the 'Format Data Series' option for the bars of a bar chart

First, left click on any one of the bars in the chart (to ensure all of them are selected) and then right click on one of the bars in the chart. Select 'Format Data Series'.

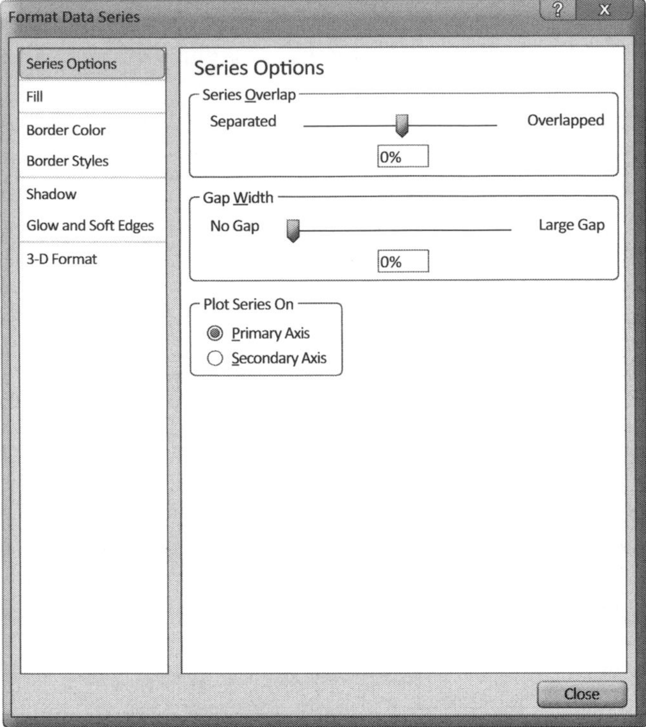

Figure 2.24: The 'Format Data Series' options for the bar chart – changing 'Gap Width'

Select 'Series Options' from the right-hand side pane and then change the 'Gap Width' to 0% by moving the slider all the way to the left.

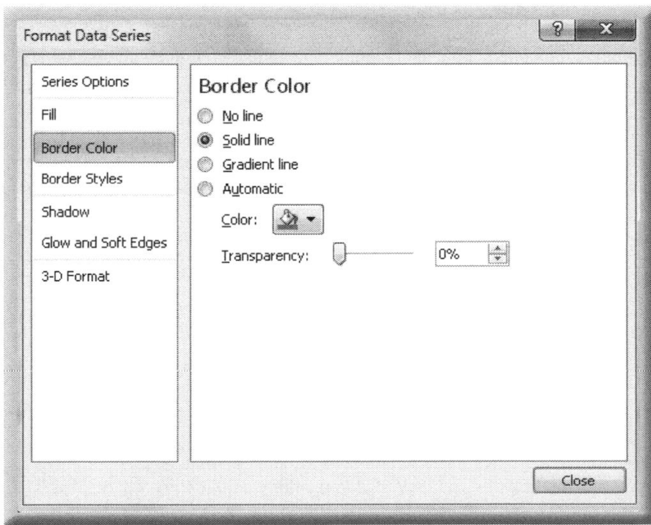

Figure 2.25: The 'Format Data Series' options for the bar chart – changing 'Border Color'

Next, select 'Border Color' from the right-hand side pane and then change the 'Border Color' to a solid line and change the colour to black. Click the 'Close' button. The resulting histogram is shown in Figure 2.26.

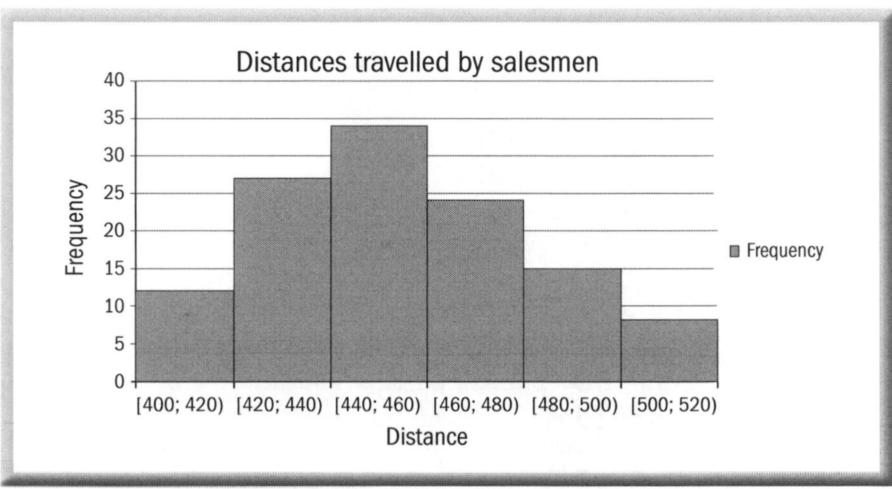

Figure 2.26: The histogram produced by Excel for the data in Example 2.5

NOTE

MANUAL SOLUTION

The data variable 'distance travelled' is grouped to form the class intervals. We construct the histogram as follows.

Table 2.27: Construction of the frequency table

DISTANCE TRAVELLED	CLASS WIDTH	CLASS MIDPOINTS	FREQUENCY (f)
[400; 420)	20	410	12
[420; 440)	20	430	27
[440; 460)	20	450	34
[460; 480)	20	470	24
[480; 500)	20	490	15
[500; 520)	20	510	8
Total			$\sum_{j=1}^{6} f_j = 120$

You can see from Table 2.27 that all the class widths are all equal to 20 (constant class width = $UCB - LCB$). In this case, we can construct the histogram so that the height of the bar represents the frequency of occurrence.

To construct the histogram, plot frequency (y-axis) against score (x-axis) with the boundary between the bars determined by the upper and lower class bounds (see Figure 2.27).

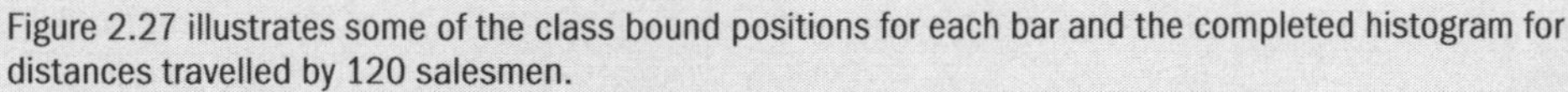
Figure 2.27 illustrates some of the class bound positions for each bar and the completed histogram for distances travelled by 120 salesmen.

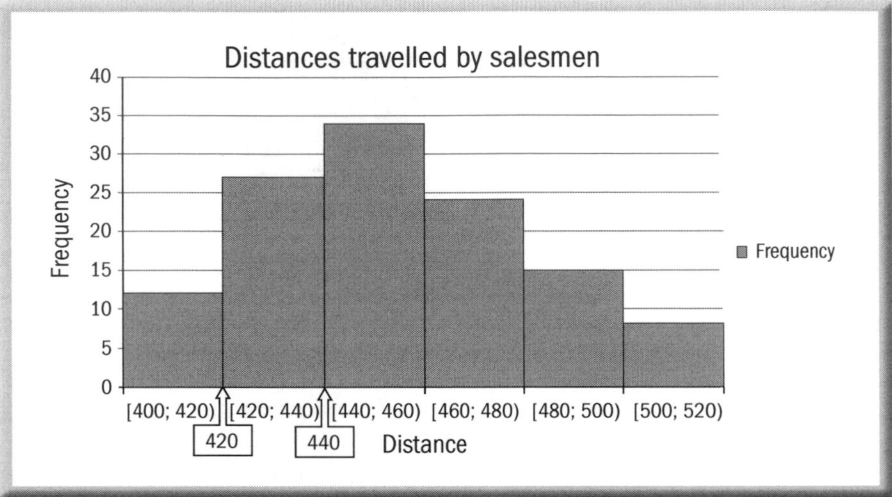

Figure 2.27: How to plot the vertical lines of the histogram

To construct the histogram we draw rectangles with heights equal to the specific class's frequency. For example, the rectangle for the second class, [420; 440), is constructed by drawing vertical lines at the class boundaries 420 and 440. The horizontal line is drawn at the frequency value of 27 (as shown in Figure 2.27).

2.5.7 Frequency polygons

A frequency polygon is formed from a histogram by joining the midpoints of the top of the rectangles with straight lines. The midpoints of the first and last classes are joined to the x-axis at either side at a distance equal to half the class interval of the first and last classes.

$$\text{Midpoint of class} = \frac{UCB + LCB}{2}$$

UCB = upper class boundary and LCB = lower class boundary.

WORKED EXAMPLES

EXAMPLE 2.13

Table 2.28 shows the table used to construct the frequency polygon for the data set from Example 2.5.

Table 2.28: Frequency table of the distances travelled by 120 salesmen

CLASS	CLASS MIDPOINT	FREQUENCY (*f*)
[400; 420)	410	12
[420; 440)	430	27
[440; 460)	450	34
[460; 480)	470	24
[480; 500)	490	15
[500; 520)	510	8

You construct the frequency polygon by plotting the class midpoints against the frequency values and then joining the consecutive points with straight lines. Figure 2.28 illustrates the frequency polygon for the distances travelled by the salesmen.

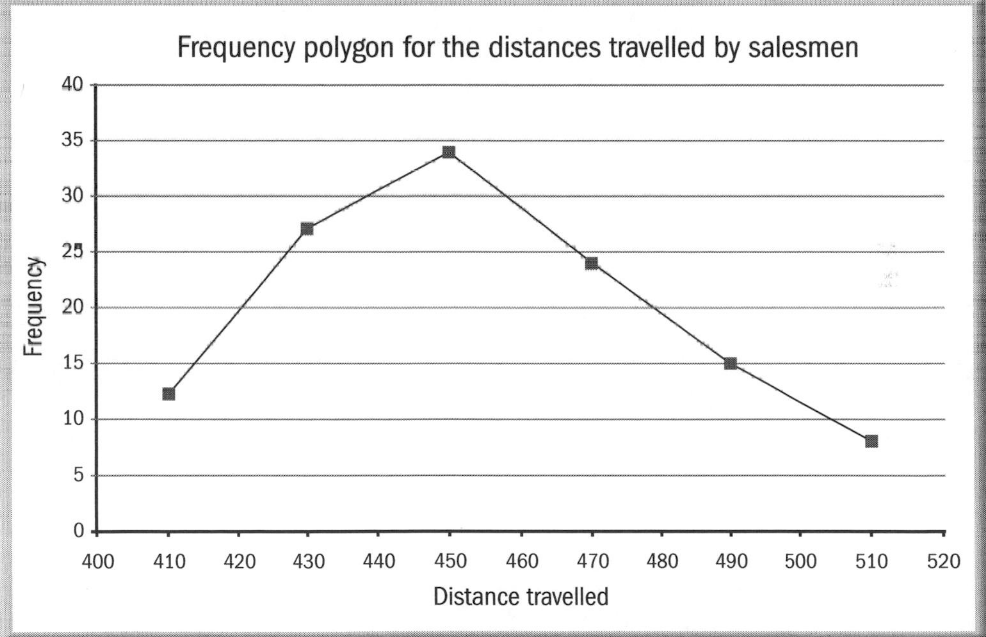

Figure 2.28: The frequency polygon constructed from the data in Example 2.5

2.5.8 Excel spreadsheet solution – frequency polygon using data from Example 2.5

Work through the following steps to obtain the Excel spreadsheet solution using the data from Example 2.5.

Step 1: Create a column that contains the class midpoints. The values that need to be typed in are shown in Figure 2.29.

	A	B	C	D
113				
114	Distance	Class midpoints	Frequency	
115	[400; 420)	410	12	
116	[420; 440)	430	27	
117	[440; 460)	450	34	
118	[460; 480)	470	24	
119	[480; 500)	490	15	
120	[500; 520)	510	8	
121				

Figure 2.29: The frequency table with midpoints in an Excel spreadsheet

EXCEL FUNCTION METHOD

Class midpoint: Cells B114:B120 (includes data label)

Frequency: Cells C114:C120 (includes data label)

Step 2: Highlight cells B114:C120 to create the scatter plot.

	A	B	C
113			
114	Distance	Class midpoints	Frequency
115	[400; 420)	410	12
116	[420; 440)	430	27
117	[440; 460)	450	34
118	[460; 480)	470	24
119	[480; 500)	490	15
120	[500; 520)	510	8
121			

Figure 2.30: Selecting the 'Scatter with straight lines and markers' plot in Excel

Select the 'Insert' ribbon tab and press the 'Scatter' button in the 'Charts' group. Select the scatter plot that joins the points with *straight lines* (as shown in Figure 2.30).

Step 3: Change the format of the scatter plot.

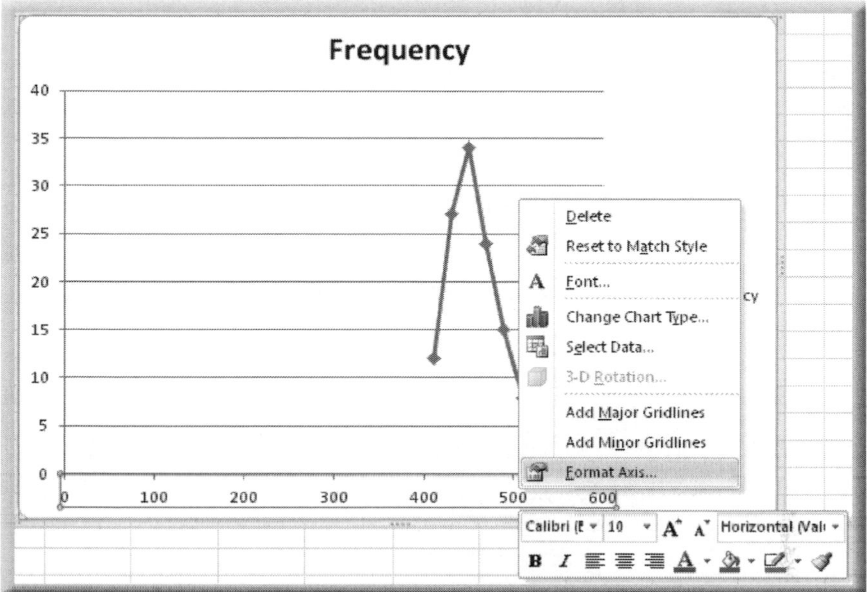

Figure 2.31: The 'Scatter with Straight Lines and Markers' plot – selecting to 'Format Axis'

Right click on the x-axis of the scatter plot produced and select 'Format Axis'.

Step 4: Alter the extreme values of the x-axis.

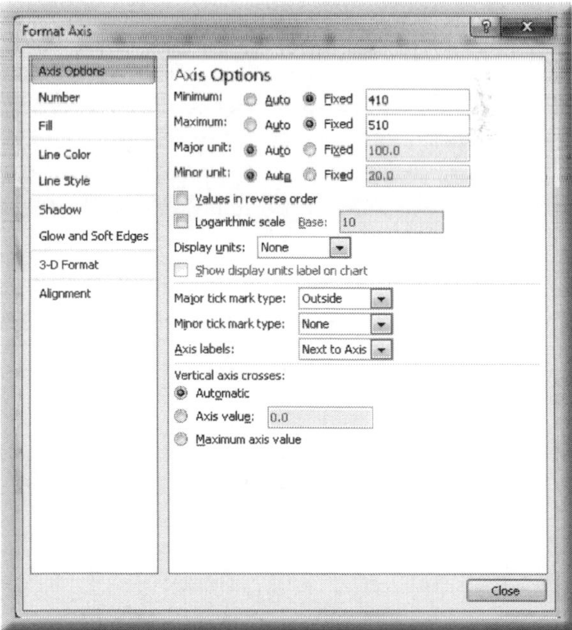

Figure 2.32: The 'Format Axis' options

Select the 'Axis Options' from the left-hand side pane and change the 'Minimum' and 'Maximum' values to 'Fixed'. Specify the minimum and maximum class midpoints for these two fixed values (in this case it will be 410 and 510).

Step 5: Alter the axis labels. Change the axis labels and chart title by first making the plot the active component in the sheet (by clicking on it) and then selecting the 'Layout' ribbon tab. The buttons that can alter the titles and labels are found in the 'Labels' group of buttons. Change the chart title to 'Frequency polygon for the distance travelled by salesmen', and change the *x*-axis label to 'Distance travelled' and the *y*-axis label to 'Frequency'.

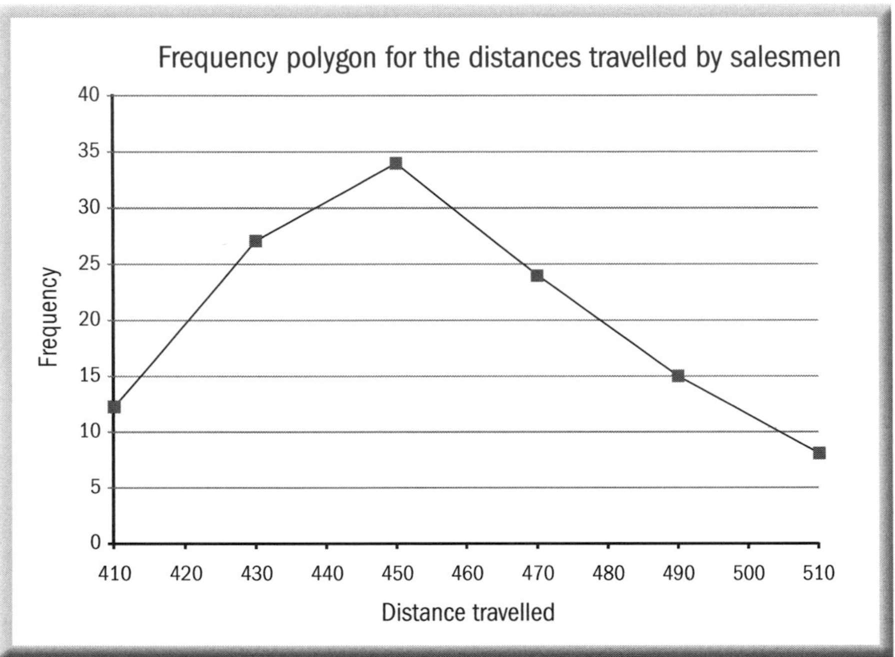

Figure 2.33: The frequency polygon created in Excel for the data from Example 2.5

Figure 2.33 shows the frequency polygon produced by Excel after some minor reformatting (for example, the legend was removed).

2.5.9 The ogive or cumulative frequency polygon

A cumulative frequency table can be represented graphically using a cumulative frequency polygon (also called an **ogive**).

Ogive (or cumulative frequency polygon) A distribution curve in which the frequencies are cumulative.

Constructing this graph is relatively simple if you have already constructed the cumulative frequency table (see Section 2.4 page 33).

Step 1: Set the horizontal axis to represent the cumulative class bounds and set the vertical axis to represent the cumulative frequencies.

Step 2: Plot the values of the cumulative frequency class bound values against their associated cumulative frequencies.

Step 3: Connect the points with straight lines.

Example 2.8 illustrates how to construct this graph using the information from Example 2.8.

WORKED EXAMPLES

EXAMPLE 2.14

Table 2.29 is the cumulative frequency table constructed from the data in Example 2.8 on page 36.

Table 2.29: Cumulative frequency table of the weekly expenses of a small business over a 12-week period

CLASS INTERVAL	CUMULATIVE FREQUENCIES (F_i)
< 600	0
< 800	1
< 1 000	8
< 1 200	11
< 1 400	12

Use this table to construct the ogive (cumulative frequency polygon).

Follow these steps to construct the ogive.

Step 1: Set the horizontal axis to describe the 'Expenses' variable and the vertical axis to represent the cumulative frequencies.

Step 2: Plot the values of the cumulative frequency class bound against their associated cumulative frequencies:

- Plot the point 600 on the horizontal axis against the point 0 on the vertical axis.
- Plot the point 800 on the horizontal axis against the point 1 on the vertical axis.
- Plot the point 1 000 on the horizontal axis against the point 8 on the vertical axis.
- Plot the point 1 200 on the horizontal axis against the point 11 on the vertical axis.
- Plot the point 1 400 on the horizontal axis against the point 12 on the vertical axis.

Step 3: Connect the points with straight lines. The result is shown in Figure 2.34.

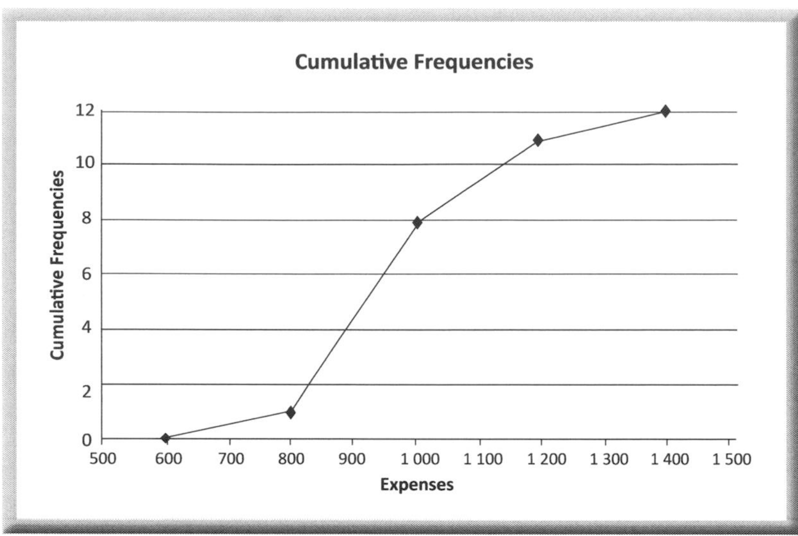

Figure 2.34: Ogive for the cumulative frequency table in Table 2.29

2.5.10 Excel spreadsheet solution

We can obtain the Excel spreadsheet solution for constructing a cumulative frequency polygon using the following steps. We have used the data from examples 2.8 and 2.14.

Step 1: Create two columns: one that contains the cumulative class upper bounds and one that contains the cumulative frequencies. The values that you need to type are shown in Figure 2.35.

	A	B	C
4		Class upper bounds (expenses)	Cumulative frequencies (F)
5		600	0
6		800	1
7		1000	8
8		1200	11
9		1400	12
10			

Figure 2.35: A cumulative frequency table in an Excel spreadsheet

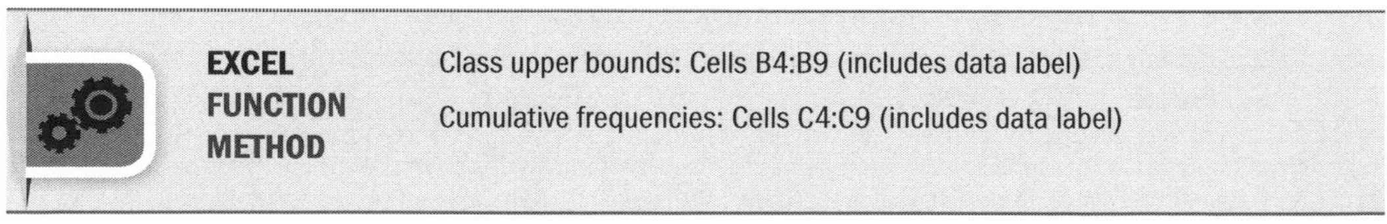

Step 2: Highlight cells B4:C9 and create the scatter plot.

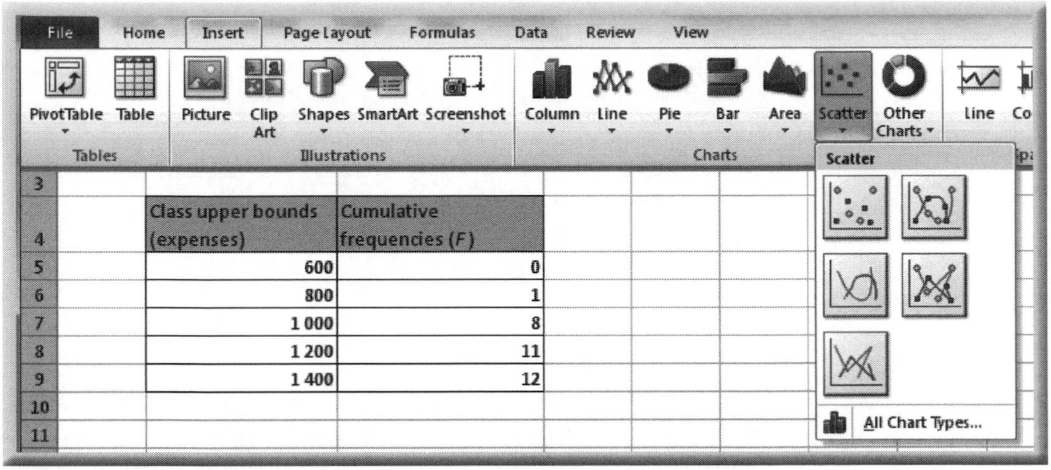

Class upper bounds (expenses)	Cumulative frequencies (F)
600	0
800	1
1 000	8
1 200	11
1 400	12

Figure 2.36: Selecting the 'Scatter with Straight Lines and Markers' plot in Excel

Select the 'Insert' ribbon tab and press the 'Scatter' button in the 'Charts' group. Select the scatter plot that joins the points with *straight lines* (as shown in Figure 2.36). This will produce a basic frequency polygon.

Step 3: Change the format of the scatter plot.

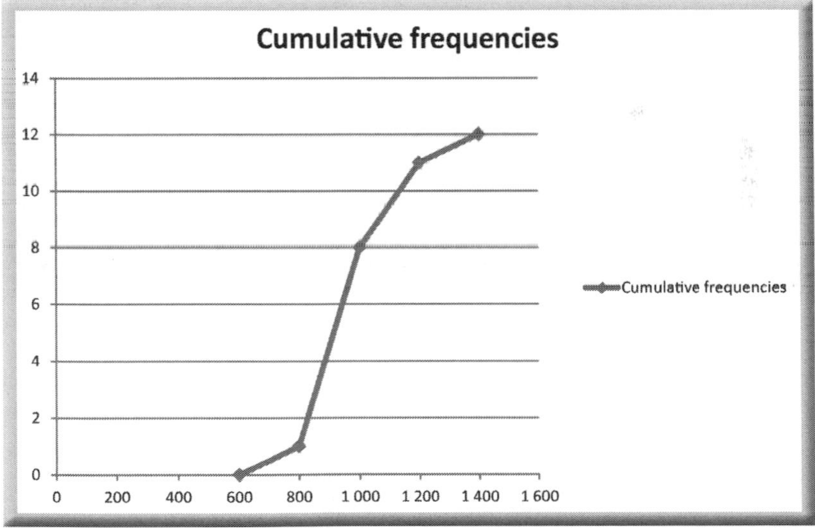

Figure 2.37: The 'Scatter with straight lines and markers' plot – selecting to 'Format Axis'

Right click on the x-axis of the scatter plot produced and select 'Format Axis'.

Step 4: Alter the extreme values of the x-axis.

Figure 2.38: The 'Format Axis' options

Select the 'Axis Options' from the left-hand side pane and change the 'Minimum' and 'Maximum' values to 'Fixed'. Specify the minimum and maximum class midpoints for these two fixed values. In this case, they were changed to 500 and 1 500.

Step 5: Alter the axis labels. Change the axis labels by first making the plot the active component in the sheet (by clicking on it) and then selecting the 'Layout' ribbon tab. The buttons that can alter the labels are found in the 'Labels' group of buttons. Change the x-axis label to 'Expenses' and the y-axis label to 'Cumulative frequency'.

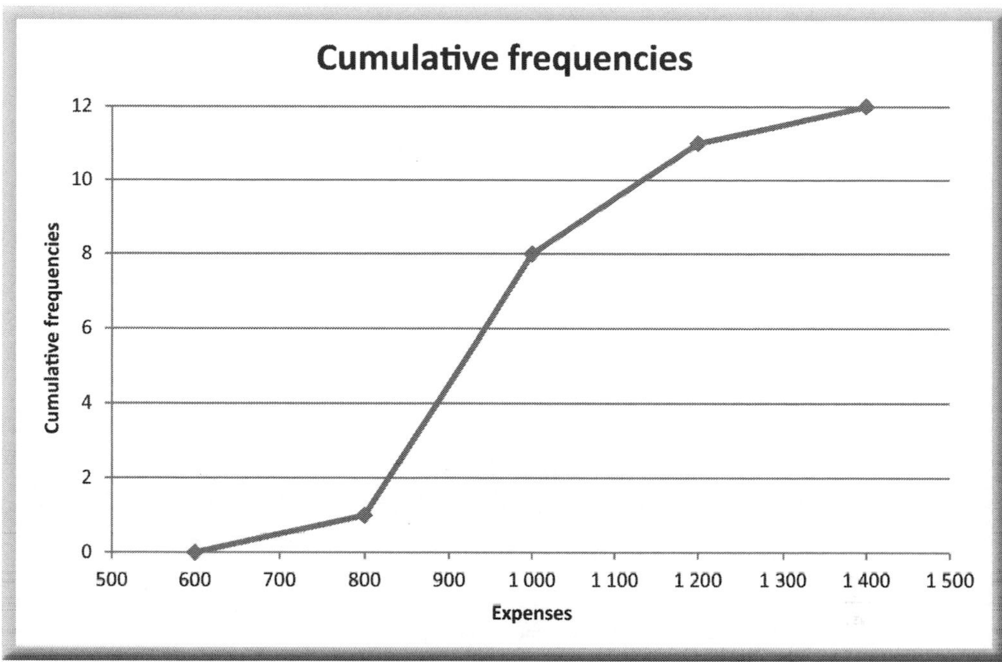

Figure 2.39: The cumulative frequency polygon created in Excel from the data in Example 2.5

Figure 2.39 illustrates the frequency polygon produced by Excel after some minor reformatting (for example, the legends and main title were removed).

SUMMARY

The methods discussed in this chapter are very useful for describing data using a variety of tables and graphs. These methods allow you to make sense of data by constructing visual representations of numbers within a data set. Table 2.30 provides a summary of which table or graph to construct depending on the data type.

Table 2.30: Which table or chart to use

	QUANTITATIVE DATA	QUALITATIVE OR CATEGORICAL DATA
Tables	Frequency distribution tables and grouped frequency distribution tables	Frequency distribution tables
Graphs	Histogram Frequency polygons	Bar charts Pie charts

KEY TERMS

Bar chart
Continuous variable
Cumulative frequency table
Frequency polygon
Frequency table
Histogram
Interval-scaled variable
Nominal-scaled variable
Ogive
Ordinal-scaled variable
Pie chart
Qualitative or categorical variable
Quantitative variable
Ratio-scaled variable
Raw data
Variable

EXERCISES

2.1 Table 2.31 shows the information obtained from $n = 2\ 000$ separate metal castings produced at a local foundry. The clients who received this table felt that the table did not display any intelligent information. Do you agree? What criticism (if any) can you level at this frequency table?

Table 2.31: Table displaying information obtained from a foundry

CASTINGS	WEIGHT OF METAL	FOUNDRY
Up to 4 tonnes	60	210
Up to 10 tonnes	100	640
All other weights	110	800
Other	20	85
Total	290	2 000

2.2 The data in Table 2.32 represents the number of customers that entered a small electronics store each day, over a period of 80 days.

Table 2.32: Number of customers entering an electronics store each day for 80 days

68	64	75	82	68	60	62	88	76	93	73	79	88	73	60	93
71	59	85	75	61	65	75	87	74	62	95	78	63	72	66	78
82	75	94	77	69	74	68	60	96	78	89	61	75	95	60	79
83	71	79	62	67	97	78	85	76	65	71	75	65	80	73	57
88	78	62	76	53	74	86	67	73	81	72	63	76	75	85	77

a) Use Excel to construct a grouped frequency distribution from the above data set and indicate the stated limits. Start the first class interval at 50, with a class width of 5.

b) Create a suitable histogram to represent the number of customers that entered the store over the 80-day period.
c) Create a frequency polygon (line graph) for the data in Table 2.32.

2.3 Use Excel to construct a suitable bar chart for the data summarised in Table 2.33.

Table 2.33: Industrial sources for consumption and investment demand (thousand million)

PRODUCING INDUSTRY	CONSUMPTION	INVESTMENT
Agriculture, mining	1.1	0.1
Metal manufacturers	2.0	2.7
Other manufacturing	6.8	0.3
Construction	0.9	2.7
Gas, electricity & water	1.2	0.2
Services	16.5	0.8
Total	28.5	7.8

2.4 3 600 people who work in Johannesburg were asked about the means of transport they used for their daily commute. The data collected are shown in Table 2.34.

Table 2.34: Frequency table of the types of transport used by 3 600 workers in Johannesburg

TYPE OF TRANSPORT	FREQUENCY OF RESPONSE
Private car	1 790
Taxi	1 010
Other	800

a) Present this information as a pie chart.
b) Present this information as a bar chart.
c) What conclusions can you make from these graphs?

2.5 The results of the voting in a small town election are shown in Table 2.35.

Table 2.35: Frequency table of the votes each party received

PARTY	VOTES
Democratic Conservatives	2 045
Republican Alliance	4 238
African National Party	8 605
The People for Africa Party	12 012

a) Present this information as a pie chart.
b) Present this information as a bar chart.
c) What conclusions can you draw from these graphs?

2.6 Use the data in Table 2.36 to create a suitable histogram to represent the amount of money spent on snacks for a random sample of 50 university students in the first week of final exams.

Table 2.36: Rand value of money spent on snacks by university students during final exams

169.10	96.50	226.08	124.50	182.40	117.90	64.80	129.30	72.50	130.20
81.00	32.50	90.00	99.00	128.70	175.00	100.50	274.30	160.10	66.30
147.30	85.90	65.00	203.05	88.40	134.50	187.50	241.00	135.70	91.80
95.00	71.40	104.10	128.00	320.90	67.40	113.80	179.50	72.50	43.20
83.10	65.00	138.00	98.70	62.90	145.90	192.50	57.40	49.50	159.00

TECHNIQUES IN PRACTICE

2.7 AfriSoft supplies a range of computer software to 50 schools within Limpopo province. When AfriSoft won the contract, the issue of customer service was considered to be central to the company being successful at the final bidding stage. The company has now requested that its customer service director creates a series of graphical representations of the data to illustrate customer satisfaction with the service. The data in Table 2.37 has been collected during the past six months and measures the time to respond to complaints (days).

Table 2.37: The time taken to respond to complaints (days)

5	24	34	6	61	56	38	32
87	78	34	9	67	4	54	23
56	32	86	12	81	32	52	53
34	45	21	31	42	12	53	21
43	76	62	12	73	3	67	12
78	89	26	10	74	78	23	32
26	21	56	78	91	85	15	12
15	56	45	21	45	26	21	34
28	12	67	23	24	43	25	65
23	8	87	21	78	54	76	79

a) Construct a frequency table from these data.
b) Use the frequency table in part (a) to construct a histogram.
c) Do the results suggest that there was a large variation in the time taken to respond to customer complaints?
d) What conclusions can you draw from these results?

2.8 Bakers Ltd runs a chain of bakery shops and is famous for the quality of its pies. The management of the company are concerned about the number of complaints from a particular branch about the amount of time that it takes to serve customers. The motto of the company is 'Have your pies in 2 minutes.' The manager of the branch concerned has been told to provide data on the time it takes for customers to enter the shop and be served by the staff.

Table 2.38: Time taken for a sample of n = 100 customers to be served (minutes)

0.37	1.18	0.51	1.93	1.83	1.33	0.22	0.97	0.91	1.08
0.19	1.83	0.66	1.14	0.78	1.38	0.89	1.57	1.56	0.37
1.21	0.71	0.81	1.22	0.65	0.86	1.08	1.53	1.14	0.44
0.59	0.89	1.08	1.05	2.33	0.88	1.64	0.85	0.83	1.20
1.35	0.52	1.10	0.28	1.00	1.93	0.96	0.63	0.39	2.07
1.08	0.77	0.55	1.14	1.90	0.63	1.16	1.52	0.63	1.33
0.70	1.39	1.31	0.62	0.41	0.48	1.11	0.93	1.42	0.80
0.31	1.28	0.86	0.06	0.54	0.85	0.09	1.07	1.54	1.49
1.12	0.48	0.67	0.97	1.34	1.15	1.64	0.36	0.72	1.38
1.24	1.23	1.70	0.56	1.47	0.37	1.09	0.43	0.33	1.78

a) Construct a frequency table from these data.
b) Use the frequency table from part (a) to construct the histogram.
c) Do the results suggest that there was a large variation in the amount of time it took to serve customers?
d) What conclusions can you draw from these results?

2.9 Home-Made Beers Ltd is a brewery that is undergoing a major expansion after a being bought out by a large national brewery. Home-Made Beers Ltd produces a small range of beers and stouts, but is renowned for the quality of its beers – having won a number of prizes at trade fairs. The new parent company is reviewing the quality-control mechanisms of Home-Made Beers Ltd and is concerned by the quantity of the lager contained in the bottles produced at the brewery. These bottles should contain a mean of 330 ml with a standard deviation of 15 ml. The bottling plant manager provided the parent company with quantity measurements from 100 bottles for analysis (Table 2.39).

Table 2.39: Quantity of beer in n = 100 randomly selected bottles of beer

348	343	337	333	324	349	348	352	335	374
337	346	347	333	315	346	356	362	340	348
354	356	343	337	356	322	361	352	360	354
344	341	324	339	339	353	342	336	331	355
355	345	345	334	349	331	351	343	346	339
339	351	318	363	334	348	336	332	375	365
328	350	330	367	316	350	345	336	322	329
351	328	343	349	361	337	325	328	360	347
360	358	365	354	326	341	360	342	346	351
360	350	338	324	342	333	338	340	350	335

a) Construct a frequency table from these data.
b) Use the frequency table from part (a) to construct the histogram.
c) Do the results suggest that there is a large variation in the quantity of beer in the bottles?
d) What conclusions can you draw from these results?

CHAPTER 3

DATA DESCRIPTORS

CHAPTER CONTENTS

OVERVIEW

This chapter looks at statistical measures that enable us to describe and summarise a data set using values calculated from the data set.

We will distinguish between values that are calculated from samples and values that are calculated from entire populations.

The central tendency of a data set indicates the centre or middle location of values. We use it to indicate what the typical values in a data set are. There are a number of different measures of central tendency, including the mean (or *average*), the median and the mode. Each of these can be calculated for both *ungrouped* (individual data values) and *grouped* (data values within class intervals) data sets.

The dispersion (or *variation*) of a data set indicates the degree of spread of the data values about the centre values. There are a number of different measures of dispersion, including the range, the interquartile range, the semi-interquartile range, the standard deviation and the variance, all of which can be calculated for both ungrouped and grouped data sets.

The *shape* of the distribution is the pattern within the data set. We can classify this shape according to whether the distribution is symmetrical (or *skewed*) and whether there is evidence that the shape is *peaked*. We define skewness as a measure of the lack of symmetry in a distribution and kurtosis as a measure of the degree of peakedness in the distribution.

We can use exploratory data analysis to explore data sets and provide answers to questions that involve central tendency, spread, skewness and the presence of outliers.

LEARNING OBJECTIVES

On completing this chapter, you should be able to:

- understand the concept of central tendency
- recognise the three possible measures of central tendency (mean, mode and median), and calculate them using a variety of graphical and formulaic methods in ungrouped data and grouped data (frequency table) form
- recognise when to use different measures of central tendency
- understand the concept of dispersion
- recognise and calculate the measures of dispersion (range, interquartile range, semi-interquartile range, standard deviation and variance)
- understand the idea of distribution shape and calculate a value for symmetry and peakedness
- apply exploratory data analysis to a data set(s)
- use Excel to calculate data descriptors.

3.1 Measures of central tendency

Although tables, diagrams and graphs provide easy-to-assimilate summaries of data, they only go part way in describing data. Often, a concise numerical description is preferable, as it allows us to interpret the significance of the data. Measures of **central tendency** (or location) attempt to quantify what we mean when we think of the 'typical' or 'average' value for a particular data set. The concept of central tendency is *extremely important* and we come across it every day. For example:

- What is the average CO_2 emission for a particular car compared to other similar cars?
- What is the typical mark received by students in a Maths class?
- How much money would a new graduate typically expect to earn as a starting salary?
- What is the average amount of money a family spends on groceries every month?

Central tendency The location of the middle or centre of a distribution.

The central tendency allows us to assign a value to what is the most representative value of the group. This value is usually somewhere in the middle of the group, and as such, is the best approximation of all other values. The **mean** (also called an *average*, an *arithmetic average* or an *arithmetic mean*), **mode** and **median** are different measures of central tendency. In the next few sections, we explore various properties of these measures, and discuss how to calculate these measures for ungrouped and grouped data.

Mean A measure of the average data value for a data set.

Median The value in the middle of an ordered data set.

Mode The most frequently occurring value in a set of discrete data.

3.1.1 The mean

The mean (sometimes also called the *average*) is one of the most common measures of central tendency. Most of you will be familiar with the concept because it is often used to summarise your performance at school, i.e. your average or mean mark is usually calculated at the end of each semester. The mean, like all measures of central tendency, can represent the 'middle' or 'centre' of a group of values.

If the mean is calculated from the entire population of a data set, then the mean is called the **population mean** (we use the notation μ to denote population mean). Unfortunately, since the entire population is usually unobservable (for reasons given in Chapter 1), we typically use the mean calculated from a sample drawn from the population. This mean is called the **sample mean** (We use the notation $\overline{X}$ to denote the mean of a sample).

Population mean The mean value of all possible values.

Sample mean The mean or average of the variable recorded for the items in a sample. It is calculated as the sum of the values of the items in a sample divided by the number of items in the sample.

We calculate the population and sample mean of raw data using the same formula:

$$\text{mean} = \frac{\text{sum of data values}}{\text{total number of data values}}$$

We can express the sample mean in terms of the mathematical notation presented in the appendix of this book as the following.

SAMPLE MEAN

$$\overline{X} = \frac{1}{n}\sum_{i=1}^{n} X_i = \frac{X_1 + X_2 + \ldots + X_n}{n} \tag{3.1}$$

n is the number of items in the sample, and $X_1, X_2, \ldots, X_n$ are the values of the n observations in the sample data set.

For example, a market research company is interested in the mean or average number of successful telephone sales made by its salespeople in one week. A sample of $n = 5$ salespeople is used and the number of successful sales made in the week is recorded. The figures for each of the five salespeople are $X_1 = 10$, $X_2 = 19$, $X_3 = 28$, $X_4 = 8$ and $X_5 = 17$. From this sample, we can calculate the sample mean number of successful telephone sales using formula (3.1) as:

$$\overline{X} = \frac{1}{5}\sum_{i=1}^{5} X_i = \frac{10 + 19 + 28 + 8 + 17}{5} = \frac{82}{5} = 16.4$$

Based on the sample of five salespeople, you can see that they only make 16.4 successful sales calls in a week, on average. This is a very simple example based on raw data (data that is not arranged in a frequency table). In the next few sections, we discuss more examples, specifically ones in which we calculate the mean for raw data (ungrouped data) and the mean for data arranged in frequency tables (grouped data).

Properties of the mean

The mean is a very popular measure of central tendency, and is widely used because it is easy to understand and easy to calculate.

- *The mean can only be calculated for quantitative data*: We can only calculate the mean of numerical, quantitative data. It does not apply to qualitative data, or even qualitative data that has been numerically coded.
- *The mean makes use of all observations*: When calculating a mean, whether it is a sample mean or a population mean, we make use of every available observation value. This implies that the mean makes use of all available information to determine the central tendency of the data (in fact, of the three measures of central tendency discussed, it is the only one that makes use of all the available information).

- *Each variable in a data set will have only one mean value*: The mean is unique to a collection of data, in that there can only be one mean value per variable in an observed data set.
- *The mean is sensitive to outliers*: Unfortunately, since the mean is based on *all* data points, it can easily be influenced by values that have been erroneously recorded or are simply unusually large or small. These extreme values are called **outliers** and they have a tendency to skew the data distribution. In data sets that have outliers, we would use a different measure to calculate the value of central tendency. For example, in the market research example given above, if we included a sixth salesperson, and that salesperson's number of sales was recorded as $X_6 = 182$ (which is very large compared to that of the other five salespeople), we would find that the mean of the new data set would be:

$$\overline{X} = \frac{1}{6}\sum_{i=1}^{6} X_i = \frac{10 + 19 + 28 + 8 + 17 + 182}{6} = \frac{264}{6} = 44$$

Clearly, introducing this outlier significantly increases the sample mean.

Outlier An observation in a data set that is far removed in value from the other values in the data set.

WORKED EXAMPLES

EXAMPLE 3.1

A lecturer in a Statistics class wants to determine the average mark obtained by her first-year students in an exam that they recently took. The marks obtained in the Statistics examination by the 13 students in her first-year class are given in Table 3.1.

Table 3.1: Raw data of the Statistics marks of 13 students

24	27	36	48	52	52	53	53	59	60	85	90	95

She can describe the overall performance of these 13 students by calculating an 'average' score using the sample mean.

To calculate the sample mean of this data set, we simply apply formula (3.1):

$$\begin{aligned}\overline{X} &= \frac{1}{13}\sum_{i=1}^{13} X_i \\ &= \frac{24 + 27 + 36 + 48 + 52 + 52 + 53 + 53 + 59 + 60 + 85 + 90 + 95}{13} \\ &= \frac{734}{13} \\ &= 56.4615\end{aligned}$$

In Excel, we can calculate the sample mean using the Excel spreadsheet functions 'COUNT' (to determine the total number of observations, n) and 'SUM' (to determine the sum of the observations, $\left(\sum_{i=1}^{n} X_i\right)$. However, we can more easily calculate the mean by using the Excel spreadsheet function 'AVERAGE'. Both methods are shown in Figure 3.1.

	A	B	C	D	E	F	G
1	**Example 3.1: Marks obtained in a Statistics exam by 13 students**						
2		**Statistics marks**					
3		24		**Excel function method**			
4		27					
5		36		n =	13	=COUNT(B3:B15)	
6		48		sum X =	734	=SUM(B3:B15)	
7		52					
8		52		mean =	56.4615384615	=E6/E5	
9		53					
10		53		**Excel function method**			
11		59					
12		60		mean =	56.4615384615	=AVERAGE(B3:B15)	
13		85					
14		90					
15		95					
16							

Figure 3.1: Excel spreadsheet calculations for Example 3.1 – the sample mean

Figure 3.1 illustrates both Excel solutions for calculating the sample mean. The data series has been input into cells B3:B15

The Excel function method involves the following steps:

1. Select cell E12.
2. In this cell, type '=AVERAGE(B3:B15)'. Alternately, type '=AVERAGE('. Then use the mouse to select cells B3:B15, and close the brackets by typing ')'.

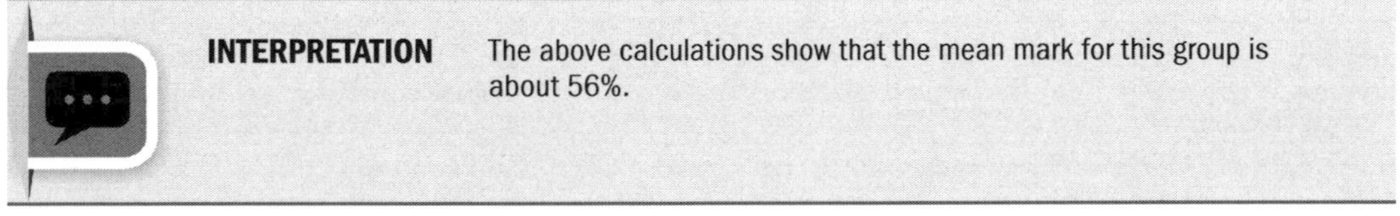

INTERPRETATION The above calculations show that the mean mark for this group is about 56%.

The mean for frequency table data

In this section, we extend the calculation of data descriptors for a set of numbers to data that are arranged in frequency tables. A frequency table, as discussed in the previous chapter, is a simple data table that shows how many times entities fall into every category (i.e. the frequencies of the entities).

We will consider two types of frequency tables: tables constructed from discrete data and tables constructed from continuous data.

- A table constructed from discrete data is a frequency table in which the data values are discrete in nature and the classes are simply the unique values in the data set. Table 3.2 shows the general form of a frequency table based on discrete data. There are k unique values (or classes) in this table and the unique values are denoted by m_i. The number of times that the value m_i occurs is denoted by the frequency f_i. Note that the sum of the f_i-values is equal to n, the sample size, i.e. $\sum_{i=1}^{k} f_i = n$.

Table 3.2: General form of a frequency table based on discrete data

CLASS (UNIQUE VALUES OF DISCRETE DATA)	FREQUENCIES
m_1	f_1
m_2	f_2
$\vdots$	$\vdots$
m_k	f_k

- A table constructed from continuous data is a frequency table in which the data are continuous in nature and the classes are intervals of values. Table 3.3 below shows the general form of this type of table. There are k class intervals in which the data points might lie, each with its own class midpoint, m_i, and associated class frequency, f_i. Note that the sum of the f_i-values is equal to n, the sample size, i.e. $\sum_{i=1}^{k} f_i = n$.

Table 3.3: General form of a frequency table based on continuous data

CLASS INTERVAL	CLASS MIDPOINT	FREQUENCIES
Class interval 1	m_1	f_1
Class interval 2	m_2	f_2
$\vdots$	$\vdots$	$\vdots$
Class interval k	m_k	f_k

In both of these frequency tables, the calculation of the mean is based on the same idea: we have to convert the grouped frequency table *back* into raw data and then calculate the mean from the new raw data. We do this by creating a new raw data set consisting of the values m_i, each one repeated f_i times. This is handled differently for each type of table.

Creating approximate raw data from frequency tables

- For frequency tables in which the data values are discrete in nature, we can create a raw data set by repeating each of the unique values f_i times. For example, suppose our data are based on the variable 'number of children in a household' collected from $n = 10$ households. For the observed data, this variable only has the unique values 0, 1, 2 and 3, and is given in the frequency table below (Table 3.4).

Table 3.4: Frequency table of the number of children in a household

UNIQUE VALUES (NUMBER OF CHILDREN)	FREQUENCY
0	3
1	4
2	1
3	2

We can easily convert this frequency table into the following raw data set:

0	0	0	1	1	1	1	2	3	3

Note that each unique item, m_i, occurs f_i times. The sample mean is then calculated as:

$$\begin{aligned} \overline{X} &= \frac{0+0+0+1+1+1+1+2+3+3}{10} \\ &= \frac{(0 \times 3)+(1 \times 4)+(2 \times 1)+(3 \times 2)}{10} \\ &= \frac{12}{10} \\ &= 1.2 \end{aligned}$$

The sample mean number of children in the 10 households is therefore 1.2.

- For frequency tables in which the data are continuous in nature, each class is an interval of potential values, and as a result, we do not know the exact values of the f_i data points that lie in the intervals. For example, suppose that we have a frequency table based on the variable 'weekly expenses in rand' collected from a small business over an $n = 12$ week period. The data are summarised in the table below (Table 3.5).

Table 3.5: Frequency table created from the weekly expenses of a small business over 12 weeks

CLASS INTERVAL (EXPENSES IN RAND)	CLASS MIDPOINT	FREQUENCIES
[600; 800)	700	1
[800; 1 000)	900	7
[1 000; 1 200)	1 100	3
[1 200; 1 400)	1 300	1

In this table, we see that there are, for example, three observed data points in the interval [1 000; 1 200). Unfortunately, we do not know the exact values of these three observations (the original data values could have been anything between R1 000 and R1 199,99). In this case, *we must make the assumption* that all three observations are equal to a specific value; the most logical choice being the class midpoint. Therefore, when we convert this table into a raw data set, we get:

700	900	900	900	900	900	900	900	1 100	1 100	1 100	1 300

Note that each class midpoint, m_i, is repeated f_i times.

The sample mean is then calculated as:

$$\begin{aligned}\overline{X} &= \frac{700 + 900 + 900 + 900 + 900 + 900 + 900 + 900 + 1\,100 + 1\,100 + 1\,100 + 1\,300}{12} \\ &= \frac{(700 \times 1) + (900 \times 7) + (1\,100 \times 3) + (1\,300 \times 1)}{12} \\ &= \frac{11\,600}{12} \\ &= 966.67\end{aligned}$$

The sample mean expenditure for one week in this sample of 12 weeks is therefore R966.67.

SAMPLE MEAN FOR FREQUENCY TABLE DATA

In general, the formula for the mean of frequency table data is given by:

$$\overline{X} = \frac{m_1 f_1 + m_2 f_2 + \ldots + m_k f_k}{n} = \frac{1}{n}\sum_{i=1}^{k} m_i f_i \qquad (3.2)$$

$f_1, f_2, \ldots, f_k$ = the observed frequencies in each class.

$m_1, m_2, \ldots, m_k$ = the class midpoints in each class.

k = the number of classes in the table.

$n = \sum_{i=1}^{k} f_i$ = the size of the sample.

Note that in formula (3.2), and in the examples shown above, we need to calculate the product $m_i f_i$ for each class. The following example illustrates a structured method for doing these calculations by hand and with Excel.

WORKED EXAMPLES

EXAMPLE 3.2

A small insurance company records the number of claims it receives each day for a period of 40 days. They are concerned that the number of claims being processed by their offices is unusually high, and they would like to determine what the average or typical number of claims per day is. The frequency table of insurance claims processed each day is given in Table 3.6.

Table 3.6: Frequency table of insurance claims processed each day

CLAIMS	1	2	3	4	5	6	7	8	9	10
FREQUENCY	3	4	4	5	5	7	5	3	3	1

To determine the typical number of claims per day, we calculate the sample mean number of insurance claims processed each day from this table.

We can calculate the mean for this data set by hand using formula (3.2) above. However, to simplify the calculation, we can first calculate all of the products $m_i f_i$ in a table, as shown in Table 3.7.

Table 3.7: Calculation of the products $m_i f_i$ for Example 3.2

CLAIMS (m_i)	FREQUENCY (f_i)	$m_i f_i$
1	3	3
2	4	8
3	4	12
4	5	20
5	5	25
6	7	42
7	5	35
8	3	24
9	3	27
10	1	10
	$n = \sum_{i=1}^{10} f_i = 40$	$\sum_{i=1}^{10} m_i f_i = 206$

Therefore, from formula (3.2), the sample mean is given by:

$$\begin{aligned}\overline{X} &= \frac{1}{40}\sum_{i=1}^{10} m_i f_i \\ &= \frac{206}{40} \\ &= 5.15\end{aligned}$$

We can do this calculation more easily and efficiently in Excel using the 'SUMPRODUCT' and 'SUM' functions. Figure 3.2 illustrates the Excel solution.

	A	B	C	D	E	F	G
1	**Example 3.2: Claims received each day**						
2	**Claims per day, *m***	**Frequency, *f***	***mf***				
3	1	3	3	=A3*B3	**Formula method**		
4	2	4	8	=A4*B4			
5	3	4	12	=A5*B5	sum *f* =	40	=SUM(B3:B12)
6	4	5	20	=A6*B6	sum *mf* =	206	=SUM(C3:C12)
7	5	5	25	=A7*B7			
8	6	7	42	=A8*B8	mean =	5.15	=F6/F5
9	7	5	35	=A9*B9			
10	8	3	24	=A10*B10	**Excel function method**		
11	9	3	27	=A11*B11			
12	10	1	10	=A12*B12	mean =	5.15	=SUMPRODUCT(A3:A12,B3:B12)/SUM(B3:B12)
13							
14							

Figure 3.2: Excel spreadsheet calculations for Example 3.2 – the sample mean for frequency table data

The claims per day have been input into cells A3:A12 and the frequencies into cells B3:B12. The Excel function method involves the following steps:

1. Select cell F12.
2. In this cell, type '=SUMPRODUCT(A3:A12,B3:B12)/SUM(B3:B12)'.

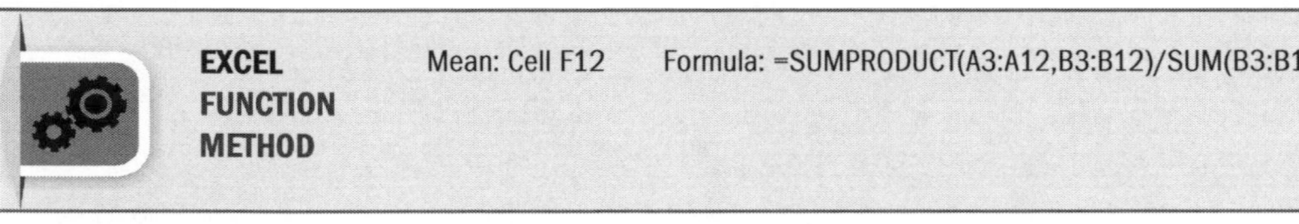

EXCEL FUNCTION METHOD Mean: Cell F12 Formula: =SUMPRODUCT(A3:A12,B3:B12)/SUM(B3:B12)

INTERPRETATION The value of the summary statistic, the mean, is:

Mean = 5.15 (Cells F8 and F12)

The mean number of claims per day is 5.15.

Example 3.2 made use of a frequency table constructed from discrete data. The next example looks at what happens when the frequency table is constructed from continuous data.

WORKED EXAMPLES

EXAMPLE 3.3

Consider the frequency table of distances travelled by 120 salesmen.

Table 3.8: Frequency table of the distances travelled by 120 salesmen

CLASS (DISTANCE TRAVELLED IN km)	CLASS MIDPOINT, (m_i)	FREQUENCY (f_i)
[400; 420)	410	12
[420; 440)	430	27
[440; 460)	450	34
[460; 480)	470	24
[480; 500)	490	15
[500; 520)	510	8
		$n = \sum_{i=1}^{6} f_i = 120$

Calculate the sample mean distance travelled by the 120 salesmen.

We can calculate the mean of this data set by first calculating the products, $m_i f_i$, shown in Table 3.9.

Table 3.9: Calculating the products $m_i f_i$ for the frequency table in Example 3.3

CLASS	CLASS MIDPOINT, (m_i)	FREQUENCY (f_i)	$m_i f_i$
[400; 420)	410	12	4 920
[420; 440)	430	27	11 610
[440; 460)	450	34	15 300
[460; 480)	470	24	11 280
[480; 500)	490	15	7 350
[500; 520)	510	8	4 080
		$n = \sum_{i=1}^{6} f_i = 120$	$\sum_{i=1}^{6} m_i f_i = 54\,540$

Using formula (3.2), the sample mean is then given by:

$$\begin{aligned}\overline{X} &= \frac{1}{120}\sum_{i=1}^{6} m_i f_i \\ &= \frac{54\,540}{120} \\ &= 454.5\end{aligned}$$

Figure 3.3 illustrates how we can obtain the same answer using the Excel functions 'SUMPRODUCT' and 'SUM'.

	A	B	C	D	E	F	G	H	I
1	Example 3.3: Distances travelled by salesmen								
2	Classes	Class midpoints, m	Frequency, f	mf					
3	[400; 420)	410	12	4920	=B3*C3		Formula method		
4	[420; 440)	430	27	11610	=B4*C4				
5	[440; 460)	450	34	15300	=B5*C5		sum f=	120	=SUM(C3:C8)
6	[460; 480)	470	24	11280	=B6*C6		sum mf=	54540	=SUM(D3:D8)
7	[480; 500)	490	15	7350	=B7*C7				
8	[500; 520)	510	8	4080	=B8*C8		mean=	454.5	=H6/H5
9									
10							Excel function method		
11									
12							mean=	454.5	=SUMPRODUCT(B3:B8,C3:C8)/SUM(C3:C8)
13									

Figure 3.3: Excel spreadsheet calculations for Example 3.3 – the sample mean for frequency table data

The class midpoints have been input into cells B3:B8 and the frequencies into cells C3:C8. The Excel function method involves the following steps:

1. Select cell H12.
2. In this cell, type '=SUMPRODUCT(B3:B8,C3:C8)/SUM(C3:C8)'.

EXCEL FUNCTION METHOD Mean: Cell H12 Formula: =SUMPRODUCT(B3:B8,C3:C8)/SUM(C3:C8)

INTERPRETATION The mean distance travelled by the 120 salesmen is 454.5 km.

3.1.2 The median

An alternative method of calculating the measure of central tendency is the *median*. The median is literally the 'middle' number *if you list the numbers in order of size.* As a result, the median is the observation in the data set situated such that 50% of the observations are smaller than it and 50% of the observations are larger. We use the notation $\widetilde{X}$ to denote the sample median.

We usually use the median instead of the mean when there might be outliers in the data set. This is because the median is robust against extreme values.

WORKED EXAMPLES

EXAMPLE 3.4

The variable 'amount of time spent in the casino (hours)' is recorded from seven patrons visiting the Sun City resort and casino. The data collected from the n = 7 patrons is *first sorted* (or ordered) and then displayed as shown in Table 3.10.

Table 3.10: Data describing the amount of hours spent in a casino

$X_1 = 1.5$	$X_2 = 2$	$X_3 = 3$	$X_4 = 5.5$	$X_5 = 7$	$X_6 = 8$	$X_7 = 42$

Determine the typical amount of time that patrons spend in the casino.

It is clear from the data set that patron number 7 has spent a lot more time in the casino than the other patrons, and we can consider this value to be an outlier (when compared to the other values). The sample mean for these data is approximately 9.86 hours, which is perhaps not a typical amount of time that people spend in casinos. (Notice that this measure of location is higher than all but one of the observations in the data set.) To calculate the median (a measure of central tendency that is not influenced by outliers), we have to find the 'middle' value in the *ordered* data set. We determine the middle value by calculating the index at which it occurs. The *index* value of the median (the middle value) is equal to $\frac{(n+1)}{2}$. Therefore, we can express the median as:

The median, $\widetilde{X}$, is the $\frac{n+1}{2}$th value in an ordered data set.

For our example, $\frac{(n+1)}{2} = \frac{(7+1)}{2} = \frac{8}{2} = 4$, and so the median is the 4th value in the ordered data set, i.e. $\widetilde{X} = 5.5$. Note that in this example, the value of n is an *odd number* and the middle value of the data set is easy to find. The next example will show how to determine the median when the sample size, n, is an *even number*.

WORKED EXAMPLES

EXAMPLE 3.5

A butcher working in a Shoprite store has a special mix that he uses in his boerewors sausage. However, the ingredients are very expensive and he needs to reduce the quantities of these ingredients in his recipe. Of course, he is concerned that changing the recipe will affect the sales of the sausage. So, over the next 10 days he records the quantities sold. The data set in Table 3.11 represents the variable 'quantity of sausages sold per day (kilograms)' over a 10-day period (the data have been sorted already).

Table 3.11: Data set describing the amount of boerewors sausage sold over 10 days

7.3	7.4	8.1	8.7	8.8	9.4	9.5	10.9	11.4	12.0

Determine the median amount of boerewors sausage sold over the 10-day period.

To determine the median of the amount of sausage sold, we note first that $n = 10$ and that the median is the $\frac{(n+1)}{2} = \frac{(10+1)}{2} = 5.5$th value in the ordered data set. Unfortunately, the index is a fraction, so do we use the 5th value or the 6th value as the median? We in fact use the average of the 5th and 6th values. The median for this ordered data set is then:

$$\begin{aligned}\widetilde{X} &= \frac{\text{5th ordered value} + \text{6th ordered value}}{2} \\ &= \frac{8.8 + 9.4}{2} \\ &= 9.1\end{aligned}$$

The median quantity of sausage sold is therefore 9.1 kg.

Properties of the median

- *The median can only be calculated for quantitative data*: Like the mean, we can only calculate the mean of numerical, quantitative data. The median does not apply to qualitative data, even qualitative data that has been numerically coded.
- *The median does not make use of all observations*: As the median is only the 'middle' value in an ordered data set, it is not based on every observation.
- *Each variable in a data set will have only one median value*: There will only be one median value for a collection of data. It is unique in the data set.
- *The median is not sensitive to outliers*: As we do not use all of the values in a data set to calculate the median (particularly because it uses only the middle value), it is not influenced by outlier values.

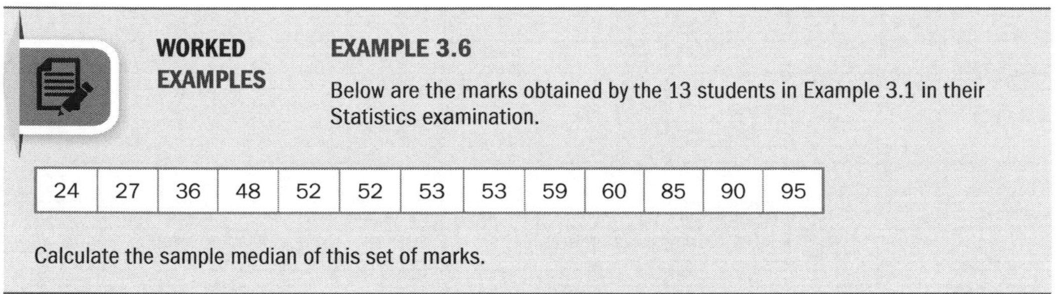

WORKED EXAMPLES

EXAMPLE 3.6

Below are the marks obtained by the 13 students in Example 3.1 in their Statistics examination.

24	27	36	48	52	52	53	53	59	60	85	90	95

Calculate the sample median of this set of marks.

We obtain the median for these marks by first noting that the marks have been sorted from smallest to largest, and then by calculating the index of the median:

$$\tilde{X} = \frac{n+1}{2}\text{th value in the ordered data set}$$
$$= \frac{13+1}{2}\text{th value in the ordered data set}$$
$$= 7\text{th value in the ordered data set}$$
$$= 53$$

The median mark is therefore 53%.

We can also use the Excel spreadsheet function 'MEDIAN' to calculate the median of this data set. The example is illustrated in Figure 3.4.

	A	B	C	D	E	F
1	**Example 3.1: Marks obtained in a Statistics exam by 13 students**					
2		**Statistics marks**				
3		24				
4		27		**Excel function method**		
5		36				
6		48		median =	53	=MEDIAN(B3:B15)
7		52				
8		52				
9		53				
10		53				
11		59				
12		60				
13		85				
14		90				
15		95				

Figure 3.4: Excel spreadsheet calculations for Example 3.1 – the sample median

The data has been input into cells B3:B15. The Excel function method involves the following steps:

1. Select cell E6.
2. In this cell, type '=MEDIAN(B3:B15)'

EXCEL FUNCTION METHOD

Median: Cell E6 Formula: =MEDIAN(B3:B15)

INTERPRETATION

From the ordered list of numbers, you can see that the median Statistics examination mark is 53%. In this example, the mean and median are reasonably close (56% compared to 53%), and the distance between the lowest mark and the median (53 – 24 = 29) is less than the distance between the largest value and the median (95 – 53 = 42). Note that the median is not influenced by the presence of very small or very large data values in the data set (extreme values or outliers). If there were a small number of these extreme values (or outliers), we would use the median instead of the mean to represent the measure of central tendency. We will explore this issue in greater detail when we discuss measuring *skewness* in Section 3.3.

NOTE

In this example, the median was calculated to be the 7th number in the ordered list of data values. If an extra value is introduced into the data set, the calculation would be a little more complex. For example, a 14th student is introduced who received a mark of 16%, in which case, the data set would become (n = 14).

Table 3.12: Raw data of the Statistics marks of 14 students

16	24	27	36	48	52	52	53	53	59	60	85	90	95

The median would then be:

$$\tilde{X} = \frac{n+1}{2}\text{th value in the ordered data set}$$

$$= \frac{14+1}{2}\text{th value in the ordered data set}$$

$$= 7.5\text{th value in the ordered data set}$$

The position of the median would now be the 7.5th number in the ordered data set. To help you understand what this means, we can rewrite this into a slightly different form:

$$\tilde{X} = \frac{\text{8th ordered value + 7th ordered value}}{2}$$

$$= \frac{53+52}{2}$$

$$= 52.5$$

The median statistics examination mark would then be 52.5%.

The median for frequency table data

We will start the discussion on calculating the sample median from a frequency table by first looking at a frequency table constructed from continuous data. To find these values, we need to use a *cumulative frequency distribution* and *cumulative frequency polygon* (ogive). We can approximate the median either by a formal calculation or by using a graphical method.

- The **formula method** involves first identifying the 'median class', i.e. the class in the frequency table that contains the $\frac{(n+1)}{2}$th observation. Once you have identified this, you can use formula (3.3) below to estimate the median.

SAMPLE MEDIAN FOR FREQUENCY DATA

$$\tilde{X} = L + \frac{C\left(\frac{(n+1)}{2} - F_{below}\right)}{f_{med}} \tag{3.3}$$

- L = the lower class boundary of the median class
- C = the median class width
- F_{below} = the cumulative frequency before the median class (i.e. the number of observations less than the lower bound of the 'median class')
- f_{med} = the frequency within the median class
- n = the total frequency

- The **graphical method** involves using the ogive to read off the median value. To read the value off the graph, begin on the vertical axis at the position $\frac{n}{2}$ and then find the value on the horizontal axis associated with the value on the vertical axis, as illustrated in Figure 3.5.

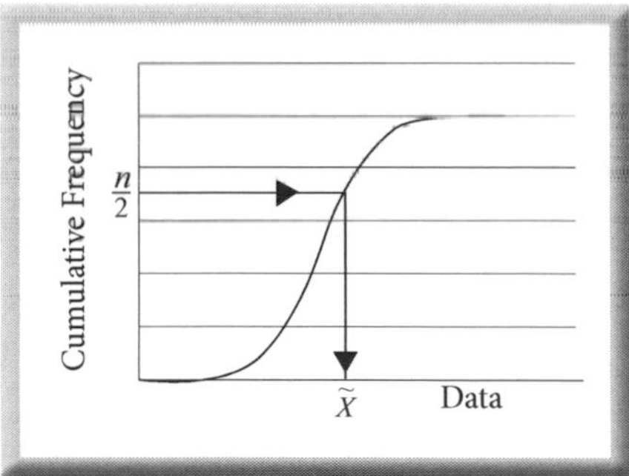

Figure 3.5: General graphical method for approximating the median

WORKED EXAMPLES

EXAMPLE 3.7

Table 3.8 in Example 3.3 gave the distances travelled by 120 salesmen. Calculate the sample median distance travelled by the salesmen using both the formula and graphical method.

You find the median by first constructing the cumulative frequency table (see Table 3.13) from the frequency table in Table 3.8.

Table 3.13: Cumulative frequency table based on Table 3.8 in Example 3.3

CLASS LIMIT	CUMULATIVE FREQUENCY (F_i)
< 400	0
< 420	12
< 440	39
< 460	73
< 480	97
< 500	112
< 520	120

We know that the median value will lie at $\frac{(n+1)}{2} = \frac{(120+1)}{2} = 60.5$th ordered value in the data set. From the cumulative frequency table, we see that the 60.5th value lies between the class boundaries 440 and 460, i.e. the median class is [440; 460). We can also identify the elements used in formula (3.3) from the cumulative frequency table. We find the following values:

- $L = 440$
- $C = 459.5 - 439.5 = 20$
- $F_{\text{below}} = 39$
- $f_{\text{med}} = 34$
- $n = 120$

Using formula (3.3), we can determine the median as:

$$\tilde{X} = L + \frac{C\left(\frac{(n+1)}{2} - F_{\text{below}}\right)}{f_{\text{med}}}$$

$$= 440 + \frac{20\left(\frac{(120+1)}{2} - 39\right)}{34}$$

$$= 452.6$$

The sample median distance travelled is therefore 452.6 km. This is quite close to the value we obtained for the sample mean (454 km). We should expect this because the histogram for the distance travelled looks *symmetrical*. We will explore the concept of symmetry and how symmetrical a distribution is when we discuss the concept of skewness (see Section 3.3).

To use the graphical method to calculate the sample median, first construct the ogive from the cumulative frequency table as shown in the example below. Next, calculate the value of $\frac{n}{2} = \frac{120}{2} = 60$ and read off the value from the vertical axis to find the corresponding value on the horizontal axis as shown in Figure 3.6. By reading off the graph in this way, we find that the median is approximately equal to 452 km.

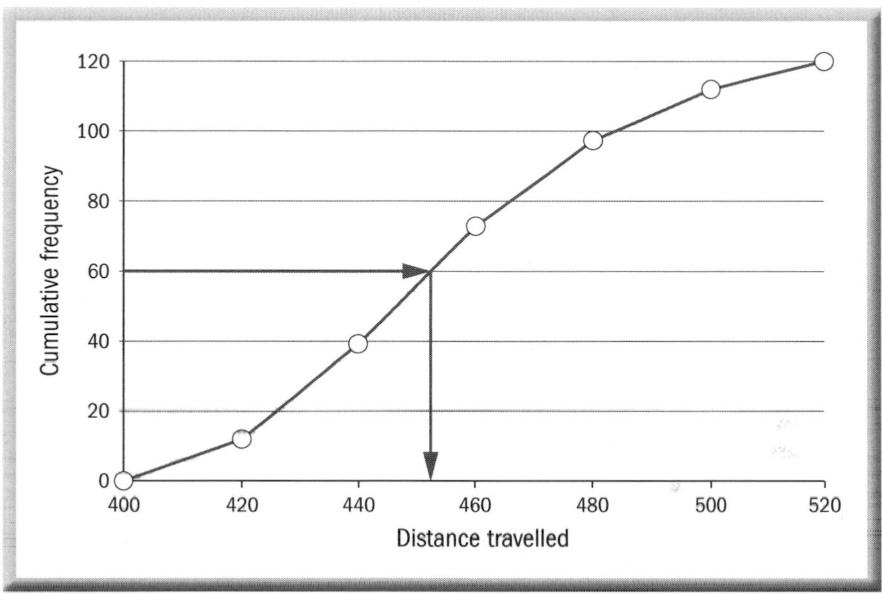

Figure 3.6: Ogive based on Table 3.8 in Example 3.3 with arrows indicating the location of the median

3.1.3 The mode

The final method that we can use to determine the central tendency of the data is the *mode*. The mode is defined as the value that occurs most frequently in a data set. It can be used for both numerical (quantitative) and categorical (qualitative) data variables.

Properties of the mode

- *The mode can be calculated for quantitative or qualitative data*: Since the mode represents the value that occurs the most often, we can use it for both qualitative and quantitative data sets.
- *Each variable in a data set can have more than one mode*: The value that occurs most often in a data set does not have to be unique, i.e. two or three separate values could all appear in the data set the same number of times, resulting in multiple modes.
- *The mode is not sensitive to outliers*: Outlier values are, by definition, very rare and so will not influence the mode since they occur the *least* often in a data set. Outliers do not usually affect the occurrence of the most frequent values in a data set, and so the mode is not influenced by these extreme values at all.

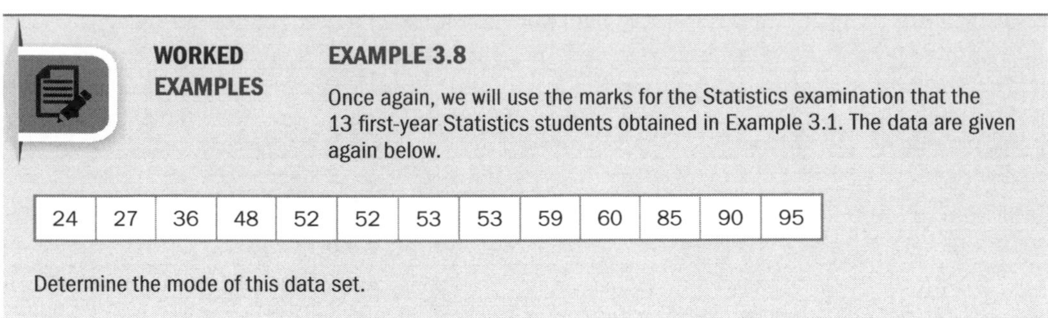

WORKED EXAMPLES

EXAMPLE 3.8

Once again, we will use the marks for the Statistics examination that the 13 first-year Statistics students obtained in Example 3.1. The data are given again below.

24	27	36	48	52	52	53	53	59	60	85	90	95

Determine the mode of this data set.

You should be able to see from this simple data set that the values 52 and 53 occur the most frequently. This data set thus exhibits two modal values: 52 and 53.

The Excel spreadsheet solution uses the Excel function 'MODE.SNGL' to determine the mode. You could also use the 'MODE' function, but it is deprecated in newer versions of Excel.

	A	B	C	D	E	F	G
1	**Example 3.1: Marks obtained in a Statistics exam by 13 students**						
2		**Statistics marks**					
3		24		**Excel function method**			
4		27					
5		36		mode =	52	=MODE.SNGL(B3:B15)	
6		48					
7		52					
8		52					
9		53					
10		53					
11		59					
12		60					
13		85					
14		90					
15		95					

Figure 3.7: Excel spreadsheet calculations for Example 3.1 – the sample mode

Figure 3.7 shows how the data from Table 3.1 were inserted into an Excel spreadsheet in the cells B3:B15. The Excel solution for the mode is also shown. The Excel function method involves the following steps:

1. Select cell E6
2. In this cell, type '=MODE.SNGL(B3:B15)'

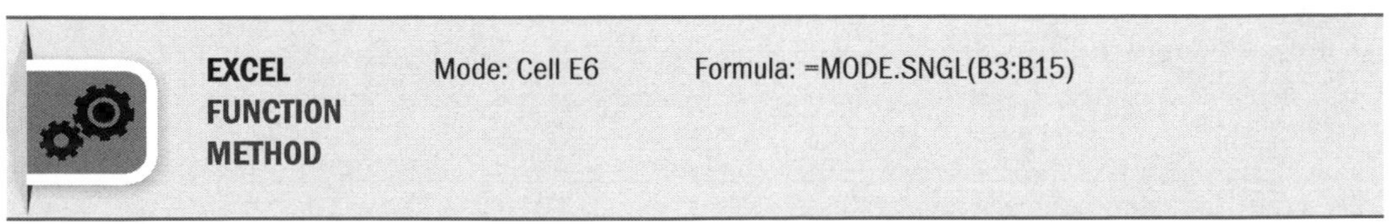

EXCEL FUNCTION METHOD

Mode: Cell E6 Formula: =MODE.SNGL(B3:B15)

NOTE

As you can see, Excel provides only one solution for the mode (52), even though there are two modal values in the data set (52 and 53).

The mode for frequency table data

Using the data in Example 3.3, we will now explain the methods that we can use to calculate the mode for frequency table data. Note that since we define the mode as the value that occurs most often in a data set (i.e. the value with the highest corresponding frequency), it can be determined directly from a frequency distribution or a histogram. Consider the frequency table in Example 3.3. You can see that the most frequently occurring class is the class '[440; 460)'. This class is known as the *modal class*. If we look at the histograms associated with this example, the modal class is very apparent, i.e. it is the class with the tallest rectangle. After you have identified the modal class, you can now approximate the mode using a formula or a graphical method

Using the formula method, we estimate the mode using formula (3.4).

SAMPLE MODE FOR FREQUENCY DATA

$$\text{Mode} = L + \left(\frac{f_{\text{mod}} - f_{\text{below}}}{2f_{\text{mod}} - f_{\text{below}} - f_{\text{above}}}\right)C \qquad (3.4)$$

- L = the lower class boundary of the modal class
- f_{below} = the frequency of the class below the modal class
- f_{mod} = the frequency of the modal class
- f_{above} = the frequency of the class above the modal class
- C = the modal class width

NOTE

This formula only works if the modal class and the two adjacent classes are of equal width.

Using the information in Example 3.3, $L = 439.5$, $f_{\text{below}} = 27$, $f_{\text{mod}} = 34$, $f_{\text{above}} = 24$ and $C = 20$. Substituting these values into formula (3.4) we get the approximate value of the mode:

$$\text{Mode} = L + \left(\frac{f_{\text{mod}} - f_{\text{below}}}{2f_{\text{mod}} - f_{\text{below}} - f_{\text{above}}}\right)\text{C}$$

$$= 440 + \left(\frac{34 - 27}{2(34) - 27 - 24}\right) \times 20$$

$$= 448.24$$

Therefore, the modal distance travelled is approximately 448 km.

Construct the first line from the top left corner of the modal class's rectangle to the right side (stopping at the level of the next class's height). The second line is drawn from the top right of the rectangle to the left side (stopping at the level of the previous class's height).

Alternatively, we can estimate the mode graphically using the histogram and then construct lines to approximate the mode. From the histogram created from the data in Example 3.3, you can see that class [440; 460) is the modal class, meaning that the mode will lie within this class. We can then use the frequencies of the two adjacent classes ([420; 440) and [460; 480)) to estimate the value of the mode as follows:

- Construct the two crossed diagonals (the dashed lines in Figure 3.8). Construct the first line from the top left corner of the modal class's rectangle to the right side (stopping at the level of the next class's height). The second line is drawn from the top right of the rectangle to the left side (stopping at the level of the previous class's height).
- Drop a perpendicular from where these two lines meet down to the horizontal axis.
- Read the estimate value for the mode from the horizontal axis.

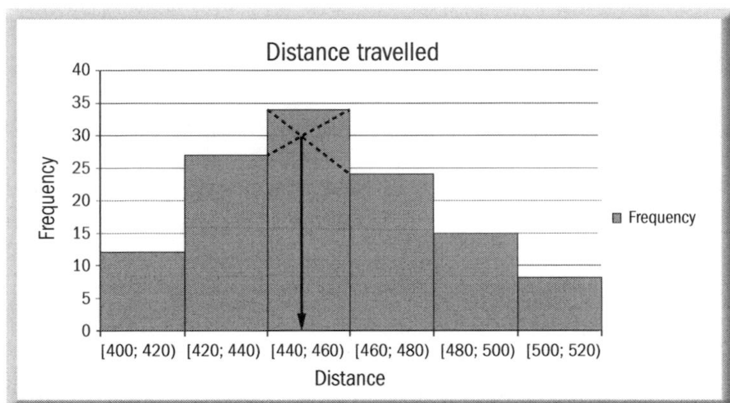

Figure 3.8: Using the histogram from Example 3.3 to approximate the mode

Figure 3.8 illustrates the graphical solution to estimating the modal value. From the histogram, the estimated value of the distance travelled is approximately 445 km.

3.1.4 The percentiles and quartiles

The final measures of location that we will discuss are percentiles and quartiles.

Quartiles are three statistics that we can use to divide a sample into four equal groups:

- The first quartile is the value such that 25% of the observations in the data set are smaller than the value and 75% are larger than the value. It is denoted by Q_1. The first quartile is sometimes also called the *lower quartile.*
- The second quartile is the value such that 50% of the observations in the data set are smaller than the value and 50% are larger than the value. The second quartile is equal to the median, and so it is denoted by either Q_2 or $\widetilde{X}$.

Quartiles Values that divide a sample of data into four groups, each containing an equal number of observations.

- The third quartile is the value such that 75% of the observations in the data set are smaller than the value and 25% are larger than the value. It is denoted Q_3. The third quartile is sometimes also called the *upper quartile.*

Percentiles divide a sample into 100 equal-sized groups and the xth percentile is defined as the value in the data set such that x% of the observations are smaller than it, and $(100 - x)$% of the observations are larger than it. It is denoted by P_x. For example, the 33% percentile is denoted by P_{33}.

Clearly, the quartiles (and the median) are simply special cases of percentiles. For example, the 50% percentile is the same as the median (or the second quartile), i.e. $P_{50} = Q_2 = \widetilde{X}$, the 25% percentile is equal to the first quartile, i.e. $P_{25} = Q_1$, and the 75% percentile is equal to the third quartile, i.e. $P_{75} = Q_3$.

As we can express all of these values in terms of percentiles, we will only focus on calculating the percentile values and then use the above relationships to determine the quartiles and the median. Calculating these percentiles is similar to the calculations we use to determine the median, except that they use different index values for each one.

To determine the value of the xth percentile in a data set, it is important *to first sort or order the data set from the smallest value to the largest value.* Once sorted, we can obtain the xth percentile, P_x, using the expression:

$$P_x = \frac{x}{100}(n+1)^{\text{th}} \text{ value in the ordered data set}$$

For example, in a sample of $n = 30$, the 15% percentile, P_{15}, will be the $\frac{15}{100}(30 + 1) = 4.65$th value in the ordered data set.

As with the median, the index value $\frac{x}{100}(n + 1)$ can result in a fraction. In order to determine the correct value associated with this index, you will need to carry out a further step.

The index value $\frac{x}{100}(n + 1)$ is a fraction value number that can be broken down into two parts:

- A 'whole number' part (for example, 0, 1, 2, 3, ... etc.) denoted by w
- A 'decimal' part (for example, 0.12, 0.67, 0.78, etc.) denoted by d

For example, the index number 7.85 can be broken up into $w = 7$ and $d = 0.85$ (note that $w + d = 7 + 0.85 = 7.85$). We can use this partitioning of the index value to find the percentile value from a set of ordered data values $X_1, X_2, X_3, \ldots, X_n$ as follows.

If the index $\frac{x}{100}(n + 1)$ is equal to a fraction with value $w + d$, then the $\frac{x}{100}(n + 1)$th value in the ordered data set (i.e. the xth percentile) is given by the following.

SAMPLE PERCENTILES

$$P_x = X_w + d \times (X_{w+1} - X_w) \tag{3.5}$$

- X_w = the wth ordered value in the data set.
- X_{w+1} = the $(w + 1)^{th}$ ordered value in the data set.
- w and d = the 'whole number' and 'decimal' part of the index number $\frac{x}{100}(n + 1)$, respectively (as described above).

WORKED EXAMPLES

EXAMPLE 3.9

Using the data in Example 3.1 again (given below), determine the sample 25% percentile (first quartile), the 33% percentile and the third quartile of this data set.

24	27	36	48	52	52	53	53	59	60	85	90	95

We obtain the 25% percentile (or first quartile) from this sorted data set by first calculating the index $\frac{25}{100}(n+1) = \frac{25}{100}(13+1) = \frac{25}{100}(14) = 3.5$

Note that we can express this index in terms of a whole number, $w = 3$ and a decimal number $d = 0.5$

Now, since $w = 3$ and $w + 1 = 4$, we must find the values $X_w = X_3 = 36$ and $X_{w+1} = X_4 = 48$. From formula (3.5), the 25% percentile is then:

$$\begin{aligned} Q_1 = P_{25} &= X_w + d \times (X_{w+1} - X_w) \\ &= X_3 + 0.5 \times (X_4 - X_3) \\ &= 36 + 0.5 \times (48 - 36) \\ &= 42 \end{aligned}$$

The first quartile Statistics examination mark is 42%.

INTERPRETATION You interpret the 25th percentile value of 42 as follows: 25% of students obtained a mark of less than or equal to 42.

Similarly, to obtain the 33% percentile, we first determine the index of the value: $\frac{33}{100}(n+1) = \frac{33}{100}(13+1) = \frac{33}{100}(14) = 4.62$. The index number expressed in terms of a whole number and a decimal is $w + d = 4 + 0.62 = 4.62$, i.e. $w = 4$ and $d = 0.62$. Note that $X_w = X_4 = 48$ and $X_{w+1} = X_5 = 52$. The 33% percentile is then:

$$\begin{aligned} P_{33} &= X_w + d \times (X_{w+1} - X_w) \\ &= X_4 + 0.62 \times (X_5 - X_4) \\ &= 48 + 0.62 \times (52 - 48) \\ &= 50.48 \end{aligned}$$

INTERPRETATION The 33rd percentile value of 50.48 indicates that 33% of the class obtained marks lower than or equal to 50.48.

Finally, for the third quartile (or 75% percentile) we begin by calculating the index value: $\frac{75}{100}(n+1) = \frac{75}{100}(13 + 1) = \frac{75}{100}(14) = 10.5$, which we can express in the form $w + d$ with $w = 10$ and $d = 0.5$. We then obtain the third quartile by noting that $X_w = X_{10} = 60$ and $X_{w+1} = X_{11} = 85$, and so we have:

$$\begin{aligned} Q_3 = P_{75} &= X_w + d \times (X_{w+1} - X_w) \\ &= X_{10} + 0.5 \times (X_{11} - X_{10}) \\ &= 60 + 0.5 \times (85 - 60) \\ &= 72.5 \end{aligned}$$

The third quartile Statistics examination mark is 72.5%.

INTERPRETATION You interpret the 75th percentile value of 72.5 as follows: 75% of students obtained a mark of less than or equal to 72.5.

Again, we can conduct all these calculations in Excel. The function that we use to calculate the percentiles is called 'PERCENTILE.EXC'. This function accepts two arguments: the data and a value between 0 and 1 indicating which percentile to calculate. For example, for P_{33} we would specify the value 0.33.

Figure 3.9 shows the explanation of the Excel spreadsheet solution.

	A	B	C	D	E	F
1	Example 3.1: Marks obtained in a Statistics exam by 13 students					
2		Statistics marks				
3		24		Excel function method		
4		27				
5		26		Q_1 =	42	=PERCENTILE.EXC(B3:B15,0.25)
6		48		P_{33} =	50.48	=PERCENTILE.EXC(B3:B15,0.33)
7		52		Q_3 =	72.5	=PERCENTILE.EXC(B3:B15,0.75)
8		52				
9		53				
10		53				
11		59				
12		60				
13		85				
14		90				
15		95				
16						

Figure 3.9: Excel spreadsheet calculations for Example 3.1 – the sample percentiles

In Figure 3.9, the data set in Table 3.1 is input into Cells B3:B15. The Excel function method to calculate, for example, the first quartile ($Q_1 = P_{25}$), involves the following steps:

- Select cell E6
- In this cell, type '=PERCENTILE.EXC(B3:B15,0.25)'

We can similarly obtain the 33rd and 75th percentiles by simply indicating the correct value in the second argument of the 'PERCENTILE.EXC' function, i.e. add '0.33' or '0.75' as the second arguments for the 33rd and 75th percentiles, respectively.

Note that we could also have used the function 'QUARTILE.EXC' instead of 'PERCENTILE.EXC' to calculate the quartiles of the data.

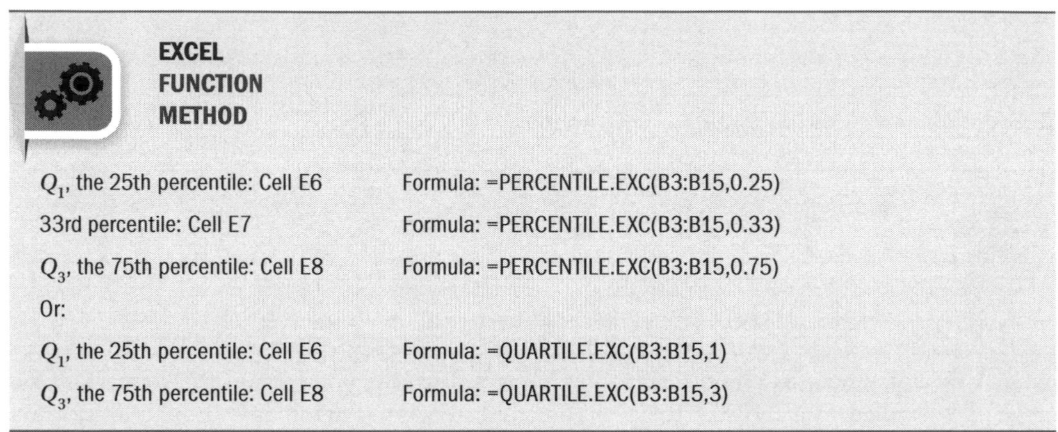

EXCEL FUNCTION METHOD

Q_1, the 25th percentile: Cell E6	Formula: =PERCENTILE.EXC(B3:B15,0.25)
33rd percentile: Cell E7	Formula: =PERCENTILE.EXC(B3:B15,0.33)
Q_3, the 75th percentile: Cell E8	Formula: =PERCENTILE.EXC(B3:B15,0.75)
Or:	
Q_1, the 25th percentile: Cell E6	Formula: =QUARTILE.EXC(B3:B15,1)
Q_3, the 75th percentile: Cell E8	Formula: =QUARTILE.EXC(B3:B15,3)

NOTE

- Remember that the 25th percentile is equivalent to the *first* quartile and the 75th percentile is equivalent to the *third* quartile.
- Unlike the median, which has a standard calculation method, there is no one standard for calculating quartiles and percentiles. There are a number of different definitions for quartiles and percentiles, which result in a number of different ways in which to calculate the value of quartiles and percentiles. Excel reflects this by providing two different functions for these calculations: 'PERCENTILE.EXC' and 'PERCENTILE.INC'. For this book, we will only make use of 'PERCENTILE.EXC', because it is identical to the procedure that we discussed to calculate percentiles by hand.

Percentiles and quartiles for frequency table data

Determining the values of individual percentiles from a frequency table is almost identical to the methods used to find the median values from a frequency table. We consider two methods to obtain these values: a formula-based numerical method and a graphical method based on the ogive. We will use Example 3.3 to illustrate these methods.

- To estimate the value of the percentile, P_x, using the formula method, begin by first determining the 'percentile class', i.e. the class that contains the $\frac{x}{100}(n+1)^{\text{th}}$ value of the data set. Once you have found the percentile class, you can use formula (3.6) to estimate the value at the xth percentile in a frequency table.

SAMPLE PERCENTILES FOR FREQUENCY TABLE DATA

$$P_x = L + \left(\frac{\frac{x}{100}(n+1) - F_{\text{before}}}{f_x} \right) \times C \quad (3.6)$$

- L = the lower class boundary of the percentile class
- C = the percentile class width
- F_{before} = the cumulative frequency before the percentile class
- f_x = the frequency within the percentile class
- n = the total frequency

To calculate the 10% percentile for Example 3.3, we find that $x = 10$, $n = 120$ and the position of the 10% percentile is the $\frac{10}{100}(120 + 1) = 12.1$th number in the data set. The percentile class is then [420; 440), and the elements of formula (3.6) are then $L = 420$, $C = 20$, $F_{\text{before}} = 12$ and $f_x = 27$. The 10% percentile is then:

$$P_{10} = L + \left(\frac{\frac{10}{100}(n+1) - F_{\text{before}}}{f_x} \right) \times C$$

$$= 420 + \left(\frac{\frac{10}{100}(120+1) - 12}{27} \right) \times 20$$

$$= 420.074$$

The 10th percentile distance travelled is approximately 420 km.

- When using the graphical method for the median, we used the cumulative frequency curve (or ogive) to find the sample median or 50% percentile. We can use the same technique to find any type of percentile. The technique rests on calculating the index used to look up values on the vertical axis. In the case of the median (50% percentile), we used the index value $\frac{n}{2} = \frac{50}{100}n$. However, generally we can find the x% percentile using the index $\frac{x}{100}n$. Once you have obtained the index, simply read off the value from the vertical axis and find the corresponding value on the horizontal axis. The result will be the approximate x% percentile, P_x.

Using the cumulative frequency table in Table 3.13, which was constructed from the data in Example 3.3, we created the cumulative frequency polygon, or ogive, in Figure 3.6. To determine the 10% percentile, P_{10}, we calculate the index $\frac{10}{100}n = \frac{10}{100}(120) = 12$, and we read this value from the vertical axis as shown in Figure 3.10.

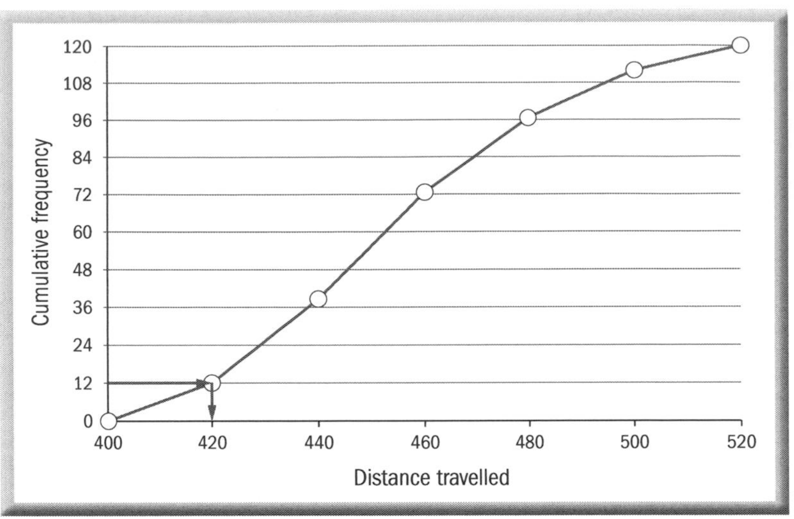

Figure 3.10: Ogive based on Table 3.8 in Example 3.3 with arrows indicating the location of P_{10}

We find that the 10% percentile, P_{10}, is approximately equal to 420 km.

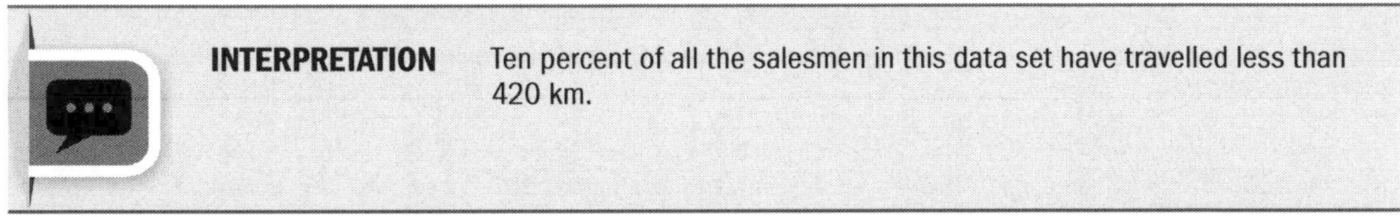

INTERPRETATION Ten percent of all the salesmen in this data set have travelled less than 420 km.

We can also estimate the two quartiles (Q_1 and Q_3) from the ogive by noting that $Q_1 = P_{25}$ and $Q_3 = P_{75}$. The index used to obtain the value of P_{25} is $\frac{25}{100}n = \frac{25}{100}(120) = 30$, and the index used to obtain the value of P_{75} is $\frac{75}{100}n = \frac{75}{100}(120) = 90$. We can read these two percentiles from the the ogive as shown in Figure 3.11.

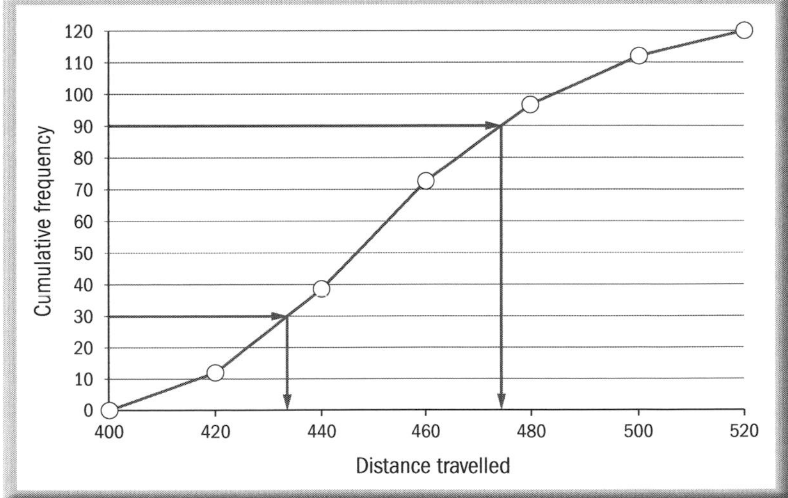

Figure 3.11: Ogive based on Table 3.8 in Example 3.3 with arrows indicating the location of Q_1 and Q_3

We observe that P_{25} (or Q_1) is approximately equal to 430 and that P_{75} (or Q_3) is approximately equal to 470.

INTERPRETATION Twenty-five percent of all the travelling salesmen in this data set have travelled less than 430 km, while 75% have travelled less than 470 km.

3.2 Measures of dispersion

In Section 3.1, we looked at the concept of central tendency, which provides a measure of the middle value of a set of data values. This, however, only gives a partial description of the distribution of a data set. We can obtain a more complete description by also obtaining a measure of **dispersion** (or spread) of the distribution. This type of measure indicates whether the values in the distribution cluster closely about an average or whether they are more dispersed. These measures of dispersion are particularly important when we want to compare distributions.

Dispersion The degree to which values are spread out on the number line.

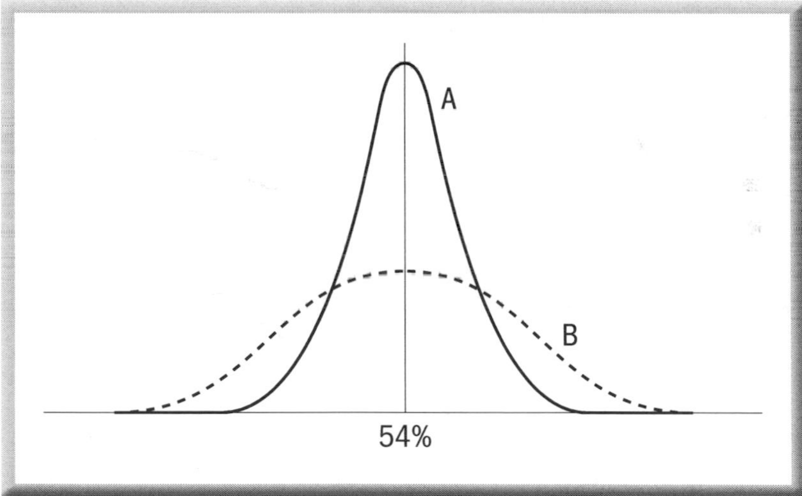

Figure 3.12: Two distributions with different dispersion patterns

Figure 13.12 shows two hypothetical distributions, which represents the distribution of final exam marks of matric students from two different high schools (A and B). You can see that the data values are both centred on the same value, i.e. the mean final exam marks of the students are both 54%, but the spread of high school B is much larger. This means that while the averages are the same for both schools, school B has a wider range of marks for its students, i.e. this school has many students that do both *very* well and *very* poorly. The marks of School A, on the other hand, are much more consistent; the majority of the students lie very close to the overall mean value with few deviations.

From Figure 3.12, we can see that both distributions, A and B, have the same mean values but distribution B is more spread out (or dispersed) than distribution A. Furthermore, distribution A is taller than distribution B. In this section, we shall explore methods we can use to put a number to this idea of dispersion. The methods we will explore include:

- range
- interquartile range
- semi-interquartile range
- variance
- standard deviation
- coefficient of variation.

Range The difference between the smallest and largest data values. It shows how widely spread the data are by considering the distance between the largest and smallest values.

Interquartile range A measure of the spread of the middle 50% of the data. It shows how widely spread the data are by considering the distance between the first and third quartiles calculated from a data set.

Variance Related to the sum of the squared distances of observations from their sample mean. This sum of squared values measures the dispersion of the observations.

Standard deviation The square root value of the variance. It measures dispersion in the same units as the original observations.

3.2.1 Range

The **range** is the simplest measure of dispersion and we use it to indicate the length of the span of values covered by the distribution. It is determined by finding the difference between the largest and smallest value in a data set.

SAMPLE RANGE

$$\text{Range} = X_{\text{max}} - X_{\text{min}} \tag{3.7}$$

- X_{min} = the smallest value in a data set
- X_{max} = the largest value in a data set

WORKED EXAMPLES

EXAMPLE 3.10

We have collected a data set consisting of observations on the mass of six laboratory rats. The collected data (in grams) are given in Table 3.14.

Table 3.14: Data collected on the mass of six laboratory rats

275	310	286	307	266	279

Determine the range of masses of the rats in the sample.

From formula (3.7), we can see that we first need to determine the smallest and largest values in the data set. The largest value in the data set is $X_{max} = 310$ and the smallest value is $X_{min} = 266$. The range of these data is then given by:

$$\begin{aligned}\text{Range} &= X_{max} - X_{min}\\ &= 310 - 266\\ &= 44\end{aligned}$$

The range is therefore equal to 44 for this simple data set.

Properties of the range

- *The range does not make use of all of the observations in the data set*: The range is based solely on the two extreme observations in the data set, and as such, it does not take into account the other values.
- *The range is heavily influenced by outliers*: Since the extreme values are used to determine the value of the range, if there is an outlier in the data set, it will appear in the calculation of the range. Unfortunately, because there are only two values used in calculating the range, this outlier will drastically affect the value of the range, making it seem as if the data are more widely spread out than they actually are.

WORKED EXAMPLES

EXAMPLE 3.11

Calculate the range of the Statistics examination data of first-year students from Example 3.1. The data are given below again.

24	27	36	48	52	52	53	53	59	60	85	90	95

The smallest and largest values in the data set are $X_{min} = 24$ and $X_{max} = 95$ respectively. The range of these data is therefore given by:

$$\begin{aligned}\text{Range} &= X_{max} - X_{min}\\ &= 95 - 24\\ &= 71\end{aligned}$$

The Excel solution involves using the functions 'MIN' and 'MAX' to obtain the smallest and largest values in the data set respectively.

	A	B	C	D	E	F
1	**Example 3.1: Marks obtained in a Statistics exam by 13 students**					
2		**Statistics marks**				
3		24				
4		27		**Excel function method**		
5		26				
6		48		Max =	95	=MAX(B3:B15)
7		52		Min =	24	=MIN(B3:B15)
8		52		Range =	71	=E6-E7
9		53				
10		53				
11		59				
12		60				
13		85				
14		90				
15		95				
16						

Figure 3.13: Excel spreadsheet calculations for Example 3.1 – the sample range

Figure 3.13 illustrates the Excel solution for the range of the data entered into cells B3:B15. The Excel function method involves the following steps:

- Select cell E6
- In this cell, type '=MAX(B3:B15)'
- Select cell E7
- In this cell, type '=MIN(B3:B15)'
- Select cell E8.
- In this cell, type '=E6–E7'

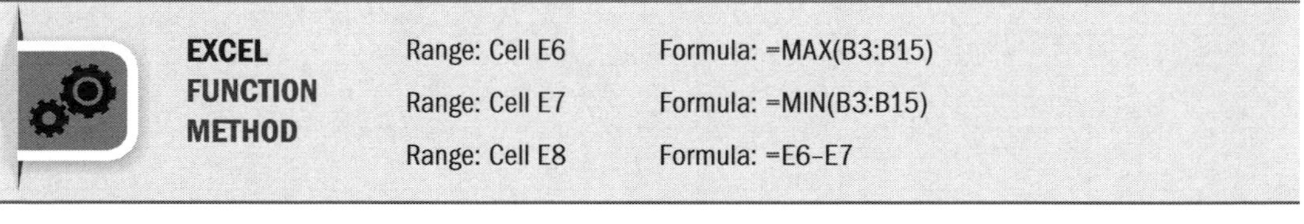

EXCEL FUNCTION METHOD		
	Range: Cell E6	Formula: =MAX(B3:B15)
	Range: Cell E7	Formula: =MIN(B3:B15)
	Range: Cell E8	Formula: =E6–E7

INTERPRETATION The range for the Statistics examination marks implies that the achieved marks are scattered over 71 marks between the highest and lowest mark.

The range for frequency tables

If we have data that are in the form of a grouped frequency table, then we use the values of the upper and lower class bounds of the first and last classes in the table to calculate the range. Thus, for a table with k classes, the formula is given as follows.

SAMPLE RANGE FOR FREQUENCY TABLE DATA

$$\text{Range} = UCB_k - LCB_1 \tag{3.8}$$

- LCB_1 = the lower class bound for the first class.
- UCB_k = the upper class bound for the kth (or last) class.

In Example 3.3 (distances travelled by salesmen) there are $k = 6$ classes, and the lower bound of the first class is $LCB_1 = 400$ and the upper bound of the last class is $UCB_6 = 520$. From formula (3.8), the range is thus:

$$\begin{aligned}\text{Range} &= UCB_6 - LCB_1\\ &= 520 - 400\\ &= 120\end{aligned}$$

The range of values for the distances travelled by the salesmen is thus 120 km.

3.2.2 Interquartile range and semi-interquartile range

We mentioned above that the range is sensitive to outlier values, i.e. outliers cause the value of the range to increase, which gives a false impression of the spread of the data. Two measures of dispersion that are more suitable when the data contain outliers are the interquartile range and semi-interquartile range. We calculate the interquartile range by taking the difference between the third and first quartile. We use this range to provide a measure of spread within a data set that contains extreme data values. The interquartile range is not greatly affected by extreme data values in the data set and it is considered to be a good measure of spread for skewed distributions. The interquartile range is denoted *IQR*.

SAMPLE INTERQUARTILE RANGE

$$IQR = Q_3 - Q_1 \tag{3.9}$$

- Q_1 = the sample first quartile
- Q_3 = the sample third quartile

The semi-interquartile range (denoted *SIQR*) is another measure of spread. It is one-half of the interquartile range.

SAMPLE SEMI-INTERQUARTILE RANGE

$$SIQR = \frac{IQR}{2} = \frac{Q_3 - Q_1}{2} \tag{3.10}$$

- IQR = the sample interquartile range
- Q_1 = the sample first quartile
- Q_3 = the sample third quartile

Properties of the interquartile range and semi-interquartile range

- *The IQR and SIQR do not make use of all of the observations in the data set*: Like the range, only two observations are used to calculate the *IQR* and *SIQR*, meaning that not all of the observations are considered.
- *The IQR and SIQR are robust against outliers*: The fact that the smallest 25% of the data set and the largest 25% of the data set are 'trimmed' off in calculating these ranges means that extreme values like outliers are almost entirely ignored. The *IQR* and the *SIQR* provide a better idea of the spread of the data by only focusing on how much variation there is in the middle 50% of the data.

WORKED EXAMPLES

EXAMPLE 3.12

Calculate the interquartile range and the semi-interquartile range of the marks obtained in the Statistics examination from Example 3.1. The data are given below.

24	27	36	48	52	52	53	53	59	60	85	90	95

Obtaining the *IQR* and *SIQR* for this data set is trivial because we have already calculated Q_1 and Q_3 in a previous example. In that example, we found that $Q_1 = 42$ and $Q_3 = 72.5$. Therefore, the *IQR* is:

$$\begin{aligned} IQR &= Q_3 - Q_1 \\ &= 72.5 - 42 \\ &= 30.5 \end{aligned}$$

The semi-interquartile range is then:

$$SIQR = \frac{IQR}{2} = \frac{30.5}{2} = 15.25$$

We can use Excel to calculate the *IQR* and *SIQR* by first calculating the quartiles using the function PERCENTILE.EXC, and then subtracting the values from one another and dividing by 2. Figure 3.14 shows the explanation of the Excel spreadsheet solution.

	A	B	C	D	E	F	G	H
1	**Example 3.1: Marks obtained in a Statistics exam by 13 students**							
2		**Statistics marks**						
3		24						
4		27		**Excel function method**				
5		26						
6		48		Q_1 =	42	=PERCENTILE.EXC(B3:B15,0.25)		
7		52		Q_3 =	72.5	=PERCENTILE.EXC(B3:B15,0.75)		
8		52		*IQR* =	30.5	=E6-E7		
9		53		*SIQR* =	15.25	=E8/2		
10		53						
11		59						
12		60						
13		85						
14		90						
15		95						
16								

Figure 3.14: Excel spreadsheet calculations for Example 3.1 – the sample interquartile and semi-interquartile range

The data are inserted into cells B3:B15 to calculate the interquartile range and semi-interquartile range from Table 3.1. The Excel function method involves the following steps:

- Select cell E6
- In this cell, type '=PERCENTILE.EXC(B3:B15,0.25)'
- Select cell E7
- In this cell, type '=PERCENTILE.EXC(B3:B15,0.75)'
- Select cell E8
- In this cell, type '=E7–E6'
- Select cell E9
- In this cell, type '=E8/2'

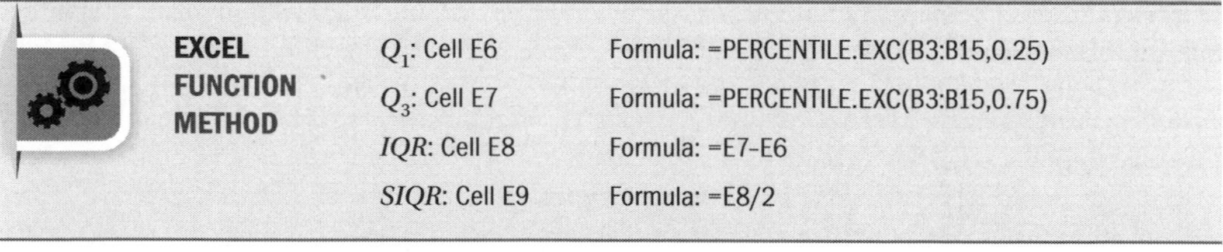

EXCEL FUNCTION METHOD

Q_1: Cell E6	Formula: =PERCENTILE.EXC(B3:B15,0.25)
Q_3: Cell E7	Formula: =PERCENTILE.EXC(B3:B15,0.75)
IQR: Cell E8	Formula: =E7-E6
SIQR: Cell E9	Formula: =E8/2

INTERPRETATION The interquartile range is a measure of variation that ignores the extremes and focuses on the middle 50% of the data, i.e. only the data between Q_3 and Q_1.

3.2.3 Standard deviation and variance

Standard deviation and variance are the measures of spread that we most commonly use in statistics to measure dispersion, since they provide a measure of how dispersed the data values (X) are about the mean value ($\overline{X}$).

The variance and standard deviation are both based on the idea that we can describe the variation in a data set by comparing all observed values to the mean and then determining how 'far away' each point is from the mean, on average. If the distance of these points from the mean is large (on average), this means that the data are widely scattered, but if the average distance of each point from the mean is small, then the observed values all lie tightly clustered around the mean.

Note that if we calculated the difference between each data value and the mean, i.e. $(X_i - \overline{X})$, some differences would be positive and some negative. If we were to then sum all these differences, we would find that $\sum_{i=1}^{n}(X_i - \overline{X}) = 0$, i.e. the positive and negative values cancel out resulting in a zero sum. To avoid this problem, we square each individual difference before summing the differences (thereby making all the values positive). The sum would then become $\sum_{i=1}^{n}(X_i - \overline{X})^2$. If we were to divide this sum by n, where $X_1, X_2, \ldots, X_n$ represents *population data,* we would obtain the mean squared distance of each data point from the mean. The result is the **population variance** (denoted by σ^2). However, when $X_1, X_2, \ldots, X_n$ represents *sample data* (as is usually the case) we need to divide the sum of the squared differences by $n - 1$ to obtain the **sample variance**. The sample variance, denoted S^2, is therefore given by:

$$S^2 = \frac{1}{n-1}\sum_{i=1}^{n}(X_i - \overline{X})^2 \tag{3.11}$$

The exact reasoning for dividing by $n - 1$ and not by n in the expression for the sample variance is beyond the scope of this textbook, but it is necessary to produce a more reliable and accurate expression for the variance.

We can obtain the standard deviation, denoted S, by simply taking the square root of the variance, i.e.

$$S = \sqrt{S^2} = \sqrt{\frac{1}{n-1}\sum_{i=1}^{n}(X_i - \overline{X})^2}$$

The sample standard deviation is sometimes preferred to the variance, because it is measured in the same units as the original observations. For example, if we had a data set describing the heights of trees measured in metres, then the standard deviation could be expressed in terms of metres, but the variance could not.

To calculate the variance and/or standard deviation, we can use an alternative but equivalent expression of formula (3.11). The alternative expression, formula (3.12) below, is easier to use when performing the calculation by hand.

SAMPLE VARIANCE

$$S^2 = \frac{1}{n-1}\left[\sum_{i=1}^{n}X_i^2 - n(\overline{X})^2\right] \tag{3.12}$$

- $X_1, X_2, \ldots, X_n$ = the observed values from the sample
- $\overline{X}$ = the sample mean
- n = the sample size

This form of the equation is easier to use when doing the calculation by hand, because we only have to determine the sum of the squares of X_i and not the sum of the squares of $(X_i - X)$. As before, we can obtain the sample standard deviation by taking the square root of this sample variance.

Properties of the variance and standard deviation

- *The variance and standard deviation can only be calculated for quantitative data.*
- *The variance and standard deviation are sensitive to outliers*: These measures of dispersion use all of the available data to determine the dispersion in the data set and are thus influenced by outlier values.

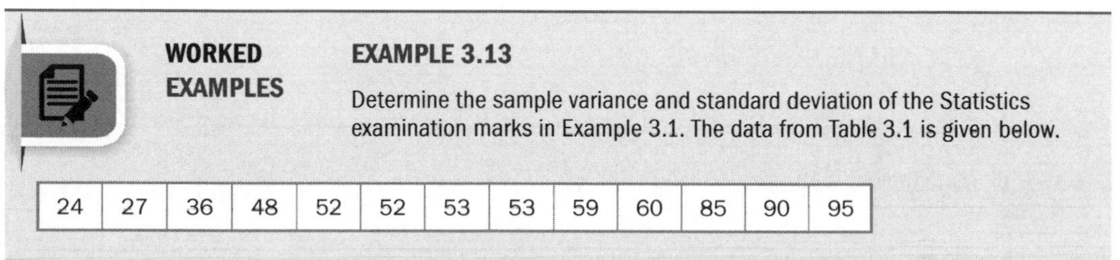

WORKED EXAMPLES

EXAMPLE 3.13

Determine the sample variance and standard deviation of the Statistics examination marks in Example 3.1. The data from Table 3.1 is given below.

24	27	36	48	52	52	53	53	59	60	85	90	95

Begin calculating the variance by using formula (3.12). We first need to calculate the mean and the square of each of the items in the data set. These squared values are summarised in Table 3.15.

Table 3.15: Example 3.1 – the examination marks and their squares

X	X^2
24	576
27	729
36	1 296
48	2 304
52	2 704
52	2 704
53	2 809
53	2 809
59	3 481
60	3 600
85	7 225
90	8 100
95	9 025
$\sum_{i=1}^{13} X_i = 734$	$\sum_{i=1}^{13} X_i^2 = 47\ 362$

The sample mean is:

$$\begin{aligned}\overline{X} &= \frac{1}{13}\sum_{i=1}^{13} X_i \\ &= \frac{1}{13}(734) \\ &= 56.46153846\end{aligned}$$

We can then calculate the sample variance using formula (3.12):

$$\begin{aligned}S^2 &= \frac{1}{13-1}\left[\sum_{i=1}^{n} X_i^2 - (13)(\overline{X})^2\right] \\ &= \frac{1}{12}[47\,362 - (13)(56.46153846)^2] \\ &= 493.27\end{aligned}$$

The sample standard deviation is then simply:

$$S = \sqrt{S^2} = \sqrt{493.27} = 22.21$$

The Excel solution shown in Figure 3.15 uses the 'VAR.S' function to calculate the sample variance, and the 'STDEV.S' function to obtain the square root of the variance (resulting in the standard error).

	A	B	C	D	E	F
1	**Example 3.1: Marks obtained in a Statistics exam by 13 students**					
2		**Statistics marks**				
3		24				
4		27		**Excel function method**		
5		26				
6		48		S^2 =	493.27	=VAR.S(B3:B15)
7		52		S =	22.21	=STDEV.S(B3:B15)
8		52				
9		53				
10		53				
11		59				
12		60				
13		85				
14		90				
15		95				
16						

Figure 3.15: Excel spreadsheet calculations for Example 3.1 – the sample variance and standard deviation

Figure 3.15 shows the Excel calculation of the variance and standard deviation of the data in Table 3.1 (given in cells B3:B15). The Excel function method involves the following steps:

- Select cell E6
- In this cell, type '=VAR.S(B3:B15)'
- Select cell E7
- In this cell, type '=STDEV.S(B3:B15)'

EXCEL FUNCTION METHOD

S^2: Cell E6 Formula: =VAR.S(B3:B15)

S: Cell E7 Formula: =STDEV.S(B3:B15)

INTERPRETATION

The variance describes how much the data values are scattered around the mean value or, how tightly the data values are grouped around the mean. In a way, the smaller the variance, the more representative the mean value is.

Unfortunately the variance does not have the same 'unit' as the data set or the mean. In other words, if the values are percentages, centimetres, degrees Celsius or any other unit of measurement, the variance is not expressed in the same values, because it is expressed in squared units. To ensure that the variance has the same units as the data set, we need to calculate the standard deviation. Although the standard deviation is less susceptible than the range to extreme values, it is still more sensitive than the semi-interquartile range. If there is a possibility that there will be outliers in the data set, then you should supplement the standard deviation with the semi-interquartile range.

NOTE

It is very important to note that Excel contains two different functions to calculate the value of the variance: VAR.S and VAR.P (similarly, there are two functions for the standard deviation: STDEV.P and STDEV.S). The function that you choose to use will depend on whether the data set represents the complete *population* or is a *sample* from the population being measured.

- If the data set is the complete population, then the population variance, σ^2, is given by the Excel function VAR.P. Similarly, the function STDEV.P is used for the population standard deviation, σ.
- If the data set is a sample from the population, then the sample variance, S^2, is given by the Excel function VAR.S. Similarly, the function STDEV.S is used for the sample standard deviation, S.

We will explore these issues in greater detail in Chapters 8 and 9 when we discuss sampling from populations and estimating population values from the sample data.

The variance and standard deviation for frequency table data

Extending the calculations for the sample variance and standard deviation to frequency table data is almost identical to the procedure used when calculating the sample mean. We will focus on the case where the frequency table is based on continuous data and has class intervals spanning multiple values.

If you remember, we mentioned earlier that for frequency tables with classes, we need to assume that the observed data values are all equal to the class midpoints m_i and that these class midpoints each occur f_i times. Intuitively, we can convert the formula used to calculate the sample variance for raw data into a formula that we can use for the frequency table as follows.

SAMPLE VARIANCE FOR FREQUENCY TABLE DATA

$$S^2 = \frac{1}{n-1}\sum_{i=1}^{k} f_i(m_i - \overline{X})^2 \quad (3.13)$$

- $f_1, f_2, ..., f_k$ = the observed frequencies in each class
- $m_1, m_2, ..., m_k$ = the class midpoints in each class
- $\overline{X}$ = the sample mean (calculated using equation (3.2))
- k = the number of classes in the table
- $n = \sum_{i=1}^{k} f_i$ = the size of the sample

However, as with the formula for sample variance for raw data, there is also an alternative version of the formula for the sample variance that is slightly more manageable and easier to work with.

SAMPLE VARIANCE FOR FREQUENCY TABLE DATA (EASIER TO CALCULATE)

$$S^2 = \frac{1}{n-1}\left[\sum_{i=1}^{k} f_i m_i^2 - n(\overline{X})^2\right] \quad (3.14)$$

- $f_1, f_2, ..., f_k$ = the observed frequencies in each class
- $m_1, m_2, ..., m_k$ = the class midpoints in each class
- $\overline{X}$ = the sample mean (calculated using the methods discussed earlier in the chapter)
- k = the number of classes in the table
- $n = \sum_{i=1}^{k} f_i$ = the size of the sample

The sample standard deviation is then:

$$S = \sqrt{S^2} = \sqrt{\frac{1}{n-1}\sum_{i=1}^{k} f_i(m_i - \overline{X})^2} = \sqrt{\frac{1}{n-1}\left[\sum_{i=1}^{k} f_i m_i^2 - n(\overline{X})^2\right]}$$

To illustrate how we calculate these values, we will apply them to the data in Example 3.3.

WORKED EXAMPLES

EXAMPLE 3.14

Using the data from Example 3.3, determine the sample variance and standard deviation of the distances travelled by the salesmen.

The data are shown in Table 3.8, as well as in Table 3.16 below.

In order to calculate the sample variance of the distances travelled by the salesmen, first determine the sample mean and the values of the $f_i m_i^2$ elements used in the formula. A table such as the one below can help you with these calculations.

Table 3.16: Frequency table of the distances travelled by 120 salesmen

CLASS	CLASS MIDPOINT (m_i)	FREQUENCY (f_i)	$f_i m_i$	$f_i m_i^2$
[400; 420)	410	12	4 920	2 017 200
[420; 440)	430	27	11 610	4 992 300
[440; 460)	450	34	15 300	6 885 000
[460; 480)	470	24	11 280	5 301 600
[480; 500)	490	15	7 350	3 601 500
[500; 520)	510	8	4 080	2 080 800
		$n = \sum_{i=1}^{6} f_i = 120$	$\sum_{i=1}^{6} f_i m_i = 54\,540$	$\sum_{i=1}^{6} f_i m_i^2 = 24\,878\,400$

The sample mean in this case is:

$$\overline{X} = \frac{1}{120}\sum_{i=1}^{6} f_i m_i = \frac{1}{120}(54\,540) = 454.5$$

And so, using formula (3.14), the sample variance is:

$$\begin{aligned} S^2 &= \frac{1}{120-1}\left[\sum_{i=1}^{6} f_i m_i^2 - (120)(\overline{X})^2\right] \\ &= \frac{1}{119}[24\,878\,400 - (120)(454.5)^2] \\ &= 756.05 \end{aligned}$$

The sample standard deviation is $S = \sqrt{S^2} = \sqrt{756.05} = 27.496$ km.

You can do these calculations in Excel, as illustrated in Figure 3.16 below.

	A	B	C	D	E	F	G
1	**Example 3.3: Distances travelled by salesmen**						
2	**Classes**	**Class midpoints, *m***	**Frequency, *f***	***mf***		***m^2f***	
3	[400; 420)	410	12	4920	=B3*C3	2017200	=B3^2*C3
4	[420; 440)	430	27	11610	=B4*C4	4992300	=B4^2*C4
5	[440; 460)	450	34	15300	=B5*C5	6885000	=B5^2*C5
6	[460; 480)	470	24	11280	=B6*C6	5301600	=B6^2*C6
7	[480; 500)	490	15	7350	=B7*C7	3601500	=B7^2*C7
8	[500; 520)	510	8	4080	=B8*C8	2080800	=B8^2*C8
9							
10	**Formula method**						
11							
12	sum *f* =	120	=SUM(C3:C8)				
13	sum *mf* =	54540	=SUM(D3:D8)				
14	sum m^2f =	24878400	=SUM(F3:F8)				
15	mean =	454.5	=B13/B12				
16	*Var* =	756.05	=(B14-B12*B15^2)/(B12-1)				
17	SD =	27.496	=SQRT(B16)				

Figure 3.16: Excel spreadsheet calculations for Example 3.3 – the sample variance and standard deviation

3.2.4 The coefficient of variation

The final measure of dispersion that we will consider is the **coefficient of variation**. This measure is simply the ratio of the sample standard deviation and the sample mean. It is a useful statistic for comparing the degree of variation from one data series to another. Standard deviations are not always suitable for this because they vary according to the size of values in the distribution and may not even be in the same unit of measurement. For example, the value of the standard deviation of a set of weights will be different, depending on whether they are measured in pounds or kilograms. The coefficient of variation, however, will be the same in both cases as it does not depend on the unit of measurement. The coefficient of variation, V, is typically expressed as a percentage and is calculated using formula (3.15), given below.

Coefficient of variation Measures the spread of a set of data relative to its mean.

SAMPLE COEFFICIENT OF VARIATION

$$V = \frac{S}{\overline{X}} \times 100\% \qquad (3.15)$$

- S = the sample standard deviation
- $\overline{X}$ = the sample mean

For example, if the coefficient of variation is 10%, this indicates that the standard deviation is equal to 10% of the sample mean. For some measures, the standard deviation changes as the average changes. In this case, the coefficient of variation is the best way to summarise the variation.

WORKED EXAMPLES

EXAMPLE 3.15

The following compares the mean weekly salaries for employees working in a Burger Baron restaurant in South Africa and employees working in equivalent positions in a Burger Baron restaurant in Australia:

- Mean earnings in the South African Burger Baron are R1 300 per month with a standard deviation of R230.
- Mean earnings in the Australian Burger Baron are $705 per week with a standard deviation of $170.

For the local Burger Baron, the coefficient of variation is:

$$V = \frac{230}{1\,300} \times 100\% = 17.69\%$$

For the Australian Burger Baron, the coefficient of variation is:

$$V = \frac{170}{705} \times 100\% = 24.11\%$$

INTERPRETATION

Even though the standard deviation of the South African Burger Baron earnings appears to be larger than the Australian value, the coefficient of variation shows that the variation or spread of the earnings in Australia is actually greater than the spread in South Africa.

3.3 Measures of skewness

A fundamental task in many statistical analyses is to characterise the location and variability of a data set. We have discussed these two characteristics of data at length in the previous two sections. Two further characterisations of data include **skewness** and kurtosis. Skewness is a measure of the degree of **symmetry** or asymmetry of a distribution and kurtosis is a measure of whether the data are peaked or flat relative to a normal distribution. A histogram is an effective graphical technique for showing both the skewness and kurtosis of a data set. Consider the following three distributions A, B and C as illustrated in Figure 3.17.

Symmetry A data set is symmetrical when the data values are distributed in the same way above and below the middle value.

Skewness Refers to the asymmetry of the distribution of data values. Distributions can be positively skewed or negatively skewed.

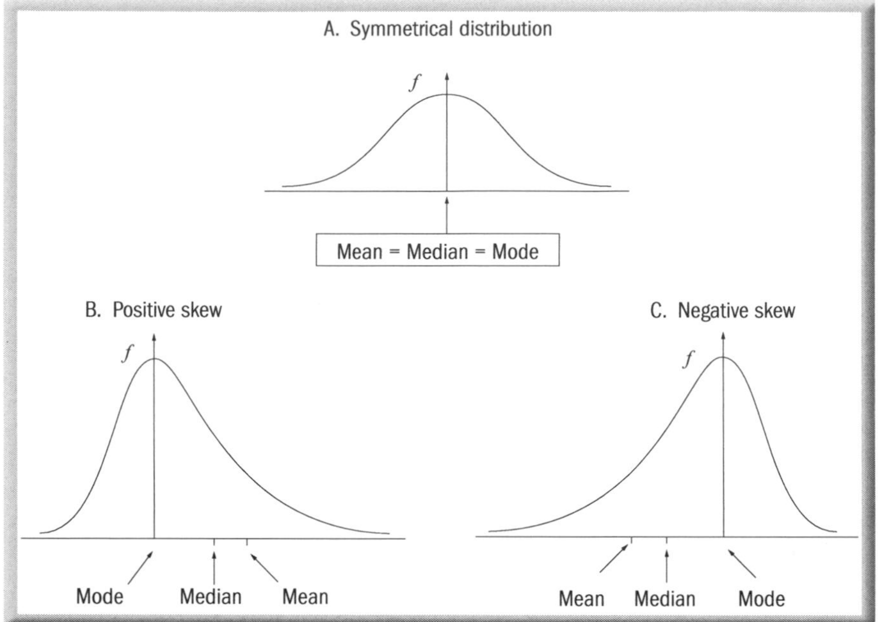

Figure 3.17: Graph representing different types of skewness and symmetry

- Distribution A is symmetrical, as the mean, median and mode all have the same value, and thus coincide at the same point of the distribution.
- Distribution B has a high frequency of relatively low values and a low frequency of relatively high values. Consequently, the mean is 'dragged' towards the right of the distribution (and the distribution has a long tail to the right). This is called a right or positively skewed distribution.
- Distribution C has a high frequency of relatively high values and a low frequency of relatively low values. Consequently, the mean is 'dragged' towards the left of the distribution (and the distribution has a long tail to the left). This is called a left or negatively skewed distribution.

The skewness of a frequency distribution can be an important consideration. For example, if your data set is 'salary', you would probably prefer a situation that led to a positively skewed distribution of salary to one that was negatively skewed. Positive skewness is more common than negative skewness.

One measure of skewness is *Pearson's coefficient of skewness*. This is defined as follows.

PEARSON'S COEFFICIENT OF SKEWNESS

$$PCS = \frac{3(\bar{X} - \tilde{X})}{S} \quad (3.16)$$

- $\bar{X}$ = the sample mean
- $\tilde{X}$ = the sample median
- S = the sample standard deviation

With skewed data, the mean is not a good measure of central tendency, because it is sensitive to the extreme values that skewed the distribution. In cases like this, we would use the median to provide the measure of central tendency.

Properties of Pearson's coefficient of skewness

- *For symmetry PCS = 0*: For symmetric distributions (i.e. $\bar{X} = \tilde{X}$), the value for skewness is zero.
- *For negatively skewed distributions PCS < 0*: If the sample mean is smaller than the sample median (i.e. $\bar{X} < \tilde{X}$), then *PCS* is negative and the distribution is negatively skewed.
- *For positively skewed distributions PCS > 0*: If the sample mean is larger than the sample median (i.e. $\bar{X} > \tilde{X}$), then *PCS* is positive and the distribution is positively skewed.
- *PCS is independent of the units being measured*: Pearson's coefficient of skewness statistic cannot be expressed in terms of the units of the observed data; it is 'unitless'.

Excel also uses another measure of skewness called *Fisher's skewness coefficient,* denoted *FSC*.

FISHER'S SKEWNESS COEFFICIENT

$$FSC = \frac{n}{(n-1)(n-2)}\sum_{i=1}^{n}\left(\frac{X_i - \bar{X}}{S}\right)^3 \quad (3.17)$$

- $X_1, X_2, \ldots, X_n$ = the set of observed sample data
- n = the sample size
- $\bar{X}$ = the sample mean
- S = the sample standard deviation

We can use the Excel function 'SKEW' to calculate this coefficient. Note that while the values of Fisher and Pearson's coefficients of skewness will occasionally be somewhat different from one another, they are both interpreted in the same way, that is, positive values indicate positive skewness, negative values indicate negative skewness, and a zero value indicates symmetry.

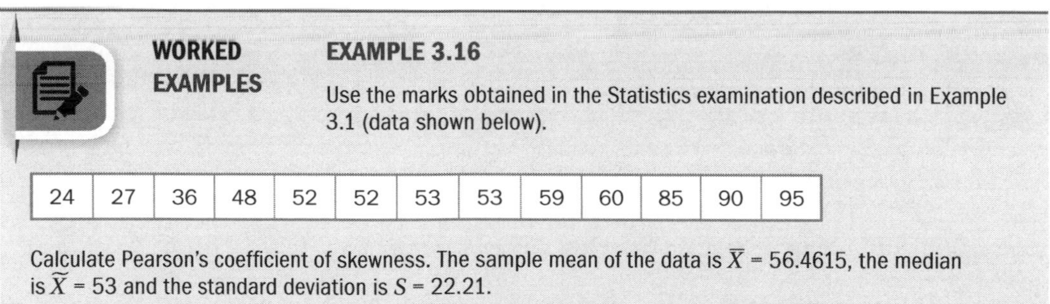

WORKED EXAMPLES

EXAMPLE 3.16

Use the marks obtained in the Statistics examination described in Example 3.1 (data shown below).

24	27	36	48	52	52	53	53	59	60	85	90	95

Calculate Pearson's coefficient of skewness. The sample mean of the data is $\bar{X} = 56.4615$, the median is $\tilde{X} = 53$ and the standard deviation is $S = 22.21$.

We calculate Pearson's correlation coefficient as follows:

$$PCS = \frac{3(56.4615 - 53)}{22.21}$$
$$= 0.4676$$

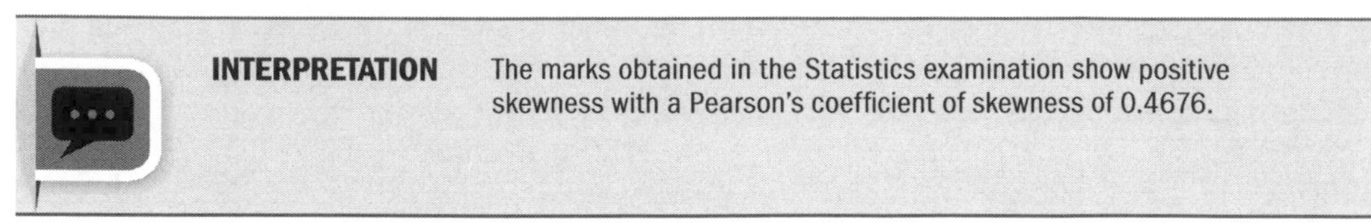

INTERPRETATION The marks obtained in the Statistics examination show positive skewness with a Pearson's coefficient of skewness of 0.4676.

Figure 3.18 illustrates the Excel solution.

	A	B	C	D	E	F
1	**Example 3.1: Marks obtained in a Statistics exam by 13 students**					
2		**Statistics marks**				
3		24		**Formula method**		
4		27				
5		26		mean =	56.4615384615385	=AVERAGE(B3:B15)
6		48		median =	53	=MEDIAN(B3:B15)
7		52		*S* =	22.2096652556771	=STDEV.S(B3:B15)
8		52		PCS =	0.467571900119518	=3*(D5-D6)/D7
9		53		FCS =	0.440986665530062	=SKEW(B3:B15)
10		53				
11		59				
12		60				
13		85				
14		90				
15		95				
16						

Figure 3.18: Excel spreadsheet calculations for Example 3.1 – Pearson's skewness and Fisher's skewness

The explanation for the Excel spreadsheet solution is as follows.

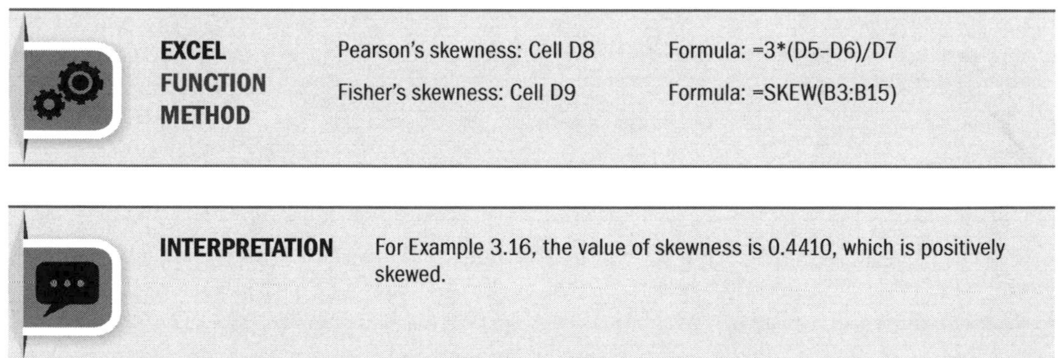

EXCEL FUNCTION METHOD

Pearson's skewness: Cell D8	Formula: =3*(D5–D6)/D7
Fisher's skewness: Cell D9	Formula: =SKEW(B3:B15)

INTERPRETATION For Example 3.16, the value of skewness is 0.4410, which is positively skewed.

NOTE

Skewness values greater than $\pm 2\sqrt{\frac{6}{n}}$ (where n is the sample size), indicate severe skewness. In the previous example, $n = 13$ and error measurement $\pm 2\sqrt{\frac{6}{13}} = \pm 1.36$. The measured value of skewness, 0.4676, lies within the region ±1.36 and not outside it. Therefore, we can conclude that the distribution is not significantly skewed.

3.4 Measures of kurtosis

Kurtosis A measure of the 'peakedness' and/or 'flatness' of a distribution.

Kurtosis measures how 'peaked' the distribution of data is. A standard normal distribution (which we will discuss in greater detail in Chapter 7) has a kurtosis of zero. Positive kurtosis indicates a 'peaked' distribution and negative kurtosis indicates a 'flat' distribution. Consider the two distributions in Figure 3.19. You can see from the two distributions that distribution A is more peaked than distribution B, but the means and standard deviations are approximately the same.

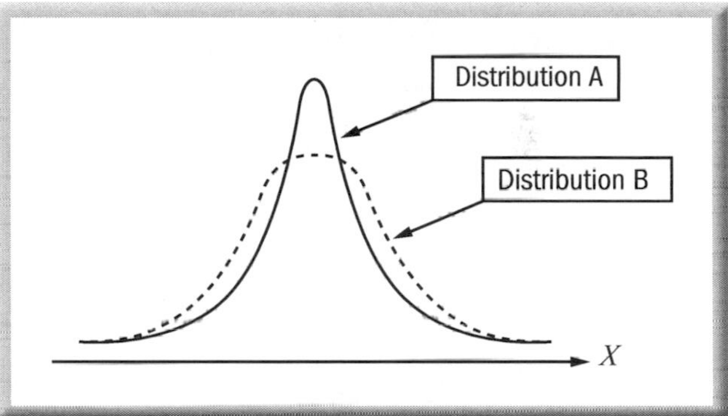

Figure 3.19: Graph representing kurtosis

A measure of whether the curve of a distribution is bell-shaped (Mesokurtic), peaked (Leptokurtic) or flat (Platykurtic) is provided by Fisher's measure of kurtosis given by formula (3.18).

FISHER'S MEASURE OF KURTOSIS

$$\text{Kurtosis} = \frac{n(n+1)}{(n-1)(n-2)(n-3)}\sum_{i=1}^{n}\left(\frac{X_i - \overline{X}}{S}\right)^4 - \frac{3(n-1)^2}{(n-2)(n-3)} \qquad (3.18)$$

- $X_1, X_2, \ldots, X_n$ = the set of observed sample data
- n = the sample size
- $\overline{X}$ = the sample mean
- S = the sample standard deviation

This equation is used by Excel in its KURT function to provide an estimate of kurtosis.

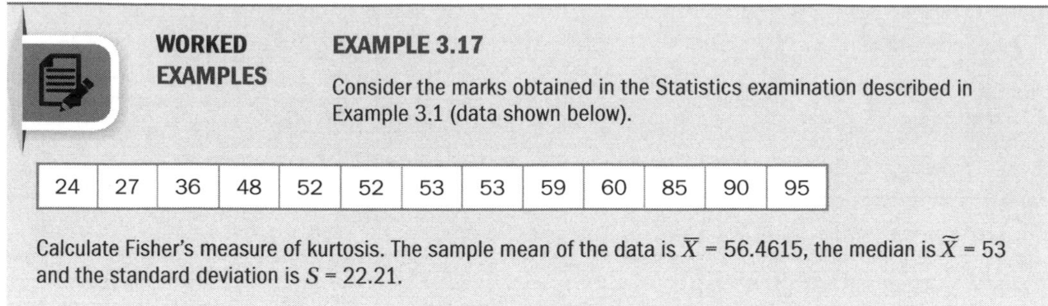

WORKED EXAMPLES

EXAMPLE 3.17

Consider the marks obtained in the Statistics examination described in Example 3.1 (data shown below).

24	27	36	48	52	52	53	53	59	60	85	90	95

Calculate Fisher's measure of kurtosis. The sample mean of the data is $\overline{X} = 56.4615$, the median is $\widetilde{X} = 53$ and the standard deviation is $S = 22.21$.

The Excel solution for the kurtosis, using the KURT function, is shown in Figure 3.20.

	A	B	C	D	E	F
1	**Example 3.1: Marks obtained in a Statistics exam by 13 students**					
2		**Statistics marks**				
3		24		**Formula method**		
4		27				
5		26		mean=	56.4615384615385	=AVERAGE(B3:B15)
6		48		median=	53	=MEDIAN(B3:B15)
7		52		*S*=	22.2096652556771	=STDEV.S(B3:B15)
8		52				
9		53		Kurt=	-0.42531924186981	=KURT(B3:B15)
10		53				
11		59				
12		60				
13		85				
14		90				
15		95				
16						

Figure 3.20: Excel spreadsheet calculations for Example 3.1 – Fisher's kurtosis

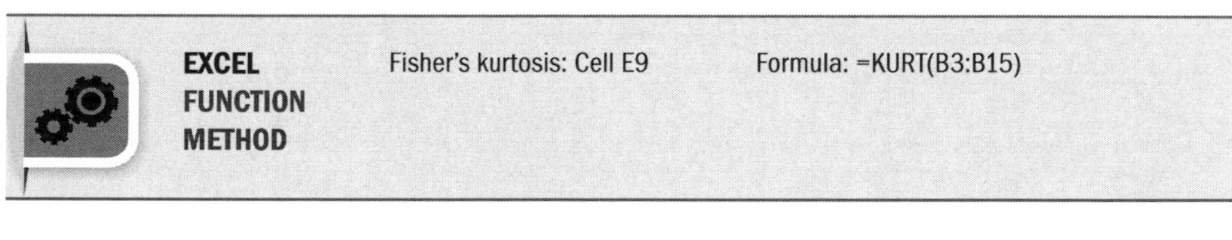

EXCEL FUNCTION METHOD

Fisher's kurtosis: Cell E9 Formula: =KURT(B3:B15)

NOTE

Kurtosis values greater than $\pm 2\sqrt{\frac{24}{n}}$ (where n is the sample size) indicate severely 'peaked' kurtosis. For Example 3.1, $n = 13$ and error measurement is $\pm 2\sqrt{\frac{24}{13}} = \pm 2.72$. The measured value of kurtosis calculated for Example 3.1 in Figure 3.20 is –0.4253, which lies within the region ±2.72 and not outside it. Therefore, we can conclude that the distribution does not have a significantly 'peaked' kurtosis.

3.5 Exploratory data analysis

In the previous sections, we explored ways in which we can describe a data set by computing measures of average, spread and shape. In this section, we explore exploratory data analysis techniques, including **five-number summary**, box plots and using the Excel ToolPak add-in to calculate descriptive statistics.

Five-number summary Is especially useful when there are so many data that it is sufficient to present a summary of the data rather than the whole data set.

3.5.1 Five-number summary

The five-number summary is a simple method that provides measures of average and spread, with the added bonus of giving us an idea of the shape of the distribution. This five-number summary consists of the following numbers in the data set:

- Smallest value, X_{min}
- First quartile, Q_1
- Median, $\widetilde{X}$
- Third quartile, Q_3
- Largest value, X_{max}

For symmetrical distributions, the following rule holds:

- Q_3 - median = median - Q_1
- largest value - $Q_3 = Q_1$ - smallest value
- median = midhinge = midrange

The midrange is the average of the largest and smallest data values (i.e. the range divided by 2), and the midhinge is the average of the first and third quartiles (i.e. the *SIQR*). For non-symmetrical distributions, the following rule holds:

- Right-skewed distributions: largest value - Q_3 greatly exceeds Q_1 - smallest value
- Left-skewed distributions: Q_1 - smallest value greatly exceeds largest value - Q_3

WORKED EXAMPLES

EXAMPLE 3.18

Suppose we have a data set with the following values for the five-number summary:

- Q_1 = first quartile = 15
- X_{min} = minimum = 8
- $\widetilde{X}$ = median = 33
- X_{max} = maximum = 88
- Q_3 = third quartile = 62

You can see from these summary statistics that the data distribution is not symmetrical:

- The distance from Q_3 to the median (62 – 33 = 29) is not the same as between Q_1 and the median (33 – 15 = 18).
- The distance from Q_3 to the largest value (88 – 62 = 26) is not the same as the distance between Q_1 and the smallest value (15 – 8 = 7).
- The median (33), the midhinge $\left(\frac{(62+15)}{2} = 38.5\right)$ and the midrange $\left(\frac{(88+8)}{2} = 48\right)$ are not equal.

The summary numbers indicate right skewness, because the distance between Q_3 and the largest number (88 – 62 = 26) is larger than the distance between Q_1 and the smallest value (15 – 8 = 7). The minimum and maximum points are identified and enable us to identify any extreme values (or outliers).

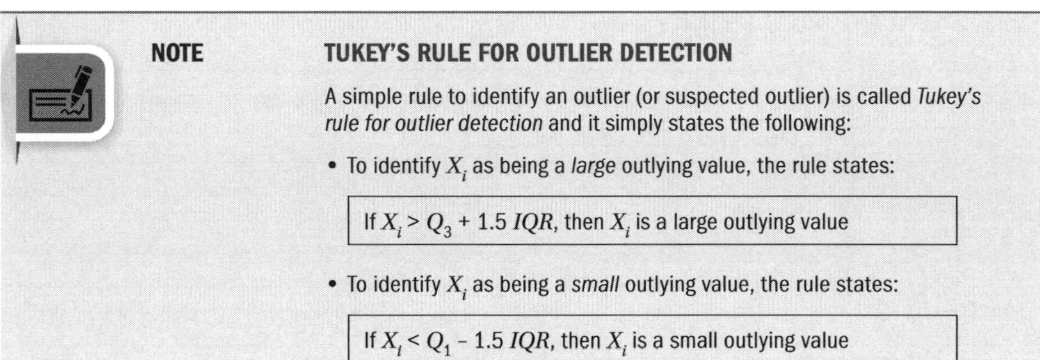

NOTE **TUKEY'S RULE FOR OUTLIER DETECTION**

A simple rule to identify an outlier (or suspected outlier) is called *Tukey's rule for outlier detection* and it simply states the following:

- To identify X_i as being a *large* outlying value, the rule states:

If $X_i > Q_3 + 1.5\ IQR$, then X_i is a large outlying value

- To identify X_i as being a *small* outlying value, the rule states:

If $X_i < Q_1 - 1.5\ IQR$, then X_i is a small outlying value

We usually use this rule to determine whether the maximum and minimum values observed in the data set are actually outliers or not. If, for example, the maximum value in the data set is identified as an outlier, then we would mark that value as being an outlier and use the next largest value in the data set as the sample maximum in our calculations. The same applies if we identify a minimum value as an outlier. Treat outlier values marked in this way carefully, as they may be important values that provide meaningful information to the study, or they may be the result of observation or measurement error. For this reason, you should never automatically ignore or delete outliers when you encounter them. Instead, you should carefully study them to determine their nature.

3.5.2 Using the Excel ToolPak add-in

You can use the *descriptive statistics* procedure in the Excel ToolPak add-in to provide a set of summary statistics, including the mean, median, mode, standard deviation, sample variance, kurtosis, skewness, range, minimum, maximum, sum, count, and largest and smallest number. You can use the skewness and kurtosis values to provide information about the shape of the distribution. The output contains much more than the five-number summary described above, but since they are all there, it is not difficult to extract the relevant ones.

WORKED EXAMPLES

EXAMPLE 3.19

If we consider the data from Example 3.1, then the descriptive statistics procedure in the Excel ToolPak add-in would give the following results.

Steps used to obtain descriptive statistics using the Excel ToolPak add-in

Step 1: Select the 'Data' ribbon tab.

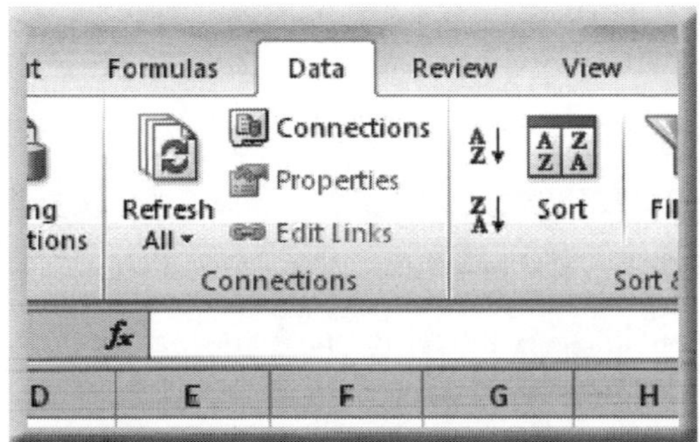

Step 2: Click on the 'Data Analysis' button (on the far right).

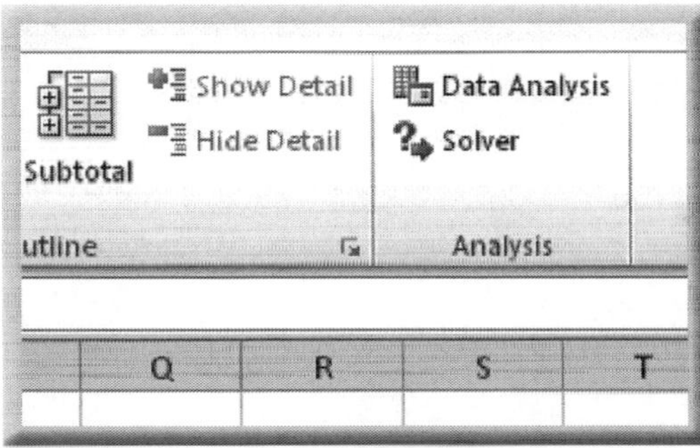

Step 3: Select 'Descriptive Statistics' and click OK.

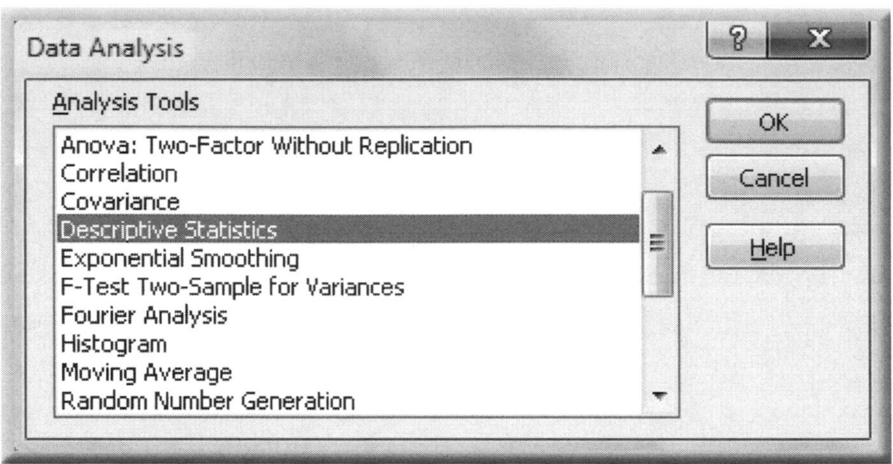

Step 4: In the 'Descriptive Statistics' window, do the following:

- Set the input range to B3:B15.
- Set the output range to D3.
- Check the 'Summary statistics' check box.
- Click OK.

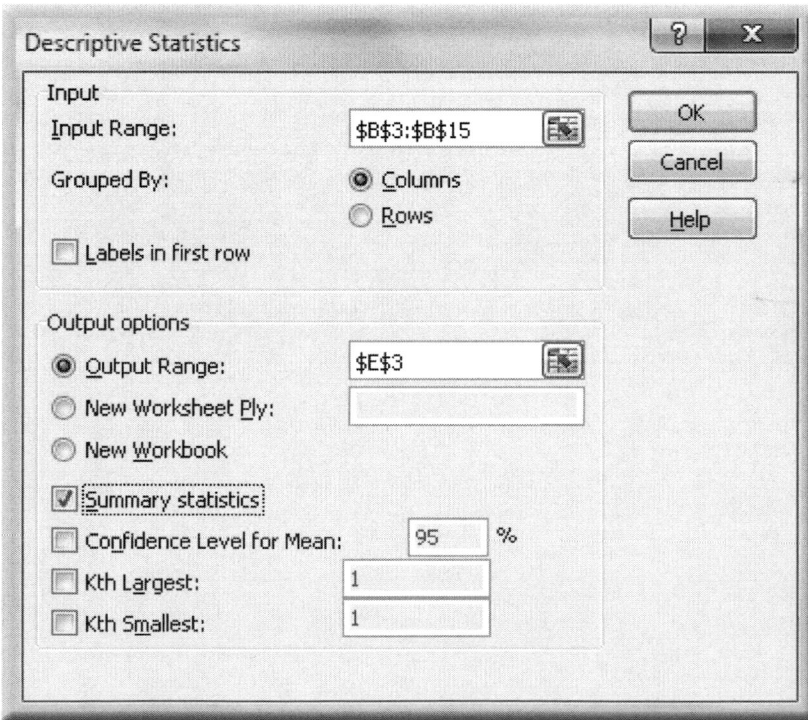

Step 5: The Excel results are then calculated and printed out in the Excel worksheet as shown below.

	A	B	C	D	E
1	**Example 3.1: Marks obtained in a Statistics exam by 13 students**				
2		**Statistics marks**			
3		24			**Column 1**
4		27			
5		26		Mean	56.4615384615
6		48		Standard error	6.1598528771
7		52		Median	53
8		52		Mode	52
9		53		Standard Deviation	22.2096652556
10		53		Sample Variance	493.269230769
11		59		Kurtosis	-0.4253192418
12		60		Skewness	0.44098666553
13		85		Range	71
14		90		Minimum	24
15		95		Maximum	95
16				Sum	734
17				Count	13
18					

SUMMARY

This chapter extends your knowledge from using tables and charts to summarising data using measures of central location, dispersion and shape. The mean is the most commonly calculated measure of central location, but this measurement uses all the data within the calculation and therefore outliers affect it. This can Imply that the value of the mean may not be representative of the underlying data set. If outliers are present in the data set, then you can either eliminate these values or use the median instead of the mean. Once you are satisfied that the measure of central tendency (or middle value) has been adequately described, the next calculation to perform is a measure of the spread of the data within the distribution. The standard deviation is the most common type of measure of dispersion (or spread), but like the mean, the standard deviation is influenced by the presence of outliers within a data set. If outliers are present, then you can reduce the effect these values by using the semi-interquartile range to represent the degree of dispersion. You can estimate the degree of skewness in a data set by calculating Pearson's coefficient of skewness (or use Fisher's skewness equation), and the degree of peakedness by calculating the kurtosis statistic.

This chapter also explored the calculation process for raw data and frequency distributions. It is important to note that the graphical method will not be as accurate as the raw data method when calculating the summary statistics.

KEY TERMS

Central tendency
Coefficient of variation
Cumulative frequency distribution
Dispersion
Extreme value
Five-number summary
Interquartile range
Kurtosis
Left-skewed
Mean
Median
Mode
Outlier
Population mean
Population standard deviation
Population variance
Q_1: first quartile
Q_2: second quartile
Q_3: third quartile
Quartiles
Range
Right-skewed
Sample mean
Skewness
Standard deviation
Symmetry
Variance
Variation

FORMULA SUMMARY

$$\overline{X} = \frac{1}{n}\sum_{i=1}^{n} X_i = \frac{X_1 + X_2 + \ldots + X_n}{n} \tag{3.1}$$

$$\overline{X} = \frac{m_1 f_1 + m_2 f_2 + \ldots + m_k f_k}{n} = \frac{1}{n}\sum_{i=1}^{k} m_i f_i \tag{3.2}$$

$$\widetilde{X} = L + \frac{C\left(\frac{(n+1)}{2} - F_{\text{below}}\right)}{f_{\text{med}}} \tag{3.3}$$

$$\text{Mode} = L + \left(\frac{f_{\text{mod}} - f_{\text{below}}}{2f_{\text{mod}} - f_{\text{below}} - f_{\text{above}}}\right)C \tag{3.4}$$

$$P_x = X_w + d \times (X_{w+1} - X_w) \tag{3.5}$$

$$P_x = L + \left(\frac{\frac{x}{100}(n+1) - F_{\text{before}}}{f_x}\right) \times C \tag{3.6}$$

$$\text{Range} = X_{\max} - X_{\min} \tag{3.7}$$

$$\text{Range} = UCB_k - LCB_1 \tag{3.8}$$

$$IQR = Q_3 - Q_1 \tag{3.9}$$

$$SIQR = \frac{IQR}{2} = \frac{Q_3 - Q_1}{2} \tag{3.10}$$

$$S^2 = \frac{1}{n-1}\sum_{i=1}^{n}(X_i - \overline{X})^2 \tag{3.11}$$

$$S^2 = \frac{1}{n-1}\left[\sum_{i=1}^{n}X_i^2 - n(\overline{X})^2\right] \tag{3.12}$$

$$S^2 = \frac{1}{n-1}\sum_{i=1}^{k} f_i(m_i - \overline{X})^2 \tag{3.13}$$

$$S^2 = \frac{1}{n-1}\left[\sum_{i=1}^{k} f_i m_i^2 - n(\overline{X})^2\right] \tag{3.14}$$

$$V = \frac{S}{\overline{X}} \times 100\% \tag{3.15}$$

$$PCS = \frac{3(X - \widetilde{X})}{S} \tag{3.16}$$

$$FSC = \frac{n}{(n-1)(n-2)}\sum_{i=1}^{n}\left(\frac{X_i - \overline{X}}{S}\right)^3 \tag{3.17}$$

$$\text{Kurtosis} = \frac{n(n+1)}{(n-1)(n-2)(n-3)}\sum_{i=1}^{n}\left(\frac{X_i - \overline{X}}{S}\right)^4 - \frac{3(n-1)^2}{(n-2)(n-3)} \tag{3.18}$$

EXERCISES

3.1 In 12 consecutive innings, a cricket batsman's scores were:
6, 13, 16, 45, 93, 0, 62, 87, 136, 25, 14, 31

a) Find his mean score and the median.
b) Determine the standard deviation and interquartile range for the data.
c) Calculate the skewness coefficient for the data.
d) What conclusions can you draw regarding the statistics calculated above?

3.2 The following are the IQs of 12 people:
115, 89, 94, 107, 98, 87, 99, 120, 100, 94, 100, 99
It is claimed that the average person in the group has an IQ of over 100. Is this a reasonable assertion?

3.3 A sample of six components was tested to destruction to establish how long they would last. The times to failure (in hours) during testing were:
40, 44, 5, 55, 64, 69
Which would be the most appropriate measure of central tendency to describe the life of these components? What are the consequences of your choice?

3.4 Find the mean, median, first quartile, third quartile and mode of this set of data:
1, 1, 1, 1, 1, 2, 2, 2, 2, 2, 2, 3, 3, 3, 3, 3, 4, 4, 4, 4, 5, 5, 5, 5, 5

3.5 The average salary paid to graduates in three companies is R700 000, R600 000 and R900 000 p.a. respectively. If the respective number of graduates in these companies is 5, 12 and 3, find the mean and median salary paid to the 20 graduates. What is the standard deviation of the salary?

3.6 AccRek Ltd, a major accounting firm, employs a leading consultant company based in Pretoria to help organise and expand the catering facilities it provides to its employees. The initial research by the company identified the following weekly spend (R) by individual employees.

Table 3.17: Amount of money spent weekly by AccRek employees in the firm's cafeteria

220	160	260	330	330	370	90	230	320	170
0	130	120	180	190	100	210	220	50	20
220	220	340	240	230	210	380	310	410	200

a) Plot the histogram and comment on the shape of the weekly expenditure. Hint: Use a class width of 50.
b) Calculate the values of the mean and median.
c) Calculate the values of the range, interquartile range and standard deviation.
d) Use descriptive statistics in conjunction with the histogram to comment on weekly expenditure.

3.7 Form a frequency distribution of the data in Table 3.18 with intervals centred at 10, 15, 20, 25, 30, 35 and 40. Calculate the mean from the raw data in Table 3.18 and calculate the mean from the frequency table that you constructed. Comment on the values of these two means.

Table 3.18: Data for Question 3.7

9	26	33	24	41	24	37	39	30	28	34	19	32
24	42	17	26	18	33	40	28	31	20	23	18	21
32	21	39	25	16	17	26	11	30	28	24	27	40

3.8 Table 3.19 shows the frequency distribution of the length of a sample of 98 nails, measured to the nearest 0.1 mm.

Table 3.19: Lengths of n = 98 nails

LENGTH	FREQUENCY (f)
[4.0; 4.3)	4
[4.3; 4.6)	9
[4.6; 4.9)	13
[4.9; 5.2)	20
[5.2; 5.5)	34
[5.5; 5.8)	18

a) Find the mean length of this sample by hand and using an Excel spreadsheet.
b) Construct the cumulative frequency polygon (ogive) and use this to estimate the median.
c) Check the value of the median using the formula method.

3.9 Table 3.20 shows the distribution of marks of 400 candidates in a matric Mathematics exam.

Table 3.20: Marks of n = 400 students

MARKS	FREQUENCY (f)
[0; 10)	6
[10; 20)	15
[20; 30)	31
[30; 40)	80
[40; 50)	93

MARKS	FREQUENCY (f)
[50; 60)	69
[60; 70)	54
[70; 80)	33
[80; 90)	12
[90; 100)	7

a) Calculate the mean value.
b) Construct the cumulative frequency polygon (ogive) and estimate the median, and lower and upper quartile values.

3.10 Over a one-month period (31 days), the number of vacant beds in a Polokwane hospital was surveyed. Table 3.21 shows the resulting frequency distribution.

Table 3.21: Frequency table of the number of hospital beds vacant per day (31 days)

BEDS VACANT	0	2	3	5	6	8
FREQUENCY	4	8	12	4	2	1

Determine the mean number of beds vacant each day. What is the standard deviation of the number of beds vacant?

3.11 In a small town, the distance of a sample of 122 randomly selected houses from the entrance to the town's main supermarket was measured to the nearest metre. Table 3.22 shows this information.

Table 3.22: Distances from houses to the supermarket

DISTANCE	[57; 60)	[60; 63)	[63; 66)	[66; 69)	[69; 72)	[72; 75)	[75; 78)
FREQUENCY	9	10	18	42	27	11	5

Determine the range, mean and standard deviation.

3.12 In a debate on altering the traffic system in a city centre, measurements of the number of cars per minute were taken at two intersections during the hour between 07h00 and 08h00 (when the roads were most busy). The results are shown in Table 3.23.

Table 3.23: The volume of traffic recorded each minute at two intersections between 07h00 and 08h00

NUMBER OF CARS PER MINUTE	INTERSECTION A	INTERSECTION B
[10; 15)	0	5
[15; 10)	3	8
[20; 25)	13	10
[25; 20)	24	12
[30; 35)	17	14
[35; 30)	3	5
[40; 45)	0	3
[45; 40)	0	3
Total	60	60

Compare the two distributions by plotting their frequency polygons and determining the means, standard deviations and coefficients of variation.

3.13 Greendelivery.com has recently decided to review the weekly distance travelled of its delivery vehicles that are used to deliver shopping purchased online to customer homes from a central parcel depot. The sample data collected is part of the first stage in analysing the economic benefit of potentially moving all vehicles to bio fuels from diesel. Table 3.24 shows the results obtained.

Table 3.24: Distances travelled by delivery vehicles

80	165	159	143	140
136	138	118	120	124
159	131	93	146	109
163	136	163	142	80
106	111	123	161	179
144	145	91	112	146
170	105	131	141	122
137	152	109	122	126
114	155	92	143	165

a) Use Excel to construct a frequency distribution and plot the histogram with class intervals of 10 and classes [75; 85), [85; 94), ..., [175; 185). Comment on the pattern in distance travelled by the company vehicles.

b) Use the raw data to determine the mean, median, standard deviation and semi-interquartile range.

c) Comment on which measure you would use to describe the average and measure of dispersion. Explain using your answers to parts (a) and (b).
d) Calculate the measure of skewness and kurtosis, and comment on the distribution shape.

3.14 The manager at BIG JIMS restaurant is concerned by the time it takes to process credit card payments at the counter by staff. The manager has collected the processing time data (time in minutes) in Table 3.25 and requested that summary statistics are calculated.

Table 3.25: Time taken to process credit cards

1.57	1.38	1.97	1.52	1.39
1.09	1.29	1.26	1.07	1.76
1.13	1.59	0.27	0.92	0.71
1.49	1.73	0.79	1.38	2.46
0.98	2.31	1.23	1.56	0.89
0.76	1.23	1.56	1.98	2.01
1.40	1.89	0.89	1.34	3.21
0.76	1.54	1.78	4.89	1.98

a) Calculate a five-number summary for this data set.
b) Is there any evidence for a symmetric distribution?
c) Use the Excel Analysis ToolPak to calculate descriptive statistics.
d) Which measures would you use to provide a measure of average and spread?

3.15 The director of housing in the municipal region of East London is conducting a study of the housing developments in the area. One economic variable that is thought to be pertinent in reflecting the economic well-being of the community is the total yearly income in each household. Table 3.26 shows this information for 50 households.

Table 3.26: Yearly income of n = 50 households

89 194	191 129	203 431	101 668	18 1079
217 319	270 141	253 564	250 349	238 891
159 726	141 654	218 777	98 994	106 816
104 942	154 710	186 509	177 497	92 833
195 171	233 321	272 487	211 744	157 440
136 102	166 109	136 767	75 558	113 271
125 225	109 870	110 750	147 995	101 700
117 407	121 447	148 243	79 197	205 008
88 393	191 186	154 794	142 689	91 889
183 197	179 457	265 620	189 012	144 272

a) Calculate a five-number summary.
b) Is there any evidence of a symmetric distribution?
c) Use the Excel Analysis-ToolPak to calculate descriptive statistics.
d) Which measures would you use to provide a measure of central tendency and dispersion?

TECHNIQUES IN PRACTICE

3.16 AfriSoft supplies a range of computer software to 50 schools within Limpopo province. When AfriSoft won the contract, they thought that the issue of customer service was central in the company being successful at the final bidding stage. The company has now requested that its customer service director creates a series of graphical representations of the data to illustrate customer satisfaction with the service. The data in Table 3.27 was collected during the past six months and measures the time to respond to a received complaint (days).

Table 3.27: The time taken to respond to complaints (in days)

5	24	34	6	61	56	38	32
87	78	34	9	67	4	54	23
56	32	86	12	81	32	52	53
34	45	21	31	42	12	53	21
43	76	62	12	73	3	67	12
78	89	26	10	74	78	23	32
26	21	56	78	91	85	15	12
15	56	45	21	45	26	21	34
28	12	67	23	24	43	25	65
23	8	87	21	78	54	76	79

The customer service director has analysed these data to create a grouped frequency table and plotted the histogram. From this, he made a series of observations regarding the time to respond to customer complaints. He now wants to extend the analysis to use numerical methods to describe these data.

a) From the data set, calculate the mean and median.
b) Repeat the analysis to calculate the standard deviation, quartiles (Q_1, Q_2 and Q_3), quartile range and semi-interquartile range.
c) Describe the shape of the distribution. Do the results suggest that there is a great deal of variation in the time taken to respond to customer complaints?
d) Which measures would you recommend the customer service manager uses to describe the variation in the time taken to respond to customer complaints?
e) What conclusions can you draw from these results?

3.17 Bakers Ltd runs a chain of bakery shops and is famous for the quality of its pies. The management of the company are concerned by the number of complaints from customers saying that it takes too long to serve customers at a particular branch. The motto of the company is 'Have your pies in 2 minutes'. The manager of the branch concerned has been told to provide data on the time it takes for customers to enter the shop and be served by the staff. The data collected is shown in Table 3.28.

Table 3.28: Time taken for a sample of n = 100 customers to be served (in minutes)

0.37	1.18	0.51	1.93	1.83	1.33	0.22	0.97	0.91	1.08
0.19	1.83	0.66	1.14	0.78	1.38	0.89	1.57	1.56	0.37
1.21	0.71	0.81	1.22	0.65	0.86	1.08	1.53	1.14	0.44
0.59	0.89	1.08	1.05	2.33	0.88	1.64	0.85	0.83	1.20
1.35	0.52	1.10	0.28	1.00	1.93	0.96	0.63	0.39	2.07
1.08	0.77	0.55	1.14	1.90	0.63	1.16	1.52	0.63	1.33
0.70	1.39	1.31	0.62	0.41	0.48	1.11	0.93	1.42	0.80
0.31	1.28	0.86	0.06	0.54	0.85	0.09	1.07	1.54	1.49
1.12	0.48	0.67	0.97	1.34	1.15	1.64	0.36	0.72	1.38
1.24	1.23	1.70	0.56	1.47	0.37	1.09	0.43	0.33	1.78

a) From the data set, calculate the mean and median.
b) Repeat the analysis to calculate the standard deviation, quartiles (Q_1, Q_2 and Q_3), quartile range and semi-interquartile range.
c) Describe the shape of the distribution. Do the results suggest that there is a great deal of variation in the time taken to serve customers?
d) Which measures would you recommend the shop manager uses to describe the variation in the time taken to serve customers?
e) What conclusions can you draw from these results?

3.18 Home-Made Beers Ltd is a brewery that is undergoing a major expansion after being bought out by a large national brewery. Home-Made Beers Ltd produces a small range of beers and stouts, but is renowned for the quality of its beers, having won a number of prizes at trade fairs. The new parent company is reviewing the quality control mechanisms operated by Home-Made Beers Ltd and are concerned about the quantity of lager contained in the bottles produced at the brewery. The bottles should contain a mean of 330 ml with a standard deviation of 15 ml. The bottling plant manager provided the parent company with quantity measurements from 100 bottles for analysis (Table 3.29).

Table 3.29: Quantity of beer in n = 100 randomly selected bottles of beer

348	343	337	333	324	349	348	352	335	374
337	346	347	333	315	346	356	362	340	348
354	356	343	337	356	322	361	352	360	354
344	341	324	339	339	353	342	336	331	355
355	345	345	334	349	331	351	343	346	339
339	351	318	363	334	348	336	332	375	365
328	350	330	367	316	350	345	336	322	329
351	328	343	349	361	337	325	328	360	347
360	358	365	354	326	341	360	342	346	351
360	350	338	324	342	333	338	340	350	335

a) From the data set, calculate the mean and median.
b) Repeat the analysis to calculate the standard deviation, quartiles (Q_1, Q_2 and Q_3), quartile range and semi-interquartile range.
c) Describe the shape of the distribution. Do the results suggest that there is a great deal of variation in quantity in the bottle measurements? Compare the assumed bottle average and spread with the measured average and spread.
d) What conclusions can you draw from these results?

CHAPTER 4

PROBABILITY

CHAPTER CONTENTS

OVERVIEW

The concept of probability is an important aspect in the study of statistics. In this chapter, we introduce some of the concepts that are relevant to probability calculations.

LEARNING OBJECTIVES

On completing this chapter, you should be able to:

- understand the following terms and concepts: experiment, outcome, sample space, relative frequency and sample probability
- understand when events are mutually exclusive and independent
- use the basic probability laws to solve simple problems
- understand the concept of conditional probability
- use tree diagrams (or decision trees) to help calculate conditional probabilities.

4.1 Introduction to probability

There are a number of terms that encapsulate the basic concept of probability, for example, chance, probable, odds, and so on. Each of these describe the degree of uncertainty in terms of the likelihood of a particular event happening. Statistically, these terms are too vague to use, and so we need some numerical measure of the likelihood of an event occurring. This measure is called **probability** and it is measured on a scale between 0 and 1. In some cases, probability is expressed as a percentage between 0% and 100%.

Probability A way of expressing the likely occurrence of a particular event as a number between 0 and 1.

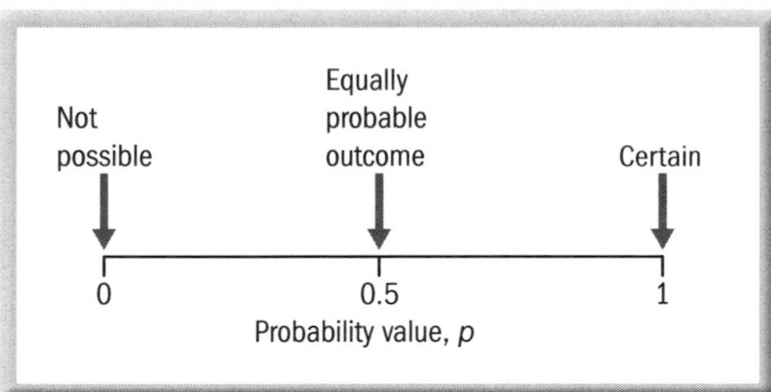

Figure 4.1: Values that probability can assume

From Figure 4.1, you can see that probability values lie between 0 and 1, with 0 representing no possibility of the outcome occurring and 1 representing the probability that the outcome is certain. Usually, the value of a probability will lie between 0 and 1.

4.1.1 Probability theory in practice

The calculation of probabilities has a number of practical applications. We now discuss some of these practical applications.

Decision making

Probability calculations allow us to quantify uncertainty, i.e. they allow us to express our uncertainty numerically. These numerical representations can inform many decisions made in business, industry, gambling and in everyday situations that require us to weigh up the possibility of risks occurring. If we know our options and the probability associated with each option, we can make decisions that are more intelligent.

For example, a man standing at a supermarket checkout counter has the opportunity to buy a lottery scratch card. The ticket costs R5 and can potentially pay out R1 000. However, the man needs the R5 to buy his groceries, but thinks that a R1 000 prize would also be quite nice. The shop assistant tells him that the probability of winning the R1 000 is only 0.01 (or 1%) and the probability of losing is 0.99 (or 99%). The man now has enough information to make a decision:

- If he buys the ticket, he could possibly lose his money and leave with nothing.
- Alternatively, if he buys the ticket he could win (unlikely) and he would have enough money for his groceries and much more.
- Finally, he could decide not to buy the ticket, in which case he would certainly leave with his groceries (and nothing else).

The probability of winning or losing will help him to make his decision, but ultimately it is his own decision to make. A conscientious person placed in this situation would realise that the safest option would be to avoid buying the scratch card, since that decision ensures that he will at least return home with his groceries.

In this chapter, we will discuss some of the techniques required to calculate probabilities such as the one given in the above example. We will also discuss some of the basic concepts and laws related to probability calculations. The chapters that follow will discuss some standard probability distributions that we can also use in probability calculations.

Statistics and inference

Statistics encompasses many aspects of data analysis, but many of the techniques that you will encounter later in this book rely rather heavily on probability theory.

In previous chapters, we were mainly concerned with summarising, describing, analysing and interpreting sample data. However, as we described in Section 1.1.3 of Chapter 1, at some point we need to extend our sample results in order to say something meaningful about population quantities.

We call the idea of extending sample results to the population *statistical inference*, i.e. we infer properties about a population based on sample properties. However, since the properties of a population are unknown, our conclusions about the properties must reflect our degree of uncertainty in the results that we report. Probability theory is the tool that allows us to quantify our uncertainty when reporting conclusions about a population.

Typical applications of statistical inference include estimators for population parameters such as the population mean. For example, we calculate the sample mean of a set of sample data and find that it is 17.3. By cleverly applying probability theory, we might be able to say that the *true population mean* lies between 16.3 and 18.3, with a probability of 0.65, i.e. we are 65% confident that the true population mean lies between the values 16.3 and 18.3 (this is called a *confidence interval* and we will discuss it in later chapters).

Applying probability theory in this example allowed us to make a claim about the much larger, unobserved population, based on information contained within an observed sample, in such a way that the level of certainty of our claim is clear.

4.1.2 The anatomy of probability problems

Every probability problem that we discuss in this book can be broken down into a few elementary components. You need to identify these components in order to calculate the probability of interest. These components include the:

- random experiment
- outcomes and sample space
- event of interest.

Random experiments

In order to determine any probability, you first need to obtain data. You can obtain data through, for example, experience, observation or experimentation. The procedure or situation that gives rise to a clearly defined result is called a **random experiment**, and the clearly defined results of these experiments are called **outcomes**. The term 'experiment' is perhaps misleading in this context, because these procedures or situations can refer to almost anything where the outcome is unknown beforehand, i.e. it does not only refer to experiments conducted by a researcher.

Random experiment A situation, procedure or activity that will give rise to a clearly defined result.

Outcome The potential result of a random experiment. The exact value is unknown before the experiment, but known after the experiment has been conducted.

Sample space

An exhaustive list of all possible outcomes of a certain type for a given experiment is called the **sample space** of an experiment. We use the symbol Ω to denote this complete set or sample space. For example, consider a simple random experiment in which we toss two coins. The outcomes measured in this experiment are the values that appear face up on the two coins after they have landed. The sample space (or complete set of possible outcomes) for this experiment is given by:

$$\Omega = \{\text{heads \& heads, heads \& tails, tails \& heads, tails \& tails}\}$$

Note the use of the curly braces to denote a set of values.

Sample space An exhaustive list of all the possible outcomes of an experiment.

An event

In typical probability calculations, we are usually interested in the probability that a particular condition is satisfied or that one or more of the outcomes listed in the sample space occurs. We call these conditions or occurrences '**events**'. The formal definition of 'events' is a collection of one or more outcomes from an experiment that satisfies some predetermined condition, i.e. events are subsets of the sample space. We will use uppercase letters to denote these subsets or events, i.e. *A*, *B*, *C*, and so on.

> **Event** Any subset of the collection of outcomes of an experiment, i.e. it is a subset of the sample space. We are usually interested in determining the probability of an event occurring.

In an experiment, you are likely to be interested in determining the probability of any one of a myriad of potential events that might occur. Going back to the random experiment in which we tossed two coins, one potential event that we could be interested in is whether at least one head appeared on the two coins. We can express this event as the following set of values:

$$A = \{\text{heads \& tails, heads \& heads, tails \& heads}\}$$

This event contains three of the four outcomes that appeared in the sample space Ω.

Another event that we might be interested in is both coins showing the same value. We can express this event in set notation as:

$$B = \{\text{heads \& heads, tails \& tails}\}$$

This event contains two of the four outcomes that appeared in the sample space Ω.

Yet another event might be that the first coin is 'tails' and the second coin is 'heads (i.e. a specific outcome of the experiment):

$$C = \{\text{tails \& heads}\}$$

This event contains only one of the four outcomes that appeared in the sample space Ω.

Note: You need to be able to distinguish between the concept of an *event* and an *individual outcome*. We define an event as a set of elements, and outcomes as the elements that make up a set. Therefore, an event is a set that contains multiple individual outcomes, but it can also contain only a single outcome. The event *C* above is an illustration of an event that only contains one outcome.

For every experiment, we observe a type of outcome (for example, with the coins, we observed the face of the coins after they landed). However, some experiments can produce many different types of outcomes, but usually we are only interested in one of these types. Table 4.1 lists some examples of random experiments, the types of outcomes that could be observed, the sample spaces for the outcome type and an example of an event for that particular outcome type in the experiment.

Table 4.1: Examples of random experiments, outcomes, sample spaces and possible events

EXPERIMENT	TYPE OF OUTCOME MEASURED	SAMPLE SPACE (Ω)	EXAMPLE OF AN EVENT
Rolling a six-sided die	The number showing on the die	$\Omega = \{1, 2, 3, 4, 5, 6\}$	Roll an even number: $A = \{2, 4, 6\}$
Playing the lottery	Whether you win or lose The amount of money won (the prizes are R1 000 or R2 000)	$\Omega = \{\text{win, lose}\}$ $\Omega = \{0, \text{R1 000}, \text{R2 000}\}$	Win something: $B = \{\text{win}\}$ Win R1 000 or less: $C = \{0, \text{R1 000}\}$
Drawing a card from a deck of 52 cards	The value of a single card drawn	$\Omega = \{A♦, 2♦, 3♦, ..., K♦,$ $A♥, 2♥, 3♥, ..., K♥,$ $A♣, 2♣, 3♣, ..., K♣,$ $A♠, 2♠, 3♠, ..., K♠\}$	Draw any card from the 'hearts' suit: $D = \{A♥, 2♥, ..., K♥\}$
Playing a football game	Whether you win, lose or draw The number of goals scored The number of red cards given	$\Omega = \{\text{win, lose, draw}\}$ $\Omega = \{0, 1, 2, ...\}$ $\Omega = \{0, 1, 2, ..., 23\}$	Lose the match: $E = \{\text{lose}\}$ Score less than three goals: $F = \{0, 1, 2\}$ Get either one or two red cards: $G = \{1, 2\}$
Inspecting products produced in a factory for defects	The product is either defective or is not	$\Omega = \{\text{defective, working}\}$	The product is defective: $H = \{\text{defective}\}$
Selling 30 bags of potatoes at a stall along the side of the road	The number of bags of potatoes sold in a day The amount of money earned (if each bag is sold for R60)	$\Omega = \{0, 1, 2, ..., 30\}$ $\Omega = \{0, \text{R60}, \text{R120}, ..., \text{R1 800}\}$	Sell all the bags of potatoes: $I = \{30\}$ Earn more than R1 600: $J = \{\text{R1 620}, \text{R1 680}, \text{R1 740}, \text{R1 800}\}$

The examples in Table 4.1 are all random experiments, because they satisfy the following characteristics of random experiments:

- Each experiment is repeatable.
- The value of the outcome is unknown before the experiment is conducted, but known and easily observable afterwards.
- All possible outcomes can be described before the experiment is conducted.
- Although individual outcomes appear haphazard, continually repeating the experiment will produce a regular pattern.

We use these definitions in the next section to calculate the probabilities of events.

4.2 Calculating probabilities

In this section, we discuss how to calculate the probabilities of certain events of an experiment. We distinguish between two different scenarios:

- The outcomes of the experiment are all assumed to be equally likely.
- The outcomes each have their own unique, unknown probability.

The first scenario is the simplest, but requires the assumption that the probability of each outcome occurring is the same. This assumption is not always reasonable, and so we cannot always apply this method. The second scenario makes no such assumption and so we will use information from repeated observations of an experiment in order to determine the probabilities associated with each outcome.

Notation

Before we begin looking at how probabilities are calculated, you need to know the notation that we use to represent the probability of events. The probability of event A is denoted by $P(A)$ and can be calculated as the sum of the probabilities of the individual outcomes in A. For example, if we define the sample space of an experiment as $\Omega = \{a_1, a_2, a_3, a_4\}$ and the event A as $A = \{a_1, a_3\}$, then the probability of event A would be:

$$P(A) = P(\{a_1\}) + P(\{a_3\})$$

$P(\{a_1\})$ and $P(\{a_3\})$ are the probabilities of the events that contain only the individual outcomes a_1 and a_3.

Note the following outcomes and their associated probabilities:

- The probability of each *individual outcome* lies between 0 and 1.
- The *sum of the probabilities of the outcomes* in the sample space equals 1.

These two properties imply that the probability of any *event* also lies between 0 and 1.

4.2.1 Determining probabilities when outcomes are equally probable

We can simplify the calculation of probabilities of events if we assume that the outcomes that make up the events are all equally likely. If it is reasonable to assume that the outcomes all have an equal probability of occurring, then you first need to determine the probability common to all outcomes. You can obtain this probability by using the following formula:

$$\text{Probability of each outcome} = \frac{1}{\#(\Omega)}$$

$\#(\Omega)$ = the number of unique outcomes in the sample space.

In the previous section, we tossed two coins and observed the outcome. The sample space was:

$$\Omega = \{\text{heads \& heads, heads \& tails, tails \& heads, tails \& tails}\}$$

Therefore, $\#(\Omega) = 4$ for this experiment and so the probability of any one of the four outcomes is:

$$\frac{1}{\#(\Omega)} = \frac{1}{4} = 0.25$$

The probability of an event (a set of individual outcomes from the sample space) is then simply the sum of the probabilities of the individual outcomes in that set. For example, suppose for the coin toss example we define the event as 'both coins have the same value showing', that is:

$$A = \{\text{heads \& heads, tails \& tails}\}$$

Then, the probability of this event is the sum of the probabilities of each individual outcome (which we know are each equal to 0.25):

$$P(A) = P(\{\text{heads \& heads}\}) + P(\{\text{tails \& tails}\}) = 0.25 + 0.25 = 0.5$$

In other words, the probability that both coins show the same value when we assume that the outcomes are equally probable is 0.5 or 50%.

In general, these probability calculations essentially resolve into a counting exercise, i.e. we need to count how many unique items there are in the sample space and how many outcomes there are in the event.

We can summarise the probability calculation for some event A (where the outcomes in the sample space are equally probable) as:

$$P(A) = \frac{\#(A)}{\#(\Omega)} \tag{4.1}$$

- $\#(A)$ = the number of unique outcomes in event A.
- $\#(\Omega)$ = the number of unique outcomes in the sample space Ω.

WORKED EXAMPLES

EXAMPLE 4.1

A gambler plays a game called 'guess the card' in which he pays R2 and then has to correctly guess the value of the card randomly drawn from the deck. If he guesses correctly, he wins R1 000.

1. What is the probability that the gambler draws a diamond?
2. What is the probability that he draws a queen?

1. The experiment here is drawing the card. The possible outcomes that form the sample space are:

$$\begin{aligned}\Omega = \{&A\blacklozenge, 2\blacklozenge, 3\blacklozenge, 4\blacklozenge, 5\blacklozenge, 6\blacklozenge, 7\blacklozenge, 8\blacklozenge, 9\blacklozenge, 10\blacklozenge, J\blacklozenge, Q\blacklozenge, K\blacklozenge,\\ &A\heartsuit, 2\heartsuit, 3\heartsuit, 4\heartsuit, 5\heartsuit, 6\heartsuit, 7\heartsuit, 8\heartsuit, 9\heartsuit, 10\heartsuit, J\heartsuit, Q\heartsuit, K\heartsuit,\\ &A\clubsuit, 2\clubsuit, 3\clubsuit, 4\clubsuit, 5\clubsuit, 6\clubsuit, 7\clubsuit, 8\clubsuit, 9\clubsuit, 10\clubsuit, J\clubsuit, Q\clubsuit, K\clubsuit,\\ &A\spadesuit, 2\spadesuit, 3\spadesuit, 4\spadesuit, 5\spadesuit, 6\spadesuit, 7\spadesuit, 8\spadesuit, 9\spadesuit, 10\spadesuit, J\spadesuit, Q\spadesuit, K\spadesuit\}\end{aligned}$$

The event of interest is the occurrence of a 'diamond'. We will denote this event A and define it as:

$$A = \{A\blacklozenge, 2\blacklozenge, 3\blacklozenge, 4\blacklozenge, 5\blacklozenge, 6\blacklozenge, 7\blacklozenge, 8\blacklozenge, 9\blacklozenge, 10\blacklozenge, J\blacklozenge, Q\blacklozenge, K\blacklozenge\}$$

If we assume that each card drawn is equally probable, then the number of items in the sample space is $\#(\Omega) = 52$ and the number of items in the event A is $\#(A) = 13$. The probability of drawing a diamond is therefore:

$$\text{P}(A) = \frac{\#(A)}{\#(\Omega)} = \frac{13}{52} = 0.25$$

2. The event, now given by B, is defined as:

$$B = \{Q\blacklozenge, Q\blacktriangledown, Q\clubsuit, Q\spadesuit\}$$

The number of items in event B is $\#(B) = 4$ and so the probability of drawing a queen is then:

$$P(B) = \frac{\#(B)}{\#(\Omega)} = \frac{4}{52} = 0.076923076$$

4.2.2 Determining probabilities when outcomes are not equally probable: relative frequencies

In cases where it is not reasonable to assume that the individual outcomes of a sample space are equally likely, we need to use a different method to determine the probability of events. In this section, we briefly describe an approximation method that we can use to obtain these probabilities. We will begin by considering a simple example.

Suppose we have a die that we suspect is 'loaded', i.e. the die has been tampered with so that it is more likely to land on one number than the other five. To approximate the probabilities of each number appearing on the die, we perform an experiment in which we throw the die and record the value that appears face up. We repeat the experiment a large number of times (1 000 times) and note the number of times each value appears. For each number, we calculate the ratio of these two numbers:

- The total number of times that outcome or event occurs (m)
- The total number of times the experiment was repeated ($n = 1\,000$)

This ratio is called the **relative frequency**. In general, if event A occurs m times, then the relative frequency that A will occur is:

$$\text{Relative frequency of } A = \frac{m}{n} \tag{4.2}$$

Relative frequency The ratio of the frequency of occurrence of each outcome or event (m) to the total number of times the experiment was repeated (n).

Here, m represents the frequency or the number of times a particular number occurs on the die (an outcome). Table 4.2 shows the result of the die experiment.

Table 4.2: A relative frequency table of the number of times each value is obtained on 1 000 rolls of a die

VALUE ON DIE	1	2	3	4	5	6
FREQUENCY OBSERVED	173	168	167	161	172	159
RELATIVE FREQUENCY	0.173	0.168	0.167	0.161	0.172	0.159

The relative frequency gives us a way of *approximating* the probability of an event. As the number of times the experiment is repeated increases, the relative frequency stabilises and approaches the true probability of the event. Thus, if the die was 'fair' (each side appearing is equally probable), and we had performed the experiment 1 000 000 times, we might expect in the long run that the frequencies of all the scores would approach 0.167, i.e. $P(\{1\}) = 0.167$, $P(\{2\}) = 0.167$, $P(\{3\}) = 0.167$, and so on. We can derive probabilities using this empirical approach for many situations. For example, if a manufacturer indicates that he is 99% certain (0.99) that an electric light bulb will last for 200 hours, he will have arrived at this figure by testing numerous samples of light bulbs. If we are told that the probability of rain on a particular day in June is 0.42, this figure will have been determined by studying rainfall records for June over, for example, the past 20 years, among other factors.

4.3 Basic probability rules

Now that we have defined methods that you can use to obtain probabilities of events, we can look at how to manipulate the probabilities using set notation, algebraic notation and other basic techniques.

4.3.1 Venn diagrams and set notation: visualising probability

We begin this section by introducing the concept of Venn diagrams. These diagrams are helpful in visualising events and sample spaces so that we can more easily understand complex set notation and probability algebra.

A set that contains every single outcome (sample space or *universal set* in general terms) is denoted by Ω. The set that contains no elements is denoted by $\emptyset$.

The following figures use Venn diagrams to illustrate various set notation that we use in the algebra of probability calculations.

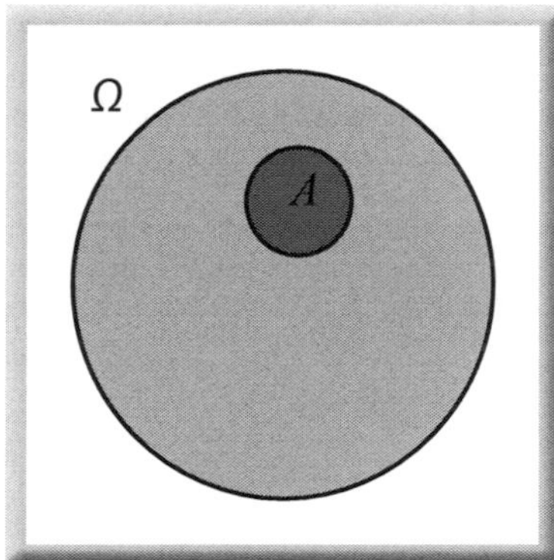

Figure 4.2: Venn diagram depicting $A \subset \Omega$

The Venn diagram in Figure 4.2 represents a sample space Ω and an event (**subset**) A. Note that A is completely contained within the sample space. We use the following set notation to indicate that A is completely contained within Ω.

$$A \subset \Omega$$

The Venn diagram in Figure 4.3 depicts two subsets, *A* and *B*, contained within the sample space Ω. However, *A* is also completely contained within *B*. In this case, we write:

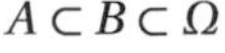

$$A \subset B \subset \Omega$$

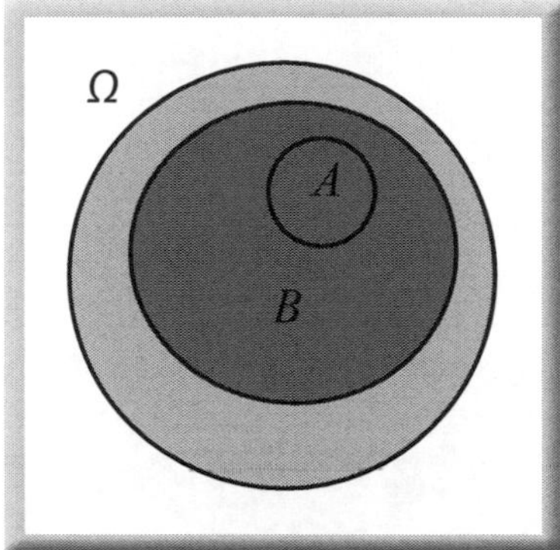

Figure 4.3: Venn diagram depicting $A \subset B \subset \Omega$

In Figure 4.4, you can see that subsets *A* and *B* overlap, but that one event is not completely contained within the other. The shaded area of the diagram represents the **union** of these two subsets and is denoted by:

$$A \cup B$$

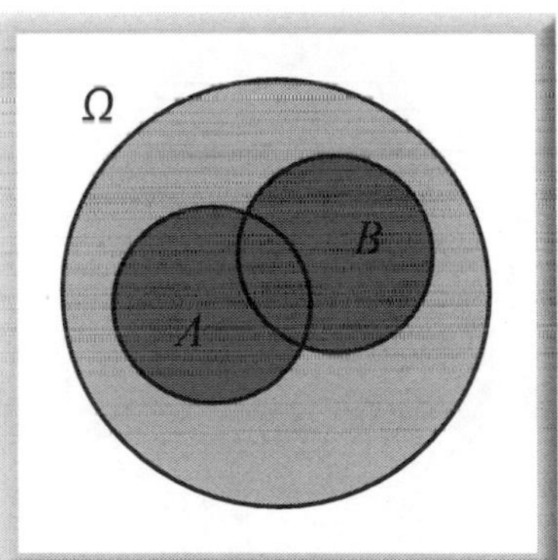

Figure 4.4: Venn diagram depicting $A \cup B$

Note that the shaded area is also a subset of the sample space and thus is also an event.

When discussing the union of events, we often use the word 'or', i.e. we refer to the union of two events as '*A* or *B*'. Intuitively, this means that the event produced by the union of *A* and *B* will occur if the outcomes associated with either *A or B* occur.

The situation in Figure 4.5 is similar to that in Figure 4.4, except that in this Venn diagram, the shaded area represents the portion of the two subset that overlap. This area of overlap is called the **intersection** of the two subsets and is denoted by:

$$A \cap B$$

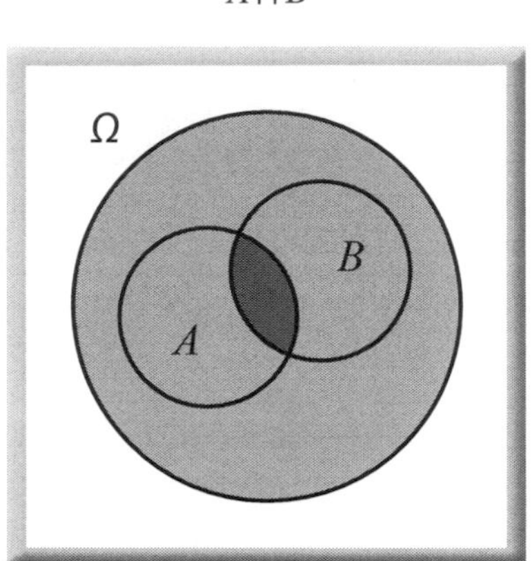

Figure 4.5: Venn diagram depicting $A \cap B$

Note again that this intersection of the events is also a subset of the sample space and is thus also an event.

We use the word 'and' when referring to intersections, i.e. we refer to the intersection of two events as 'A and B'. Intuitively, we can say that the event formed by the intersection of two events A and B will only occur if the outcomes that are associated with both A *and* B occur.

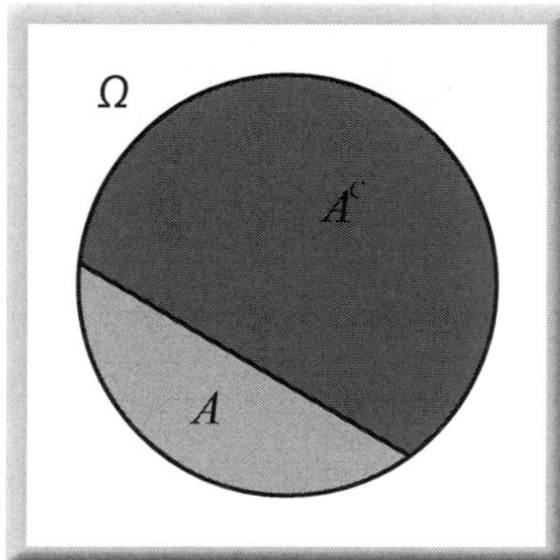

Figure 4.6: Venn diagram depicting A^C the complement of A

Figure 4.6 depicts a subset A of Ω and the dark shaded area represents A^C, the **complement** of A. These two events are disjointed from one another (i.e. A is not a subset of A^C). The sets A and A^C together form the *complete* sample space Ω (the word *complement* is related to the word *complete*: A needs A^C to complete the whole space).

Note that $A \cup A^C = \Omega$ and that $A \cap A^C = \emptyset$. The notation A^C is sometimes read '*not* A' or 'A does not occur'.

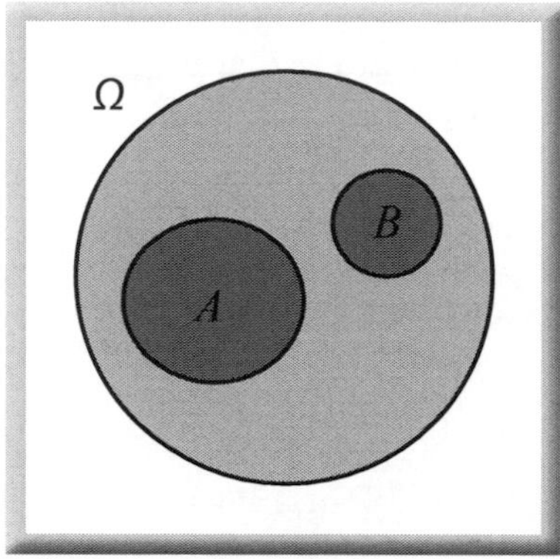

Figure 4.7: Venn diagram depicting two mutually exclusive events

Two events A and B are said to be **mutually exclusive** if they do not intersect in any way, i.e. if $A \cap B = \emptyset$. Figure 4.7 shows two events, A and B, that are mutually exclusive.

4.3.2 Probability rules

The preceding Venn diagrams will now help us to discuss some basic probability rules that apply to events, unions of events, intersection of events and complements of events. Refer back to the relevant Venn diagrams where necessary in order to grasp these concepts intuitively.

The probability that one outcome listed in the sample space will occur is certain, i.e. if Ω represents the sample space that contains all possible outcomes of an experiment, then the probability that any one of these outcomes occurs is certain. We write this as:

$$P(\Omega) = 1 \tag{4.3}$$

The probability that nothing happens is zero:

$$P(\emptyset) = 0 \tag{4.4}$$

In other words, one of the outcomes listed in the sample space *must* occur.

The additive rule for mutually exclusive events

If two events, A and B, are mutually exclusive, then the probability of the union of the two events is equal to the sum of the probabilities of the two individual events:

$$P(A \cup B) = P(A) + P(B) \tag{4.5}$$

You can see this relationship in Figure 4.7 (in contrast to Figure 4.4), in which we have two mutually exclusive events.

The complement rule

We can apply the above additive rule and replace the mutually exclusive events A and B with the mutually exclusive events A and A^C. We then find the following:

$$P(A \cup A^C) = P(A) + P(A^C)$$

However, we know from the definition of A and A^C that $A \cup A^C = \Omega$, and so therefore we have:

$$P(\Omega) = P(A) + P(A^C)$$

Finally, since we also know that $P(\Omega) = 1$ we can write:

$$1 = P(A) + P(A^C)$$

Or:

$$P(A) = 1 - P(A^C) \tag{4.6}$$

This rule is also evident from Figure 4.6.

The general additive rule

If the events A and B are *not* mutually exclusive (as in Figure 4.4), then finding the probability of their union is complicated by the fact that each event has a section that overlaps with the other. The overlapping section, $A \cap B$, is common to both A and B, so this portion of the event appears twice in the union between A and B. To compensate for this, we subtract the portion that appears twice from the sum of the probability of the two events. The general additive rule is then:

$$P(A \cup B) = P(A) + P(B) - P(A \cap B) \tag{4.7}$$

Figure 4.8 illustrates the union of two events that are not mutually exclusive using Venn diagrams.

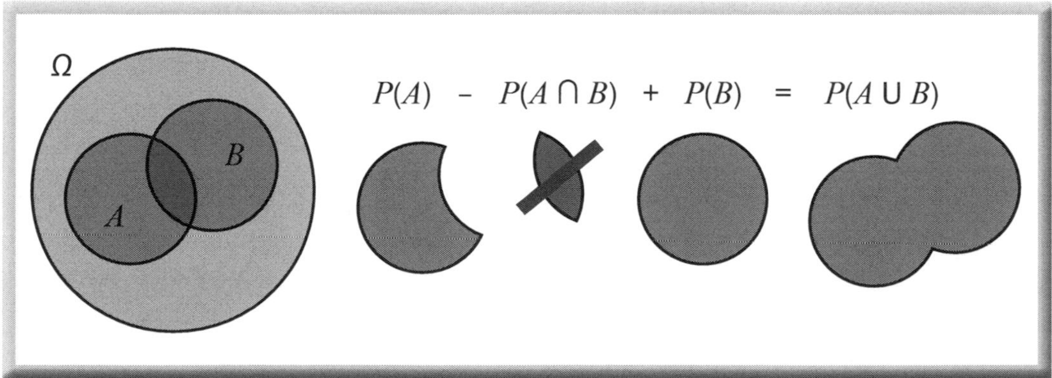

Figure 4.8: Venn diagram depicting the general additive rule

WORKED EXAMPLES

EXAMPLE 4.2

To illustrate the above three rules, consider a sample space from an experiment in which a die is rolled. The sample space is:

$$\Omega = \{1, 2, 3, 4, 5, 6\}$$

Let event A represent the event of rolling an odd number, let B represent the event of rolling a number less than or equal to 4, and let C be the event that a 4 or 6 is rolled:

$$A = \{1, 3, 5\} \qquad B = \{1, 2, 3, 4\} \qquad C = \{4, 6\}$$

Note that events A and B overlap, whereas events A and C are mutually exclusive.

1. Calculate the probabilities that A *and* B both occur when the die is rolled.

   The 'and' in the question tells us that we need to use the '∩' symbol. Therefore, we need to calculate:

   $$P(A \cap B) = P(\{1, 3, 5\} \cap \{1, 2, 3, 4\}) = P(\{1, 3\}) = \frac{2}{6} = 0.333$$

2. Calculate the probability that C does not occur when the die is rolled.

   The question asks for the probability that C does 'not' occur, so we need to calculate the probability of the complement of C:

   $$P(C^C) = 1 - P(C) = 1 - \frac{2}{6} = \frac{4}{6} = 0.667$$

3. Calculate the probability that A *or* B occur when the die is rolled.

   The 'or' in the question tells us we need to use the '∪' symbol, and thus we use the additive rule:

   $$P(A \cup B) = P(A) + P(B) - P(A \cap B) = \frac{3}{6} + \frac{4}{6} - \frac{2}{6} = \frac{5}{6} = 0.833$$

WORKED EXAMPLES

EXAMPLE 4.3

A card is chosen from an ordinary pack of cards. Let events A and B represent the events of obtaining an ace card and a black card respectively:

$$A = \{A\diamondsuit, A\heartsuit, A\clubsuit, A\spadesuit\}$$

and:

$$B = \{A\clubsuit, 1\clubsuit, 2\clubsuit, 3\clubsuit, 4\clubsuit, 5\clubsuit, 6\clubsuit, 7\clubsuit, 8\clubsuit, 9\clubsuit, 10\clubsuit, J\clubsuit, Q\clubsuit, K\clubsuit, A\spadesuit, 1\spadesuit, 2\spadesuit, 3\spadesuit, 4\spadesuit, 5\spadesuit, 6\spadesuit, 7\spadesuit, 8\spadesuit, 9\spadesuit, 10\spadesuit, J\spadesuit, Q\spadesuit, K\spadesuit\}$$

The sample space Ω is given in Example 4.1.

Write down the probabilities of obtaining the following cards.

a) A black card and an ace

$$P(B \cap A) = \frac{\#(\{A♣, A♠\})}{\#(\Omega)} = \frac{2}{52} = 0.0385$$

b) A black card or an ace

$$P(B \cup A) = P(B) + P(A) - P(B \cap A) = \frac{26}{52} + \frac{4}{52} - \frac{2}{52} = \frac{28}{52} = 0.538462$$

c) Neither a black card nor an ace

$$\begin{aligned} P(\text{neither } B \text{ nor } A) &= P((B \cup A)^C) \\ &= 1 - P(B \cup A) \\ &= 1 - 0.5385 = 0.4615 \end{aligned}$$

4.3.3 Independent events

Earlier in this section, we discussed mutually exclusive events, i.e. events that cannot occur at the same time, but what about completely **independent events**? An example of an independent event is rolling a die twice. The fact that we get a 6 on the first roll does not influence the outcome of the second roll. Similarly, if we pick a ball from a bag and replace it in the bag before picking another ball, nothing changes because the sample space remains the same on both draws. Drawing the first ball (and then replacing it) cannot affect the probability of the outcome of the next selection. These are both examples of independent events.

Independent events Two events are independent if the occurrence of one of the events has no influence on the occurrence of the other event.

If two (or more) events are independent, then the general multiplication law applies:

$$P(A \cap B) = P(A) \times P(B) \tag{4.8}$$

If the probability $P(A \cap B) \neq P(A) \times P(B)$, then events A and B are said to be dependent on one another.

NOTE

The terms 'independent' and 'mutually exclusive' are different and apply to different things. If A and B are events with non-zero probabilities, then we can show that:

- $P(A \cap B) = 0$, if mutually exclusive (but only if $P(A) \neq 0$ and $P(B) \neq 0$). Mutually exclusive events cannot occur at the same time.
- $P(A \cap B) = P(A) \times P(B) \neq 0$, if the events are independent (but only if $P(A) \neq 0$ and $P(B) \neq 0$). Independent events do not influence each other.

WORKED EXAMPLES

EXAMPLE 4.4

Suppose a pair of fair dice are tossed. Let A be the event that the first die shows an even number and B be the event that the second die shows a 5 or 6. Events A and B are unrelated (i.e. the outcome on one die cannot affect the outcome on the second die) and are therefore independent events. Thus, the probability of A occurring is:

$$P(A) = \frac{3}{6} = 0.5$$

The probability of event B occurring is:

$$P(B) = \frac{2}{6} = 0.3$$

Thus:

$$P(A \cap B) = P(A) \times P(B) = 0.5 \times 0.3 = 0.15$$

4.4 Conditional probability

In this section, we will look at how to apply the methods just discussed to calculate probabilities of events that are conditional on the outcomes of other experiments.

4.4.1 What is conditional probability?

Conditional probabilities are probabilities calculated under the condition that something else has occurred. For example, we could be interested in the probability that a person is carrying an umbrella conditional on the fact that it had rained that morning. This example illustrates two things about conditional probabilities:

- The scenario is potentially dependent on two different sample spaces (from two different experiments the results of which could be dependent on one another). The two experiments in this example are 'determine if a person has an umbrella' and 'determine if it rained' with sample spaces {'umbrella', 'no umbrella'} and {'rained', 'didn't rain'} respectively. The resulting sample space of the joint experiment (i.e. the experiment that combines both experiments) has the sample space {'rained with umbrella', 'rained without umbrella', 'didn't rain with umbrella', 'didn't rain without umbrella'}.
- The outcome of one of the experiments has already been observed or is the sole focus of the study (other outcomes for that experiment are ignored). The other experiment, on the other hand, has not been realised yet (it is uncertain and is thus the subject of the probability calculation). In this example, we assume that we know it has rained, i.e. the experiment 'determine if it rained' yielded the outcome {'rained'}, but the outcome of the 'determine if a person has an umbrella' experiment is not yet known (we are thus interested in determining the probability of some event associated with this experiment).

Essentially, conditional probabilities are probabilities calculated in situations where the specified condition has restricted the sample space. In this example, the joint sample space of both experiments would have four outcomes: {rained with umbrella, rained without umbrella, didn't rain with umbrella, didn't rain without umbrella}. However, the sample space becomes restricted to only two outcomes with the condition: {rained with umbrella, rained without umbrella}. This sample space is linked only to the situation we are interested in: determining the probability of whether a person has an umbrella on the days that it rains. We ignore the days on which it does not rain.

The result is that the probability of the event that a person has an umbrella will potentially change under this specific condition because the sample space is smaller than usual.

The notation we use to express these conditional probabilities is $P(B|A)$, which we read as 'the probability of event B, given that event A has occurred. We express this conditional probability as:

$$P(B|A) = \frac{P(B \cap A)}{P(A)} \tag{4.9}$$

We can rewrite this equation as:

$$P(B \cap A) = P(B|A)P(A)$$

When events A and B are independent of one another, the expression for conditional probability simplifies to:

$$P(B|A) = P(B)$$

This is because if A and B are independent, then $P(B \cap A) = P(A)P(B)$.

WORKED EXAMPLES

EXAMPLE 4.5

A football team finds that the probability that they score one or more goals in any match is 0.7. They also find that they won 72 of the 120 matches in which they scored goals over the past two seasons. On the other hand, they lost 16 of the 120 games in which they did not score.

What is the probability that the team wins a match given that they scored a goal?

Let A be the event that they score one or more goals in a match. Let B be the event that they win the match. The probability that they score a goal is:

$$P(A) = 0.7$$

The probability that they score a goal and win is given as (we will use the relative frequency to approximate this probability):

$$P(A \cap B) = \frac{72}{120} = 0.6$$

Therefore, the probability that they win a match given that they have scored one or more goals is then:

$$P(B|A) = \frac{P(B \cap A)}{P(A)} = \frac{0.6}{0.7} = 0.857$$

WORKED EXAMPLES

EXAMPLE 4.6

A bag contains three red and four white balls. You draw two balls, one-by-one, from the bag and place them on the table.

What is the probability that you draw two red balls? Assume that each ball has an equal chance of being drawn.

Let A denote the event that you draw a red ball on the first attempt and let B denote the event that you draw a red ball on the second attempt.

The probability of A is:

$$P(A) = \frac{3}{7}$$

Now, if you draw a red ball on the first draw, then there are two red balls and four white balls left in the bag (six in total). The conditional probability that you draw a red ball given that you have already drawn a red ball is thus:

$$P(B|A) = \frac{2}{6}$$

Use the formula:

$$P(A \cap B) = P(B|A)\, P(A)$$

We find that the probability of drawing two red balls is (i.e. that event A and event B occurs):

$$P(A \cap B) = P(B \mid A)\, P(A) = \frac{2}{6} \times \frac{3}{7} = \frac{1}{7}$$

In the next section, we look at a method that is helpful in calculating probabilities when the joint probabilities are unknown, but we know the conditional probabilities.

4.4.2 Using tree diagrams and conditional probabilities to solve more complex probability problems

Occasionally, you will encounter probability problems that involve joint probabilities that are too complex to solve easily using the tools we have presented up to now. In this section, we briefly discuss using tree diagrams and conditional probabilities as tools to determine these complex probabilities.

We construct tree diagrams by considering all of the decisions or actions that are taken during the course of an experiment. We represent these decisions with branches that stem from a single node or setting and which terminate in a different node. The node represents a particular experimental setting. Each branch of the tree diagram is associated with a specific probability calculated under the conditions stipulated by the node. We then need to add or multiple the probabilities associated with branches on pathways that link the origin node to some specified end target node(s).

For example, suppose that a bag contains two green balls and three orange balls. You conduct an experiment in which you draw two balls from the bag one-at-a-time and place them on the table next to the bag. Let A_1 be the event that you draw a green ball on the first draw (i.e. A_1^C is the event that an orange ball is drawn). Figure 4.9 shows the tree diagram that represents the first action in this experiment. The probability that you draw a green ball is $P(A_1) = \frac{\#(A_1)}{\#(\Omega)} = \frac{2}{5}$, and the probability that you draw an orange ball is equal to the probability that a green ball is *not* drawn, i.e. $P(A_1^C) = 1 - P(A_1) = 1 - \frac{2}{5} = \frac{3}{5}$.

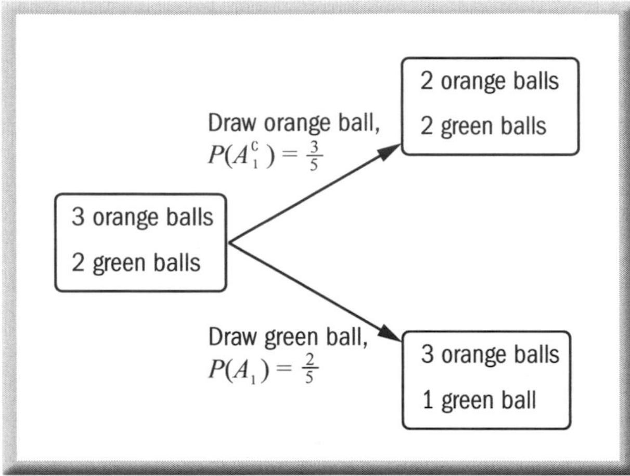

Figure 4.9: A first action of a tree diagram (initially a bag with two green balls and three orange balls)

In the second stage of the experiment, you draw another ball, but now the previous action has changed the sample space. Each of the possible two outcomes of the previous action has resulted in a new starting condition and so the probabilities you calculate at this stage are *conditional* probabilities, i.e. conditional on the event that happened in the previous step. Let A_2 denote the event that you draw a green ball on the second draw.

- The probability that you draw an orange ball given that the previous ball was orange is:

$$P(A_2^C|A_1^C) = \frac{2}{4} = \frac{1}{2}$$

- The probability that you draw a green ball given that the previous ball was orange is:

$$P(A_2|A_1^C) = \frac{2}{4} = \frac{1}{2}$$

- The probability that you draw an orange ball given that the previous ball was green is:

$$P(A_2^C|A_1) = \frac{3}{4}$$

- The probability that you draw a green ball given that the previous ball was green is:

$$P(A_2|A_1) = \frac{1}{4}$$

Figure 4.10 shows the tree diagram after the second step.

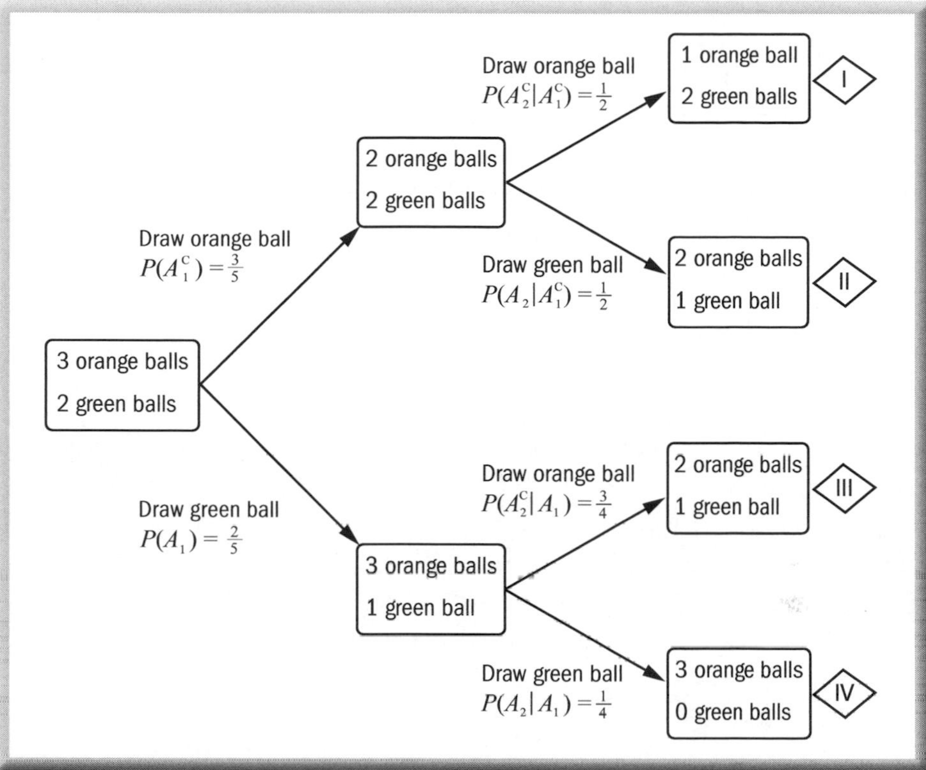

Figure 4.10: A second action of a tree diagram (initially a bag with three green balls and two orange balls)

Using this tree diagram, you can answer a number of probability questions such as the following:

- What is the probability that you draw two green balls?
- What is the probability that you are left with only one green ball at the end of the experiment?
- What is the probability that you draw an orange ball on the second draw?

You can answer each of these questions by examining the tree diagram, identifying which of the terminal nodes match the question being asked, and then tracing the path from these terminal nodes back to the original node, multiplying the probabilities along the path, and summing up the resulting products at the end.

For example (refer to Figure 4.10):

- What is the probability that you draw two green balls?
  The terminal node associated with this event is node IV. You obtain the answer by multiplying the probabilities along the path from node IV to the origin node, i.e. $P(A_1 \cap A_2) = \frac{1}{4} \times \frac{2}{5} = \frac{1}{10}$. Note that you can also do this calculation using formula (4.1), i.e. $P(A_1 \cap A_2) = P(A_2|A_1)P(A_1) = \frac{1}{4} \times \frac{2}{5} = \frac{1}{10}$.
- What is the probability that you are left with only one green ball at the end of the experiment?
  The terminal nodes that are associated with this event are nodes II and III. Once again, you determine the probability by multiplying the probabilities along the path from the terminal node to the origin, and then adding up all of the results. The product of the probabilities along the path from node II to the origin is $\frac{1}{2} \times \frac{3}{5} = \frac{3}{10}$. The product of the probabilities along the path

from node III to the origin is $\frac{3}{4} \times \frac{2}{5} = \frac{3}{10}$. The probability is thus $\left(\frac{1}{2} \times \frac{3}{5}\right) + \left(\frac{3}{4} \times \frac{2}{5}\right) = \frac{3}{10} + \frac{3}{10} = \frac{6}{10} = \frac{3}{5}$. You can also calculate this probability using the formula $P(A_1 \cap A_2^C) + P(A_1^C \cap A_2) = \left(\frac{1}{2} \times \frac{3}{5}\right) + \left(\frac{3}{4} \times \frac{2}{5}\right) = \frac{3}{10} + \frac{3}{10} = \frac{6}{10} = \frac{3}{5}$.

- What is the probability that you draw an orange ball on the second draw?
  Nodes I and III are associated with the event that you draw an orange ball on the second draw. The probability is thus the sum of the products of the probabilities along the paths from nodes I and III to the origin. The path for node I is $\frac{1}{2} \times \frac{3}{5} = \frac{3}{10}$. The path for node III is $\frac{3}{4} \times \frac{2}{5} = \frac{6}{20} = \frac{3}{10}$. The sum of these two paths is then $\frac{3}{10} + \frac{3}{10} = \frac{6}{10}$. You can also calculate this probability using the formula $P(A_2^C \cap A_1) + P(A_2^C \cap A_1^C) = \left(\frac{1}{2} \times \frac{3}{5}\right) + \left(\frac{3}{4} \times \frac{2}{5}\right) = \frac{3}{10} + \frac{6}{20} = \frac{6}{10} = \frac{3}{5}$.

WORKED EXAMPLES

EXAMPLE 4.7

A certain school in the Free State has three Grade 8 class groups, namely class group 8a, class group 8b, and class group 8c, with 86, 75 and 69 students respectively (there are a total of 230 Grade 8 students).

At the end of the semester it is found that 5 of the 86 students from class group 8a failed, 3 of the 75 students from class group 8b failed, and 8 of the 69 students from class group 8c failed.

a) What is the probability that a randomly chosen Grade 8 student failed?

b) What is the probability that randomly chosen student came from class group 8c, given that they failed?

To answer these questions begin by constructing the tree diagram:

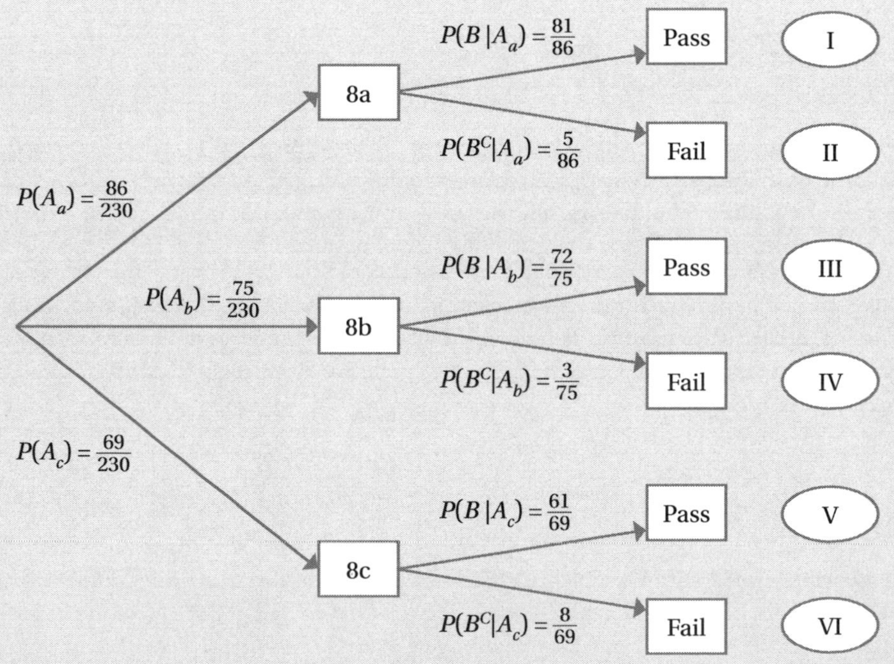

Where A_a, A_b and A_c denote the events that students come from class groups 8a, 8b and 8c respectively, and let B denote the event that they pass.

The answers to the probability questions stated are:

a) The terminal nodes associated with failing are nodes II, IV and VI. The probability that a student fails is thus

$$P(B^C) = \underbrace{P(B^C|A_a) \times P(A_a)}_{\text{From node II to origin}} + \underbrace{P(B^C|A_b) \times P(A_b)}_{\text{From node IV to origin}} + \underbrace{P(B^C|A_c) \times P(A_c)}_{\text{From node VI to origin}}$$

$$= \left(\frac{5}{86} \times \frac{86}{230}\right) + \left(\frac{3}{75} \times \frac{75}{230}\right) + \left(\frac{8}{69} \times \frac{69}{230}\right)$$

$$= \frac{8}{115}$$

This probability could also have been more easily obtained by noting that 16 of the 230 students failed.

b) To answer this question, we begin by noting that the conditional probability of interest is given by:

$$P(A_c|B^C) = \frac{P(A_c \cap B^C)}{P(B^C)}$$

The probability $P(B^C)$was shown in the previous calculation to be equal to $\frac{8}{115}$, so for this calculation we only need to calculate $P(A_c \cap B^C)$ from the tree diagram, i.e. we need to get the probability that the student was in class group 8c and failed. We can get this probability by first noting that node VI is associated with students that failed in class 8c and so we can calculate this probability by following the path from node VI to the origin of the tree diagram:

$$P(A_c \cap B^C) = \underbrace{P(B^C|A_c)P(A_c)}_{\text{From node VI to origin}} = \frac{8}{69} \times \frac{69}{230} = \frac{8}{230} = \frac{4}{115}$$

Therefore, the probability $P(A_c|B^C)$ is given by:

$$P(A_c|B^C) = \frac{P(A_c \cap B^C)}{P(B^C)} = \frac{\frac{4}{115}}{\frac{8}{115}} = \frac{4}{8} = 0.5$$

4.4.3 Probability rules involving conditional probabilities

In the previous section, we introduced conditional probability calculations by making use of tree diagrams, but these calculations can also be done by using some simple formulae. In this section, we will briefly discuss the *Law of Total Probability* and also *Bayes' Theorem* for conditional probability. These two concepts will be demonstrated by using the situation described in Example 4.7.

First, we look at the Law of Total Probability: this law allows us to write the probability of an event A as the sum of conditional probabilities.

Suppose that we have k mutually exclusive events $B_1, B_2, \ldots, B_k$, such that the union of these events is the entire sample space, i.e. $B_1 \cup B_2 \cup \ldots \cup B_k = \Omega$. As a consequence of these events forming the entire sample space, any other event, say A, will naturally intersect with some of these B_k events. Therefore, the probability of event A can simply be written as the sum of all these intersections:

$$P(A) = P(A \cap B_1) + P(A \cap B_2) + \cdots + P(A \cap B_k)$$

Figure 4.11 illustrates how this sum can be visualised.

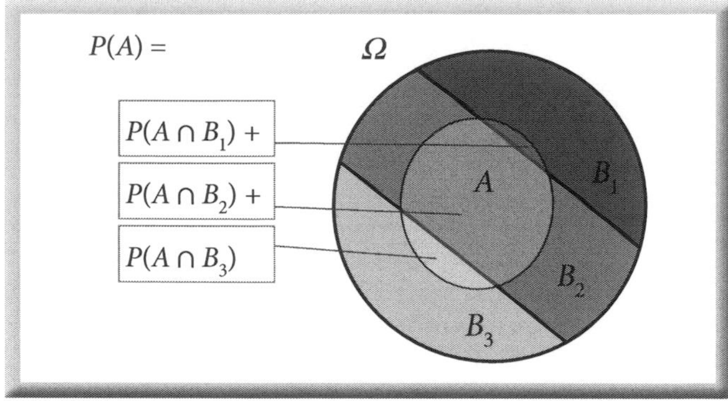

Figure 4.11: Illustration of the Law of Total Probability: Calculation of $P(A)$ where $B_1 \cup B_2 \cup B_3 = \Omega$

Now, since the conditional probability $P(A|B_i)$ can be written as $\frac{P(A \cap B_i)}{P(B_i)}$ using formula (4.9), it stands to reason that we can rearrange that equation and rewrite $P(A \cap B_i)$ as follows:

$$P(A \cap B_i) = P(A|B_i)P(B_i) \tag{4.10}$$

Using the result in formula (4.10), we can now state the Law of Total Probability.

LAW OF TOTAL PROBABILITY

Suppose that we have k mutually exclusive events $B_1, B_2, ..., B_k$, such that the union of these events is the entire sample space, i.e. $B_1 \cup B_2 \cup ... \cup B_k = \Omega$. The probability of some event A is then:

$$P(A) = P(A \cap B_1) + P(A \cap B_2) + \cdots + P(A \cap B_k) \tag{4.11}$$

Or, by using the result in (4.10), we can write:

$$P(A) = P(A|B_1)P(B_1) + P(A|B_2)P(B_2) + \cdots + P(A|B_k)P(B_k) \tag{4.12}$$

Next, we will look at Bayes' Theorem, which allows us to relate the conditional probability $P(A|B)$ to the conditional probability $P(B|A)$, i.e. it shows how we are able to switch the order of the conditioning.

BAYES' THEOREM

Bayes' Theorem states that the conditional probability of event A given event B can be written as:

$$P(A|B) = \frac{P(B|A)P(A)}{P(B)} \tag{4.13}$$

These two concepts will now be illustrated using the situation first discussed in Example 4.7.

WORKED EXAMPLES

EXAMPLE 4.8

Continuing with Example 4.7, calculate the probability that

a) a randomly chosen Grade 8 student failed, i.e. $P(B^C)$?

b) a randomly chosen student came from class group 8c, given that they failed, i.e. $P(A_c|B^C)$?

In Example 4.7, we calculated these probabilities using tree diagrams; we will now see how these same probabilities can be calculated using formula (4.11), (4.12) and (4.13).

a) To answer this question, first note that $A_a \cup A_b \cup A_c = \Omega$. We can then make use of the Law of Total Probability, formula (4.12):

$$\begin{aligned} P(B^C) &= P(B^C|A_a)P(A_a) + P(B^C|A_b)P(A_b) + P(B^C|A_c)P(A_c) \\ &= \frac{5}{86} \times \frac{86}{230} + \frac{3}{75} \times \frac{75}{230} + \frac{8}{69} \times \frac{69}{230} \\ &= \frac{8}{115} \end{aligned}$$

b) First note that the conditional probabilities provided in the example are of the form $P(B|A)$, but we need to calculate a probability of the form $P(A|B)$, and also note that, in this example, $A_a \cup A_b \cup A_c = \Omega$. These two characteristics indicate that we can apply Bayes' Theorem in formula (4.13):

$$\begin{aligned} P(A_c|B^C) &= \frac{P(B^C|A_c)P(A_c)}{P(B^C)} \\ &= \frac{\frac{8}{69} \times \frac{69}{230}}{\frac{8}{115}} \\ &= 0.5 \end{aligned}$$

Recall that we calculated $P(B^C) = \frac{8}{115}$ above.

SUMMARY

In this chapter, we provided an overview of the concept of probability and its associated rules of addition and multiplication to solve a range of probability problems. To help solve these problems, we introduced the idea of using a visual display (tree diagram) to enable the events contributing to the solution to be identified.

KEY TERMS

Event
Independent events
Outcome
Mutually exclusive
Probability
Random experiment
Relative frequency
Sample space
Tree diagram

FORMULA SUMMARY

$$P(A) = \frac{\#(A)}{\#(\Omega)} \tag{4.1}$$

$$\text{Relative frequency of } A = \frac{m}{n} \tag{4.2}$$

$$P(\Omega) = 1 \tag{4.3}$$

$$P(\emptyset) = 0 \tag{4.4}$$

$$P(A \cup B) = P(A) + P(B) \tag{4.5}$$

$$P(A) = 1 - P(A^C) \tag{4.6}$$

$$P(A \cup B) = P(A) + P(B) - P(A \cap B) \tag{4.7}$$

$$P(A \cap B) = P(A) \times P(B) \tag{4.8}$$

$$P(B|A) = \frac{P(B \cap A)}{P(A)} \tag{4.9}$$

$$P(A \cap B_i) = P(A|B_i)P(B_i) \tag{4.10}$$

$$P(A) = P(A \cap B_1) + P(A \cap B_2) + \cdots + P(A \cap B_k) \quad (4.11)$$

$$P(A) = P(A|B_1)P(B_1) + P(A|B_2)P(B_2) + \cdots + P(A|B_k)P(B_k) \quad (4.12)$$

$$P(A|B) = \frac{P(B|A)P(A)}{P(B)} \quad (4.13)$$

EXERCISES

4.1 Give an appropriate sample space for each of the following experiments:

a) A card is chosen at random from a pack of cards.

b) A person is chosen at random from a group containing five females and six males.

c) A football team records the results of each of two games as 'win', 'draw', or 'lose'.

4.2 A dart is thrown at a board and is likely to land on any one of eight squares numbered 1 to 8 inclusive. *A* represents the event the dart lands in square 5 or 8. *B* represents the event the dart lands in square 2, 3 or 4. *C* represents the event the dart lands in square 1, 2, 5 or 6. Which two events are mutually exclusive?

4.3 How would you approximate the probability of a 25-year-old passing their driving test on the first attempt?

4.4 Table 4.3 provides information about 200 school leavers and their destination after leaving school.

Table 4.3: Table depicting the number of learners that leave school and seek employment

	LEAVE SCHOOL AFTER GRADUATING GRADE 10	LEAVE SCHOOL AFTER GRADUATING GRADE 12
Full-time education, (*E*)	14	18
Full-time job, (*J*)	96	44
Other	15	13

Determine the following probabilities that a person selected at random:

a) went into full-time education

b) went into a full-time job

c) either went into full-time education or went into a full-time job

d) left school after graduating Grade 10

e) left school after graduating Grade 10 and went into full-time education.

4.5 Susan takes examinations in Mathematics, English and History. The probability that she passes Mathematics is 0.7, and the corresponding probabilities for English and History are 0.8 and 0.6. Given that her performances in each subject are independent, draw a tree diagram to show the possible outcomes. Use this tree diagram to calculate the following probabilities: (a) she fails all three examinations and (b) she fails just one examination.

CHAPTER 5

RANDOM VARIABLES

CHAPTER CONTENTS

OVERVIEW

This chapter broadly defines and relates the concepts of random variables to their associated probability distributions using generic, data-based examples for both continuous and discrete data types. The chapters that follow introduce you to random variables described by *theoretical probability distributions* (continuous and discrete). So, the random variables in the next few chapters will have theoretical formulae that describe their probability structure, whereas in this chapter, we only discuss the probability distributions using tables (not formulae) in an attempt to illustrate the ideas more easily.

General properties of random variables such as 'expected value' and 'variance' will be explored in this chapter.

LEARNING OBJECTIVES

On completing this chapter, you should be able to:

- understand the concept of the following terms: random variable, relative frequency, sample probability distribution, population (true) probability distribution, population parameter, sample statistic, expected value and population variance
- understand how a population probability distribution relates to a random variable
- calculate the expected value and variance of a random variable given the true population distribution
- understand the concept of a discrete random variable
- understand the concept of a continuous random variable
- calculate expected values and variances using Microsoft Excel.

5.1 Introduction to random variables

In this section, we will discuss the concepts of random variables and how they differ from the outcomes of experiments discussed in the previous chapter. We will see that while they appear to be very similar, they are two distinct concepts.

5.1.1 Random variables

A **random variable** is a variable that provides a measure of the possible numerical values obtainable from a quantitative experiment and is usually denoted by an uppercase letter, for example, X. The numerical values of a random variable are associated with the measurable outcomes of an experiment and thus have specific probabilities of occurrence. For example, consider the following two experiments and the outcomes related to these experiments.

- Roll a single fair die and observe the value that appears.
  In this first example, the experiment can produce any one of six outcomes, which we can represent numerically as 1, 2, 3, 4, 5 or 6. If the die was fair, then on each toss of the die, each possible number (or outcome) would have an equal chance of occurring. The numbers 1, 2, 3, 4, 5 and 6 simultaneously represent the potential values that the random variable can assume and the outcomes for this experiment. We can denote this random variable by, for example, Y.

- Measure the amount of weight lost by people who have been involved in a new diet programme for the past two weeks.
  In this second example, the possible measured values that we could obtain from the experiment could be any number of kilograms that a dieter loses during the two weeks of the diet, for example, any value between 0 kg and 300 kg. If we denote this random variable Z, then Z could potentially take on *any* value between 0 kg and 300 kg with some probability

It is important to note that the first example shows values that are whole numbers (1, 2, 3, 4, 5 and 6), and so Y is an example of a **discrete random variable**. The second example consists of numbers that can take any value within a range of values with specified accuracy (for example, the weight loss could be measured as 1.4 kg, or 1.41 kg, or 1.414 kg, and so on, depending on the accuracy of the measurement device), and so Z is an example of a **continuous random variable**.

Random variable A variable that assumes numerical values associated with the outcomes or events from an experiment (each outcome or event having a particular probability of occurrence). We use uppercase letters such as X, Y or Z to denote random variables.

Discrete random variable A variable that can assume a countable number of values, each with a specified probability.

Continuous random variable A random variable that can potentially take on an infinite (or uncountable) number of values within a specified range of values.

5.1.2 Random variables and outcomes of experiments

The distinct concepts of the 'outcome of an experiment' and 'random variable' are easy to confuse because they appear to be very similar, especially when we consider the two examples presented above, and indeed there are instances where the definitions of the two overlap. To understand the difference between these two concepts, we need to remember that a random variable *always* takes on numerical values (either discrete or continuous), whereas the outcome of an experiment is *occasionally* (but not always) somewhat more abstract.

To illustrate this difference, consider Example 5.1.

WORKED EXAMPLES

EXAMPLE 5.1

An experiment is conducted in which three coins are tossed. If we denote a heads with the letter H and a tails with the letter T, then the eight possible outcomes that form the sample space Ω of this experiment are:

$$\Omega = \{\text{HHH, HHT, HTH, HTT, THH, THT, TTH, TTT}\}$$

The outcome HTH means the first coin was heads, the second coin was tails and the third coin was heads.

Note that the outcome of this experiment is represented by an abstract representation of *H*s and *T*s, and is not actually numeric in nature. Note also that, if the coins were 'fair' (the probability of getting 'heads' and 'tails' are equal), then each of the eight outcomes is equally probable. A possible discrete *random variable* associated with this experiment could be the numerical value 'number of heads obtained', denoted X. The possible values for X are $\{0, 1, 2, 3\}$ (Note that the number of unique values of X differs from the number of unique outcomes.) The probabilities associated with the occurrence of each numeric value of X will not be the same, as was the case for unique outcomes. (We can see this by noting that the probability of getting a 2 for X is larger than the probability of getting a 3 for X because '2 heads' occurs more frequently in the original sample space Ω than '3 heads'.)

The random variable in Example 5.1 assigns a numerical value to the abstract concept of obtaining a number of heads from a physical experiment of tossing coins. We do not know the specific value of the realised random variable (similar to the resulting outcome) before the experiment is conducted, but we can (approximately) determine the *probability* of specific values occurring by using the techniques discussed in the previous chapter.

NOTE

The experiment in Example 5.1 can have many numerical random variable interpretations of the outcomes, that is, we could link other random variables to it. For example, we could define a new random variable, W, as the number of tails obtained.

However, there are experiments in which the outcomes are already expressed numerically (consider the two random variables, Y and Z, which represented the value on a die and the weight lost by people on a diet, at the beginning of the chapter). In cases where the outcome is already numerical, then there is little to distinguish between the outcome of the experiment and a random variable – they are essentially the same thing.

In the next section, we consider the probability distributions (presented in a table format) associated with general discrete and continuous random variables.

5.2 Probability distributions and random variables

The probability distribution of random variables differ depending on whether the random variable is discrete or continuous. In this section, we briefly consider the probability distribution of discrete and continuous random variables, and in the next section we look at some properties of these distributions.

5.2.1 Discrete random variables and probability distributions

Discrete random variables, as defined in the previous section, are random variables that take on a set of countable whole numbers (that is, typically no fraction values) and each of these values has an associated probability. For these random variables, it is usually possible to enumerate every possible value that the variable can assume and, if there is enough information, we can also determine the probability of each of these values occurring. A *comprehensive* list of these discrete random variable values and their associated probability values is called a **probability distribution** (or simply a distribution).

The form of a probability distribution for discrete random variables is very similar to the frequency tables for discrete values that were constructed in Chapter 2. In general, we denote the unique values of a discrete random variable X by $x_1, x_2, \ldots, x_k$, and we define $p(x_i)$ as the probability that the random variable equals x_i:

$$p(x_i) = P(X = x_i)$$

Table 5.1 gives the general form of a probability distribution of a discrete random variable.

Table 5.1: General form of a probability distribution of a discrete random variable, X

VALUE OF X	PROBABILITY
x_1	$p(x_1) = P(X = x_1)$
x_2	$p(x_2) = P(X = x_2)$
$\vdots$	!
x_k	$p(x_k) = P(X = x_k)$
	$\sum_{i=1}^{k} p(x_i) = 1$

Note that the value $p(x_i)$ is referred to as the *mass function* of the discrete random variable X. This mass function has two very basic (but important) properties.

- $p(x_i)$, like all probability values, is always larger than 0 and smaller than 1:

$$0 \leq p(x_i) \leq 1$$

- The sum of the $p(x_i)$-values for all unique values of x_i is equal to 1:

$$\sum_{i=1}^{k} p(x_i) = 1$$

This is intuitively logical, because the probability that at least one of the x_i-values occurs in the experiment is a certainty.

We will now use the discrete random variable X, defined in Example 5.1, to illustrate how to construct a probability distribution.

WORKED EXAMPLES

EXAMPLE 5.2

Consider the situation in Example 5.1, in which three coins were tossed. The possible values for X (the number of heads showing) were {0, 1, 2, 3}. The coins used in the experiment were 'fair', and the sample space of the experiment was defined as:

$$\Omega = \{\text{HHH, HHT, HTH, HTT, THH, THT, TTH, TTT}\}$$

To construct the probability distribution of X, we need to determine the probabilities of the events $X = 0$, $X = 1$, $X = 2$ and $X = 3$.

The probability $P(X = 0)$ corresponds to the probability of the event A_0 = 'heads does not occur'. The probability of this event is then:

$$P(X = 0) = P(A_0) = \frac{\#(A_0)}{\#(\Omega)} = \frac{\#(\{\text{TTT}\})}{\#(\Omega)} = \frac{1}{8}$$

Similarly, for $X = 1$, which corresponds to the event A_1 = 'heads occurs exactly once in the three tosses':

$$P(X = 1) = P(A_1) = \frac{\#(A_1)}{\#(\Omega)} = \frac{\#(\{\text{HTT, THT, TTH}\})}{\#(\Omega)} = \frac{3}{8}$$

For $X = 2$, which corresponds to the event A_2 = 'heads occurs exactly twice in the three tosses':

$$P(X = 2) = P(A_2) = \frac{\#(A_2)}{\#(\Omega)} = \frac{\#(\{\text{HHT, HTH, HHT}\})}{\#(\Omega)} = \frac{3}{8}$$

Finally, for $X = 3$, which corresponds to the event A_3 = 'all three coins are heads':

$$P(X = 3) = P(A_3) = \frac{\#(A_3)}{\#(\Omega)} = \frac{\#(\{\text{HHH}\})}{\#(\Omega)} = \frac{1}{8}$$

Table 5.2 shows the probability distribution of X.

Table 5.2: Probability distribution of X

NUMBER OF HEADS OBTAINED (X)	PROBABILITY
0	$p(0) = P(X = 0) = \frac{1}{8}$
1	$p(1) = P(X = 1) = \frac{3}{8}$
2	$p(2) = P(X = 2) = \frac{3}{8}$
3	$p(3) = P(X = 3) = \frac{1}{8}$

Once we have determined the probability distribution of a random variable, we can then easily answer questions about the probability structure of the random variable using the distribution and the rules given in Chapter 4. Example 5.3 illustrates some of these calculations.

WORKED EXAMPLES

EXAMPLE 5.3

Let Y denote the random variable that represents the number of students that fail a particular exam (assuming that only five students write the exam). The random variable Y has the following probability distribution. (Do not worry about the construction of this probability distribution yet, we will discuss it in the next chapter.)

Table 5.3: Probability distribution of Y

NUMBER OF STUDENTS THAT FAIL (Y)	PROBABILITY
0	$p(0) = P(Y = 0) = 0.03125$
1	$p(1) = P(Y = 1) = 0.15625$
2	$p(2) = P(Y = 2) = 0.3125$
3	$p(3) = P(Y = 3) = 0.31250$
4	$p(4) = P(Y = 4) = 0.15625$
5	$p(5) = P(Y = 5) = 0.03125$

Note that the each of the events listed in this table are mutually exclusive (that is, we cannot simultaneously have exactly one student fail and have exactly four students fail).

a) What is the probability that either everyone passes or everyone fails?

b) What is the probability that less than three students fail the exam?

c) What is the probability that three or more students fail the exam?

Answers

a) First note that we can express the event we are investigating as $\{Y = 0\} \cup \{Y = 5\}$. Recall that we read the symbol '∪' as 'or'. Since these two events are mutually exclusive, we can apply the *additive rule for mutually exclusive events* (see Section 4.3.2):

$$\begin{aligned} P(\{Y = 0\} \cup \{Y = 5\}) &= P(Y = 0) + P(Y = 5) \\ &= 0.03125 + 0.03125 = 0.0625 \end{aligned}$$

This means that the probability that either no one fails or everyone fails is 0.0625 (or 6.25%).

b) The event we are interested in for this question is $\{Y < 3\}$, which we can also express as $\{Y \leq 2\}$ or even $\{Y = 0\} \cup \{Y = 1\} \cup \{Y = 2\}$. Once again, applying the additive rule for mutually exclusive events we get:

$$\begin{aligned} P(Y < 3) &= P(Y \leq 2) \\ &= P\{Y = 0\} \cup \{Y = 1\} \cup \{Y = 2\} \\ &= P(Y = 0) + P(Y = 1) + P(Y = 2) \\ &= 0.03125 + 0.15625 + 0.31250 = 0.5 \end{aligned}$$

There is thus a 0.5 (or 50%) probability that less than three students will fail.

c) The event we are now interested is $\{Y \geq 3\}$. We can express this event as $\{Y = 3\} \cup \{Y = 4\} \cup \{Y = 5\}$, and so the probability is (using the additive rule):

$$\begin{aligned} P(Y \geq 3) &= P\{Y = 3\} \cup \{Y = 4\} \cup \{Y = 5\} \\ &= P(Y = 3) + P(Y = 4) + P(Y = 5) \\ &= 0.31250 + 0.15625 + 0.03125 = 0.5 \end{aligned}$$

Note, however, that it is simpler to see that $\{Y \geq 3\}$ is the *complement* of the event $\{Y < 3\}$ and so, using the *complement rule*, we could have said:

$$\begin{aligned} P(Y \geq 3) &= 1 - P(Y < 3) \\ &= 1 - 0.5 = 0.5 \end{aligned}$$

Once we have the probability distribution of a random variable, we can easily do many other calculations, such as the expected value and variance of the random variable. We discuss these concepts later in the chapter. In the next chapter, you will see probability distributions that are described by *theoretical mass functions*, which have explicit *mathematical expressions* (as opposed to mass functions that can only be expressed as simple tables, such as the ones presented in this chapter). The properties of the probabilities of discrete random variables that we have discussed in this chapter will carry over directly to the theoretical distributions and mass functions in the next chapter.

5.2.2 Continuous random variables

As with discrete random variables, continuous random variables also have associated probability distributions. However, as these random variables can potentially take on infinitely many possible values within a specified interval, constructing probability distributions using the methods described for discrete random variables is too complex. For this reason, constructing a probability distribution follows approximate methods using techniques similar to those used to construct frequency distributions (as discussed in Chapter 2). Additionally, we approximate the probabilities associated with these random variables by using the *relative frequency* approach (as discussed in Section 4.2.2). Throughout this discussion, we will point out the link between frequencies, relative frequencies and probabilities.

Relative frequency is one way to approximate the probabilities associated with the values of a continuous random variable. For a given data set, we use the relative frequency (or proportion) that a case falls within an interval as an estimate of the probability that the random variable falls within the stated interval. In this respect, formula (5.1) provides a frequency approximation of the probability that the values of a continuous random variable X fall within an interval between a and b.

$$P(a < X < b) \approx \frac{\text{number of cases between } a \text{ and } b}{\text{total number of cases}} \tag{5.1}$$

Note that we do not calculate quantities of the form $P(X = a)$ using this definition, because the continuous nature of the variable means that the probability that X is *exactly* equal to a specific value is negligibly small. This definition of probability is only an approximate answer. It only becomes completely accurate as the total number of cases becomes *very* large.

WORKED EXAMPLES

EXAMPLE 5.4

A store accounts manager collects data about the reported sales figures from the sales people. The sales figures reported by each sales person are a continuous random variable (even though the value is only recorded up to two decimal places) and is denoted by X. The manager would like to determine the probability that a sales person reports a value of less than R1 000.

To estimate this probability, she obtains sales figures of 250 randomly selected sales people. She finds that 3 of the 250 individuals have reported values between R0 and R1 000. So, from formula (5.1), the relative frequency (or approximate probability) of a sales person reporting between R0 and R1 000 is:

$$P(0 < X < 1\,000) \approx \frac{3}{250} = 0.012 \text{ or } 1.2\%$$

We will now combine this relative frequency approximation of a probability with a frequency distribution to approximate the probability distribution of a continuous random variable. Example 5.5 illustrates how to construct this distribution using the example of travelling salesmen first encountered in Chapter 2.

WORKED EXAMPLES

EXAMPLE 5.5

The following frequency distribution represents the distance travelled by 120 salesmen (the original data can be found in Table 2.9 in Example 2.5). Let X denote the distance travelled by a salesman. From Table 5.4, we can easily calculate the relative frequencies by simply dividing each frequency by the total sample size n = 120.

Table 5.4: Frequency table – distance travelled by 120 salesmen

DISTANCE TRAVELLED (km) (X)	FREQUENCY (f)
[400; 420)	12
[420; 440)	27
[440; 460)	34
[460; 480)	24
[480; 500)	15
[500; 520)	8

(Recall from Chapter 2 that the square brackets used in Table 5.4 represent 'inclusion' and the round brackets represent 'exclusion', that is, the class [440; 460) represents all the values starting with, and including, 440 up to, but excluding, 460.)

By dividing each frequency by 120, we get the *relative frequency* table below, which represents the estimated probability distribution of the random variable X.

Table 5.5: Relative frequency table – distance travelled by 120 salesmen

DISTANCE TRAVELLED (km) (X)	RELATIVE FREQUENCY (r)
[400; 420)	$\frac{12}{120} = 0.100$
[420; 440)	$\frac{27}{120} = 0.225$
[440; 460)	$\frac{34}{120} = 0.283$
[460; 480)	$\frac{24}{120} = 0.200$
[480; 500)	$\frac{15}{120} = 0.125$
[500; 520)	$\frac{8}{120} = 0.067$

We can use the spreadsheet shown in Figure 5.1 to calculate these probabilities in Excel.

	A	B	C	D	E	F
1	**Probability distribution**					
2						
3		**Distance travelled by salesmen (km)**	**Frequency, *f***	**Relative frequency, *r***		
4		[400; 420)	12	0.1000000	=C4/$C$11	
5		[420; 440)	27	0.2250000	=C5/$C$11	
6		[440; 460)	34	0.2833333	=C6/$C$11	
7		[460; 480)	24	0.2000000	=C7/$C$11	
8		[480; 500)	15	0.1250000	=C8/$C$11	
9		[500; 520)	8	0.0666667	=C9/$C$11	
10						
11		Total =	120	1		
12			=SUM(C4:C9)	=SUM(D4:D9)		
13						

Figure 5.1: Excel spreadsheet calculation of relative frequencies

Figure 5.1 illustrates the calculation process. From Figure 5.1, we can see that the relative frequency for 440–460 km travelled is 0.283333. This implies that we have a chance or probability of $\frac{34}{120}$ that the distance travelled lies within this class.

EXCEL SOLUTION

Distance data: Cells B4:B9	Values
Frequency, f: Cells C4:C9	Values
Relative frequency, r: Cells D4:D9	Formula: =C4/$C$11
	Copy formula from D4:D9
Total f: Cell C11	Formula: =SUM(C4:C9)
Total relative frequency: Cell D11	Formula: =SUM(D4:D9)

NOTE

Relative frequencies provide estimates of the probability of that class, or interval of values, occurring. If we were to plot the histogram of relative frequencies, we would in fact be plotting the estimated probabilities for each event.

We can use this relative frequency to draw the following graph of the probability distribution.

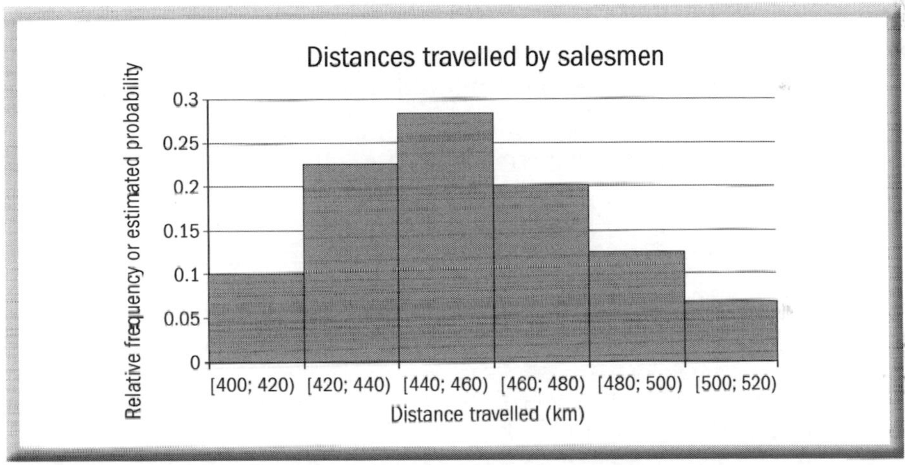

Figure 5.2: The probability distribution of the distances travelled by 120 salesmen

The distribution of relative frequencies (or estimated probabilities) in Table 5.5 and Figure 5.2 are different ways of illustrating the probability distribution.

Given a particular probability distribution, we can determine almost any probability for any event associated with it (depending on the classes chosen for the frequency distribution). For example, if X is the continuous random variable that represents the distance travelled by the salesmen, then we can estimate the probability that an individual salesman travels between 400 km and 460 km by:

$$\begin{aligned} P(400 < X < 460) &= P(400 < X < 420) + P(420 < X < 440) + P(440 < X < 460) \\ &= 0.10 + 0.225 + 0.283 \\ &= 0.608 \end{aligned}$$

Thus, the probability estimate of a salesman travelling between 400 km and 460 km is 61%.

NOTE

A point to note about this type of probability distribution (that is, derived from continuous data) is that if we decreased the class limits and increased the sample size, the associated polygon of the distribution would begin to approximate a curve called the *probability density function.* We discuss this function in more detail in Chapter 7.

5.3 Expected values and variance

We now explore two properties that random variables and their probability distributions exhibit: **expected values** and **variances**. The expected value is essentially the mean value of a distribution, whereas the variance is a measure of how much the values can vary (that is, it means the same as the variance discussed in Chapter 3). In practice, these values are unknown if the probability distribution is unknown. In these cases, we refer to them as the 'population' or 'unknown' expected value or variance. When we have to estimate the probability distribution with relative frequencies (that is, when the probability distribution is unknown), we will refer to the expected value as the 'sample' expected value (or simply the sample mean), and the variance as the sample variance.

Expected value Represents the population mean or average value for the random variable associated with the probability distribution.

Variance Represents the population variance or measure of variation for the random variable associated with the probability distribution.

5.3.1 Expected value

The mean of a probability distribution of a random variable X is called the *expected value* of X and is denoted by $E(X)$.

Discrete random variables

For a *discrete random variable, X,* we can calculate the true population value of $E(X)$ using formula (5.2):

$$E(X) = \sum_{i=1}^{k} x_i P(X = x_i) \tag{5.2}$$

Note that we can only determine this population expression if we have the exact probabilities $P(X = x_i)$. If we cannot obtain the exact probabilities, we can approximate them with relative frequencies from the data. However, this results in an estimated or sample version of the expected value. Note that formula (3.2) for the sample mean of grouped data employs this idea exactly.

Continuous random variables

The meaning of the expected value of continuous random variables is identical to that of discrete random variables, that is, it represents the population mean of the probability distribution. Unfortunately, while we can calculate the exact *population,* expected values of continuous random variables in a similar way to the discrete random variables, the calculations require advanced integral calculus, which is beyond the scope of this text.

We focus only on calculating the population expected value of discrete random variables (if the values of $P(X = x_i)$ can be obtained), and using sample estimators to *approximate* the population expected value of continuous random variables (and for discrete random variables with unknown probability distributions). These approximate versions of the expected values are simply equal to the sample means ($\overline{X}$) of grouped frequency data.

5.3.2 Variance

The variance of the probability distribution of a random variable follows the same lines of thought used to develop the expected value of X. We denote the variance of a random variable X by *Var*(X), and we once again distinguish between a case in which we use the true probabilities $P(X = x_i)$ and a case in which $P(X = x_i)$ must be estimated by relative frequencies from the data.

Discrete random variables

We can determine the true population *Var*(X) of the probability distribution of a discrete random variable X from formula (5.3):

$$Var(X) = \sum_{i=1}^{k} x_k^2 P(X = x_i) - \left[\sum_{i=1}^{k} x_i P(X = x_i)\right]^2 \tag{5.3}$$

We can calculate the standard deviation of X (denoted *SD*(X)) from formula (5.3) using the relationship given in formula (5.4):

$$SD(X) = \sqrt{Var(X)} \tag{5.4}$$

As before, if the probability distribution must be estimated from relative frequencies, then formulae (5.3) and (5.4) revert to the sample variance and standard deviation calculated from a sample frequency table, as discussed in Chapter 3.

Continuous random variables

Due to the mathematical complexity of the expressions, we will not discuss the true population variance of continuous variables. However, we can easily obtain the *estimated* variances using the sample variances discussed in Chapter 3.

We now consider a few examples of expected values of random variables.

WORKED EXAMPLES

EXAMPLE 5.6

A stall at a fete is running a game of chance. The game consists of a customer taking turns to choose three balls from a bag that contains 3 white and 17 red balls without replacing them. For a customer to win, he has to choose 3 white balls, 2 white balls or 1 white ball, with winnings of R5, R2 and R0.50 respectively. On the day of the fete, 2 000 customers played the game. How much money may have been paid out to each customer?

The expected value of the random variable Z represents the amount of money that a player can win in the game (that is, Z can take on the values 5, 2, 0.5 or 0).

To calculate this expected value, we first need to obtain the probability distribution, that is, we need to calculate the associated probabilities of choosing 3, 2, 1 and 0 white balls. We can calculate these probabilities using the tree diagrams discussed in Section 4.4.2 (see Figure 5.3). Finally, we calculate the associated expected value, as we know what the winnings are for 3, 2, 1 and 0 white balls.

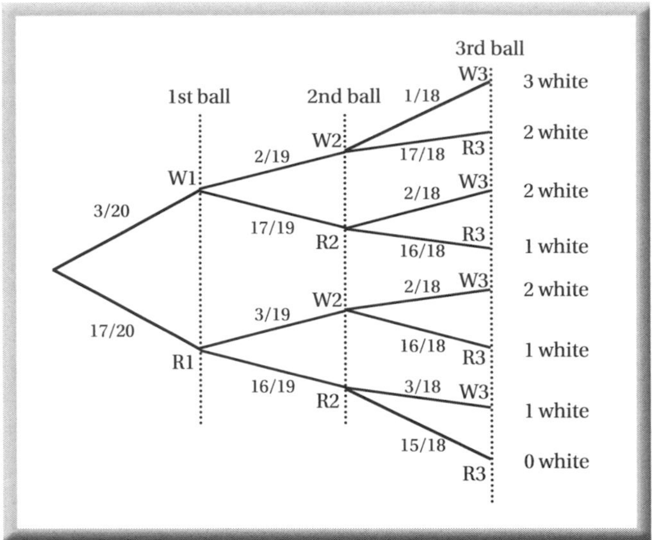

Figure 5.3: The tree diagram used to calculate the probabilities in Example 5.6

From the tree diagram in Figure 5.3, we can identify the different probabilities of choosing 3, 2, 1 and 0 white balls.

- The probability of choosing 3 white balls (the probability of winning R5) is obtained by looking at the terminal nodes that correspond to '3 white' (there is only one terminal node like this) and then multiplying all the probabilities along the path from the terminal node to the origin to obtain:

$$P(Z = \text{R}5.00) = \frac{3}{20} \times \frac{2}{19} \times \frac{1}{18} = 0.0009$$

- The probability of choosing 2 white balls (the probability of winning R2) requires that we identify all of the paths that terminate in '2 whites' (there are three scenarios that give rise to this) and then, for each path, multiplying the probabilities from the terminal node to the origin and finally adding up all the results:

$$\begin{aligned} P(Z = \text{R}2.00) &= \left(\frac{3}{20} \times \frac{2}{19} \times \frac{17}{18}\right) + \left(\frac{3}{20} \times \frac{17}{19} \times \frac{2}{18}\right) + \left(\frac{17}{20} \times \frac{3}{19} \times \frac{2}{18}\right) \\ &= 0.0447 \end{aligned}$$

- The probability of choosing 1 white ball (the probability of winning R0.50) corresponds to three terminal nodes in Figure 5.3. As above, the probability is:

$$\begin{aligned} P(Z = \text{R}0.50) &= \left(\frac{3}{20} \times \frac{17}{19} \times \frac{16}{18}\right) + \left(\frac{17}{20} \times \frac{3}{19} \times \frac{16}{18}\right) + \left(\frac{17}{20} \times \frac{16}{19} \times \frac{3}{18}\right) \\ &= 0.3579 \end{aligned}$$

- Finally, the probability of choosing 0 white balls (the probability of winning nothing) is:

$$P(Z = \text{R}0.00) = \frac{17}{20} \times \frac{16}{19} \times \frac{15}{18} = 0.5965$$

The probability distribution of the winnings (summarised in Table 5.6) allows us to calculate the expected winnings of the game.

Table 5.6: Probability distribution of the winnings – Example 5.6

WINNINGS (Z)	PROBABILITY, $P(Z = z)$
R0.00	$P(Z=$ R0.00$) = 0.5965$
R0.50	$P(Z=$ R0.50$) = 0.3579$
R2.00	$P(Z=$ R2.00$) = 0.0447$
R5.00	$P(Z=$ R5.00$) = 0.0009$

The calculation to find this expected value using formula (5.2) is shown below, and the Excel solution is shown in Figure 5.4.

From formula (5.2) we have:

$$\begin{aligned} E(Z) &= \sum_{i=1}^{4} z_i P(Z = z_i) \\ &= 0.00 \times P(Z = 0.00) + 0.50 \times P(Z = 0.50) + 2.00 \times P(Z = 2.00) + 5.00 \times P(Z = 5.00) \\ &= 0.5 \times 0.3579 + 2 \times 0.0447 + 5 \times 0.0009 \\ &= 0.27285 \end{aligned}$$

The expected winnings from each game is approximately R0.27. The Excel solution produces the same result.

	A	B	C	D	E	F
1	**Example 5.6**					
2						
3		**Number of white balls chosen**	**Amount won, *Z***	**Probability, *P*(*Z*=*z*)**	***z** *P*(*Z*=*z*)**	
4		3	R5.00	0.0009	R0.00450	=C4*D4
5		2	R2.00	0.0447	R0.08940	=C5*D5
6		1	R0.50	0.3579	R0.17895	=C6*D6
7		0	R0.00	0.5965	R0.00000	=C7*D7
8						
9				*E*(*Z*)=	R0.27285	=SUM(E4:E7)
10				Total=	R545.70	=2000*E9
11						

Figure 5.4: The Excel spreadsheet calculation of the expected value of the random variable Z for Example 5.6

EXCEL SOLUTION

Number of white balls: Cells B4:B7	Values
Amount won, Z: Cells C4:C7	Values
Probability, $P(Z = z)$: Cells D4:D7	Values
$zP(Z = z)$: Cells E4:E7	Formula: =C4*D4
	Copy formula from E4:E7
$E(Z)$: Cell E9	Formula: =SUM(E4:E7)
Total: Cell E10	Formula: =2000*E9

INTERPRETATION

From Excel, we can see that the expected winnings for each game played is $E(Z) = \sum z \times P(Z = z) = 0.27285$ (or R0.27 to the nearest cent). Given that we have $n = 2\ 000$ players (or games played) then the total winnings is R545.70 ($= n \times E(Z) = 2\ 000 \times 0.27285$) to the nearest cent.

WORKED EXAMPLES

EXAMPLE 5.7

A small butchery makes, packages and sells small packets of biltong. The cost to manufacture each packet differs depending on the prices he pays his supplier for the meat, among other factors. However, the butcher decides to sell all the biltong packets at R6.00 per unit. He estimates the following probabilities:

- Sales demand, X: The butcher thinks that the demand for 5 000 packets will be reasonable, the demand for 6 000 packets will be most likely and that the demand for 8 000 packets will be low. The butcher estimates these probabilities and summarises them in Table 5.7.
- Cost per unit, Y: The butcher determines that each packet could cost him R3.00, R3.50, R4.00 or R4.50. Using data collected at his butchery, he calculates and summarises the probability distribution of these values in Table 5.8.

Table 5.7: Sales demand

SALES DEMAND (X)	PROBABILITY $P(X = x)$
5 000	0.3
6 000	0.6
8 000	0.1

Table 5.8: Variable cost per unit

COST PER UNIT (RAND) (Y)	PROBABILITY $P(Y = y)$
3.0	0.1
3.5	0.3
4.0	0.5
4.5	0.1

If we assume that the miscellaneous fixed cost for running his business is R10 000, determine the expected profit.

We determine the expected profit from the following equation:

expected profit = expected sales – expected costs – fixed costs

We only need to calculate the 'expected sales' and the 'expected costs' in order to find the 'expected profit'.

The expected sales demand is calculated using formula (5.2) with the probability distribution in Table 5.7.

Table 5.9: Calculation of expected demand, $E(X)$

SALES DEMAND (X)	PROBABILITY $P(X = x)$	$x P(X = x)$
5 000	0.3	1 500
6 000	0.6	3 600
8 000	0.1	800
	Total =	5 900

We find that the expected value of the 'sales demand' variable is then:

$$E(X) = \sum_{i=1}^{3} x_i P(X = x_i) = 5\,900 \text{ units}$$

In other words, the butcher expects that there will be a demand for 5 900 packets of biltong.

We also calculate the expected value of the 'cost per unit' variable using formula (5.2) with the probability distribution in Table 5.8.

Table 5.10: Calculation of cost per unit, $E(Y)$

COST PER UNIT (RAND) (Y)	PROBABILITY $P(Y = y)$	$yP(Y = y)$
3	0.1	0.30
3.5	0.3	1.05
4	0.5	2.00
4.5	0.1	0.45
	Total =	3.80

The expected value per unit is then:

$$E(Y) = \sum_{i=1}^{4} y_i P(Y = y_i) = \text{R}3.80$$

Using the results of these calculations, we can now calculate the overall value of sales, variable costs and expected profit as follows:

- Total expected sales = 5 900 × R6.00 = R35 400.00 (assuming he sells all packets for R6.00)
- Expected costs = 5 900 × R3.80 = R22 420.00
- Fixed costs = R10 000.00
- Expected profit:

$$\begin{aligned}\text{expected profit} &= \text{expected sales} - \text{expected costs} - \text{fixed costs} \\ &= \text{R}35\,400.00 - \text{R}22\,420.00 - \text{R}10\,000.00 \\ &= \text{R}2\,980.00\end{aligned}$$

The expected profit is R2 980.00 if the butcher decides to sell the biltong packets at R6.00.

WORKED EXAMPLES

EXAMPLE 5.8

We will again use Example 2.5 of the distances travelled by salesmen.

Table 5.11: Distances travelled by salesmen data

DISTANCE TRAVELLED	CLASS MIDPOINTS	FREQUENCY (f)
[400; 420)	410	12
[420; 440)	430	27
[440; 460)	450	34
[460; 480)	470	24
[480; 500)	490	15
[500; 520)	510	8
	Total	$\sum_{j=1}^{6} f_i = 120$

Determine the population expected number and population variance of the kilometres travelled by a salesman.

Unfortunately, since the probabilities associated with these classes are unknown, we must estimate them using relative frequencies. Then, we are simply calculating the estimated population expected value (the sample mean) and the estimated population variance (the sample variance). We have already done these calculations in Section 3.2.3 in Example 3.3.

Figure 5.5 shows the Excel solution to determine the estimated expected value and estimated variance. We used Excel to automate the following manual calculations.

Expected value: $E(X) = \sum_{i=1}^{k} x_i P(X = x_i) = 454.5$

Variance: $Var(X) = \sum_{i=1}^{k} x_i^2 P(X = x_i) - \left[\sum_{i=1}^{k} x_i P(X = x_i)\right]^2 = 207\,320 - (454.5)^2 = 749.75$

Standard deviation: $SD(X) = \sqrt{Var(X)} = \sqrt{749.75} = 27.38$

	A	B	C	D	E	F	G	H	I	J	K	L
2	**Expectation and Variance**											
3												
4												
5	**Distance travelled by salesmen (km)**	**Frequency, f**	LCB	UCB	**Class midpoint**		**Relative frequency, r**		$x*P(X=x)$		$x^2P(X=x)$	
6	[400; 420)	12	400	420	410	=(C5+D5)/2	0.1000000	=B6/$C$15	41.000	=E6*G6	16810.00	=E6^2*G6
7	[420; 440)	27	420	440	430	=(C6+D6)/2	0.2250000	=B7/$C$15	96.750	=E7*G7	41602.50	=E7^2*G7
8	[440; 460)	34	440	460	450	=(C7+D7)/2	0.2833333	=B8/$C$15	127.500	=E8*G8	57375.00	=E8^2*G8
9	[460; 480)	24	460	480	470	=(C8+D8)/2	0.2000000	=B9/$C$15	94.000	=E9*G9	44180.00	=E9^2*G9
10	[480; 500)	15	480	500	490	=(C9+D9)/2	0.1250000	=B10/$C$15	61.250	=E10*G10	30012.50	=E10^2*G10
11	[500; 520)	8	500	520	510	=(C10+D10)/2	0.0666667	=B11/$C$15	34.000	=E11*G11	17340.00	=E11^2*G11
12												
13												
14												
15		**Summary statistics**										
16		$n=\Sigma f=$	120	=SUM(B6:B11)								
17		$\Sigma xP(X=x)=$	454.500	=SUM(I6:I11)								
18		$\Sigma x^2P(X=x)=$	207320	=SUM(K6:K11)								
19		Mean =	454.500	=C16								
20		Variance =	749.75	=C17-C18^2								
21		Stnd. Dev =	27.38	=SQRT(C19)								

Figure 5.5: The Excel spreadsheet calculation of the expected value of the random variable X for Example 5.8

EXCEL SOLUTION

Distance travelled: Cells A6:A11	Values
Frequency, f: Cells B6:B11	Values
LCB: Cells C6: C11	Values
UCB: Cells D6: D11	Values
Class midpoint: Cells E6:E11	Formula: =(C6+D6)/2
	Copy formula from E6:E11
Relative frequency: Cells G6:G11	Formula: =B6/$C$15
	Copy formula from G6:G11
$x*P(X=x)$: Cells I6:I11	Formula: =E6*G6
	Copy formula from I6:I11
$x^2*P(X=x)$: Cells K6:K11	Formula: =E6^2*G6
	Copy formula from K6:K11
$n=\sum f$: Cell C15	Formula: =SUM(B6:B11)
$\sum xP(X=x)$: Cell C16	Formula: =SUM(I6:I11)
$\sum x^2P(X=x)$: Cell C17	Formula: =SUM(K6:K11)
Mean: Cell C18	Formula: =C16
Variance: Cell C19	Formula: =C17-C18^2
Standard deviation: Cell C20	Formula: =C19^0.5

INTERPRETATION From Excel, the estimated expected value is 454.5 km travelled, with a sample standard deviation of 27.38 km.

SUMMARY

In this chapter, we briefly discussed the fundamental concepts underlying most of the random variables and their related probability distributions that you will encounter in later chapters. This included properties related to the probabilities in the probability distributions (such as the probabilities in a probability distribution must sum to 1) and other properties of the random variables themselves, such as the expected value and variance.

In the next few chapters, we discuss very specific discrete and continuous random variables (and their probability distributions).

KEY TERMS

Continuous probability distribution
Discrete probability distribution
Expected value
Expected value of a discrete variable
Probability
Standard deviation of a discrete variable

FORMULA SUMMARY

$$P(a < X < b) \approx \frac{\text{number of cases between } a \text{ and } b}{\text{total number of cases}} \quad (5.1)$$

$$E(X) = \sum_{i=1}^{k} x_i P(X = x_i) \quad (5.2)$$

$$Var(X) = \sum_{i=1}^{k} x_k^2 P(X = x_i) - \left[\sum_{i=1}^{k} x_i P(X = x_i)\right]^2 \quad (5.3)$$

$$SD(X) = \sqrt{Var(X)} \quad (5.4)$$

EXERCISES

5.1 A bag contains six white and four red counters. Three counters are drawn at random without replacement. If X can take on the values of 0, 1, 2 and 3 (denoting the number of red counters drawn), construct the probability distribution of X. If the experiment was repeated 60 times, how many times would you expect to draw more than one red counter?

5.2 You are considering putting money into one of two investments: A and B. Each investment can potentially yield net profits ranging from R8 000 to R12 000 at the end of the term of the investment, depending on the market conditions. The probabilities of each amount differs from one investment to the next. The net profits for identical periods and probabilities of success for investments A and B are given in Table 5.12.

Table 5.12: Probability distributions

NET PROFITS	PROBABILITY OF RETURN FOR INVESTMENT A	PROBABILITY OF RETURN FOR INVESTMENT B
R8 000	0.0	0.1
R9 000	0.3	0.2
R10 000	0.4	0.4
R11 000	0.3	0.2
R12 000	0.0	0.1

a) Which investment is expected to yield a higher net profit?
b) Which of the two investments has the greater variance?
c) Can you make a decision on which investment is better, given this extra information?

TECHNIQUES IN PRACTICE

5.3 AfriSoft is concerned about the time taken to react to customer complaints and has implemented a new set of procedures for its support centre staff (see the 'Techniques in practice' section in Chapter 3). The customer service director plans to reduce the mean time taken to respond to customer complaints to 28 days and collected the following sample data after implementing the new procedures.

Table 5.13: Raw data for 5.3 (in days)

20	33	33	29	24	30
40	33	20	39	32	37
32	50	36	31	38	29
15	33	27	29	43	33

31	35	19	39	22	21
28	22	26	42	30	17
32	34	39	39	32	38

a) Estimate the expected time to react to customer complaints.
b) Estimate the probability that the mean time to react is less than 28 days.

5.4 Bakers Ltd is currently in the process of reviewing the credit line available to supermarkets that are defined as a 'good' or 'bad' risk. Based on a R100 000 credit line, the profit is estimated to be R25 000. If the company accepts a 'bad risk' credit request, it will lose R8 000. If it rejects a 'good risk' it will lose R500 in good will, but gains or loses nothing by rejecting a 'bad risk'.

a) Complete the following profit and loss table for this situation.

		DECISION	
		ACCEPT	**REJECT**
TYPE OF RISK	**GOOD**		
	BAD		

b) The credit manager assesses that the probability that a particular applicant is a 'good risk' is $\frac{4}{10}$ and a 'bad risk' as $\frac{6}{10}$. What would the expected profits for each of the two decisions be? Consequently, what decision should be made regarding the applicant?

5.5 Home-Made Beers Ltd is developing a low-calorie lager with a mean calorie count of 43 calories per 100 ml. The new product development team are having problems with the production process and have collected an independent random sample to assess whether the target calorie count is being met.

Table 5.14: Calorie counts of n = 22 randomly selected low-calorie beer bottles

49.7	45.2	37.7	31.9	34.8	39.8
45.9	40.5	40.6	41.9	51.4	54.0
34.3	47.8	63.1	26.3	41.2	31.7
41.4	45.1	41.1	47.9		

a) Estimate the mean and variance based on this sample data.
b) State the interval of acceptable calorie count values, if the production manager wants this interval to be 43 ± 5%.
c) Estimate the probability that the calorie count lies between 43 ± 5%. (Assume that your answers to part (a) represent the population values.)

CHAPTER 6

DISCRETE PROBABILITY DISTRIBUTIONS

CHAPTER CONTENTS

OVERVIEW

We introduced the concept of a general discrete probability distribution in the previous chapter. This chapter deals with theoretical distributions (specifically the binomial and Poisson distributions) that we can use to describe the probabilities of a number of scenarios. The benefit of using a theoretical distribution is that we can calculate probability using an equation (as opposed to the observation-based methods discussed in the previous chapter). Section 6.1 will briefly introduce the theoretical discrete probability distributions, and Sections 6.2 and 6.3 will discuss the binomial and Poisson probability distributions respectively. We also describe the interpretation, application and properties of these two distributions in each section.

Discrete probability distribution If a random variable is a discrete variable, its probability distribution is called a discrete probability distribution.

LEARNING OBJECTIVES

On completing this chapter, you should be able to:

- distinguish between theoretical discrete distributions and discrete distributions constructed from observations
- describe a probability using mass functions
- understand when to apply the binomial distribution
- solve simple problems using both tree diagrams and the binomial mass function
- understand when to apply the Poisson distribution
- solve simple problems using the Poisson mass function
- solve problems using Microsoft Excel.

6.1 Introduction

In this section, we shall explore theoretical probability distributions when dealing with discrete random variables. Two specific distributions discussed are the **binomial** and **Poisson probability distributions** (a number of other distributions also exist, but we will only discuss these two common ones). If a random variable's probability distribution is described by the binomial or Poisson probability distribution, then that random variable is called a **binomial random variable** or a **Poisson random variable**, respectively. These distributions have explicit functions that describe the true (or theoretical) probability occurrence of individual values. We can then use these functions to solve a myriad of probability problems for random variables that are either binomial or Poisson type random variables. In order to distinguish between these types of random variable, we need to look at various characteristics of the random variable being studied, such as the values it can assume, among others. We will discuss these characteristics for each random variable to help you identify the type of variable being used.

6.2 Binomial probability distribution

6.2.1 Introduction to the binomial probability distribution

One of the most elementary discrete random variables – the *binomial* – is associated with questions that only allow 'Yes' or 'No' type answers, a classification such as male or female, or recording a component as defective or not defective. In general, we will refer to one of these two outcomes as a 'success' (even if the outcome does not seem so 'successful', for example, if the scenario concerns the occurrence of a disease in patients, we can choose the outcome 'yes, has the disease' to be the 'successful' outcome). Specifically, binomial random variables describe the *number of successes within a fixed number of independent trials* or runs of an experiment. (The trials are independent if the possibility of a success in one trial does not affect the possibility of success in any other trial.)

Consider the example of a supermarket that runs a two-week television campaign in an attempt to increase the volume of trade at the supermarket. During the campaign, n customers are asked if they came to the supermarket because of the television advert. Each customer's response can be classified as either 'Yes' or 'No' (success or failure). At the end of the campaign, the proportion of customers that responded 'Yes' is determined. For this study, the *experiment* is the process of asking customers if they came to the supermarket because of the television advert. The binomial *random variable, X,* is defined as the number of customers that responded 'Yes' (that is, it is the number of successes from n independent individuals). Clearly, the random variable can assume only the values 0, 1, 2, 3, ..., n, where n is the total number of customers. Consequently, the random variable is *discrete* in nature.

Next, we consider the characteristics of a binomial random variable to better help us identify them in scenarios.

Binomial random variable A discrete random variable that describes the number of successful outcomes of n simple independent trials that can either succeed or fail. The probability of success for each simple trial is the same and is denoted by p.

Binomial probability distribution A probability distribution that describes the probabilities of occurrence of a binomial random variable.

6.2.2 Identifying binomial random variables

The following are the characteristics that define binomial experiments.

CHARACTERISTICS OF BINOMIAL RANDOM VARIABLES

a) The experiment consists of n identical trials.
b) Each trial results in one of two outcomes, which we can define as either a *success* or a *failure.*
c) The outcomes from trial to trial are *independent.*
d) The probability of *success* (p) is the same for each trial. (The probability of *failure* is thus given by $q = 1 - p$.)
e) The *random variable* equals the number of successes in the n trials, and can only take on whole number values between 0 and n.

These five characteristics define the *binomial experiment* and apply to situations of sampling from *finite* populations with replacement or sampling from *infinite* populations with or without replacement.

To be able to identify whether a random variable follows a binomial probability distribution, it is helpful to look out for any tell-tale phrases that allude to the five characteristics mentioned above. Finding phrases such as '...each run of the experiment succeeds with probability 0.6...' (alluding to characteristics (b) and (d)) or '...the experiment was independently conducted five times...' (alluding to characteristics (a) and (c)) is always helpful. Unfortunately, due to the wide range of possible scenarios that can be modelled with binomial random variables, it is often difficult to identify the actual 'experiment' from a written statement, and so there are a myriad of ways in which these phrases can be formulated.

Finally, once we are satisfied that the scenario describes a binomial experiment, it is important to be able to determine the values of n and p from the information provided. To identify these values, we simply need to remember that n represents the number of trials, and so we should look for a simple success/failure type of experiment that is repeated n times. The value of p can be expressed in a number of ways, but it always refers to the probability of success of an *individual* success/failure type of experiment. Consider the following two examples of possible binomial experiments and random variables. The first scenario describes an experiment that can be modelled using a binomial random variable, and the second scenario describes an experiment that cannot be described by a binomial random variable. For each scenario, we will comment on each of the five characteristics of a binomial experiment and indicate whether it has been satisfied or not.

SCENARIO I

AN EXAMPLE OF A SITUATION THAT *CAN* BE MODELLED WITH A BINOMIAL RANDOM VARIABLE

From previous experience, we know that one in every 10 ants usually dies from exposure to a particular insecticide. Twenty randomly selected ants are exposed to this insecticide and (at the end of the experiment) the number of dead ants is recorded. The characteristics of the binomial experiment *are* present in this scenario:

a) The experiment consists of $n = 20$ near identical ants, that is, we are repeating a simple success/failure type of experiment 20 times (once for each ant in the study), and therefore $n = 20$.

b) Each individual trial results in one of two outcomes: 'dead' or 'alive'.

c) The outcomes for each trial are *independent* (it is reasonable to assume that randomly selected ants will not influence each other's chances of success in this experiment).

d) The probability of being 'dead' is assumed to be the same for each trial. Specifically, the probability of being 'dead' for each of the individual experiments is stated as being 'one in every 10' and so, $p = \frac{1}{10} = 0.1$. (The probability of being 'alive' is thus given by $q = 1 - p = 1 - 0.1 = 0.9$.)

e) The random variable x is the number of the original 20 ants that died by the end of the experiment, and so it can only take on the values 0, 1, 2, 3, ..., 20.

SCENARIO II

AN EXAMPLE OF A SITUATION THAT *CANNOT* BE MODELLED WITH A BINOMIAL RANDOM VARIABLE

The number of 'stars' or 'merits' that a hotel accreditation organisation assigns to a hotel is equal to the number of 'tests' that that hotel passes. There are five tests that each hotel must attempt to pass: the cleanliness of rooms, room service efficiency, quality of entertainment facilities, quality of food services and sanitation of bathrooms. It is found that each test is passed or failed with probabilities 10%, 20%, 20%, 30% and 40%, respectively. The characteristics of the binomial experiment are *not* present in this scenario:

a) The experiment consists of $n = 5$ tests. Unfortunately, the tests are *not all the same*. This *violates* the characteristics of a binomial experiment.

b) Each individual trial results in one of two outcomes: 'pass' or 'fail'. This is the only characteristic that this scenario shares with a binomial experiment.

c) The outcomes for each trial are potentially *dependent*. The probabilities of any of the two tests may depend on one another (for example, the probabilities of passing 'cleanliness of rooms' and 'sanitation of bathrooms' are potentially related, but both will differ from the probability of passing the 'quality of food services' test).

d) The probability of success of each test differs, which *violates* the characteristics stated for binomial distributions.

e) The random variable x is the number of 'stars' earned by the hotel, and so it can only take on the values 0, 1, 2, 3, 4 and 5. Therefore it is discrete, but a binomial distribution cannot be used to describe the probability distribution of this discrete random variable.

Some other discrete random variable (other than the binomial) would be appropriate for this variable.

The examples presented later in this section each provide illustrations of binomial experiments. In each case, we indicate the characteristics of the binomial experiment, and values of n and p, to facilitate identification.

6.2.3 The binomial probability distribution and the binomial mass function

In this section, we discuss the probability distribution of a binomial random variable by first showing how we obtain these probabilities using methods that were discussed in Chapter 4, and then by introducing the concept of a *mass function*, which we can use to obtain these probabilities using a simple mathematical expression.

We begin this discussion by looking at how to obtain the probabilities associated with a binomial experiment using a tree diagram, as illustrated in Example 6.1.

WORKED EXAMPLES

EXAMPLE 6.1

A marksman shoots three rounds at a target. His probability of getting a bullseye in any *one* of his shots is 0.3. Develop the probability distribution for getting 0, 1, 2 or 3 bullseyes. This experiment can be modelled by a binomial distribution since:

- there are three identical trials ($n = 3$)
- each trial can result in either a bullseye (success) or not a bullseye (failure)

- the outcome of each trial is independent
- the probability of a success (P(a bullseye) $= p = 0.3$) is the same for each trial
- the random variable is discrete.

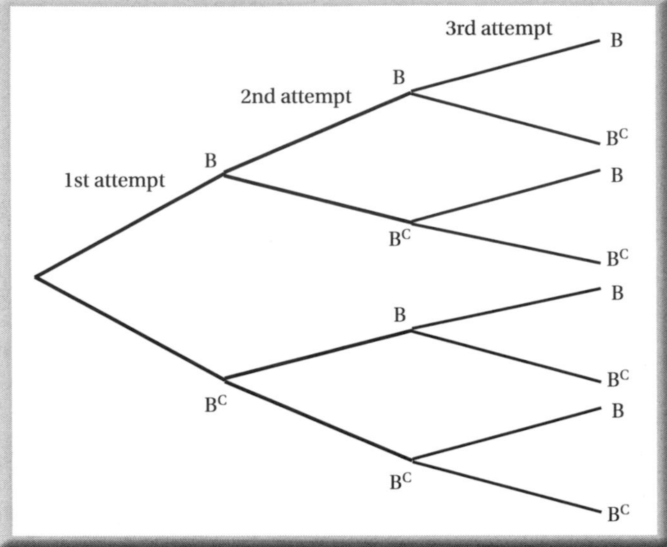

Figure 6.1: Tree diagram for the probabilities of obtaining bullseyes

Figure 6.1 shows the tree diagram that represents the described experiment.

- Let B represent the event that the marksman hits the bullseye and B^C represent the event that the marksman misses the bullseye in any single attempt on the target.
- The corresponding individual event probabilities are $P(B) = 0.3$ and $P(B^C) = 1 - P(B) = 1 - 0.3 = 0.7$.
- Let X denote the total number of bullseyes that the marksman obtains after firing three rounds (X thus follows a binomial distribution).

From this tree diagram, we can determine the probabilities of obtaining 0, 1, 2 or 3 bullseye hits by identifying the possible routes for these outcomes (as described in Chapter 4).

To determine the probability that the marksman does not hit a single the bullseye in his three shots is:

$$\begin{aligned} P(\text{no bullseye hit}) &= P(X = 0) \\ &= P(B^C \cap B^C \cap B^C) \\ &= 0.7 \times 0.7 \times 0.7 \\ &= (0.7)^3 = 0.343 \end{aligned}$$

Note how we can use the tree diagram to calculate an individual probability, but also note that the overall probability of the event differs from the probability of success of the individual trials, p. We observe that $P(\text{no bullseye hit}) = (0.7)^3 = q^3$.

Continuing the calculation, we need to find the probability that one of the three shots was successful. Unfortunately, the successful shot could have been the first, second or third shot, and so the probability needs to reflect this:

$$\begin{aligned} P(1 \text{ bullseye hit}) &= P(X = 1) \\ &= P([B \cap B^C \cap B^C]) \cup [B^C \cap B \cap B^C] \cup [B^C \cap B^C \cap B]) \\ &= (0.3 \times 0.7 \times 0.7) + (0.7 \times 0.3 \times 0.7) + (0.7 \times 0.7 \times 0.3) \\ &= (0.3 \times (0.7)^2) + (0.3 \times (0.7)^2) + (0.3 \times (0.7)^2) \\ &= 3 \times 0.3 \times (0.7)^2 = 0.441 \end{aligned}$$

Therefore, $P(1 \text{ bullseye hit}) = 3pq^2$.

The probability that two bullseyes are hit must also take into account the order in which the successes (or failures) occurred within the three shots taken. It turns out that there are three ways in which the marksman could get exactly two successful bullseyes: hit the first and second shots, hit the first and third shots, or hit the second and third shots. These outcomes are reflected in the following probability:

$$\begin{aligned} P(2 \text{ bullseye hits}) &= P(X = 2) \\ &= P([B \cap B \cap B^C]) \cup [B \cap B^C \cap B] \cup [B^C \cap B \cap B]) \\ &= (0.3 \times 0.3 \times 0.7) + (0.3 \times 0.7 \times 0.3) + (0.7 \times 0.3 \times 0.3) \\ &= (0.3)^2 \times 0.7 + (0.3)^2 \times 0.7 + (0.3)^2 \times 0.7 \\ &= 3 \times (0.3)^2 \times 0.7 = 0.189 \end{aligned}$$

Therefore, $P(2 \text{ bullseyes hits}) = 3p^2q$.

Finally, the probability that all three shots are bullseye shots can be calculated as:

$$\begin{aligned} P(3 \text{ bullseyes hits}) &= P(X = 3) \\ &= P(B \cap B \cap B) \\ &= 0.3 \times 0.3 \times 0.3 \\ &= (0.3)^3 = 0.027 \end{aligned}$$

Therefore, $P(3 \text{ bullseyes hits}) = p^3$

From these calculations, we can now note the probability distribution for this experiment (see Table 6.1).

Table 6.1: The probability distribution for the binomially distributed variable, *X*, the number of successful bullseye shots out of three attempts

x	$P(X = x)$
0	0.343
1	0.441
2	0.189
3	0.027
Total =	1.000

This probability distribution is illustrated in Figure 6.2.

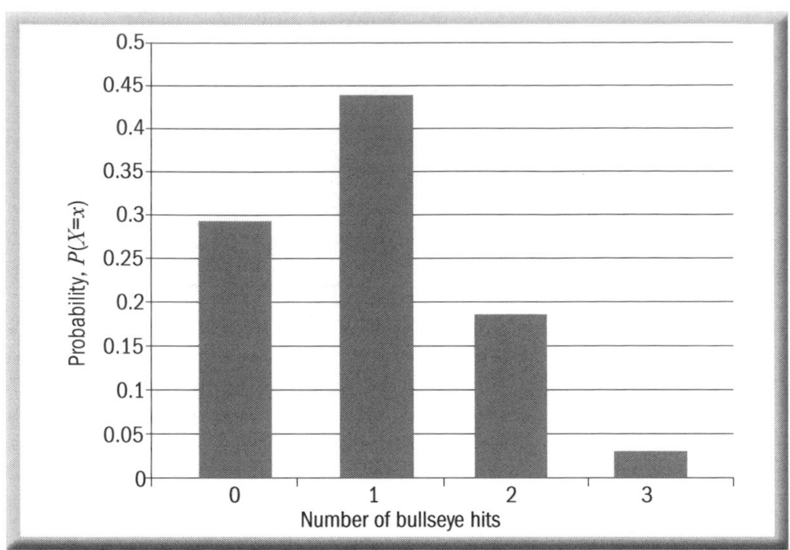

Figure 6.2: A bar chart of the probability distribution of the binomial random variable described in Example 6.1

NOTE

From the probability distribution, we observe that the total probability (the sum of the probabilities of all of the possible outcomes) equals 1. This is expected, since the total probability would represent the total experiment.

$$\text{Total probability} = \sum_{i=1}^{n} P(X = x_i) = 1 \tag{6.1}$$

If we increase the size of the experiment (for example, increase the number of attempts the marksman is allowed to make in Example 6.1), then it becomes quite difficult to calculate the event probabilities. To make these situations simpler, we will rely on a formula to calculate binomial probabilities.

If the experiment was repeated for increasing values of n, we would eventually find that a clear pattern emerges that we can use to develop an equation to calculate the general probability of r, successes given n, attempts of the experiment, that is, $P(X = r)$. Forgoing any detailed mathematical derivations, we find that the expression for this probability is:

THE MASS FUNCTION OF A BINOMIAL RANDOM VARIABLE

$$P(X = r) = \binom{n}{r} p^r q^{n-r}, \qquad r = 0, 1, 2, \ldots, n \tag{6.2}$$

We call these types of functions **mass functions**. Mass functions are mathematical expressions for the probability $P(X = r)$ of discrete random variables. They enable us to calculate probabilities for these specific random variables without always having to rely on complicated probability calculation procedures such as tree diagrams.

Mass function A theoretical function that describes the probability $P(X = r)$, where X is some discrete random variable (for example, for the binomial mass function, X is a binomial random variable).

NOTE

- The term $\binom{n}{r}$ in formula (6.2), which is read 'n combination r', is also discussed in Appendix A, Section A.1.7.

- We define $\binom{n}{r}$ as follows:

$$\binom{n}{r} = \frac{n!}{r!(n-r)!} \tag{6.3}$$

where $n!$ (which is read 'n factorial') is defined as:

$$n! = n \times (n-1) \times \ldots \times 2 \times 1$$

- The term $\binom{n}{r}$ is used to determine the number of possible ways that we can obtain r successes from n attempts of the experiment. For example, to count the number of ways we can obtain two successes if we make five attempts, we calculate:

$$\binom{5}{2} = \frac{5!}{2!(5-2)!} = \frac{5!}{2!(3)!}$$

But:

$$5! = 5 \times 4 \times 3 \times 2 \times 1 = 120$$
$$3! = 3 \times 2 \times 1 = 6$$

And:

$$2! = 2 \times 1 = 2$$

Therefore:

$$\binom{5}{2} = \frac{5!}{2!(3)!} = \frac{120}{6 \times 2} = \frac{120}{12} = 10$$

That is, there are 10 possible ways of obtaining two successes from five attempts.

- Note that $1! = 1$ and $0! = 1$.

- We can use the Excel function COMBIN for combination calculations and the function FACT for factorial calculations.

It can be shown that the mean (expected value) and variance for a random variable X that follows a binomial distribution are given by formulae (6.4) and (6.5) respectively:

$$\text{Mean of binomial distribution, } E(X) = np \tag{6.4}$$

$$\text{Variance of binomial distribution, } Var(X) = npq \tag{6.5}$$

Reconsidering Example 6.1, we note that $n = 3$, $p = 0.3$ and $q = 1 - p = 0.7$. Substituting these values into formula (6.2) gives:

$$P(\text{no bullseyes}) = P(X = 0) = \binom{3}{0}(0.3)^0(0.7)^3$$

Using formula (6.3) we find that:

$$\binom{3}{0} = \frac{3!}{0!(3\text{-}0)!} = \frac{3!}{0!3!} = \frac{3 \times 2 \times 1}{1 \times 3 \times 2 \times 1} = 1$$

And so substituting this value back into the equation produces:

$$\begin{aligned} P(\text{no bullseyes}) &= P(X = 0) \\ &= \binom{3}{0}(0.3)^0(0.7)^3 \\ &= 1 \times 1 \times (0.7)^3 = 0.343 \end{aligned}$$

We see here that we obtain the same solution that we obtained using the tree diagram in Example 6.1. To verify this result, we can calculate the remaining values of the probability distribution in Example 6.1 using formula (6.3):

$$P(X = 1) = \binom{3}{1}(0.3)^1(0.7)^2 = \frac{3 \times 2 \times 1}{1 \times 2 \times 1} \times 0.3 \times 0.49 = 0.441$$

$$P(X = 2) = \binom{3}{2}(0.3)^2(0.7)^1 = \frac{3 \times 2 \times 1}{2 \times 1 \times 1} \times 0.09 \times 0.7 = 0.189$$

$$P(X = 3) = \binom{3}{3}(0.3)^3(0.7)^0 = \frac{3 \times 2 \times 1}{3 \times 2 \times 1 \times 1} \times 0.027 \times 1 = 0.027$$

Naturally, we cannot be expected to calculate these probabilities by hand every time, and so the Excel solution for the probability calculations in Example 6.1 is illustrated in Figure 6.3.

	A	B	C	D	E	F
1	**Binomial distribution**					
2	**Example 6.1**					
3			Number of trials n =	3		
4			Probability of hitting the bullseye p =	0.3		
5			Probability of missing the bullseye q =	0.7	=1-D4	
6						
7	Let X represent the number of bullseye hits (r) out of n attempts					
8						
9			**Probability distribution**	r	$P(X = r)$	
10				0	0.343	=BINOM.DIST(D10,$D$3,$D$4,FALSE)
11				1	0.441	=BINOM.DIST(D11,$D$3,$D$4,FALSE)
12				2	0.189	=BINOM.DIST(D12,$D$3,$D$4,FALSE)
13				3	0.027	=BINOM.DIST(D13,$D$3,$D$4,FALSE)
14				Total =	1	=SUM(E10:E13)
15						
16			**Number of combinations**	r	n combination r	
17				0	1	=COMBIN($D$3,D17)
18				1	3	=COMBIN($D$3,D18)
19				2	3	=COMBIN($D$3,D19)
20				3	1	=COMBIN($D$3,D20)
21						
22			**Factorials**	r	$r!$	
23				0	1	=FACT(D23)
24				1	1	=FACT(D24)
25				2	2	=FACT(D25)
26				3	6	=FACT(D26)

Figure 6.3: Excel solution for Example 6.1

Note that Excel has many built-in functions for calculating binomial probabilities.

- BINOM.DIST(): Used to calculate probabilities of the form $P(X = r)$ and $P(X \leq 4)$ relatively easily, where X is a binomial random variable with parameters n and p. This function accepts four arguments:
  - The value of r to be used in the probability
  - The value of n
  - The value of p
  - An indicator value: If the value is TRUE, then the function calculates the probability $P(X \leq r)$. If it is FALSE, then it calculates the probability $P(X = r)$. For example, to calculate $P(X \leq 4)$, where $n = 10$ and $p = 0.2$, we would type BINOM.DIST(4,10,0.2,TRUE). To calculate $P(X = 4)$, where $n = 10$ and $p = 0.2$, we would type BINOM.DIST(4,10,0.2,FALSE).
- COMBIN(): Used to calculate the binomial coefficients $\binom{n}{r}$ or n combination r. It accepts two arguments: the value of n and the value of r. For example, to calculate $\binom{6}{2}$, 6 combination 2, we would type COMBIN(6,2).
- FACT(): Used to calculate the factorial values, $n!$. This function accepts one argument: the value of n. For example, to calculate 7! we would type FACT(7).

EXCEL SOLUTION

Number of trials: Cell D3	Value
Probability of hitting bullseye, p: Cell D4	Value
Probability of missing bullseye, q: Cell D5	Formula: =1-D4
Probability distribution, r: Cells D10:D13	Values
$P(X = r)$: Cells E10:E13	Formula: =BINOM.DIST(D10,$D$3,$D$4,FALSE) Copy formula from E10:E13
Total: Cell E14	Formula: =SUM(E10:E13)
Number of combinations, r: Cells D17:D20	Values
n combination r: Cells E17:E20	Formula: =COMBIN($D$3,D17) Copy formula from E17:E20
Factorials, $r!$: Cells E23:E26	Values Formula: =FACT(D23) Copy formula from E23:E26

6.2.4 Using the binomial probability distribution with probability rules

In Chapter 4, we discussed probability rules such as the 'additive probability rule for mutually exclusive events' and the 'complement rule'. We can now apply these rules to calculate probabilities from the binomial probability distribution. We need these rules, as the probability mass function in formula (6.3) only provides an expression for probabilities of the form $P(X = r)$. So, if were interested in calculating probabilities such as $P(X \leq r)$ or $P(X > r)$, then we encounter some difficulty.

Fortunately, since the outcomes of a binomial random variable are discrete and mutually exclusive, these probabilities are relatively easy to obtain. We now discuss some important points to consider when calculating these probabilities, which we follow with some examples of how to calculate these probabilities.

- The probability that a discrete binomial random variable is *smaller than or equal to* some number, for example, 3 (i.e. $P(X \leq 3)$), is equal to the probability that the variable is equal to 0 or equal to 1 or equal to 2 or equal to 3 (i.e. $P\{(X = 0) \cup (X = 1) \cup (X = 2) \cup (X = 3)\}$). Note that the $\leq$ symbol implies that the last value – the number 3 in this case – is *included* in the probability calculation. Since these events are mutually exclusive, we apply the additive rule and find:

  $$\begin{aligned} P(X \leq 3) &= P\{(X = 0) \cup (X = 1) \cup (X = 2) \cup (X = 3)\} \\ &= P(X = 0) + P(X = 1) + P(X = 2) + P(X = 3) \end{aligned}$$

  Each of the values for the probabilities $P(X = r)$ is easily obtained from the mass function in formula (6.2).

- The probability that a discrete binomial random variable is *strictly smaller than* some number, for example, 2 (i.e. $P(X < 2)$), is equal to the probability that the variable is equal to 0 or equal to 1 (i.e. $P\{(X = 0) \cup (X = 1)\}$). Note that the strict inequality symbol $<$ implies that the last value – the number 2 in this case – is *excluded* from the probability calculation. Since these events are mutually exclusive, we apply the additive rule and find:

  $$\begin{aligned} P(X < 2) &= P\{(X = 0) \cup (X = 1)\} \\ &= P(X = 0) + P(X = 1) \end{aligned}$$

  Again, each of the values for the probabilities $P(X = r)$ is easily obtained from the mass function in formula (6.2).

- The probability that a discrete binomial random variable is *greater than or equal to* some number, for example, 2 (i.e. $P(X \geq 2)$), can be obtained by using the complement rule, that is, the probability can be written as:

  $$P(X \geq 2) = 1 - P(X < 2)$$

  Note that the $\geq$ symbol changes to a $<$ symbol when we apply the complement rule. We can thus obtain the answer to this probability by first calculating the probability $P(X < 2)$ as discussed above. Similarly, we can also obtain the probability that a discrete binomial random variable is *strictly greater than* some number, for example, 3 (i.e. $P(X > 3)$), using the complement rule:

  $$P(X > 3) = 1 - P(X \leq 3)$$

  Note that the $>$ symbol changes to a $\leq$ symbol. We obtain the probability by first calculating $P(X \leq 3)$.

For example, if X is a binomial random variable with parameters $n = 7$ and $p = 0.8$, then the probability that X is strictly greater than 1 can be expressed as $P(X > 1)$. Using the *complement rule*, we find that:

$$P(X > 1) = 1 - P(X \leq 1)$$

The probability $P(X \leq 1)$, according to the *additive rule*, is:

$$\begin{aligned} P(X \leq 1) &= P\{(X = 0) \cup (X = 1)\} \\ &= P(X = 0) + P(X = 1) \end{aligned}$$

We obtain the individual probabilities from the binomial mass function, formula (6.3):

$$P(X = 0) = \binom{7}{0}(0.8)^0(0.2)^7 = 0.0000128$$

$$P(X = 1) = \binom{7}{1}(0.8)^1(0.2)^6 = 0.0003584$$

The probability $P(X \leq 1)$ is then:

$$P(X \leq 1) = 0.0000128 + 0.0003584 = 0.0003712$$

And, the probability $P(X > 1)$ is:

$$P(X > 1) = 1 - P(X \leq 1) = 1 - 0.0003712 = 0.9996288$$

Example 6.2 illustrates how we calculate these probabilities by hand and by using Excel.

WORKED EXAMPLES

EXAMPLE 6.2

A market research company is hired to determine the commuting preferences of the people in a small town. There are two taxi companies competing for fares in the area (Boitumelo's Brilliant Taxis (BBT) and Taxi Ride Co.), but both offer different types of services. The initial analysis suggests that 1 in 5 people travel with Boitumelo's Brilliant Taxis.

If five randomly selected people are interviewed, then what is the probability that:

a) exactly three prefer travelling with Boitumelo's Brilliant Taxis ($P(X = 3)$)

b) three or more prefer travelling with Boitumelo's Brilliant Taxis ($P(X \geq 3)$)

c) less than three prefer travelling with Boitumelo's Brilliant Taxis ($P(X < 3)$)?

The random variable, X, represents the number of people travelling with Boitumelo's Brilliant Taxis out of the five people interviewed.

From the information given:

$$P(success) = P(\text{prefer Boitumelo's Brilliant Taxis}) = p = \frac{1}{5} = 0.2$$

$$P(failure) = 1 - p = q = 0.8$$

The number of identical trials is $n = 5$.

This experiment can be modelled using a binomial distribution because we can identify the five characteristics of binomial experiments in the given information:

- Five identical trials (that is, five people randomly selected individuals are interviewed, $n = 5$).
- Each trial can result in either a person travelling with Boitumelo's Brilliant Taxis (a success) or not (a failure).
- The outcome of each trial is independent of the others.
- The probability of a success (P travels with Boitumelo's Brilliant Taxis) $= P = \frac{1}{5} = 0.2$) is the same for each trial.
- The random variable (number of people) is discrete.

Using the fact that the variable follows a binomial distribution, we can use Excel's BINOM.DIST function and the probability rules discussed above to answer the probability questions in Example 6.2.

The Excel solution is illustrated in Figure 6.4. For the sake of simplicity, we will abbreviate Boitumelo's Brilliant Taxis to BBT.

	A	B	C	D	E	F
1	**Binomial distribution**					
2	**Example 6.2**					
3			Number of trials n=	5		
4			Probability of taking BBT=	0.2		
5			Probability of not taking BBT=	0.8	=1-D4	
6						
7	Let X represent the number of commuters travelling with					
8	BBT (r) out of the n individuals interviewed.					
9			**Probability Distribution**	r	$P(X=r)$	
10				0	0.32768	=BINOM.DIST(D10,$D$3,$D$4,FALSE)
11				1	0.4096	=BINOM.DIST(D11,$D$3,$D$4,FALSE)
12				2	0.2048	=BINOM.DIST(D12,$D$3,$D$4,FALSE)
13				3	0.0512	=BINOM.DIST(D13,$D$3,$D$4,FALSE)
14				4	0.0064	=BINOM.DIST(D14,$D$3,$D$4,FALSE)
15				5	0.00032	=BINOM.DIST(D15,$D$3,$D$4,FALSE)
16						
17				Total=	1	=SUM(E10:E15)
18						
19				r	Prob	
20	(a) $P(X=3)$ = 0.0512			3	0.0512	=BINOM.DIST(D20,$D$3,$D$4,FALSE)
21	(b) $P(X>=3)$ = 0.05792			2	0.05792	=1-BINOM.DIST(D21,$D$3,$D$4,TRUE)
22	(c) $P(X<3)$ = $P(X<=2)$=0.94208			2	0.94208	=BINOM.DIST(D22,$D$3,$D$4,TRUE)

Figure 6.4: Excel solution for Example 6.2

EXCEL SOLUTION

Number of trials, n: Cell D3	Value
Probability of travelling with BBT, p: Cell D4	Value
Probability of not travelling with BBT, q: Cell D5	Formula: =1-D4
r: Cells D10:C15	Values
$P(X=r)$: Cells E10:E15	Formula: =BINOM.DIST(D10,$D$3,$D$4,FALSE)
	Copy formula from E10:E15
Total: Cell E17	Formula: =SUM(E10:E15)
r: Cells D20:D22	Values
a) $P(X=3)=0.0512$	
$P(X=r)$: Cell E20	Formula: =BINOM.DIST(D20,$D$3,$D$4,FALSE)
b) $P(X>=3)=0.05792$	
$P(X=r)$: Cell E21	Formula: =1-BINOM.DIST(D21,$D$3,$D$4,TRUE)
c) $P(X<3)=P(X<=2)=0.94208$	
$P(X=r)$: Cell E22	Formula: =BINOM.DIST(D22,$D$3,$D$4,TRUE)

INTERPRETATION

a) What is the probability that exactly three of the interviewed people prefer travelling with BBT?

To answer this, we calculate $P(X=3)$ using formula (6.3) in Excel:

$$\begin{aligned} P(\text{exactly three prefer BBT}) &= P(X=3) \\ &= 0.0512 \end{aligned}$$

b) What is the probability that three or more prefer travelling with BBT?

To answer this question, we are required to determine the probability that three, four or five people prefer to travel with BBT. We calculate these individual probabilities and, using the additive rule of mutually exclusive, events we get:

$$\begin{aligned} P(\text{three or more prefer BBT}) &= P(X \geq 3) \\ &= P\{(X=3) \cup (X=4) \cup (X=5)\} \\ &= P(X=3) + P(X=4) + P(X=5) \\ &= 0.0512 + 0.0064 + 0.00032 \\ &= 0.05792 \end{aligned}$$

c) What is the probability that less than three prefer travelling with BBT?

We can easily obtain this answer from the previous answer and by making use of the complement rule of probability:

$$\begin{aligned} P(\text{less than three prefer BBT}) &= P(X < 3) \\ &= 1 - P(X \geq 3) \\ &= 1 - 0.05792 \\ &= 0.94208 \end{aligned}$$

Alternatively, we could answer this question the same way that we answered part (b) (that is, by using the additive rule of probability for mutually exclusive events). The probability would be equivalent to the probability that none, one or two preferred BBT:

$$\begin{aligned} P(\text{less than three prefer BBT}) &= P(X < 3) \\ &= P\{(X = 0) \cup (X = 1) \cup (X = 2)\} \\ &= P(X = 0) + P(X = 1) + P(X = 2) \\ &= 0.32768 + 0.4096 + 0.2048 \\ &= 0.94208 \end{aligned}$$

WORKED EXAMPLES

EXAMPLE 6.3

A manufacturing company regularly conducts quality control checks at specified periods on all products manufactured by the company. A new order for 2 000 light bulbs is due to be delivered to a large franchise hardware store. Historically, the manufacturing record has a failure rate of 15% and the sample to be tested consists of four randomly selected light bulbs that are drawn from the delivery consignment. From this information, estimate the following probabilities.

a) Find the probability distribution for 0, 1, 2, 3 and 4 defective light bulbs in the sample of four drawn.

b) Calculate the probability that at least three will be defective.

c) Determine the mean and variance of the distribution.

Note that this example illustrates a situation in which the elements are drawn *without replacement*. This would typically imply *dependent sampling* (since the probabilities of selecting items not selected change when items are drawn and not replaced). However, since the population size is sufficiently large, the effect on the sample space (and selection probabilities) can be considered negligible, and therefore we will consider the events as independent.

Let the random variable X represent the number of defective light bulbs from the random sample. This value of X can take the values of zero defective from four bulbs or one defective from four bulbs, or two defective from four bulbs, or three defective from four bulbs, or all four bulbs are defective.

This can be written as $X = 0, 1, 2, 3, 4$. For this example, we have $p = P(success) = P(\text{defective bulb}) = 0.15$, $q = P(failure) = 1 - p = 0.85$ and $n = 4$.

We will once again use Excel's BINOM.DIST function to calculate these probabilities. The Excel solution is illustrated in Figure 6.5 below.

	A	B	C	D	E	F	G	H	I
1	**Binomial distribution**								
2	**Example 6.3**								
3			Number of trials n=	4					
4			Probability of defective bulb p =	0.15					
5			Probability of working bulb q=	0.85	=1-D4				
6									
7	Let X represent the number of defective bulbs (r) out of the n in the sample								
8									
9	**(a) Probability Distribution**			r	$P(X=r)$				
10				0	0.52201	=BINOM.DIST(D10,$D$3,$D$4,FALSE)			
11				1	0.36848	=BINOM.DIST(D11,$D$3,$D$4,FALSE)			
12				2	0.09754	=BINOM.DIST(D12,$D$3,$D$4,FALSE)			
13				3	0.01148	=BINOM.DIST(D13,$D$3,$D$4,FALSE)			
14				4	0.00051	=BINOM.DIST(D14,$D$3,$D$4,FALSE)			
15									
16				Total=	1	=SUM(E10:E14)			
17									
18	**(b) $P(X>=3)$ = 0.0119813**			r	$P(X<=r)$				
19				2	0.011981	=1-BINOM.DIST(D19,$D$3,$D$4,TRUE)			
20									
21	**(c) mean and variance**			r	$P(X=r)$	$r \times P(X=r)$		$r^2 \times P(X=r)$	
22				0	0.52201	0	=D22*E22	0	=E22*D22^2
23				1	0.36848	0.368475	=D23*E23	0.368475	=E23*D23^2
24				2	0.09754	0.195075	=D24*E24	0.39015	=E24*D24^2
25				3	0.01148	0.034425	=D25*E25	0.103275	=E25*D25^2
26				4	0.00051	0.002025	=D26*E26	0.0081	=E26*D26^2
27									
28				E(X)=	0.6	=SUM(F22:F26)			
29				Var(X)=	0.51	=SUM(H22:H26)-E28^2			
30				np=	0.6	=D3*D4			
31				npq=	0.51	=D3*D4*D5			

Figure 6.5: Excel solution for Example 6.3

EXCEL SOLUTION

Number of trials n: Cell D3	Value
Probability of obtaining a defective bulb, p: Cell D4	Value
Probability of obtaining a working bulb, q: Cell D5	Formula: =1-D4
a) Probability distribution	
r: Cells D10:D14	Value
$P(X = r)$: Cells E10:E14	Formula: =BINOM.DIST(D10,$D$3,$D$4,FALSE) Copy formula from E10:E14
Total: Cell E16	Formula: =SUM(E10:E14)
b) $P(X >= 3) = P(X = 3) + P(X = 4) = 1 - P(X < 3) = 1 - P(X <= 2) = 0.0119813$	
r: Cell D19	Value
$P(X = 4)$: Cell E19	Formula: =BINOM.DIST(D22,$D$3,$D$4,FALSE) Copy formula from E22:E26
c) Mean and variance	
r: Cells D22:D26	Values
$P(X = r)$: Cells E22:E26	Formula: =BINOM.DIST(D22,$D$3,$D$4,FALSE) Copy formula from E22:E26
$r \times P(X = r)$: Cells F22:F26	Formula: =D22*E22 Copy formula from F22:F26
$r^2 \times P(X = r)$: Cells H22:H26	Formula: =D22^2*F22 Copy formula from H22:H26
$E(x)$: Cell E28	Formula: =SUM(F22:F26)
$VAR(X)$: Cell E29	Formula: =SUM(H22:H26)-E28^2
np: Cell E30	Formula: =D3*D4
npq: Cell E31	Formula: =D3*D4*D5

INTERPRETATION

a) The probability distribution is shown in Table 6.2.

Table 6.2: Probability distribution of the number of defective light bulbs in a sample of four light bulbs drawn from a consignment

r	$P(X = r)$
0	0.52201
1	0.36848
2	0.09754
3	0.01148
4	0.00051

b) The probability of at least three (that is, three or more) defective bulbs from the sample of four light bulbs is $P(X \geq 3) = 0.0119813$.

c) The mean (or expected value) and variance for the probability distribution can be obtained using formulae (6.5) and (6.6). Recall that we have $n = 4$, $p = 0.15$ and $q = 0.85$, therefore, we find $E(X) = np = 4 \times 0.15 = 0.6$ and $Var(X) = npq = 4 \times 0.15 \times 0.85 = 0.51$. These answers agree with the Excel sheet.

6.3 Poisson probability distribution

6.3.1 Introduction to the Poisson probability distribution

In the previous section, we explored the concept of a binomial distribution: a discrete probability distribution, which enables us to calculate the probability of achieving r successes from n independent experiments. Each experiment (or event) had two possible outcomes (success or failure), and the probability of success (p) was known. The *Poisson distribution*, developed by Siméon Poisson (1781 to 1840), is another discrete probability distribution that describes the probability of r events to occur during a specified interval (time, distance, area or volume), if the average occurrence is known and the events are independent of the specified interval since the last event occurred. Random variables associated with the Poisson distribution are called **Poisson random variables**. We can use Poisson random variables to describe phenomena such as product demand, demands for service, numbers of accidents, numbers of traffic arrivals, and numbers of defects in various types of lengths or objects.

Poisson random variable A discrete random variable that describes the number of occurrences over a particular interval (times, distance, area, volume, and so on). The mean number of occurrences over an interval is denoted by λ.

In contrast to the binomial distribution, which requires a known number of trials resulting in successes and failures, we use the Poisson distribution in situations where the number of trials is either unknown or where it would not be possible to know how many failures occurred. For example, if we watch a football match, we can report the number of goals scored (number of successes), but we cannot say how many were *not* scored (number of failures). In such cases, we are dealing with isolated cases in a continuum of space and time, where the number of experiments (n), probability of success (p) and failure (q) cannot be clearly defined. What we can do, however, is divide the interval (time, distance, area or volume) into very small sections and calculate the mean number of occurrences in the interval.

Poisson probability distribution A probability distribution that describes the probabilities of occurrence of a Poisson random variable.

6.3.2 The Poisson probability distribution and mass function

This gives rise to the Poisson mass function defined by formula (6.6).

THE MASS FUNCTION OF A POISSON RANDOM VARIABLE

$$P(X=r)=\frac{e^{-\lambda}\lambda^{r}}{r!}, \qquad r=0, 1, 2, \ldots, \tag{6.6}$$

The important elements in formula (6.6) are the following:

- $P(X=r)$ is the probability that r events occurred.
- The symbol r represents the number of occurrences of an event, and can take on any whole numbered value between 0 and $+\infty$ (positive infinity).
- $r!$ is the factorial of r (calculated using the Excel function FACT()).
- λ is a positive real number that represents the expected number of occurrences for a given interval.
- The symbol e represents the base of the natural logarithm ($e = 2.71828 \ldots$).

We say that a random variable is a Poisson random variable if we can describe the probability distribution of that distribution by the mass function in formula (6.6). As with the binomial distribution, we can use the Poisson mass function to calculate a myriad probabilities related to Poisson random variables.

6.3.3 Properties of the Poisson distribution and identifying Poisson random variables

Unlike other distributions, the mean and variance of the Poisson distribution are identical (in practice however, the sample mean and variance will typically not be identical, but will be very close to one another). In other words, if we determine the mean and the variance, either by using the frequency distribution or the probability distribution, we would find that the variance and expected value (mean) of the Poisson distribution are the same:

$$\lambda = Var(X) = E(X) \tag{6.7}$$

This property leads us to a simple list of characteristics that can be used to identify Poisson random variables based on evidence from a given scenario and the given data.

Typically, things that can be *counted* can be described by a Poisson distribution, but the following characteristics should hold in order to confirm it:

- The mean should be equal to the variance. (As noted in the above example, these quantities will only be approximately equal for any given observed sample.)
- The events are discrete and are randomly distributed in time and space.
- The mean number of events in a given interval is constant.
- Events are independent.
- Two or more events cannot occur simultaneously.

NOTE

Once you have identified that the mean and variance have the same numerical value, ensure that the other conditions above are satisfied, which then indicates that the sample data will most likely follow the Poisson distribution. Note, however, that this is not a definitive way to identify whether the distribution is Poisson. In the next example, we attempt to determine if the data comes from a Poisson distribution using the characteristics described above. However, this will not be sufficient to come to a concrete conclusion. In the section that follows, we look at a more reliable method of identifying Poisson distributions.

In the following example, we consider an observed frequency distribution, and calculate its mean and variance to determine if they are roughly equal (and thus if the random variable being considered is approximately Poisson distributed). We then use the theoretical probability mass function in formula (6.6) to construct a theoretical frequency table with the same mean and variance (that is, the theoretical frequency table will indicate what the observed frequency table should look like if it came from a Poisson distribution).

WORKED EXAMPLES

EXAMPLE 6.4(A)

The data in Table 6.3, derived over the past 100 years, concerns the number of times a river floods in a given year's wet season.

Check if the distribution may be modelled using the Poisson distribution by first considering the characteristics of Poisson random variables.

Table 6.3: Frequency table representing the frequency of flooding over 100 years

NUMBER OF FLOODS PER YEAR (x)	NUMBER OF THE 100 YEARS WITH x FLOODS (f)
0	24
1	35
2	24
3	12
4	4
5	1
Total =	100

To determine if the random variable 'number of floods per year' follows a Poisson distribution, we must first consider the five characteristics of Poisson distributions discussed earlier:

a) *The mean should be equal to the variance*: To test this characteristic, we will need to calculate the sample mean and variance (done below).
b) *The events are discrete and are randomly distributed in time and space*: The event in this case is the occurrence of floods, which is discrete, and the interval over which we count the occurrence is one year, and the events are assumed to be randomly distributed in this interval. This characteristic of Poisson random variables is satisfied.
c) *The mean number of events in a given interval is constant*: If it is reasonable to assume that the mean number of floods per year does not increase (or decrease) over time, we can assume that this characteristic also holds.
d) *Events are independent*: If we assume that the occurrence of one flood does not affect another one, we can assume that this characteristic also holds.
e) *Two or more events cannot occur simultaneously*: Two floods cannot occur at the same time (and even if they did, it would only be counted as a single big flood). We will accept that this characteristic is satisfied.

From this, we see that we only need to confirm point (a) (that is, that the mean and variance of the data are the same) in order to confirm whether the random variable in question has the same characteristics of a Poisson distribution.

In the Excel solution below, we calculate the mean and variance of this frequency table. If they are roughly equal to one another, it provides some more evidence that the data are Poisson distributed. However, please note that simply identifying these characteristics in the data is not sufficient to decisively conclude a Poisson distribution for the data.

Excel solution is provided in Figure 6.6.

	A	B	C	D	E	F	G	H	I
1	POISSON PROBABILITY DISTRIBUTION EXAMPLE								
2		Example 6.4	(a) Calculate frequency distribution mean and variance						
3									
4									
5		Number of floods	Number of years with *x* floods						
6		*x*	*f*	*xf*		x^2		fx^2	
7		0	24	0	=B7*C7	0	=B7^2	0	=C7*F7
8		1	35	35	=B8*C8	1	=B8^2	35	=C8*F8
9		2	24	48	=B9*C9	4	=B9^2	96	=C9*F9
10		3	12	36	=B10*C10	9	=B10^2	108	=C10*F10
11		4	4	16	=B11*C11	16	=B11^2	64	=C11*F11
12		5	1	5	=B12*C12	25	=B12^2	25	=C12*F12
13		Total =	100	140				328	
14			=SUM(C7:C12)	=SUM(D7:D12)				=SUM(H7:H12)	
15									
16		Mean =	1.4	=D13/C13					
17		Variance =	1.32	=H13/C13-C16^2					

Figure 6.6: Excel solution for Example 6.4(a)

The first stage is to estimate the number of floods per year, λ, based on the sample data.

EXCEL SOLUTION **Calculate frequency distribution mean and variance**

Number of floods X: Cells B7:B12	Values
Number of years with X floods: Cells C7:C12	Values
Xf: Cells D7:D12	Formula: =B7*C7
	Copy formula from D7:D12
Totals	
$\sum X$: Cell C13	Formula: =SUM(C7:C12)
$\sum Xf$: Cell D13	Formula: =SUM(D7:D12)
X^2: Cells F7:F12	Formula: =B7^2
	Copy formula from F7:F12
fX^2: Cells H7:H12	Formula: =C7*F7
	Copy formula from H7:H12
Mean: Cell D16	Formula: =D13/C13
Variance: Cell D17	Formula: =H13/C13–C16^2

The average number of floods per year, λ, and the variance is calculated from this frequency distribution:

$$\text{Mean: } \lambda = \frac{\sum_{i=1}^{n} f_i x_i}{\sum_{i=1}^{n} f_i} = \frac{140}{100} = 1.4 \text{ floods per year}$$

$$\text{Variance: } Var(X) = \frac{\sum_{i=1}^{n} f_i x_i^2}{\sum_{i=1}^{n} f_i} - (\text{mean})^2 = 1.32$$

INTERPRETATION The average number of floods, that is, the mean, is 1.4 floods per year with a variance of 1.32. They seem to be in close agreement (only 5.7% difference), which is one of the characteristics of the Poisson distribution. The mean and variance of the Poisson distribution have the same numerical value, and given the closeness of the two values in this numerical example, we would be inclined to conclude that the Poisson distribution should be a good model for the sample data.

In the next section, we continue with this example and look at what the frequency table should look like if the data came from a theoretical Poisson distribution with the same mean. If the observed frequency table closely matches the theoretical frequency table, it will support the conclusion that the data are Poisson distributed.

6.3.4 Calculating probabilities associated with Poisson random variables and applying probability rules

Once it is clear that a random variable follows a Poisson distribution, we can easily calculate probabilities associated with that random variable by using the mass function given in formula (6.6) and the probability rules discussed in Chapter 4. The rules for calculating probabilities such as $P(X < 2)$ or $P(X \geq 4)$ are identical to the rules discussed in Section 6.2.4, except that the calculation of the individual probabilities, for example, $P(X = 1)$ or $P(X = 4)$, is calculated using the Poisson mass function in formula (6.6).

For example, if X is a Poisson random variable with parameter $\lambda = 2$, then the probability that X is less than 3 is $P(X < 3)$ and, according to the *additive rule*, we would calculate:

$$\begin{aligned} P(X < 3) &= P\{(X = 0) \cup (X = 1) \cup (X = 2)\} \\ &= P(X = 0) + P(X = 1) + P(X = 2) \end{aligned}$$

We obtain the individual probabilities from the Poisson mass function, formula (6.6):

$$P(X = 0) = \frac{2^0 e^{-2}}{0!} = e^{-2} = 0.1353$$

$$P(X = 1) = \frac{2^1 e^{-2}}{1!} = 2 \times e^{-2} = 0.2707$$

$$P(X = 2) = \frac{2^2 e^{-2}}{2!} = \frac{4 \times e^{-2}}{2} = 0.2707$$

The probability $P(X < 3)$ is then:

$$P(X < 3) = 0.1353 + 0.2707 + 0.2707 = 0.6767$$

If the question changed to 'what is the probability that X is greater than or equal to 3', expressed as $P(X \geq 3)$, then we could simply apply the *complement rule* and find that:

$$P(X \geq 3) = 1 - P(X < 3) = 1 - 0.6767 = 0.3233$$

Excel provides a function called 'POISSON.DIST', which we can use to calculate probabilities of the form $P(X = r)$ and $P(X \leq r)$ relatively easily. This function accepts three arguments:

- The value of r to be used in the probability
- The value of λ (the mean and variance of the Poisson random variable)
- An indicator value: If the value is TRUE, then the function calculates the probability $P(X \leq r)$. If it is FALSE, then it calculates the probability $P(X = r)$. For example, to calculate $P(X = 6)$, where $\lambda = 0.4$, we would type POISSON.DIST(6,0.4,FALSE). To calculate $P(X \leq 6)$, where $\lambda = 0.4$, we would type POISSON.DIST(6,0.4,TRUE).

WORKED EXAMPLES

EXAMPLE 6.4(B)

Continuing with the 'flood' data presented in Example 6.4(a), determine the frequencies we may have expected to see for the 100-year period, if the random variable is Poisson distributed with a mean of 1.4 (as calculated in Example 6.4).

To do this, first calculate the probabilities of 0, 1, 2, 3, 4 and 5 floods occurring, assuming that the number of floods is Poisson distributed with $\lambda = 1.4$. Next, obtain the theoretical frequencies by multiplying the probabilities by 100.

Continuing with the Excel spreadsheet used in Example 6.4(a), we can now determine the probability distribution using formula (6.6) as illustrated in Figure 6.7.

	J	K	L	M	N
1					
2		**Example 6.4**			
3		**(b) Calculate the Poisson probabilities and expected frequencies**			
4					
5				**Expected frequency**	
6	r	$P(X=r)$			
7	0	0.2466	=POISSON.DIST(J7,$C$16,FALSE)	24.66	=$C$13*K7
8	1	0.3452	=POISSON.DIST(J8,$C$16,FALSE)	34.52	=$C$13*K8
9	2	0.2417	=POISSON.DIST(J19,$C$16,FALSE)	24.17	=$C$13*K9
10	3	0.1128	=POISSON.DIST(J10,$C$16,FALSE)	11.28	=$C$13*K10
11	4	0.0395	=POISSON.DIST(J11,$C$16,FALSE)	3.95	=$C$13*K11
12	5	0.0111	=POISSON.DIST(J12,$C$16,FALSE)	1.11	=$C$13*K12
13					
14	Total =	0.9968		99.68	
15		=SUM(K7:K12)		=SUM(M7:M12)	

Figure 6.7: Excel solution for Example 6.4(b)

EXCEL SOLUTION **Calculate the Poisson probabilities and expected frequencies**

r: Cells J7:J12	Values
$P(X = r)$: Cells K7:K12	Formula: =POISSON.DIST(J7,$C$16,FALSE)
Total: Cell K14	Formula: =SUM(K7:K12)
Expected frequencies: Cells M7:M12	Formula: =$C$13*K7
	Copy formula from M7:M12
Total: Cell M14	Formula: =SUM(M7:M12)

INTERPRETATION

The probability distribution is given in Table 6.4.

Table 6.4: The Poisson probability distribution of the number of floods

r	$P(X = r)$
0	0.2466
1	0.3452
2	0.2417
3	0.1128
4	0.0395
5	0.0111

To check how well the Poisson probability distribution fits the data set, we have to compare the observed frequencies given in the original table with the expected frequencies calculated by multiplying the total sample size, $n = \sum_{i=1}^{k} f_i$ with the theoretical Poisson probabilities calculated from the mass function, that is, the expected frequencies are obtained using the following formula:

$$\text{Expected frequency} = \left(\sum_{i=1}^{k} f_i\right) \times P(X = r)$$

The summary of the solution is presented in Table 6.5.

Table 6.5: Observed frequencies and frequencies expected under the Poisson distribution

r	$P(X = r)$	OBSERVED FREQUENCY	EXPECTED FREQUENCY
0	0.2466	24	24.66
1	0.3452	35	34.52
2	0.2417	24	24.17
3	0.1128	12	11.28
4	0.0395	4	3.95
5	0.0111	1	1.11
	Totals =	100	99.68

Note that the expected frequencies are *approximately* equal to the observed frequency values. This strongly suggests that the observed data comes from a Poisson distribution.

Table 6.6 illustrates the calculation of the Poisson probability values for $\lambda = 1.4$ by applying formula (6.6).

Table 6.6: The theoretical Poisson probabilities calculated using formula (6.6)

r	POISSON VALUE	EXCEL
0	$P(X=0)=\frac{1.4^0 e^{-1.4}}{0!}=0.2466$	=POISSON.DIST(J7,$C$16,FALSE)
1	$P(X=1)=\frac{1.4^1 e^{-1.4}}{1!}=0.3452$	=POISSON.DIST(J8,$C$16,FALSE)
2	$P(X=2)=\frac{1.4^2 e^{-1.4}}{2!}=0.2417$	=POISSON.DIST(J9,$C$16,FALSE)
3	$P(X=3)=\frac{1.4^3 e^{-1.4}}{3!}=0.1128$	=POISSON.DIST(J10,$C$16,FALSE)
4	$P(X=4)=\frac{1.4^4 e^{-1.4}}{4!}=0.0395$	=POISSON.DIST(J11,$C$16,FALSE)
5	$P(X=1)=\frac{1.4^5 e^{-1.4}}{5!}=0.0111$	=POISSON.DIST(J12,$C$16,FALSE)

Figure 6.8 illustrates a bar chart of the Poisson probabilities for the 'number of floods' example. You can clearly see the skewed nature of the distribution.

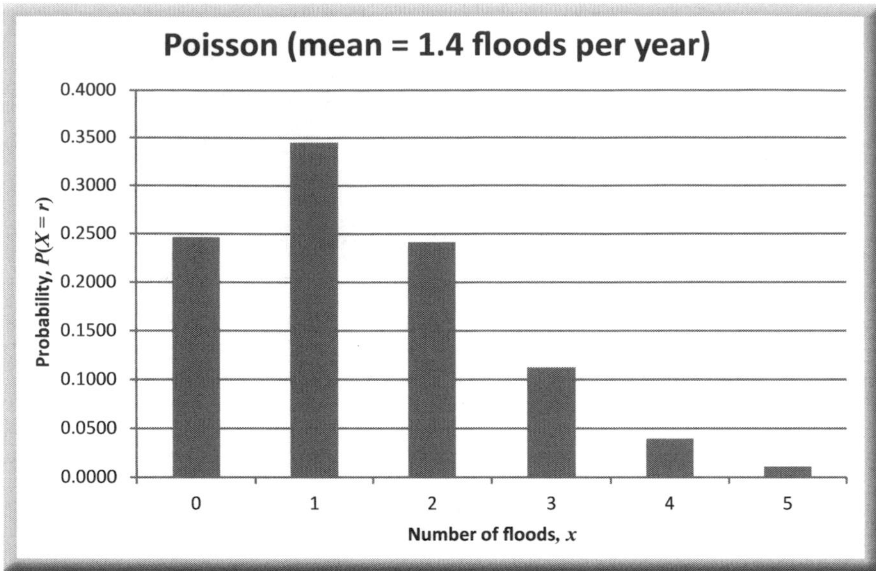

Figure 6.8: A bar chart representing the Poisson probability distribution for Example 6.4

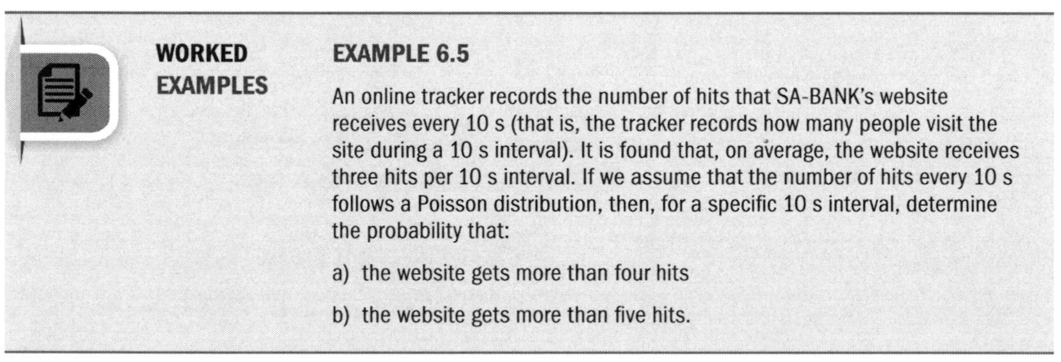

WORKED EXAMPLES

EXAMPLE 6.5

An online tracker records the number of hits that SA-BANK's website receives every 10 s (that is, the tracker records how many people visit the site during a 10 s interval). It is found that, on average, the website receives three hits per 10 s interval. If we assume that the number of hits every 10 s follows a Poisson distribution, then, for a specific 10 s interval, determine the probability that:

a) the website gets more than four hits

b) the website gets more than five hits.

To obtain these answers, we need to calculate the probabilities $P(X > 4)$ and $P(X > 5)$, where X is a Poisson-distributed random variable with $\lambda = 3$. Unfortunately, determining these probabilities by hand can be rather tedious, so we will rely on Excel's POISSON.DIST function and some probability rules to obtain the answers more easily.

The Excel solution is illustrated in Figure 6.9.

	A	B	C	D
1	**Example 6.5**			
2				
3		$\lambda = 3$		
4				
5		r	$P(X = r)$	
6		0	0.049787068	=POISSON.DIST(B6,$C$3,FALSE)
7		1	0.149361205	=POISSON.DIST(B7,$C$3,FALSE)
8		2	0.224041808	=POISSON.DIST(B8,$C$3,FALSE)
9		3	0.224041808	=POISSON.DIST(B9,$C$3,FALSE)
10		4	0.168031356	=POISSON.DIST(B10,$C$3,FALSE)
11				
12		$P(X <= 4) =$	0.815263245	=POISSON.DIST(B10,$C$3,FALSE)
13		$P(X <= 4) =$	0.815263245	=SUM(C6:C10)
14				
15		$P(X >= 4) =$	0.18473755	=1-C12
16				
17		$P(X > 5) =$	0.083917942	=1-POISSON.DIST(5,C3,TRUE)

Figure 6.9: Excel solution for Example 6.5

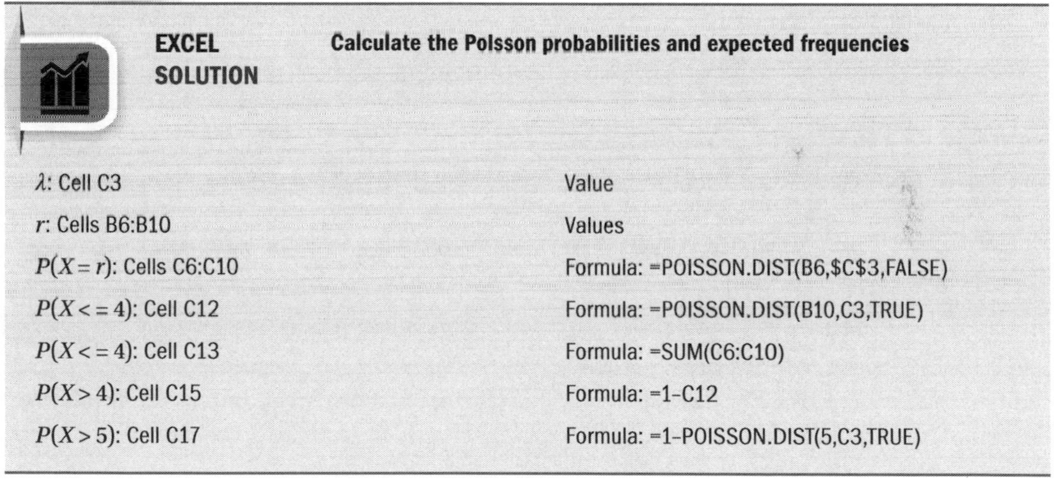

EXCEL SOLUTION **Calculate the Poisson probabilities and expected frequencies**

λ: Cell C3	Value
r: Cells B6:B10	Values
$P(X = r)$: Cells C6:C10	Formula: =POISSON.DIST(B6,$C$3,FALSE)
$P(X < = 4)$: Cell C12	Formula: =POISSON.DIST(B10,C3,TRUE)
$P(X < = 4)$: Cell C13	Formula: =SUM(C6:C10)
$P(X > 4)$: Cell C15	Formula: =1–C12
$P(X > 5)$: Cell C17	Formula: =1–POISSON.DIST(5,C3,TRUE)

INTERPRETATION

a) The probability that the website gets more than four hits in 10 s is:

$$\begin{aligned}&P(X>4)\\&=1-P(X\leq 4)\\&=1-[P\{(X=0)\cup(X=1)\cup(X=2)\cup(X=3)\cup(X=4)\}]\\&=1-[P(X=0)+P(X=1)+P(X=2)+P(X=3)+P(X=4)]\end{aligned}$$

From the Excel spreadsheet calculation, we have $P(X>4)=0.185263245$ or 18.5%. The probability that there are more than four visitors in a 10-s interval is 18.5% (that is, this event happens in 18.5% of the 10-s intervals).

b) The probability the website gets more than five hits in 10 s is:

$$\begin{aligned}&P(X>5)\\&=1-P(X\leq 5)\\&=1-[P\{(X=0)\cup(X=1)\cup(X=2)\cup(X=3)\cup(X=4)\cup(X=5)\}]\\&=1-[P(X=0)+P(X=1)+P(X=2)+P(X=3)+P(X=4)+P(X=5)]\end{aligned}$$

From Excel, $P(X>5)=0.083917942$ or 8.4%.

Table 6.7 illustrates calculating the Poisson probability values for $\lambda = 3$, by applying formula (6.6).

Table 6.7: The probability distribution for the Poisson random variable, X, the number of hits SA-BANK's website receives every 10 s

r	POISSON VALUE	EXCEL
0	$P(X=0)=\frac{3^0e^{-3}}{0!}=0.0498$	=POISSON.DIST(B6,$C$3,FALSE)
1	$P(X=1)=\frac{3^1e^{-3}}{1!}=0.1494$	=POISSON.DIST(B7,$C$3,FALSE)
2	$P(X=2)=\frac{3^2e^{-3}}{2!}=0.2240$	=POISSON.DIST(B8,$C$3,FALSE)
3	$P(X=3)=\frac{3^3e^{-3}}{3!}=0.0498$	=POISSON.DIST(B9,$C$3,FALSE)
4	$P(X=4)=\frac{3^4e^{-3}}{4!}=0.1680$	=POISSON.DIST(B10,$C$3,FALSE)

6.4 Other discrete probability distributions

Other types of discrete probability distributions include the *hypergeometric* and *negative binomial* discrete probability distribution. These distributions measure, like the binomial distribution, the number of successes observed in an experiment. However, they differ from the binomial distribution in a number of respects, for example, the hypergeometric distribution involves sampling without replacement, making the probability of success (p) dependent on the outcome of the previous run of the experiment (unlike the binomial distribution). The negative binomial distribution also differs in that the total number of trials being conducted is typically not known, because these experiments continue until the first success is obtained (therefore the process can continue for a large number of times if the probability of success of each individual success/failure experiment is very low). Unfortunately, these topics are beyond the scope of this textbook.

SUMMARY

In this chapter, we considered two very important discrete random variables and their associated probability mass functions: the binomial random variable and the Poisson random variable. We briefly discussed methods of identifying these variables in various situations and then went on to look at how the mass functions could be used to calculate probabilities pertaining to the random variables.

KEY TERMS

Binomial probability distribution
Binomial random variable
Discrete probability distribution
Expected value of a discrete variable
Mean of the binomial distribution
Mean of the Poisson distribution
Poisson probability distribution
Poisson random variable
Variance of binomial distribution
Variance of poisson distribution

FORMULA SUMMARY

$$\text{Total probability} = \sum_{i=1}^{n} P(X = x_i) = 1 \tag{6.1}$$

$$P(X = r) = \binom{n}{r} p^r q^{n-r}, \qquad r = 0, 1, 2, \ldots, n \tag{6.2}$$

$$\binom{n}{r} = \frac{n!}{r!(n-r)!} \tag{6.3}$$

$$\text{Mean of binomial distribution, } E(X) = np \tag{6.4}$$

$$\text{Variance of binomial distribution, } Var(X) = npq \tag{6.5}$$

$$P(X = r) = \frac{e^{-\lambda}\lambda^r}{r!}, \qquad r = 0, 1, 2, \ldots \tag{6.6}$$

$$\lambda = Var(X) = E(X) \tag{6.7}$$

EXERCISES

6.1 A binomial random variable, X, has $n = 4$ and $p = 0.6$.

a) Find the probabilities of each of the five possible outcomes (that is, $P(X = 0)$, $P(X = 1), \ldots, P(X = 4)$).

b) Construct a bar chart of these data.

6.2 Attendance at a cinema has been analysed and shows that audiences for a particular film consist of 60% men and 40% women. If a random sample of six people were selected from the audience during a performance, find the following probabilities that:

a) all women are selected

b) three men are selected

c) less than three women are selected.

6.3 A quality control system selects a sample of three items from a production line. If one or more is defective, a second sample is taken (also three items), and if one or more of these are defective, then the whole production line is stopped. Given that the probability of a defective item is 0.05, what is the probability that the second sample is taken? What is the probability that the production line is stopped?

6.4 Five people in seven voted in an election. If four of those on the roll are interviewed, what is the probability that at least three voted?

6.5 A small tourist resort has a weekend traffic problem and is considering whether to provide emergency services to help mitigate the congestion that results from an accident or breakdown. Past records show that the probability of a breakdown or an accident on any given day of a four-day weekend is 0.25. The cost to the community caused by congestion resulting from an accident or breakdown is as follows.

- A weekend with one accident day costs R20 000.
- A weekend with two accident days costs R30 000.

- A weekend with three accident days costs R60 000.
- A weekend with four accident days costs R125 000.

As part of its contingency planning, the resort needs to know:

a) the probability that a weekend will have no accidents
b) the probability that a weekend will have at least two accidents
c) the expected cost that the community will have to bear for an average weekend period
d) whether to accept a tender from a private firm for emergency services of R20 000 for each weekend during the season.

6.6 Calculate the probability that a Poisson random variable, X, with mean 1.2, is equal to 0, 1, 2, 3, 4, 5, 6 and more than 6. Using this probability distribution, determine the mean and variance.

6.7 In a machine shop, the average number of machines out of operation is two. Assuming a Poisson distribution for machines out of operation, calculate the probability that at any one time there will be:

a) exactly one machine out of operation
b) more than one machine out of operation.

6.8 A factory estimates that 0.25% of its production of small components is defective. The components are sold in packets of 200. Calculate the percentage of the packets containing one or more defective components.

6.9 The average number of faults in 1 m of cloth produced by a particular sewing machine is 0.1. The line manager assumes that the number of faults per metre of cloth follows a Poisson distribution.

a) What is the probability that a length of 4 m is free from faults?
b) How long would a piece of cloth have to be before the probability that it contains no flaws is less than 0.95?
c) Is there enough evidence to support the notion that the number of faults follows a Poisson distribution?

6.10 A garage has three cars available for daily hire. Calculate the following if the variable is a Poisson variable with a mean of 2.

a) Find the probability that on any given day exactly none, one, two and three cars will be hired, and determine the mean number of cars hired per day.
b) The cost of hiring a car is R25 per day, and the total outgoings per car, irrespective of whether or not it is hired, are R5 per day. Determine the expected daily profit from hiring these three cars.

6.11 Accidents occur in a factory randomly, on average at a rate of 2.6 per month. Assuming a Poisson distribution, what is the probability that in a given month:

a) no accidents will occur
b) more than one accident will occur?

CHAPTER 7

CONTINUOUS PROBABILITY DISTRIBUTIONS

CHAPTER CONTENTS

OVERVIEW

We briefly mentioned continuous probability distributions in Chapter 5. However, in the examples in Chapter 5, we focused on values from a continuous random variable to construct 'empirical' or observed distributions. In this chapter, we consider the situation where the theoretical distribution of these continuous random variables are described by mathematical formulae (we consider the uniform, normal, chi-squared and F-distributions). As with discrete distributions, we can use these mathematical functions to calculate various probabilities associated with the corresponding continuous random variable. This method differs from the method discussed in Chapter 5 (where we had to use large amounts of sample data to approximate these probabilities) because, if we are correct in assuming that the random variable follows a specified distribution, then the theoretical functions allow for accurate probability calculations.

The interpretation, application and properties of these distributions will also be described in each section.

LEARNING OBJECTIVES

On completing this chapter, you should be able to:

- distinguish between theoretical continuous distributions and continuous distributions constructed from observations
- describe probabilities using density functions
- have a basic understanding of the uniform distribution
- use the normal distribution to calculate the values of a variable that correspond to a particular probability
- use the normal distribution to calculate the probability that a variable has a value between specific limits
- understand when to apply the normal distribution
- have a basic understanding of the Student's t-distribution
- have a basic understanding of the chi-squared distribution
- have a basic understanding of the F-distribution
- solve problems using Microsoft Excel.

7.1 Introduction to continuous probability distributions

7.1.1 Introduction

In the previous chapter, we explored different types of theoretical discrete random variables and their associated probability functions (which we called *mass functions*). We now begin the discussion on continuous random variables and their associated theoretical probability functions (called **density functions**). We use these theoretical functions to describe the probability structure of a continuous random variable in much the same way that we used the histograms and probability distribution tables in Chapter 5, except that now these functions have regular, predictable forms that will allow us to calculate probabilities easily. In this chapter, we explore the concept of a **continuous probability distribution** with the focus on introducing you to the concept of a normal probability distribution. We also briefly discuss a few other important continuous distributions.

Density functions Describe the distribution of the potential values of a continuous random variable, X. This function is denoted by $f_X(x)$ and is used to determine probabilities associated with continuous random variables.

Continuous probability distribution If a random variable is a continuous variable, its probability distribution is called a continuous probability distribution.

7.1.2 Continuous probability distributions and density functions

When considering the *randomness* of a continuous random variable, it is always tempting to believe that all the potential values occur with equal probability. Unfortunately, this *equal* probability scenario for these values is only one of many possible forms that the probability distribution of a random variable can assume. In Figure 7.1 below, we see a number of different shapes for symmetric probabilities and Figure 7.2 shows some asymmetric probability structures. (These shapes are analogous to the different forms of a histogram.)

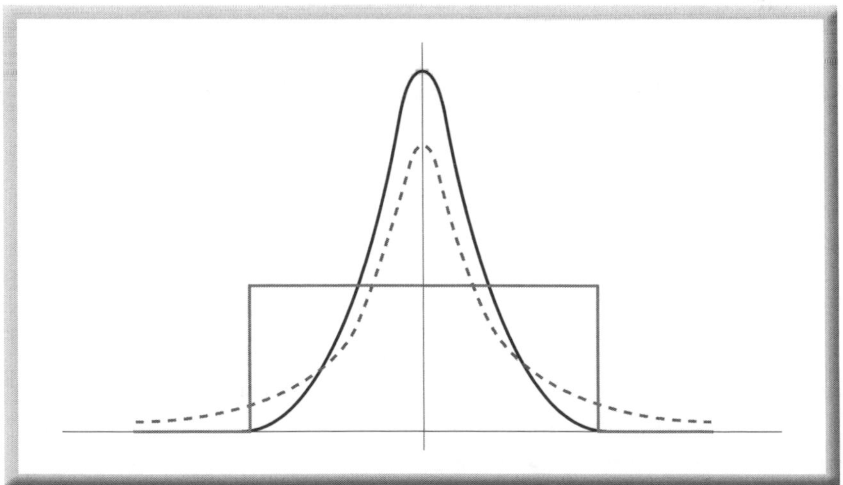

Figure 7.1: Symmetric theoretical continuous probability structures (density functions)

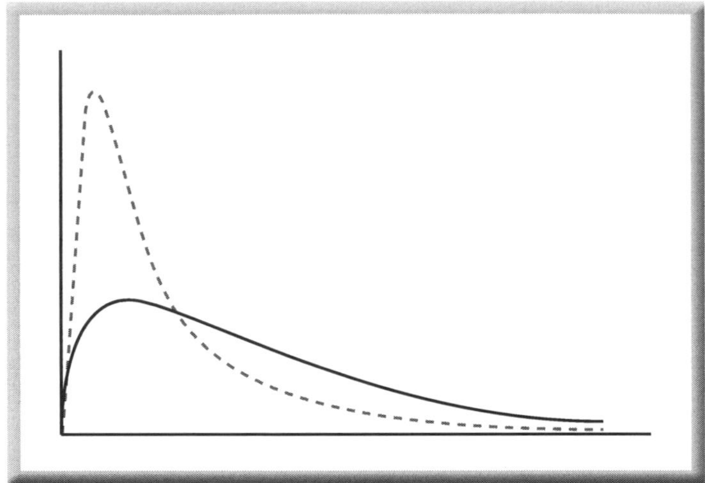

Figure 7.2: Asymmetric theoretical continuous probability structures (density functions)

These forms are called density functions, and they describe the *density* of potentially observable values on a number line, for example, we find that a random variable more commonly assumes values on the number line where the function bulges and we rarely find values from a random variable when the function is close to the horizontal axis.

Where applicable, we define the mathematical form of the density function and, using this mathematical form, we attempt to calculate probabilities for the associated random variable.

NOTE

Density functions have a number of important properties:

- The density function associated with a random variable X will typically be denoted by a continuous function $f_X(x)$.
- The density function is always larger than, or equal to, zero, that is, $f_X(x) \geq 0$.
- The total area under a density function is equal to 1.
- The probability $P(x_1 < X < x_2)$ can be determined by simply calculating the area under the density function between the points x_1 and x_2.

7.1.3 Probability calculations using density functions

To illustrate how we can use density functions to calculate probabilities, we will use one of the simplest density functions, the uniform density function, shown in Figure 7.3. However, we first need to define the uniform distribution and density function.

We say that a continuous random variable, X, that takes on values between a and b has a uniform distribution if the probability structure of this variable is constant over this interval. The density function of a continuous uniform random variable is given by formula (7.1).

THE DENSITY FUNCTION OF A UNIFORM RANDOM VARIABLE

$$f_X(x) = \frac{1}{b-a} \text{ if } a < x < b \text{ and zero otherwise} \tag{7.1}$$

Uniform density functions have a *rectangular* form, as illustrated in Figure 7.3. As with all density functions, the area under this rectangle is equal to 1. The total area corresponds to the total probability. We now show how we can use the area under this density function to calculate simple probabilities for continuous uniform random variables.

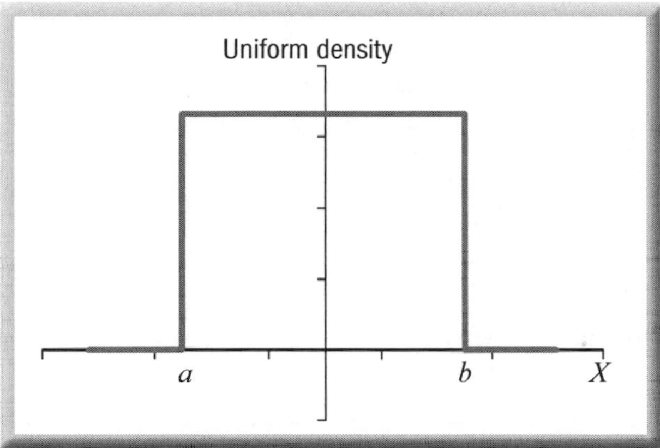

Figure 7.3: The uniform density between *a* and *b*

Suppose that we define the variable X as being uniform over the interval between $a = 0$ and $b = 4$. (Suppose that X represents the mass of a newborn baby measured in kilograms.) If we assume that X is uniform over the interval 0 to 4, then Figure 7.4 shows the shape of this density, and the density function is given by the following formula:

$$f_X(x) = \frac{1}{4-0} = \frac{1}{4} = 0.25, \text{ if } 0 < x < 4 \text{ and zero otherwise}$$

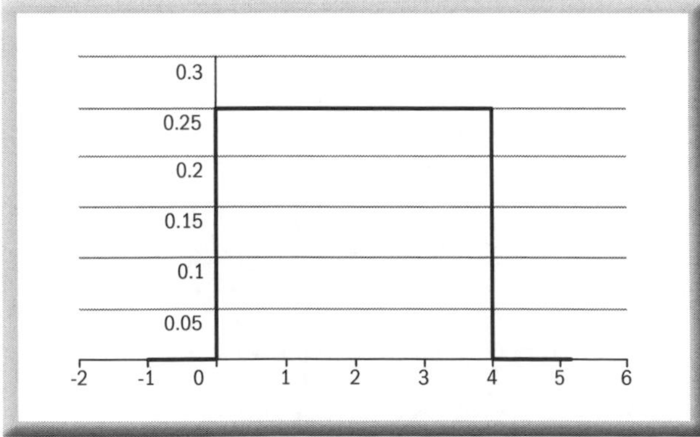

Figure 7.4: The uniform density that describes the probability distribution of the mass of new born babies

Now, if we were interested in determining the probability that the mass of a newborn baby is between 2 kg and 3 kg, $P(2 < X < 3)$, then we could use the property of the density function that states that the probability between any two values is simply the area under the density function between these two values.

Therefore, to calculate $P(2 < X < 3)$, we simply calculate the area shown in Figure 7.5.

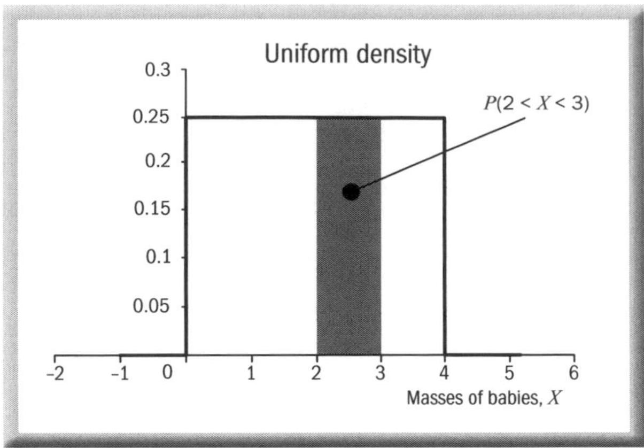

Figure 7.5: The shaded area represents the probability $P(2 < X < 3)$

The area of this rectangle turns out to be equal to:

$$\begin{aligned} \text{Area} &= \text{length} \times \text{height} \\ &= (3 - 2) \times 0.25 \\ &= 0.25 \end{aligned}$$

Therefore, the probability that a newborn baby's mass lies between 2 kg and 3 kg is 0.25, that is, $P(2 < X < 3) = 0.25$.

NOTE

The above probability is based on a rather strict assumption that the distribution of the variable X is uniformly distributed on 0 and 4. However, this might not actually be the case, and in practice, we usually perform numerical tests to decide whether assumptions like these are reasonable. For the remainder this chapter, we will assume that the specified distribution is correct for the random variables discussed.

NOTE

The probability of a continuous random variable being exactly equal to some value is zero:

$$P(X = x) = 0, \text{ if } X \text{ is a continuous random variable}$$

This is because the actual area of a specific point under the density function is zero. In other words, the area under the continuous density function, between x and x, is zero.

For this reason, we will only consider probabilities of the form $P(X < x)$, $P(X > x)$ or $P(x_1 < X < x_2)$, and so on for continuous random variables.

In the next few sections, we discuss a number of other continuous distributions and how to perform probability calculations for each one.

7.2 The normal distribution

The uniform distribution discussed in the previous section is one of the simplest continuous distributions (and thus also one of the simplest density functions), but it is not very common. This section focuses on one of the most common continuous probability distributions: the **normal distribution**. Probability calculations for the normal distribution are analogous to the probability calculated above but, since the normal distribution's density function is not rectangular like the uniform distribution, the probability calculations are somewhat more complex. Fortunately, Excel provides functions for these calculations.

Normal distribution A symmetric, bell-shaped curve, centred at its expected value.

7.2.1 A description of the normal distribution

When a variable is continuous, and its value is affected by a large number of chance factors, none of which predominates, then it will frequently appear as a normal distribution. This distribution does occur frequently and is probably the most widely used statistical distribution. Some real-life variables that have a normal distribution can be found, for example, in industry (the weights of steel girders manufactured, the time required to build a single car, the total monthly printing expenses of an office, and so on) or can be associated with the human population (people's heights, the IQ of students, the annual salary of accountants, and so on). The distribution of a normally distributed random variable *X* is governed by the normal density function given in formula (7.2).

THE DENSITY FUNCTION OF A NORMAL RANDOM VARIABLE

$$f_X(x) = \frac{1}{\sigma\sqrt{2\pi}} \exp\left(-\frac{(x-\mu)^2}{2\sigma^2}\right) \qquad (7.2)$$

NOTE

The term 'exp', used in the density function in formula (7.2) means that the term in brackets is the exponent of the constant *e*. For example, $\exp(1.253) = e^{1.253} = 3.50083$. Recall that the constant *e* is approximately equal to 2.71183.

The *population mean* and *population standard deviation* are represented by the notation μ and σ respectively (the *population variance* is denoted by σ^2).

This distribution is *symmetrical* around the value μ, that is, the distribution is a mirror image on either side of the value μ.

The parameter μ controls the centre position of the density function and σ controls how widely spread out it is.

For the normal distribution, the mean, median and mode all have the same numerical value.

If the values of a random variable X vary in the same way as described by a normal distribution (with mean μ and variance σ^2), then we would use the following short-hand notation to indicate that it is normally distributed with mean μ and variance σ^2: $X \sim N(\mu, \sigma^2)$.

As with all density functions, the total area under the curve represents the total probability of all events occurring, which is equal to 1.

Similarly, the area under the curve between any two points x_1 and x_2 is the probability $P(x_1 < X < x_2)$.

This density function is plotted in Figure 7.6 and illustrates the symmetrical and 'bell-shaped' characteristics of the normal distribution.

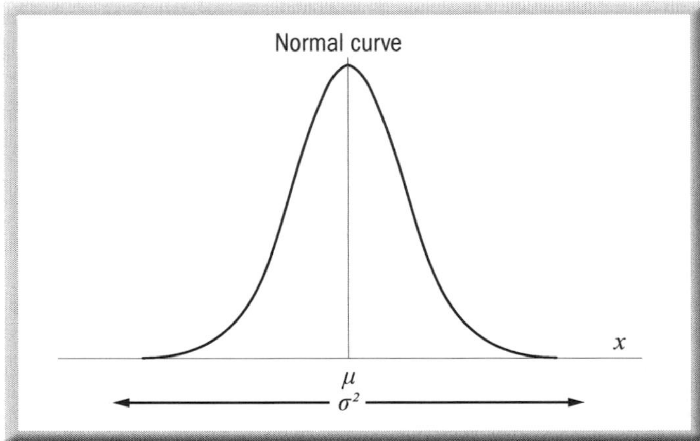

Figure 7.6: The normal density function with mean μ and variance σ^2

7.2.2 Standardisation of normal random variables

We address the probability calculations that we need to perform for the normal distribution in the next section, but before we can discuss those calculations, we must first introduce the concept of **standardisation**. Standardisation is a way to *rescale* or *standardise* values from normal populations so that they have a standard mean and variance, and also to remove the unit of measurement of the variable (for example, instead of being measured in kilograms, meters or seconds, the standardised values have no unit). By standardising a normal random variable X with mean μ and standard deviation σ, we create a random variable Z that has a **standard normal distribution**. The standard normal distribution is a specific type of normal distribution, the mean of which is $\mu = 0$ and the standard deviation is $\sigma = 1$. Any random variable with a normal distribution can be transformed to a standard normal distribution by formula (7.3):

$$Z = \frac{(X - \mu)}{\sigma} \tag{7.3}$$

X, μ and σ are the variable score value, population mean and population standard deviation respectively, taken from the original normal distribution. We will call Z a **standard normal random variable**.

Standardisation The calculation performed to convert a $N(\mu, \sigma^2)$ normal random variable X into a $N(0, 1)$ normal random variable Z that is, $Z = \frac{(X - \mu)}{\sigma}$.

Standard normal random variable A normal random variable with mean equal to 0 and standard deviation equal to 1. We denote these random variables by $Z \sim N(0, 1)$.

NOTE

The advantages of standardisation include the following:

- The Z-values are unitless, that is, they do not depend on the units of the original data. This is helpful when comparing values from two normal distributions with wildly different scales and locations.
- Another benefit of the standard scale is that it allows us to construct generic tables of Z-values and their corresponding areas under the curve (that is, probabilities). The result is that it prevents the need to create a table for every possible type of normal distribution. For example, without standardised variables, we would need a table for a $N(19, 2)$-distribution, a $N(-9, 17)$-distribution, an $N(0.5, 2.8)$-distribution, and so on. By standardising the normal random variable, we only need to create a table of probabilities for the $N(0, 1)$-distribution, because any other type of normal distribution can be converted to a $N(0, 1)$ through standardisation formula (7.3).

To illustrate this, suppose that the weight of the garbage collected over one week by a garbage truck is a random variable X that follows a normal distribution with mean $\mu = 9$ tonnes and standard deviation $\sigma = 3$ tonnes, that is, $X \sim N(9, 3^2)$. If we want to calculate the probability that the weight of garbage collected is less than 9.5 ($P(X < 9.5)$), then we should first standardise the variable X so that it becomes a standard normal random variable. However, if we standardise the variable X, we *also have to standardise the other values in the probability expression.* In this case, it means we also have to standardise the value 9.5. The probability that needs to be calculated is then:

$$\begin{aligned} P(X < 9.5) &= P\left(\frac{X-9}{3} < \frac{9.5-9}{3}\right) \\ &= P(Z < 0.167) \end{aligned}$$

The standardised values in this new probability are unitless, that is, they are no longer measured in tonnes. Also, please note that the standardisation formula (7.3) is done *within* the probability operator $P(.)$ and on *both* sides of the < symbol. We can now easily determine the probability $P(Z < 0.167)$ from the tables in Appendix C or by using Excel functions. We discuss these calculations next.

7.2.3 Calculating probabilities associated with the normal distribution

To calculate the probability of a particular value of a normally distributed random variable X, we only need to calculate the appropriate area under the curve in Figure 7.6 by using either the tables provided in Appendix C or an Excel function. We now discuss these two procedures for determining probabilities. The first method can be done by hand and we will use it to highlight some basic considerations when determining probabilities. We also require these considerations when using the Excel functions.

Normal probability calculations using tables

The tables given in Appendix C, which we will use for probability calculations involving normal random variables, are specifically set out to present probabilities in the form $P(Z < z)$, where z is the score value and Z is a **standard normal random variable**, that is, a normal random variable with $\mu = 0$ and $\sigma^2 = 1$ or $Z \sim N(0, 1)$. The area or probability depicted by these tables is illustrated in Figures 7.7 and 7.8. Note that the area calculated is to the *left* of the specified z point.

The two tables provided in Appendix C distinguish between positive and negative score values. If the score value is negative, use Table C.1; otherwise, if the score value is positive, use Table C.2.

To use the tables to calculate $P(Z < z)$, we need to split the score value z into two parts:

- The first part contains the units and the tenths.
- The second part contains the hundredths.

For example, the score value $z = 1.96$ would be split into:

- 1.9 (the units and the tenths)
- 0.06 (the hundredths).

We then find the probability by looking in Table C.2 (since $z = 1.96$ is positive) for the row that corresponds to 1.9 and the column that corresponds to 0.06.

Figures 7.7 and 7.8 represent the probabilities provided by Tables C.1 and C.2 respectively.

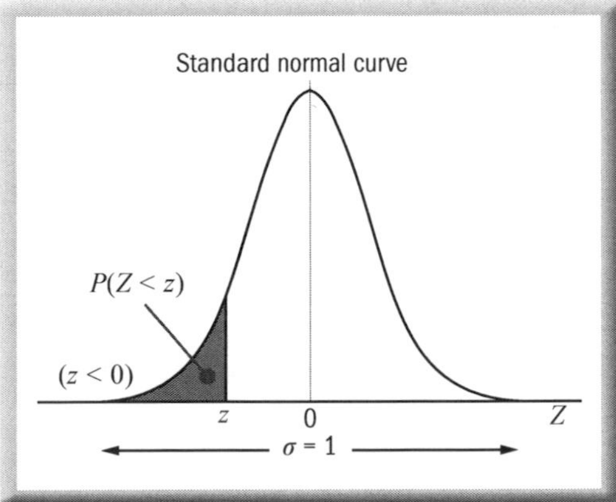

Figure 7.7: The area under the standard normal density to the left of a negative score z, i.e. $P(Z < z)$

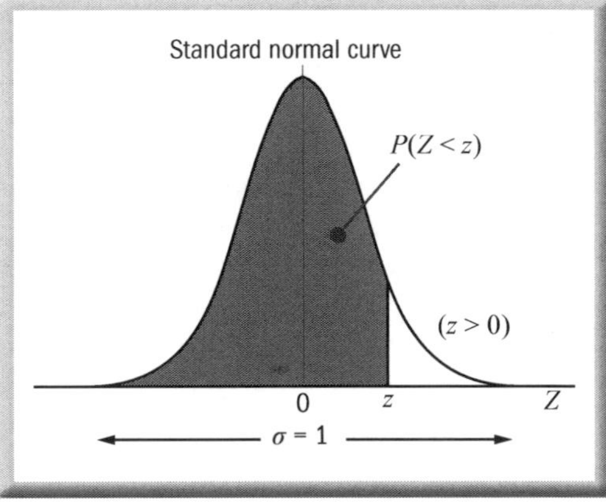

Figure 7.8: The area under the standard normal density to the left of a positive score z, i.e. $P(Z < z)$

In Figure 7.7, we see the probability $P(Z < z)$ (with $z < 0$) represented as an area under the standard normal density curve. We can obtain these probability values from Table C.1. For example, if $z = -1.65$ then, to determine $P(Z < -1.65)$, we split the score value into -1.6 (which indicates which row to use) and 0.05 (which indicates which column to use). The probability value in Table C.1 that corresponds to row -1.6 and column 0.05 is 0.0495, that is, $P(Z < -1.65) = 0.0495$.

Figure 7.8 represents the type of probabilities provided by Table C.2, that is, the probabilities $P(Z < z)$ if $z > 0$. We use this table in the same way as Table C.1. For example, to calculate $P(Z < 1.96)$, we first find the row that corresponds to 1.9 and then find the column that corresponds to 0.06. The value in Table C.2 that corresponds to that particular row and column is 0.9750, that is, $P(Z < 1.96) = 0.9750$.

Normal probability calculations using Excel

By using Excel, we can easily obtain the same results as given in the tables of Appendix C. The standard normal probabilities can be calculated using the function NORM.S.DIST(x,TRUE).

This function accepts only two arguments:

- The value of x (this can be any positive or negative number)
- The value TRUE or FALSE. If TRUE, then it will return the probability $P(Z < z)$. If FALSE, it will return the standard normal density function value evaluated in the point x.

As in the standard normal table, this function only calculates probabilities in the form $P(Z < x)$, where $Z \sim N(0, 1)$.

To illustrate how this function works, the calculation of the probabilities $P(Z < -1.65)$ and $P(Z < 1.96)$ are shown in Figure 7.9.

	A	B	C	D	
1					
2		z =	-1.65		
3		P(Z < −1.65) =	0.04947	=NORM.S.DIST(C2,TRUE)	
4					
5		z =	1.96		
6		P(Z < 1.96) =	0.975	=NORM.S.DIST(C5,TRUE)	
7					

Figure 7.9: The NORM.S.DIST function used to calculate probabilities of the form $P(Z < z)$ in Excel

Another function, called NORM.DIST, can calculate probabilities in the form $P(X < x)$, where $X \sim N(\mu, \sigma^2)$. This function uses the following syntax: NORM.DIST(x, μ, σ, TRUE), that is, it accepts four arguments in Excel:

- The value of x (this can be any positive or negative number).
- The value of the mean, μ (this can be any positive or negative number).
- The value of the standard deviation, σ (note that you must specify the value of the standard deviation σ and not the variance σ^2; this value must be positive).
- Finally, a binary indicator that can be TRUE or FALSE. Choose the value TRUE if you want to determine the probability$P(X < x)$. If you specify FALSE, it will return the value of the density function$f_X(x)$ in formula (7.2). This is not the same as the probability (the area under the density function is a probability, but the actual *value* of the density function at the point x is not).

Since Table C.1, Table C.2 and the Excel function NORM.S.DIST only present probabilities in the form $P(Z < z)$ (in the case of the NORM.DIST Excel function, it only supplies the probabilities of the form $P(X < x)$), it is not always straight-forward to calculate probabilities of different forms, for example, $P(Z > z)$ or $P(z_1 < Z < z_2)$. Fortunately, these problems can be resolved by using the properties of the normal density and the probability rules discussed in Chapter 4.

To determine the probability in each case, simply use the properties of the normal distribution and apply the probability rules to the probability expression so that we can reduce it to contain expressions that look like $P(Z < z)$. We do this because the tables only supply probabilities in this form, so it is useful to reduce our problem to one that we can look up in these tables. The final step is then to calculate these separate probabilities and collect the results.

In the discussion that follows, we look at how to calculate probabilities in the form $P(Z > z)$ and $P(z_1 < Z < z_2)$.

Calculation of $P(Z > z)$

To calculate $P(Z > z)$ (shown in Figures 7.10 and 7.11), we simply apply the complement rule of Chapter 4, that is, $P(A^C) = 1 - P(A)$. In this situation, the event A is defined as $A = (Z > z)$ and the complement is $A^C = (Z < z)$, and so applying the complement rule we get:

$$P(Z > z) = 1 - P(Z < z) \tag{7.4}$$

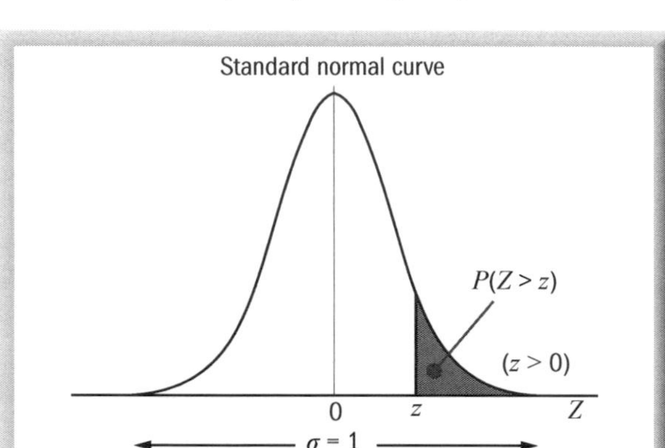

Figure 7.10: The area under the standard normal density to the right of a positive score z, i.e. $P(Z > z)$

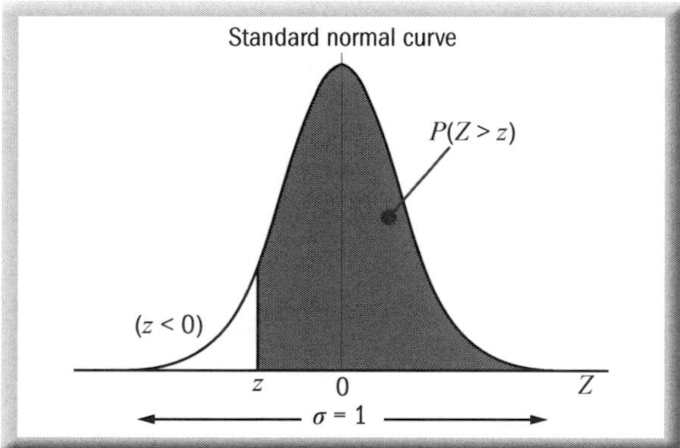

Figure 7.11: The area under the standard normal density to the right of a negative score z, i.e. $P(Z > z)$

Formula (7.4) allows us to use the tables in Appendix C, because it contains expressions provided by these tables, that is, $P(Z < z)$. For example, if we want to calculate the probability $P(Z > 1.65)$, that is, the probability that a standard normal random variable is larger than $z = 1.65$, we can apply formula (7.4) and the probabilities in Table C.2 to obtain:

$$\begin{aligned} P(Z > 1.65) &= 1 - P(Z < 1.65) \\ &= 1 - 0.9505 \\ &= 0.0495 \end{aligned}$$

In the same way, if we want to calculate the probability that a standard normal random variable is larger than $z = -0.17$, $(P(Z > -0.17))$ then, by applying formula (7.4) and using Table C.1, we get:

$$\begin{aligned} P(Z > -0.17) &= 1 - P(Z < -0.17) \\ &= 1 - 0.4325 \\ &= 0.5675 \end{aligned}$$

We can visualise formula (7.4) by considering the probability (the area under the graph) shown in Figure 7.10. We obtain the expression given in formula (7.4) by subtracting the areas depicted in Figure 7.12. (Recall that the entire area under the normal density is equal to 1.)

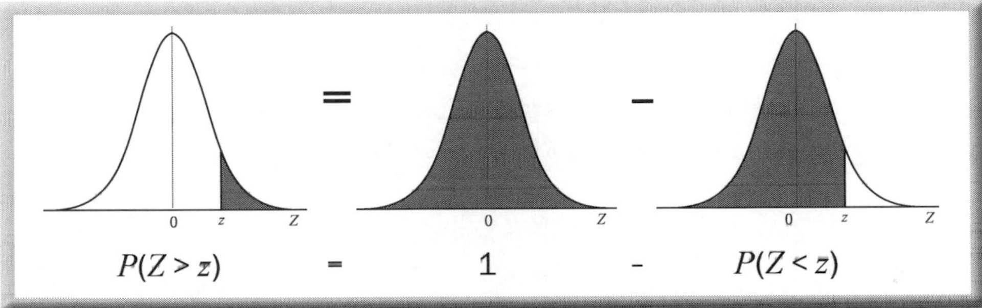

Figure 7.12: Graphical representation of the complement rule applied to $P(Z > z)$ in formula (7.4)

Calculation of $P(z_1 < Z < z_2)$

To calculate the probability that the standard normal random variable lies between two numbers z_1 and z_2, first calculate the probabilities $P(Z < z_1)$ and $P(Z < z_2)$, and then simply subtract the smaller probability from the larger one. The actual order of subtraction is easy to determine if we consider the form of the area being calculated (see, for example, the three different forms presented in Figures 7.13, 7.14 and 7.15). In all three cases, the formula used to determine the probability if $z_2 > z_1$ is:

$$P(z_1 < Z < z_2) = P(Z < z_2) - P(Z < z_1) \tag{7.5}$$

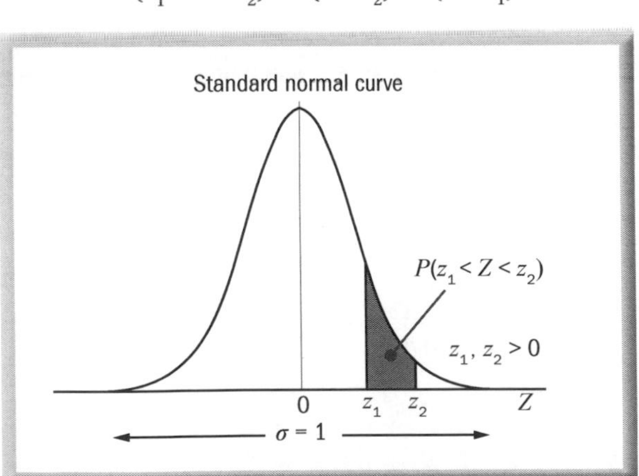

Figure 7.13: The area under the standard normal density between two positive scores z_1 and z_2, i.e. $P(z_1 < Z < z_2)$

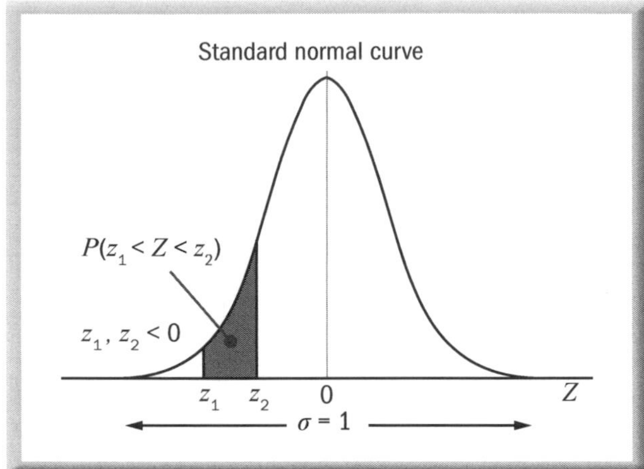

Figure 7.14: The area under the standard normal density between two negative numbers z_1 and z_2, i.e. $P(z_1 < Z < z_2)$

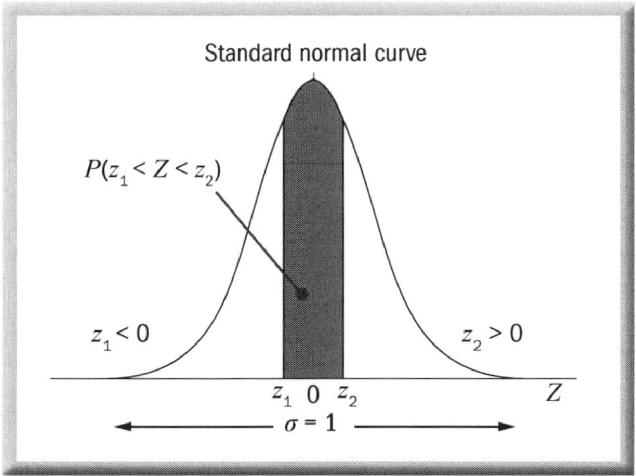

Figure 7.15: The area under the standard normal density between a negative number, z_1, and a positive number, z_2, i.e. $P(z_1 < Z < z_2)$

Suppose, for example, we want to calculate the probability $P(0.15 < Z < 2.11)$. This is the same as the scenario in Figure 7.13. Applying formula (7.5) and using Table C.2 (because both z_1 and z_2 are positive), we get:

$$\begin{aligned} P(0.15 < Z < 2.11) &= P(Z < 2.11) - P(Z < 0.15) \\ &= 0.9826 - 0.5596 \\ &= 0.4230 \end{aligned}$$

Note that in this example, $z_1 = 0.15$ and $z_2 = 2.11$.

In the case where both z_1 and z_2 are negative values, we can also use formula (7.5), but then we use Table C.1 to calculate the probabilities (since both values are negative). For example, to calculate the probability $P(-0.66 < Z < -0.11)$:

$$\begin{aligned} P(-0.66 < Z < -0.11) &= P(Z < -0.11) - P(Z < -0.66) \\ &= 0.7454 - 0.5438 \\ &= 0.2016 \end{aligned}$$

Note that in this example, we have $z_1 = -0.66$ and $z_2 = -0.11$.

Finally, if one z-value is negative and the other is positive, we use both Table C.1 and Table C.2 with formula (7.5). For example, to calculate $P(-1.28 < Z < 2.00)$:

$$\begin{aligned} P(-1.28 < Z < 2.00) &= P(Z < 2.00) - P(Z < -1.28) \\ &= 0.9772 - 0.1003 \\ &= 0.8769 \end{aligned}$$

We use Table C.1 to determine $P(Z < -1.28)$ and we use Table C.2 to determine $P(Z < 2.00)$.

A graphical motivation for the equality in formula (7.5) is illustrated in Figure 7.16 below.

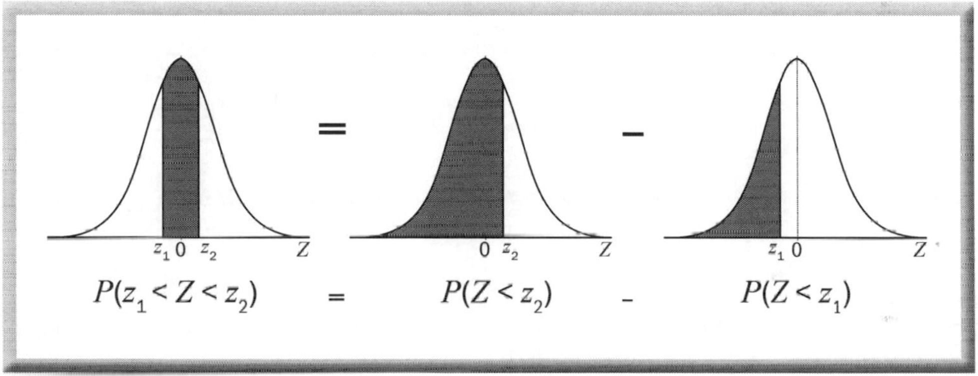

Figure 7.16: Graphical representation of formula (7.5)

We now consider some practical examples of these probability calculations, using the tables and the Excel functions to perform these calculations.

WORKED EXAMPLES

EXAMPLE 7.1

A manufacturing firm quality assures tubes manufactured in a factory and, historically, the length of a tube is found to be normally distributed with a population mean of 100 cm and a standard deviation of 5 cm. Calculate the probability that a randomly selected tube will have a length of at least 110 cm. From the information provided, we define X as the tube length in centimetres, population mean $\mu = 100$ and standard deviation $\sigma = 5$. We can represent this using the notation $X \sim N(100, 5^2)$.

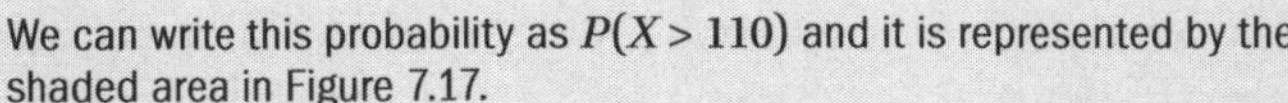
We can write this probability as $P(X > 110)$ and it is represented by the shaded area in Figure 7.17.

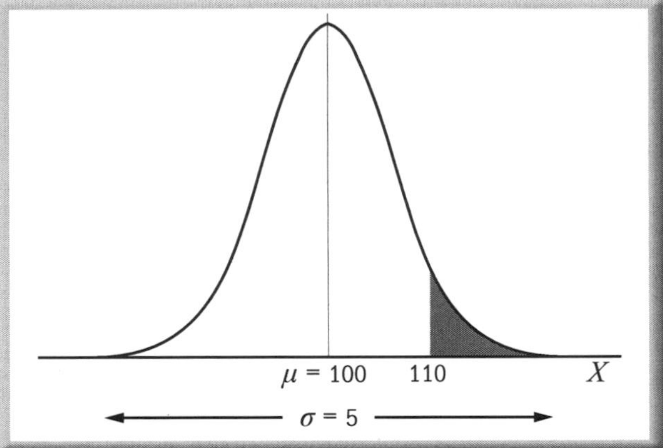

Figure 7.17: An $N(100, 5^2)$ normal curve depicting the probability that X is greater than 110

The probability in this question is similar to, but not exactly the same as, the one shown in Figure 7.10. The main difference between the form shown in Figure 7.10 and the form shown here is that the probability in this case is not based on a standard normal random variable, Z.

We now calculate this probability using the tables in Appendix C, the Excel function NORM.S.DIST and the Excel function NORM.DIST.

Before we obtain this probability using the tables in Appendix C or NORM.S.DIST, first note that the expression $P(X > 110)$ is not written in terms of a standardised normal random variable Z. To standardise all the terms in the expression, we use formula (7.3):

$$P(X > 110) = P\left(\frac{X - 100}{5} > \frac{110 - 100}{5}\right)$$
$$= P(Z > 2)$$

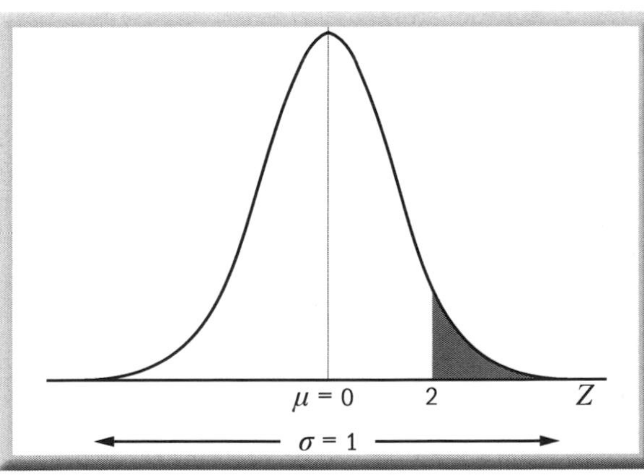

Figure 7.18: The probability from Figure 7.17 expressed on the standardised scale

Figure 7.18 represents the probability on the standardised scale. Compare this to the graph in Figure 7.17. We can use formula (7.4) and Table C.2 to calculate the answer:

$$\begin{aligned} P(X > 110) &= P(Z > 2) \\ &= 1 - P(Z < 2) \\ &= 1 - 0.9772 \\ &= 0.0228 \end{aligned}$$

Next, we show that the same result can be obtained using the Excel functions NORM.S.DIST and NORM.DIST.

The Excel solution is illustrated in Figure 7.19.

	A	B	C	D	E
1	**Example 7.1**				
2					
3		**Normal distribution**			
4					
5		Mean μ =	100		
6		Standard deviation σ =	5		
7					
8		z =	110		
9					
10		$P(X < 110)$ =	0.97725	=NORM.DIST(C8,C5,C6,TRUE)	
11					
12		$P(X > 110)$ =	0.02275	=1-C10	
13					
14		Z =	2	=(C8-C5)/C6	
15		$P(Z < 2)$ =	0.97725	=NORM.S.DIST(C14,TRUE)	
16		$P(Z > 2)$ =	0.02275	=1-C15	

Figure 7.19: Excel solution for Example 7.1

In Excel, we can use the NORM.S.DIST function to mimic the above calculation. We do this by first obtaining the standardised z score (shown in cell C14) and then calculating the probability $P(Z < 2)$ (shown in cell C15). The final result is obtained by calculating $1 - P(Z < 2)$ as shown in cell C16.

The function NORM.DIST() can also calculate this probability, but it can do this without having to resort to standardisation. Using this function, we can calculate general probabilities in the form $P(X < x)$, where $X \sim N(\mu, \sigma^2)$. In this case, $\mu = 100$ and $\sigma = 5$, and so the probability $P(X < 110)$ (shown in cell C10) is easily obtained (note that this probability is the same as the probability $P(Z < 2)$ in cell C15). As with the standardised probability, we can calculate the probability $P(X > 110)$ using the complement rule: $P(X > 110) = 1 - P(X < 110) = 1 - 0.97725 = 0.02275$ as shown in cell C12.

EXCEL SOLUTION

Mean μ: Cell C5	Value
Standard deviation σ: Cell C6	Value
x: Cell C8	Value
$P(X < 110)$: Cell C10	Formula: =NORM.DIST(C8,C5,C6,TRUE)
$P(X > 110)$: Cell C12	Formula: =1-C10
z: Cell C14	Formula: =(C8-C5)/C6
$P(Z < 2)$: Cell C15	Formula: =NORM.S.DIST(C14,TRUE)
$P(Z > 2)$: Cell C16	Formula: =1-C15

INTERPRETATION We observe that the probability that an individual tube is at least 110 cm long is 0.02275 or 2.3% ($P(X > 110) = 0.02275$).

WORKED EXAMPLES

EXAMPLE 7.2

Calculate the probability that the tube length, X, lies between 85 cm and 105 cm for the problem in Example 7.1.

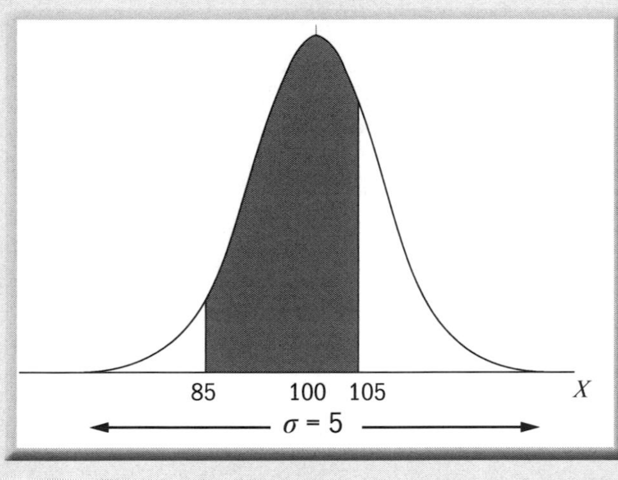

In this example, we are required to calculate $P(85 < X < 105)$, which is represented by the shaded area in Figure 7.20.

Once again, we have to standardise the quantities and then use the tables in Appendix C or the Excel function NORM.S.DIST() to calculate this probability.

Alternatively, we could also use the Excel function NORM.DIST() without having to standardise.

Figure 7.20: An $N(100, 5^2)$ normal curve depicting the probability that X lies between 85 cm and 105 cm

We begin by first obtaining the standardised values in the probability expression using formula (7.3):

$$
\begin{aligned}
P(85 < X < 105) &= P\left(\frac{85 - 100}{5} < \frac{X - 100}{5} < \frac{105 - 100}{5}\right) \\
&= P(-3 < Z < 1)
\end{aligned}
$$

Figure 7.21: The probability from Figure 7.20 expressed on the standardised scale

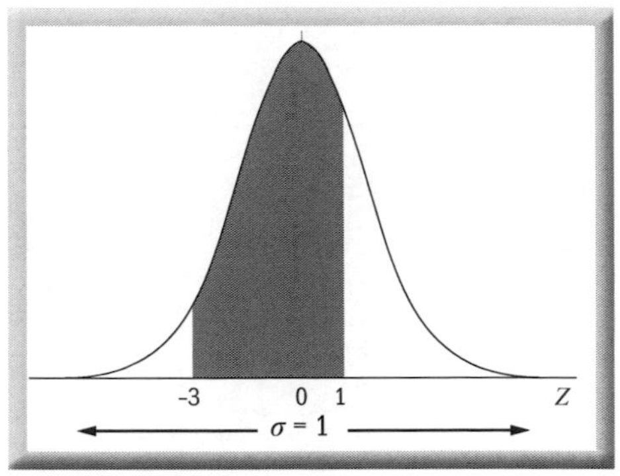

After standardising, we obtain the region shown in Figure 7.21. Compare this to the graph in Figure 7.20. We now use formula (7.5), and both Tables C.1 and C.2 to calculate the answer:

$$\begin{aligned} P(85 < X < 105) &= P(-3 < Z < 1) \\ &= P(Z < 1) - P(Z < -3) \\ &= 0.8413 - 0.0013 \\ &= 0.84 \end{aligned}$$

Next, we show that the same result can be obtained using the Excel functions NORM.S.DIST and NORM.DIST.

The Excel solution is illustrated in Figure 7.22.

	A	B	C	D
1	**Example 7.2**			
2				
3		**Normal distribution**		
4				
5		Mean μ =	100	
6		Standard deviation σ =	5	
7				
8		x_1 =	85	
9		x_2 =	105	
10				
11		$P(85 < X < 105) = P(X < 105) - P(X < 85)$		
12				
13		$P(X < 185)$ =	0.00135	=NORM.DIST(C8,C6,C6,TRUE)
14		$P(X < 105)$ =	0.841345	=NORM.DIST(C9,C5,C6,TRUE)
15				
16		$P(85 < X < 105)$ =	0.839995	=C14-C13
17				
18		z_1 =	-3	=(C8-C5)/C6
19		z_2 =	1	=(C9-C5)/C6
20				
21		$P(85 < X < 105) = P(-3 < Z < 1) = P(Z < 1) - P(Z < -3)$		
22				
23		$P(Z < -3)$ =	0.00135	=NORM.S.DIST(C18,TRUE)
24		$P(Z < 1)$ =	0.841345	=NORM.S.DIST(C19,TRUE)
25				
26		$P(85 < X < 10)$ =	0.839995	=C24-C23

Figure 7.22: Excel solution for Example 7.2

This Excel solution is similar to the solution from the tables in which we first calculated $P(Z < -3)$ and $P(Z < 1)$ (seen in cells C23 and C24). We then subtracted one from the other (seen in cell C26).

To use the NORM.DIST function (without standardisation) in this case requires that we first calculate $P(X < 85)$ and $P(X < 105)$ (shown in cells C13 and C14), and then subtract the smaller value from the larger one. The final result of this subtraction is given in cell C16. Note that the answer obtained with standardisation is the same as the answer obtained without standardisation.

EXCEL SOLUTION

Mean μ: Cell C5	Value
Standard deviation σ: Cell C6	Value
x_1: Cell C8	Value
x_2: Cell C9	Value
$P(85 < X < 105)$: $P(X < 105) - P(X < 85)$	
$P(X < 85)$: Cell C13	Formula: =NORM.DIST(C8,C5,C6,TRUE)
$P(X < 110)$: Cell C14	Formula: =NORM.DIST(C9,C5,C6,TRUE)
$P(85 < X < 105)$: $P(Z < 1) - P(Z < -3)$	
$P(Z < -3)$: Cell C23	Formula: =NORM.S.DIST(C18,TRUE)
$P(Z < 1)$: Cell C24	Formula: =NORM.S.DIST(C19,TRUE)
$P(85 < X < 105)$: Cell C26	Formula: =C24-C23

INTERPRETATION

We observe that the probability that an individual tube length lies between 85 cm and 105 cm is 0.839995 or 84.0%.

NOTE

From calculations, we can show that the proportion of values between ±1, ±2 and ±3 population standard deviations from the population mean of zero is 68%, 95% and 99.7% respectively.

WORKED EXAMPLES

EXAMPLE 7.3

A local municipality installs 2 000 electric street lamps in an urban area. The lifetime or life expectancy of these lamps, measured in hours (X), follows a normal distribution with a mean of 1 000 hours and a variance of 40 000, that is, $X \sim N(1\,000, 40\,000)$.

Use this information to answer the following questions.

a) What number of lamps might be expected to fail within the first 700 hours?

b) What number of lamps may be expected to fail between 900 and 1 300 hours?

We can answer these questions using the tables in Appendix C, or the NORM.DIST or NORM.S.DIST Excel functions.

a) This question can be split into two parts: (i) calculate the probability that one lamp will fail in the first 700 hours, and (ii) calculate the number of lamps from the 2 000 that we expect to fail in the first 700 hours.

The solution requires that we calculate the probability $P(X < 700)$, because we are interested in the probability that the lifetime of any single lamp is less than 700 hours (that is, it will fail within 700 hours). By standardising the probability and using Table C.1, we get:

$$\begin{aligned} P(X < 700) &= P\left(\frac{X - 1\,000}{\sqrt{40\,000}} < \frac{700 - 1\,000}{\sqrt{40\,000}}\right) \\ &= P(Z < -1.5) \\ &= 0.0668 \end{aligned}$$

Note, we divide by $\sqrt{40\,000}$ in the above expression because the scenario provides the variance, σ^2 and not the standard deviation, σ.

Finally, to find the answer to the question 'What number of lamps might be expected to fail within the first 700 hours?', we simply multiply the probability obtained with the total number of lamps, $n = 2\,000$:

$$n \times P(X < 700) = 2\,000 \times 0.0668 \approx 134$$

Therefore, approximately 134 of the 2 000 lamps will fail within 700 hours.

We can easily obtain the same solution using Excel. The Excel solution is shown in Figure 7.23.

	A	B	C	D
1	**Example 7.3(a)**			
2				
3		**Normal distribution**		
4				
5		Mean μ =	1000	
6		Variance σ^2 =	40000	
7		Standard deviation σ =	200	=SQRT(C6)
8				
9		x =	700	
10				
11		$P(X < 700)$ =	0.066807	=NORM.DIST(C9,C5,C7,TRUE)
12				
13		z =	−1.5	=(C9-C5)/C7
14				
15		$P(Z < -1.5)$ =	0.066807	=NORM.S.DIST(C13,TRUE)
16		$nP(X < 700)$ =	133.6144	=2000*C11

Figure 7.23: Excel solution for Example 7.3(a)

EXCEL SOLUTION

Mean μ: Cell C5	Value
Variance σ^2: Cell C6	Value
Standard deviation σ: Cell C7	Formula: =SQRT(C6)
x: Cell C9	Value
$P(X < 700)$: Cell C11	Formula: =NORM.DIST(C9,C5,C7,TRUE)
z: Cell C13	Formula: =(C9–C5)/C7
$P(Z < -1.5)$: Cell C14	Formula: =NORM.S.DIST(C13,TRUE)
$nP(X < 700)$: Cell C16	Formula =2000*C11

INTERPRETATION This problem involves determining the probability $P(X < 700)$. Using the NORM.DIST or NORM.S.DIST functions, we find out that the probability is 0.0668 and so, of the 2 000 lamps, approximately $2\,000 \times 0.0668 = 134$ lamps are expected to fail within the first 700 hours.

b) For this part of the problem, we need to calculate the probability that X lies between 900 and 1 300 hours, and estimate the number of lamps from 2 000 that will fail between these limits. In other words, we need to calculate the probability $P(900 < X < 1\,300)$. Standardising, we get:

$$
\begin{aligned}
P(900 < X < 1\,300) &= P\left(\frac{900 - 1\,000}{\sqrt{40\,000}} < \frac{X - 1\,000}{\sqrt{400\,000}} < \frac{1\,300 - 1\,000}{\sqrt{40\,000}}\right) \\
&= P(-0.5 < Z < 1.5)
\end{aligned}
$$

This standardised probability has a form similar to the one in Figure 7.15. So, to obtain the probability, we need to use formula (7.4), and Tables C.1 and C.2:

$$
\begin{aligned}
P(900 < X < 1\,300) &= P(-0.5 < Z < 1.5) \\
&= P(Z < 1.5) - P(Z < -0.5) \\
&= 0.9332 - 0.3085 \\
&= 0.6247
\end{aligned}
$$

To determine the number of lamps with lifetimes between 900 and 1 300 hours, we multiply the total number of lamps (n = 2 000) by the probability that a single lamp's lifetime lies in that interval:

$$n \times P(900 < X < 1\,300) = 2\,000 \times 0.6247 \approx 1\,249$$

We can expect 1 249 of the 2 000 lamps to last between 900 and 1 300 hours.

The Excel solution is given in Figure 7.24.

	A	B	C	D
1	**Example 7.3(b)**			
2				
3		**Normal distribution**		
4				
5		Mean μ =	1000	
6		Variance σ^2 =	40000	
7		Standard deviation σ =	200	=SQRT(C6)
8				
9		x_1 =	900	
10		x_2 =	1300	
11				
12		$P(X < 900)$ =	0.308538	=NORM.DIST(C9,C5,C7,TRUE)
13		$P(X < 1300)$ =	0.933193	=NORM.DIST(C10,C5,C7,TRUE)
14		$P(900 < X < 1300)$ =	0.624655	=C13-C12
15		$nP(900 < X < 1300)$ =	1249.311	=2000*C14
16				
17				
18		z_1 =	–0.5	=(C9-C5)/C7
19		z_2 =	1.5	=(C10-C5)/C7
20				
21		$P(Z < -0.5)$ =	0.308538	=NORM.S.DIST(C18,TRUE)
22		$P(Z < 1.5)$ =	0.933193	=NORM.S.DIST(C19,TRUE)
23		$P(-0.5 < Z < 1.5)$ =	0.624655	=C22-C21
24		$nP(-0.5 < Z < 1.5)$ =	1249.311	=2000*C23

Figure 7.24: Excel solution for Example 7.3(b)

EXCEL SOLUTION

Mean μ: Cell C5	Value
Variance σ^2: Cell C6	Value
Standard deviation σ: Cell C7	Formula: =SQRT(C6)
x_1: Cell C9	Value
x_2: Cell C10	Value
$P(X < 900)$: Cell C12	Formula: =NORM.DIST(C9,C5,C7,TRUE)
$P(X < 1\,300)$: Cell C13	Formula: =NORM.DIST(C10,C5,C7,TRUE)
$P(900 < X < 1\,300)$: Cell C14	Formula: =C13-C12
$nP(900 < X < 1\,300)$: Cell C15	Formula: =2000*C14
z_1: Cell C18	Formula: =(C9-C5)/C7
z_2: Cell C19	Formula: =(C10-C5)/C7
$P(Z < -0.5)$: Cell C21	Formula: =NORM.S.DIST(C18,TRUE)
$P(Z < 1.5)$: Cell C22	Formula: =NORM.S.DIST(C19,TRUE)
$P(-0.5 < Z < 1.5)$: Cell C23	Formula: =C22-C21
$nP(900 < X < 1\,300)$: Cell C24	Formula: =2000*C23

INTERPRETATION This problem involves calculating $P(900 < X < 1\,300)$. Using the NORM.DIST() function, we find that out of the 2 000 lamps, 1 249 lamps are expected to last between 900 and 1 300 hours.

7.2.4 Calculating quantiles associated with the normal distribution

In the previous section, we were interested in calculations where a probability that a normal random variable X is smaller than some value x, that is, $P(X < x)$. In those calculations, the value of x was provided, and we used tables and Excel functions to determine the associated probability. In this section, we reverse the problem and provide the probability value and have to determine the corresponding value of x. The value x we are looking for in these problems is called a **quantile**. A quantile is a number or score associated with a specific probability of a random variable. For example, if $P(X < q) = 0.95$, then q is the quantile value larger than 95% of all other values.

Quantile A number with a known probability associated with it. Formally we define a quantile q_α associated with the probability α of the distribution of a random variable X as the value that satisfies the expression $P(X < q_\alpha) = \alpha$.

Typically, we will formulate these quantile problems as 'Find the value of x such that the probability is equal to p' or, using the probability notation we could simply write, 'Given the value of p, determine x where $P(X < x) = p$.' To obtain the solution to these normal quantile problems, we can use the tables in Appendix C, but it is much easier to use the functions that Excel provides: NORM.INV and NORM.S.INV. In this section, we will only use the Excel functions.

Note that it is also possible to solve quantile problems using standardised normal random variables, but it requires a number of extra steps.

- Suppose we have a standardised variable $Z = \frac{(X - \mu)}{\sigma}$.
- To find x for the probability $P(X < x) = p$, we must first find z for the probability $P(Z < z) = p$, where $z = \frac{(x - \mu)}{\sigma}$ (note that the same p is used). This can be done using the Excel function NORM.S.INV. Once we know the value of z, we can simply rearrange $z = \frac{(x - \mu)}{\sigma}$ to solve for x: $x = z\sigma + \mu$.

Naturally, this solution is only feasible if the values of μ and σ are known.

The Excel functions NORM.INV and NORM.S.INV for obtaining these quantiles are described below.

We call the NORM.INV function with the code: NORM.INV(p, μ, σ).

- p is a probability value (this number must be between 0 and 1).
- μ is the mean of the normal population.
- σ is the standard deviation of the normal population.

We use the function NORM.S.INV when using standardised normal distributions. It is similar to the NORM.INV function, except that it only accepts the argument p defined above.

WORKED EXAMPLES

EXAMPLE 7.4

We will use the information given in Example 7.3 again of the local municipality that wants to install 2 000 electric street lamps, the lifetimes of which follow a normal distribution with a mean of 1 000 hours and a variance of 40 000.

After how many hours would we expect 10% of the lamps to fail?

We can also state this question as: 'If the number of lamps that are expected to fail within the first x hours is $2\,000 \times 0.1 = 200$, what is the value of x?'

We can answer this question by using the NORM.INV or NORM.S.INV Excel functions.

This part of the problem involves calculating the number of hours for the first 10% to fail. This corresponds to calculating the value of x where $P(X < x) = 0.1$. This type of question is the reverse of what was asked in Example 7.3, in which we were given a score value and asked to calculate a probability value. In this question, we are given a probability value and are asked to calculate the corresponding score value.

To obtain this value, we need to solve for x in the equation:

$$P(X < x) = 0.1$$

Or, equivalently, solve for z in the standardised equation:

$$P(Z < z) = P\left(\frac{X - 1\,000}{\sqrt{40\,000}} < \frac{x - 1\,000}{\sqrt{40\,000}}\right) = 0.1$$

Where $z = \dfrac{(x - 1\,000)}{\sqrt{40\,000}}$.

To obtain x from z, note that:

$$x = z \times \sqrt{40\,000} + 1\,000$$

The Excel solution is given in Figure 7.25.

	A	B	C	D	E
1	**Example 7.3 (c)**				
2					
3		**Normal distribution**			
4					
5		Mean μ =	1000		
6		Variance σ^2 =	40000		
7		Standard deviation σ =	200	=SQRT(C6)	
8					
9		$P(X < x)$ =	0.1		
10					
11		x =	743.6897	=NORM.INV(C9,C5,C7)	
12					
13		z =	-1.28155	=NORM.S.INV(C9)	
14		$x = z\sigma + \mu$ =	743.6897	=C13*C7+C5	

Figure 7.25: Excel solution for Example 7.4

EXCEL SOLUTION

Mean μ: Cell C5	Value
Variance σ^2: Cell C6	Value
Standard deviation σ: Cell C7	Formula: =SQRT(C6)
$P(X < x)$: Cell C9	Value
x: Cell C11	Formula: =NORM.INV(C9,C5,C7)
z: Cell C13	Formula: =NORM.S.INV(C9)
$x = z\sigma + \mu$: Cell C14	Formula: = C13*C7+C5

INTERPRETATION

In Excel, we can use the NORM.INV or NORM.S.INV function to calculate the number of hours for 10% to fail. From Excel, the number of hours obtained for 10% to fail is $x = 744$ hours.

The expected number of hours for 10% of the lamps to fail is 744 hours.

NOTE

This problem corresponds to finding the value of x such that $P(X < x) = 0.1$ (or $P(Z < z) = 0.1$, where $z = \frac{x-\mu}{\sigma}$). From Excel, we find that the value of z that satisfies the equation $P(Z < z) = 0.1$ is $z = -1.28$. However, since $z = \frac{x-\mu}{\sigma}$, we can rearrange the terms to get $x = z\sigma + \mu = -1.28 \times 200 + 1\,000 \approx 744$.

The Excel function NORM.INV calculates the quantile value of x from a normal distribution for the specified probability p, mean μ, and standard deviation σ.

The Excel function NORM.S.INV calculates the quantile value z from a standard normal distribution for the specified probability value p.

In the next few sections, we briefly discuss three other continuous probability distributions, namely the Student's t-distribution, the chi-squared distribution and the F-distribution.

7.3 The Student's *t*-distribution

The *Student's t-distribution* is a distribution that you will meet again in later chapters when we start to test the statistical significance of hypotheses made about the population mean and when we start to construct interval estimators for population means.

The Student's t-distribution is completely governed by one parameter: the degrees of freedom. The degree of freedom parameter changes the spread of this distribution, but does not affect the location (the centre of the t-distribution is always 0). Other important properties of the t-distribution include the following:

- The t-distribution is symmetrical around 0
- The mean of the t-distribution is always equal to 0

- The values of the *t*-distribution range between $-\infty$ and $+\infty$
- Compared to the standard normal distribution, the *t*-distribution has heavier tails (see Figure 7.26)
- When the degrees of freedom become *very* large, the *t*-distribution approaches the shape of the standard normal distribution.

We will use the notation $T \sim t_{df}$ to indicate that the random variable T follows a *t*-distribution with *df* degrees of freedom.

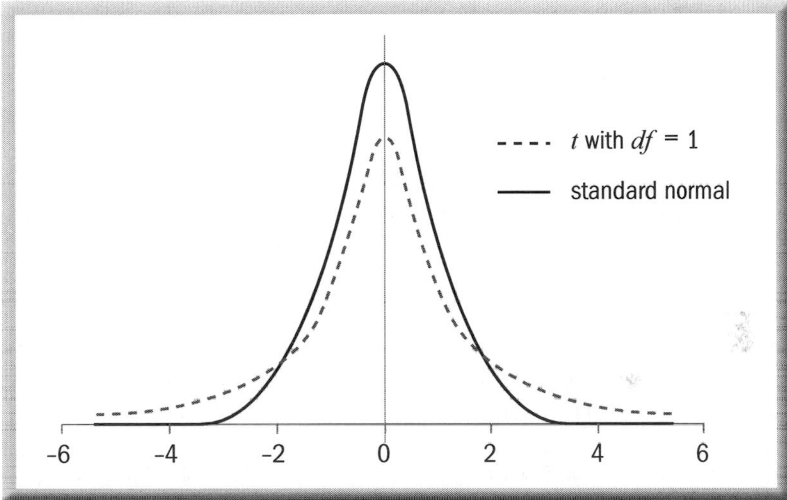

Figure 7.26: Comparison of the standard normal and *t*-distributions

For now, we will only look at how to calculate some basic probabilities and quantiles for this distribution. The Excel functions that we will use to do this are T.DIST and T.INV.

7.3.1 Calculating probabilities associated with the *t*-distribution

We use the function T.DIST to calculate probabilities of the form $P(T < x)$, where T follows a *t*-distribution with *df* degrees of freedom. This function uses the following syntax:

T.DIST(*x*,*df*,TRUE)

The arguments to the function are the following:

- *x* is the value specified in the probability $P(T < x)$
- *df* is the degrees of freedom
- The final argument should be set to TRUE to calculate $P(T < x)$ and FALSE if you want to evaluate the *t* density function in the point *x*.

For example, suppose we wanted to calculate the probability $P(T < 1.68)$ where $T \sim t_{10}$, that is, it is a random variable with a *t*-distribution with $df = 10$ degrees of freedom. The code used to calculate this probability is given in Figure 7.27.

Figure 7.27: Excel calculation of $P(T < 1.68)$ where $T \sim t_{10}$

	A	B	C	D
1				
2		*t*-distribution		
3				
4		*df* =	10	
5		*x* =	1.68	
6				
7		*P*(*T* < 1.68)=	0.938061	=T.DIST(C5,C4,TRUE)

Therefore, the probability that T is smaller than 1.68 is:

$$P(T < 1.68) = 0.938061$$

7.3.2 Calculating quantiles associated with the *t*-distribution

To calculate quantiles for this distribution, we use the function T.INV. The syntax is:

T.INV(*p*,*df*)

- *p* is the specified probability value.
- *df* is the degrees of freedom.

To illustrate how we can use this function, we will attempt to use it to determine the quantile of a *t*-distributed random variable with $df = 7$ degrees of freedom associated with the probability $p = 0.90$. In other words, we want to determine the value of x that satisfies the expression $P(T < x) = 0.9$, where $T \sim t_7$.

The Excel code used to determine this quantile is given in Figure 7.28 below.

	A	B	C	D	E
1					
2		*t*-distribution			
3					
4		*df* =	7		
5					
6		*p* = *P*(*T* < *x*) =	0.9		
7					
8		*x* =	1.414924	=T.INV(C6,C4)	
9					

Figure 7.28: Excel calculation of the quantile x in $P(T < x) = 0.9$ where $T \sim t_7$

Therefore, the quantile that satisfies the expression $P(T < x) = 0.9$ for $T \sim t_7$ is $x = 1.41492$.

7.4 The chi-squared distribution

The *chi-squared distribution* (χ^2-distribution) is a popular distribution that is used to solve statistical inference problems involving contingency tables and assessing the goodness of fit of a model to sample data.

Some properties of the chi-squared distribution include the following:

- The distribution is skewed to the right (see Figure 7.29).
- The values of this distribution are all greater than or equal to 0.
- The only parameter in this distribution is the degrees of freedom, which is denoted by *df*.

If a random variable X follows a chi-squared distribution with *df* degrees of freedom, we indicate it using the shorthand notation $X \sim \chi^2_{df}$

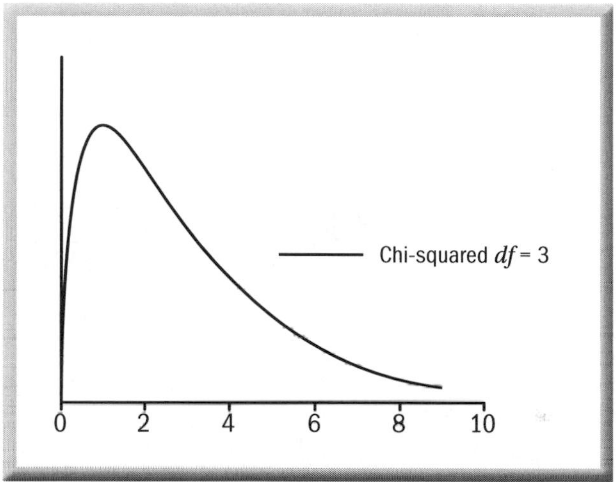

Figure 7.29: Graph of a chi-squared density curve with *df* = 3 degrees of freedom

As with the *t*-distribution, we will only look at how to calculate probabilities and quantiles for the distribution using Excel functions. In this case, the Excel functions are called CHISQ.DIST and CHISQ.INV.

7.4.1 Calculating probabilities associated with the χ^2-distribution

We can use the CHISQ.DIST function to calculate $P(X < x)$, where $X \sim \chi^2_{df}$. The syntax and arguments of this function are:

$$\text{CHISQ.DIST}(x, df, \text{TRUE})$$

- x is the value specified in the probability $P(X < x)$.
- *df* is the degrees of freedom.
- The final argument should be set to TRUE to calculate $P(X < x)$ and FALSE if you want to evaluate the chi-squared density function in the point x.

The following Excel spreadsheet illustrates how we can calculate the probability that some chi-squared random variable X with 3 degrees of freedom is less than 3.9, that is, we will calculate $P(X < 3.9)$. The Excel spreadsheet used to calculate this probability is shown in Figure 7.30.

Figure 7.30: Excel calculation of $P(X < 3.9)$ where $X \sim \chi^2_3$

	A	B	C	D
1				
2		Chi-squared distribution		
3				
4		*df* =	3	
5		*x* =	3.9	
6				
7		*P*(*X* < 3.9) =	0.727533	=CHISQ.DIST(C5,C4,TRUE)

Therefore, the probability that X is smaller than 3.9 is:

$$P(X < 3.9) = 0.72753324$$

7.4.2 Calculating quantiles associated with the χ^2-distribution

For chi-squared quantiles the function is:

$$\text{CHISQ.INV}(p,df)$$

- p is the specified probability value.
- df is the degrees of freedom.

The next example shows how we can obtain the quantile of a χ^2_9-distribution associated with the probability 0.99, that is, find x such that $P(X < x) = 0.99$, where $X \sim \chi^2_9$

The Excel spreadsheet is given in in Figure 7.31.

	A	B	C	D
1				
2		Chi-squared distribution		
3				
4		*df* =	9	
5		*p* = *P*(*X* < *x*) =	0.99	
6				
7		*x* =	21.666	=CHISQ.INV(C5,C4)

Figure 7.31: Excel calculation of the quantile x in $P(X < x) = 0.99$ where $X \sim \chi^2_9$

Therefore, the quantile that satisfies the expression $P(X < x) = 0.99$ for $X \sim \chi^2_9$ is $x = 21.666$

7.5 The *F*-distribution

The *F-distribution* is another distribution that will crop up when we start to perform statistical hypothesis tests. In particular, we use this distribution when testing whether the ratios of two population variances from normally distributed populations are statistically different, and when attempting to determine if multiple population means are equivalent.

Some important properties of the *F*-distribution include the following:

- Like the chi-squared distribution, the *F*-distribution is also skewed to the right (see Figure 7.32).

- The shape of this distribution depends on two degrees of freedom denoted df_1 and df_2.
- The values of the F-distribution are all greater than or equal to 0.

We write $X \sim F_{df_1,df_2}$ to indicate that X has an F-distribution with degrees of freedom df_1 and df_2.

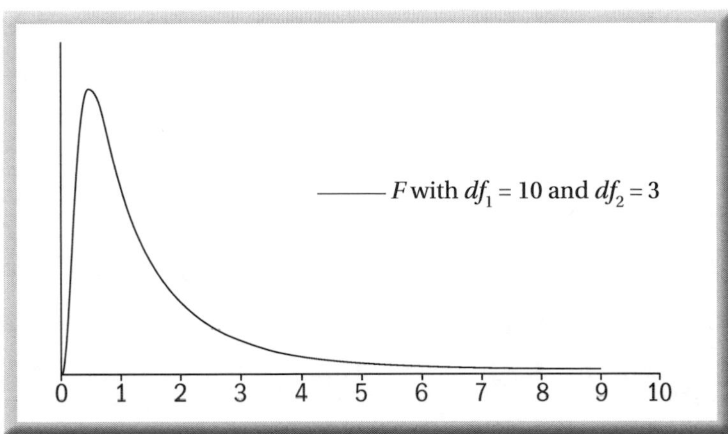

Figure 7.32: Graph of the F-density curve with $df_1 = 10$ and $df_2 = 3$ degrees of freedom

The two Excel functions that we use to determine probabilities and quantiles for the F-distribution are F.DIST and F.INV.

7.5.1 Calculating probabilities associated with the *F*-distribution

The probability calculator function we use to calculate probabilities of the form $P(X < x)$ where $X \sim F_{df_1,df_2}$ is:

$$\text{F.DIST}(x, df_1, df_2, \text{TRUE})$$

- x is the value specified in the probability $P(X < x)$.
- df_1 and df_2 are the two degrees of freedom.
- The final argument should be set to TRUE to calculate $P(X < x)$ and FALSE if you want to evaluate the F-density function in the point x.

For example, to calculate the probability $P(X < 5.1)$ if $X \sim F_{19,2}$ we use the Excel spreadsheet shown in Figure 7.33.

Therefore, the probability that X is smaller than 5.1 is $P(X < 5.1) = 0.82359009$

	A	B	C	D
1				
2		*F*-distribution		
3				
4		df_1 =	19	
5		df_2 =	2	
6		x=	5.1	
7				
8		$P(X < 5.1)$ =	0.82359009	=F.DIST(C6,C4,C5,TRUE)

Figure 7.33: Excel calculation of $P(X < 5.1)$ where $X \sim F_{19,2}$

7.5.2 Calculating quantiles associated with the *F*-distribution

For *F* quantiles, the function is:

$$\text{F.INV}(p,df_1,df_2)$$

- p is the specified probability value.
- df_1 and df_2 are the two degrees of freedom.

The 0.85 probability quantile of a $F_{8,5}$ distributed random variable, X, is calculated with the help of the F.INV function in Figure 7.34.

	A	B	C	D	E
1					
2		*F*-distribution			
3					
4		df_1 =	8		
5		df_2 =	5		
6					
7		*P*(*X* < *x*) =	0.85		
8					
9		*x* =	2.63911	=F.INV(C7,C4,C5)	

Figure 7.34: Excel calculation of the quantile x in $P(X<x)=0.85$ where $X \sim F_{8,5}$

Therefore, the quantile that satisfies the expression $P(X<x)=0.85$ for $X \sim F_{8,5}$ is $x=2.63911$

SUMMARY

In this chapter, we considered calculating probabilities and quantiles for continuous random variables. Particular attention was given to the calculation of normal probabilities and quantiles, because these values will be very important in the later chapters on inferential statistics.

KEY TERMS

Continuous probability distribution
Chi-squared distribution
Density functions
F-distribution
Mean of the normal distribution
Normal distribution
Quantile
Standard deviation
Standardisation
Standardised normal random variable
Student's *t*-distribution
Uniform distribution

FORMULA SUMMARY

$$f_x(x) = \frac{1}{b-a} \text{ if } a < x < b \text{ and zero otherwise} \tag{7.1}$$

$$f_X(x) = \frac{1}{\sigma\sqrt{2\pi}} \exp\left(-\frac{(x-\mu)^2}{2\sigma^2}\right) \tag{7.2}$$

$$Z = \frac{(X-\mu)}{\sigma} \tag{7.3}$$

$$P(Z > z) = 1 - P(Z < z) \tag{7.4}$$

$$P(z_1 < Z < z_2) = P(Z < z_2) - P(Z < z_1) \tag{7.5}$$

EXERCISES

7.1 Use NORM.DIST to calculate the following probabilities, $X \sim N(100, 25)$. For each probability, identify the region to be found by shading the area on the normal probability distribution.

a) $P(X \leq 95)$
b) $P(95 \leq X \leq 105)$
c) $P(105 \leq X \leq 115)$
d) $P(93 \leq X \leq 99)$

7.2 Use NORM.S.DIST to calculate the following probabilities, $X \sim N(100, 25)$. In each case, convert X to Z. Compare your answers to those from question 7.1.

a) $P(X \leq 95)$
b) $P(95 \leq X \leq 105)$
c) $P(105 \leq X \leq 115)$
d) $P(93 \leq X \leq 99)$

7.3 Given that a normal random variable has a mean of 10 and a variance of 25, calculate the probability that a member chosen at random is:

a) greater than 11
b) less than 11
c) less than 5
d) greater than 5
e) between 5 and 11.

7.4 The lifetimes of certain types of car battery are normally distributed with a mean of 1 248 days and standard deviation of 185 days. If the supplier guarantees them for 1 080 days, what proportion of batteries will be replaced under guarantee?

7.5 Electrical resistors have a design resistance of 500 ohms. The resistors are produced by a machine with an output that is normally distributed $N(501, 9)$. Resistance below 498 ohms and above 508 ohms are rejected. Find:

a) the proportion that will be rejected
b) the proportion that would be rejected if the mean was adjusted to minimise the proportion of rejects
c) how much the standard deviation would need to be reduced by (leaving the mean at 501 ohms) so that the proportion of rejects below 498 ohms would be halved.

7.6 Suppose that we have three random variables, W, X and Y, defined as follows:

- W follows a *t*-distribution with 7 degrees of freedom.
- X follows a chi-square distribution with 10 degrees of freedom.
- Y follows an *F*-distibution with 2 and 5 degrees of freedom.

Use Excel functions to calculate the following probabilities:

a) $P(W < 1)$
b) $P(-1 < W < 0.5)$
c) $P(X < 10)$
d) $P(X > 5)$
e) $P(4 < X < 9)$
f) $P(Y < 1.5)$
g) $P(Y > 0.2)$

CHAPTER 8

SAMPLING AND SAMPLING DISTRIBUTIONS

CHAPTER CONTENTS

OVERVIEW

In Chapters 5, 6 and 7, we introduced the concept of a probability distribution through the idea of relative frequency, and introduced two distinct types of distributions: discrete and continuous. In this chapter, we explore the concept of taking a sample from a population, and discuss the distributional properties of the sample mean and sample proportion calculated from these samples. To this end, we begin the discussion by first considering different methods of obtaining representative samples from a population and then move onto the concept of a sampling distribution. The idea behind the sampling distribution of a statistic is linked to the fact that the sample statistic's value will vary from one sample to the next, leading to a variation in the values of a statistic. We define the sampling distribution of the mean in this chapter and discuss various properties relating to the sampling distribution. In particular, we note that the sample mean is normally distributed when the underlying data are normally distributed. We also show that the Central Limit Theorem allows us to assume a normal distribution approximation for the sampling distribution of the mean, even if the population is *not normally distributed*. This result is one of the main tools that we will use in later chapters.

LEARNING OBJECTIVES

On completing this chapter, you should be able to:

- distinguish between the concept of a population and sample
- recognise different types of sampling: probability (simple, systematic, stratified, cluster) and non-probability (purposive, quota, snowball, convenience)
- understand the concept of a sampling distribution: mean and proportion
- understand sampling from a normal population
- understand sampling from a non-normal population: Central Limit Theorem
- solve problems using Microsoft Excel.

8.1 Sampling

In Chapter 1, we briefly discussed the differences between the concepts of a sample and a population. In the subsequent chapters, we looked at various calculations that could be performed using the information acquired from these samples (which we called sample statistics). This chapter relates to some technical aspects regarding these sample statistics, specifically probability calculations related to sample statistics. These calculations will be used in the next few chapters in which we apply statistical inference to comment on population properties using the information obtained from a sample. However, all of the theory that we discuss is based on the assumption that the sample drawn from the population is *good*. In this section, we look at various techniques that we can use to draw representative samples from populations; the choice between these techniques is typically determined by the problem being considered.

Types of sampling methods

There are a number of different methods that we could use to create a representative sample from a population, but these methods can generally be grouped into one of two categories: *probability samples* or *non-probability samples.*

8.1.1 Probability sampling

The idea behind probability sampling is *random* selection, and for this reason we typically call these **random samples**. More specifically, each item in the population of interest that could potentially be included in a sample has a known probability of selection under a given sampling scheme.

> **Random sample** A sampling technique where we select an element from a population of interest using some random mechanism and where the probability that a single element from the population will be included in the sample is known beforehand.

There are four categories of probability samples as illustrated in Figure 8.1.

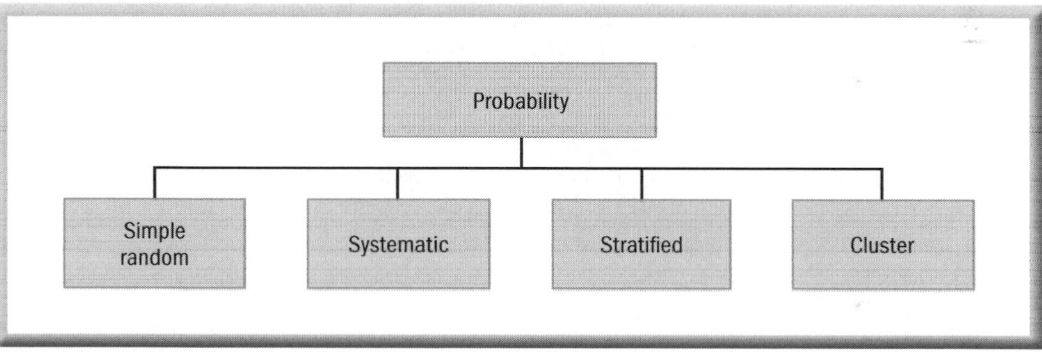

Figure 8.1: The different types of probability sampling schemes

Simple random sampling

The most widely used type of a random sample is the ***simple random sample.*** This type of sampling is characterised by the fact that the probability of selection is the same for every case in the population, that is, the probability of selecting an element to be included in the sample is *equal* for all elements. Simple random sampling is then a method used to select n items from a population of size N, such that every possible sample of size n has an equal chance of being drawn.

> **Simple random sampling** A random sampling technique that selects any element from a population with equal probability.

WORKED EXAMPLES

EXAMPLE 8.1

A marketing researcher needs to select a random sample of 200 shoppers who shop at a supermarket during a particular time period. The supermarket would like to know the views of its customers on a proposed redevelopment of the store. The total footfall (the number of people vising a shop or a chain of shops in a period of time) within this time period is 10 000. With a footfall (or population) of this size, we could employ a number of methods to select an appropriate sample of 200 from the potential 10 000. For example, we could place 10 000 consecutively numbered pieces of paper (number 1 to 10 000) in a box, draw a number at random from the box, shake the box, and then select another number to maximise the chances of the second pick being random. We would then continue the process until all 200 numbers are selected. These numbers would then be used to select a customer entering the store, with the customer being chosen based on the number selected from the random process. These 200 customers would form our sample, with each number in the selection having the same probability of being chosen. When collecting data by random sampling, we generally find it difficult to devise a selection scheme that guarantees a random sample. For example, when selecting from a population, it may not be the whole population that we wish to measure, or, during the time period when the survey is conducted, we may find that the customers sampled are unrepresentative of the population due to unforeseen circumstances.

Systematic random sampling

With **systematic random sampling**, we create a list of every element in the population and number them from 1 to N (where N is the total population size). From the list, we randomly select the first sample element from the first υ number values on the population list. Thereafter, we select every υ^{th} value on the list.

Systematic random sampling A random sampling technique that randomly selects an initial element from the first υ elements in a population list, and thereafter systematically selects every υ^{th} element to be included in the sample, where $\upsilon = \frac{N}{n}$, and where n is the size of the sample.

The procedure of drawing the n sample element from the N elements in a population list is as follows.

- Divide the number of cases in the population, N, by the desired sample size, n, that is, calculate $\upsilon = \frac{N}{n}$. For example, if the population size is $N = 10\ 000$ and the desired sample size is $n = 6$, then $\upsilon = \frac{10\ 000}{6} = 1\ 666.67$ or roughly $\upsilon \approx 1\ 667$ (rounded off to a whole number).
- Select a random number, k, between one and υ. For example, if $\upsilon = 1\ 667$, then we could potentially choose $k = 28$ (or any number between 1 and 1 667).
- Starting with the case number chosen in the previous step, select every subsequent υ^{th} element in the list to be included in the sample. For example, if we have $N = 10\ 000$, $n = 6$, $\upsilon = 1\ 667$ and $k = 28$, then the numbers of the elements that will be included in the sample are the elements numbered 28, 1 695, 3 362, 5 029, 6 696 and 8 363. (Note that if we randomly chose $k = 1\ 667$ in this example, then the number of the last element chosen would have been 10 002. In this case,

we would *wrap around* to the beginning of the list and choose element number 2, because 10 002 is 2 more than the total population size.)

The advantage of systematic sampling compared to simple random sampling is that the sample is easier to draw from the population. The disadvantage is that the sample points are not equally likely and, if there are patterns in the list (if, for example, every 1 667th item in the list has a particular property not shared by the rest of the items), then this method will possibly select a biased sample.

Stratified random sampling

With **stratified random sampling**, the population is divided into two or more mutually exclusive strata (or groups). Each stratum contains relatively homogenous elements (the elements are relatively similar to one another when considering the variable being studied). For example, if we were looking at the working conditions of people, a natural stratification would be to group the people according to high, medium and low income. The stratified sampling procedure involves organising the population into homogenous subsets and then drawing a simple random sample from each group. The advantage of this method is that it guarantees that every group within the population is selected and provides an opportunity to undertake group comparisons.

Stratified random sampling A random sampling technique that randomly selects elements from a stratified population. The proportion of elements in each strata of the population is reflected in the sample.

If we use simple random sampling in populations that are stratified, then we may not obtain a representative sample. This is because the simple random sampling procedure could (randomly) not select elements from one or more strata (this would typically happen if one or more stratum size is small relative to the rest). In these cases, we would employ stratified random sampling to ensure that appropriate numbers of sample values are drawn from each group in proportion to the percentage of the population as a whole. Stratified sampling offers several advantages over simple random sampling:

- It guards against an unrepresentative sample.
- It provides sufficient group data for separate group analysis.
- It does not require very large sample sizes in order to be representative.
- Greater precision is achievable compared to simple random sampling for a sample of the same size.

Stratified random sampling nearly always results in a smaller variance for the estimated mean or other population parameters of interest. The main disadvantage of a stratified sample is that it may be more costly to collect and process the data compared to a simple random sample.

Two different categories of stratified random sampling are available: proportionate and disproportionate stratification.

- *Proportionate stratification*: With proportionate stratification, the stratum size in the sample is proportionate to the stratum size in the population. This method provides greater precision than simple random sampling with the same sample size, and this precision is better when dealing with characteristics that are the same (homogeneous) strata.

- *Disproportionate stratification*: With disproportionate stratification, the proportion of elements required from each stratum may differ from the proportions observed in the population. If differences are explored in the characteristics being measured across strata, then disproportionate stratification can provide better precision than proportionate stratification when the sample points are correctly allocated to strata. In general, given similar costs, you would always choose proportionate stratification.

WORKED EXAMPLES

EXAMPLE 8.2

An employment company wishes to draw a sample from its pool of past clients to conduct a study on the salaries of the people that they have placed in jobs around the country. Over the years, they have found employment for $N = 1\ 389$ people, but they only need to draw a sample of $n = 25$ individuals for this study. To obtain a representative sample, they decide to stratify the population according to the variable 'highest level of education' that the clients report on their curriculum vitae (CV). This variable takes on the values 'No higher education', 'University degree or college diploma' and 'Post-graduate degree'. It is thought that this will be a good way to stratify the population of clients, because it should group the clients into similar (homogeneous) groups with respect to their salary. The following information is recorded from the population (we will use the notation N_1, N_2 and N_3 to denote the stratum sizes of the education groups in the *population*):

- $N_1 = 347$ of the $N = 1\ 389$ clients reported their education level as 'No higher education' (24.98% of the clients).
- $N_2 = 601$ of the $N = 1\ 389$ clients reported their education level as 'University degree or college diploma' (43.27% of the clients).
- $N_3 = 441$ of the $N = 1\ 389$ clients reported their education level as 'Post-graduate degree' (31.75% of the clients).

Using *proportionate stratification*, we first need to determine the number of people that we will need to draw from each education group. To maintain the same proportions that appear in the population, in a sample of size $n = 25$, we need to draw the following number of people from each education group (we will use the notation n_1, n_2 and n_3 to denote the stratum sizes of the education groups in the *sample*):

- We need $n_1 = 6$ people (roughly 24.98%) from the 'No higher education' group.
- We need $n_2 = 11$ people (roughly 43.27%) from the 'University degree or college diploma' group.
- We need $n_3 = 8$ people (roughly 31.75%) from the 'Post-graduate degree' group.

Note that $n_1 + n_2 + n_3 = n = 25$. We would then treat each stratum as a population and apply simple random sampling to obtain the appropriate number of people from each stratum to form our representative sample.

Cluster sampling

Cluster sampling is a sampling technique in which the entire population of interest is divided into K groups, or clusters, and a sample of k of these clusters are randomly selected (where k is some number smaller than K). Each cluster must be mutually exclusive and, when all clusters are combined, they must form the entire population. Once the clusters have been selected, we have the choice of performing either *one-stage cluster sampling* or *two-stage cluster sampling*.

Cluster sampling A sampling technique where we group the population into K (heterogeneous) natural clusters, draw k of these clusters and then either use all the elements in this cluster (one-stage), or randomly select elements from within each cluster (two-stage) to form your sample.

- One-stage cluster sampling involves including *all* the elements in the selected cluster into the sample (none of the elements in the clusters that were not chosen will be included in the sample).
- Two-stage cluster sampling involves selecting the k clusters and then performing a second level of sampling whereby only some elements are randomly drawn from these chosen clusters to be included in the sample.

The cluster sampling method differs from the stratified sampling method in the following ways:
- In stratified samples, *all* the groups are used and not just a random selection of the groups as in cluster sampling.
- Stratified sampling forms *homogeneous* groups in the population, based on some variable of interest, whereas cluster sampling groups the population into *heterogeneous* groups, based on *natural* groupings of elements. For example, if we were sampling people, then a *cluster* could be a region within a city. Then, all individuals that live in that region belong to that cluster.

Cluster sampling can also be conducted in three or more stages, in which case it is then called **multistage cluster sampling**. The main reason for using cluster sampling is that it is usually much cheaper and more convenient to sample the population in clusters than sampling individuals. In some cases, constructing a sampling frame that identifies every population element is too expensive or impossible. Cluster sampling can also reduce costs when the population elements are scattered over a wide area.

Multistage sampling

With multistage sampling, we select a sample by using combinations of different sampling methods. For example, in stage 1, we might use cluster sampling to choose clusters from a population. Then, in stage 2, we might use simple random sampling to select a subset of elements from each chosen cluster for the final sample.

8.1.2 Non-probability sampling

In many situations, it is not possible to select the types of probability samples used in large-scale surveys. For example, we may have to seek the views of local family-run businesses that experienced financial difficulties during the bank credit crunch of 2007–2009. In this situation, there are no easily accessible lists of businesses that experienced difficulties or a list may never have been created or made available. In this situation, we can obtain a sample by using *non-probability sampling* methods to collect the required sample data.

Figure 8.2 illustrates the four primary types of non-probability sampling methods.

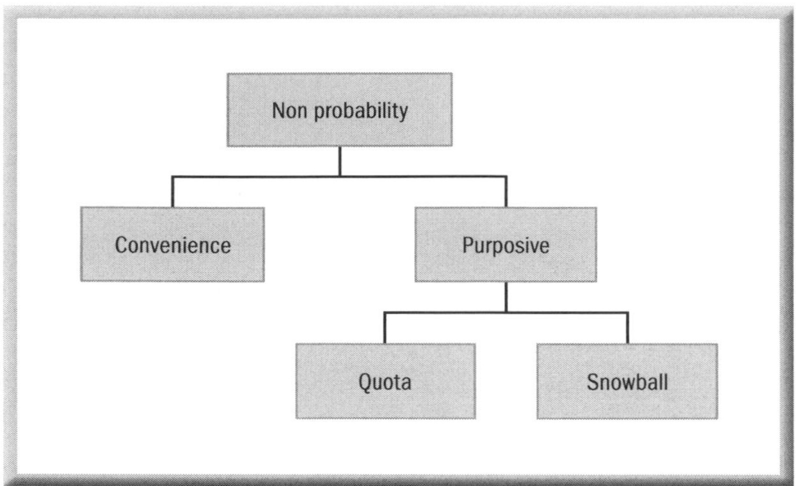

Figure 8.2: Types of non-probability sampling techniques

We can divide non-probability sampling methods into two broad types: *convenience* or *purposive.*

Convenience sampling

Convenience (or availability) *sampling* is a method of choosing subjects who are available or easy to find. This method is also sometimes called haphazard, accidental or availability sampling. The primary advantage of this method is that it is very easy to carry out relative to other methods. The main problem with using this survey method is that you cannot guarantee that the sample is representative of the population. Convenience sampling is a popular method with researchers and provides some data that can be analysed, but the type of statistics that can be applied to the data is compromised by uncertainties regarding the nature of the population that the survey data represents.

Purposive sampling

Purposive sampling is a sampling method in which elements are chosen based on the purpose of the study. Purposive sampling can involve studying the entire population of some limited group (for example, the accounts department at a local engineering firm) or a subset of a population (for example, chartered accountants). As with other non-probability sampling methods, purposive sampling does not produce a sample that is representative of a larger population, but it can be exactly what is needed in some cases, for example, when studying an organisation, community or some other clearly defined and relatively limited group. Examples of two popular purposive sampling methods include *quota sampling* and *snowball sampling.*

- *Quota sampling* is designed to overcome the most obvious flaw of availability sampling. Rather than taking just anyone, you set quotas to ensure that the sample you collect represents certain characteristics in proportion to their prevalence in the population. Note that for this method, you have to know something about the characteristics of the population ahead of time. There are two types of quota sampling: proportional and non-proportional.

- In *proportional quota sampling*, you want to represent the major characteristics of the population by sampling a proportional amount of each. For example, if you know the population is made up of 25% women and 75% men, and that you want a total sample size of 400, you will continue sampling until you get those percentages and then you stop. So, if your sample already contains the 100 women, but not the 300 men, you will continue to sample men. However, even if legitimate women respondents come along, you will not sample them because you have already met your quota. The primary problem with this type of sampling is that even when we know that a quota sample is representative of the particular characteristics for which quotas have been set, we have no way of knowing if the sample is representative in terms of any other characteristics. For example, if we set quotas for age, our sample will likely be representative for age, but it may not be in terms of gender, education or other pertinent factors.
- In *non-proportional quota sampling*, you specify the minimum number of sampled data points you want in each category. In this case, you are not concerned with having the correct proportions, but with achieving the numbers in each category. This method is the non-probabilistic analogue of stratified random sampling, in that it is typically used to ensure that smaller groups are adequately represented in your sample.

Finally, researchers often introduce bias when allowed to self-select respondents, which is usually the case in this type of survey research. For example, if the study involves choosing males, interviewers are more likely to choose those that are better-dressed, or seem more approachable or less threatening. That may be understandable from a practical point of view, but it introduces bias into research findings.

- In *snowball sampling*, you begin by identifying someone who meets the criteria for inclusion in your study. You then ask them to recommend others who they may know who also meet the criteria. Thus, the sample group appears to grow like a rolling snowball. This sampling technique is often used in hidden populations that are difficult for researchers to access, including firms with financial difficulties or students struggling with their studies. The method creates a sample with questionable representativeness, and it can be difficult to judge how a sample compares to a larger population. Furthermore, an issue arises in who the respondents refer you to, for example, friends will refer you to friends but are less likely to refer people that they do not consider friends, for whatever reason. This creates a further bias within the sample that makes it difficult to say anything about the population.

NOTE The primary difference between probability methods of sampling and non-probability methods is that in the latter, you do not know the likelihood that any element of a population will be selected for study.

The rest of this chapter will focus on samples that have been randomly selected and the associated statistical techniques that we can apply to a randomly selected data set.

8.2 Sampling distributions

Sampling distribution Describes how a sample statistic varies when calculated from all samples of size n drawn from a single population.

8.2.1 Introduction

The main issue that we explore in the next chapter is using a sample (or samples) from a population to provide an estimate of population parameters (such as the population mean, population standard deviation or population proportion) by using the sample statistic value (that is, the sample mean, sample standard deviation or sample proportion). Fundamental to this, is the idea that the sample statistic will change when calculated from different samples. For example, a breakfast cereal manufacturer may wish to estimate the true (or population) mean quantity of breakfast cereal that is placed in each bag during the manufacturing process. To accomplish this, they collect a sample of, for example, 80 boxes of breakfast cereal and then calculate the sample mean of this one sample of 80 boxes. However, as you will see later, to answer this type of question properly, the manufacturer also needs to know how the estimator for the parameter (the sample mean in this case) varies from one sample of 80 breakfast cereal boxes to the next. The manner in which the sample statistic changes from one sample to another is called the **sampling distribution** of the statistic. This concept is directly related to the probability distributions discussed in Chapters 5, 6 and 7, and we will see that the only thing that changes is that we now consider the sample mean of values to be the *random variable* of interest (with associated probability distribution).

In Figure 8.3, the concept of a sampling distribution is roughly illustrated for some statistic of interest based on samples of size $n = 3$ from a population of individuals. In this figure, J samples of size 3 are drawn from the population and the statistic of interest is calculated for each one. The statistic calculated is then recorded and a frequency distribution (histogram) is constructed for the statistic values obtained. The resulting frequency distribution in this example is then an approximation of the true sampling distribution of the statistic. The approximation will become more accurate if we increase J, the number of samples drawn.

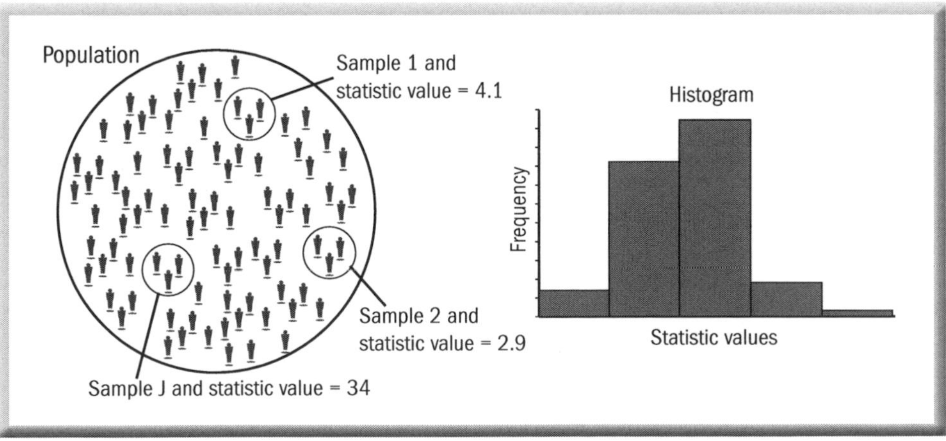

Figure 8.3: Graphical representation of the sampling distribution of a statistic based on samples of size $n = 3$

In the next few sections, we discuss the sampling distribution of the *mean.*

8.2.2 Properties of the sampling distribution of the mean

In this section, we briefly discuss some distributional properties of the *sampling distribution of the mean.* Consider the following example. We have a population of baby seals and the population mean weight of these seals is $\mu = 133.6$ kg. A sample of size 200 is drawn from this population and the sample mean weight of the baby seals in this first sample is calculated to be 135.5 kg. Another sample is drawn and the mean weight of this new sample is calculated to be 132.5 kg. By repeating this process a large number of times, we find that the individual sample means calculated differ from sample to sample, but we also encounter a very *interesting property* of the sample mean, namely, the mean of all the sample means is equal to the original population's mean.

Stated more formally: If the population mean of a random variable X is μ, then the expected value (see Chapter 5) of the sample mean $\overline{X}$ is also μ:

$$E(\overline{X}) = \mu$$

This is an important result because it states that the population mean of the sample data is exactly the same as the population mean (expected value) of the sampling distribution of the mean.

NOTE A *sample mean* is an **unbiased** estimator for the population mean μ, because the mean (expected value) of all sample means of size n selected from the population is equal to the population mean, μ.

Unbiased When the mean (expected value) of the sampling distribution of a statistic is equal to a population parameter, that statistic is said to be an unbiased estimator of that parameter, that is, on average, the statistic estimates the correct value.

Another important property of the sampling distribution of the mean is that the variance of the sampling distribution of the mean is also related to the population variance of the sample data. Formally, if the variance of the variable X is σ^2, then the variance of the sample mean $\overline{X}$, denoted by $\sigma^2_{\overline{X}}$, is given by:

$$\sigma^2_{\overline{X}} = Var(\overline{X}) = \frac{\sigma^2}{n}$$

In other words, the variance of the sample mean is equal to the variance of the sample variable divided by the sample size. One consequence of this is that if the sample size increases, then the true variance of $\overline{X}$ becomes smaller.

The standard deviation of $\overline{X}$ (which is also referred to as the **standard error** of $\overline{X}$) is denoted by the symbol $\sigma_{\overline{X}}$ and is given by:

$$\sigma_{\overline{X}} = \sqrt{Var(\overline{X})} = \frac{\sigma}{\sqrt{n}} \qquad (8.1)$$

NOTE The standard deviation of the sample means is also called the ***standard error*** of the sample means.

Standard error The standard deviation of a statistic. We use the term standard error (instead of standard deviation) to indicate that we are referring to the square root of the variance of a statistic.

In the next two sections, we introduce some concepts that will allow us to calculate probabilities of the form $P(\overline{X} < x)$ by incorporating the properties discussed above. This may seem strange to want to calculate the probability that the sample mean is smaller or larger than a specific value, but keep in mind that, before the sample is observed, the value of the mean is unknown and can potentially take on many values. We want to quantify our uncertainty regarding the value of the sample mean by calculating these probabilities. In the discussion that follows, we consider two scenarios: one in which the underlying variable in the study is *assumed to be normally distributed* and one in which we *make no assumptions about the distribution* of the underlying variable.

8.2.3 Sampling from a normal population

If we select a random variable X from a population that is normally distributed with population mean μ and standard deviation σ, then we could state this relationship using the notation $X \sim N(\mu, \sigma^2)$ (as discussed in Chapter 7).

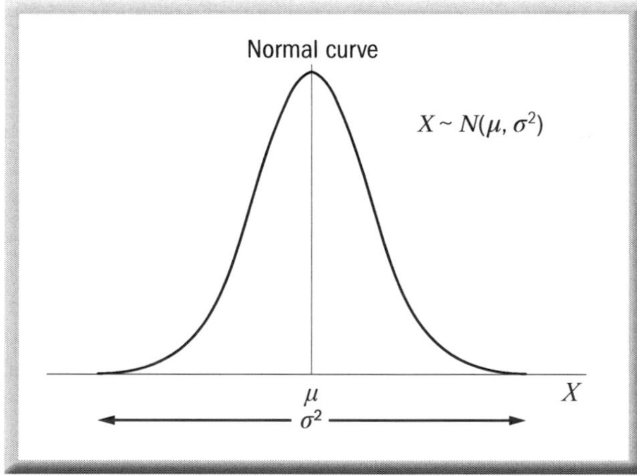

Figure 8.4: The normal density function with mean μ and variance σ^2

If we now draw samples of n-values from this normal population and calculate the sample means, then we can show that the sample means are *also* normally distributed with a mean of μ and a standard deviation given by formula (8.1), where n is the sample size on which the sampling distribution was based.

In other words, if $X \sim N(\mu, \sigma^2)$, then the random variable $\overline{X} = \frac{1}{n}\sum_{i=1}^{n} X_i$ is also normally distributed as shown in formula (8.2):

$$\overline{X} \sim N\left(\mu, \frac{\sigma^2}{n}\right) \quad (8.2)$$

Consequently, the standardised sample mean Z-value is given by formula (8.3):

$$Z = \frac{\overline{X} - \mu}{\frac{\sigma}{\sqrt{n}}} \sim N(0, 1) \tag{8.3}$$

Given that we now know that the sample mean is normally distributed if the underlying values are normally distributed, we can solve a range of problems using the methods to be described in Chapter 9.

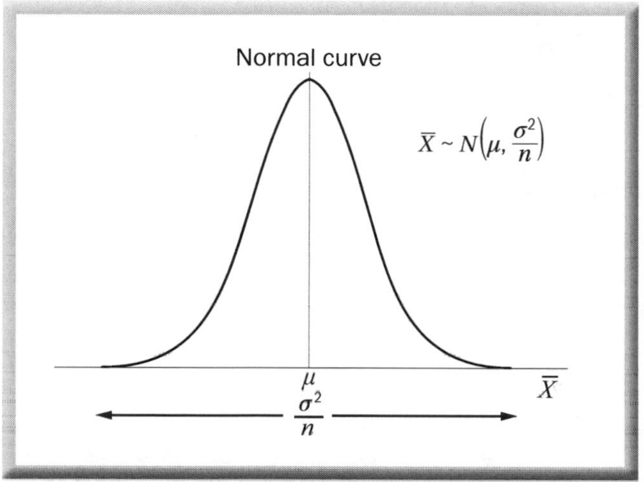

Figure 8.5: Normal density function of the sampling distribution of the mean

The following example intuitively illustrates the above results pertaining to the distribution of the sample mean by drawing multiple samples from a normally distributed population, calculating the means for each of these samples, and then constructing histograms for the mean.

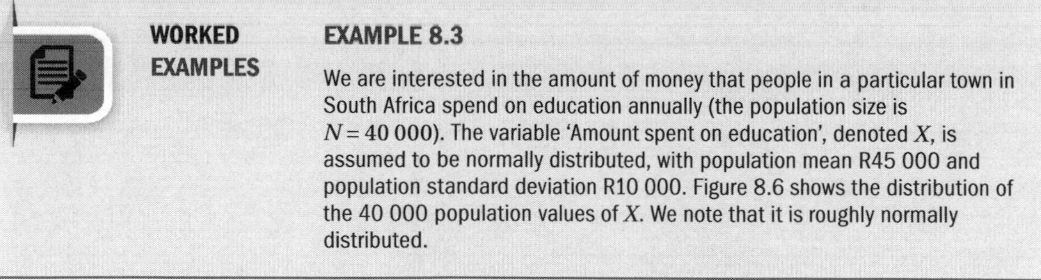

WORKED EXAMPLES

EXAMPLE 8.3

We are interested in the amount of money that people in a particular town in South Africa spend on education annually (the population size is $N = 40\,000$). The variable 'Amount spent on education', denoted X, is assumed to be normally distributed, with population mean R45 000 and population standard deviation R10 000. Figure 8.6 shows the distribution of the 40 000 population values of X. We note that it is roughly normally distributed.

Now, consider the problem of selecting 1 000 random samples of sizes n from the normally distributed population and then calculating the mean for each of these samples. We will create samples of size $n = 40$, $n = 10$, $n = 5$ and $n = 2$. The sampling distribution of the mean of the 1 000 samples for each different sample size is shown in Figures 8.7(a), (b), (c) and (d).

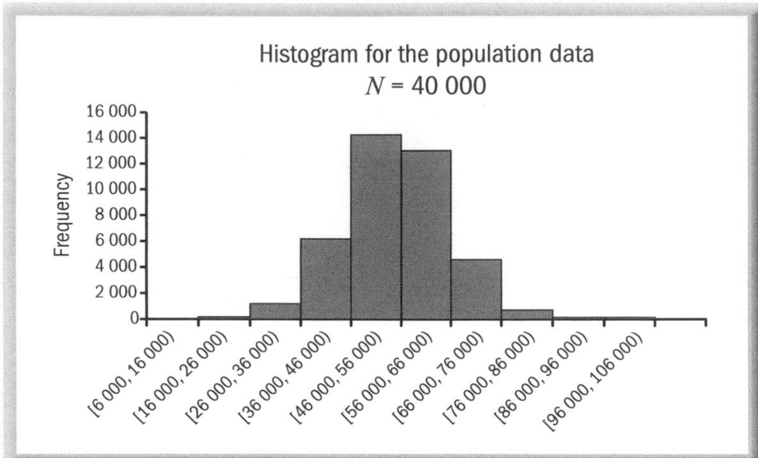

Figure 8.6: The histogram for the values of the variable, 'Amount spent on education' for the population

If we now sample 1 000 data points from this population, where each sample is of size n, then we can see from Figure 8.7 that the sampling distributions of the mean is approximately normal for sample distributions of size $n = 2, 5, 10$ and 40. From the histograms, we can see that the sample means are less spread out about the mean as the sample sizes increase.

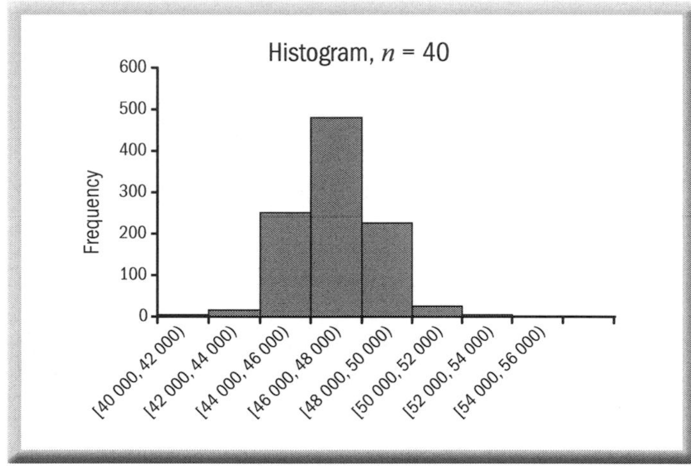

Figure 8.7(a): The histogram for the 1 000 values of the sample mean calculated from samples of size $n = 40$

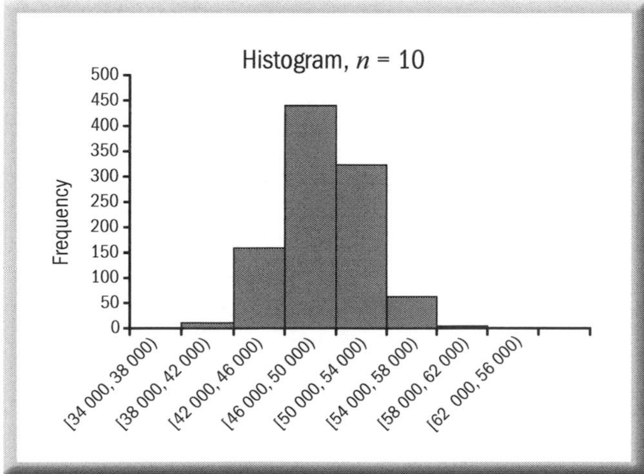

Figure 8.7(b): The histogram for the 1 000 values of the sample mean calculated from samples of size $n = 10$

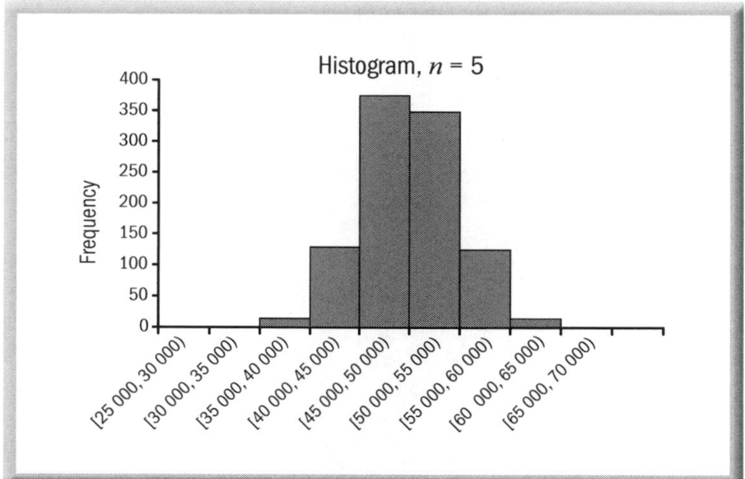

Figure 8.7(c): The histogram for the 1 000 values of the sample mean calculated from samples of size $n = 5$

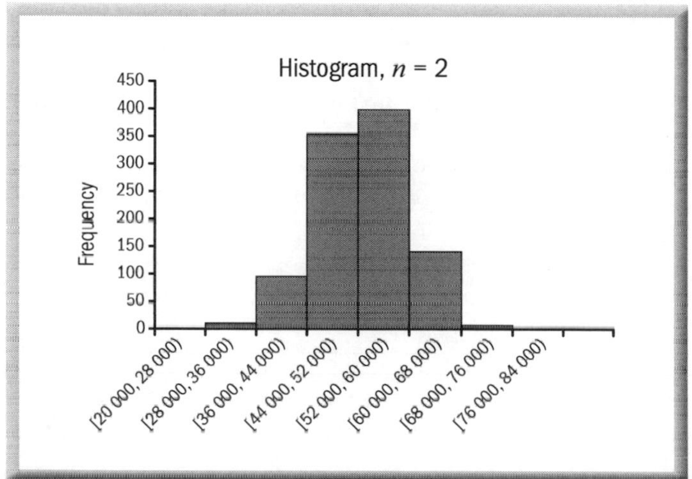

Figure 8.7(d): The histogram for the 1 000 values of the sample mean calculated from samples of size $n = 2$

NOTE

From this output, we can see that if we sample from a population that is normally distributed with mean μ and standard deviation σ, that is, $\overline{X} \sim N(\mu, \sigma^2)$, then:

- the sample distribution of the sample mean is also *approximately normally distributed*
- the expected value of the sampling distribution is approximately the same as the population mean of the sample data, μ
- the standard error of the sampling distribution gets smaller as the sample size increases.

These observations all agree with what we stated earlier: the sample mean's distribution is $\overline{X} \sim N\left(\mu, \frac{\sigma^2}{n}\right)$.

We have intuitively seen that the sample mean, $\overline{X}$, follows a normal distribution when the underlying data are also normal, so we now move on to probability calculations for the mean.

Probability calculations for the sample mean – samples drawn from a normal population

The probability calculations that we will discuss are almost identical to the calculations discussed in Section 7.2, except that the normally distributed variable is the sample mean and the variance of the variable is given by $\sigma_{\overline{X}}^2 = \frac{\sigma^2}{n}$. We now consider some examples of these probabilities.

WORKED EXAMPLES

EXAMPLE 8.4

Chubby Chuckers, a weight-loss society for the morbidly obese, runs a number of weight reduction centres in Gauteng province. From historical data, it is found that the weight of participants is normally distributed with a mean of 150 kg and a standard deviation of 25 kg. This can be written in mathematical notation as $X \sim N(150, 25^2)$, where X denotes the weight of an individual.

Calculate the probability that the average sample weight is greater than 160 kg when 25 participants are randomly selected for the sample.

The following information is given in this example: the population mean ($\mu = 150$), population standard deviation ($\sigma = 25$), sample size ($n = 25$) and standard error ($\sigma_{\overline{X}} = \frac{\sigma}{\sqrt{n}} = \frac{25}{\sqrt{25}} = 5$).

Figure 8.8 illustrates the probability that we need to determine in this example. We can use either the tables in Appendix C, or Excel's NORM.DIST() or NORM.S.DIST() functions to obtain this probability.

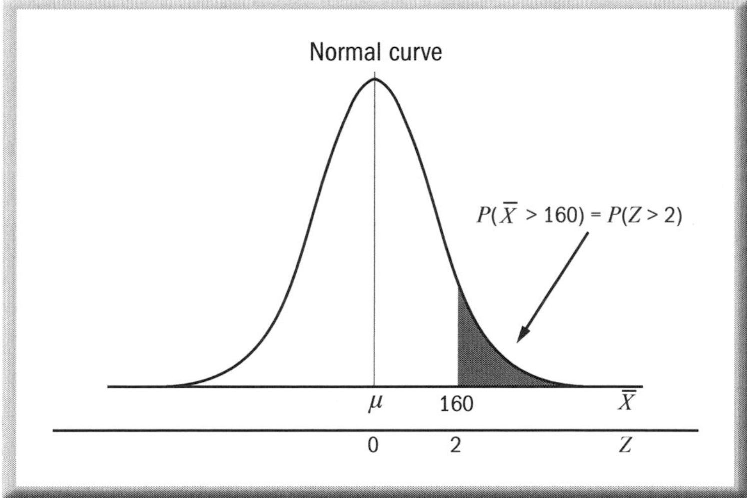

Figure 8.8: Graphical depiction of the probability $P(\overline{X} > 160)$

Note that we can calculate this probability because it states that the underlying variable, X, is normally distributed, that is, $X \sim N(150, 25^2)$. The sample mean based on $n = 25$ observations will therefore also be normally distributed with mean $\mu = 150$ and variance $\sigma_{\overline{X}}^2 = \frac{\sigma^2}{n} = \frac{25^2}{25} = 25$:

$$X \sim N\left(150, \frac{25^2}{25}\right)$$

We need to determine the probability that the sample mean weight is greater than 160 kg, so the probability of interest is $P(\overline{X} > 160)$. As with the probability calculations in Chapter 7, we first need to standardise this probability in order to use the tables given in Appendix C:

$$\begin{aligned} P(\overline{X} > 160) &= P\left(Z > \frac{160 - 150}{\sqrt{\frac{25^2}{25}}}\right) \\ &= P(Z > \frac{10}{5}) \\ &= P(Z > 2) \\ &= 1 - P(Z < 2) && \text{(using formula (7.4))} \\ &= 1 - 0.9772 && \text{(from Appendix C)} \\ &= 0.0228 \end{aligned}$$

Note that the standardisation in this example uses $\sigma_{\overline{X}}^2 = \frac{\sigma^2}{n}$ and not just σ^2. We can conclude that the probability that the sample mean of the 25 participants will exceed 160 kg is 0.0228.

As before, we can also use Excel's NORM.DIST() and NORM.S.DIST() functions to calculate these probabilities.

Figure 8.9 illustrates the Excel solution.

	A	B	C	D	E
1	**Sampling distribution - Example 8.4**				
2					
3		$P(\overline{X} > 160)$			
4					
5		Population:	$X \sim N(150, 25^2)$		
6					
7			Mean μ =	150	
8			Standard deviation =	25	
9					
10		Sample:			
11			n =	25	
12			$\overline{X}$ =	160	
13			$\sigma_{\overline{X}}$ =	5	=D8/D11^0.5
14					
15			z =	2	=(D12-D7)/D13
16			z =	2	=STANDARDIZE(D12,D7,D13)
17					
18			$P(\overline{X} > 160)$ =	0.022750132	=1-NORM.DIST(D12,D7,D13,TRUE)
19			$P(\overline{X} > 160)$ =	0.022750132	=1-NORM.S.DIST(D16,TRUE)
20					

Figure 8.9: Excel solution to Example 8.4

EXCEL SOLUTION

Population mean: Cell D7	Value
Population standard deviation: Cell D8	Value
Sample size n: Cell D11	Value
Sample mean: Cell D12	Value
Standard error of mean: Cell D13	Formula: =D8/D11^0.5
Z: Cell D15	Formula: =(D12-D7)/D13
Z: Cell D16	Formula: =STANDARDISE(D12,D7,D13)
$P(\overline{X} > 160)$: Cell D18	Formula: =1-NORM.DIST(D12,D7,D13,TRUE)
$P(\overline{X} > 160)$: Cell D19	Formula: =1-NORM.S.DIST(D16,TRUE)

NOTE

We have already described both Excel functions NORM.DIST() and NORM.S.DIST() in the previous chapter. In this example, they result in the same value, but make sure that you do not confuse them.

The Excel solutions can be obtained using either of the following two methods.

- **Method 1:** Use the NORM.DIST() function: =NORM.DIST(x,μ,$\sigma_{\overline{X}}$,TRUE). From Excel:

$$\begin{aligned} P(\overline{X} > 160) &= 1 - \text{NORM.DIST}\,(x,\mu,\sigma_{\overline{X}},\text{TRUE}) \\ &= 1 - \text{NORM.DIST}\,(160,150,5,\text{TRUE}) \\ &= 0.022750132. \end{aligned}$$

- **Method 2:** Use the NORM.S.DIST() function: =NORM.S.DIST(z,TRUE). From formula (8.3) we have:

$$z = \frac{160 - \mu}{\frac{\sigma}{\sqrt{n}}} = \frac{160 - 150}{\frac{25}{\sqrt{25}}} = \frac{10}{5} = 2$$

From Excel:

$$\begin{aligned} P(\overline{X} > 160) &= P(Z > 2) \\ &= 1 - \text{NORM.S.DIST}(z) \\ &= 1 - \text{NORM.S.DIST}(2) \\ &= 0.022750132 \end{aligned}$$

As expected, both methods result in the same answer to the problem of calculating the required probability.

INTERPRETATION Based on a random sample, the probability that the sample mean is greater than 160 kg is 0.0228 or 2.28%.

WORKED EXAMPLES

EXAMPLE 8.5

Calculate the probability that the sample mean lies between 140 kg and 158 kg for the population distribution described in Example 8.4.

Once again, the following information is provided for this example: the population mean is $\mu = 150$ and the population standard deviation is $\sigma_{\overline{X}} = \frac{\sigma}{\sqrt{n}} = \frac{25}{\sqrt{25}} = 5$. This example requires that we find the probability $P(140 < \overline{X} < 158)$.

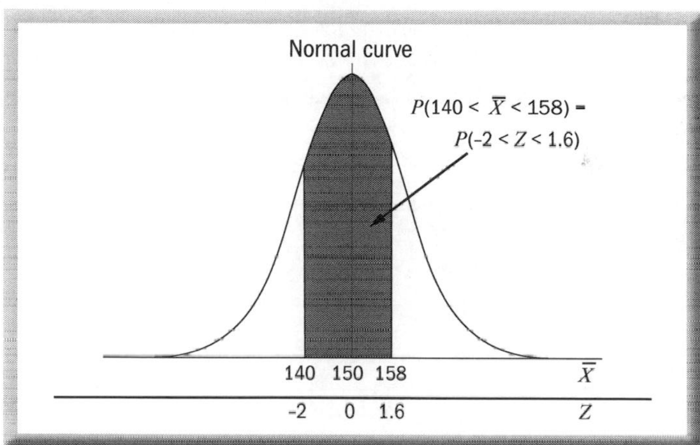

Figure 8.10: Graphical depiction of the probability $P(140 < \overline{X} < 158)$

Using the techniques discussed in Chapter 7 and the tables in Appendix C, we obtain the probability as follows:

$$P(140 < \overline{X} < 158) = P\left(\frac{140 - 150}{\frac{25}{\sqrt{25}}} < Z < \frac{158 - 150}{\frac{25}{\sqrt{25}}}\right)$$

$$= P\left(\frac{-10}{5} < Z < \frac{8}{5}\right)$$

$$= P(-2 < Z < 1.6)$$

$$= P(Z < 1.6) - P(Z < -2) \quad \text{(from formula (7.5))}$$

$$= 0.9452 - 0.0228 \quad \text{(from Appendix C)}$$

$$= 0.9224$$

In other words, the probability that the sample mean of the 25 participants will lie between 140 kg and 158 kg is 0.9224.

Figure 8.11 illustrates the Excel solution.

	A	B	C	D	E
1	**Sampling distribution - Example 8.5**				
2					
3		$P(140 < \overline{X} < 158)$			
4					
5		Population:	Mean μ =	150	
6		$X \sim N(150, 25^2)$	Standard deviation =	25	
7					
8		Sample:	n =	25	
9			$\sigma_{\overline{X}}$ =	5	=D6/D8^0.5
10			x_1 =	140	
11			x_2 =	158	
12			z_1 =	−2	=(D10-D5)/D9
13			z_2 =	1.6	=(D11-D5)/D9
14					
15			$P(140 < \overline{X} < 158)$ =	0.922450576	=NORM.DIST(D11,D5,D9,TRUE)-NORM.DIST(D10,D5,D9,TRUE)
16			$P(-2 < Z < 1.6)$ =	0.922450576	=NORM.S.DIST(D13,TRUE)-NORM.S.DIST(D12,TRUE)

Figure 8.11: Excel solution to Example 8.5

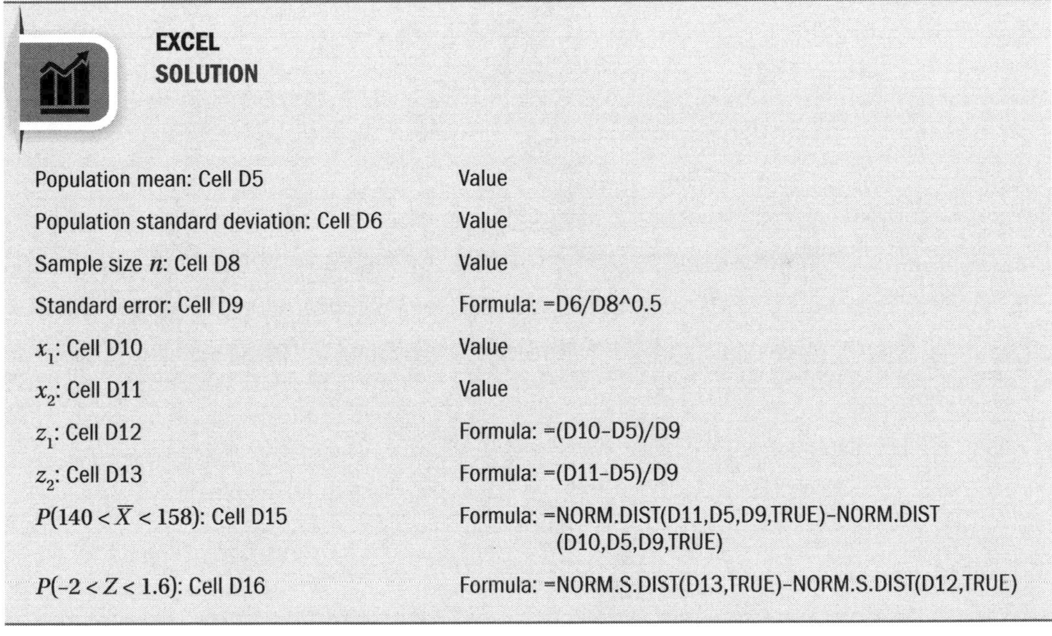

EXCEL SOLUTION

Population mean: Cell D5	Value
Population standard deviation: Cell D6	Value
Sample size n: Cell D8	Value
Standard error: Cell D9	Formula: =D6/D8^0.5
x_1: Cell D10	Value
x_2: Cell D11	Value
z_1: Cell D12	Formula: =(D10-D5)/D9
z_2: Cell D13	Formula: =(D11-D5)/D9
$P(140 < \overline{X} < 158)$: Cell D15	Formula: =NORM.DIST(D11,D5,D9,TRUE)-NORM.DIST (D10,D5,D9,TRUE)
$P(-2 < Z < 1.6)$: Cell D16	Formula: =NORM.S.DIST(D13,TRUE)-NORM.S.DIST(D12,TRUE)

Figure 8.11 illustrates the probability that we are required to calculate for this example. Again, we can use Excel to obtain this probability by using either the NORM.DIST() or NORM.S.DIST() functions:

- **Method 1**: Using the NORM.DIST() function: =NORM.DIST(x,μ,$\sigma_{\overline{X}}$,TRUE). From Excel:

$$P(140 < \overline{X} < 158) = \text{NORM.DIST}\ (x,\mu,\sigma_{\overline{X}},\text{TRUE}) - \text{NORM.DIST}\ (x,\mu,\sigma_{\overline{X}},\text{TRUE})$$
$$= 0.922450576$$

- **Method 2**: Using the NORM.S.DIST() function: =NORM.S.DIST(Z). From formula (8.3) we have:

$$z_1 = \frac{140 - \mu}{\frac{\sigma}{\sqrt{n}}} = \frac{140 - 150}{\frac{25}{\sqrt{25}}} = \frac{-10}{5} = -2$$

And:

$$z_2 = \frac{158 - \mu}{\frac{\sigma}{\sqrt{n}}} = \frac{158 - 150}{\frac{25}{\sqrt{25}}} = \frac{8}{5} = 1.6$$

From Excel:

$$P(140 < \overline{X} < 158) = P(-2 < Z < 1.6)$$
$$= \text{NORM.S.DIST}(1.6) - \text{NORM.S.DIST}(-2)$$
$$= 0.922450576$$

Both methods provide the same answer to the problem of calculating the required probability.

INTERPRETATION Based on a random sample, the probability that the sample mean is between 140 kg and 158 kg is 0.9224 or 92.24%.

8.2.4 Sampling from a non-normal population

In the previous section, we sampled from a population that was normally distributed. We stated that the sampling distribution of the sample means will be normally distributed with mean μ and standard deviation $\sigma_{\overline{X}}$. However, what if the data does not come from the normal distribution? It can be shown that if we select a random sample from a non-normal distribution, then the *sampling mean will be approximately normal* with mean μ and standard deviation $\sigma_{\overline{X}}$ if the sample size (n) is sufficiently large. In most cases, the value of n should be at least 30 for non-symmetric distributions and at least 20 for symmetric distributions, before we trust this approximation. This relationship is already represented by formula (8.2).

This leads to an important concept in statistics called the **Central Limit Theorem.** The Central Limit Theorem provides us with a shortcut to determining the sampling distribution of the mean. It does this by providing the distribution and other properties of this sampling distribution (usually the mean and the standard error, which is computed from the sampling variance). Using this information, we can then also obtain probabilities associated with the sample means.

NOTE

THE CENTRAL LIMIT THEOREM

The Central Limit Theorem states that if we draw our samples from a population with mean μ and variance σ^2, and *any arbitrary population distribution*, the sampling distribution of the sample means will be approximately normal when the sample size, n, is large:

$$\overline{X} \sim N\left(\mu, \frac{\sigma^2}{n}\right), \text{ if } n \text{ is large}$$

Or alternatively:

$$Z = \frac{\overline{X} - \mu}{\frac{\sigma}{\sqrt{n}}} \sim N(0, 1), \text{ if } n \text{ is large}$$

(Increasing the sample size improves the approximation to the normal distribution.)

Central Limit Theorem Whenever a random sample is taken from any distribution with mean μ and variance σ^2 then the sample mean will be approximately normally distributed with mean μ and variance $\frac{\sigma^2}{n}$.

Probability calculations for the sample mean – samples drawn from a non-normal population

If the mean is approximately normally distributed, we can solve a range of problems using the methods described in Chapter 7. The standardised sample mean Z-value is already given by formula (8.3).

WORKED EXAMPLES

EXAMPLE 8.6

Consider drawing a sample of 50 electrical components from a production run and then testing the lifetime of these components. Historically, the components' average lifetime was found to be 950 hours with a standard deviation of 25 hours. The population data are right-skewed and therefore cannot be considered to be normally distributed. Calculate the probability that the sample mean is less than 958 hours.

Since the sample size is reasonably large (in this case $n = 50$), we will apply the Central Limit Theorem and assume that the sampling mean distribution is approximately normally distributed. From formula (8.2), we have $\overline{X} \sim N(\mu, \frac{\sigma^2}{n}) = N(950, \frac{25^2}{50})$.

We now need to determine the probability $P(\overline{X} < 958)$ using the information provided: the population mean is $\mu = 950$, the population standard deviation is $\sigma = 25$, the sample size is $n = 50$ and the standard error of the mean must therefore be $\sigma_{\overline{X}} = \frac{\sigma}{\sqrt{n}} = \frac{25}{\sqrt{50}} = 3.535533906$. Figure 8.12 illustrates the probability that we need to find in this example.

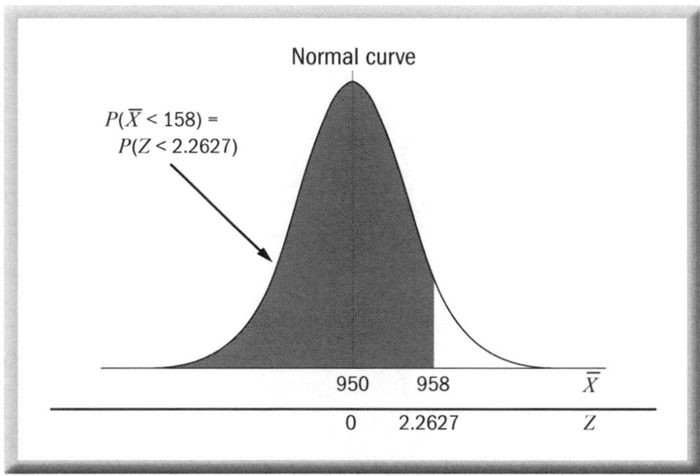

Figure 8.12: Graphical depiction of the probability $P(\overline{X} < 958)$

By standardising the probability $P(\overline{X} < 958)$ using the information provided and then using the tables in Appendix C, we can arrive at the probability:

$$P(\overline{X} < 958) = P\left(Z < \frac{958 - 950}{\frac{25}{\sqrt{50}}}\right)$$

$$= P(Z < 2.26) \qquad \text{(using Appendix C)}$$

$$= 0.9881$$

The probability that the mean lifetime of any 50 randomly selected components is less than 958 hours is thus 0.9881.

	A	B	C	D	E
1	**Sampling distribution – Example 8.6**				
2		$P(\overline{X} < 958)$			
3		Population:	Mean μ =	950	
4		$\overline{X} \sim N\left(950, \frac{25^2}{50}\right)$	Standard deviation, σ =	25	
5					
6		Sample:	n =	50	
7			$\sigma_{\overline{X}}$ =	3.5355339	=D4/D6^0.5
8			$\overline{X}$ =	958	
9			Z =	2.2627417	=(D8-D3)/D7
10					
11			$P(\overline{X} < 958)$ =	0.9881742	=NORM.DIST(D8,D3,D7,TRUE)
12			$P(Z < 2.2627417)$ =	0.9881742	=NORM.S.DIST(D9,TRUE)

Figure 8.13: Excel solution to Example 8.6

EXCEL SOLUTION

Population mean: Cell D3	Value
Population standard deviation: Cell D4	Value
Sample size n: Cell D6	Value
Standard error: Cell D7	Formula: =D4/D6^0.5
Sample mean: Cell D8	Value
Z: Cell D9	Formula: =(D8–D3)/D7
$P(\overline{X} < 958)$: Cell D11	Formula: =NORM.DIST(D8,D3,D7,TRUE)
$P(Z < 2.2627417)$: Cell D12	Formula: =NORM.S.DIST(D9,TRUE)

The Excel solution for this probability is found by using either one of the following two methods.

- **Method 1**: Using the NORM.DIST() function: =NORM.DIST(958,μ,$\sigma_{\overline{X}}$,TRUE). From Excel:

$$P(\overline{X} < 958) = \text{NORM.DIST}\ (958,\mu,\sigma_{\overline{X}},\text{TRUE}) \\ = 0.988174192$$

- **Method 2**: Using the NORM.S.DIST() function: =NORM.S.DIST(z). From formula (8.3) we have:

$$z = \frac{958 - \mu}{\frac{\sigma}{\sqrt{n}}} = \frac{958 - 950}{\frac{25}{\sqrt{50}}} = \frac{8}{3.535533906} = 2.2627417$$

From Excel:

$$P(\overline{X} < 958) = P(Z < 2.2627417) \\ = \text{NORM.S.DIST}(2.2627417) \\ = 0.988174192$$

Both methods provided the same answer to the problem of calculating the required probability.

INTERPRETATION Based on a random sample, the probability that the sample mean is less than 958 hours is 0.988174192 or 98.82%.

8.2.5 Sampling distribution of the proportion

Suppose that we are interested in a variable that has only two possible values, for example, the variable might be the following question in a consumer survey: 'Do you like product A?' The response for this variable is only yes or no, and we want to determine the proportion of respondents that choose yes and the proportion that choose no. From exhaustive historical data, it is found that 40% of the people surveyed preferred product A. We will define this as the *population proportion*, π, of people who prefer product A. If we then took a random sample from this population, it would be unlikely that exactly 40% would choose product A but, given sampling error, it is likely that this proportion would only be slightly less or slightly more than 40%. If we continued to draw samples from this population and calculated the sample proportions, each sample would have its own individual sample proportion value. If we collected all these proportion values calculated from the multiple samples drawn from the population, it would form the sampling distribution of the sample proportion of people that chose product A.

The sampling distribution for the sample proportion (denoted p) is also approximated using the normal distribution where formula (8.4) represents the *mean of the sampling distribution for the proportion*:

$$\mu_p = \pi \tag{8.4}$$

Formula (8.5) represents the standard deviation of the sampling distribution for the proportion:

$$\sigma_p = \sqrt{\frac{\pi(1-\pi)}{n}} \tag{8.5}$$

This normal approximation for the sampling distribution of the proportion is typically only valid if:

- the probability of success, π, is not too close to 0 or 1
- the sample size, n, is reasonably large
- the products $n\pi$ and $n(1-\pi)$ are at least 5.

If these conditions hold, the sample proportion's approximate distribution can be expressed as:

$$p \sim N\left(\pi, \frac{\pi(1-\pi)}{n}\right) \tag{8.6}$$

The standardised sample mean Z-value is given by modifying formula (8.3) to give formula (8.7):

$$Z = \frac{p-\pi}{\sqrt{\frac{\pi(1-\pi)}{n}}} \tag{8.7}$$

Probability calculations for the sample proportion

We can now conduct probability calculations for the sample proportion in the same way as for the sample mean.

WORKED EXAMPLES

EXAMPLE 8.7

It is known that 25% of workers in a factory own a personal computer. Find the probability that at least 26% of a *random sample of 80 workers* will own a personal computer. In this example, we have the population proportion $\pi = 0.25$ and sample size $n = 80$. The problem requires you to calculate $P(p > 0.26)$.

From formula (8.5), the standard error for the sampling distribution of the proportion is:

$$\sigma_p = \sqrt{\frac{\pi(1-\pi)}{n}} = \sqrt{\frac{0.25(1-0.25)}{80}} = 0.04841$$

Substituting this value into formula (8.7) gives the standardized version of the value 0.26:

$$z = \frac{0.26 - \pi}{\sqrt{\frac{\pi(1-\pi)}{n}}} = \frac{0.26 - 0.25}{0.04841} = 0.206559$$

We therefore have that $p \sim N\left(\pi, \frac{\pi(1-\pi)}{n}\right) = N(0.25, (0.04841)^2)$ and the probability is then:

$$\begin{aligned} P(p > 0.26) &= P\left(Z > \frac{0.26 - 0.25}{0.04841}\right) \\ &= P(Z > 0.21) \\ &= 1 - P(Z < 0.21) && \text{(from formula (7.4))} \\ &= 1 - 0.5832 && \text{(from Appendix C)} \\ &= 0.4168 \end{aligned}$$

This answer required that we round the Z score off to two decimal places. To obtain a more accurate answer we use Excel. The Excel solution is shown in Figure 8.14.

	A	B	C	D	E
1	**Sampling distribution - Example 8.7**				
2		$P(p > 0.26)$			
3		Population:	π =	0.25	
4					
5		Sample:	p =	0.26	
6			n =	80	
7					
8			σ_p =	0.048412292	=SQRT(D3*(1-D3)/D6)
9					
10			z =	0.206559111	=(D5-D3)/D8
11					
12			$P(p > 0.26)$ =	0.418177098	=1-NORM.DIST(D5,D3,D8,TRUE)
13					
14			$P(Z > 0.206559111)$ =	0.418177098	=1-NORM.S.DIST(D10,TRUE)

Figure 8.14: Excel solution to Example 8.7

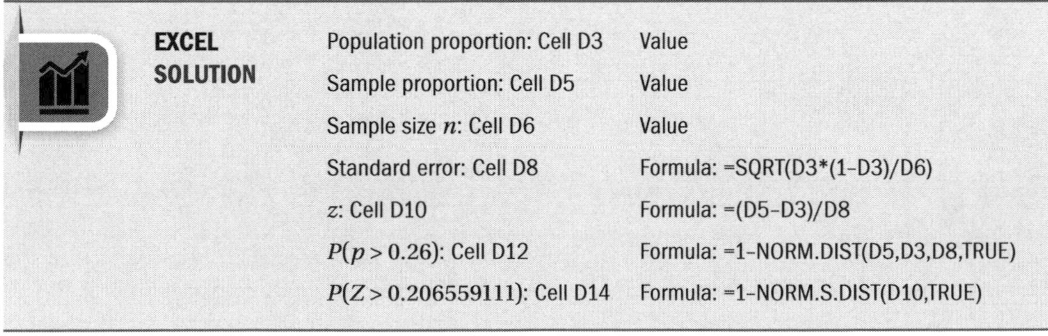

EXCEL SOLUTION

Population proportion: Cell D3	Value
Sample proportion: Cell D5	Value
Sample size n: Cell D6	Value
Standard error: Cell D8	Formula: =SQRT(D3*(1-D3)/D6)
z: Cell D10	Formula: =(D5-D3)/D8
$P(p > 0.26)$: Cell D12	Formula: =1-NORM.DIST(D5,D3,D8,TRUE)
$P(Z > 0.206559111)$: Cell D14	Formula: =1-NORM.S.DIST(D10,TRUE)

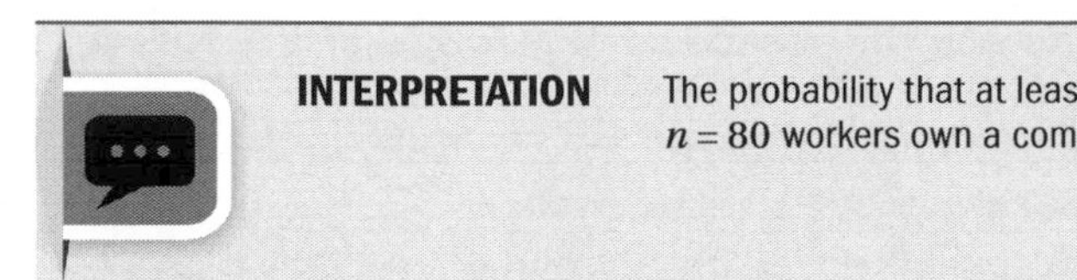

INTERPRETATION The probability that at least 26% of a randomly selected sample of $n = 80$ workers own a computer is 41.82%.

8.3 Using Excel to generate a sample from a sampling distribution

We can use Excel to generate random samples from a range of probability distributions, including uniform, normal, binomial and Poisson distributions. To generate a random sample, select the 'Data' tab and then select 'Data Analysis' in the 'Analysis' group. This will bring up the 'Data Analysis' toolkit as illustrated in Figure 8.15.

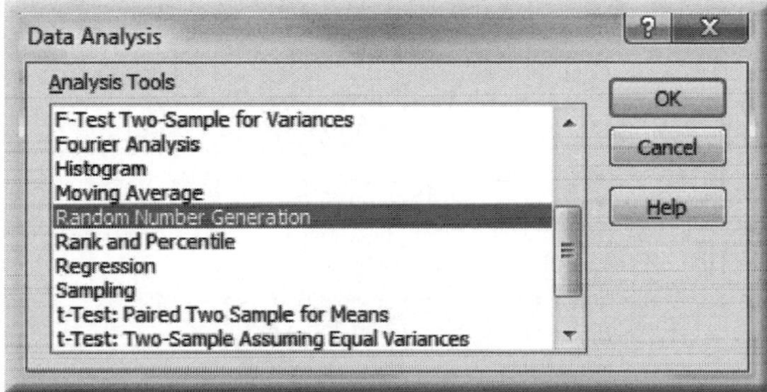

Figure 8.15: Excel's 'Data analysis' toolkit – selecting 'Random Number Generation'

In the 'Data Analysis' toolkit, select 'Random Number Generation' and click OK. You will then see the window displayed in Figure 8.16. From this window, we can select various options to generate random variates from specified distributions.

Figure 8.16: Excel's 'Data Analysis' toolkit – the 'Random Number Generation' window

The procedure to generate random variates using the 'Random number generation' window in Figure 8.16 is as follows:

- Input the number of variables (or samples) in the 'Number of Variables' field. This will indicate how many *columns* of random numbers are generated in the output.
- Input the number of data values in each sample in the 'Number of Random Numbers' field. This will indicate how many *rows* of random numbers are generated in the output.
- Using the 'Distribution' drop-down list, you can select the distribution from which you want to generate values. Possible distributions include the uniform, normal, binomial and Poisson distributions.
- Depending on the distribution chosen, a different number of fields will appear in which you can type the parameters of that distribution. For example, if you choose 'Normal', two fields will appear where you can specify the values of μ and σ.
- Decide on where the results should appear (output range).
- Click OK.

In the next example, we look at how we can use these random number generation tools to artificially generate values from a specified distribution. We then use this to explore an artificial way of sampling from a population of values to illustrate the sampling distribution of the mean.

WORKED EXAMPLES

EXAMPLE 8.8

Consider the problem of sampling from a population that consists of the salaries of public sector employees employed by some government agency. Historical data suggests that the population annual salary is normally distributed with mean of R45 000 and standard deviation of R1 000. We can use Excel to generate $J = 1\ 000$ random samples; each sample containing $n = 10$ data values. To visualise the sampling distribution of the mean in this scenario, we will perform the following calculations.

a) For each sample generated, calculate the mean of the sample of values.

b) Plot a histogram of the sample means calculated in the previous step. This represents the approximate sampling distribution for the sample mean.

a) Generate a data set with $J = 1\ 000$ rows (each row represents a sample drawn from the population) and $n = 10$ columns (each column represents the individual in the sample). To generate this many rows and columns, we will specify the values as shown in Figure 8.17.

Note that for this example we interpret the labels 'Number of Variables' and 'Number of Random Variables' listed on the window to mean columns and rows, respectively.

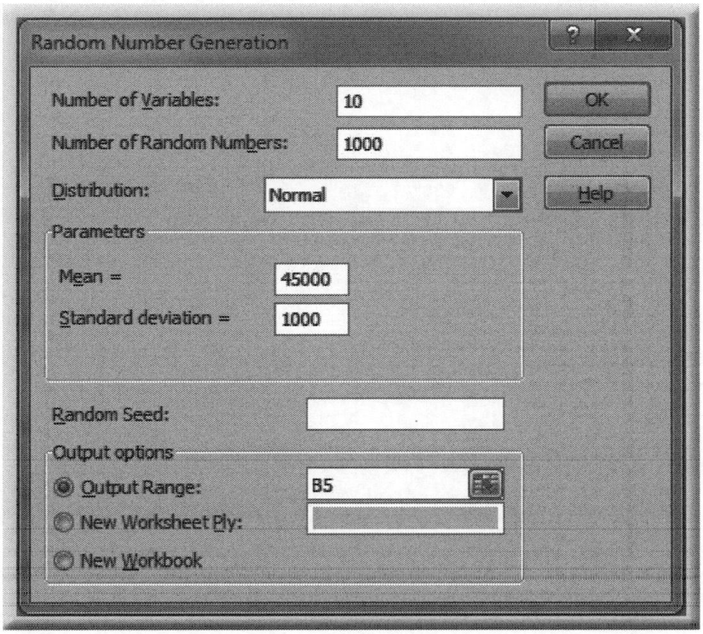

Random Number Generation

Number of Variables:	10	OK
Number of Random Numbers:	1000	Cancel
Distribution:	Normal	Help
Parameters		
Mean =	45000	
Standard deviation =	1000	
Random Seed:		
Output options		
Output Range:	B5	
New Worksheet Ply:		
New Workbook		

Figure 8.17: Generate $J = 1\,000$ rows and $n = 10$ columns from a $N(45\,000, 1\,000^2)$ distribution

From Excel, select the 'Data' tab, select 'Data Analysis' and then 'Random Number Generation'. Specify the values $n = 10$ in the 'Number of Variables' (the columns) and $J = 1\,000$ in the 'Number of Random Numbers' (the rows).

Select 'Normal' from the 'Distribution' drop-down list and specify mean = 45 000 and standard deviation = 1 000.

Set the output range to Cell B5 and finally click OK.

The J samples are located in the rows of the table of values, for example, Sample 1: B5:K5, Sample 2: B6:K6 and Sample 1 000: B1004:K1004.

b) Calculate J sample means:
Calculate the sample mean using the Excel function AVERAGE(), for example, from Sample 1: mean = average(B5:K5), Sample 2: mean = average(B6:K6) and up to Sample 1 000 mean = average(B1004:K1004).

Figure 8.18 illustrates the first four samples and their sample means.

	A	B	C	D	E	F	G	H	I	J	K	L	M
1	Sampling distribution - Example 8.8												
2													
3		Population											
4												Sample means	
5	Sample 1	45719.23	44242.39	44579.55	43604.84	44768.57	45924.6	45436.89	45115.12	43837.27	46284.81	44951.33	=AVERAGE(B5:K5)
6	Sample 2	43966.96	45915.49	45081.68	45822.52	45330.38	44481.99	43875.67	44926.92	44694.72	43935.8	44803.21	=AVERAGE(B6:K6)
7	Sample 3	43138.58	44687.9	44077.04	44003.32	46109.2	46232.94	45209.33	43723.7	45230.49	42862.2	44527.47	=AVERAGE(B7:K7)
8	Sample 4	44917.56	44140.32	44980.61	44978.92	44531.84	44635.73	44050.72	46774.81	44633.69	47270.23	45091.44	=AVERAGE(B8:K8)

Figure 8.18: The randomly generated samples and their sample means

c) Create histogram bins and plot the histogram of the sample means:

	L	M	N	O	P
4	**Sample means**				
5	44951.33	=AVERAGE(B5:K5)			
6	44803.21	=AVERAGE(B6:K6)	Min =	44084.78	=MIN(L5:L1004)
7	44527.47	=AVERAGE(B7:K7)	Max =	46430.19	=MAX(L5:L1004)
8	45091.44	=AVERAGE(B8:K8)			
9	45219.39	=AVERAGE(B9:K9)	**BIN**		
10	44986.64	=AVERAGE(B10:K10)	44000		
11	45319.73	=AVERAGE(B11:K11)	44500		
12	44805.16	=AVERAGE(B12:K12)	45000		
13	44552.05	=AVERAGE(B13:K13)	45500		
14	45518.99	=AVERAGE(B14:K14)	46000		
15	45356.63	=AVERAGE(B15:K15)	46500		
16	⋮	⋮			

Figure 8.19: The bins used in creating the frequency distribution and histogram of the sampling distribution of the mean

We can see from the Excel spreadsheet that the smallest and largest sample means are 44 084.78 and 46 430.19 respectively. Based on these two values, we then determine the histogram bin size as 44 000 with step size of 500 (that is, 44 000, 44 500, ..., 46 500), as illustrated in Figure 8.19.

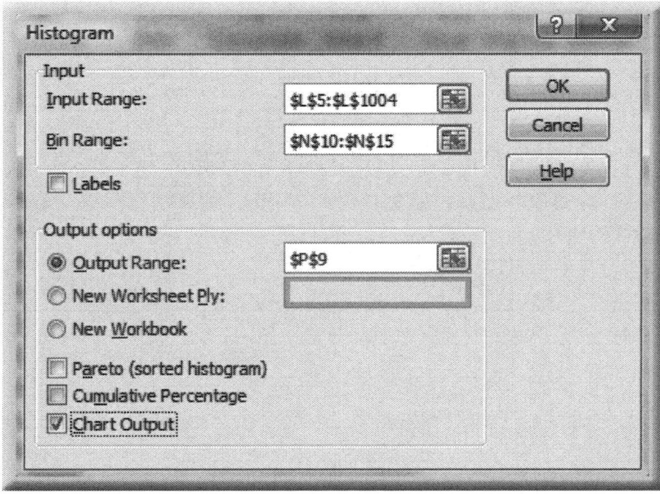

Figure 8.20: The histogram window for in the 'Data Analysis' toolkit

To create the frequency distribution, select 'Data Analysis' under the 'Data' tab, click on 'Histogram' and select the values as illustrated in Figure 8.20.

Figures 8.21 and 8.22 illustrate the frequency distribution and corresponding histogram.

	M	N	O	P	Q	R
5						
6		MIN =	44084.78	=MIN(L5:L1004)		
7		MAX =	46430.19	=MAX(L5:L1004		
8						
9		**BIN**		*Bin*	*Frequency*	
10		44000		44000	2	
11		44500		44500	57	
12		45000		45000	460	
13		45500		45500	428	
14		46000		46000	52	
15		46500		46500	1	
16				More	0	
17						

Figure 8.21: The frequency distribution for the means: the approximate sampling distribution of the sample mean

For the bar chart to look like a histogram, set the bar gap width equal to zero.

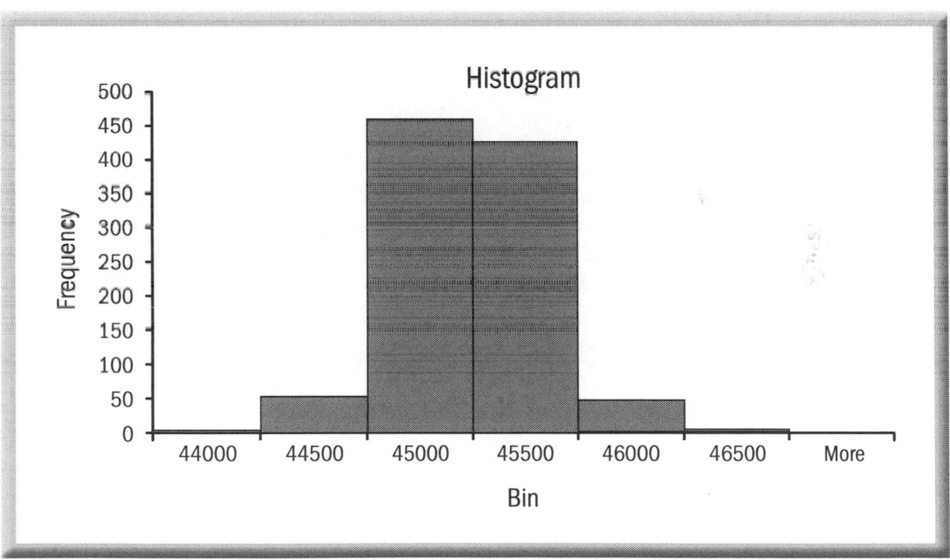

Figure 8.22: The histogram of the sample means

From the histogram, we can see that the histogram values are centred about the population mean value of R45 000. If we repeated this exercise for different sample sizes, *n*, we would find that the range/variation of the sample mean values calculated would reduce as the sample sizes increase.

SUMMARY

In this chapter, we introduced the important statistical concept of sampling and explored methods that will be useful for constructing estimators in the next chapter. We have shown that the Central Limit Theorem is a very important theorem that allows us to apply a range of statistical tests.

We showed how the Central Limit Theorem can eliminate the need to construct a sampling distribution by examining all possible samples that might be drawn from a population. The Central Limit Theorem allows us to determine the sampling distribution by using the population mean and variance values, or estimates of these, obtained from a sample.

From the Central Limit Theorem, we know that the sampling distribution can be approximated by the normal distribution.

Using the sampling distribution of the sample mean, we can answer questions pertaining to the probabilities related to the potential values of the sample mean. We will implement these probability concepts in a practical way in the next few chapters. These concepts form the basis for constructing and calculating confidence intervals and hypothesis tests for the population mean.

KEY TERMS

Central Limit Theorem
Cluster sampling
Random sample
Sampling distribution
Sampling distribution of the mean
Sampling distribution of the proportion
Sampling distribution of the variance
Sampling error
Simple random sampling
Standard error of the mean
Standard error of the proportion
Stratified random sampling
Systematic random sampling
Unbiased

FORMULA SUMMARY

$$\sigma_{\overline{X}} = \frac{\sigma}{\sqrt{n}} \tag{8.1}$$

$$\overline{X} \sim N\left(\mu, \frac{\sigma^2}{n}\right) \tag{8.2}$$

$$Z = \frac{\overline{X} - \mu}{\frac{\sigma}{\sqrt{n}}} \tag{8.3}$$

$$\mu_p = \pi \tag{8.4}$$

$$\sigma_p = \sqrt{\frac{\pi(1-\pi)}{n}} \tag{8.5}$$

$$p \sim N\left(\pi, \frac{\pi(1-\pi)}{n}\right) \tag{8.6}$$

$$Z = \frac{p-\pi}{\sqrt{\frac{\pi(1-\pi)}{n}}} \tag{8.7}$$

EXERCISES

8.1 The following five people made claims for the amounts shown in Table 8.1.

Table 8.1: Insurance claims for five people

PERSON	1	2	3	4	5
INSURANCE CLAIM (RAND)	500	400	900	1 000	1 200

Assume that these five people form the *entire population* of individuals with insurance claims. A sample of two people is to be taken at random, with replacement, from the five. Derive the sampling distribution of the mean and confirm the following.

a) Show that μ is equal to the mean of all the $\overline{X}$ statistics calculated from each possible sample drawn.

b) Show that the population standard deviation of the sample mean, $\sigma_{\overline{X}}$, is equal to the population standard deviation of the population divided by the square root of n, i.e. show that $\sigma_{\overline{X}}, = \frac{\sigma}{\sqrt{n}}$.

8.2 If X is a normal random variable with mean 10 and standard deviation 2, i.e. $X \sim N(10, 4)$. State the sampling distribution of the sample mean $\overline{X}$ for samples of the following size. Compare these three distributions with one another. What do you notice?

a) 2

b) 4

c) 16

8.3 If X is any random variable with mean = 63 and standard deviation = 10, state the sampling distribution of the sample mean $\overline{X}$ for samples of the following size.

a) 40

b) 60

c) 100

8.4 Use an Excel spreadsheet to generate a random sample of 100 observations from a normal distribution with a mean of 10 and a standard deviation of 4. Calculate the sample mean and standard deviation. Why are these values different from the population values?

8.5 The weights of 10 000 items are normally distributed and the distribution has a mean of 115 kg and a standard deviation of 3 kg.

a) Estimate how many items have weights of between 115 kg and 118 kg.
b) If you have to pick one item at random from the whole 10 000 items, how confident would you be in predicting that its value would lie between 112 kg and 115 kg?
c) If a sample of 10 items were drawn from the 10 000 items, what would be the standard error of the sample mean? What would be the standard error if the sample consisted of 40 items?

8.6 A sample of 100 was taken from a population with $\pi = 0.5$. Find the probability that the sample proportion will lie between:

a) 0.4 and 0.6
b) 0.35 and 0.65
c) 0.5 and 0.65.

8.7 From a parliamentary constituency, a sample of 100 were asked whether they would vote for the African National Party or Democratic Conservatives. It is thought that 40% of the constituency will favour the African National Party. Find the approximate probability that in an election, the African National Party will win (assume only a two party vote and that a party wins if they collect more than 50% of the vote).

8.8 The annual income of doctors constitutes a highly positive skewed distribution. The population has an unknown mean and a standard deviation of R10 000. An estimate of the population mean is to be made using the sample mean. This estimate must be within R1 000 either side of the true mean.

a) If $n = 100$, find the probability that the estimate will meet the desired accuracy.
b) If $n = 625$, find the probability that the estimate will meet the desired accuracy.

8.9 The average number of Xerox copies made in a working day in a certain office is 356 with a standard deviation of 55. It costs the firm 3c per copy. During a working period of 121 days, what is the probability that the average cost per day is more than R11.10?

CHAPTER 9

ESTIMATION: POINT ESTIMATORS AND CONFIDENCE INTERVALS

CHAPTER CONTENTS

OVERVIEW

In this chapter, we discuss the concept of estimating population parameters by using sample information. We briefly discuss these estimators' properties and define the two main types of estimators: *point estimators* (estimators that estimate the population quantity using only one value) and *interval estimators* (estimators that estimate population quantities using a range or interval of possible values). The calculation of the point estimators will be familiar since many of these statistics are simply the sample versions of their population counterparts and were encountered in earlier chapters. The intervals, on the other hand, are new and will require the tools developed in Chapters 6, 7 and 8, specifically the concepts of the sampling distribution and standard errors of statistics.

LEARNING OBJECTIVES

On completing this chapter, you should be able to:

- calculate point estimates for population parameters from one or two populations
- calculate confidence intervals when the population standard deviation is known and unknown
- determine sample sizes
- solve problems using Microsoft Excel.

9.1 An introduction to estimation

9.1.1 Introduction

In the previous chapters, we explored the sampling distribution of the sample mean and proportion, and stated that we can consider the distributions of these quantities to be normal with population parameters μ and σ^2. For many populations, it is likely that we do not know the value of the population mean (or proportion). Fortunately, we can use the sample mean (or proportion) to provide an estimate of the population value, i.e. we can estimate these population quantities using information provided in a sample. This is called **estimation**. The objective of estimation is to determine the approximate value of a population parameter on the basis of a sample statistic. The two methods described in this section are *point* estimates and *interval* estimates.

- **Point estimators** are sample statistics that attempt to express the value of the population parameter using only a single number.
- **Confidence interval estimates** provide a range of possible values that the true parameter value can assume along with the degree of confidence that the parameter value lies within the interval. For example, we often talk about a 95% or 90% confidence interval for a parameter value, i.e. the probability that the parameter value lies within the given interval is 0.95 or 0.9, respectively. This method of estimation relies on the sampling distribution of the statistics being used.

Figure 9.1 illustrates how the unknown population mean, μ, is estimated by a point estimator and also by a confidence interval estimator. Note in the figure that the point estimator, $\overline{X}$, based on sample data is not exactly the same as the true population value. This is because $\overline{X}$ is only a sample approximation of the true value, μ. Note also that the value of $\overline{X}$, and the position and width of the interval estimator, will change from one sample to another.

Estimate An indication of the value of an unknown population quantity based on sample values.

Point estimate Any single quantity calculated from the sample data that is used to provide information about a population parameter.

$(1 - \alpha) \times 100\%$ confidence interval Provides an estimated range of values that includes an unknown population parameter with probability $1 - \alpha$.

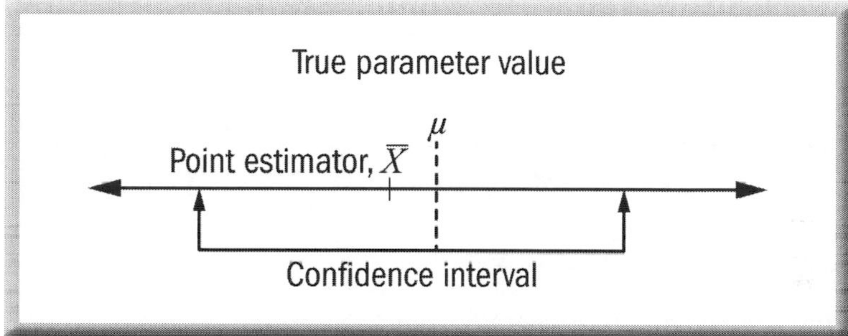

Figure 9.1: Graphical representation of a point estimator, $\overline{X}$, and an interval estimator for the population parameter μ

Suppose that we want to find the population mean of the amount of money that shoppers spent on holiday gifts in December 2012. Due to practical constraints, we were unable to obtain all the information in this population (we could not access the spending details of all the people that spent money on holiday gifts), but we were able to select a random sample of 250 shoppers and interview them to determine the amount of money they spent. From Chapter 8, we know that the sampling distribution of the mean is approximately normally distributed for large sample sizes and that we can consider the sample mean to be an unbiased estimator of the population mean. After the sampling, we establish that the mean amount of money spent in the sample of 250 shoppers is R1 880. This number is then the *point estimate* of the population mean. If we know that the population standard deviation σ is equal to 560, then we could construct an interval such that we were 95% certain that the true population mean of the money spent on gifts lies in the resulting interval. In this example, the interval would be [R1 810.58; R1 949.42], i.e. we are 95% certain that the true population mean of money spent on gifts lies somewhere between R1 810.58 and R1 949.42. To obtain this interval, we need to manipulate the quantity in formula (8.3) to incorporate the variability of the sample mean around the population mean to provide the interval estimate for the population mean (we will discuss the detail behind this procedure in Section 9.3). This interval estimate is called the *confidence interval* for the population mean.

In this chapter we shall consider the following topics:

- Types of estimates (point and interval)
- Criteria for a good estimator

- Point estimates of the:
  - population mean, μ
  - **population variance**, σ^2
  - population standard error of the sample mean, $\overline{X}$
  - population proportion, π
  - population standard error of the sample proportion, p
- Confidence interval estimates of the:
  - population mean μ when σ is known
  - population mean μ when σ is unknown and $n \geq 30$
  - population mean μ when σ is unknown and $n < 30$
  - population proportion
- The appropriate choice of the sample size when constructing confidence intervals

9.1.2 Types of estimates

To recap, a *point estimate* is a sample statistic that we use to estimate an unknown population parameter. An *interval estimate* is a range of values we use to estimate a population parameter.

9.1.3 Criteria for a good estimator

Qualities desirable in estimators include unbiasedness, consistency and efficiency.

- An *unbiased estimator* of a population parameter is an estimator that has an expected value equal to the parameter. As we already know, the sample mean, $\overline{X}$, is an unbiased estimator of the population mean, μ, because the expected value of the sample mean equals the population mean:

$$E(\overline{X}) = \mu \tag{9.1}$$

- An unbiased estimator is said to be *consistent* if the difference between the estimator and the parameter grows smaller as the sample size grows larger. The sample mean, $\overline{X}$, is a consistent estimator of the population mean, μ. If n grows larger, the value of the variance of the sample mean grows smaller, i.e. the estimator exhibits less variation as the sample size increases. We can see this in formula (9.2), which is a restatement of formula (8.1):

$$Var(\overline{X}) = \frac{\sigma^2}{n} \tag{9.2}$$

  (Note what happens to $Var(\overline{X})$ as n increases and σ stays constant.)
- If there are two unbiased estimators of a parameter, the one with the smaller variance is said to be more *efficient*. For example, both the sample mean and median are unbiased estimators of the population mean. Which one should we use? The sample median has a greater variance than the sample mean, so we prefer the sample mean, since it is *relatively efficient* when compared to the sample median.

NOTE

If you see a population parameter with a *hat*, it denotes an estimator for that parameter.

For example, we often use the notation $\hat{\mu}$ to denote an estimator for the parameter μ, the estimator for σ will be denoted by $\hat{\sigma}$, and the estimator for π will be denoted by $\hat{\pi}$.

9.2 Point estimators

9.2.1 Point estimate of the population mean, μ

A *point estimator* estimates the value of an unknown population parameter by using a single point or value. The sample mean is the best estimator of the population mean, because it possesses all the desirable qualities of *good* estimators discussed above: it is unbiased, consistent and the most efficient estimator, as long as the sample from which it was obtained:

- is drawn from a normal population, or
- if the population was not normal, but the sample was sufficiently large so that the sampling distribution can be approximated by the normal distribution.

Thus, a point estimate of the population mean, μ, is given by formula (9.3):

$$\hat{\mu} = \overline{X} = \frac{1}{n}\sum_{i=1}^{n} X_i \tag{9.3}$$

We expect the point estimator to get closer and closer to the true population value as the sample size increases. The degree of variability or uncertainty of the estimator is not reflected by the point estimator, but we can employ the concept of the interval estimator to assign a probability to the value of the population parameter lying between two values, with the middle value being represented by the point estimator. Section 9.3 will discuss the concept of an interval estimate or confidence interval.

9.2.2 Point estimate of the population standard deviation, σ

The most frequently used estimate of the unknown population standard deviation, σ, is the sample standard deviation (S). The form of the sample standard deviation that we will use was already given in Chapter 3:

$$\hat{\sigma} = S = \sqrt{\frac{1}{n-1}\sum_{i=1}^{n}(X_i - \overline{X})^2} \tag{9.4}$$

The estimator, S, is an unbiased estimator for σ and is calculated in Excel using the function STDEV.S().

NOTE

The estimator, S_b, is defined as:

$$S_b = \sqrt{\frac{1}{n}\sum_{i=1}^{n}(X_i - \overline{X})^2}$$

It is a *biased* estimator for σ (note that the only difference between S and S_b is that S_b divides by n and S divides by $n - 1$). This statistic is called the population standard deviation and should only ever be calculated if we have *all* of the population data. We calculate this value in Excel using the function STDEV.P().

When n is large, then $\hat{\sigma} = S \approx S_b$

9.2.3 Point estimate of the standard error of $\overline{X}$, $\sigma_{\overline{X}} = \dfrac{\sigma}{\sqrt{n}}$

We now discuss the point estimator for the parameter $\sigma_{\overline{X}}$, the standard error of the sample mean, $\overline{X}$. We saw in the previous chapter and in formula (9.2) that this standard error is defined as $\frac{\sigma}{\sqrt{n}}$; the estimator for this quantity can now be expressed as:

$$\hat{\sigma}_{\overline{X}} = \frac{\hat{\sigma}}{\sqrt{n}} = \frac{S}{\sqrt{n}} \qquad (9.5)$$

Note that to obtain the estimator for $\sigma_{\overline{X}}$, we simply replaced the σ term in formua (9.2) with its unbiased estimate, S.

WORKED EXAMPLES

EXAMPLE 9.1

An experiment is conducted in which students in a Grade 10 class are asked to measure and then cut a rod of wood to a length of one metre. The wooden rods of five randomly selected students are then collected and measured with a precision device. The measurement yielded the following results: 1.010 m, 1.012 m, 1.008 m, 1.013 m and 1.011 m. Calculate the unbiased estimates of the population mean and variance of possible measurements, and give an estimate for the standard error of your estimate of the mean.

The value of the unbiased estimates of the population mean, variance and standard error of the mean are provided by using formulae (9.3), (9.4) and (9.5). We begin by noting that the following information can be obtained from the sample:

Sample size $n = 5$

Sample mean, $\overline{X} = \dfrac{1.010 + 1.012 + 1.008 + 1.013 + 1.011}{5} = 1.0108$

Unbiased sample standard deviation, $S = \sqrt{\dfrac{1}{n-1}\sum_{i=1}^{n}(X_i - \overline{X})^2}$

$= 0.0019235$

We then use these values to obtain the population estimates:

- Estimate of population mean $\hat{\mu} = \overline{X} = 1.0108$
- Estimate of population standard deviation $\hat{\sigma} = S = 0.019235$
- Estimate of population standard error of the mean $\hat{\sigma}_{\overline{X}} = \frac{\hat{\sigma}}{\sqrt{n}} = \frac{S}{\sqrt{n}} = 0.0008602$

Figure 9.2 illustrates the Excel solution.

	A	B	C	D	E	F	G	H
1	Point Estimates, Example 9.1							
2								
3		Sample Data				Summary Statistic		
4		X_1	$(X_i - \overline{X})^2$			$n =$	5	=COUNT(B5:B9)
5		1.01	0.00000064	=(B5-GG19)^2		$\sum_{i=1}^{n} X_i =$	5.054	=SUM(B5:B9)
6		1.012	0.00000144	=(B6-GG19)^2		$\sum_{i=2}^{n}(X_i - \overline{X})^2 =$	0.000015	=SUM(C5:C9)
7		1.008	0.00000784	=(B7-GG19)^2				
8		1.013	0.00000048	=(B8-GG19)^2				
9		1.011	0.00000004	=(B9-GG19)^2		Formula Solution		
10						Sample mean =	1.0108	=G5/G4
11						Sample variance =	0.0000037	=G6/(G4-1)
12						Sample standard deviation =	0.0019235	=G11^0.5
13						Estimate of population mean =	1.0108	=G10
14						Estimate of population standard deviation =	0.0019235	=G12
15						Estimate of standard error of mean =	0.0008602	=G14/G4^0.5
16								
17								
18						Function Solution		
19						$\overline{X} =$	1.0108	=AVERAGE(B5:B9)
20						Sample variance =	0.0000037	=VAR.S(B5:B9)
21						Sample standard deviation =	0.0019235	=STDEV(B5:B9)
22						Estimate of population mean =	1.0108	=G19
23						Estimate of population standard deviation =	0.0019235	=G21
24						Estimate of standard error of mean =	0.0008602	=G23/G4^0.5

Figure 9.2: The Excel solution for Example 9.1

EXCEL SOLUTION

X: Cells B5:B9	Values
$(X_i - \overline{X})^2$: Cell C5	Formula: =(B5-$G$9)^2
	(Copy formula C5:C9)
n: Cell G4	Formula: =COUNT(B5:B9)
$\sum X$: Cell G5	Formula: =SUM(B5:B9)
$\sum(X - \overline{X})^2$: Cell G6	Formula: =SUM(C5:C9)
Formula solution	
Sample mean: Cell G10	Formula: =G5/G4
Sample variance: Cell G11	Formula: =G6/(G4-1)
Sample standard deviation: Cell G12	Formula: =G11^0.5

Estimate of population mean: Cell G13	Formula: =G10
Estimate of population standard deviation: Cell G14	Formula: =G12
Estimate of the standard error of the mean: Cell G15	Formula: =G14/(G4^0.5)
Function solution	
$\overline{X}$: Cell G19	Formula: =AVERAGE(B5:B9)
Sample variance: Cell G20	Formula: =VAR.S(B5:B9)
Sample standard deviation: Cell G21	Formula: =STDEV.S(B5:B9)
Estimate of population mean: Cell G22	Formula: =G19
Estimate of population standard deviation: Cell G23	Formula: =G21
Estimate of the standard error of the mean: Cell G24	Formula: =G23/(G4^0.5)

INTERPRETATION The value of the unbiased estimates of the mean, variance and standard error are 1.0108, 0.0019235 and 0.0008602 respectively.

9.2.4 Point estimates for the population proportion, π and the standard error of p, $\sqrt{\frac{\pi(1-\pi)}{n}}$

In the previous section, we provided the equations to calculate the point estimate for the population mean based on the sample data. Another parameter that we will investigate is the population proportion and, like the mean, we can estimate this parameter using sample data.

The sample proportion is a point estimate of the population proportion. Formulae (9.6) and (9.7) provide unbiased estimates of the population proportion and standard error of the sample proportion:

$$\text{Estimate of population proportion, } \hat{\pi} = p \tag{9.6}$$

$$\text{Estimate of standard error of the proportion, } \hat{\sigma}_p = \sqrt{\frac{\hat{\pi}(1-\hat{\pi})}{n}} = \sqrt{\frac{p(1-p)}{n}} \tag{9.7}$$

WORKED EXAMPLES

EXAMPLE 9.2

In a sample of 400 platinum mine workers, 184 expressed dissatisfaction regarding a prospective plan to modify working conditions. Provide a point estimate for the *population* proportion of total workers who would be dissatisfied and give an estimate for the standard error of your estimate.

We get the value of the unbiased estimates of the population mean and standard error of the mean by applying formulae (9.6) and (9.7). We can obtain the following information from the sample:

- Sample size, $n = 400$
- Number of miners dissatisfied, $X = 184$
- Sample proportion, $p = \frac{X}{n} = \frac{184}{400} = 0.46$

We then use these values to obtain the population estimates:

- Estimate of population proportion, $\hat{\pi} = p = 0.46$
- Estimate of population standard error $\hat{\sigma}_p = \sqrt{\frac{\hat{\pi}(1-\hat{\pi})}{n}} = \sqrt{0.46 \times \frac{(1-0.46)}{400}} = 0.0249$

Excel solution – Example 9.2

Figure 9.3 illustrates the Excel solution.

	A	B	C	D	E	F
1	Point Estimates, Example 9.2					
2						
3		Sample Data				
4						
5			Total In sample, n =	400		
6			Number dissatisfied, X =	184		
7						
8			Sample proportion, p =	0.46	=D6/D5	
9						
10		Population				
11						
12			Estimated population proportion =	0.46	=D8	
13			Estimated population proportion standard error =	0.02491987	=SQRT(D12*(1-D12)/D5)	

Figure 9.3: Excel solution for Example 9.2

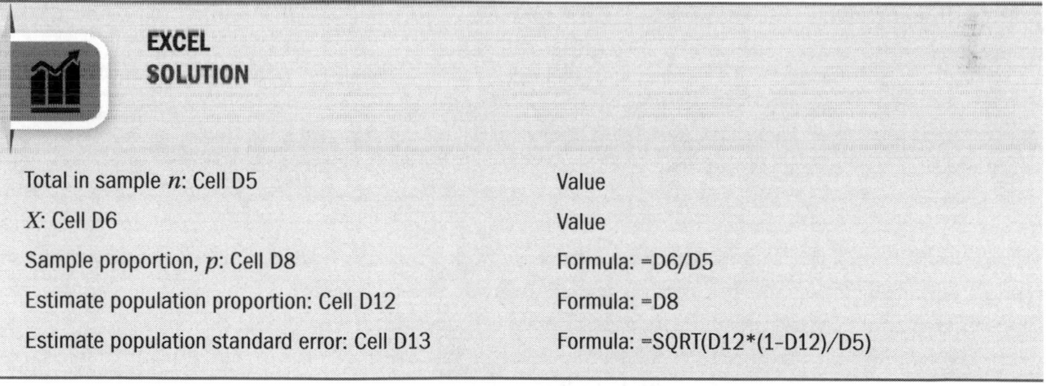

EXCEL SOLUTION

Total in sample n: Cell D5 — Value

X: Cell D6 — Value

Sample proportion, p: Cell D8 — Formula: =D6/D5

Estimate population proportion: Cell D12 — Formula: =D8

Estimate population standard error: Cell D13 — Formula: =SQRT(D12*(1-D12)/D5)

INTERPRETATION The value of the unbiased estimates of the population proportion of miners dissatisfied with the proposed changes is 0.46 with an estimated standard error of 0.0249.

9.2.5 Pooled estimates

If we take more than one sample from a population, then we can combine the resulting sample statistics to provide *pooled estimates* for the population mean, variance and proportion.

The following pooled sample mean of two sample means provides an estimate of the population mean:

$$\overline{X} = \frac{n_1\overline{X}_1 + n_2\overline{X}_2}{n_1 + n_2} \tag{9.8}$$

The following pooled sample variance of two sample variances provides an estimate of the population variance:

$$\hat{\sigma}^2 = \frac{n_1 s_1^2 + n_2 s_2^2}{n_1 + n_2 - 2} \tag{9.9}$$

The following pooled sample proportion of two sample proportions provides an estimate of the population proportion:

$$\hat{\pi} = \frac{n_1\hat{\pi}_1 + n_2\hat{\pi}_2}{n_1 + n_2} = \frac{n_1 p_1 + n_2 p_2}{n_1 + n_2} \tag{9.10}$$

9.3 Confidence intervals

9.3.1 Introduction to confidence intervals for the population mean

We can estimate the population mean of a sample from a population, and our knowledge of the sampling distribution of the sample mean allows us to also describe the likely variability of this estimate. If we assume that the sampling distribution of the sample means is normally distributed, we can provide a measure of this variability in such a way that it describes the probability that the value of the population mean will lie within a specified interval. (The probability that a parameter lies in these intervals is dentoted by $1 - \alpha$ and is referred to as the confidence level).

Confidence level The probability value $(1 - \alpha)$ associated with a confidence interval, i.e. the interval contains the specified parameter with probability $(1 - \alpha)$.

This interval is called an *interval estimate* (or *confidence interval*). Note that when we construct confidence intervals for the population mean under these assumptions, the interval is centred at the point estimate for the population mean, i.e. it is centred on $\overline{X}$.

In this section, we discuss three different scenarios that we encounter when attempting to construct confidence intervals for the population mean:

- When σ is known and the data are normally distributed.
- When σ is unknown, the data are normally distributed and $n < 30$.
- When σ is unknown and $n \geq 30$ (data can be normally distributed or not).

Each of these scenarios leads to slight modifications in the way in which we construct the interval.

We begin the discussion by looking at the simplest situation: when the data are normal and the value of σ is known.

9.3.2 Confidence interval estimate for the population mean, μ (σ is known and the data are normally distributed)

Recall from Chapter 7 that if a random sample of size n is taken from a normal population $N(\mu, \sigma^2)$, the sampling distribution of the sample means will also be normal, $\overline{X} \sim N(\mu, \frac{\sigma^2}{n})$. If the value σ is known, we can use this concept to construct a confidence interval by first noting that the standardised statistic, Z, is defined as:

$$Z = \frac{\overline{X} - \mu}{\frac{\sigma}{\sqrt{n}}} \tag{9.11}$$

From Chapter 7, we know that this standardised statistic follows a standard normal distribution, i.e. $Z \sim N(0, 1)$. We can now find quantiles $z_{\alpha/2}$ and $-z_{\alpha/2}$ such that:

$$P(-z_{\alpha/2} < Z < z_{\alpha/2}) = 1 - \alpha.$$

For example, if $\alpha = 0.05$, we can find quantiles $z_{0.025}$ and $-z_{0.025}$ such that:

$$P(-z_{0.025} < Z < z_{0.025}) = 1 - 0.05 = 0.95$$

Using the tools developed in Chapter 7 or the Excel function NORM.S.INV(), we can easily show that the value of $z_{0.025} = 1.96$ satisfies this expression, that is, we can show that:

$$P(-1.96 < Z < 1.96) = 0.95 \tag{9.12}$$

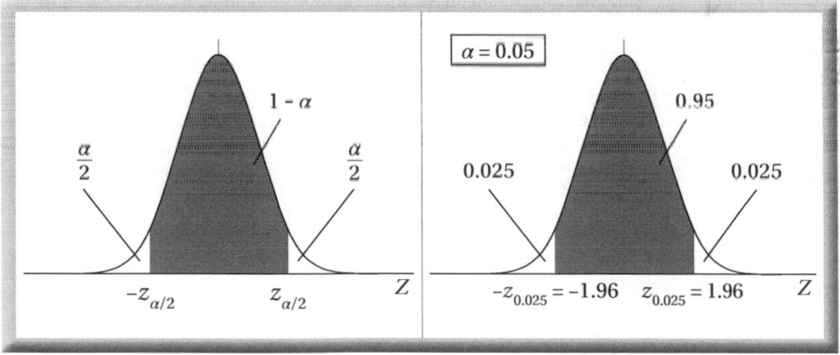

Figure 9.4: Graphical illustration of the probabilities and quantiles used in constructing a confidence interval

In its current form, formula (9.12) is not very helpful for determining the confidence interval for μ, because the parameter μ does not appear in this expression. However, if we substitute (9.11) into (9.12) we get:

$$P\left(-1.96 < \frac{\overline{X} - \mu}{\frac{\sigma}{\sqrt{n}}} < 1.96\right) = 0.95$$

Rearranging these terms so that μ remains in the middle of the inequality we get:

$$P\left(\overline{X} - 1.96 \times \frac{\sigma}{\sqrt{n}} < \mu < \overline{X} + 1.96 \times \frac{\sigma}{\sqrt{n}}\right) = 0.95 \quad (9.13)$$

Note that the probability 0.95 does not change, no matter how much we rearrange the terms within the probability operator.

We can then interpret formula (9.13) as follows: We are 95% certain that the population mean, μ, lies between the values $\overline{X} - 1.96 \times \frac{\sigma}{\sqrt{n}}$ and $\overline{X} + 1.96 \times \frac{\sigma}{\sqrt{n}}$, i.e. we are 95% confident that μ is in the interval $[\overline{X} - 1.96 \times \frac{\sigma}{\sqrt{n}}; \overline{X} + 1.96 \times \frac{\sigma}{\sqrt{n}}]$.

These two values, called the *upper and lower confidence bounds*, are all we need to define a confidence interval.

In general, we will write a $100 \times (1 - \alpha)\%$ confidence interval (CI) for μ as:

$$\left[X - z_{\alpha/2} \times \frac{\sigma}{\sqrt{n}} \quad ; \quad \overline{X} + z_{\alpha/2} \times \frac{\sigma}{\sqrt{n}}\right] \quad (9.14)$$

$z_{\alpha/2}$ is the standard normal quantile defined such that $P(Z > z_{\alpha/2}) = \frac{\alpha}{2}$, or $P(Z < z_{\alpha/2}) = 1 - \frac{\alpha}{2}$. We can obtain these normal quantile values by using the Excel function NORM.S.INV().

WORKED EXAMPLES

EXAMPLE 9.3

Eight bolts of cloth, randomly selected from a factory production line at a textile factory, are each tested for their tearing strength (the amount of force required to tear the cloth, measured in kilograms). These bolts of cloth are sampled from a population in which the tearing strength is normally distributed with known population standard deviation $\sigma = 0.2$. Calculate a 95% confidence interval for the population mean based on the following sample of eight observations:

4.9 kg, 4.7 kg, 5.1 kg, 5.4 kg, 4.7 kg, 5.2 kg, 4.8 kg, 5.1 kg

In order to calculate this interval, we need to use formula (9.14). To simplify the calculation, we break the interval down into its three main components.

- **The sample mean, $\overline{X}$:** From the data provided, it is clear that the sample mean is:

$$\overline{X} = \frac{1}{n}\sum_{i=1}^{n} X_i = \frac{1}{8}(4.9 + 4.7 + 5.1 + 5.4 + 4.7 + 5.2 + 4.8 + 5.1) = \frac{39.9}{8} = 4.9875$$

- **The standard error of $\overline{X}$, $\frac{\sigma}{\sqrt{n}}$:** The information provided in the sample states that the population standard deviation is $\sigma = 0.2$ and the sample size is known to be $n = 8$. The standard error is therefore $\frac{\sigma}{\sqrt{n}} = \frac{0.2}{\sqrt{8}} = 0.070710678$.
- **The standard normal quantile,** $z_{\alpha/2}$: To obtain this quantile, we first note that the requested interval is a 95% confidence interval. This means that $\alpha = 0.05$, because
$(1 - \alpha) \times 100\% = (1 - 0.05) \times 100\% = 0.95 \times 100\% = 95\%$.
We now need to find the value $z_{\alpha/2} = z_{0.025}$ that satisfies the expression $P(Z > z_{0.025}) = 0.025$.
Using the Excel function NORM.S.INV, we can see that this value is approximately $z_{0.025} = 1.96$.

We can now combine these three elements into formula (9.14) to get the interval:

$$\left[\overline{X} - z_{\alpha/2} \times \frac{\sigma}{\sqrt{n}} ; \overline{X} + z_{\alpha/2} \times \frac{\sigma}{\sqrt{n}}\right]$$
$$\Rightarrow [4.99875 - 1.96 \times 0.070710678 ; 4.9875 + 1.96 \times 0.070710678]$$
$$\Rightarrow [4.86016 ; 5.1373]$$

Excel provides a number of functions that will help with this calculation:

- The function AVERAGE(X) calculates the sample mean, $\overline{X}$.
- The function NORM.S.INV($1 - \frac{\alpha}{2}$) allows us to calculate $z_{\alpha/2}$, the quantiles of the standard normal distribution.
- The function CONFIDENCE.NORM(α,σ,n) will calculate the quantity $\frac{\sigma}{\sqrt{n}} \times z_{\alpha/2}$. This function accepts three arguments: the value of α the standard deviation, σ and the sample size n, respectively. We obtain the confidence interval from this function by adding or subtracting it from the sample mean.

Figure 9.5 illustrates the Excel solution.

	A	B	C	D	E	F	G
1	**Confidence interval for μ - population standard deviation known**						
2	**Example 9.3**						
3							
4		**Sample Data**			Population standard deviation σ =	0.2	Known
5		X	X^2		95% confidence interval =	0.05	Chosen 5%
6		4.9	24.01	=B6^2	confidence interval, α =	0.975	=1-F5/2
7		4.7	22.09	=B7^2	$z\alpha/2$ =	1.959964	=NORM.S.INV(F6)
8		5.1	26.01	=B8^2	**Sample Data**		
9		5.4	29.16	=B9^2	Sample mean =	4.9987	=C19/C18
10		4.7	22.09	=B10^2	Estimate of population mean =	4.9987	=F9
11		5.2	27.04	=B11^2	Standard error of the mean =	0.0707107	=F4/C17^0.5
12		4.8	23.04	=B12^2	CI lower bound =	4.860156	=F9-F7*F11
13		5.1	26.01	=B13^2	CI upper bound =	5.137290	=F9+F7*F11
14							
15		**Sample Data**			**Sample Data**		
16					Sample mean =	4.9987	=AVERAGE(B6:B13)
17		n =	8	=COUNT(B6:B13)	Estimate of population mean =	4.9987	=F16
18		$\sum_{i=1}^{n} X_i$ =	39.9	=SUM(B6:B13)	Standard error of the mean =	0.0707107	=F4/C17^0.5
19		$\sum_{i=1}^{n} X_i^2$ =	199.45	=SUM(C6:C13)	CI lower bound =	4.860156	=F16-CONFIDENCE.NORM(F5,F4,C17)
20					CI upper bound =	5.137290	=F16+CONFIDENCE.NORM(F5,F4,C17)

Figure 9.5: The Excel solution for Example 9.3

EXCEL SOLUTION

X: Cells B6:B13	Values
X^2: Cells C6:C13	Formula: =B6^2
	(Copy formula C6:C13)
n: Cell C17	Formula: =COUNT(B6:B13)
$\sum X$: Cell C18	Formula: =SUM(B6:B13)
$\sum X^2$: Cell C19	Formula: =SUM(C6:C13)
Population standard deviation σ: Cell F4	Values
95% confidence interval: Cell F5	Values
Confidence interval, α: Cell F6	Formula: =1-F5/2
$z_{\alpha/2}$: Cell F7	Formula: =NORMSINV(F6)
Formula solution	
Sample mean: Cell F9	Formula: =C19/C18
Estimate of population mean: Cell F10	Formula: =F9
Standard error of the mean: Cell F11	Formula: =F4/C17^0.5
CI lower bound: Cell F12	Formula: =F9-F7*F11
CI upper bound: Cell F13	Formula: =F9+F7*F11
Function solution	
Sample mean: Cell F16	Formula: =AVERAGE(B6:B13)
Estimate of population mean: Cell F17	Formula: =F16
Standard error of the mean: Cell F18	Formula: =F4/C17^0.5
CI lower bound: Cell F19	Formula: =F16-CONFIDENCE(F5,F4,C17)
CI upper bound: Cell F20	Formula: =F16+CONFIDENCE(F5,F4,C17)

INTERPRETATION We are 95% confident that, on the basis of this sample, the population mean tearing strength of the bolts of cloth manufactured in the factory lies between 4.8489 and 5.1261.

In the next two sections, we relax the assumption that the population standard deviation, σ, is known.

9.3.3 Confidence interval estimate of the population mean, μ (σ is unknown, the data are normally distributed and $n < 30$)

The previous example calculated the point and interval estimates when the population was normally distributed but the population standard deviation was known. However, in most cases, the population standard deviation would be an unknown value and we would have to use the sample value to estimate the population value. We still estimate the population mean by the sample mean, but what about the confidence interval? In the previous example, we used the sample mean and size to provide this interval, but in this new case, we have an extra unknown quantity we have to estimate from the sample data in order to determine this confidence interval: the standard deviation.

NOTE The scenario described above is one that you will most likely encounter in research projects: a situation with small sample sizes and where the population standard deviation is unknown.

This interval requires that we use the *t*-distribution. This was discovered by W.S. Gossett, who determined that when data are normally distributed, the distribution of the mean, when divided by an estimate of the standard error, i.e. $\frac{\hat{\sigma}}{\sqrt{n}} = \frac{S}{\sqrt{n}}$, follows what he called the *Student's t-distribution* with $n - 1$ degrees of freedom:

$$T = \frac{\overline{X} - \mu}{\frac{S}{\sqrt{n}}} \sim t_{n-1} \qquad (9.15)$$

NOTE Formula (9.15) is very similar to the *standardised* statistic, Z, in formula (9.11). However, when we alter the statistic in this way (by dividing by the *estimated* standard error of the mean instead of the *true* standard error), we call the result a *studentised* statistic.

Refer to Chapter 7, Section 7.3 for a brief review of the *t*-distribution. Recall that this distribution is very similar to the normal probability distribution when the estimate of the variance is based on many **degrees of freedom** ($df = n - 1$), but the left and right tails are *fatter* when compared to the normal distribution.

Degrees of freedom Refers to the number of independent observations in a sample minus the number of population parameters that must be estimated from sample data.

Figure 9.6 shows the *t*-distribution with one degree of freedom and the standard normal distribution. Clearly, the *t*-distribution is *thinner* in the middle and *fatter* in the tails than the normal distribution (it is said to be *leptokurtic*).

Since the *t*-distribution is leptokurtic, the percentage of the distribution within 1.96 standard deviations of the mean is less than the 95% for the normal distribution.

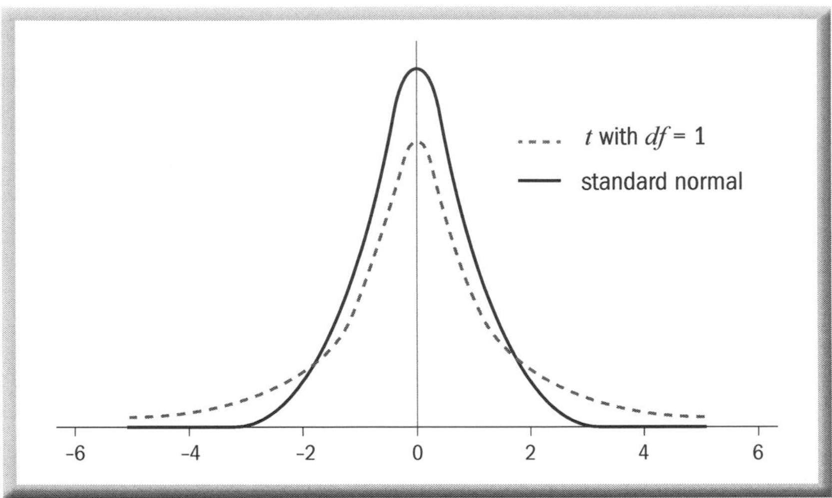

Figure 9.6: Comparison of the standard normal and t_1-distributions

However, if the number of degrees of freedom (*df*) is large ($df = n - 1 \geq 30$), then there is very little difference between the two probability distributions.

Note also that, like the normal distribution, the *t*-distribution is symmetrical.

The fact that the statistic *t* in formula (9.15) follows a *t*-distribution, with $n - 1$ degrees of freedom, means that the construction of the confidence interval for μ will now differ: it will require that the calculation of the quantiles $t_{df,\alpha/2}$ and $-t_{df,\alpha/2}$ such that

$$P(-t_{df,\alpha/2} < T < t_{df,\alpha/2}) = 1 - \alpha.$$

For example, if $\alpha = 0.05$ and $n = 20$ ($df = n - 1 = 19$), then we can find quantiles $t_{19,0.025}$ and $-t_{19,0.025}$ such that

$$P(-t_{19,0.025} < T < t_{19,0.025}) = 1 - 0.05 = 0.95$$

Using the Excel function T.INV(), as discussed in Chapter 7, we can find the value of $t_{19,0.025} = 2.093$ satisfies this expression. We can show that:

$$P(-2.093 < T < 2.093) = 0.95$$

Note that this quantile, unlike the standard normal quantile, depends on both the degrees of freedom (or sample size) and the value of α.

We can then convert the formula above into a confidence interval for μ by substituting it in formula (9.15):

$$P\left(-2.093 < \frac{\overline{X} - \mu}{\frac{S}{\sqrt{n}}} < 2.093\right) = 0.95$$

We then rearrange the terms so that μ remains in the middle of the inequality:

$$P\left(\overline{X} - 2.093 \times \frac{S}{\sqrt{n}} < \mu < \overline{X} + 2.093 \times \frac{S}{\sqrt{n}}\right) = 0.95$$

In general, the confidence interval for μ when $n < 30$ and the data are normally distributed, is given by:

$$\left[\overline{X} - t_{df,\alpha/2} \times \frac{S}{\sqrt{n}}; \overline{X} + t_{df,\alpha/2} \times \frac{S}{\sqrt{n}}\right] \quad (9.16)$$

$t_{df,\alpha/2}$ is the quantile of the t-distribution with df degrees of freedom defined such that $P(T > t_{df,\alpha/2}) = \frac{\alpha}{2}$, or $P(T < t_{df,\alpha/2}) = 1 - \frac{\alpha}{2}$, where $T \sim t_{df}$.

WORKED EXAMPLES

EXAMPLE 9.4

A random sample of eight German Shepard police dogs is drawn from the population of SAPS police dogs. Each of the dogs is weighed producing the following observations:

10.3 kg, 12.4 kg, 11.6 kg, 11.8 kg, 12.6 kg, 10.9 kg, 11.2 kg, 10.3 kg

The mass (in kilograms) of the dogs in the population is known to be normally distributed, but the population mean and variance are unknown.

Calculate a point estimator and a 95% confidence interval estimator for the population mean mass of the dogs.

The values of the lower and upper limits of the confidence interval are given by formula (9.16). We once again break the problem down to its three components.

- **The sample mean, $\overline{X}$:**

$$\overline{X} = \frac{1}{n}\sum_{i=1}^{n} X_i = \frac{1}{8}(10.3 + 12.4 + 11.6 + 11.8 + 12.6 + 10.9 + 11.2 + 10.3)$$
$$= \frac{91.1}{8}$$
$$= 11.3875$$

- **The estimated standard error of $\overline{X}$, $\frac{S}{\sqrt{n}}$:** To obtain the estimated standard error, we first need to calculate the sample standard deviation, S. We use formula (9.4), and find that the unbiased sample standard deviation is:

$$S = \sqrt{\frac{1}{n-1}\sum_{i=1}^{n}(X_i - \overline{X})^2} = 0.8741322$$

The estimated standard error of $\overline{X}$ is then $\sigma_{\overline{X}} = \frac{S}{\sqrt{n}} = \frac{0.8741322}{\sqrt{8}} = 0.3090524$

- **The t quantile, $t_{df,\alpha/2}$:** Since this question requires a 95% interval, it implies that $\alpha = 0.05$ (because $(1 - \alpha) \times 100\% = (1 - 0.05) \times 100\% = 95\%$). The degrees of freedom are calculated to be $df = n - 1 = 8 - 1 = 7$. Finally, we can obtain the $\frac{\alpha}{2}$ quantile for the t-distribution with $df = 7$ degrees of freedom ($t_{7,0.025}$) by using the Excel function T.INV($1 - \frac{\alpha}{2}$, df). In this case, we find it to be equal to $t_{7,0.025} = 2.3646243$.
This is the value that satisfies the expression $P(T > t_{7,0.025}) = 0.025$, where $T \sim t_7$.

- We can now combine these three elements into formula (9.16) to get the interval:

$$\left[\overline{X} - t_{df,\alpha/2} \times \frac{S}{\sqrt{n}}; \overline{X} + t_{df,\alpha/2} \times \frac{S}{\sqrt{n}}\right]$$

$$\Rightarrow [11.3875 - 2.3646243 \times 0.3090524; 11.3875 + 2.3646243 \times 0.3090524]$$

$$\Rightarrow [10.6567; 12.1183]$$

Excel provides a number of functions that help with this calculation:

- The function AVERAGE() calculates the sample mean, $\overline{X}$.
- The function T.INV($1 - \frac{\alpha}{2}$, df) allows us to calculate $t_{df,\alpha/2}$, the quantiles of the t-distribution with df degrees of freedom.
- The function CONFIDENCE.T(α,σ,n) calculates the quantity $\frac{\sigma}{\sqrt{n}} \times t_{df,\alpha/2}$. This function accepts three arguments: the value of α, the standard deviation, σ, and the sample size n, respectively. We obtain the confidence interval from this function by adding and subtracting it from the sample mean.

Figure 9.7 illustrates the Excel solution.

	A	B	C	D	E	F	G	H
1	Confidence interval for μ – population standard deviation unknown, n small							
2	Example 9.4							
3								
4		Sample Data				95% confidence interval, α =	0.05	**Chosen 5%**
5		X_i				$df = n - 1$ =	7	=C18-1
6		10.3				$t_{\alpha/2}$ =	2.3646243	=T.INV(1-G4/2,G5)
7		12.4						
8		11.6				Formula solution		
9		11.8				Sample mean =	11.3875	=AVERAGE(B6:B13)
10		12.6				Sample standard deviation =	0.8741322	=STDEV.S(B6:B13)
11		10.9				Estimate of population mean =	11.388	=G9
12		11.2				Standard error of the mean =	0.3090524	=G10/C18^0.5
13		10.3				CI lower bound =	10.656707	=G9-G6*G12
14						CI upper bound =	12.118293	=G9+G6*12
15								
16		Summary Statistics				Function solution		
17						Sample mean =	11.3875	=AVERAGE(B6:B13)
18		n =	8	=COUNT(B6:B13)		Sample standard deviation =	0.8741322	=STDEV.S(B6:B13)
19		$\sum_{i=1}^{n} X_i$ =	91.1	=SUM(B6:B13)		CI lower bound =	10.656707	=G17-CONFIDENCE.T(G4,G18,C18)
20						CI upper bound =	12.118293	=G17+CONFIDENCE.T(G4,G18,C18)

Figure 9.7: Excel solution for Example 9.4

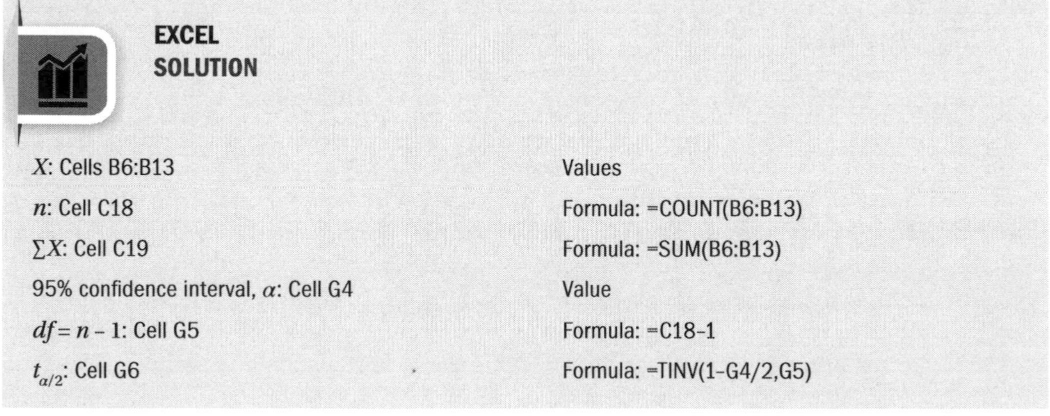

EXCEL SOLUTION

X: Cells B6:B13	Values
n: Cell C18	Formula: =COUNT(B6:B13)
$\sum X$: Cell C19	Formula: =SUM(B6:B13)
95% confidence interval, α: Cell G4	Value
$df = n - 1$: Cell G5	Formula: =C18-1
$t_{\alpha/2}$: Cell G6	Formula: =TINV(1-G4/2,G5)

Formula solution

Sample mean: Cell G9	Formula: =AVERAGE(B6:B13)
Sample standard deviation: Cell G10	Formula: =STDEV.S(B6:B13)
Estimate of population mean: Cell G11	Formula: =G9
Standard error of the mean: Cell G12	Formula: =G10/C18^0.5
CI lower bound: Cell G13	Formula: =G9-G6*G12
CI upper bound: Cell G14	Formula: =G9+G6*G12

Function solution

Sample mean: Cell G17	Formula: =AVERAGE(B6:B13)
Sample standard deviation: Cell G18	Formula: =STDEV.S(B6:B13)
CI lower bound: Cell G19	Formula: =G19-CONFIDENCE.T(G4,G18,C18)
CI upper bound: Cell G20	Formula: =G19+CONFIDENCE.T(G4,G18,C18)

INTERPRETATION We are 95% confident that, on the basis of the sample, the true population mean mass of the police dogs lies between 10.6567 kg and 12.1183 kg.

9.3.4 Confidence interval estimate of the population mean, μ (σ is unknown and $n \geq 30$)

Recall from Chapter 8, Section 8.2.4, that for large samples ($n \geq 30$), the sampling distribution of the sample mean is approximately normal with the population variance being estimated from the sample variance ($\sigma^2 \approx S^2$). Substituting this approximation into formula (9.11) gives the new expression for Z in formula (9.17). This new Z now has an approximate standard normal distribution (from the Central Limit Theorem, since n is large):

$$Z = \frac{\overline{X} - \mu}{\frac{S}{\sqrt{n}}} \sim N(0, 1) \tag{9.17}$$

The standard normal approximation means that the resulting confidence interval in formula (9.18) uses the standard normal quantiles (but also uses the estimated standard deviation, S):

$$\left[\overline{X} - z_{\alpha/2} \times \frac{S}{\sqrt{n}}; \overline{X} + z_{\alpha/2} \times \frac{S}{\sqrt{n}}\right] \tag{9.18}$$

$z_{\alpha/2}$ is the standard normal quantile defined such that $P(Z > z_{\alpha/2}) = \frac{\alpha}{2}$, or $P(Z < z_{\alpha/2}) = 1 - \frac{\alpha}{2}$

WORKED EXAMPLES

EXAMPLE 9.5

Similar to the situation described in Example 9.3, a factory is interested in determining the population mean of the tearing strength of the bolts of cloth produced on the production line. In this study, 40 bolts of cloth are randomly selected and the tearing strength of each one is measured. However, in this study, we do not assume that the tearing strength is normally distributed.

Calculate a 99% confidence interval for the population mean based on the following sample of 40 observations.

4.8	4.2	4.6	5.5	5.0	4.1	4.9	3.7
3.9	4.5	4.6	4.6	4.4	4.7	4.7	3.8
3.7	3.9	5.5	3.3	4.6	5.2	5.1	4.2
5.6	5.1	3.8	4.2	4.9	4.8	5.4	5.1
5.0	3.2	5.8	5.1	4.2	5.1	5.4	4.5

The values of the lower and upper limits of the confidence interval are given by formula (9.18). The calculation of the three components in the interval yields are as follows.

- The sample mean, $\overline{X}$: $\overline{X} = 4.6175$
- The estimated standard error of $\overline{X}$, $\frac{S}{\sqrt{n}}$: The unbiased sample standard deviation is calculated as $S = 0.64087$, and so the estimated standard error is $\hat{\sigma}_{\overline{X}} = \frac{S}{\sqrt{n}} = \frac{0.64087}{\sqrt{40}} = 0.10133$
- The standard normal quantile, $z_{\alpha/2}$: In this example, we need to obtain a 99% confidence interval, and so $\alpha = 0.01$ because $(1 - \alpha) \times 100\% = (1 - 0.01) \times 100\% = 99\%$. The standard normal quantile in this case is the value $z_{0.005}$ defined such that $P(Z > z_{0.005}) = 0.005$. The value that satisfies this expression is $z_{0.005} = 2.576$
- Substituting these values into formula (9.18) gives:

$$\left[\overline{X} - z_{\alpha/2} \times \frac{S}{\sqrt{n}} ; \overline{X} + z_{\alpha/2} \times \frac{S}{\sqrt{n}}\right]$$

$$\Rightarrow [4.6175 - 2.576 \times 0.10133 ; 4.6175 + 2.576 \times 0.10133]$$

$$\Rightarrow [4.356 ; 4.879]$$

As before, the Excel solution for these intervals is presented in Figure 9.8.

	A	B	C	D	E	F	G	H	I	J	K	L	M
1	Confidence interval for μ – large sample, Example 9.5												
2													
3		Sample Data									95% confidence interval, α =	0.01	Chosen 1%
4											$1-\alpha/2$ =	0.995	=1-L3/2
5		4.8	4.2	4.6	5.5	5	4.1	4.9	3.7		$z_{\alpha/2}$ =	2.5758293035489	=NORM.S.INV(L4)
6		3.9	4.5	4.6	4.6	4.4	4.7	4.7	3.8				
7		3.7	3.9	3.3	3.3	4.6	5.2	5.1	4.2		Sample statistics		
8		5.6	5.1	4.2	4.2	4.9	4.8	5.4	5.1		n =	40	=COUNT(B5:I9)
9		5.1	3.2	5.1	5.1	4.2	5.1	5.4	4.5		$\sum_{i=1}^{n} X_i$ =	184.7	=SUM(B5:I9)
10											Sample mean, $\overline{X}$ =	4.6175	=AVERAGE(B5:I9)
11											Sample standard deviation =	0.640867801	=STDEV.S(B5:I9)
12											Estimate of standard error of mean =	0.101330097523878	=L11/L8^0.5
13													
14											Function solution		
15											Sample mean =	4.35649096804236	=L10-L5*L12
16											Sample standard deviation =	4.87850903195764	=L10+L5*L12
17													
18											Function solution		
19											CI lower bound =	4.35649096804236	=L10-CONFIDENCE.NORM(L3,L11,L8)
20											CI upper bound =	4.87850903195764	=L10+CONFIDENCE.NORM(L3,L11,L8)

Figure 9.8: Excel solution for Example 9.5

EXCEL SOLUTION

X: Cells B5:I9	Values
n: Cell L8	Formula: =COUNT(B5:I9)
$\sum X$: Cell L9	Formula: =SUM(B5:I9)
$\overline{X}$: Cell L10	Formula: =AVERAGE(B5:I9)
Sample standard deviation: Cell L11	Formula: =STDEV.S(B5:I9)
Standard error of the mean: Cell L12	Formula: =L11/L8^0.5
99% confidence interval, α: Cell L3	Value
$1 - \frac{\alpha}{2}$: Cell L4	Formula: =1-L3/2
$z_{\alpha/2}$: Cell L5	Formula: =NORM.S.INV(L4)
Formula solution	
CI lower bound	Formula: =L10–L5*L12
CI upper bound	Formula: =L10+L5*L12
Formula solution	
CI lower bound	Formula: =L10–CONFIDENCE.NORM(L3,L11,L8)
CI upper bound	Formula: =L10+CONFIDENCE.NORM(L3,L11,L8)

INTERPRETATION The 99% confidence interval for the population mean tearing strength is 4.356 kg to 4.879 kg.

9.3.5 Confidence interval estimate of a population proportion

If the population is normally distributed or the sample size is large, the sample proportion will follow an approximate normal distribution and we obtain the confidence interval for the population proportion π using this fact. By manipulating formula (8.7) in much the same way as before, we obtain the interval in formula (9.19), where the population proportion, π, is estimated by the sample proportion, p:

$$\left[p - z_{\alpha/2} \times \sqrt{\frac{p(1-p)}{n}}; p + z_{\alpha/2} \times \sqrt{\frac{p(1-p)}{n}}\right] \tag{9.19}$$

WORKED EXAMPLES

EXAMPLE 9.6

In Example 8.7, we stated that 25% of workers in a factory own a personal computer. If this was not known, we can use the idea of a confidence interval to put a confidence level on the population proportion based on the sample data collected. The sample data resulted in a sample proportion = 0.26 with a sample size = 80.

The values of the lower and upper limits of the confidence interval are given by formula (9.19). The following components are needed to calculate this interval.

- **The sample proportion, *p*:** The sample proportion is given to be equal to $p = 0.26$.
- **The estimated standard error,** $\sqrt{\frac{p(1-p)}{n}}$**:** The estimated standard error of the sample proportion p is given by

$$\hat{\sigma}_p = \sqrt{\frac{p(1-p)}{n}} = \sqrt{\frac{0.26(1-0.26)}{80}} = 0.0490408.$$

- **The standard normal quantile,** $z_{\alpha/2}$**:** Once again, we need to determine a 95% confidence interval and so $\alpha = 0.05$, and the corresponding standard normal quantile is $z_{0.025} = 1.96$.

Substituting these values into (9.20) yields:

$$\left[p - z_{\alpha/2} \times \sqrt{\frac{p(1-p)}{n}}; p + z_{\alpha/2} \times \sqrt{\frac{p(1-p)}{n}}\right]$$

$$\Rightarrow [0.26 - 1.96 \times 0.0490408; 0.26 + 1.96 \times 0.0490408]$$

$$\Rightarrow [0.1639; 0.3561]$$

Figure 9.9 illustrates the Excel solution.

	A	B	C	D
1	**Confidence interval for the population proportion, π, n large**			
2	**Example 9.6**			
3				
4				
5		Sample proportion, p =	0.26	
6		Sample size, n =	80	
7				
8		Point estimate of population proportion, π =	0.26	
9				
10		95% confidence interval, α =	0.05	
11		$\frac{\alpha}{2}$ =	0.025	=C10/2
12		$z_{\alpha/2}$ =	1.959964	=NORM.S.INV(1-C11)
13				
14		Estimate of standard error =	0.0490408	=SQRT(C5*(1-C5)/C6)
15				
16		CI lower bound =	0.1638818	=C5-C12*C14
17		CI upper bound =	0.3561182	=C5+C12*C14

Figure 9.9: The Excel solution for Example 9.6

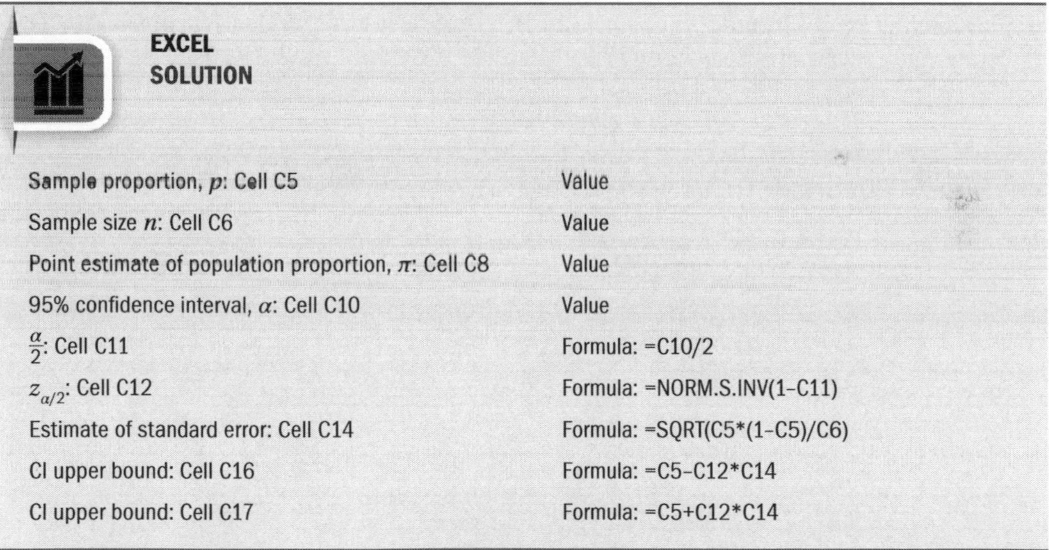

EXCEL SOLUTION

Sample proportion, p: Cell C5	Value
Sample size n: Cell C6	Value
Point estimate of population proportion, π: Cell C8	Value
95% confidence interval, α: Cell C10	Value
$\frac{\alpha}{2}$: Cell C11	Formula: =C10/2
$z_{\alpha/2}$: Cell C12	Formula: =NORM.S.INV(1-C11)
Estimate of standard error: Cell C14	Formula: =SQRT(C5*(1-C5)/C6)
CI upper bound: Cell C16	Formula: =C5-C12*C14
CI upper bound: Cell C17	Formula: =C5+C12*C14

INTERPRETATION The 95% confidence interval for the proportion of people who own a personal computer in the whole population is between 16.39% and 35.61%.

9.4 Calculating sample sizes

Typically, when constructing confidence intervals, we want the interval to be as narrow as possible. This is because narrow intervals allow us to be more *precise* in our estimations. Very wide intervals are not helpful when attempting to say something meaningful about a population parameter (for example, if someone reported that the 95% confidence interval for the population mean of the IQ of children in South Africa was [0 ; 200], it would not be very informative since we would be saying that the population mean can lie anywhere between 0 and 200). Precise intervals are thus highly sought after in statistical analysis.

If we look at formulae (9.14), (9.16), (9.18) and (9.19), we notice that there are a number of factors that will influence the width (or precision) of the interval. For example, looking at the interval in formula (9.14), we note that if we decrease the level of confidence for the interval from 99% to 95%, then the value of $z_{\alpha/2}$ will also decrease from 2.576 to 1.96, which in turn will make the interval narrower. Unfortunately, decreasing the confidence level is not really a viable method of reducing the width of the interval, because it also reduces our confidence in the interval's ability to estimate the parameter. If we could reduce the value of σ in formula (9.14), it would also lead to narrower intervals, but this is also not practical because we cannot change the population standard deviation's value. The only practical way to ensure narrower intervals is to control the sample size, n.

Note that in all of the intervals discussed in this chapter, the interval width will *decrease* if we *increase* the sample size. However, this too is a double-edged sword, because obtaining large samples can be difficult, costly, time consuming, and so on. We now discuss a method with which we can determine the smallest possible sample to achieve a desired width for a confidence interval for the population mean.

This method begins by noting that the width of a confidence interval for the population mean (using the confidence interval in formula (9.14)) can be given by formula (9.20):

$$\text{Interval width} = 2 \times z_{\alpha/2} \times \frac{\sigma}{\sqrt{n}} \tag{9.20}$$

The reason why the interval width can be expressed in this form is shown in Figure 9.10.

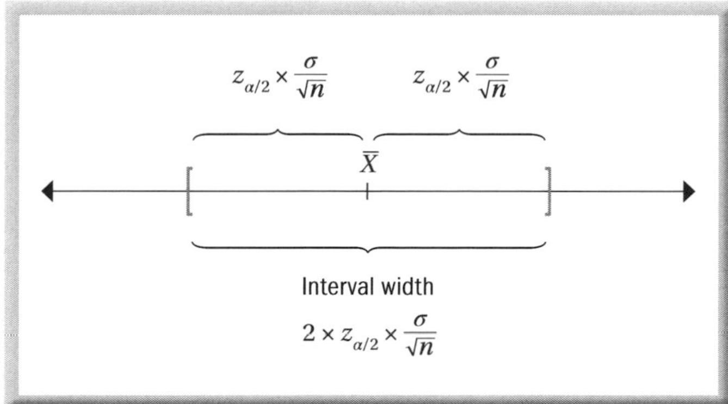

Figure 9.10: Illustration of the formula for the width of the confidence interval for the mean

Now, we need to be provided with:

- a particular interval width

- the value of $z_{\alpha/2}$ (used as an indication of the level of confidence, because α is contained in this term)
- the value of σ (σ could be known or it could be estimated from data).

With these values, we can easily find the sample size, *n*, associated with these values. We obtain the value of *n* that will satisfy the specified interval width, variance and level of confidence by solving for *n* in formula (9.20). The expression for *n* is then given by formula (9.21):

$$n = \left(\frac{2 \times z_{\alpha/2} \times \sigma}{\text{interval width}}\right)^2 \tag{9.21}$$

Interval width is the desired width of the interval and can be defined as

$$\text{interval width} = \text{CI upper bound} - \text{CI lower bound}.$$

For example, if we want to create a 95% confidence interval for the population mean based on a normally distributed population with $\sigma = 2$, and we specify that we do not want to be more than 0.25 units away from the true mean, i.e. the *margin of error* is 0.25, this means that the specified width of the interval should be no larger than 0.25 + 0.25 = 0.5. The appropriate sample size to achieve this interval width is then:

$$n = \left(\frac{2 \times z_{\alpha/2} \times \sigma}{\text{interval width}}\right)^2 = \left(\frac{2 \times 1.96 \times 2}{0.5}\right)^2 = 245.8624 \approx 246$$

Therefore, we need a sample size of *at least* 246 items in order to achieve a 95% confidence interval that has a width of 0.5.

WORKED EXAMPLES

EXAMPLE 9.7

A market researcher working for a large shoe retailer wants to estimate the population mean length of customers' feet. He knows from experience that the population is normally distributed with variance, $\sigma^2 = 0.04$. He wants to develop a 98% confidence interval to estimate this population mean, but he has decided that his margin of error can be no more than ±0.05 units (the total width of his interval must be no more than 0.05 + 0.05 = 0.1).

Determine the size of the sample he would need to collect in order to obtain this level of precision in his 98% confidence interval for the population mean foot length of customers.

To obtain this sample size, we simply need to use formula (9.21). The components of this equation are the following.

- **Interval width:** The margin of error is specified to be 0.05, meaning that the interval can deviate 0.05 above the point estimator and it can deviate 0.05 below the point estimator. This means that the total amount of deviation (or width) of the interval is 0.05 + 0.05 = 0.1.
- **Population standard deviation,** σ: The population variance is given as $\sigma^2 = 0.04$. The population standard deviation is then simply $\sigma = \sqrt{\sigma^2} = \sqrt{0.04} = 0.2$.

- **The standard normal quantile** $z_{\alpha/2}$: The requested interval is a 98% interval, which means that $\alpha = 0.02$. The standard normal quantile, $z_{\alpha/2} = z_{0.01}$ is then $z_{0.01} = 2.326347874$.

By substituting these values into formula (9.21), we get the appropriate sample size.

$$n = \left(\frac{2 \times z_{\alpha/2} \times \sigma}{\text{Interval width}}\right)^2 = \left(\frac{2 \times 2.326347874 \times 0.2}{0.1}\right)^2 = 86.59 \approx 87$$

Figure 9.11 illustrates the Excel solution.

	A	B	C	D
1	Example 9.7: Calculating sample size			
2				
3				
4		Specified interval width =	5	
5		Population standard deviation, σ =	4	
6				
7		98% confidence interval, α =	0.02	
8		Proportion in right and left tails =	0.01	=C7/2
9		$z_{\alpha/2}$ =	2.326348	=NORM.S.INV(1-C8)
10				
11		Sample size n =	13.85445	=(2*C9*C5/C4)^2

Figure 9.11: Excel solution for Example 9.7

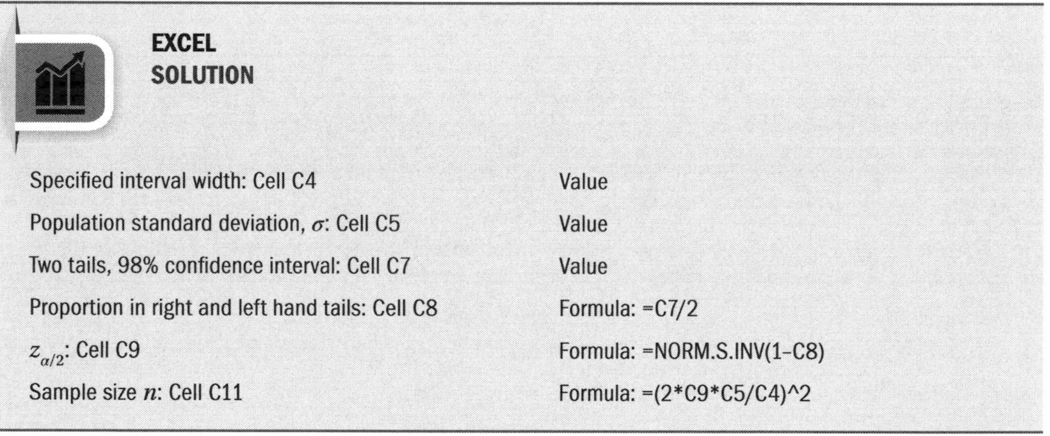

EXCEL SOLUTION

Specified interval width: Cell C4	Value
Population standard deviation, σ: Cell C5	Value
Two tails, 98% confidence interval: Cell C7	Value
Proportion in right and left hand tails: Cell C8	Formula: =C7/2
$z_{\alpha/2}$: Cell C9	Formula: =NORM.S.INV(1-C8)
Sample size n: Cell C11	Formula: =(2*C9*C5/C4)^2

INTERPRETATION Thus, to produce a 98% confidence interval estimate of the population mean foot length of customers, we need a sample size of at least 87 individuals.

NOTE

To see what impact the selection of the interval width and confidence interval has on the sample size, we present a small study using the data from Example 9.7.

Table 9.1: Study of sample sizes by changing the confidence level and maintaining the precision (interval width) of the estimator

INTERVAL WIDTH	0.10	0.10	0.10	0.10
CONFIDENCE LEVELS	90%	95%	98%	99%
SAMPLE SIZE	43	61	87	106

In Table 9.1, we have kept the specified interval width constant, but changed the confidence level. Note how the sample sizes change. Effectively, we need to increase the sample size almost two-and-a-half times if we want our confidence level to increase from 90% to 99%.

Let us now keep the confidence level constant, at 90%, and instead change the specified interval width.

Table 9.2: Study of sample sizes by maintaining the confidence level and changing the precision (interval width) of the estimator

INTERVAL WIDTH	0.10	0.05	0.03	0.01
CONFIDENCE LEVEL	90%	90%	90%	90%
SAMPLE SIZE	43	173	481	4 329

As we can see in Table 9.2, the interval width specified also has a tremendous impact on the sample size. To increase the precision (decrease the width of the interval) we need to increase the sample size over a hundredfold, which, in some cases, can be prohibitively expensive, time consuming or difficult to do.

SUMMARY

In this chapter, we introduced the important statistical concept of estimation. This concept is tremendously useful in practice and it also forms an important first step towards understanding the concepts of statistical inference, which we discuss in later chapters.

KEY TERMS

Confidence interval
Confidence level
Degrees of freedom
Estimate
Level of confidence
Point estimate
Point estimate for the mean
Point estimate for the proportion
Point estimate for the variance
Population variance
Unbiased

FORMULA SUMMARY

$$E(\overline{X}) = \mu \tag{9.1}$$

$$Var(\overline{X}) = \frac{\sigma^2}{n} \tag{9.2}$$

$$\mu = \overline{X} = \frac{1}{n}\sum_{i=1}^{n} X_i \tag{9.3}$$

$$\hat{\sigma} = S = \sqrt{\frac{1}{n-1}\sum_{i=1}^{n}(X_i - \overline{X})^2} \tag{9.4}$$

$$\hat{\sigma}_{\overline{X}} = \frac{\hat{\sigma}}{\sqrt{n}} = \frac{S}{\sqrt{n}} \tag{9.5}$$

$$\hat{\pi} = p \tag{9.6}$$

$$\hat{\sigma}_p = \sqrt{\frac{\hat{\pi}(1-\hat{\pi})}{n}} = \sqrt{\frac{p(1-p)}{n}} \tag{9.7}$$

$$\overline{X} = \frac{n_1\overline{X}_1 + n_2\overline{X}_2}{n_1 + n_2} \tag{9.8}$$

$$\hat{\sigma}^2 = \frac{n_1 s_1^2 + n_2 s_2^2}{n_1 + n_2 - 2} \tag{9.9}$$

$$\hat{\pi} = \frac{n_1\hat{\pi}_1 + n_2\hat{\pi}_2}{n_1 + n_2} = \frac{n_1 p_1 + n_2 p_2}{n_1 + n_2} \tag{9.10}$$

$$Z = \frac{X - \mu}{\frac{\sigma}{\sqrt{n}}} \tag{9.11}$$

$$P(-1.96 < Z < 1.96) = 0.95 \tag{9.12}$$

$$P\left(\overline{X} - 1.96 \times \frac{\sigma}{\sqrt{n}} < \mu < \overline{X} + 1.96 \times \frac{\sigma}{\sqrt{n}}\right) = 0.95 \quad (9.13)$$

$$\left[X - z_{\alpha/2} \times \frac{\sigma}{\sqrt{n}}; \overline{X} + z_{\alpha/2} \times \frac{\sigma}{\sqrt{n}}\right] \quad (9.14)$$

$$T = \frac{\overline{X} - \mu}{\frac{S}{\sqrt{n}}} \sim t_{n-1} \quad (9.15)$$

$$\left[\overline{X} - t_{df,\alpha/2} \times \frac{S}{\sqrt{n}}; [\overline{X} + t_{df,\alpha/2} \times \frac{S}{\sqrt{n}}\right] \quad (9.16)$$

$$Z = \frac{\overline{X} - \mu}{\frac{S}{\sqrt{n}}} \sim N(0, 1) \quad (9.17)$$

$$\left[\overline{X} - z_{\alpha/2} \times \frac{S}{\sqrt{n}}; \overline{X} + z_{\alpha/2} \times \frac{S}{\sqrt{n}}\right] \quad (9.18)$$

$$\left[p - z_{\alpha/2} \times \sqrt{\frac{p(1-p)}{n}}; p + z_{\alpha/2} \times \sqrt{\frac{p(1-p)}{n}}\right] \quad (9.19)$$

$$\text{Interval width} = 2 \times z_{\alpha/2} \times \frac{\sigma}{\sqrt{n}} \quad (9.20)$$

$$n = \left(\frac{2 \times z_{\alpha/2} \times \sigma}{\text{interval width}}\right)^2 \quad (9.21)$$

EXERCISES

9.1 A random sample of five values was taken from a population: 8.1, 9.5, 4.9, 7.3, 5.9. Estimate the population mean and standard deviation, and the standard error of the estimate for the population mean.

9.2 The mean of 10 readings of a variable was 8.7 with standard deviation of 0.3. A further five readings were taken: 8.6, 8.5, 8.8, 8.7, 8.9. Calculate the mean and standard deviation of the set of all 15 data readings (the original 10 and the 5 new values collected), using all the information available.

9.3 Two samples are drawn from the same population:

- Sample 1: 0.4, 0.2, 0.2, 0.4, 0.3, 0.3
- Sample 2: 0.2, 0.2, 0.1, 0.4, 0.2, 0.3, 0.1

Determine the best unbiased estimates of the population mean and variance.

9.4 A factory produces metal rods used in construction work. A random sample of 100 rods from the production line were measured and found to have a mean length of 12.132 cm with a standard deviation of 0.11 cm. A further sample of 50 were then taken. Using the information obtained from the first sample, estimate the probability that the sample mean length of this sample of 50 rods will be between 12.12 cm and 12.14 cm. What assumptions do you need to make to answer this question?

9.5 The students in a large school were asked a logic question. In a random sample of 20 students, it was found that only 12 answered the question correctly. Estimate the proportion of students in the school who answered correctly and the standard error of this estimate.

9.6 A random sample of 500 fish is taken from a lake, marked and released back into the lake. After a suitable interval, a second sample of 500 is taken and 25 of these are found to be marked. By considering the second sample, estimate the number of fish in the lake.

9.7 The standard deviation for a method of measuring the concentration of nitrate ions in water is known to be 0.05 parts per million (ppm). If 100 measurements give a mean of 1.13 ppm, calculate the 90% confidence limits for the true mean.

9.8 In trying to determine the sphere of influence of a shopping centre, a random sample of 100 shoppers was taken. The sample showed that the mean distance travelled by the shoppers (denoted d) was 10 km with a standard deviation of 3 km. If the population mean distance travelled is denoted by D then:

a) What are the 90% confidence limits for D?
b) What sample size would be required to ensure that the confidence interval for D was 0.5 km at the 95% level?

9.9 The masses, in grams, of 13 ball bearings taken at random from a batch are 21.4, 23.1, 25.9, 24.7, 23.4, 24.5, 25.0, 22.5, 29.9, 29.4, 25.8, 23.2, 21.9. Calculate a 95% confidence interval for the mean mass of the population, supposed normal, from which these masses were drawn.

9.10 A business analyst has been asked by the managing director of a national supermarket chain to conduct a business review of the company. One of the key objectives is to assess the level of spending of shoppers who historically have weekly mean levels of spending of R168 with a standard deviation of R15.65. Calculate the size of a random sample to produce a 98% confidence interval for the population mean spend, given that the width of the interval is R30. Is the sample size appropriate given the practical factors?

TECHNIQUES IN PRACTICE

9.11 AfriSoft is concerned about the time taken to react to customer complaints and has implemented a new set of procedures for its support centre staff. The customer service director has asked that a suitable test is applied to a new sample to assess whether the new target mean time for responding to customer complaints is 28 days.

Table 9.3: The time taken to respond to complaints (in days)

20	33	33	29	24	30
40	33	20	39	32	37
32	50	36	31	38	29
15	33	27	29	43	33
31	35	19	39	22	21
28	22	26	42	30	17
32	34	39	39	32	38

a) Construct a point estimate for the mean time to respond.
b) What are the model assumptions for question (a)?
c) Construct a 95% confidence interval for the mean time.
d) Is there any evidence to suggest that the mean time to respond to complaints is greater than 28 days?

9.12 Bakers Ltd is currently undertaking a review of the delivery vans used to deliver products to customers. The company runs two types of delivery van (type A – recently purchased – and type B – at least three years old), which are supposed to be capable of achieving 20 km per litre of petrol. A new sample has now been collected as shown in Table 9.4.

Table 9.4: Fuel consumption figures (km/ℓ) for the two van types; 15 for van type A and 21 for B

VAN TYPE A	VAN TYPE B
17.68	15.8
18.72	39.1
29.49	9.3
29.64	12.3
9.31	15.5
22.38	40.1
20.23	20.4
28.80	3.7

VAN TYPE A	VAN TYPE B
29.42	34.8
25.22	19.8
13.52	15.0
14.01	28.9
	33.9
	27.1
	19.8
	23.6

VAN TYPE A	VAN TYPE B	VAN TYPE A	VAN TYPE B
17.57	13.6		29.7
9.13	35.1		28.2
20.98	33.3		

a) Construct a point estimate for the mean fuel consumption for both van types.
b) What are the model assumptions for question (a)?
c) Construct a 95% confidence interval for the mean fuel consumption for van type A.
d) Construct a 90% confidence interval for the mean fuel consumption for van type B.
e) Assuming that the fuel consumption varies as per a normal distribution for each van type, do we have any evidence to suggest that the two types of delivery vans differ in their mean fuel consumption?
f) Based on your analysis, do we have any evidence that the new delivery vans meet the mean average of 20 km per litre?

9.13 Home-Made Beers Ltd is developing a low-calorie lager with a mean designed calorie count of 43 calories per 100 ml. The new product development team are having problems with the production process and have collected two independent random samples to assess whether the target calorie count is being met (assume the population of calorie count values is normally distributed).

Table 9.5: Calorie counts of two samples (A and B) of beer bottles; each sample consists of 22 bottles.

SAMPLE A	SAMPLE B	SAMPLE A	SAMPLE B
49.7	39.4	45.2	34.5
45.9	49.5	40.5	43.5
37.7	39.2	31.9	37.8
40.6	49.7	41.9	39.7
34.8	39.5	39.8	41.1
51.4	45.4	54.0	33.6
34.3	38.2	47.8	35.8
63.1	44.1	29.3	44.6
41.2	58.7	31.7	38.4
41.4	47.1	45.1	29.1
41.1	59.7	47.9	30.7

a) Construct a point estimate for the calorie count using all 44 beer bottle values.
b) What assumption is necessary for question (a) to produce an appropriate estimate?
c) Construct a 95% confidence interval for the population mean calorie count.
d) Is it likely that the target average number of calories is being achieved?

CHAPTER 10

PARAMETRIC HYPOTHESIS TESTING: ONE POPULATION

CHAPTER CONTENTS

OVERVIEW

Experiments, surveys and pilot projects are often carried out with the objective of testing a theory or hypothesis about the nature of population parameters under investigation. Since we cannot observe population parameters, we need to rely on sample information to come to conclusions about hypotheses made concerning their values. This procedure of using sample information to conclude whether a hypothesis concerning a population parameter should be rejected is called hypothesis testing and requires the use of the probability theory covered in earlier chapters.

In this chapter, we explore hypothesis tests for hypotheses made on parameters from a single population.

LEARNING OBJECTIVES

On completing this chapter, you should be able to:

- understand the concept of null and alternative hypotheses
- identify appropriate tests
- explain what is meant by a significance level
- understand the concept of a test statistic
- identify the appropriate test statistic for a given hypothesis test
- determine the sampling distribution of a test statistic
- understand the difference between left-sided, right-sided and two-sided tests
- distinguish between type I and II errors
- understand the concept of a *p*-value
- understand the concept of a critical value
- understand the use of the *p*-value and critical values in making decisions
- identify and apply a step-by-step procedure for solving hypothesis-related problems
- conduct one-sample hypothesis tests for the sample mean and proportion
- solve hypothesis test problems using Microsoft Excel.

10.1 An introduction to hypothesis testing

We begin our discussion by introducing the basic concepts surrounding hypotheses and hypothesis testing. In general, a hypothesis is a proposition (made by, for example, a researcher or analyst) concerning the nature or value of some unknown population quantity. For example, a person conducting wildlife research might propose, based on new evidence, that the population mean lifespan of adult tsetse flies is 750 hours. However, we cannot simply accept these hypotheses; they need to be substantiated using real data. In this tsetse fly example, we would not simply take the researcher's word that the population mean lifespan of adult tsetse flies was 750 hours; we would collect data in an attempt to refute or confirm the hypothesis.

The process of testing these hypotheses using sample data is called *statistical hypothesis testing* and it involves, among other things, probability theory to come to conclusions about the stated hypothesis (such as whether the statement should be rejected).

10.1.1 Hypothesis testing procedure

We will encounter many different types of hypotheses throughout the course of this textbook and, since each one will require us to perform different calculations and use different types of data, it may become cumbersome to memorise the specific process for each test separately. Therefore, to simplify implementing hypothesis testing, we present here a generic **hypothesis test procedure** that can be used in most of the hypothesis tests that you will be confronted with in this and later chapters. This generic step-by-step procedure is given below.

Hypothesis test procedure A series of five steps used to determine whether we reject a null hypothesis based on sample data.

GENERIC HYPOTHESIS TESTING PROCEDURE

Step 1: Provide the formal hypothesis statements: H_0 and H_1.

Step 2: Determine the appropriate test for the given hypothesis statement.

Step 3: Specify the level of significance, α.

Step 4: Calculate the relevant test statistic.

Step 5: Make a decision.

Before we begin the detailed discussion of these five steps, we must first introduce and briefly define some concepts that are necessary to understand the progression of the steps.

- *Null and alternative hypotheses*: The **null** and **alternative hypotheses** are two competing statements concerning the population parameters of interest. These statements inform the entire testing procedure. The null hypothesis is denoted by H_0 and the alternative hypothesis by H_1.

Null hypothesis (H_0) Represents a theory regarding population parameters that has been put forward but has not been proved.

Alternative hypothesis (H_1) Contains specific alternative values for the population parameters stated in H_0 and as such serves as a contrasting statement for H_0.

- *Significance level, α*: The **significance level** of a statistical hypothesis test is a fixed probability of making the error of *rejecting the null hypothesis, H_0, even though it is true*. This probability is specified by the researcher and represents the degree of accuracy that the test should exhibit. For example, if we choose $\alpha = 0.05$, we are saying that we would like to make the mistake of incorrectly rejecting H_0 in, at most, 5% of the cases where this test is conducted.
- *Test statistic*: A **test statistic** is a quantity calculated from sample data. It is used to determine if H_0 should be rejected. This statistic is always calculated under the assumption that H_0 is true.
- *Critical value*: The **critical value** is a quantile (related to the probability α) from the sampling distribution of the test statistic. Critical values define the range of values for the test statistic for which we do not reject H_0, i.e. if the observed value of the test statistic lies in the *rejection region* defined by the critical values, then we reject H_0.

- p-*value*: The ***p*-value** is the probability of getting a value of the test statistic as extreme as, or more extreme than, that observed by chance alone, if the null hypothesis is true. Typically, if p-value $< \alpha$ we will reject the null hypothesis.

Using these concepts as a basic foundation, we now continue the discussion of the five steps of the hypothesis testing procedure in greater detail.

Significance level, α A specified probability of incorrectly rejecting the null hypothesis, H_0, if it is in fact true.

p-value The probability of getting a value of the test statistic as extreme as or more extreme than that observed by chance alone, if the null hypothesis is true.

Critical value A quantile associated with α and the sampling distribution of the test statistic. It defines the range of possible values of the test statistic for which we will reject H_0.

Test statistic A quantity calculated from our sample of data that is used to measure the *distance* between a sample statistic and a hypothesised parameter.

Step 1: Provide the hypothesis statements H_0 and H_1

When dealing with a hypothesis test, we have to formulate our initial research hypothesis into *two* statements, which can then be evaluated: the null hypothesis and the alternative hypothesis.

- The null hypothesis (denoted by H_0) is called the hypothesis of *no difference* and is typically a very specific statement about the population parameters (at least for this chapter and the next). For example, the formal statement of the null hypothesis regarding the population lifespan of the adult tsetse flies (discussed in the opening paragraph) could be written as H_0:$\mu = 750$, where μ denotes the population mean lifespan of adult tsetse flies. For this chapter and the next, we always use the equals sign (=) in a null hypothesis statement.
- The alternative hypothesis (denoted by H_1) opposes the null hypothesis by providing an alternative value or set of alternative values for the population parameter stated in the null hypothesis. For example, if the null hypothesis states that the population mean lifespan of adult tsetse flies is 750 hours, the alternative hypothesis could state that the population mean lifespan is every length of time *except* 750 hours: H_1:$\mu \neq 750$. This alternative is more general, since it provides infinitely many other possibilities for the value of μ. Other choices of this alternative hypothesis could be that μ will be strictly greater than 750: H_1:$\mu > 750$. Or, perhaps the researchers are interested in the alternatives where μ is strictly less than 750: H_1:$\mu < 750$.

When the symbols $\neq$, $<$ or $>$ appear in the alternate hypothesis, we refer to the hypothesis as being **two-sided**, **left-sided** or **right-sided**, respectively. In general, these hypotheses have the following forms.

- Two-sided hypothesis in general:

  H_0: population parameter = specified value
  vs
  H_1: population parameter $\neq$ specified value

For example, if the population parameter of interest is the population mean IQ of school children, μ, and it is claimed that μ is equal to 105, versus the alternative that it is not 105, then this will result in the following two-sided hypothesis statement:

H_0: $\mu = 105$
vs
H_1: $\mu \neq 105$

- Left-sided hypothesis in general:

H_0: population parameter = specified value
vs
H_1: population parameter < specified value

For example, if the population parameter of interest is the population proportion of families in South Africa that own televisions, π, and it is claimed that π is equal to 0.85, versus the alternative that it is less than 0.85, then this will result in the following left-sided hypothesis statement:

H_0: $\pi = 0.85$
vs
H_1: $\pi < 0.85$

- Right-sided hypothesis in general:

H_0: population parameter = specified value
vs
H_1: population parameter > specified value

For example, if the population parameter of interest is the population variance of the distances travelled by truck drivers working for a logistics company, σ^2, and it is claimed that σ^2 is greater than 116 km, then this will result in the following right-sided hypothesis statement:

H_0: $\sigma^2 = 116$ km
vs
H_1: $\sigma^2 > 116$ km

The choice between a left-sided, right-sided or two-sided hypothesis depends on the problem being considered. It will also affect the subsequent steps in the hypothesis testing procedure, so it is therefore important that this is correctly specified.

Two-sided test A statistical hypothesis test in which the values that can reject the null hypothesis, H_0, are located in both tails of the test statistic's probability distribution.

Left-sided (or right-sided) tests Tests in which the values that can reject the null hypothesis, H_0, are entirely in the left (or right) tails of the test statistic's probability distribution.

NOTE

Decisions in hypothesis tests are always formulated in terms of the null hypothesis, for example, we typically report the final decision of a hypothesis test as either 'Reject the null hypothesis' or 'Do not reject the null hypothesis'.

We never say 'Accept the null hypothesis', because not rejecting the null hypothesis cannot be taken as conclusive proof that the null hypothesis is true. It is rather interpreted as a piece of evidence that increases our belief in the truth of the null hypothesis.

Step 2: Choosing an appropriate test statistic

The second step of the hypothesis testing procedure involves deciding on the appropriate test statistic to test the stated hypotheses.

To understand the concept of a test statistic, we briefly describe a few properties shared by all test statistics.

PROPERTIES OF TEST STATISTICS

Test statistics are calculated under the assumption that H_0 is true: A test statistic is a statistic that assumes that the conditions stipulated in H_0 are true. This assumption is usually reflected in the statistic by replacing the symbols that represent hypothesised values with the value given in H_0.

For example, if our null hypothesis states H_0: $\mu = 750$, and we want to use the statistic, $\frac{\sqrt{n}(\overline{X} - \mu)}{S}$, for this test, then in order for this statistic to be considered as a *test statistic*, we need to replace μ with the value given in H_0. For this example, the test statistic will therefore be $\frac{\sqrt{n}(\overline{X} - 750)}{S}$.

Test statistics measure the distance between a hypothesised population parameter and a sample statistic: A test statistic can be interpreted as a measure of *distance* between a *sample statistic* and the *parameter value specified in H_0*.

For example, if the null hypothesis states H_0: $\mu = 750$, then a test statistic for this hypothesis will attempt to measure the difference between the sample mean, $\overline{X}$, and the hypothesised population mean value, $\mu = 750$. For this example, the test statistic might require us to calculate (among other things) the following difference: $\overline{X} - 750$.

The sampling distribution of a test statistic is completely known: The final property that test statistics must possess is that their *sampling distribution must be completely* known if H_0 is assumed to be true.

For example, consider the quantity $\overline{X} - 750$ stated above, and suppose that we have a very large sample. Even though this statistic can be interpreted as a distance, and even though we partially know its distribution (it follows a normal distribution under H_0 for large samples according to the Central Limit Theorem), it still does not qualify as a test statistic because we do not know the variance of this normal distribution, i.e. the distribution is not *fully* known. It turns out, in this case, that if we slightly modify the statistic to $\frac{\sqrt{n}(\overline{X} - 750)}{S}$, the result is a test statistic, because this new statistic follows a t-distribution with $n - 1$ degrees of freedom (there are no unknown parameters in the sampling distribution of this new statistic). Refer to Section 9.3.3 to see a motivation for using the t-distribution in this situation.

Over the course of the next few chapters, we will encounter a number of different scenarios in which we apply hypothesis testing. Determining which test statistic will be most appropriate can be tricky. In each of the hypothesis testing scenarios, a different test statistic must be calculated and different rules for rejecting or not rejecting the null hypothesis must be applied. Therefore, in order to decide which test statistic to use, the following aspects of a study need to be determined.

- *The number of populations in the study*: Is the sample data from a single population or are they from two or more populations? Typically, if multiple populations were used, it will have produced multiple sets of sample data. Similarly, if the data were from a single population, there will typically only be one set of sample data. Note that this chapter deals with single population tests and the next chapter with two population tests.
- *The research question*: What is the nature of the research question? The research question will dictate the type of test to be conducted. For example, in Chapter 14, we will encounter research questions concerning the association between variables. We will have to use the appropriate test statistics that measure these associations. In this chapter and the next, we mainly consider research questions related to the value of population parameters (for example, the population mean, the population proportion or the population variance), and for each of these population parameters, we will need different statistics.
- *Assumptions underlying the test*: Once we have decided what the nature of the research question is, we can decide which test statistic to use. However, some test statistics require certain assumptions to be satisfied before we can apply them. For example, in this chapter, we encounter a test statistic that has a sampling distribution that relies on the assumption that the sample data used in its calculation were obtained from a normally distributed population. If this assumption is made but is not true, it will adversely affect the conclusions concerning the hypotheses. It is thus important to confirm whether the assumptions are true or not. If they are true, we can continue using the test, but if they are false, we may need to find a more appropriate test statistic.

Step 3: Specify the significance level

When making a decision in hypothesis testing, we distinguish between two types of possible errors: **type I** and **type II errors**. A type I error is committed when we reject a null hypothesis when it is true, whereas a type II error occurs when we do not reject a null hypothesis when it is not true. These errors are summarised in Table 10.1.

Table 10.1: Types of error

		TRUTH	
		H_0 IS TRUE	H_1 IS TRUE
DECISION	REJECT H_0	Type I error	Correct
	DO NOT REJECT H_0	Correct	Type II error

From Table 10.1, we can see that a type I error occurs when we reject a null hypothesis that is actually true. The *probability of a type I error* is called the *level of significance* and is denoted by the Greek letter *alpha*, α.

NOTE

The type II error is only an error in the sense that an opportunity to reject the null hypothesis correctly was lost. The *probability of a type II error* is denoted by the Greek letter *beta, β*.

Type I error Occurs when the null hypothesis is rejected when it is in fact true.

Type II error Occurs when the null hypothesis, H_0, is not rejected when it is in fact false.

Alpha, *α* Also called the level of significance, refers to the probability of committing a type I error.

Beta, *β*: Refers to the probability of committing a type II error.

The *level of significance, α,* is a value that the analyst specifies, and it represents the acceptable amount of risk when making a decision concerning the null hypothesis. For example, if the analyst specifies a very small value for α, for example, $\alpha = 0.0001$ (or 0.01%), then the hypothesis test will only ever reject H_0 incorrectly in 0.01% of the cases. Unfortunately, this value is overly conservative in most tests, because if we specify an α-value this small, then we will almost always *not* reject null hypotheses, even in situations in which it would reasonably be rejected. On the other hand, if an analyst specifies $\alpha = 0.999$, then we will almost *always* reject H_0 (both correctly and incorrectly), because the probability of a type I error is 99.9%.

Typically, the value of α is chosen to be 5% (0.05) or 1% (0.01), but this value depends on how sure we want to be that our decisions are an accurate reflection of the true population relationship.

Step 4: Calculate the relevant test statistic

We will deal with calculating the appropriate test statistic in each section where we introduce each new test. This step will typically be carried out using Excel.

Step 5: Make a decision

The final step in the hypothesis testing procedure is to decide whether the null hypothesis should be rejected. We do this by deciding whether the test statistic is *large*, that is, whether the distance between a sample statistic and a hypothesised parameter is large (see Step 4). That is, based on the value of the test statistic, we can determine if the sample statistic is *close* to the hypothesised parameter (in which case we will *not* reject H_0), or if it is *far away* from the hypothesised parameter (in which case we will reject H_0). To facilitate this interpretation, we consider two different approaches that we can use to decide what constitutes far away and what is close. We can use either of the following two approaches:

- Using critical values
- Using *p*-values

In both approaches, the way in which we make these decisions depends on the nature of the alternative hypothesis (whether it is right-sided, left-sided or two-sided). We now consider both approaches and indicate how we test the hypothesis for right-sided, left-sided and two-sided tests.

The critical value approach

A critical value is simply a quantile based on the level of significance, α, and the sampling distribution of a test statistic. We use critical values to define **regions of rejection** for the observed value of the test statistic. In other words, if the observed value of the test statistic falls in the rejection region, we reject H_0.

Region of rejection The range of values that leads to rejection of the null hypothesis.

Intuitively, we can say that the critical values are thresholds that indicate when a test statistic's value is close to zero or not. If the test statistic exceeds the critical value, its value is far away from zero (there is a large distance between the sample statistic and the hypothesised parameter). If the test statistic lies anywhere else, then it is close to zero (the distance between the sample statistic and the hypothesised parameter is small enough to be considered negligible).

To illustrate how critical values and rejection regions are defined, we consider testing whether the population mean is equal to 100:

$$H_0: \mu = 100$$

The test statistic selected for this test follows a standard normal distribution if we assume that the sample data used in this test is obtained from a normally distributed population with known variance, σ^2. The test statistic is:

$$Z = \frac{\overline{X} - 100}{\frac{\sigma}{\sqrt{n}}} \overset{H_0}{\sim} N(0, 1)$$

That is, Z follows a standard normal distribution if the conditions stated in the null hypothesis are true (we usually shorten this by simply saying '*Z has a standard normal distributed under H_0*').

Note that we distinguish between the random variable Z and the actual calculated value of the test statistic by denoting the calculated value by z_{cal}.

We will select $\alpha = 0.05$ for all of the examples.

- **Left-sided test:** The hypothesis statement for a left-sided test that tests whether the population mean is 100 versus the alternative that it is less than 100 is:

  $$H_0: \mu = 100 \quad \text{vs} \quad H_1: \mu < 100$$

  The critical value for this test is then just the *lower* $\alpha = 0.05$ quantile for the standard normal distribution: it will be $-z_\alpha = -z_{0.05} = -1.645$. (This value was obtained using the Excel function NORM.S.INV.) If the observed value of the test statistic is smaller than this critical value (if it falls in the rejection region), then we reject H_0. In other words, if $z_{cal} < z_\alpha$ reject H_0.

  The critical value and rejection region are illustrated in Figure 10.1.

- **Right-sided test:** The hypothesis statement for a right-sided test that tests whether the population mean is 100 versus the alternative that it is greater than 100 is:

  $$H_0: \mu = 100 \quad \text{vs} \quad H_1: \mu > 100$$

  The critical value for this test is the *upper* $\alpha = 0.05$ quantile for the standard normal distribution: it will be $z_\alpha = z_{0.05} = 1.645$. (Again, this value was obtained using the Excel function NORM.INV.) If the observed value of the test statistic is greater than this critical value (if it falls in the rejection region), then we reject H_0. In other words, if $z_{cal} > z_\alpha$, reject H_0.

  The critical value and rejection region are illustrated in Figure 10.2.

- **Two-sided test:** The hypothesis statement for a two-sided test used to test whether the population mean is 100 versus the alternative that it is not 100 is:

  $$H_0: \mu = 100 \quad \text{vs} \quad H_1: \mu \neq 100$$

  There are two critical values in this test: the lower $\frac{\alpha}{2} = 0.025$ quantile and the upper $\frac{\alpha}{2} = 0.025$ quantile, both for the standard normal distribution, i.e. they will be $-z_{\alpha/2} = -z_{0.025} = -1.96$ and $z_{\alpha/2} = z_{0.025} = 1.96$. If the observed value of the test statistic is greater than $z_{\alpha/2}$ or is less than $-z_{\alpha/2}$, then we reject H_0. In other words, if $z_{cal} < -z_{\alpha/2}$ or if $z_{cal} > z_{\alpha/2}$, reject H_0.

  The critical values and rejection region are illustrated in Figure 10.3.

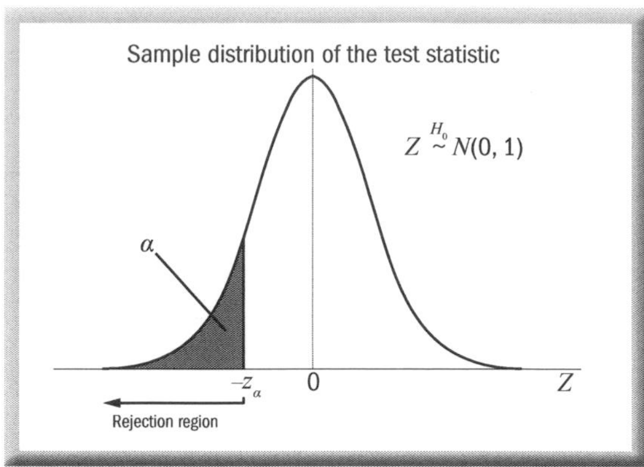

Figure 10.1: Critical value and rejection region for a left-sided test

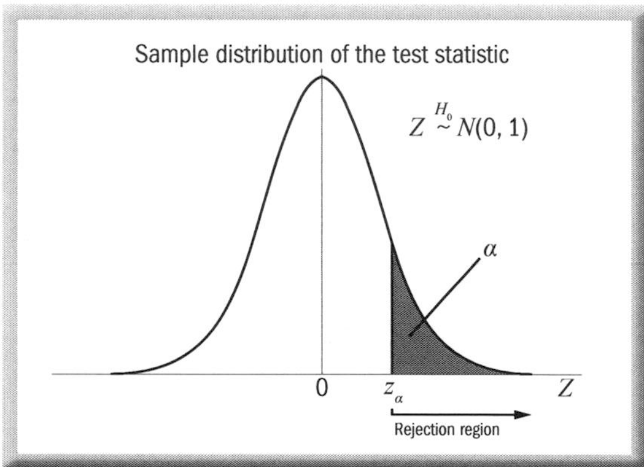

Figure 10.2: Critical value and rejection region for a right-sided test

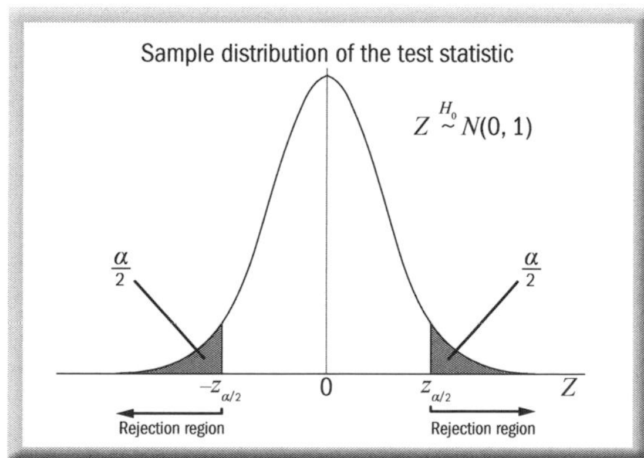

Figure 10.3: Critical value and rejection region for a two-sided test

In the above examples, we used a normally distributed test statistic. However, during this course, we also encounter test statistics that follow the *t*-, chi-squared, and *F*-distributions. See the discussion in Chapter 7 on how to calculate quantiles for these distributions.

NOTE

If a test statistic lies within the rejection region defined by the critical values, then we reject the null hypothesis H_0.

Specifically, this approach uses a direct comparison of the calculated test statistic and the critical value. For the different types of tests we have:

- Left-sided test: Reject H_0 if the calculated test statistic < critical value.
- Right-sided test: Reject H_0 if the calculated test statistic > critical value.
- Two-sided test: Reject H_0 if the calculated test statistic < *lower* critical value, or if the calculated test statistic > *upper* critical value.

We can use Excel to calculate the critical values for the tests in this chapter and the next. We present the Excel solutions for each test as they are discussed.

The *p*-value approach

The *p*-value approach is directly related to the critical value approach, except that instead of basing the decision on the test statistic's actual value, we base it on a probability associated with the test statistic, called the *p*-value. We then compare the *p*-value to the level of significance, α, specified for the test, to make a decision between rejecting or not rejecting the null hypothesis, H_0.

Once again, the nature of the alternative hypothesis will affect the way in which we make the decision. We now consider the left-sided, right-sided and two-sided tests using the same test and test statistic we used for the critical value approach, i.e. we will test H_0: $\mu = 100$ using the test statistic $Z = \frac{\sqrt{n}(\bar{X} - 100)}{\sigma} \overset{H_0}{\simeq} N(0, 1)$.

- **Left-sided test:** The hypothesis statement for a left-sided test that tests whether the population mean is 100 versus the alternative that it is less than 100 is:

  $$H_0: \mu = 100 \quad \text{vs} \quad H_1: \mu < 100$$

  We calculate the *p*-value using the formula:

  $$p\text{-value} = P(Z < z_{\text{cal}}) \tag{10.1}$$

  To make a decision concerning H_0, we compare the *p*-value to α. If the *p*-value is smaller than α, reject H_0.

  Figure 10.4 shows two scenarios for a left-sided test. Scenario I shows the case in which the test statistic lies in the rejection region and scenario II shows the case in which the test statistic lies in the do not reject H_0 region.

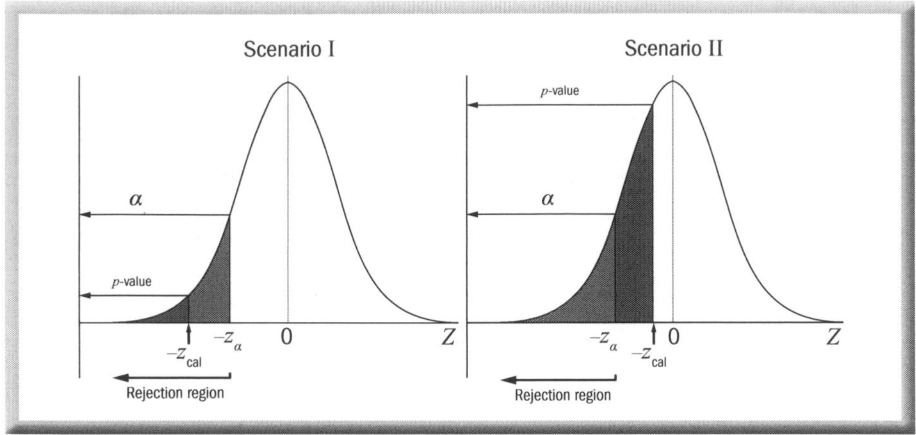

Figure 10.4: p-values for a left-sided test: Scenario I, H_0 is rejected; scenario II, H_0 is not rejected

- **Right-sided test:** The hypothesis statement for a right-sided test that tests whether the population mean is 100 versus the alternative that it is greater than 100 is:

  $H_0: \mu = 100 \quad \text{vs} \quad H_1: \mu > 100$

  We calculate the p-value using the formula:

  $$p\text{-value} = P(Z > z_{cal}) \tag{10.2}$$

  To make a decision concerning H_0, we compare the p-value to α. If the p-value is smaller than α, reject H_0.

  Figure 10.5 below shows two scenarios for a right-sided test: Scenario I shows the case in which the test statistic lies in the rejection region and scenario II shows the case in which the test statistic lies in the do not reject H_0 region.

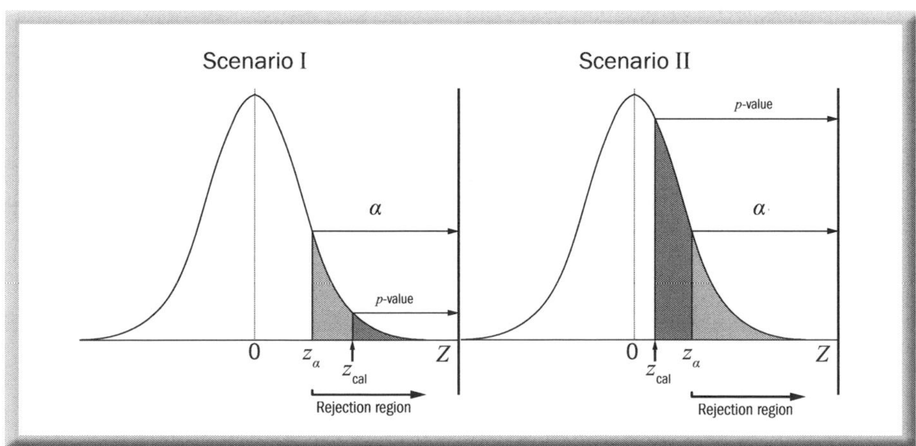

Figure 10.5: p-values for a right sided test: Scenario I, H_0 is rejected; scenario II, H_0 is not rejected

- **Two-sided test:** The hypothesis statement for a two-sided test that tests whether the population mean is 100 versus the alternative that it is not 100 is:

$H_0: \mu = 100$ vs $H_1: \mu \neq 100$

If the calculated value of the test statistic z_{cal} is positive, then the p-value is calculated using the formula:

$$p\text{-value} = P(Z < -z_{cal}) + P(Z > z_{cal}) = 2 \times P(Z > z_{cal}) \quad (10.3)$$

If the calculated value of the test statistic z_{cal} is negative, then the p-value is calculated using the formula:

$$p\text{-value} = P(Z > -z_{cal}) + P(Z < z_{cal}) = 2 \times P(Z < z_{cal}) \quad (10.4)$$

Note that this calculation differs from the previous two because we need to calculate the probability to the left and the right. This probability calculation is illustrated in Figure 10.6. Once again, to make a decision concerning H_0, we compare the p-value to α. If the p-value is smaller than α, reject H_0.

The two scenarios in Figure 10.6 show how the p-value is split into two parts. This is necessary because the statistic can be significantly smaller than zero or it can be significantly greater than zero. Scenario I shows the case in which the test statistic lies in the rejection region and scenario II shows the case in which the test statistic lies in the do not reject H_0 region.

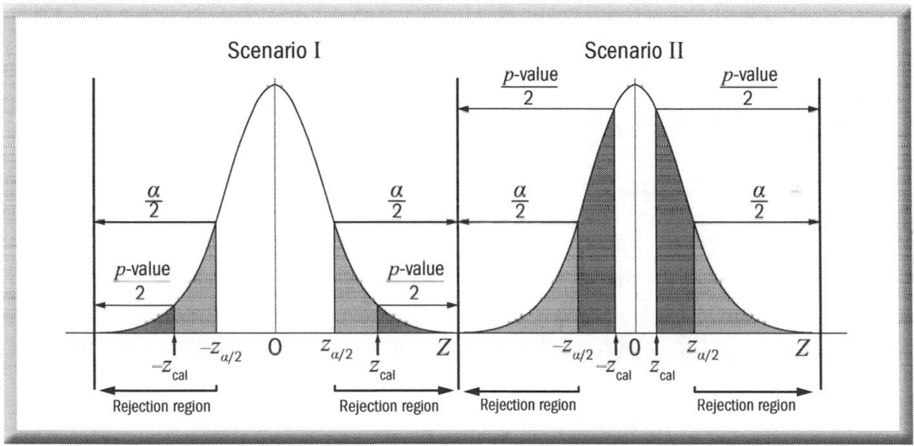

Figure 10.6: p-values for a two-sided test: Scenario I, H_0 is rejected; scenario II, H_0 is not rejected

Note that in *all* cases, the p-value is only smaller than α when the calculated test statistic lies in the rejection region.

NOTE If $p < \alpha$, we reject the null hypothesis, H_0.

We can also use Excel to calculate a *p*-value depending on the sampling distribution of the test statistic.

NOTE

We can summarise the differences between the critical value approach and the *p*-value approach as follows:

- The critical value approach directly compares the test statistic to a critical value to decide whether to reject H_0.
- The *p*-value approach compares a *probability associated with the test statistic* (the *p*-value) to a *probability associated with the critical value* (the significance level α) to decide whether to reject H_0

Now that we have briefly described the five different steps common to all different hypothesis tests, we continue with tests for specific population parameters under different circumstances.

10.2 One sample Z-test for the population mean

The first test we will explore is the one sample Z-test for the population mean. The null hypothesis for this test is always $H_0: \mu = \mu_0$ where μ_0 is some value specified in the null hypothesis. The alternative hypothesis can be left-sided, right-sided or two-sided:

$H_1: \mu < \mu_0$ (left-sided) $\quad$ $H_1: \mu > \mu_0$ (right-sided) $\quad$ or $\quad$ $H_1: \mu \neq \mu_0$ (two-sided)

Examples of hypotheses statements are therefore:

A two-sided test with μ_0 specified as 100, or:

$$H_0: \mu = 100 \quad \text{vs} \quad H_1: \mu \neq 100$$

A right-sided test with μ_0 specified as 0.067:

$$H_0: \mu = 0.067 \quad \text{vs} \quad H_1: \mu > 0.067$$

The test statistic that we use in this situation is:

$$Z = \frac{\overline{X} - \mu_0}{\frac{\sigma}{\sqrt{n}}} \overset{H_0}{\sim} N(0, 1) \tag{10.5}$$

σ is the *known* population standard deviation, n is the sample size and μ_0 is the value of μ specified in H_0.

In order to use this test statistic, at *least one* of the following two assumptions should hold:

- The sample data are randomly collected from a population that is normally distributed and the value of the population standard deviation, σ, is *known*.
- The value of the population standard deviation, σ, is *known* but the sample size, n, is large enough that we can apply the Central Limit Theorem (typically we consider a sample to be large if $n \geq 30$).

These assumptions ensure that the test statistic stated in formula (10.5) follows a standard normal distribution. If the assumptions are not satisfied, we cannot assume a standard normal distribution.

The following example illustrates how these types of tests can be formulated and solved in Excel.

WORKED EXAMPLES

EXAMPLE 10.1

Each employee of a meat packing factory can correctly pack 100 packets of lamb chops every hour (on average) with a standard deviation of 20 packets. A new employee is tested on 36 randomly chosen separate occasions and is found to have an output of 90 packs per hour. Does this indicate that the new employee's output is significantly different from the average output? Test the hypothesis at a significance level of 5%.

To arrive at a conclusion regarding the new employee, we use the five-step hypothesis testing procedure discussed in Section 10.1.

Step 1: Provide the hypothesis statements H_0 and H_1

- *Null hypothesis*: H_0: $\mu = 100$, i.e. the population mean is hypothesised to be equal to 100 packets per hour.
- *Alternative hypothesis*: H_1: $\mu \neq 100$.
  The wording of the problem does not state that the analysts are interested in the population mean being larger or smaller than 100 packets per hour, but rather they are only interested in whether it *differs* from 100 packets per hour, hence the use of the $\neq$ sign in H_1. Recall that this implies a two-sided test.

Step 2: Choose an appropriate test statistic

We now need to choose an appropriate statistical test for testing H_0. From the information provided we note the following.

- *The number of populations in the study*: A sample from one population is being considered.
- *The research question*: The research question concerns the value of a population mean, μ. Our test statistic will therefore need to measure the distance between the sample mean ($\overline{X} = 90$) and the hypothesised population mean ($\mu_0 = 100$).
- *Assumptions underlying the test*: The information provided states that the population standard deviation is known ($\sigma = 20$), but it does not indicate that the data came from a normally distributed population. Fortunately, the size of the sample is large enough ($n = 36$), thus satisfying the assumption for the Z-test in formula (10.5).

The one sample Z-test statistic for population means given in formula (10.5) is thus an appropriate test statistic.

Step 3: Specify the significance level

The significance level is specified as $\alpha = 0.05$ (or 5%).

Step 4: Calculate the relevant test statistic

The sample mean is given as $\overline{X} = 90$, the sample size is $n = 36$, the hypothesised population mean is $\mu_0 = 100$ and the population standard deviation is given as $\sigma = 20$, so the calculated value of the test statistic in formula (10.5) becomes:

$$z_{cal} = \frac{\overline{X} - \mu_0}{\frac{\sigma}{\sqrt{n}}} = \frac{90 - 100}{\frac{20}{\sqrt{36}}} = -\frac{10}{\frac{20}{6}} = -3$$

Step 5: Make a decision

We use both the critical value approach and the p-value approach to make a decision for this test.

- *Critical value approach*: The significance level was chosen to be $\alpha = 0.05$, the sampling distribution of the chosen test statistic is standard normal and the test is a two-sided test, so the critical values of the test are the values $-z_{\alpha/2}$ and $z_{\alpha/2}$ defined such that $P(Z > z_{\alpha/2}) = P(Z < -z_{\alpha/2}) = \frac{\alpha}{2}$, where $Z \sim N(0, 1)$. Using Excel's NORM.S.INV function, we find that $z_{\alpha/2} = z_{0.025} = 1.96$ and $-z_{\alpha/2} = -z_{0.025} = -1.96$. Does the calculated value of the test statistic, $z_{cal} = -3$, lie in the rejection region? Yes, because $z_{cal} = -3 < -z_{\alpha/2} = -1.96$ and $-z_{cal} = 3 > z_{\alpha/2} = 1.96$. *Therefore we reject H_0*. The rejection region is shown in Figure 10.7.
- p-*value approach*: The p-value for this test is calculated using formula (10.4):

$$\begin{aligned} p\text{-value} &= 2 \times P(Z < z_{cal}) \\ &= 2 \times P(Z < -3) \\ &= 2 \times (0.0013) = 0.0026 \end{aligned}$$

The p-value is smaller than the specified significance level $\alpha = 0.05$, *therefore reject H_0*. Figure 10.7 shows the p-values relative to the significance level.

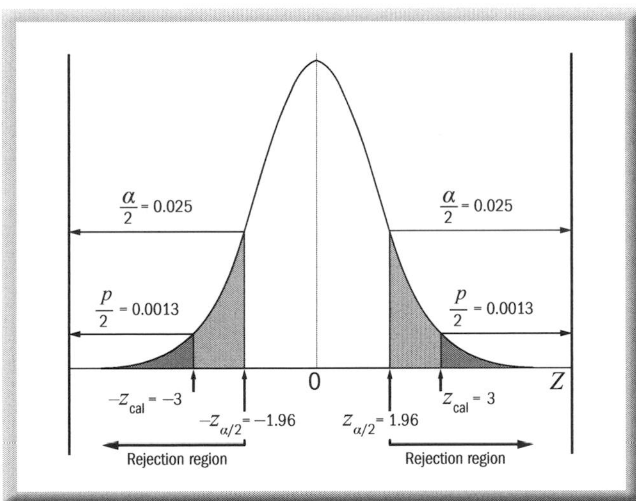

Figure 10.7: Graphical representation of the critical values, test statistic value and p-value of the test in Example 10.1

The Excel solution for this example is given in Figure 10.8.

	A	B	C	D	E	F
1	**Hypohesis testing example – one sample Z-test of the population mean**					
2						
3				H_0 : Population mean $\mu = 100$		
4			**1. State hypothesis**	H_1 : Population mean $\mu \neq 100$		
5				Two-sided test		
6						
7				One sample Z-test for the population mean		
8			**2. Selected test**	Population distribution unknown, but n is large		
9				Population standard deviation σ, is known		
10						
11			**3. Set level of significance**	Significance $\alpha =$	0.05	
12						
13				Population		
14				Mean, $\mu =$	100	
15				Standard deviation, $\sigma =$	20	
16				Sample		
17				$n =$	36	
18				$\overline{X} =$	90	
19			**4. Calculate test statistic**	$\sigma/\sqrt{n} =$	3.3333333	=E15/SQRT(E17)
20				$z_{cal} =$	-3	=(E18-E14)/E19
21				p-value and critical value		
22				Two-sided p-value =	0.002699796	=2*(NORM.S.DIST(E20,TRUE))
23				$-z_{\alpha/2} =$	-1.959964	=NORM.S.INV(E11/2)
24				$z_{\alpha/2} =$	1.959964	=NORM.S.INV(1-E11/2)
25						
26			**5. Decision**	Test statistic compared to critical value $z_{cal} < -z_{\alpha/2}$		Reject H_0
27				p-values compared to significance level $p < \alpha$		Reject H_0

Figure 10.8: Excel solution for Example 10.1

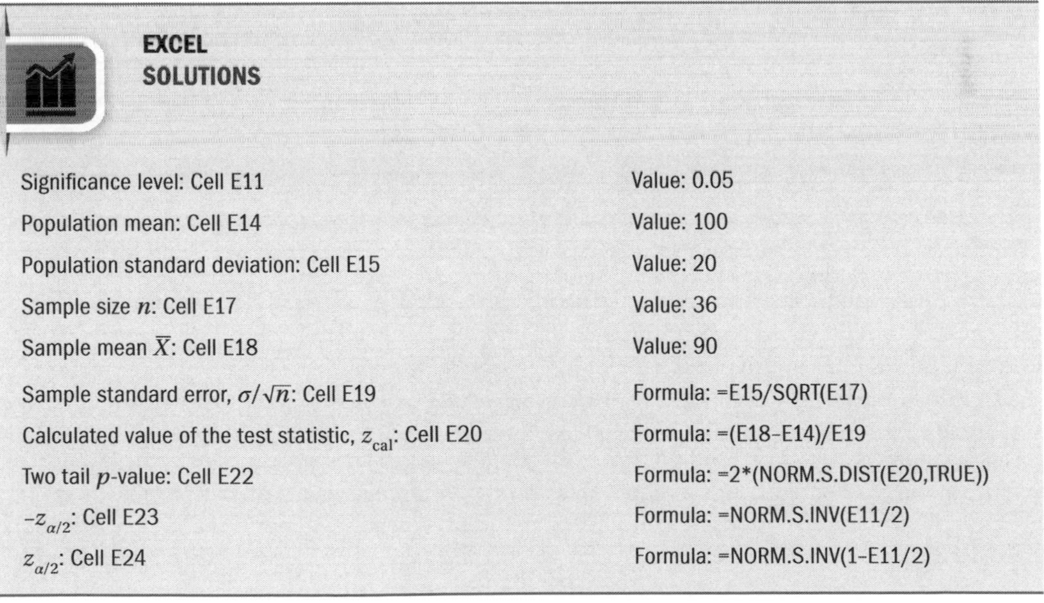

EXCEL SOLUTIONS

Significance level: Cell E11	Value: 0.05
Population mean: Cell E14	Value: 100
Population standard deviation: Cell E15	Value: 20
Sample size n: Cell E17	Value: 36
Sample mean $\overline{X}$: Cell E18	Value: 90
Sample standard error, $\sigma/\sqrt{n}$: Cell E19	Formula: =E15/SQRT(E17)
Calculated value of the test statistic, z_{cal}: Cell E20	Formula: =(E18-E14)/E19
Two tail p-value: Cell E22	Formula: =2*(NORM.S.DIST(E20,TRUE))
$-z_{\alpha/2}$: Cell E23	Formula: =NORM.S.INV(E11/2)
$z_{\alpha/2}$: Cell E24	Formula: =NORM.S.INV(1-E11/2)

INTERPRETATION We conclude that there is a significant difference, at the 0.05 level, between the new employee's output and the packing factory's existing average employee output. In other words, the sample mean value (90 units per hour) is not close enough to the population mean value (100 units per hour) to allow us to assume that the sample comes from a population with mean 100.

NOTE As noted earlier, the use of the p-value for comparing the calculated test statistic versus the use of the critical value for comparison is a matter of preference. Both methods yield identical results.

10.3 One sample *t*-test for the population mean

We do not usually know the value of the population standard deviation, σ, and so we do not employ the Z-test discussed in Section 10.2 very often. To overcome the difficulty associated with not knowing σ, we use the t-test. The t-test statistic is similar to the Z-test, except that it estimates the population standard deviation, σ, using the sample standard deviation, S.

The null and alternative hypotheses for this test is the same as before:

$$H_0: \mu = \mu_0$$

Versus any of the following:

$H_1: \mu < \mu_0$	$H_1: \mu > \mu_0$	$H_1: \mu \neq \mu_0$
left-sided	right-sided	two-sided

μ_0 is some value specified in the null hypothesis.

The test statistic is then:

$$T = \frac{\overline{X} - \mu_0}{\frac{S}{\sqrt{n}}} \overset{H_0}{\sim} t_{n-1} \tag{10.6}$$

S is the sample standard deviation, n is the sample size, and μ_0 is the value of μ specified in H_0. Note that the distribution of this test statistic is now a t-distribution and not a standard normal distribution. The calculated value of this test statistic is denoted t_{cal}.

We can apply this test if either of the following two sets of assumptions is satisfied:

- The sample data are randomly collected from a population that is normally distributed and the value of the population standard deviation, σ, is *unknown*.
- The value of the population standard deviation, σ, is *unknown* but the sample size, n, is large enough that we can apply the Central Limit Theorem (typically we consider a sample to be large if $n \geq 30$).

In the next example, we use this t-test to test an assertion about the value of a population mean. The solution is presented as a worked example as well as an Excel spreadsheet.

WORKED EXAMPLES

EXAMPLE 10.2

A local car dealer wants to know if the purchasing habits of buyers buying extras for their vehicles have changed. He is particularly interested in determining if male buyers are willing to spend *more* money on extras for their cars. Based on data collected over the past year, he has estimated that the distribution of the amount of money spent on extras is approximately normally distributed with an average of R2 000 per customer. To test his hypothesis, he has collected the following information concerning the amount of money that the last seven male customers have spent on extras (rands).

Table 10.2: Amount of money spent on vehicle extras by seven customers

	X_1	X_2	X_3	X_4	X_5	X_6	X_7
AMOUNT SPENT ON EXTRAS (R)	2 300	2 386	1 920	1 578	3 065	2 312	1 790

Test, at a 5% level of significance, whether there is any evidence to suggest that the population average amount spent on extras has increased.

We once again use the five-step hypothesis testing procedure to reach our decision.

Step 1: Provide the hypothesis statements: H_0 and H_1

- *Null hypothesis*: H_0: $\mu = 2\,000$, i.e. the population mean is hypothesised to be equal to R2 000.
- *Alternative hypothesis*: H_1: $\mu > 2\,000$

  The salesman is interested in the alternative that the spending habits have increased. Hence, we test the right-sided hypothesis.

Step 2: Choose an appropriate test statistic

From the information provided we note the following.

- *The number of populations in the study*: A sample from one population is being considered.
- *The research question*: The research question concerns the value of a population mean, μ. Our test statistic will therefore need to measure the distance between the sample mean (which we will calculate shortly) and the hypothesised population mean ($\mu_0 = 2\,000$).
- *Assumptions underlying the test*: The sample size is very small ($n = 7$), but the description states that the data are randomly drawn from a normally distributed population.

The above conditions permit the use of the t-test statistic in formula (10.6), since the conditions required for this test are satisfied.

Step 3: Specify the significance level

The significance level is specified as $\alpha = 0.05$ (or 5%).

Step 4: Calculate the relevant test statistic

To calculate the test statistic, we first need to calculate $\overline{X}$ and S:

$$\overline{X} = \frac{1}{7}\sum_{i=1}^{n} X_i$$
$$= \frac{1}{7}(2\,300 + 2\,300 + 2\,300 + 2\,300 + 2\,300 + 2\,300 + 2\,300)$$
$$= 2\,193$$

And:

$$S = \sqrt{\frac{1}{7-1}\sum_{i=1}^{7}(X_i - \overline{X})^2}$$
$$= \Big[\frac{1}{6}[(2\,300 - 2\,193)^2 + (2\,300 - 2\,193)^2 + (2\,300 - 2\,193)^2 + (2\,300 - 2\,193)^2 + (2\,300 - 2\,193)^2 + (2\,300 - 2\,193)^2 + (2\,300 - 2\,193)^2]\Big]^{\frac{1}{2}}$$
$$= 489.6267$$

Using this information and the calculated value of the test statistic in formula (10.6), t_{cal}, is:

$$t_{\text{cal}} = \frac{\overline{X} - \mu_0}{\frac{S}{\sqrt{n}}} = \frac{2\,193 - 2\,000}{\frac{489.6267}{\sqrt{7}}} = 1.042896503$$

Step 5: Make a decision

We use both the critical value approach and the p-value approach to make a decision for this test.

- *Critical value approach*: The significance level was chosen to be $\alpha = 0.05$, the sampling distribution of the chosen test statistic is $t_{n-1} = t_6$ and the test is a right-sided test. The critical value for the test is therefore the quantile $t_{6,0.05}$ defined such that $P(T > t_{6,\alpha}) = \alpha$, where $T \sim t_6$. Using the Excel output in Figure 10.10, we find that $t_{6,\alpha} = 1.94318$. Clearly the observed value of the test statistic is not greater than the critical value, i.e. $t_{\text{cal}} = 1.042896503 < t_{6,0.05} = 1.94318$, and so we **do not reject H_0**. The rejection region is shown in Figure 10.9.
- *p-value approach*: The p-value for this test is calculated using formula (10.2):

$$p\text{-value} = P(T > t_{\text{cal}})$$
$$= P(T > 1.042896503)$$
$$= 1 - P(T < 1.042896503)$$
$$= 1 - 0.8314088$$
$$= 0.1685912$$

We obtained these probabilities using Excel functions. The p-value in this example is greater than the specified significance level $\alpha = 0.05$, therefore **do not reject H_0.** Figure 10.9 shows the p-values relative to the significance level.

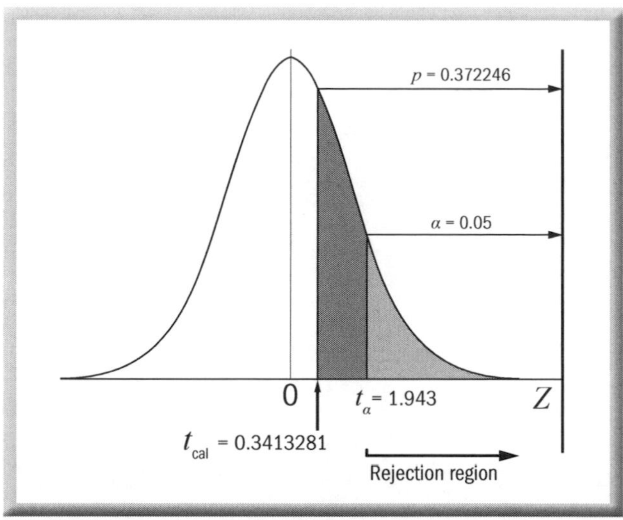

Figure 10.9: Graphical representation of the critical values, test statistic value and p-value of the test in Example 10.2

	A	B	C	D	E	F	G
1	**Hypothesis testing example - One sample t-test of the population mean**						
2							X
3			**1. State hypothesis**	H_0: μ = 2000		**Sample data: Amount spent on car extras (Rands):**	2300
4				H_1: μ > 2000			2386
5				Right-sided test			1920
6							1578
7			**2. Select test**	One sample t-test for the population mean			3065
8				Population distribution is normal, but n is small			2312
9				Population standard deviation σ is unknown			1790
10							
11			**3. Set level of significance**	Significance level, α =	0.05		
12							
13			**4. Calculate test statistic**	**Population**			
14				Mean, μ =	2000		
15				**Sample**			
16				n =	7	=COUNT(G3:G9)	
17				$\overline{X}$ =	2 193	=AVERAGE(G3:G9)	
18				S =	489.6267286	=STDEV(G3:G9)	
19				$S/\sqrt{n}$ =	185.0615084	=E18/SQRT(E16)	
20				t_{cal} =	1.0428965033	=(E17-E14)/E19	
21				**p-value and critical values**			
22				Degrees of freedom =	6	=E16-1	
23				Right-sided p-value =	0.1686	=1-T.DIST(E20,E22,TRUE)	
24				t_α =	1.943	=T.INV(1-E11,E22)	
25							
26			**5. Decision**	Test statistic compared to critical value: $t_{cal} < t_\alpha$		Do not reject H_0	
27				p-value compared to significance level: $p > \alpha$		Do not reject H_0	
28							

Figure 10.10: Excel solution for Example 10.2

EXCEL SOLUTIONS

Significance level: Cell E11	Value = 0.05
Population mean: Cell E14	Value = 2000
Sample data: Cells G4:G9	Values
Sample size: Cell E16	Formula: =COUNT(G3:G9)
Sample mean $\overline{X}$: Cell E17	Formula: =AVERAGE(G3:G9)
Sample standard deviation: Cell E18	Formula: =STDEV.S(G3:G9)
Standard error: Cell E19	Formula: =E18/SQRT(E16)
t_{cal}: Cell E20	Formula: =(E17-E14)/E19
No. of degrees of freedom: Cell E22	Formula: =E16-1
Right-sided p-value: Cell E23	Formula: =1-T.DIST(E20,E22,TRUE)
t_α: Cell E24	Formula: =T.INV(1-E11,E22)

INTERPRETATION We conclude that the population mean expenditure on car extras is *not* significantly greater than the historical population mean of R2 000 at the $\alpha = 0.05$ level.

10.4 One sample Z-test for the population proportion

We now consider a test that we can use to test hypotheses regarding the population proportion, π. This test relies heavily on the Central Limit Theorem to ensure a standard normal distribution for its test statistic, and so we can only apply it to large samples.

The null and alternative hypotheses for this test are are H_0: $\pi = \pi_0$.

H_1: $\pi < \pi_0$	H_1: $\pi > \pi_0$	H_1: $\pi \neq \pi_0$
left-sided	right-sided	two-sided

π_0 is some value specified in the null hypothesis.

The only assumption that this test requires is that the sample size be sufficiently large that the test statistic in formula (10.7) will follow a standard normal distribution. This test statistic is defined as:

$$Z = \frac{p - \pi_0}{\sqrt{\frac{\pi_0(1 - \pi_0)}{n}}} \overset{H_0}{\sim} N(0, 1) \tag{10.7}$$

p is the sample proportion, n is the sample size and π_0 is the population proportion value specified in H_0. The calculated value of this test statistic is denoted z_{cal}.

Example 10.3 illustrates this test.

WORKED EXAMPLES

EXAMPLE 10.3

The occupational health representative of a mining union has claimed that 20% of the union members employed at a platinum mine suffer from some form of breathing disorder. The mine company, hoping to prove that this number is not as high as the union claims it to be, conducts a small, discreet study on a randomly selected representative sample of its mineworkers. The study shows that 123 of the 695 mine employees included in the study suffer from some form of breathing disorder.

The mining company would like to know if they can use this result to refute the claim made by the health representative (at a $\alpha = 0.05$ level).

The five-step procedure to conduct this test progresses as follows.

Step 1: Provide the hypothesis statements H_0 and H_1

- *Null hypothesis*: H_0: $\pi = 0.2$, i.e. it was claimed that the population proportion of miners with breathing disorders is 20% or 0.2.
- *Alternative hypothesis*: H_1: $\pi < 0.2$, i.e. the mining company would like to prove that the true proportion is, in fact, lower than 0.2. The symbol < implies that a left-sided test will be used.

Step 2: Choose an appropriate test statistic

- *The number of populations in the study*: A sample from one population is being considered.
- *The research question*: Clearly the parameter of interest is the population proportion π. The test statistic will need to reflect the distance between the sample proportion ($p = \frac{123}{695} = 0.176978$) and the hypothesised population proportion ($\pi_0 = 0.2$).
- *Assumptions underlying the test*: The sample size is sufficiently large ($n = 695$) for the test in formula (10.7) to be conducted (it is larger than 30).

The information provided here allows us to use the test statistic given in formula (10.7).

Step 3: Specify the significance level

The significance level is specified as $\alpha = 0.05$ (or 5%).

Step 4: Calculate the relevant test statistic

First note that the sample proportion of miners with a breathing disorder is $p = \frac{123}{695} = 0.176978417$ and that the hypothesised value of the population proportion is given as $\pi_0 = 0.2$. Therefore, the test statistic calculated from this information and formula (10.7) is:

$$z_{cal} = \frac{p - \pi_0}{\sqrt{\frac{\pi_0(1 - \pi_0)}{n}}} = \frac{0.176978417 - 0.2}{\sqrt{\frac{0.2(1 - 0.2)}{695}}}$$
$$= -\frac{0.023021582}{\sqrt{0.000230215}}$$
$$= -1.517286501$$

Step 5: Make a decision

We will use both the critical value approach and the p-value approach to make a decision for this test.

- *Critical value approach*: Using a significance level of $\alpha = 0.05$, the critical value of a left-sided test is $-z_{\alpha} = -z_{0.05} = -1.645$ (from Excel and the tables in Appendix C). Comparing the calculated test statistic, $z_{cal} = -1.52$ to the critical value, $z_{0.05} = -1.645$, we find that the z_{cal} does not exceed the critical value. We will therefore **not reject H_0** in this case. The rejection region is shown in Figure 10.11.
- *p-value approach*: We calculate the p-value for this test using formula (10.1):

$$\begin{aligned} p\text{-value} &= P(Z < z_{cal}) \\ &= P(Z < -1.52) \\ &= 0.0643 \end{aligned}$$

The p-value is greater than the significance level ($p > \alpha$), and so we do **not reject H_0**. Figure 10.11 shows the p-values relative to the significance level.

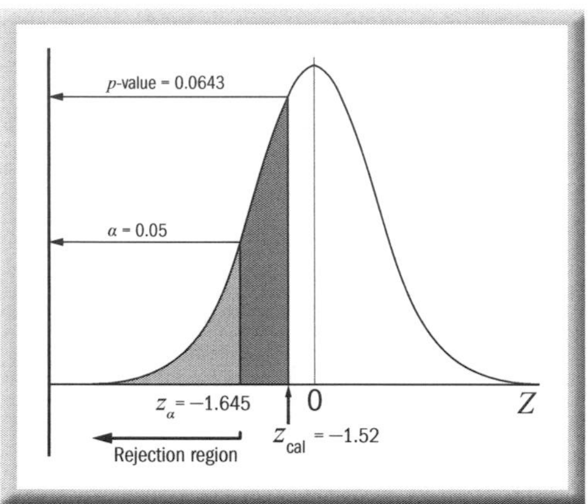

Figure 10.11: Graphical representation of the critical values, test statistic value and p-value of the test in Example 10.3

	A	B	C	D	E	F
1	**Hypothesis testing example – One sample Z-test of the population proportion**					
2						
3				$H_0: \pi = 0.2$		
4			**1. State hypothesis**	$H_1: \pi < 0.2$		
5				Left-sided test		
6						
7			**2. Select test**	One sample Z-test for the population mean		
8				n is large		
9						
10			**3. Set level of significance**	Significance level, α =	0.05	
11						
12				**Population**		
13				Proportion, π =	0.2	
14				**Sample**		
15				n =	695	
16				Number of individuals with breathing disorders =	123	
17			**4. Calculate test statistic**	p =	0.176978417	=E16/E15
18				$\sqrt{\pi_0(1-\pi_0)/n}$ =	0.015172865	=SQRT(E13*(1-E13)/E15)
19				z_{cal} =	-1.517286484	=(E17-E13)/E18
20				**p-value and criticial values**		
21				Left-sided p-value =	0.064597185	=NORM.S.DIST(E19,TRUE)
22				z_{α} =	-1.644853627	=NORM.S.INV(E10)
23						
24			**5. Decision**	Test statistic compared to critical value: $z_{cal} > z_{\alpha}$	Do not reject H_0	
25				p-value compared to significance level $p > \alpha$	Do not reject H_0	

Figure 10.12: Excel solution for Example 10.3

EXCEL SOLUTIONS

Significance level: Cell E10	Value: 0.05
Population proportion: Cell E13	Value: 0.2
Sample size: Cell E15	Value: 695
Number of individuals with breathing disorders: Cell E16	Value: 123
Sample proportion, p: Cell E17	Formula: =E16/E15
Standard error: Cell E18	Formula: =SQRT(E13*(1-E13)/E15)
z_{cal}: Cell E20	Formula: =(E17-E13)/E18
Left-sided p-value: Cell E23	Formula: =NORM.S.DIST(E19,TRUE)
z_{α}: Cell E35	Formula: =NORM.S.INV(E10)

INTERPRETATION The mining company cannot refute the claim that the population proportion of employees that suffer from breathing disorders is 20% (at a significance level of $\alpha = 0.05$).

SUMMARY

In this chapter, we introduced the important statistical concept of parametric hypothesis testing. What is important in hypothesis testing is recognising the nature of the problem and being able to convert this into two appropriate hypothesis statements (H_0 and H_1). In this chapter, we described a simple five-step procedure to help you solve this, and we focused on using Excel to solve the data problems. The main emphasis is placed on the use of the p-value, which provides a number to the probability of the null hypothesis (H_0) being rejected. Thus, if the measured p-value > α (alpha), then we would not reject H_0. Remember that the value of the p-value will depend on whether we are dealing with a two-sided, left-sided or right-sided test. So, take extra care with this concept since this is where most students slip up.

KEY TERMS

α, alpha
Alternative hypothesis (H_1)
β, beta
Critical value
Hypothesis test procedure
Left-sided test
Null hypothesis (H_0)
One sample t-test
One sample Z-test
p-value
Region of rejection
Right-sided test
Significance level (α)
Test statistic
Two-sided test
Type I error
Type II error

FORMULA SUMMARY

$$p\text{-value} = P(Z < z_{\text{cal}}) \tag{10.1}$$

$$p\text{-value} = P(Z > z_{\text{cal}}) \tag{10.2}$$

$$p\text{-value} = P(Z < -z_{\text{cal}}) + P(Z > z_{\text{cal}}) = 2 \times P(Z > z_{\text{cal}}) \tag{10.3}$$

$$p\text{-value} = P(Z > -z_{\text{cal}}) + P(Z < z_{\text{cal}}) = 2 \times P(Z < z_{\text{cal}}) \tag{10.4}$$

$$Z = \frac{\overline{X} - \mu_0}{\frac{\sigma}{\sqrt{n}}} \overset{H_0}{\sim} N(0, 1) \tag{10.5}$$

$$T = \frac{\overline{X} - \mu_0}{\frac{S}{\sqrt{n}}} \overset{H_0}{\sim} t_{n-1} \tag{10.6}$$

$$Z = \frac{p - \pi_0}{\sqrt{\frac{\pi_0 (1 - \pi_0)}{n}}} \overset{H_0}{\sim} N(0, 1) \tag{10.7}$$

EXERCISES

10.1 A supermarket is supplied by a consortium of milk producers. Recently, a quality assurance check suggested that the amount of milk supplied is significantly different from the quantity stated within the contract.

a) Define what we mean by significantly different.

b) State the null and alternative hypothesis statements.

c) For the alternative hypothesis, is it a two-sided, left-sided or right-sided test?

10.2 A business analyst is attempting to understand visually the meaning of the critical test statistic and the *p*-value. For a *z*-value of 2.5 and significance level of 5%, sketch the normal probability distribution and use the sketch to illustrate the location of the following statistics: test statistic, critical value, significance value and *p*-value. (You do not need to calculate the values of z_α or the *p*-value.)

10.3 What are the critical *z*-values for a significance level of 2% for a:

a) two-sided

b) left-sided

c) right-sided?

10.4 A marketing manager undertakes a hypothesis test to test for the difference between accessories purchased for two different products. The initial analysis has been performed and right-sided *Z*-test chosen. Given that the calculated *z*-value was 3.45, find the corresponding *p*-value. From this result, what would you conclude?

10.5 A mobile phone company is concerned about the lifetime of phone batteries supplied by a new supplier. Based on historical data, this type of battery should last for 900 days with a standard deviation of 150 days. Of a recent randomly selected sample of 40 batteries, the sample battery life was found to be 942 days. Is the population battery life significantly different from 900 days (significance level 5%)?

10.6 A local pizza restaurant advertises home-delivery times of 30 minutes. To monitor the effectiveness of this promise, the restaurant manager monitors the time that the order was received and the time of delivery. Based on historical data, the average time for delivery is 30 minutes with a standard deviation of 5 minutes. After a series of complaints from customers regarding this promise, the manager decided to analyse the last 50 data orders that resulted in an average time of 32 minutes. Conduct an appropriate test at a significance level of 5%. Should the manager be concerned?

10.7 Calculate the critical *t*-values for a significance level of 1% and 12 degrees of freedom for a:

a) two-sided

b) left-sided

c) right-sided.

10.8 After further data collection, the marketing manager (from Exercise 10.4) decides to revisit the data analysis and change the type of test to a *t*-test.

a) Explain under what conditions a *t*-test could be used rather than the *Z*-test.

b) Calculate the corresponding *p*-value if the sample size was 13 and the test statistic equal to 2.03. From this result, what would you conclude?

10.9 A tyre manufacturer conducts quality assurance checks on the tyres that it manufactures. One of the tests consists of testing their medium-quality tyres with an independent random sample of 12 types, which provided a sample mean and standard deviation of 14 500 km and 800 km respectively. Given that the historical average is 15 000 km and that the population is normally distributed, test whether the sample should be a cause for concern.

10.10 A new low-fat fudge bar is advertised as having 120 calories. The manufacturing company conducts regular checks by selecting independent random samples and testing the sample average against the advertised average. Historically, the population has a normal distribution and the most recent sample consists of the numbers 99, 132, 125, 92, 108, 127, 105, 112, 102, 112, 129, 112, 111, 102, 122. Is the population value significantly different from 120 calories (significance level 5%)?

TECHNIQUES IN PRACTICE

10.11 AfriSoft is concerned about the time taken to react to customer complaints and has implemented a new set of procedures for its support centre staff. The customer service director has asked that a suitable test is applied to a new sample to assess whether the new target mean time for responding to customer complaints is 28 days. Table 10.3 shows the recent sample of the number of days taken to respond to customer complaints.

Table 10.3: The time taken to respond to complaints (in days)

20	33	33	29	24	30
40	33	20	39	32	37
32	50	36	31	38	29
15	33	27	29	43	33
31	35	19	39	22	21
28	22	26	42	30	17
32	34	39	39	32	38

a) Describe the test to be applied with stated assumptions.

b) Conduct the required test to assess whether evidence exists that the mean time to respond to complaints is greater than 28 days.

c) What would happen to your results if the population mean time to react to customer complaints changes to 30 days?

10.12 Bakers Ltd is currently reviewing the delivery vans it uses to deliver products to customers. The company runs two types of delivery van (type A – recently purchased – and type B – at least three years old), which are supposed to achieve 20 km per litre of petrol. Table 10.4 shows the new collected sample.

Table 10.4: Fuel consumption figures (km/ℓ) for the two van types; 15 for van type A and 21 for B

VAN TYPE A	VAN TYPE B	VAN TYPE A	VAN TYPE B
17.68	15.8	29.42	34.8
18.72	39.1	25.22	19.8
29.49	9.3	13.52	15.0
29.64	12.3	14.01	28.9
9.31	15.5		33.9
22.38	40.1		27.1
20.23	20.4		19.8
28.80	3.7		23.6
17.57	13.6		29.7
9.13	35.1		28.2
20.98	33.3		

Based on your analysis, is there any evidence that the new delivery vans meet the mean of 20 km per litre?

10.13 Home-Made Beers Ltd is developing a low-calorie lager with a mean designed calorie count of 43 calories per 100 ml. The new product development team are having problems with the production process and have collected two independent random samples to assess whether the target calorie count is being met (assume the population variables are normally distributed).

Table 10.5: Calorie counts of two samples (A and B) of beer bottles (each sample consists of 22 bottles)

SAMPLE A	SAMPLE B	SAMPLE A	SAMPLE B
49.7	39.4	45.2	34.5
45.9	49.5	40.5	43.5
37.7	39.2	31.9	37.8
40.6	49.7	41.9	39.7

SAMPLE A	SAMPLE B
34.8	39.5
51.4	45.4
34.3	38.2
63.1	44.1
41.2	58.7
41.4	47.1
41.1	59.7

SAMPLE A	SAMPLE B
39.8	41.1
54.0	33.6
47.8	35.8
29.3	44.6
31.7	38.4
45.1	29.1
47.9	30.7

a) Using both samples in a combined 44 bottle sample, describe the test to be applied with stated assumptions.
b) Is it likely that the target average number of calories is being achieved?

CHAPTER 11

PARAMETRIC HYPOTHESIS TESTING: TWO POPULATIONS

CHAPTER CONTENTS

OVERVIEW

In the previous chapter, we considered the basics of hypothesis testing and applied it to situations in which we were interested in hypotheses concerning a population parameter from a single population. We now turn our attention to the situation in which we have two populations and we wish to compare the population parameters for these two populations (for example, we might be interested in testing if the population mean of population A is the same as the population mean of population B). These procedures are important because we often need to compare the parameters from data collected from different sources (i.e. different populations).

We again use the generic five-step procedure for hypothesis testing discussed in the previous chapter.

LEARNING OBJECTIVES

On completing this chapter. you should be able to:

- conduct hypothesis tests involving two independent populations for population means
- conduct hypothesis tests involving two independent populations for population proportions
- conduct hypothesis tests involving two dependent populations for population means
- conduct hypothesis tests involving two independent populations for population variances (the F-test)
- solve hypothesis test problems using Microsoft Excel.

11.1 Tests involving two populations

11.1.1 Introduction

We consider questions (or hypotheses) concerning the equality (or inequality) of two population parameters in this chapter. Throughout this chapter, we distinguish between the two populations by labelling them 'population A' and 'population B'. The hypotheses of interest will involve comparing population means, proportions and variances from these two populations.

Typical situations that give rise to these hypotheses occur when we are interested in the distributional properties of a random variable that has been observed in both populations. For example, if the variable that we are investigating is the IQ of individuals, we may want to determine if the population mean IQ of males (population A) is the same as the population mean IQ of females (population B). Alternately, we may want to determine whether the population proportion of men with IQs over 100 is the same as the population proportion of women with IQs over 100. Since these population values are unknown (unobservable unless we can observe the whole of both populations), we need to rely on hypothesis testing to come to some conclusion regarding these statements.

We can answer these types of questions using the same approach as the one in Chapter 10 (hypothesis tests concerning a single population parameter). However, since there are now two populations, we need to consider additional aspects, namely whether the populations are **independent** or **dependent**.

11.1.2 Independent and dependent populations

The majority of the tests in this chapter deal with comparing parameters from two independent populations, but we also discuss a test in which two populations are dependent. These two different scenarios can be defined as follows.

- *Independent populations*: Two populations are said to be independent if the measured values of the items observed in one population do not affect the measured values of the items observed in the other population. For example, consider the following two populations: all *unmarried* men aged 28 in South Africa (population A) and all *married* men aged 28 in South Africa (population B). The variable we are interested in measuring in all of these men is the amount of weight they have gained/lost since they were 18 years old. In this case, we would say that the two populations are *independent*, because the amount of weight gained by an individual in population A will not affect the amount of weight gained by an individual in population B (and vice versa).
- *Dependent populations*: Two populations are dependent if the measured values of the items observed in one population directly affect the measured values of the items observed in the other population. Typically, the items in two dependent populations are *paired*, in the sense that each item in one population is directly linked to a corresponding item in the other population. For example, in a study to determine the effectiveness of a headache tablet, we define population A as the population of headache sufferers *before* taking the medication and population B as the population of headache sufferers *after* taking the medication. The variable being measured is the severity of the headache (measured on a scale of 1 to 100). In this example, each item in population A is directly linked to each item in population B (the individual before medication and the *same* individual after medication). Clearly, the headache severity value after medication (population B) is somewhat reliant on the original value before medication (population A), i.e. they are dependent.

11.1.3 Notation

The notation that we use to indicate whether items were obtained from a sample from population A or from a sample from population B is as follows:

- We will refer to the sample from population A as *sample A* and the sample from population B as *sample B*.
- The sample size of sample A is denoted n_A and the sample size of sample B is denoted n_B.
- The population means of populations A and B are denoted by μ_A and μ_B respectively.
- The sample means of samples A and B are denoted $\overline{X}_A$ and $\overline{X}_B$ respectively.
- The population variances of populations A and B are denoted σ_A^2 and σ_B^2 respectively.
- The sample variances of samples A and B are denoted S_A^2 and S_B^2 respectively.
- The population proportions of populations A and B are denoted π_A and π_B respectively.
- The sample proportions of samples A and B are denoted p_A and p_B respectively.

We discuss the following tests in this chapter:

- Comparing the population mean of population A, μ_A, to the population mean of population B, μ_B, when the two populations are independent. (We discuss the situation in which the population variances are equal separately from the situation in which the population variances are unequal.)
- Determining if the difference between the population means of two dependent populations (this difference is denoted $\mu_{\text{diff}} = \mu_A - \mu_B$) has a specified value.
- Comparing the population proportion of population A, π_A, to the population proportion of population B, π_B, when the two populations are independent.
- Comparing the population variance of population A, σ_A^2, and the population variance of population B, σ_B^2.

11.2 Comparing population means from two independent populations (population variances are known)

The first hypothesis that we consider in this chapter is the comparison of two population means from two independent populations. As usual, the procedure requires that we obtain sample data from the populations to draw some conclusion regarding the two population values. In particular, we obtain one sample from each of the two populations and then calculate various statistics from each sample to ultimately construct a test statistic.

In this first test, we consider testing the equality of the population means when the population variances (σ_A^2 and σ_B^2) are known. Please note that it is not very common for the population variances to be known. However, we will use this setting to illustrate the test. In later sections, we consider the more realistic situation in which the variances are unknown.

The null hypothesis that we are interested in testing is whether the two population means are equal to one another:

$$H_0: \mu_A = \mu_B$$

Or, stated slightly differently:

$$H_0: \mu_A - \mu_B = 0$$

As with the hypotheses discussed in the previous chapter, we can formulate the alternative hypothesis as either a left-sided, right-sided or two-sided test. The alternative hypothesis for this test can thus be any one of the following:

$H_1: \mu_A < \mu_B$	$H_1: \mu_A > \mu_B$	$H_1: \mu_A \neq \mu_B$
left-sided	right-sided	two-sided

Or, stated differently:

$H_1: \mu_A - \mu_B < 0$	$H_1: \mu_A - \mu_B > 0$	$H_1: \mu_A - \mu_B \neq 0$
left-sided	right-sided	two-sided

We use the following test statistic (the *two-sample* Z-*test*) to test this hypothesis:

$$Z = \frac{\overline{X}_A - \overline{X}_B}{\sqrt{\frac{\sigma_A^2}{n_A} + \frac{\sigma_B^2}{n_B}}} \overset{H_0}{\sim} N(0, 1) \quad (11.1)$$

Note that in order for this statistic to follow a standard normal distribution, the following conditions (or assumptions) must hold:

- The population variances, σ_A^2 and σ_B^2, must be known. These two parameters may be equal or unequal to one another, but they must be known.
- One (or both) of the following two conditions must hold:
  - The sample sizes n_A and n_B must both be sufficiently large so that the Central Limit Theorem will allow us to assume that the distributions of $\overline{X}_A$ and $\overline{X}_B$ are approximately normal (typically both sample sizes must be larger than 30).
  - The distributions of populations A and B must be normally distributed.

Example 11.1 illustrates this test.

WORKED EXAMPLES

EXAMPLE 11.1

A large organisation produces electric light bulbs in each of its two factories (A and B). It is suspected that the quality of bulbs from factory A is better than those from factory B. To test this, the organisation would need to test every light bulb in each factory. However, this is not feasible because the light bulbs are destroyed in the testing process and it would not make financial sense to destroy the entire stock of light bulbs. To overcome this problem, they decide instead to collect 30 light bulbs from factory A and 32 light bulbs from factory B. These light bulbs are measured to determine how long each one works for (in hours) before they fail. The population variance of the light bulbs' lifetimes are known ($\sigma_A^2 = 52\ 783$, $\sigma_B^2 = 61\ 650$).

Conduct an appropriate test to test the hypothesis that the population mean lifetime of the light bulbs from factory A is greater than the population mean lifetime of light bulbs from factory B. Use a significance level of $\alpha = 0.05$.

The data set used in Example 11.1 is given in Table 11.1.

Table 11.1: Data set for Example 11.1

FACTORY A			
900	875	1 299	1 653
1 276	816	1 110	1 288
1 421	983	929	1 187
1 014	1 119	843	
1 246	988	1 156	
1 507	1 137	867	
975	1 227	1 454	
1 177	858	1 403	
1 246	941	1 165	

FACTORY B			
1 052	1 369	990	649
947	737	950	1 166
886	1 114	783	498
788	354	816	945
1 188	1 347	658	1 002
928	1 062	504	
983	756	1 076	
970	1 052	500	
766	754	1 025	

We will use the five-step procedure described in the previous chapter to conduct this hypothesis test.

Step 1: Provide the hypothesis statements H_0 and H_1

- *Null hypothesis*: The information provided indicates that we need to compare the two population means, μ_A and μ_B. Since the null hypothesis is always used to denote equality, we will formulate it as H_0: $\mu_A = \mu_B$ or, equivalently, H_0: $\mu_A - \mu_B = 0$.
- *Alternative hypothesis*: The alternative hypothesis should reflect the stated hypothesis that factory A light bulbs last longer on average, so we use the hypothesis statement H_1: $\mu_A > \mu_B$ or equivalently, H_1: $\mu_A - \mu_B > 0$. Recall that the greater than symbol (>) implies a right-sided test.

Step 2: Choose an appropriate test statistic

We now need to choose an appropriate statistical test for testing H_0. From the information provided we note the following.

- *The number of populations in the study*: There are two independent populations in this study: the population of light bulbs from factory A and the population of light bulbs from factory B.
- *The research question*: The question of interest is whether one population mean is larger than the other, which we can formulate as either $\mu_A > \mu_B$ or $\mu_A - \mu_B > 0$ as stated in the alternative hypothesis. We would like to measure the distance between the sample statistic, $\overline{X}_A - \overline{X}_B$, and the population parameter, $\mu_A - \mu_B$, to determine if the one population mean is larger than the other. Note that the difference $\mu_A - \mu_B$ is 0 under the null hypothesis and so we only have to determine the distance of $\overline{X}_A - \overline{X}_B$ from 0. If $\overline{X}_A - \overline{X}_B$ is 0, then there is evidence to conclude that the null hypothesis should not be rejected. However, if $\overline{X}_A - \overline{X}_B$ is *much* larger than 0, then there is evidence that the statement made by the alternative hypothesis is viable (that the population mean lifetime of light bulbs from factory A, μ_A, is greater than the population mean lifetime of light bulbs from factory B, μ_B).
- *Assumptions underlying the test*: The two assumptions for the test in formula (11.1) are satisfied, that is, both population variances are known ($\sigma_A^2 = 52\ 783$ and $\sigma_B^2 = 61\ 560$) and both samples large enough for the Central Limit Theorem to work ($n_A = 30$ and $n_B = 32$).

We can conclude that the Z-test statistic in formula (11.1) is the appropriate test statistic for this test.

Step 3: Specify the significance level

We conduct this test at a significance level of 5%, i.e. $\alpha = 0.05$.

Step 4: Calculate the relevant test statistic

The following information is provided that will enable us to calculate the test statistic in formula (11.1).

- Population/sample A: $n_A = 30$, $\overline{X}_A = 1\,135.33$ and $\sigma_A^2 = 52\,783$
- Population/sample B: $n_B = 32$, $\overline{X}_B = 894.21575$ and $\sigma_B^2 = 61\,560$

Note that we denote the calculated version of (11.1) by z_{cal}:

$$z_{\text{cal}} = \frac{\overline{X}_A - \overline{X}_B}{\sqrt{\frac{\sigma_A^2}{n_A} + \frac{\sigma_B^2}{n_B}}} = \frac{1\,135.33 - 894.21575}{\sqrt{\frac{52\,783}{30} + \frac{61\,560}{32}}} = 3.9729$$

Step 5: Make a decision

We use both the critical value approach and the p-value approach to make a decision for this test.

- *Critical value approach*: The significance level is chosen to be $\alpha = 0.05$ and the distribution of the test statistic under H_0 is $N(0, 1)$, so we will need to find the critical value $z_\alpha = z_{0.05}$ from the standard normal distribution. We use Excel's NORM.S.INV function to find that this value is $z_{0.05} = +1.645$. Comparing this critical value to the calculated test statistic, we find that $z_{\text{cal}} = 3.9729 > z_{0.05} = 1.645$ and (because it is a right-sided test) we conclude that **H_0 will be rejected**, since the test statistic lies in the rejection region.
- *p-value approach*: We can calculate the p-value of the right-sided test using formula (10.2) of the previous chapter. (Note that in this test, $Z \sim N(0, 1)$.)

$$\begin{aligned} p\text{-value} &= P(Z > z_{\text{cal}}) \\ &= P(Z > 3.97) \\ &= 1 - P(Z < 3.97) \\ &= 1 - 0.99997 \\ &= 0.00003 \end{aligned}$$

We obtained this answer using the probability tables in Appendix C, but Excel's NORM.S.DIST function provides a more accurate answer of 0.0000354957. This p-value is clearly much smaller than the prescribed significance level of $\alpha = 0.05$. Therefore, since the p-value $= 0.00003 < \alpha = 0.05$, we **reject H_0** and conclude that the population mean lifetimes of light bulbs from factory A are greater than the population mean lifetimes of those from factory B at a 5% level of significance.

INTERPRETATION We conclude that at the 0.05 (5%) level, light bulbs from factory A have significantly longer lifetimes than light bulbs from factory B.

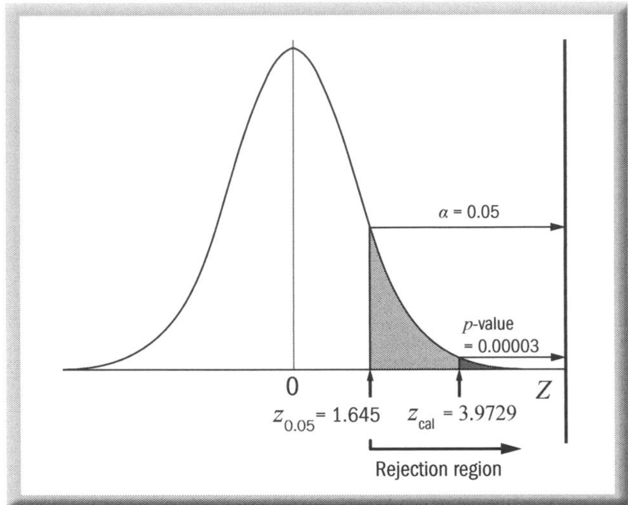

Figure 11.1: Illustration of the relationships between the p-value and α, and the test statistic and the critical values for Example 11.1

	A	B	C	D	E	F	G	H
1	Hypothesis testing example - One sample Z-test of the population proportion							
2		Factory A	Factory B					
3		900	1052		1. State hypothesis	$H_0: \mu_A = \mu_B$		
4		1276	947			$H_1: \mu_A > \mu_B$		
5		1421	886			Right-sided test		
6		1014	788					
7		1246	1188					
8		1507	928					
9		975	983		2. Select test	Two sample Z-test for two population means		
10		1177	970			Variances are known		
11		1246	766			Samples are large enough to use CLT		
12		875	1369					
13		816	737		3. Set level of significance	Significance level, α =	0.05	
14		983	1114					
15		1119	354					
16		988	1347		4. Calculate test statistic	n_A =	30	=COUNT(B3:B32)
17		1137	1062			$\bar{X}_A$ =	1135.333333	=AVERAGE(B3:B32)
18		1227	756			Population variance known σ_A^2 =	52783	
19		858	1052					
20		941	754			n_B =	32	=COUNT(C3:C34)
21		1299	990			$\bar{X}_B$ =	894.21875	=AVERAGE(C3:C34)
22		1110	950			Population variance known σ_B^2 =	61560	
23		929	783					
24		843	816			z_{cal} =	3.972938206	=(G17-G21)/SQRT((G18/(G16)+(G22/G20)))
25		1156	658			p-value and critical values		
26		867	504			p-value =	0.0000354957	=1-NORM.S.DIST(G24,TRUE)
27		1454	1076			Critical value, z_α =	1.644853627	=NORM.S.INV(1-G13)
28		1403	500					
29		1165	1025		5. Decision	Test statistic compared to critical value: $z_{cal} > z_\alpha$	Reject the null hypothesis	
30		1653	649					
31		1288	1166			p-value compared to significance level $p < \alpha$	Reject the null hypothesis	
32		1187	498					
33			945					
34			1002					

Figure 11.2: Excel solution for Example 11.1

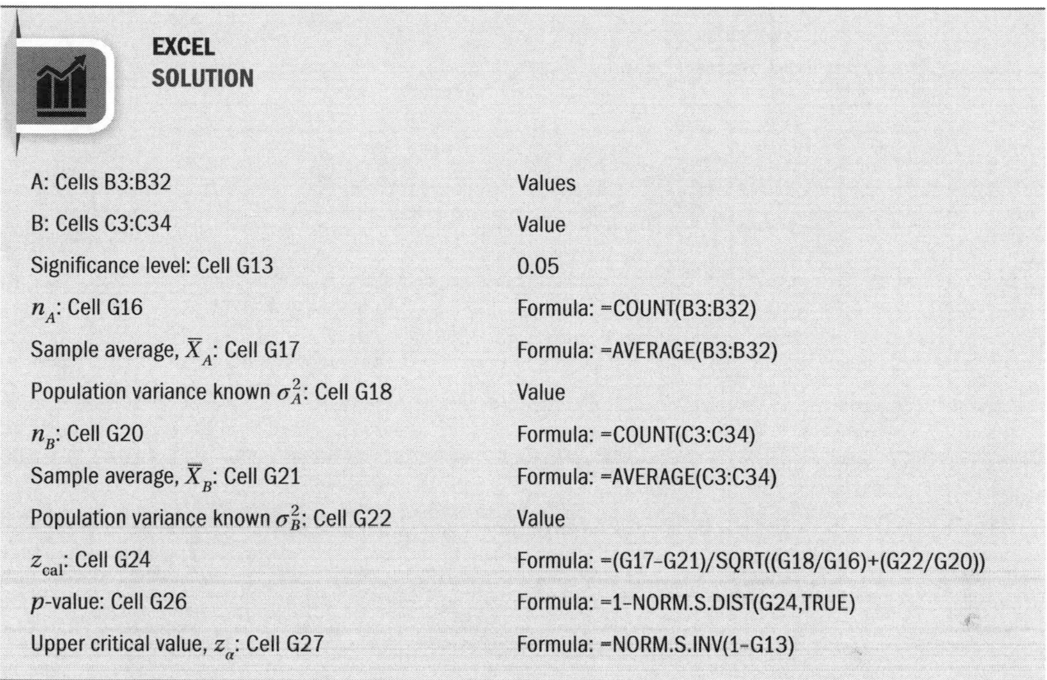

EXCEL SOLUTION

A: Cells B3:B32	Values
B: Cells C3:C34	Value
Significance level: Cell G13	0.05
n_A: Cell G16	Formula: =COUNT(B3:B32)
Sample average, $\overline{X}_A$: Cell G17	Formula: =AVERAGE(B3:B32)
Population variance known σ_A^2: Cell G18	Value
n_B: Cell G20	Formula: =COUNT(C3:C34)
Sample average, $\overline{X}_B$: Cell G21	Formula: =AVERAGE(C3:C34)
Population variance known σ_B^2: Cell G22	Value
z_{cal}: Cell G24	Formula: =(G17-G21)/SQRT((G18/G16)+(G22/G20))
p-value: Cell G26	Formula: =1-NORM.S.DIST(G24,TRUE)
Upper critical value, z_α: Cell G27	Formula: =NORM.S.INV(1-G13)

Excel Analysis ToolPak solution

As an alternative to either of the two previous methods, we can use a method embedded in Excel Analysis ToolPak. The screenshot in Figure 11.3 shows the menu of different analyses we can choose.

To access this ToolPak, click on the 'Data' tab and then click on the 'Data Analysis' button. This will bring up a window (as shown in Figure 11.3). In this window, select the 'z-test: Two Sample for Means' option and this will then bring up the analysis window shown in Figure 11.4. We can now fill the appropriate values into this window and the output (also shown in Figure 11.4) is then automatically generated. Note that the results of this procedure are identical to the Excel work sheet in Figure 11.2.

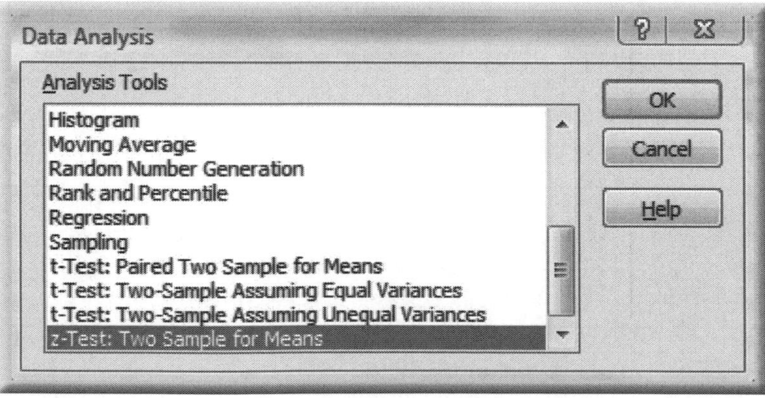

Figure 11.3: The Data Analysis window in Excel

	A	B	C	D	E	F	G	H
1	*Z*-test for two population means							
2		Factory A	Factory B		z-Test: Two Sample for Means			
3		900	1052					
4		1276	947			*Variable 1*	*Variable 2*	
5		1421	886		Mean	1135.3333333333	894.21875	
6		1014	788		Known Variance	52783	61560	
7		1246	1188		Observations	30	32	
8		1507	928		Hypothesized Mean Difference	0		
9		975	983		z	3.9729382062		
10		1177	970		P(Z<=z) one-tail	3.54957353958518E-005		
11		1246	766		z Critical one-tail	1.644853627		
12		875	1369		P(Z<=z) two-tail	7.09914707917036E-005		
13		816	737		z Critical two-tail	1.9599639845		
14		983	1114					
15		1119	354					
16		988	1347					
17		1137	1062					
18		1227	756					
19		858	1052					
20		941	754					
21		1299	990					
22		1110	950					
23		929	783					
24		843	816					
25		1156	658					
26		867	504					
27		1454	1076					
28		1403	500					
29		1165	1025					
30		1653	649					
31		1288	1166					
32		1187	498					
33			945					
34			1002					
35								

Figure 11.4: The 'z-test: Two sample for means' window and output using the data from Example 11.1

11.3 Comparing population means from two independent populations (population variances are unknown, but equal)

In the previous section, we considered the comparison of two population means from two independent populations in which the population variances were known. However, we do not usually know the values of the population variances, and so that test is not always particularly useful. In this section and the next, we consider the following two scenarios:

- The scenario in which the two population means must be compared when the population variances are unknown, but are *equal* to one another (discussed in this section).
- The scenario in which the two population means must be compared when the population variances are unknown, but are *unequal* to one another (discussed in Section 11.4).

A natural question that arises in this context is 'How do we determine if the population variances are equal?' This is important because each scenario results in slightly different test statistics. To answer the question, we employ a test that determines whether σ_A^2 differs from σ_B^2. However, we only discuss this later in this chapter (Section 11.7). For now, we assume that this information is available or easily obtainable.

We now discuss the test for equality (or inequality) of population means when the population variances are unknown, but are equal to one another. This test is sometimes called the *two-sample t-test: assuming equal variances* or the *pooled-variance t-test.*

The null hypothesis is H_0: $\mu_A = \mu_B$ or H_0: $\mu_A - \mu_B = 0$.

The alternative hypotheses are:

H_1: $\mu_A < \mu_B$	H_1: $\mu_A > \mu_B$	H_1: $\mu_A \neq \mu_B$
left-sided	right-sided	two-sided

Or equivalently:

H_1: $\mu_A - \mu_B < 0$	H_1: $\mu_A - \mu_B > 0$	H_1: $\mu_A - \mu_B \neq 0$
left-sided	right-sided	two-sided

The test statistic is:

$$T = \frac{\overline{X}_A - \overline{X}_B}{S_{\text{pool}}\sqrt{\frac{1}{n_A} + \frac{1}{n_B}}} \overset{H_0}{\sim} t_{n_A + n_B - 2} \quad (11.2)$$

Where:

$$S_{\text{pool}} = \sqrt{\frac{(n_A - 1)\, S_A^2 + (n_B - 1)\, S_B^2}{n_A + n_B - 2}} \quad (11.3)$$

Note that we use a pooled version of the standard deviation in this test statistic called S_{pool}. Technically, under the assumption that the population variances are equal, we could have used either S_A or S_B instead of S_{pool} (since all of these statistics estimate the same common population standard deviation, $\sigma = \sigma_A = \sigma_B$). However, we prefer to pool S_A and S_B into one statistic, S_{pool}, because it contains more information about the population standard deviation (σ) than either S_A or S_B on their own.

The assumptions underlying this test are the following:

- The population variances, σ_A^2 and σ_B^2, are unknown, but are equal to one another.
- The test statistic T will follow a $t_{n_A + n_B - 2}$-distribution if either of the following two assumptions hold:
  - Both samples are drawn from normally distributed populations.
  - The sample sizes are large enough (they are both at least larger than 30) so that the Central Limit Theorem will ensure the approximate normality of $\overline{X}_A$ and $\overline{X}_B$.

Fortunately, the *t*-test is quite robust to departures from normality, even for small samples, so the condition that the data are normal is not too restrictive.

Example 11.2 illustrates how to apply this test.

WORKED EXAMPLES

EXAMPLE 11.2

A company that packages and distributes 500 g sugar packets has received complaints that the weight of sugar in the packets packaged at their two different packaging plants differs. To test this statistically, two small random samples were collected from both plants (a sample of size $n_A = 18$ is collected from plant A and a sample of size $n_B = 25$ is collected from plant B).

Conduct the hypothesis test at $\alpha = 0.05$ to determine if the population means are the same.

Note that we assume that the distribution of the packet weights is normal and that the population variances for both plants are the same.

The data set used for Example 11.2 is given in Table 11.2.

Table 11.2: Data set for Example 11.2

PLANT A	
437	490
497	533
555	509
485	500
462	528
638	588
592	484
569	531
517	572

PLANT B		
418	504	495
525	489	508
581	493	605
495	483	492
489	463	514
448	484	460
455	539	491
484	439	
527	535	

We use the five-step procedure described in the previous chapter to conduct this hypothesis test.

Step 1: Provide the hypothesis statements H_0 and H_1

- *Null hypothesis*: H_0: $\mu_A = \mu_B$ or H_0: $\mu_A - \mu_B = 0$
- *Alternative hypothesis*: No information is given that states that we are interested in testing if plant A's population mean is greater than B's (or vice versa), so we simply test if the two population means are unequal: H_1: $\mu_A \neq \mu_B$ or H_1: $\mu_A - \mu_B \neq 0$.

Recall that the unequal to symbol ($\neq$) implies a two-sided test.

Step 2: Choose an appropriate test statistic

We now need to choose an appropriate statistical test for testing H_0. From the information provided we note the following:

- *The number of populations in the study*: There are two independent populations in this example: the population of sugar packets from plant A and the population of sugar packets from plant B.
- *The research question*: The question we are considering testing requires that we investigate the difference between μ_A and μ_B. To determine if there is a difference between the population parameters, we rely on the sample statistics $\overline{X}_A$ and $\overline{X}_B$. The test for this will then involve checking if $\overline{X}_A - \overline{X}_B$ is roughly the same as $\mu_A - \mu_B$ under the null hypothesis. However, since $\mu_A - \mu_B = 0$ under H_0, this means we only need to determine if $\overline{X}_A - \overline{X}_B$ is significantly different from 0.
- *Assumptions underlying the test*: Both population standard deviations are unknown, but we do know that the population values are normally distributed. Since both populations are normally distributed, the relatively small sample sizes ($n_A = 18$ and $n_B = 25$) are not a concern. The test statistic will still follow a $t_{n_A + n_B - 2}$-distribution.

The statistic in formula (11.2) satisfies all of these conditions.

Step 3: Specify the significance level
The significance level is stated as being $\alpha = 0.05$ or 5%.

Step 4: Calculate the relevant test statistic
The data in Table 11.2 allows us to calculate the quantities required to calculate the test statistic in formula (11.2).

- Sample A: $n_A = 18$, $\overline{X}_A = 527.055556$ and $S_A = 51.020725$
- Sample B: $n_B = 25$, $\overline{X}_B = 496.64$ and $S_B = 41.3872766$

Once we have calculated these statistics (using the formulae from Chapter 9), we can calculate the pooled sample standard deviation using formula (11.3):

$$S_{pool} = \sqrt{\frac{(n_A - 1)\, S_A^2 + (n_B - 1)\, S_B^2}{n_A + n_B - 2}}$$

$$= \sqrt{\frac{(18 - 1)(51.02)^2 + (25 - 1)(41.39)^2}{18 + 25 - 2}}$$

$$= 45.63$$

The calculated version of formula (11.2), denoted t_{cal}, is then:

$$t_{cal} = \frac{\overline{X}_A - \overline{X}_B}{S_{pool}\sqrt{\frac{1}{n_A} + \frac{1}{n_B}}} = \frac{572.056 - 496.64}{45.63\sqrt{\frac{1}{18} + \frac{1}{25}}} = 2.156$$

Step 5: Make a decision
We use both the critical value approach and the p-value approach to make a decision for this test.

- *Critical value approach*: The significance level is chosen to be $\alpha = 0.05$ and the distribution of the test statistic under H_0 is $t_{n_A + n_B - 2} = t_{41}$, so we need to find the critical values $t_{41,\alpha/2} = t_{41,0.025}$ and $-t_{41,\alpha/2} = -t_{41,0.025}$ from the t_{41}-distribution, i.e. find the value $t_{41,0.025}$ that satisfies $P(T > t_{41,0.025}) = 0.025$ and find the value $-t_{41,0.025}$ that satisfies $P(T < -t_{41,0.025}) = 0.025$, where $T \sim t_{41}$. We use Excel's T.INV function to obtain this value: $\pm t_{41,0.025} = \pm 2.01954$. Comparing these two critical values to the calculated test statistic, we find that $t_{cal} = 2.156 > t_{41,0.025} = 2.01954$ and $-t_{cal} = -2.156 < -t_{41,0.025} = -2.01954$. Our conclusion is that the calculated test statistic lies in the rejection region, so we **reject H_0**.

- p-*value approach:* We can calculate the p-value of the two-sided test using formula (10.3). (Note that in this test, $T \sim t_{41}$.)

$$\begin{aligned} p\text{-value} &= 2 \times P(T > t_{cal}) \\ &= 2 \times P(T > 2.156) \\ &= 2 \times (1 - P(T < 2.156)) \\ &= 2 \times (1 - 0.9815) \\ &= 2 \times (0.0185) \\ &= 0.037 \end{aligned}$$

Note that we obtained this answer using Excel's T.DIST function.

This p-value is clearly much smaller than the prescribed significance level of $\alpha = 0.05$. Therefore, since p-value $= 0.037 < \alpha = 0.05$, we **reject H_0** at a 5% level of significance.

INTERPRETATION We conclude that based on the sample data collected, we have evidence that the quantity of sugar in the 500g packets of sugar packaged at the two plants are significantly different at the 5% level of significance. It should be noted that the decision will change if you choose a 1% level of significance.

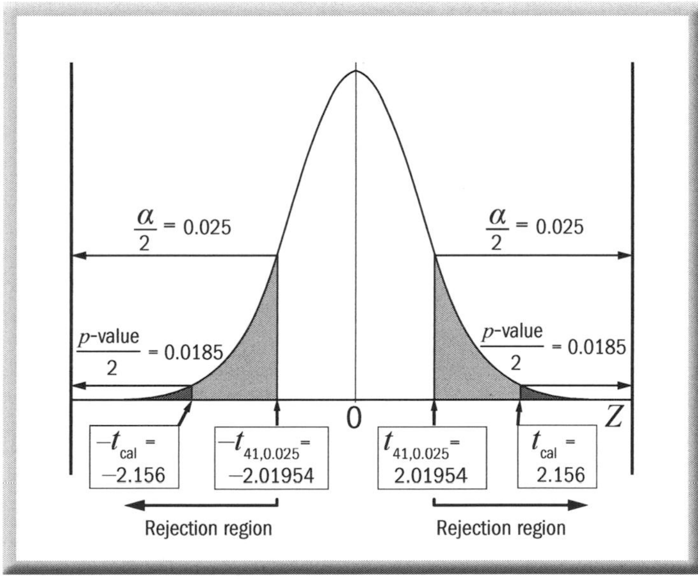

Figure 11.5: Illustration of the relationships between the p-value and α, and the test statistic and the critical values for Example 11.2

	A	B	C	D	E	F	G	H	I	J
1	*t*-test two population means (unknown and equal population variance)									
2		Plant A	Plant B							
3		437	418		1. State Hypothesis	H_0: $\mu_A = \mu_B$				
4		497	525			H_1: $\mu_A \neq \mu_B$				
5		555	581							
6		485	495			Two sample *t*-test for two population means				
7		462	489		2. Select test	Variances are unknown, but equal				
8		638	448			Samples are not large enough for CLT, but data are normal				
9		592	455							
10		569	484		3. Set level of significance	Significance level =	0.05			
11		517	527							
12		490	504							
13		533	489		4. Calculate test statistic	n_A =	18	=COUNT(B3:B20)		
14		509	493			$\overline{X}_A$ =	527.0555556	=AVERAGE(B3:B20)		
15		500	483			S_A =	51.020725	=STDEV.S(B3:B20)		
16		528	463							
17		588	484			n_B =	25	=COUNT(C3:C27)		
18		484	539			$\overline{X}_B$ =	496.64	=AVERAGE(C3:C27)		
19		531	439			S_B =	41.38727663	=STDEV.S(C3:C27)		
20		572	535							
21			495			S_{pool} =	45.62912646	=SQRT(((G13-1)*G15^2+(G17-1)*G19^2)/G13+G17-2)))		
22			508			t_{cal} =	2.156381653	=(G14-G18)/(G21*SQRT(1/G13+1/G17))		
23			605			*p*-value =	0.03697043	=2*(1-T.DIST((G22,G13+G17-2,TRUE))		
24			492			Lower critical value =	-2.01954097	=T.INV(G10/2,G17+G13-2)		
25			514			Upper crticial value =	2.01954097	=T.INV(1-G10/2,G17+G13-2)		
26			460							
27			491			Test statistic compared to the critical value:	$t_{cal} > t_{41\alpha/2}$			
28							and			
29							$-t_{cal} < -t_{41\alpha/8}$	Reject the null hypothesis		
30					5. Decision					
31						*p*-value compared to significance level				
32							$p < \alpha$	Reject the null hypothesis		

Figure 11.6: The Excel solution for Example 11.2

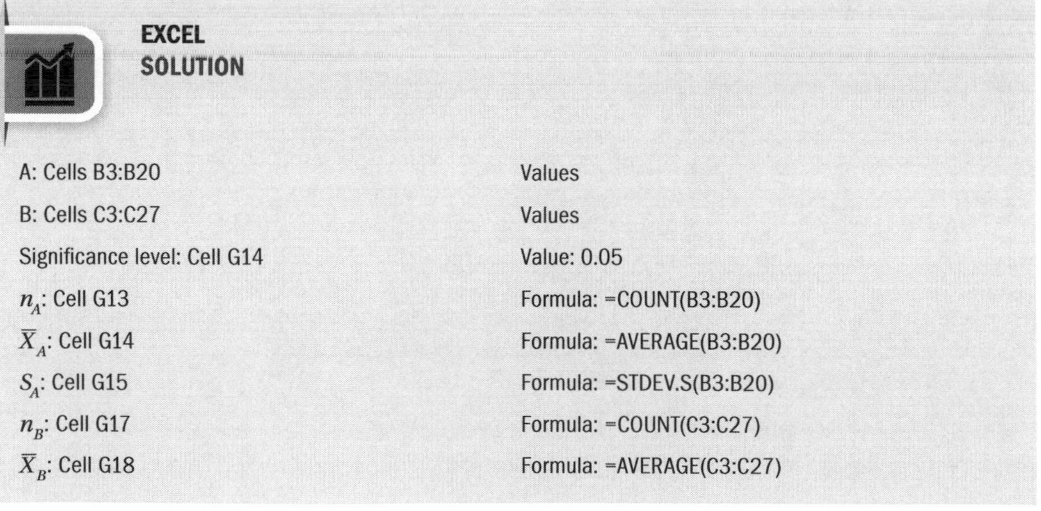

EXCEL SOLUTION

A: Cells B3:B20	Values
B: Cells C3:C27	Values
Significance level: Cell G14	Value: 0.05
n_A: Cell G13	Formula: =COUNT(B3:B20)
$\overline{X}_A$: Cell G14	Formula: =AVERAGE(B3:B20)
S_A: Cell G15	Formula: =STDEV.S(B3:B20)
n_B: Cell G17	Formula: =COUNT(C3:C27)
$\overline{X}_B$: Cell G18	Formula: =AVERAGE(C3:C27)

S_B: Cell G19	Formula: =STDEV.S(C3:C27)
Pooled standard deviation, S_{pool}: Cell G21	Formula: =SQRT((G13-1)*G15^2+(G17-1)*G19^2)/(G13+G17-2))
t_{cal}: Cell G22	Formula: =(G14-G18)/(G21*SQRT(1/G13+1/G17))
Two-sided p-value: Cell G23	Formula: =*(1-T.DIST(G22,G13+G17-2,TRUE))
Left-sided t critical value: Cell G24	Formula: =T.INV(G10/2,G17+G13-2)
Right-sided t critical value: Cell G25	Formula: =T.INV(1-G10/2,G17+G13-2)

Excel Analysis ToolPak solution

We can also use the Excel Analysis Toolpak to obtain these results. Open the Analysis ToolPak (click on the 'Data' tab and then click on the 'Data analysis' button) and select 't-test: Two sample assuming equal variances'. Figure 11.7 shows the results once the necessary information has been provided in the window.

	A	B	C	D	E	F	G	H	I	J	K	L	M	N
1		Plant A	Plant B		t-Test: Two-Sample Assuming Equal Variances									
2		437	418											
3		497	525			*Variable 1*	*Variable 2*							
4		555	581		Mean	527.0555555556	496.64							
5		485	495		Variance	2603.114379085	1712.9066666667							
6		462	489		Observations	18	25							
7		638	448		Pooled Variance	2082.0171815718								
8		592	455		Hypothesized Mean Difference	0								
9		569	484		df	41								
10		517	527		t Stat	2.1563816526								
11		490	504		P(T<=t) one-tail	0.0184852149								
12		533	489		t Critical one-tail	1.6828780026								
13		509	493		P(T<=t) two-tail	0.0369704298								
14		500	483		t Critical two-tail	2.0195409483								
15		528	463											
16		588	484											
17		484	539											
18		531	439											
19		572	535											
20			495											
21			508											
22			605											
23			492											
24			514											
25			460											
26			491											
27														

t-Test: Two-Sample Assuming Equal Variances
Input
Variable 1 Range: $B$2:$B$19
Variable 2 Range: $C$2:$C$26
Hypothesized Mean Difference: 0
Labels
Alpha: 0.05
Output options
Output Range: $E$1
New Worksheet Ply:
New Workbook
OK
Cancel
Help

Figure 11.7: The 't-test: Two sample assuming equal variances' window and output using the data from Example 11.2

11.4 Comparing population means for two independent populations (population variances are unknown and unequal)

We can now consider the situation in which we want to compare the population means of two independent populations where the variances are unknown and unequal.

As with the previous two tests, the null hypothesis is $H_0: \mu_A = \mu_B$ or $H_0: \mu_A - \mu_B = 0$.

The alternative hypotheses are:

$H_1: \mu_A < \mu_B$	$H_1: \mu_A > \mu_B$	$H_1: \mu_A \neq \mu_B$
left-sided	right-sided	two-sided

Or equivalently:

$H_1: \mu_A - \mu_B < 0$	$H_1: \mu_A - \mu_B > 0$	$H_1: \mu_A - \mu_B \neq 0$
left-sided	right-sided	two-sided

The test statistic now differs from the one in formula (11.2), because the population variances are no longer assumed to be equal. This results in using *separate* estimators for the population variances instead of a single pooled estimate. The test statistic, known as the *two sample t-test: assuming unequal variances* or the *separate-variance t-test* or *Satterthwaite's approximate t-test statistic,* is now:

$$t_{\text{cal}} = \frac{\overline{X}_A - \overline{X}_B}{\sqrt{\frac{S_A^2}{n_A} + \frac{S_B^2}{n_B}}} \overset{H_0}{\sim} t_{df_{\text{Satterthwaite}}} \qquad (11.4)$$

Where:

$$df_{\text{Satterthwaite}} = \frac{\left(\frac{S_A^2}{n_A} + \frac{S_B^2}{n_B}\right)^2}{\frac{1}{n_A - 1}\left(\frac{S_A^2}{n_A}\right)^2 + \frac{1}{n_B - 1}\left(\frac{S_B^2}{n_B}\right)^2} \qquad (11.5)$$

Note that the degrees of freedom for the *t*-distribution for this test will likely be a fraction. To overcome this problem, we will simply round off the degree of freedom to the nearest whole number.

The assumptions underlying this test are the following:

- The population variances, σ_A^2 and σ_B^2, are unknown and unequal to one another.
- The test statistic T will follow a $t_{df_{\text{Satterthwaite}}}$-distribution if either of the following two assumptions hold:
  - Both samples are drawn from normally distributed populations.
  - The sample sizes are large enough (they are both at least larger than 30) so that the Central Limit Theorem will ensure the approximate normality of $\overline{X}_A$ and $\overline{X}_B$.

Example 11.3 illustrates this test by extending Example 11.2, adding the restriction that the two population variances are now *unequal.*

WORKED EXAMPLES

EXAMPLE 11.3

We continue with Example 11.2, but now state that the population variances are unequal. How do we test whether the two population means are equal?

The data for this test is provided in Table 11.2 and we will test the hypothesis at $\alpha = 0.05$.

The five-step procedure for performing this test is given below. Note that because the same example is used, these steps will be very similar to the steps described in Example 11.2.

Step 1: Provide the hypothesis statements H_0 and H_1

Once again the null and alternative hypotheses are the following.

- *Null hypothesis*: H_0: $\mu_A = \mu_B$
- *Alternative hypothesis*: H_1: $\mu_A \neq \mu_B$

Step 2: Choose an appropriate test statistic

We now need to choose an appropriate statistical test for testing H_0. From the information provided, we note the following.

- *The number of populations in the study*: There are two independent populations: the population of sugar packets from plant A and the population of sugar packets from plant B.
- *The research question*: As before, the statistic we are interested in calculating must be able to describe the distance between $\overline{X}_A - \overline{X}_B$ and $\mu_A - \mu_B$. In this example though, the difference $\mu_A - \mu_B$ is 0 under H_0.
- *Assumptions underlying the test*: Both population standard deviations are unknown and unequal. The population values are again normally distributed, meaning that the assumptions for the test statistic in formula (11.4) are satisfied.

The test statistic in formula (11.4) is thus appropriate for this hypothesis.

Step 3: Specify the significance level

The significance level is chosen as $\alpha = 0.05$.

Step 4: Calculate the relevant test statistic

The information provided in the data set leads to the calculation of the following sample statistics, which we can use in formulae (11.4) and (11.5).

- Sample A: $n_A = 18$, $\overline{X}_A = 527.055556$ and $S_A = 51.020725$
- Sample B: $n_B = 25$, $\overline{X}_B = 496.64$ and $S_B = 41.3872766$

Using these values, the calculated version of formula (11.4) becomes:

$$t_{\text{cal}} = \frac{\overline{X}_A - \overline{X}_B}{\sqrt{\dfrac{S_A^2}{n_A} + \dfrac{S_B^2}{n_B}}} = \frac{572.055 - 496.64}{\sqrt{\dfrac{(51.02)^2}{18} + \dfrac{(41.38)^2}{25}}} = 2.083$$

We must also determine the degrees of freedom in order to determine the critical values and p-values. The degrees of freedom for this test are given by the Satterthwaite degrees of freedom calculation in formula (11.5):

$$df_{\text{Satterthwaite}} = \frac{\left(\frac{S_A^2}{n_A} + \frac{S_B^2}{n_B}\right)^2}{\frac{1}{n_A - 1}\left(\frac{S_A^2}{n_A}\right)^2 + \frac{1}{n_B - 1}\left(\frac{S_B^2}{n_B}\right)^2}$$

$$= \frac{\left(\frac{(51.02)^2}{18} + \frac{(41.38)^2}{25}\right)^2}{\frac{1}{18-1}\left(\frac{(51.02)^2}{18}\right)^2 + \frac{1}{25-1}\left(\frac{(41.38)^2}{25}\right)^2}$$

$$\approx 32$$

Step 5: Make a decision

We will use both the critical value approach and the p-value approach to make a decision for this test.

- *Critical value approach*: The significance level is chosen to be $\alpha = 0.05$ and the distribution of the test statistic under H_0 is $t_{df_{\text{Satterthwaite}}} = t_{32}$, so we will need to find the critical values $t_{32,\alpha/2} = t_{32,0.025}$ and $-t_{32,\alpha/2} = -t_{32,0.025}$ from the t_{32}-distribution, i.e. find the value $t_{32,0.025}$ that satisfies $P(T > t_{32,0.025}) = 0.025$ and find the value $-t_{32,0.025}$ that satisfies $P(T < -t_{32,0.025}) = 0.025$, where $T \sim t_{32}$. We have used Excel's T.INV function to obtain this value: $\pm t_{32,0.025} = \pm 2.03693$. Comparing these two critical values to the calculated test statistic, we find that $t_{\text{cal}} = 2.083 > t_{32,0.025} = 2.03693$ and $-t_{\text{cal}} = -2.083 < -t_{32,0.025} = -2.03693$. Our conclusion is that the calculated test statistic lies in the rejection region, so we will **reject H_0**.
- p-*value approach*: We can calculate the p-value of the two-sided test by using formula (10.3). (Note that in this test, $T \sim t_{32}$.)

$$\begin{aligned} p\text{-value} &= 2 \times P(T > t_{\text{cal}}) \\ &= 2 \times P(T > 2.083) \\ &= 2 \times (1 - P(T < 2.083)) \\ &= 2 \times (1 - 0.9773) \\ &= 2 \times (0.0227) \\ &= 0.0453 \end{aligned}$$

Note, we obtained this answer using Excel's T.DIST function.

This p-value is slightly smaller than the prescribed significance level of $\alpha = 0.05$. Therefore, since p-value $= 0.0453 < \alpha = 0.05$, we will **reject H_0**.

INTERPRETATION We conclude that based on the sample data collected, we have evidence that the weight of the 500 g sugar packets packaged at plants A and B are significantly different at the 5% level of significance. It should be noted the result in this case rests at the borderline of rejecting H_0. At this stage, a recommendation would be to revisit the data collection methods employed and increase the sample sizes.

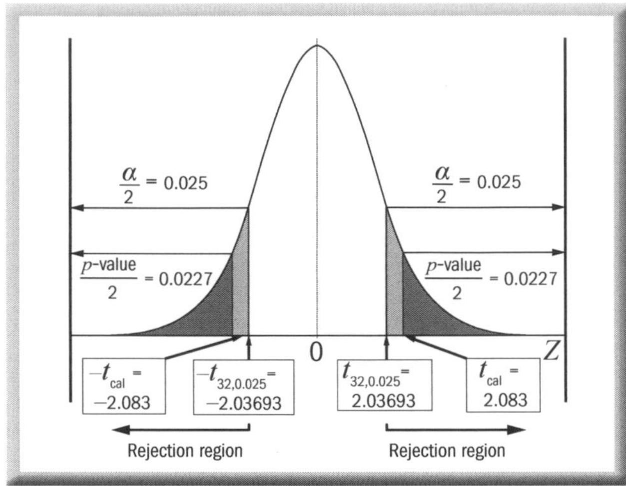

Figure 11.8: Illustration of the relationships between the p-value and α, and the test statistic and the critical values for Example 11.3

	A	B	C	D	E	F	G	H
1	**t-test two population means (unknown and equal population variance)**							
2		**Plant A**	**Plant B**					
3		437	418		**1. State hypothesis**	$H_0: \mu_A = \mu_B$		
4		497	525			$H_1: \mu_A \neq \mu_B$		
5		555	581					
6		485	495			Two sample t-test for two population means		
7		462	489		**2. Select test**	Variances are unknown and unequal		
8		638	448			Samples are not large enough to use CLT, but data are normal		
9		592	455					
10		569	484		**3. Set level of significance**	Significance level, α =	0.05	
11		517	527					
12		490	504					
13		533	489			n_A =	18	=COUNT(B3:B20)
14		509	493			$\bar{X}_A$ =	527.0555555556	=AVERAGE(B3:B20)
15		500	483			S_A =	51.0207249957	=STDEV.S(B3:B20)
16		528	463					
17		588	484			n_B =	25	=COUNT(C3:C27)
18		484	539			$\bar{X}_B$ =	496.64	=AVERAGE(C3:C27)
19		531	439			S_B =	41.3872766278	=STDEV.S(C3:C27)
20		572	535		**4. Calculate test statistic**			
21			495			df numerator =	45425.9877893046	=(G15^2/G13+G19^2/G17)^2
22			508			df denominator =	1425.8510084832	=((G15^2/G13)^2)/(G13-1)+((G19^2/G17)^2)/(G17-1)
23			605			$df_{satterthwaite}$ =	32	=ROUND(G21/G22,0)
24			492			t_{cal} =	2.0833856022	=(G14-G18)/SQRT(G15^2/G13+G19^2/G17)
25			514			p-value =	0.0452881	=2*(1-T.DIST(G24,G23,TRUE))
26			460			Lower critical value =	-2.0369333	=T.INV(G10/2,G23)
27			491			Upper critical value =	2.0369333	=T.INV(1-G10/2,G23)
28								
29						Test statistic compared to the critical value	$t_{cal} > t_{41,\alpha/2}$	
30							and	
31					**5. Decision**		$-t_{cal} < -t_{41,\alpha/2}$	Reject the null hypothesis
32								
33						p-value compared to significance level	$p < \alpha$	Reject the null hypothesis
34								
35								

Figure 11.9: The Excel solution for Example 11.3

EXCEL SOLUTION

A: Cells B3:B20	Values
B: Cells C3:C27	Values
Significance level: Cell G14	Value: 0.05
n_A: Cell G13	Formula: =COUNT(B3:B20)
$\overline{X}_A$: Cell G14	Formula: =AVERAGE(B3:B20)
S_A: Cell G15	Formula: =STDEV.S(B3:B20)
n_B: Cell G17	Formula: =COUNT(C3:C27)
$\overline{X}_B$: Cell G18	Formula: =AVERAGE(C3:C27)
S_B: Cell G19	Formula: =STDEV.S(C3:C27)
df numerator: Cell G21	Formula: =(G15^2/G13+G19^2/G17)^2
df denominator: Cell G22	Formula: =((G15^2/G13)^2)/(G13-1)+((G19^2/G17)^2)/(G17-1)
$df_{\text{Satterthwaite}}$: Cell G23	Formula: =ROUND(G21/G22,0)
t_{cal}: Cell G24	Formula: =(G14-G18)/SQRT(G15^2/G13+G19^2/G17)
p-value: Cell G25	Formula: =2*(1-T.DIST(G24,G23,TRUE))
Lower t critical: Cell G26	Formula: =T.INV(G10/2,G23)
Upper t critical: Cell G27	Formula: =T.INV(1-G10/2,G23)

Excel Analysis ToolPak solution

To obtain the same result in Excel's Analysis Toolpak, begin by opening the 'Data Analysis' window (click on the 'Data' tab and then click on the 'Data Analysis' button) and select '*t*-test: Two Sample assuming Unequal Variances'. Figure 11.10 shows the results after having provided the necessary information in the window that appears.

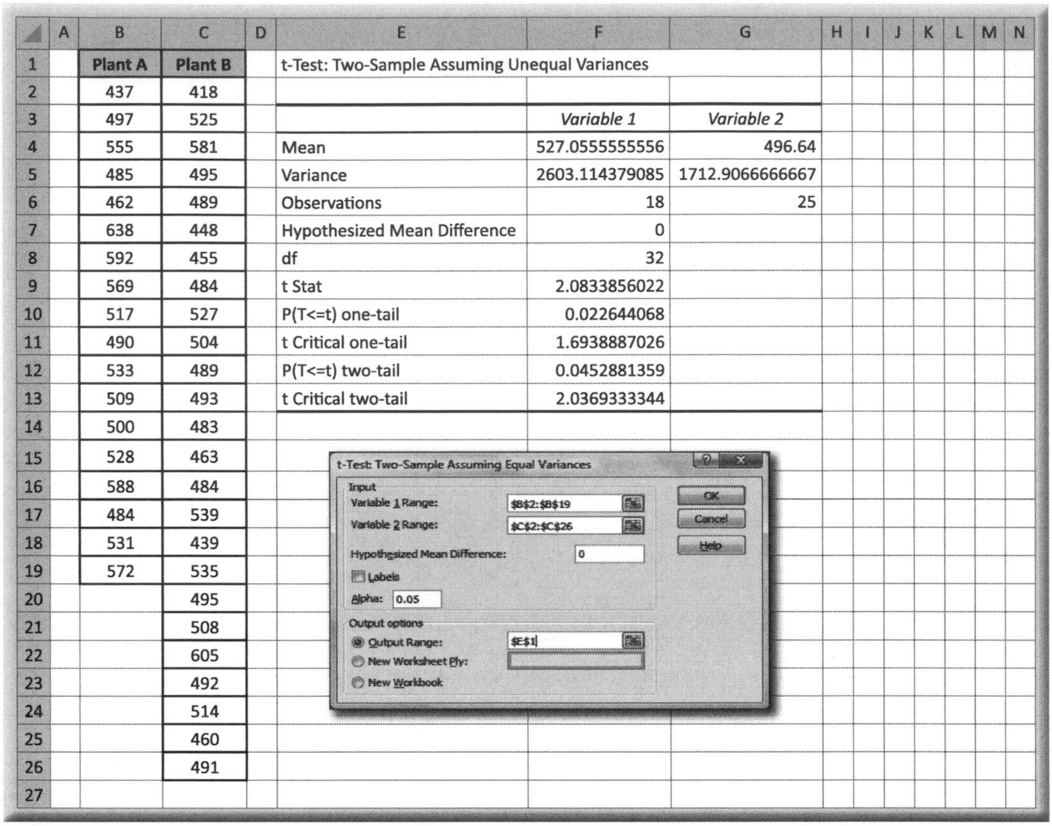

	Plant A	Plant B
1	Plant A	Plant B
2	437	418
3	497	525
4	555	581
5	485	495
6	462	489
7	638	448
8	592	455
9	569	484
10	517	527
11	490	504
12	533	489
13	509	493
14	500	483
15	528	463
16	588	484
17	484	539
18	531	439
19	572	535
20		495
21		508
22		605
23		492
24		514
25		460
26		491

t-Test: Two-Sample Assuming Unequal Variances

	Variable 1	*Variable 2*
Mean	527.0555555556	496.64
Variance	2603.114379085	1712.9066666667
Observations	18	25
Hypothesized Mean Difference	0	
df	32	
t Stat	2.0833856022	
P(T<=t) one-tail	0.022644068	
t Critical one-tail	1.6938887026	
P(T<=t) two-tail	0.0452881359	
t Critical two-tail	2.0369333344	

t-Test: Two-Sample Assuming Equal Variances
Input
Variable 1 Range: $B$2:$B$19
Variable 2 Range: $C$2:$C$26
Hypothesized Mean Difference: 0
Labels
Alpha: 0.05
Output options
Output Range: $E$1
New Worksheet Ply:
New Workbook
OK
Cancel
Help

Figure 11.10: The '*t*-test: Two Sample Assuming Unequal Variances' window and output using the data from Example 11.3

11.5 Comparing the population means of two dependent populations

As mentioned in Section 11.1, we can have independent and dependent populations when we consider two population problems. The hypothesis tests discussed so far have all dealt with the problem of testing the hypothesis of whether the population means of two *independent* populations are equal or unequal. We now consider testing the equality of population means for two *dependent* populations. However, since two dependent populations consist of paired observations (each item in population A has a direct counterpart in population B), we can reduce the problem of testing these two population means to a problem of testing a single population mean by constructing a new population of the differences between paired observations. To explain this idea, suppose that both populations A and B have N items and that $x_{i,A}$ represents the observed value of the ith item in population A and $x_{i,B}$ represents the corresponding i^{th} value in population B. We can now create a new population of values by taking the differences between these observations. We call the ith observation from this new population $x_{i,\text{diff}} = x_{i,A} - x_{i,B}$. We can base hypothesis tests for the difference in population means on this new differenced population by considering the population mean of this new population, which we denote μ_{diff}. The hypothesis procedure is then very similar to the single population hypothesis test discussed in Section 10.3: we are interested in determining if $\mu_{diff} = 0$, which is equivalent to testing that the population means for the original two dependent populations do not differ.

Table 11.3 illustrates an example where we have paired observations on a sample of athletes' heart rates *before* and *after* running a race (in beats per minute). The first two columns show the heart rate before the race and after the race, respectively, and the third column is simply the difference between these two values.

Table 11.3: Heart rates for athletes before and after a race, and the difference between these two values

ATHLETE	HEART RATE (BEFORE)	HEART RATE (AFTER)	HEART RATE DIFFERENCE: (AFTER – BEFORE)
1	50	120	70
2	52	129	77
3	56	134	78
4	53	123	70

We can now view the heart rate difference column in Table 11.3 as a sample from a single population of differenced values. We now focus our attention on this new population rather than considering the original two. A hypothesis in this example might be that the population mean heart rate after a race is more than 70 beats per minute greater than before a race: formulated as $H_0: \mu_{diff} = 70$ vs $H_1: \mu_{diff} > 70$.

As we have just illustrated, our hypotheses for this situation concerns the population mean of the differenced population, μ_{diff}. We test if this population mean is equal to some hypothesised value, which we denote $\mu_{diff,0}$. The null hypothesis is then $H_0: \mu_{diff} = \mu_{diff,0}$

The alternative hypotheses can be:

$H_1: \mu_{diff} < \mu_{diff,0}$	$H_1: \mu_{diff} > \mu_{diff,0}$	$H_1: \mu_{diff} \neq \mu_{diff,0}$
left-sided	right-sided	two-sided

The test statistic used for this hypothesis is nearly identical to the one stated in formula (10.6) and is called the *two sample* t*-test: paired sample for means*:

$$T = \frac{\bar{X}_{diff} - \mu_{diff,0}}{\frac{S_{diff}}{\sqrt{n}}} \overset{H_0}{\sim} t_{n-1} \tag{11.6}$$

Where:

$$\bar{X}_{diff} = \frac{1}{n}\sum_{i=1}^{n} X_{i,diff} \tag{11.7}$$

And:

$$S_{diff} = \sqrt{\frac{\sum_{i=1}^{n} X_{i,diff}^2 - \frac{1}{n}\left(\sum_{i=1}^{n} X_{i,diff}\right)^2}{n-1}} \tag{11.8}$$

The value $X_{i,\text{diff}}$ is simply defined as the difference between the ith pair of observations from the two dependent samples: $X_{i,\text{diff}} = X_{i,A} - X_{i,B}$, where $X_{i,A}$ represents the observed value of the ith item in sample A and $X_{i,B}$ represents the corresponding i^{th} value in the paired sample B.

Note that as these are paired samples, the sample sizes for both samples (sample A and B) will be the same: $n_A = n_B = n$.

As with the test statistic in formula (10.6), *either* of the following two assumptions must be satisfied before we can assume that it follows a t_{n-1}-distribution:

- The differenced population must be normally distributed (this will usually occur when both populations A and B are also normally distributed).
- The sample size, *n*, is large enough that the Central Limit Theorem can be applied (it is larger than 30).

In both cases, we assume that the population standard deviation of the differenced population is *unknown*.

Example 11.4 will help demonstrate the calculations and the interpretation of the test.

WORKED EXAMPLES

EXAMPLE 11.4

Super Slim, a weight loss society, is offering a weight reduction programme that they advertise will result in a more than 7 cm loss in waist size in the first 30 days of the programme. Twenty-six subjects were independently and randomly selected for a study, and their waist sizes before and after the weight loss programme were recorded (given in Table 11.4).

Test the hypothesis (at a $\alpha = 0.05$ level) that the claim made by Super Slim is valid.

Note that Super Slim have stated that the historical data shows that the populations are normally distributed.

Table 11.4: Waist sizes before and after the weight loss treatment

PERSON	1	2	3	4	5	6	7	8	9
BEFORE (cm), X_B	119	111.3	113.4	107.1	123.9	116.9	110.6	124.6	98.7
AFTER (cm), X_A	119	107.1	90.3	100.1	95.9	93.8	93.1	89.6	106.4
DIFFERENCE (cm), $X_{\text{diff}} = X_B - X_A$	0	4.2	23.1	7	28	23.1	17.5	35	–7.7

PERSON	10	11	12	13	14	15	16	17	18
BEFORE (cm), X_B	114.1	107.8	111.3	111.3	96.6	112.7	109.2	115.5	110.6
AFTER (cm), X_A	99.4	98	107.8	100.1	102.9	99.4	104.3	95.2	107.8
DIFFERENCE (cm), $X_{\text{diff}} = X_B - X_A$	14.7	9.8	3.5	11.2	–6.3	13.3	4.9	20.3	2.8

PERSON	19	20	21	22	23	24	25	26
BEFORE (cm), X_B	105.7	115.5	108.5	107.8	102.9	109.2	108.5	118.3
AFTER (cm), X_A	98	101.5	87.5	98	87.5	98.7	102.2	94.5
DIFFERENCE (cm), $X_{\text{diff}} = X_B - X_A$	7.7	14	21	9.8	15.4	10.5	6.3	23.8

We now conduct the five-step procedure for testing the hypothesis.

Step 1: Provide the hypothesis statements H_0 and H_1

The hypothesis statement implies that the population mean waist size difference between population A (the population after treatment) and B (the population before treatment) should be at least 7 cm. If $\mu_{\text{diff}} = \mu_B - \mu_A$, then we can state null and alternative hypotheses as follows (note that we choose 'before minus after' in this case because we stipulated that the difference is +7, meaning that we assume that they will be thinner after the treatment).

- *Null hypothesis*: H_0: $\mu_{\text{diff}} = 7$
- *Alternative hypothesis*: H_1: $\mu_{\text{diff}} > 7$ (or $\mu_{\text{diff}} - 7 > 0$)

The > sign implies a right-sided test.

Step 2: Choose an appropriate test statistic

We now need to choose an appropriate statistical test for testing H_0. From the information provided we note the following.

- *The number of populations in the study*: There are two dependent populations in this study: the population of individuals before treatment (population B) and the population of individuals after treatment (population A).
- *The research question*: The question concerns the centimetres lost during the programme. Specifically it asks if the population mean of the paired difference between before and after, μ_{diff}, is greater than 7. The test statistic should therefore be able to measure the difference between the observed mean paired difference, $\bar{X}_{\text{diff}}$, and the population mean paired difference, μ_{diff}.
- *Assumptions underlying the test*: Both population standard deviations are unknown and the sample sizes are relatively small ($n = n_A = n_B = 26$). However, it is stated that both populations A and B are historically normally distributed, meaning that the differenced population might possibly also be normally distributed.

In this case, the conditions required to employ the test stated in formula (11.6) have been reasonably satisfied, so we can use it.

Step 3: Specify the significance level

The significance level is given as $\alpha = 0.05$.

Step 4: Calculate the relevant test statistic

The *t*-test statistic, given by formula (11.6), relies on the calculation of the sample mean and standard deviation using formulae (11.7) and (11.8) respectively. These values are calculated to be:

$$\bar{X}_{\text{diff}} = \frac{1}{26}\sum_{i=1}^{26} X_{i,\text{diff}} = \frac{1}{26}(312.9) = 12.03462$$

And:

$$S_{\text{diff}} = \sqrt{\frac{\sum_{i=1}^{26} X_{i,\text{diff}}^2 - \frac{1}{n}\left(\sum_{i=1}^{26} X_{i,\text{diff}}\right)^2}{n-1}}$$

$$= \sqrt{\frac{6\,364.61 - \frac{1}{26}(312.9)^2}{26-1}}$$

$$= 10.19604$$

Using these two calculations, we can finally calculate the test statistic (denoted t_{cal}):

$$t_{\text{cal}} = \frac{\overline{X}_{\text{diff}} - \mu_{\text{diff},0}}{\frac{S_{\text{diff}}}{\sqrt{n}}} = \frac{12.03462 - 7}{\frac{10.19604}{\sqrt{26}}} = 2.51780$$

Step 5: Make a decision

We use both the critical value approach and the p-value approach to make a decision for this test.

- *Critical value approach*: For this example, the test statistic follows a $t_{n-1} = t_{25}$-distribution and the $\alpha = 0.05$ critical value is thus $t_{25,0.05} = 1.708141$ (obtained from the T.INV function in Excel). The test statistic's calculated value is $t_{\text{cal}} = 2.51780$. Does the calculated test statistic lie within the region of rejection? Yes it does, because this is a right-sided test and $t_{\text{cal}} = 2.51780 > t_{25,0.05} = 1.708141$, i.e. the calculated value of the test statistic exceeds the critical value for the test. Therefore, we **reject H_0**.
- p*-value approach*: We calculate the p-value of the right-sided test using formula (10.2) of the previous chapter (note that in this test $T \sim t_{n-1} = t_{25}$):

$$\begin{aligned} p\text{-value} &= P(T > t_{\text{cal}}) \\ &= P(T > 2.51780) \\ &= 1 - P(T < 2.51780) \\ &= 1 - 0.990708 \\ &= 0.009292 \end{aligned}$$

This p-value is clearly much smaller than the prescribed significance level of $\alpha = 0.05$. Therefore, since p-value $= 0.009292 < \alpha = 0.05$, we **reject H_0** at a 5% level of significance.

INTERPRETATION We conclude that the average loss in waist size is more than 7 cm at a 5% level of significance.

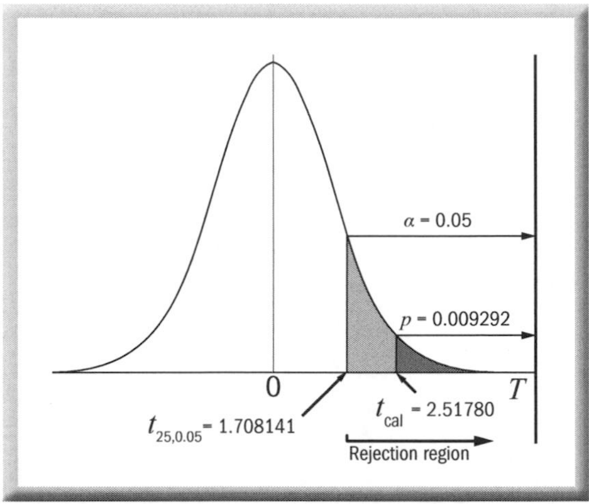

Figure 11.11: Illustration of the relationships between the p-value and α, and the test statistic and the critical values for Example 11.4

	A	B	C	D	E	F	G	H	I	J	K
1	Two sample t-test for paired populations										
2		Person	Before, X_B	After, X_A	Difference, $X_B - X_A$			1. State hypothesis	H_0: $\mu_{\text{diff}} = 7$		
3		1	119	119	0	=C3-D3			H_1: $\mu_{\text{diff}} > 7$		
4		2	111.3	107.1	4.2	=C4-D4					
5		3	113.4	90.3	23.1	=C5-D5		2. Select test	Two dependent populations		
6		4	107.1	100.1	7	=C6-D6			Both populations are normally distributed		
7		5	123.9	95.9	28	=C7-D7					
8		6	116.9	93.8	23.1	=C8-D8		3. Set level of significance	Significance level, α =	0.05	
9		7	110.6	93.1	17.5	=C9-D9					
10		8	124.6	89.6	35	=C10-D10					
11		9	98.7	106.4	-7.7	=C11-D11			n =	26	=COUNT(E3:E28)
12		10	114.1	99.4	14.7	=C12-D12			$\overline{X}_{\text{diff}}$ =	12.0346	=AVERAGE(E3:E28)
13		11	107.8	98	9.8	=C13-D13			S_{diff} =	10.1960	=STDEV.S(E3:E28)
14		12	111.3	107.8	3.5	=C14-D14		4. Calculate test statistic	t_{cal} =	2.5178	=(J12-7)/(J13/SQRT(J11))
15		13	111.3	100.1	11.2	=C15-D15					
16		14	96.6	102.9	-6.3	=C16-D16			p-value =	0.0093	=1-T.DIST(J14,J11-1,TRUE)
17		15	112.7	99.4	13.3	=C17-D17			Critical value =	1.7081	=T.INV(1-J8,J11-1)
18		16	109.2	104.3	4.9	=C18-D18					
19		17	115.5	95.2	20.3	=C19-D19			Test statistic compared to critical values	$t_{\text{cal}} > t_{25,\alpha}$	Reject the null hypothesis
20		18	110.6	107.8	2.8	=C20-D20					
21		19	105.7	98	7.7	=C21-D21		5. Decision			
22		20	115.5	101.5	14	=C22-D22			p-value compared to significance level		
23		21	108.5	87.5	21	=C23-D23				$p < \alpha$	Reject the null hypothesis
24		22	107.8	98	9.8	=C24-D24					
25		23	102.9	87.5	15.4	=C25-D25					
26		24	109.2	98.7	10.5	=C26-D26					
27		25	108.5	102.2	6.3	=C27-D27					
28		26	118.3	94.5	23.8	=C28-D28					
29											

Figure 11.12: The Excel solution for Example 11.4

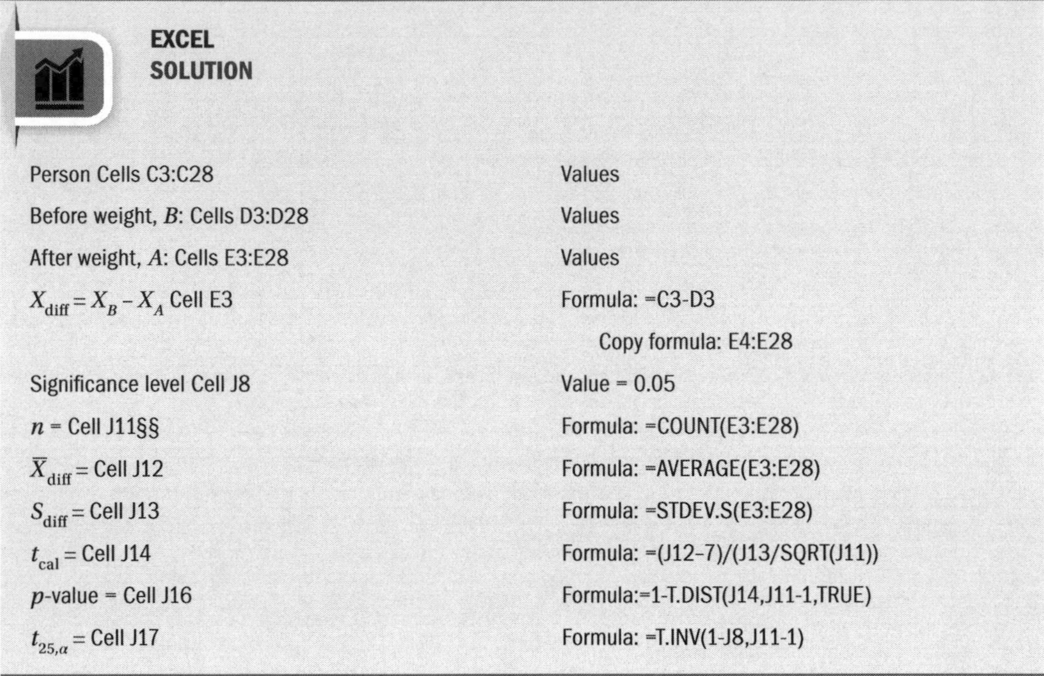

EXCEL SOLUTION

Person Cells C3:C28	Values
Before weight, B: Cells D3:D28	Values
After weight, A: Cells E3:E28	Values
$X_{\text{diff}} = X_B - X_A$ Cell E3	Formula: =C3-D3
	Copy formula: E4:E28
Significance level Cell J8	Value = 0.05
n = Cell J11§§	Formula: =COUNT(E3:E28)
$\overline{X}_{\text{diff}}$ = Cell J12	Formula: =AVERAGE(E3:E28)
S_{diff} = Cell J13	Formula: =STDEV.S(E3:E28)
t_{cal} = Cell J14	Formula: =(J12-7)/(J13/SQRT(J11))
p-value = Cell J16	Formula:=1-T.DIST(J14,J11-1,TRUE)
$t_{25,\alpha}$ = Cell J17	Formula: =T.INV(1-J8,J11-1)

Excel Analysis ToolPak solution

We can obtain the same results as in Figure 11.12 by performing this calculation using Excel's Analysis Toolpak. Click on the 'Data' tab, and then click on the 'Data Analysis' button to bring up the data analysis window. Select '*t*-Test: Paired Two-Sample for Means' and then fill in the window that appears. The resulting output is shown in Figure 11.13.

Person	Before	After
1	119	119
2	111.3	107.1
3	113.4	90.3
4	107.1	100.1
5	123.9	95.9
6	116.9	93.8
7	110.6	93.1
8	124.6	89.6
9	98.7	106.4
10	114.1	99.4
11	107.8	98
12	111.3	107.8
13	111.3	100.1
14	96.6	102.9
15	112.7	99.4
16	109.2	104.3
17	115.5	95.2
18	110.6	107.8
19	105.7	98
20	115.5	101.5
21	108.5	87.5
22	107.8	98
23	102.9	87.5
24	109.2	98.7
25	108.5	102.2
26	118.3	94.5

t-Test: Paired Two Sample for Means

	Variable 1	*Variable 2*
Mean	111.1923076923	99.1576923077
Variance	42.7551384615	50.9969384615
Observations	26	26
Pearson Correlation	-0.1092962298	
Hypothesized Mean Difference	7	
df	25	
t Stat	2.5178021761	
P(T<=t) one-tail	0.0092920879	
t Critical one-tail	1.7081407452	
P(T<=t) two-tail	0.0185841758	
t Critical two-tail	2.0595385357	

t-Test: Paired Two Sample for Means
Input
Variable 1 Range: $C$3:$C$28
Variable 2 Range: $D$3:$D$28
Hypothesized Mean Difference: 7
Labels
Alpha: 0.05
Output options
Output Range: $F$2
New Worksheet Ply:
New Workbook
OK
Cancel
Help

Figure 11.13: The '*t*-test: Paired two sample for means' window and output using the data from Example 11.4

11.6 Comparing population proportions from two independent populations

Comparing proportions from two independent populations is analogous to comparing means from two independent populations. The null hypothesis of interest is H_0: $\pi_A = \pi_B$ or H_0: $\pi_A - \pi_B = 0$.

The alternative hypotheses are:

H_1: $\pi_A < \pi_B$ (left-sided) H_1: $\pi_A > \pi_B$ (right-sided) H_1: $\pi_A \neq \pi_B$ (two-sided)

Or equivalently:

H_1: $\pi_A - \pi_B < 0$ (left-sided) H_1: $\pi_A - \pi_B > 0$ (right-sided) or H_1: $\pi_A - \pi_B \neq 0$ (two-sided)

π_A and π_B are the population proportions. Note that π_A is estimated by p_A and π_B is estimated by p_B.

The test statistic that we can use for this particular hypothesis is:

$$Z = \frac{p_A - p_B}{\sqrt{p_{\text{tot}}(1 - p_{\text{tot}})\left[\frac{1}{n_A} + \frac{1}{n_B}\right]}} \overset{H_0}{\sim} N(0, 1) \tag{11.9}$$

$p_A = \frac{x_A}{n_A}$ and $p_B = \frac{x_B}{n_B}$ are proportions for sample A and B, and $p_{\text{tot}} = \frac{x_A + x_B}{n_A + n_B}$, where x_A and x_B are the number of items that satisfy some specified condition in samples A and B respectively, and n_A and n_B are the total number of items in sample A and B respectively.

The only assumption that this test statistic must satisfy to have the stated standard normal distribution is that the sample sizes, n_A and n_B, must both be large (typically they should each contain 30 or more observations).

Example 11.5 goes through the steps of testing a hypothesis for two population proportions.

WORKED EXAMPLES

EXAMPLE 11.5

The Department of Transport (Gauteng) is concerned about the number of passengers not wearing rear seatbelts in cars in two of their large metropolitan areas. They decide to undertake a series of surveys based on these two large metropolitan areas: the City of Johannesburg Metropolitan Municipality (area A) and the City of Tshwane Metropolitan Municipality (area B). The survey consists of two independent random samples collected from these two areas: $n_A = 250$ cars were investigated in area A and $n_B = 190$ cars were investigated in area B. It was found that of the $n_A = 250$ cars in area A, only $x_A = 135$ were found with passengers using rear seatbelts, and of the $n_B = 190$ cars investigated in area B, only $x_B = 80$ were found using rear seatbelts.

The Department of Transport would like to know if the proportions of passengers wearing seatbelts in area A and area B are significantly different. Conduct an appropriate test (at significance level $\alpha = 0.05$) to test this hypothesis.

The five-step procedure for testing this hypothesis is given below.

Step 1: Provide the hypothesis statements H_0 and H_1

The problem indicates that the Department of Transport is only interested in determining if the population proportions differ, so the null and alternative hypothesis statements can be formulated as follows.

- *Null hypothesis*: H_0: $\pi_A - \pi_B = 0$
- *Alternative hypothesis*: H_1: $\pi_A - \pi_B \neq 0$

Step 2: Choose an appropriate test statistic

We now need to choose an appropriate statistical test for testing H_0. From the information provided we note the following.

- *The number of populations in the study*: There are two populations involved: the population of cars in the City of Johannesburg Metropolitan Municipality (population A) and the population of cars in the City of Tshwane Metropolitan Municipality (population B).

- *The research question*: The Department is interested in testing the distance between the sample proportion difference, $p_A - p_B$, and the population proportion difference, $\pi_A - \pi_B$ (which is 0 under H_0). The test statistic in formula (11.9) can measure this distance, and so it is a reasonable choice for this hypothesis.
- *Assumptions underlying the test*: The size of both samples is large ($n_A = 250$ and $n_B = 190$) and so the Central Limit Theorem allows the statistic in formula (11.9) to follow an approximate normal distribution.

From this information, we conduct a two-sample Z-test for proportions.

Step 3: Specify the significance level

The significance level is given as $\alpha = 0.05$.

Step 4: Calculate the relevant test statistic

Note that we can gather the following values from the information provided in Example 11.5.

- Sample A: $n_A = 250$ and $x_A = 135$
- Sample B: $n_B = 190$ and $x_B = 80$

The statistics that we need to calculate before calculating formula (11.9) are:

$$p_A = \frac{x_A}{n_A} = \frac{135}{250} = 0.54$$

$$p_B = \frac{x_B}{n_B} = \frac{80}{190} = 0.42105$$

And:

$$p_{\text{tot}} = \frac{x_A + x_B}{n_A + n_B} = \frac{135 + 80}{250 + 190} = 0.4886$$

The calculated test statistic (denoted z_{cal}) is then:

$$z_{\text{cal}} = \frac{p_A - p_B}{\sqrt{p_{\text{tot}}(1 - p_{\text{tot}})\left[\frac{1}{n_A} + \frac{1}{n_B}\right]}}$$

$$= \frac{0.54 - 0.42105}{\sqrt{0.4886 \times (1 - 0.4886) \times \left(\frac{1}{250} + \frac{1}{190}\right)}}$$

$$= 2.4725$$

Step 5: Make a decision

We use both the critical value approach and the p-value approach to make a decision for this test.

- *Critical value approach*: The critical values for this test are $z_{\alpha/2} = z_{0.025} = 1.96$ and $-z_{\alpha/2} = -z_{0.025} = -1.96$ (obtained using the NORM.S.INV function in Excel). Comparing $z_{\text{cal}} = 2.4725$ to these critical bounds, we see that it definitely lies in the rejection region of the test and so **we reject H_0**.

- p-*value approach*: We obtain the p-value by using formula (10.3) and noting that $Z \sim N(0, 1)$:

$$\begin{aligned} p\text{-value} &= 2 \times P(Z > z_{cal}) \\ &= 2 \times P(Z > 2.4725) \\ &= 2 \times (1 - P(Z < 2.4725)) \\ &= 2 \times (1 - 0.993291) \\ &= 2 \times (0.006709) \\ &= 0.013417 \end{aligned}$$

This p-value is smaller than the specified level of $\alpha = 0.05$ and so we **reject H_0** at a 5% level of significance.

INTERPRETATION We conclude that a significant difference exists between the proportions of cars with passengers wearing rear seatbelts in area A and area B. Furthermore, the evidence suggests that the proportion of cars is higher for area A. To test this, we could conduct a right-sided test to test whether the proportion for area A is significantly larger than for area B. It should also be noted that the decision will change if you choose a 1% level of significance.

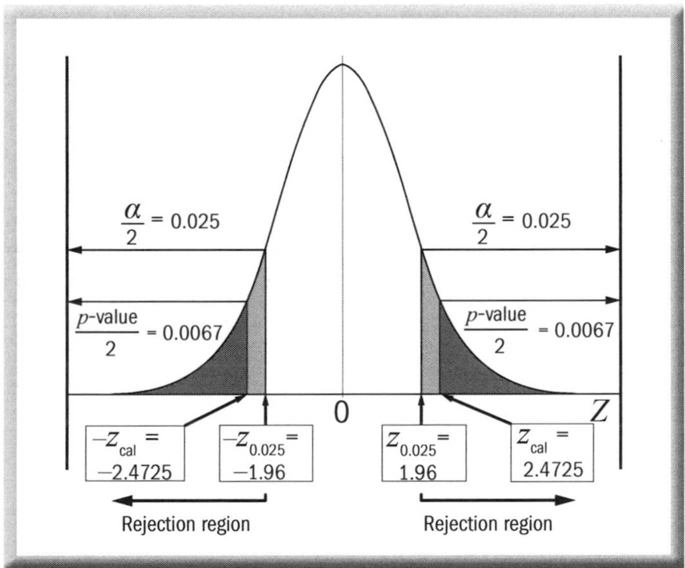

Figure 11.14: Illustration of the relationships between the p-value and α, and the test statistic and the critical values for Example 11.5

	A	B	C	D	E	F
1	Testing two population proportions					
2						
3			Area A	Area B		
4		Number wearing seat belts, x	135	80		
5		Number interviewed, n	250	190		
6						
7		1. State hypothesis	H_0: $\pi_A - \pi_B = 0$			
8			H_1: $\pi_A - \pi_B \neq 0$			
9						
10		2. Select test	Two populations - testing two population proportions			
11			Sample size is large			
12						
13		3. Set level of significance	Significance level, α =	0.05		
14						
15			n_A =	250	=C5	
16			x_A =	135	=C4	
17			n_B =	190	=D5	
18			x_B =	80	=D4	
19			p_A =	0.54	=D17/D16	
20		4. Calculate test statistic	p_B =	0.4210526316	=D19/D18	
21			p_{tot} =	0.4886363636	=(D17+D19)/(D16+D18)	
22			z_{cal} =	2.4723929255	=(D20-D21)/SQRT(D22*(1-D22)*(1/D16+1/D18))	
23			p-value =	0.013421191	=2*(1-NORM.S.DIST(D23,TRUE))	
24			Lower critical value =	-1.959963985	=NORM.S.INV(D14/2)	
25			Upper critical value =	1.959963985	=NORM.S.INV(1-D14/2)	
26						
27			Test statistic compared to critical value	$z_{cal} > z_{\alpha/2}$		
28				and		
29		5. Decision		$-z_{cal} < -z_{\alpha/2}$	Reject the null hypothesis	
30						
31			p-value compared to significance level			
32				$p < \alpha$	Reject the null hypothesis	
33						

Figure 11.15: The Excel solution for Example 11.5

EXCEL SOLUTION

n_A: Cell C5	Value
n_B: Cell D5	Value
x_A: Cell C4	Value
x_B: Cell D4	Value
Significance level: Cell D13	Value: 0.05

n_A: Cell D16	Formula: =C5
n_B: Cell D18	Formula: =D5
x_A: Cell D17	Formula: =C4
x_B: Cell D19	Formula: =D4
p_A: Cell D20	Formula: =D16/D15
p_B: Cell D21	Formula: =D18/D17
p_{tot}: Cell D22	Formula: =(D16+D18)/(D15+D17)
z_{cal}: Cell D23	Formula: =(D19-D20)/SQRT(D21*(1-D21)*(1/D15+1/D17))
p-value: Cell D24	Formula: =2*(1-NORM.S.DIST(D22,TRUE))
Lower critical value: Cell D25	Formula: =NORM.S.INV(D13/2)
Upper Z_{cri}: Cell D26	Formula: =NORM.S.INV(1-D13/2)

11.7 *F*-test for two population variances (variance ratio test)

In the previous sections, we introduced the concept of hypothesis testing to test the difference between interval-scaled variables using both *Z*- and *t*-tests. In Example 11.2, we assumed that the population variances were equal for both populations (plants A and B) and conducted a pooled two sample *t*-test. In Example 11.3, we described the corresponding *t*-test for population means when the population variances are considered to be not equal. The question that arose was 'How do we know which of these two tests to use in practice?' To decide which test is appropriate, we must first determine if the population variances are equal (or not) by conducting a separate hypothesis test for the variances. This section discusses the test for determining if two population variances are equal.

The null hypothesis for this test is H_0: $\sigma_A^2 = \sigma_B^2$ *or* H_0: $\dfrac{\sigma_A^2}{\sigma_B^2} = 1$.

The alternative hypotheses are:

H_1: $\sigma_A^2 < \sigma_B^2$	H_1: $\sigma_A^2 > \sigma_B^2$	H_1: $\sigma_A^2 \neq \sigma_B^2$
left-sided	right-sided	two-sided

Or equivalently:

H_1: $\dfrac{\sigma_A^2}{\sigma_B^2} < 1$	H_1: $\dfrac{\sigma_A^2}{\sigma_B^2} > 1$	H_1: $\dfrac{\sigma_A^2}{\sigma_B^2} \neq 1$
left-sided	right-sided	two-sided

The test statistic (called the F-*test for variance* or the *variance ratio test*) is then simply the ratio of the two sample variances:

$$F = \frac{S_A^2}{S_B^2} \overset{H_0}{\sim} F_{n_A - 1, n_B - 1} \tag{11.10}$$

S_A and S_B are the unbiased sample standard deviations for the observations in group A and group B respectively, as given by Excel function STDEV.S and formula (9.4) in Chapter 9.

The test statistic in formula (11.10) follows an F-distribution with $n_A - 1$ and $n_B - 1$ degrees of freedom if the underlying populations (populations A and B) are both normally distributed.

Example 11.6 extends from Examples 11.2 and 11.3, and we use it to determine which of the tests discussed in those two examples is appropriate if it is not known whether the population variances are equal. In other words, in this example, we compare σ_A^2 to σ_B^2. If we find that they are not equal, we will have to use the test in Example 11.3 to compare μ_A and μ_B, otherwise we can use the test described in Example 11.2.

WORKED EXAMPLES

EXAMPLE 11.6

In this example, we use the F-test to check if the two population variances in Examples 11.2 and 11.3 can be considered equal using a significance level of $\alpha = 0.05$

Step 1: Provide the hypothesis statements H_0 and H_1

The information provided in Example 11.6 indicates that we should test whether the population variances are equal, and so the null and alternative hypotheses can be stated as follows.

- Null hypothesis: H_0: $\sigma_A^2 = \sigma_B^2$
- Alternative hypothesis: H_1: $\sigma_A^2 \neq \sigma_B^2$

The $\neq$ sign implies a two-tail test.

Step 2: Choose an appropriate test statistic

We now need to choose an appropriate statistical test for testing H_0. From the information provided we note the following.

- *The number of populations in the study*: Once again, we have two populations.
- *The research question*: For this test, we need to measure the distance between σ_A^2 and σ_B^2 using the sample variances S_A^2 and S_B^2. In this case, we use the ratio of these two statistics to measure this distance (as opposed to subtracting one from the other). The two statistics are far from one another if the ratio is much larger than 1 or much smaller than 1. They are equal if the ratio is equal to 1. The statistic given in formula (11.10) is thus a good choice for measuring this distance.
- *Assumptions underlying the test*: It is assumed that both populations are normally distributed and so the small sample sizes ($n_A = 18$ and $n_B = 25$) will not cause any concern for this test. The F-test is sensitive to the normality assumption. If two samples are not normally distributed, do not use this test.

Step 3: Specify the significance level

The significance level is given as $\alpha = 0.05$.

Step 4: Calculate the relevant test statistic

Just as with the previous hypothesis test, we calculate f_{cal} and compare this to a critical value (F_α) or calculate the corresponding p-value for the F-distribution. If the two populations are independent and vary as normal distributions, then this ratio will vary as a F-distribution with two sets of degrees of freedom ($df_A = n_A - 1$ and $df_B = n_B - 1$).

With the hypothesis tests considered so far, we have been able to write the hypothesis statement as either a one- or two-tail test. With the F-test, we have a similar situation but we are dealing with variances rather than mean values.

From the calculations performed in Examples 11.2 and 11.3, we know that $S_A = 51.02$ and $S_B = 41.38$, and so the calculated version of the test statistic (denoted f_{cal}) is:

$$f_{cal} = \frac{S_A^2}{S_B^2} = \frac{51.02}{41.38} = 1.5197059$$

Step 5: Make a decision

We use both the critical value approach and the p-value approach to make a decision for this test.

- *Critical value approach*: Calculate both critical values for this test: $F_{\alpha/2, n_A - 1, n_B - 1} = F_{0.025,17,24}$ and $F_{1 - \alpha/2, n_A - 1, n_B - 1} = F_{0.925,17,24}$. Both the upper and lower critical values are needed for this test because H_1: $\sigma_A^2 \neq \sigma_B^2$, but unlike tests that use the standard normal or t-distributions, we cannot simply calculate one of these critical values and then multiply by –1 to obtain the other one. This only applies to symmetric distributions and the F-distribution is not symmetrical. Fortunately, we can find these critical F-values using Excel's F.INV function. From Excel, the upper and lower critical F-values are $F_{0.025,17,24} = F_{upper} = 2.3864801$ and $F_{0.925,17,24} = F_{lower} = 0.3906518$.
  Does the test statistic lie within the region of rejection? Compare the calculated value f_{cal} to the lower and upper critical F-values to come to a conclusion regarding H_0. In this case, $f_{cal} = 1.5197059$, which lies between the two critical values, implying that we **do not reject H_0**.
- p-*value approach:* We obtain the p-value for this test by checking the value of f_{cal}: if it is larger than 1, calculate $2 \times P(F > f_{cal})$ otherwise calculate $2 \times P(F < f_{cal})$. In this example, $f_{cal} = 1.5197059 > 1$ and so we perform the following calculation (note that in this example $F \sim F_{17,24}$):

$$\begin{aligned} p\text{-value} &= 2 \times P(F > f_{cal}) \\ &= 2 \times P(F > 1.5197059) \\ &= 2 \times (1 - P(F < 1.5197059)) \\ &= 2 \times (1 - 0.830336) \\ &= 2 \times (0.169664) \\ &= 0.339328 \end{aligned}$$

Note that we obtained these probabilities using the Excel function F.DIST.

This p-value is larger than the specified level of significance: p-value $= 0.339328 > \alpha = 0.05$, and we **do not reject H_0** at a 5% level of significance.

INTERPRETATION We conclude that based on the sample data collected, we have evidence that the population variances are not significantly different at the 5% level of significance. In this case, we would conduct the two-sample pooled t-test for population means conducted in Example 11.2 (the equal variance version of the test) rather than the unequal variances version of the test conducted in Example 11.3.

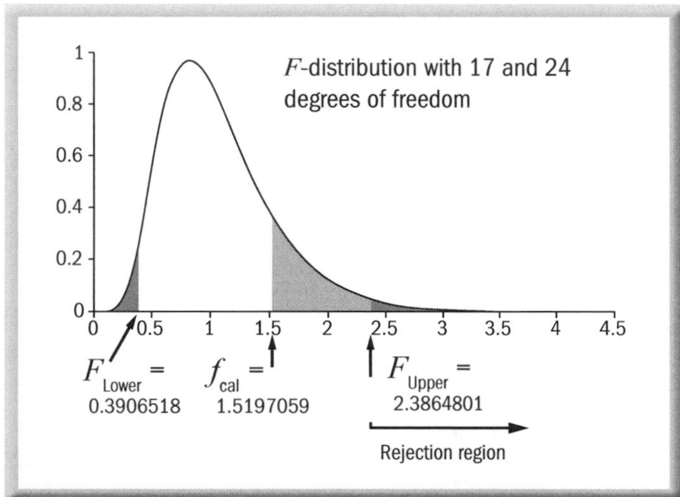

Figure 11.16: Illustration of the relationships between the test statistic and the critical values for Example 11.6

	A	B	C	D	E	F	G	
1	*F*-test for two population variances							
2		Plant A	Plant B					
3		437	418					
4		497	525		1. State hypothesis	$H_0: \sigma_A^2 = \sigma_B^2$		
5		555	581			$H_1: \sigma_A^2 \neq \sigma_B^2$		
6		485	495					
7		462	489		2. Select test	Two sample *F*-test for two population variances.		
8		638	448			Data are normal.		
9		592	455					
10		569	484		3. Set level of significance	Significance level, α =	0.05	
11		517	527					
12		490	504					
13		533	489		4. Calculate test statistic	n_A =	18	=COUNT(B3:B20)
14		509	493			S_A =	51.0207249957	=STDEV.S(B3:B20)
15		500	483					
16		528	463			n_B =	25	=COUNT(C3:E27)
17		588	484			S_B =	41.3872766	=STDEV.S(C3:B27)
18		484	539					
19		531	439			f_{cal} =	1.519706	=G14^2/G17^2
20		572	535					
21			495			*p*-value =	0.03697	=IF(G19>1,2*(1-F.DIST(G19,G13-1,G16-1,TRUE)),2*(F.DIST(G19,G13-1,G16-1,TRUE)))
22			508			Lower critical value =	0.3906518	=F.INV(G10/2,G13-1,G16-1)
23			605			Upper critical value =	2.3864801	=F.INV(1-G10/2,G13-1,G16-1)
24			492					
25			514		5. Decision	Test statistic compared to	$f_{cal} < f_{upper}$	
26			460			critical values	$f_{cal} > f_{lower}$	Do not reject the null hypothesis
27			491					
28						*p*-value compared to		
29						significance level	$p > \alpha$	Do not reject the null hypothesis
30								

Figure 11.17: The Excel solution for Example 11.6

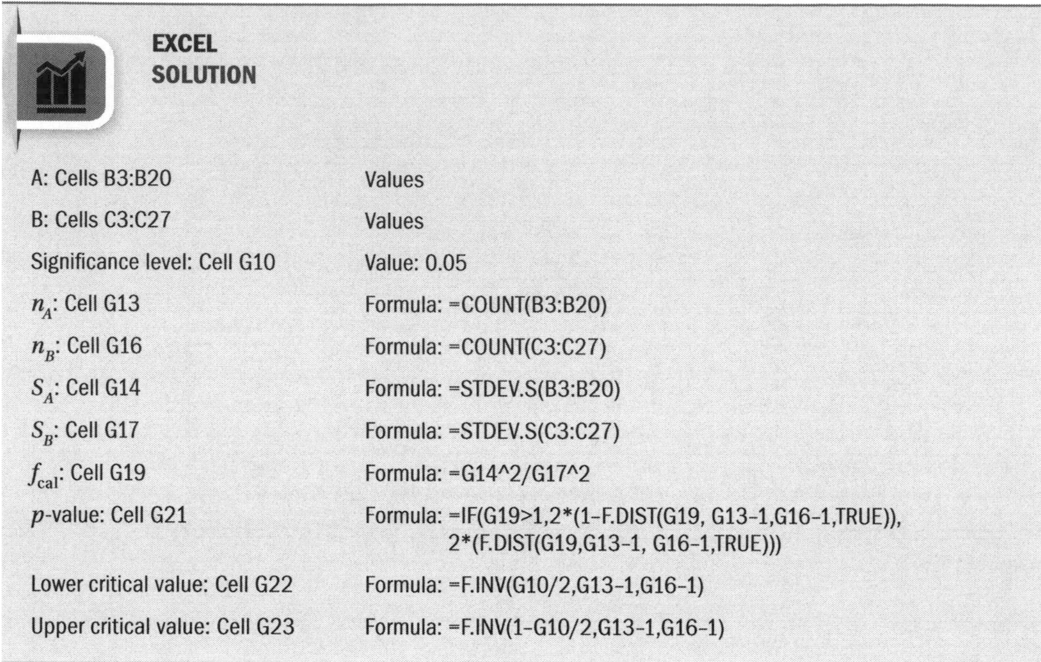

EXCEL SOLUTION

A: Cells B3:B20	Values
B: Cells C3:C27	Values
Significance level: Cell G10	Value: 0.05
n_A: Cell G13	Formula: =COUNT(B3:B20)
n_B: Cell G16	Formula: =COUNT(C3:C27)
S_A: Cell G14	Formula: =STDEV.S(B3:B20)
S_B: Cell G17	Formula: =STDEV.S(C3:C27)
f_{cal}: Cell G19	Formula: =G14^2/G17^2
p-value: Cell G21	Formula: =IF(G19>1,2*(1-F.DIST(G19, G13-1,G16-1,TRUE)), 2*(F.DIST(G19,G13-1, G16-1,TRUE)))
Lower critical value: Cell G22	Formula: =F.INV(G10/2,G13-1,G16-1)
Upper critical value: Cell G23	Formula: =F.INV(1-G10/2,G13-1,G16-1)

Excel Analysis ToolPak solution

We can more easily conduct the test for equal variances using Excel's Analysis ToolPak. However, please note that this procedure only supports the one-sided test (although, the two-sided results can still be obtained from this output). Open the data analysis window by selecting the 'Data' tab, and then clicking on the 'Data analysis' button. In the window that appears, we provide the required information needed to conduct this test. The results are shown in Figure 11.18. Note that the p-value for the one-sided test is simply half the p-value of the two-sided test calculated in Figure 11.19. So, it is possible to obtain the two-sided result from this output, but it requires an additional calculation: multiplying the p-value by 2).

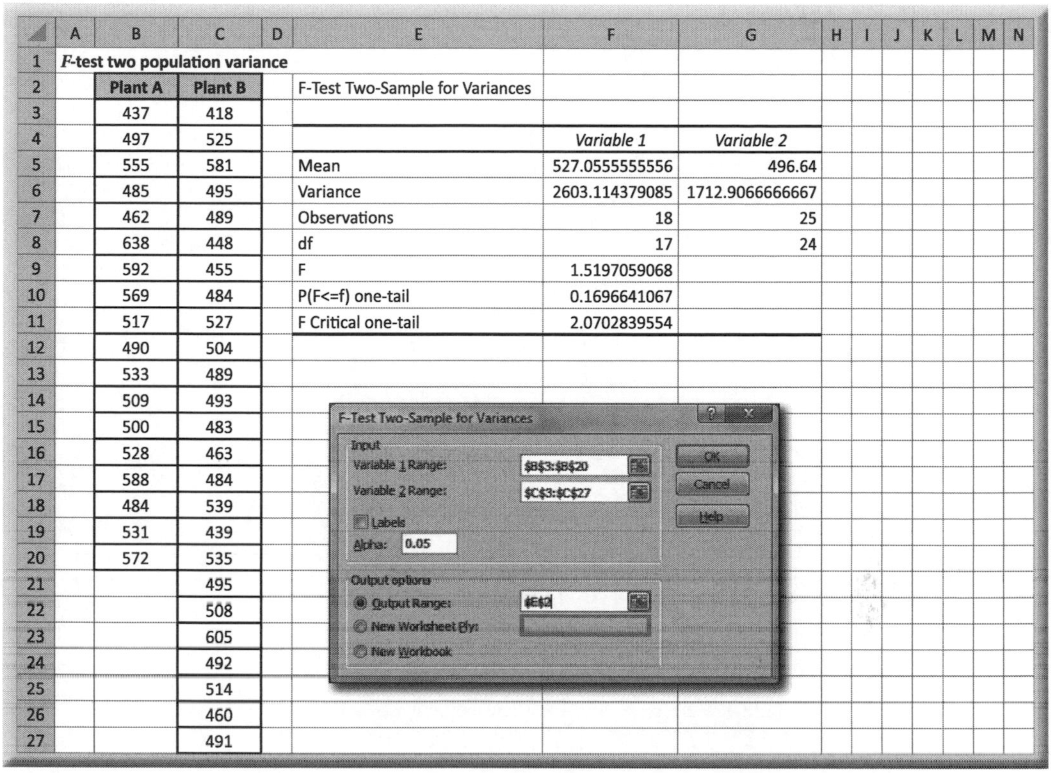

	A	B	C	D	E	F	G
1	***F*-test two population variance**						
2		**Plant A**	**Plant B**		F-Test Two-Sample for Variances		
3		437	418				
4		497	525			*Variable 1*	*Variable 2*
5		555	581		Mean	527.0555555556	496.64
6		485	495		Variance	2603.114379085	1712.9066666667
7		462	489		Observations	18	25
8		638	448		df	17	24
9		592	455		F	1.5197059068	
10		569	484		P(F<=f) one-tail	0.1696641067	
11		517	527		F Critical one-tail	2.0702839554	
12		490	504				
13		533	489				
14		509	493				
15		500	483				
16		528	463				
17		588	484				
18		484	539				
19		531	439				
20		572	535				
21			495				
22			508				
23			605				
24			492				
25			514				
26			460				
27			491				

F-Test Two-Sample for Variances
Input
Variable 1 Range: $B$3:$B$20
Variable 2 Range: $C$3:$C$27
Labels
Alpha: 0.05
Output options
Output Range: $E$2
New Worksheet Ply:
New Workbook
OK
Cancel
Help

Figure 11.18: The '*F*-test: Two-sample for variances' window and output using the data from Example 11.6

SUMMARY

In this chapter, we continued with the hypothesis testing work that began in Chapter 10. Here, however, we applied hypothesis tests to situations involving two populations. The tests we conducted included comparing population means, population proportions and population variances from two independent populations, as well as comparing the population means of two dependent populations. The test statistics, assumptions and decision rules for rejecting (or not rejecting) the null hypothesis were discussed for each one, and examples were provided.

KEY TERMS

F-test for variances
Two-sample pooled *t*-test for means
Two-sample *t*-test for dependent (or paired, repeated) samples
Two-sample *t*-test for independent samples (equal variances)
Two-sample *t*-test for independent samples (unequal variances)
Two-sample *Z*-test for population means
Two-sample *Z*-test for proportions

FORMULA SUMMARY

$$Z = \frac{\overline{X}_A - \overline{X}_B}{\sqrt{\frac{\sigma_A^2}{n_A} + \frac{\sigma_B^2}{n_B}}} \overset{H_0}{\sim} N(0, 1) \tag{11.1}$$

$$T = \frac{\overline{X}_A - \overline{X}_B}{S_{\text{pool}}\sqrt{\frac{1}{n_A} + \frac{1}{n_B}}} \overset{H_0}{\sim} t_{n_A + n_B - 2} \tag{11.2}$$

$$S_{\text{pool}} = \sqrt{\frac{(n_A - 1)\,S_A^2 + (n_B - 1)\,S_B^2}{n_A + n_B - 2}} \tag{11.3}$$

$$t_{\text{cal}} = \frac{\overline{X}_A - \overline{X}_B}{\sqrt{\frac{S_A^2}{n_A} + \frac{S_B^2}{n_B}}} \overset{H_0}{\sim} t_{df_{\text{Satterthwaite}}} \tag{11.4}$$

$$df_{\text{Satterthwaite}} = \frac{\left(\frac{S_A^2}{n_A} + \frac{S_B^2}{n_B}\right)^2}{\frac{1}{n_A - 1}\left(\frac{S_A^2}{n_A}\right)^2 + \frac{1}{n_B - 1}\left(\frac{S_B^2}{n_B}\right)^2} \tag{11.5}$$

$$T = \frac{\overline{X}_{\text{diff}} - \mu_{\text{diff},0}}{\frac{S_{\text{diff}}}{\sqrt{n}}} \overset{H_0}{\sim} t_{n-1} \tag{11.6}$$

$$\overline{X}_{\text{diff}} = \frac{1}{n}\sum_{i=1}^{n} X_{i,\text{diff}} \tag{11.7}$$

$$S_{\text{diff}} = \sqrt{\frac{\sum_{i=1}^{n} X_{i,\text{diff}}^2 - \frac{1}{n}\left(\sum_{i=1}^{n} X_{i,\text{diff}}\right)^2}{n - 1}} \tag{11.8}$$

$$Z = \frac{p_A - p_B}{\sqrt{p_{tot}(1 - p_{tot})\left[\frac{1}{n_A} + \frac{1}{n_B}\right]}} \overset{H_0}{\sim} N(0, 1) \tag{11.9}$$

$$F = \frac{S_A^2}{S_B^2} \overset{H_0}{\sim} F_{n_A - 1, n_B - 1} \tag{11.10}$$

EXERCISES

11.1 A battery manufacturer supplies a range of car batteries to car manufacturers. The 40 amp-hour battery is manufactured at two manufacturing plants and the time between charges is assumed to be normally distributed. The company regularly selects an independent random sample from the two plants, the results of which are shown in Table 11.5.

Table 11.5: Charge time (in days) of randomly selected batteries from two separate battery manufacturing plants

PLANT A			
6.72	10.13	9.31	7.83
9.83	7.38	9.36	9.23
7.15	6.93	7.23	8.70
7.72	9.32	8.32	10.65
9.20	8.70	9.32	8.09
11.36	8.50	8.86	10.06
6.38	7.99	9.34	6.62
9.57	7.23	8.91	10.74

PLANT B			
9.93	8.10	6.27	8.54
10.36	7.81	9.69	8.51
9.06	7.58	8.01	9.54
8.08	8.35	7.78	9.08
9.82	6.51	8.33	7.01
9.56	7.98	8.94	7.06
7.81	6.62	9.82	9.26
7.27	8.14	9.45	10.26

a) For the given samples, conduct an appropriate hypothesis test to test that the population variances are equal at the 5% level of significance.
b) Using the result in (a) above, conduct the appropriate test to test that the population mean values are not different at the 5% level of significance.

11.2 The manager of a pizza restaurant has employed two new delivery drivers and wants to assess their performance. The following data represent the delivery times for delivery person A and delivery person B on the same day. Based on your analysis of the two samples, is there any evidence that the population mean delivery times are different (test at 1%)? Conduct the test under both of the following two assumptions.
a) Assume the variances of both populations are equal.
b) Assume the variances of both populations are not equal.

Table 11.6: Delivery times of two pizza delivery people

PERSON A				
32.9	25.6	36.2	34.6	30.3
29.4	33.5	32.5	40.7	32.7
41.2	35.6	40.8	32.4	35.3
40.3	34.6	30.2	37.1	
39.3	36.5	35.0	32.7	
30.3	35.7	40.2	34.2	
37.5	38.0	33.4	33.2	
45.0	30.7	37.8	37.7	

PERSON B				
31.6	25.5	36.5	36.0	36.3
25.5	28.1	38.8	32.4	32.8
34.2	37.5	33.3	25.9	37.7
31.0	33.4	32.3	33.2	
35.5	32.6	31.9	36.8	
36.5	34.0	35.9	25.1	
36.1	41.4	29.0	37.6	
28.9	29.8	34.3	34.4	

11.3 During a national election, a national newspaper wanted to assess whether there was a similar voting pattern for a particular party in two towns in the Western Cape. The sample results are shown in Table 11.7. Assess whether there is a significant difference in voting intentions between town A and town B (test at 5%).

Table 11.7: Counts of individuals that stated they will vote for a particular political party in two towns in the Western Cape

	TOWN A	TOWN B
Number interviewed, (n)	$n_A = 456$	$n_B = 345$
Number that stated they will vote for the party (x)	$x_A = 243$	$x_B = 212$

11.4 A national airline keeps a record of luggage misplaced at two airports during one week in the summer of 2014. Table 11.8 is a summary of the sample data. Assess whether there is a significant difference in misplaced luggage between the two airports (test at 5%).

Table 11.8: Counts of the number of items lost by two airports

	AIRPORT A	AIRPORT B
Total number of items processed (n)	$n_A = 15\,596$	$n_B = 25\,789$
Number of items of luggage misplaced (x)	$x_A = 123$	$x_B = 167$

11.5 During an examination, Board concerns were raised concerning the marks obtained by students sitting the final papers for the Advanced Economics (AE) and the E-Marketing (EM) courses. Table 11.9 shows the marks achieved. Historically, the sample data varies as a normal distribution and the population standard deviations are approximately equal. Assess whether there is a significant difference between the two sets of results (test at 5%).

Table 11.9: Marks achieved by students for Advanced Economics (AE) and E-Marketing (EM)

AE	AE
51	63
66	35
50	9
48	39
54	35
83	44
68	68
48	36
45	

EM	EM	EM
71	68	61
69	53	59
63	65	55
66	48	66
43	63	64
34	48	58
57	47	77
58	53	73
68	64	54

11.6 A university finance department would like to compare expenses claimed by staff attending conferences. After initial data analysis, the finance director has identified two departments that seem to have very different levels of claims. Based on the data provided, conduct a suitable test to assess whether the level of claims from department A is significantly greater than that from department B. You can assume that the population expenses data are normally distributed and that the population standard deviations are approximately equal.

Table 11.10: Claims filed for conference expenses by two different university departments

DEPARTMENT A			
156.7	146.81	147.28	140.67
169.81	143.69	157.58	154.78
130.74	155.38	179.89	154.86
158.86	170.74		

DEPARTMENT B		
108.21	109.10	127.16
142.68	110.93	101.85
135.92	132.91	124.94

11.7 Choko Ltd provides training to its salespeople to help each sales person increase the value of their sales. During the last training session, 15 sales people attended and their weekly sales before and sales after are provided in Table 11.11. Assuming that the populations are normally distributed, assess whether there is any evidence that the training sessions are effective (test at 5% and 1%).

Table 11.11: Sales figures before and after a training session of Choko Ltd salespeople

x	BEFORE	AFTER
1	2 911.48	2 287.22
2	1 465.44	3 430.54
3	2 315.36	2 439.93
4	1 343.16	3 071.55
5	2 144.22	3 002.40
6	2 499.84	2 271.37
7	2 125.74	2 964.65
8	2 843.05	3 510.43
9	2 049.34	2 727.41
10	2 451.25	2 969.99
11	2 213.75	2 597.71
12	2 295.94	2 890.20
13	2 594.84	2 194.37
14	2 642.91	2 800.56
15	3 153.21	2 365.75

11.8 Concern has been raised about the standard achieved by students completing final year project reports within a university department. One of the factors identified as important is the mark achieved for the 'Research methods' module, which is studied before the students start their project. The department has now collected data for 15 students, which is shown in Table 11.12. Assuming that the populations are normally distributed, is there any evidence that the marks are different (test at 5%)?

Table 11.12: Marks achieved by students for their 'Research methods' module and the research project

STUDENT	MARK FOR THE RESEARCH METHODS MODULE	PROJECT MARK
1	38	71
2	50	46
3	51	56
4	75	44
5	58	62
6	42	65
7	54	50
8	39	51
9	48	43
10	14	62
11	38	66
12	47	75
13	58	60
14	53	75
15	66	63

11.9 In Question 11.5, we assumed that the two population variances were equal. Conduct an appropriate test to check whether the variances are equal (test at 5% and 1%).

11.10 In Question 11.6, we assumed that the two population variances were equal. Conduct an appropriate test to check whether the variances are equal (test at 5%).

11.11 Apply a two sample *t*-test to Question 11.5, but do not assume equal variance. Is there a significant difference (test at 5%)?

11.12 Apply a two sample *t*-test to Question 11.6, but do not assume equal variance. Is there a significant difference (test at 5%)?

TECHNIQUES IN PRACTICE

11.13 Bakers Ltd is currently reviewing the delivery vans used to deliver products to customers. The company runs two types of delivery van (type A – recently purchased and type B – at least three years old), which are supposed to achieve 20 km per litre of petrol. A new sample has now been collected as shown in Table 11.13. Assuming that the population distance travelled varies as a normal distribution, is there any evidence to suggest that the two types of delivery vans differ in their mean fuel consumption?

Table 11.13: Fuel consumption figures (km/ℓ) for the two van types; 15 for van type A and 21 for B

VAN TYPE A	VAN TYPE B	VAN TYPE A	VAN TYPE B
17.68	15.8	29.42	34.8
18.72	39.1	25.22	19.8
29.49	9.3	13.52	15.0
29.64	12.3	14.01	28.9
9.31	15.5		33.9
22.38	40.1		27.1
20.23	20.4		19.8
28.80	3.7		23.6
17.57	13.6		29.7
9.13	35.1		28.2
20.98	33.3		

11.14 Home-Made Beers Ltd is developing a low-calorie lager with a mean designed calorie count of 43 calories per 100 ml. The new product development team are having problems with the production process and have collected two independent random samples to assess whether the target calorie count is being met (assume the population of calorie count values is normally distributed).

Table 11.14: Calorie counts of two samples (A and B) of beer bottles (each sample consists of 22 bottles)

SAMPLE A	SAMPLE B	SAMPLE A	SAMPLE B
49.7	39.4	45.2	34.5
45.9	49.5	40.5	43.5
37.7	39.2	31.9	37.8
40.6	49.7	41.9	39.7
34.8	39.5	39.8	41.1
51.4	45.4	54.0	33.6
34.3	38.2	47.8	35.8
63.1	44.1	29.3	44.6
41.2	58.7	31.7	38.4
41.4	47.1	45.1	29.1
41.1	59.7	47.9	30.7

If sample A was drawn from the production line overseen by the new product development team, and sample B was drawn from the production line overseen by the original development team, describe the test that we could use to determine whether the population mean calorie counts of the beers in the two production lines differ significantly.

CHAPTER 12

LINEAR CORRELATION AND REGRESSION ANALYSIS

CHAPTER CONTENTS

OVERVIEW

In this chapter, we explore methods that define possible relationships, or associations, between two interval- (or ordinal-) scaled data variables. When dealing with two data variables, we can visually explore whether there is an association by plotting a scatter plot of one variable against another variable. This graphical approach does not only help to determine whether an association exists, but it also hints at the possible form of the association, for example, linear or non-linear association. We can assess the strength of this association by calculating Pearson's correlation coefficient for interval-scaled data. If the scatter plot suggests a possible linear association between the variables, we can use least squares regression to fit an appropriate linear model to the data set. In this book, we focus on linear relationships, but it is also possible to fit non-linear models. We consider the use of basic Excel functions to perform most of the simpler calculations required, but we also discuss the use of the Data Analysis ToolPak macro to perform the entire regression analysis.

LEARNING OBJECTIVES

On completing this chapter, you will be able to:

- understand the meaning of simple linear correlation and regression analysis
- apply a scatter plot to visually represent a possible relationship between two data variables
- calculate Pearson's correlation coefficient for interval-scaled data and interpret this value
- fit a simple linear regression model to the two data variables to be able to describe a dependent variable using an independent variable
- use the linear regression model to predict values for the dependent value, given values of the independent variable
- fit this simple linear model to the scatter plot
- estimate the reliability of this model fit to the dependent variable using the coefficient of determination and interpret this value
- apply suitable inference tests to the simple linear model fit (t-test)
- construct a confidence interval for the population parameters estimated in simple linear regression
- assess whether the assumptions of the linear model have been violated
- assess reliability and conduct inference tests to test suitability of the predictor variable(s)
- solve problems using Microsoft Excel.

12.1 Introduction

In the preceding chapters, we were primarily concerned with data sets that consisted of a single variable. In practice, however, it is far more common to encounter data sets consisting of multiple variables, each one describing some different aspect of the items being studied. For example, if we consider the population of South African school children aged between 7 and 12, there are many variables that could be investigated for each child, such as their height, weight, race, gender, IQ score, and so on. In these cases, the studies may not only concern individual variables, but also the association *between* variables. In the data set containing the information about South African school children, for example, we might be interested in determining how height and weight are related to one another, that is, we may want to know if there is any evidence to suggest that taller children are heavier (or vice versa). The measures of association that we consider in this chapter attempt to describe the type and strength of relationships between the variables using graphical or numerical representations of these relationships.

We will discuss a few of the techniques that we can use to measure these associations between interval-scaled and ordinal-scaled variables. (We consider the association between nominal-scaled variables in a later chapter.) The techniques included here include scatter plots of variables, Pearson's correlation coefficient for interval-scaled data and linear regression models.

- *Scatter plots of variables*: These scatter plots allow us to visually represent the possible relationship between two data variables.
- *Pearson's correlation coefficient for interval scaled data*: This coefficient is a numerical representation of the strength of the *linear* relationship between two interval-scaled data variables.
- *Linear regression models*: These are statistical/mathematical models that allow us to represent the linear relationship between two interval-scaled data variables as mathematical equations (equations that relate one variable to another). The models that we discuss can be applied to *any* given observed data, but the degree to which the chosen model fits the observed data gives an indication about whether the linear relationship described by that model is appropriate.

The true correlation coefficient and the coefficients of the models mentioned above will be estimated using sample data. It is important to note that these sample statistics are estimators for population values, for example, we calculate the sample Pearson correlation coefficient, r, from sample data, but this value is just an estimator for the true population Pearson correlation coefficient, ρ, which is unobservable. Therefore, for each of the above mentioned quantities, we will employ the confidence interval and hypothesis testing techniques from previous chapters to infer the properties of the population values from the values calculated from these samples.

Throughout the chapter, we are interested in studying the association between two variables known as the *dependent* and *independent variable*. The definitions of these two variables are as follows.

- The *dependent variable's* value relies, to a large extent, on the other variable's value, i.e. its values *depend* on, or are affected by, the values of the other variable. It is usually denoted by Y.
- The *independent variable* is the variable that provides the basis for calculating the value of the dependent variable. It is usually unaffected by the other variable in the study and is generally denoted by X.

Note that the associations described by these measures are not necessarily indicators of causal associations, i.e. simply because we know that one variable is associated with another does *not* mean that the change in one variable causes changes in the other. The relationship between the variables could be the result of a third variable that was not observed. For this reason, we should always be very careful when making statements concerning causality between variables when interpreting these measures.

We begin the discussion of determining relationships between two interval- and ordinal-scaled variables by looking at the graphical representation using scatter plots.

12.2 Scatter plots

12.2.1 Introduction to scatter plots

Scatter plots represent two data variables on a two-dimensional graph, with one variable represented on each axis, and with each point in the plot representing an individual case from the sample. These plots can potentially show how (and to what degree) one variable is related to another.

> **Scatter plot** A two-dimensional plot of one data variable against another data variable (one variable on each axis). Each observation in the data set is represented by a point on the graph.

The plots shown in Figure 12.1 illustrate some different scatter plots representing different relationships between independent and dependent variables.

- Figure 12.1(a) shows an example of a linear relationship between the variables *X* and *Y*: as *X* increases, *Y* increases and the relationship forms a straight line (roughly). Note that this relationship is both monotone and has a linear relationship.

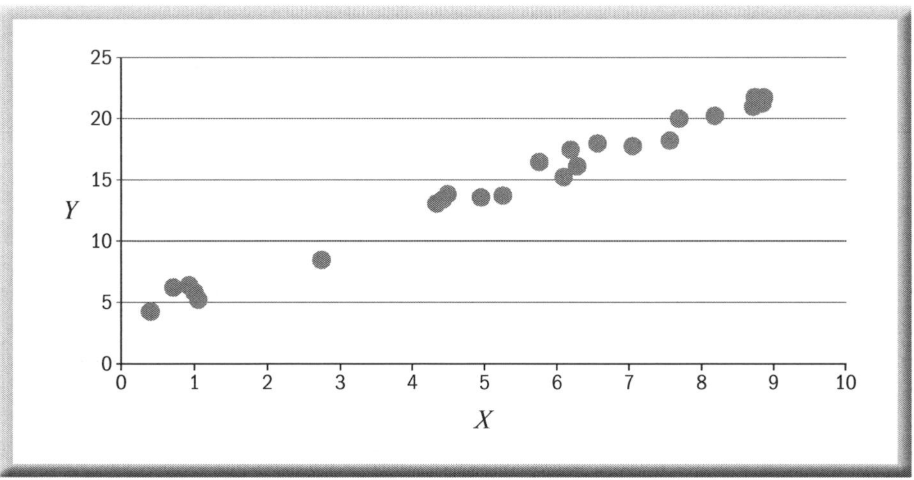

Figure 12.1(a): Scatter plot representing a rough linear relationship between the variables *X* and *Y*

- Figure 12.1(b) illustrates a tendency towards an increasing non-linear monotone relationship between *X* and *Y*. We call it non-linear, because it would not be prudent to represent this relationship with a straight line. (A curvy line would be more appropriate.) The relationship is monotone, because we find that as *X* increases, *Y* *strictly* increases (i.e. the rate of increase seems to slow, but it does not start decreasing at any point).

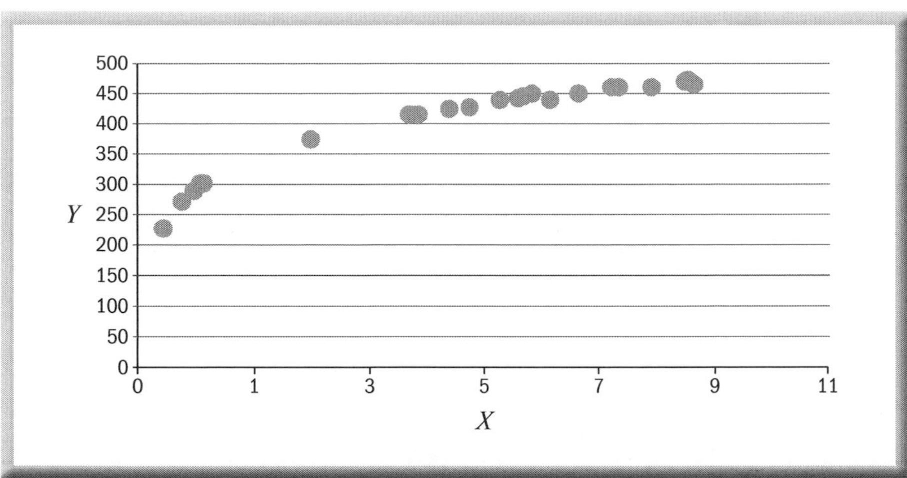

Figure 12.1(b): Scatter plot representing an increasing monotone relationship between the variables *X* and *Y*

- Similar to Figure 12.1(b), Figure 12.1 (c) also shows a tendency towards a non-linear monotone relationship, but this relationship is *decreasing*.

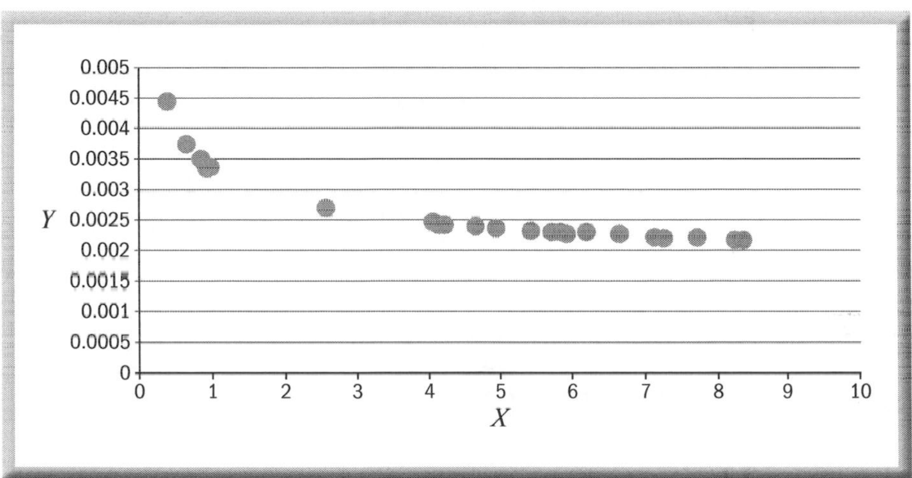

Figure 12.1(c): Scatter plot representing a decreasing monotone relationship between the variables *X* and *Y*

- A non-linear, non-monotone trend is shown in Figure 12.1(d). This relationship is non-monotone, because for smaller values of *X*, the relationship *decreases*, but as *X* becomes larger, the relationship changes to an *increasing* relationship.

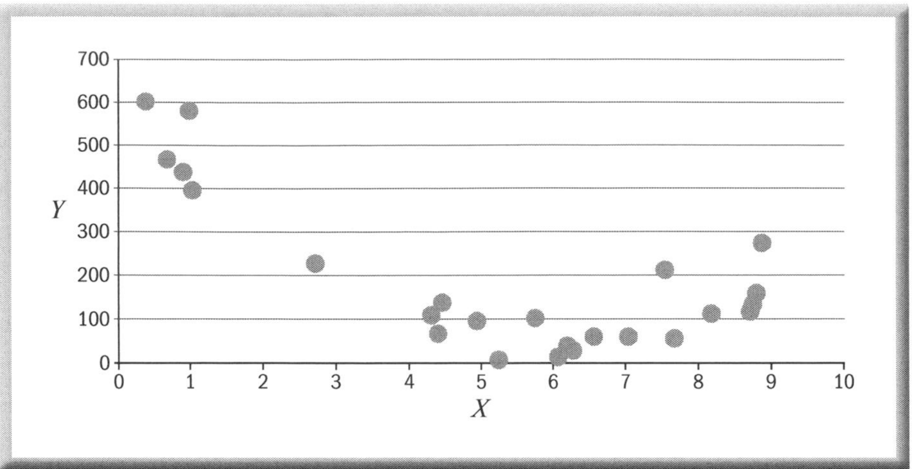

Figure 12.1(d): Scatter plot representing a rough quadratic relationship between the variables *X* and *Y*

- Finally, Figure 12.1(e) illustrates a situation in which there does not appear to be any logical relationship between *X* and *Y*. This is because the value of *X* has no discernible effect on *Y*, so as *X* increases, *Y* tends to neither decrease nor increase.

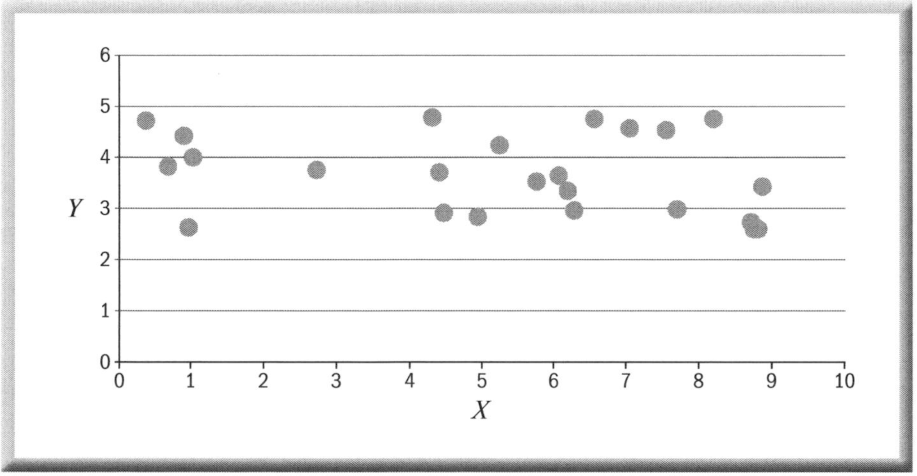

Figure 12.1(e): Scatter plot representing no discernible relationship between the variables *X* and *Y*

There are many different forms of scatter plots and each one needs to be *subjectively* interpreted.

12.2.2 Construction of scatter plots

In order to construct a scatter plot, we simply use the values of the variables as the coordinates in the plot area. For example, if we have a data set with two variables, *X* and *Y*, with data values as shown in Table 12.1, then we construct the scatter plot by using the *X*-values for the horizontal axis and the *Y*-values for the vertical axis. The scatter plot for these data is shown in Figure 12.2.

Table 12.1: Three observations made on two variables, X and Y

X	Y
12	25
25	80
3	62

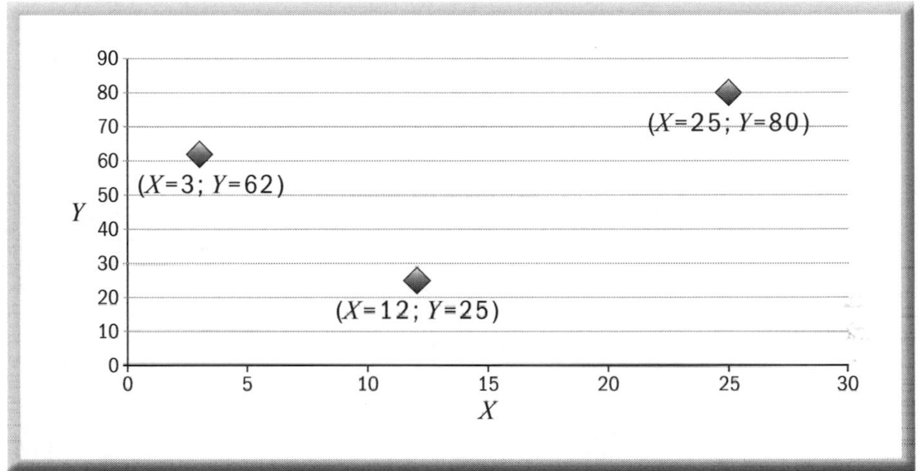

Figure 12.2: Scatter plot of the data in Table 12.1

Example 12.1 illustrates how to construct a scatter plot for a larger data set.

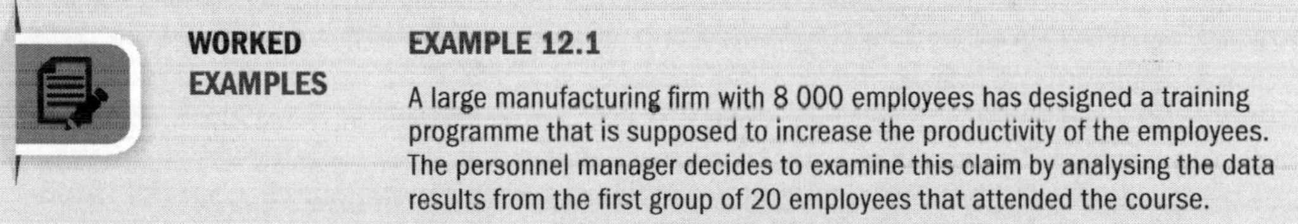

WORKED EXAMPLES

EXAMPLE 12.1

A large manufacturing firm with 8 000 employees has designed a training programme that is supposed to increase the productivity of the employees. The personnel manager decides to examine this claim by analysing the data results from the first group of 20 employees that attended the course.

Table 12.2 provides the data set with the percentage increase in productivity (Y) measured against an evaluation score to see how successful the training was (X).

Table 12.2: Table describing the variables 'evaluation score' and '% increase in productivity' for 20 employees

EMPLOYEE NUMBER	EVALUATION SCORE (X)	% INCREASE IN PRODUCTIVITY (Y)
1	47	4.2
2	71	8.1
3	64	6.8

EMPLOYEE NUMBER	EVALUATION SCORE (X)	% INCREASE IN PRODUCTIVITY (Y)
4	35	4.3
5	43	5.0
6	60	7.5
7	38	4.7
8	59	5.9
9	67	6.9
10	56	5.7
11	67	5.7
12	57	5.4
13	69	7.5
14	38	3.8
15	54	5.9
16	76	6.3
17	53	5.7
18	40	4.0
19	47	5.2
20	23	2.2

Use the information provided and construct a scatter plot of 'evaluation score' and '% increase in productivity'. Interpret the resulting scatter plot.

To construct this scatter plot, we use the values of the variables 'evaluation score' and '% increase in productivity' as the coordinates in the plot. Unfortunately, since there are so many data points, doing this by hand would be quite cumbersome. So, we rely on Excel's graphical functions to convert the data into a scatter plot.

- First, type the data into two columns of an Excel spreadsheet.
- Highlight the two columns that you need to plot.
- Select the 'Insert' tab.
- Click on the 'Scatter' button in the ribbon that appears and select the option that you would like to use (typically this will be the option with only points and no lines, i.e. the first option).

Figure 12.3 illustrates these instructions in Excel.

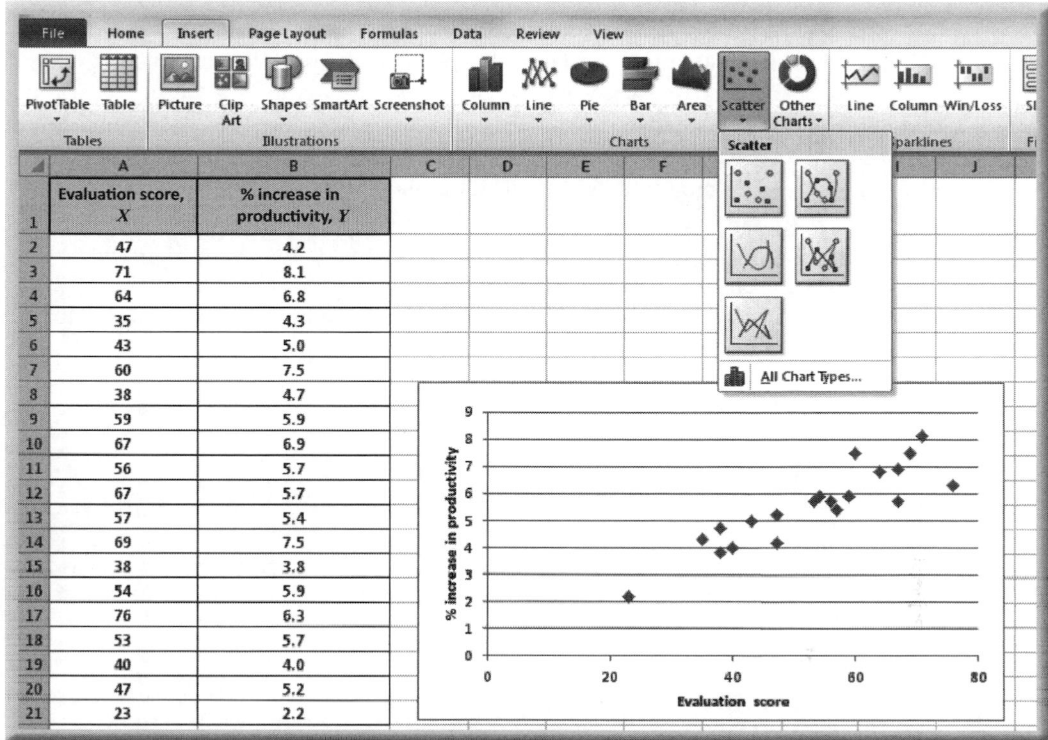

	A	B
1	Evaluation score, X	% increase in productivity, Y
2	47	4.2
3	71	8.1
4	64	6.8
5	35	4.3
6	43	5.0
7	60	7.5
8	38	4.7
9	59	5.9
10	67	6.9
11	56	5.7
12	67	5.7
13	57	5.4
14	69	7.5
15	38	3.8
16	54	5.9
17	76	6.3
18	53	5.7
19	40	4.0
20	47	5.2
21	23	2.2

Figure 12.3: Constructing a scatter plot in Excel for Example 12.1

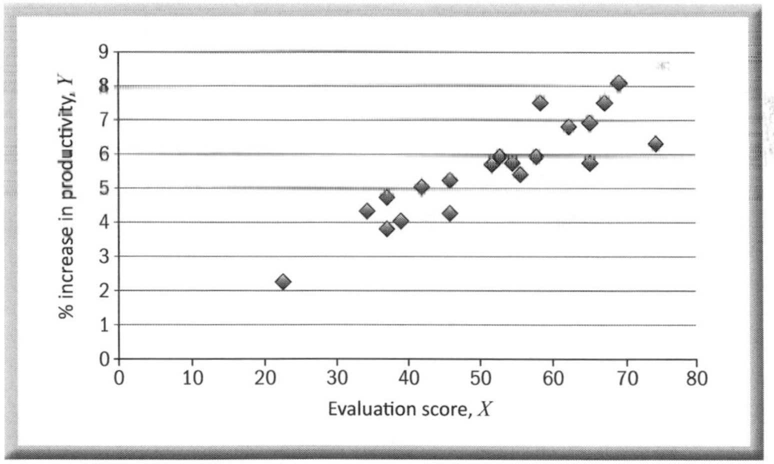

Figure 12.4: Scatter plot of evaluation scores vs. % increase in productivity for 20 employees

As you can see from the scatter plot in Figure 12.4, there seems to be some form of linear relationship between the dependent variable (% increase in productivity) and independent variable (evaluation score), because as 'evaluation score' increases, there is a tendency for '% increase in productivity' to increase.

12.2.3 Using scatter plots to detect outliers

As well as using scatter plots to identify the relationship between the dependent and independent variables, we can also use them to determine if there are any *outliers* in the data. Outliers, last mentioned in Chapter 3, are values in a data set that are extreme, i.e. they are either too small or too large when compared to typical values in the data set. Outliers could be the result of erroneous observations (true outliers) or they could simply be naturally occurring large or small values. In this context of two variables, we only consider outliers of the Y-variable (the dependent variable). These outliers have a large impact on the analyses and so it is important that we are able to detect them.

In Figure 12.5, you can see an outlier that was introduced to the data found in Example 12.1 to illustrate how we can use scatter plots to detect outliers. The outlying Y-value that was introduced, is approximately equal to 22.

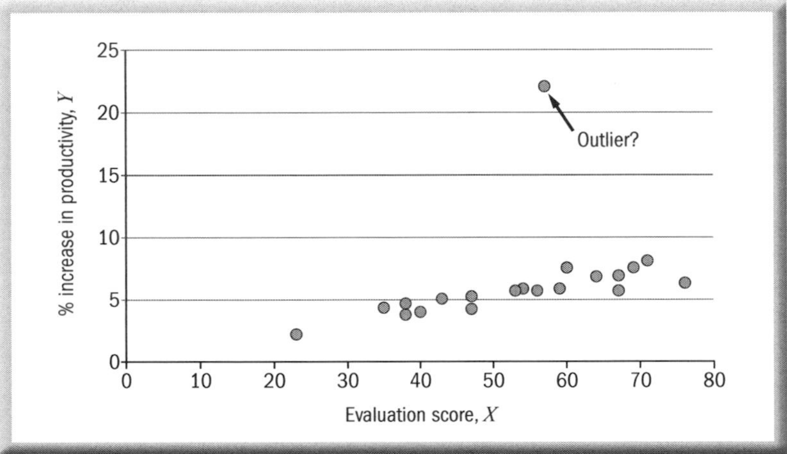

Figure 12.5: Scatter plot of evaluation scores vs % increase in productivity (with an outlier)

From Figure 12.5, we can identify the outlier, since its Y-value is far greater than any other observation. Typically, outliers will be those values that are extreme (with respect to the vertical axis) and thus stray from the general cluster of observations.

As previously mentioned, the outlying value can cause problems during the analyses, which we will discuss in the next few sections. Once identified, we can attempt to rectify the problems resulting from the presence of the outlier.

Possible solutions include the following:

- Simply deleting the observation containing the outlier from the data set.
- Replacing the Y-value with the estimated expected value of Y for the given X-value.

For this second technique, we need to fit a model that can return this estimated Y-value. We discuss models like this in Section 12.4.

However, it might occasionally be that the item identified is not a true outlier but rather just an extreme value of whatever you are measuring (i.e the large or small value could be a valid, naturally occurring observation). It is also possible that, if we have a small sample, we can misdiagnose values as being outliers simply because we do not have enough information to determine what typical values look like.

To decide on the type of relationship that exists between two variables, we need to provide a numerical method to assess the strength of this potential relationship, rather than relying on just the subjective evaluation of a scatter plot. The next few sections will explore a method that we can use to measure the relationship between data values: **Pearson's coefficient of correlation**.

Pearson's coefficient of correlation Measures the linear association between two variables that have been measured on interval or ratio scales.

12.3 Linear correlation analysis

Most analysts hope to find a linear relationship between two variables, because it is one of the simplest types of relationships to describe and work with. In this section, we discuss numerical measures that can quantify the degree of linear relationship between two variables.

12.3.1 Pearson's correlation coefficient, *r*

The *Pearson's correlation coefficient* is one of the most commonly used measures of *linear association* between two interval-scaled variables. This measure, like most other quantities discussed in this book, can have both a population value (a value calculated using the entire population's data) and a sample value (a value calculated from sample data). The sample value of Pearson's correlation coefficient, denoted r, is then an estimator for the population quantity, denoted ρ.

The sample version of Pearson's correlation coefficient (also called the *Pearson product moment correlation coefficient* or just the *correlation coefficient*), r, is defined as:

$$r = \frac{S_{XY}}{S_X S_Y} \tag{12.1}$$

S_X is the standard deviation of the X data and S_Y is the standard deviation of the Y data, i.e. from formula (3.10) in Chapter 3:

$$S_X = \sqrt{\frac{1}{n-1}\left[\sum_{i=1}^{n} X_i^2 - n(\bar{X})^2\right]} \quad \text{and} \quad S_Y = \sqrt{\frac{1}{n-1}\left[\sum_{i=1}^{n} Y_i^2 - n(\bar{Y})^2\right]} \tag{12.2}$$

S_{XY} is the sample *covariance* between X and Y:

$$S_{XY} = \frac{1}{n-1}\left[\sum_{i=1}^{n} X_i Y_i - \frac{1}{n}\sum_{i=1}^{n} X_i \sum_{i=1}^{n} Y_i\right] \tag{12.3}$$

n is the number of paired observations in the data set (typically n is the number of rows in a data set).

NOTE

COVARIANCE

Covariance is a measure that describes the manner and degree to which two variables vary with respect to one another. The covariance can take on either positive or negative values, depending on whether the two variables move in the same or opposite directions.

- If Y tends to increase as X increases, the covariance will be positive.
- If Y tends to decrease as X increases, the covariance will be negative.
- If the covariance value is 0, or close to 0, the two variables do not vary with respect to one another at all (Y has neither the tendency to decrease nor increase as X increases).

The covariance is related to the correlation coefficient, since they provide very similar information. The sign (positive or negative) of the covariance is always the same as the sign of the correlation coefficient.

However, the primary difference between the *correlation* and the *covariance* is that the correlation is scaled to lie between –1 and +1, whereas the covariance has no upper or lower bounds. The scaling allows us to interpret the *magnitude* of the linear association between the variables when using the correlation, but not when using covariance.

Combining the definitions provided in formulae (12.2) and (12.3), we can rewrite the sample correlation coefficient given in formula (12.1) as follows:

$$r = \frac{\sum_{i=1}^{n} X_i Y_i - \frac{1}{n}\sum_{i=1}^{n} X_i \sum_{i=1}^{n} Y_i}{\sqrt{\left[\sum_{i=1}^{n} X_i^2 - n(\overline{X})^2\right]\left[\sum_{i=1}^{n} Y_i^2 - n(\overline{Y})^2\right]}} \quad (12.4)$$

This statistic measures the degree of *linear* association between the variables X and Y, and ranges between the values –1 and +1.

We now briefly discuss the interpretation of the correlation coefficient, r, and how this measure is related to the intuitive concepts that were discussed for scatter plots.

Interpreting Pearson's correlation coefficient, r

As noted, the correlation coefficient's value lies between –1 and +1, but how do we interpret these values? We consider possible values for r and then briefly discuss how these values can be interpreted. We use the graphs in Figure 12.6 to illustrate how the correlation coefficient's value is tied to the graphical representation of a scatter plot.

- *r is close to 0*: A value of r close to 0 indicates there is very little *linear* relationship between X and Y. However, this does not necessarily mean that there is absolutely no relationship between X and Y; it simply means that there is no *linear* relationship (i.e. a non-linear relationship might be appropriate). A situation in which there is almost no association is illustrated in Figure 12.6(a), with r equal to –0.08192, and Figure 12.6(b) shows a situation in which there is a strong quadratic relationship between the variables, also resulting in r having a value close to 0, since there is no *linear* relationship. We usually expect that the value of r will lie between -0.3 and +0.3 for non-linear relationships.

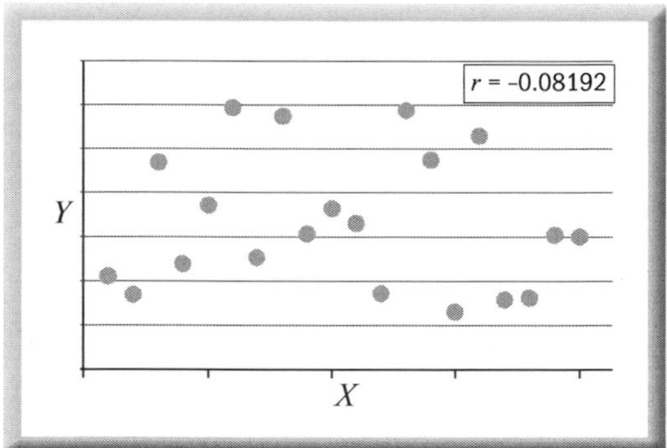

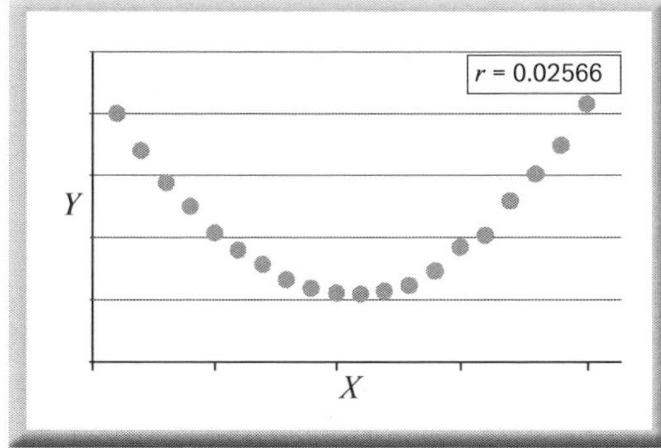

Figure 12.6(a) and (b): Examples of near 0 correlations, $r \approx 0$; no linear relationship

- *r in the range* +0.3 *to* +0.5 *or* –0.5 *to* –0.3: If the value of r lies between +0.3 and +0.5, or between -0.5 and -0.3, then this indicates a *weak* linear relationship between the variables. This is illustrated in Figures 12.6(c) and (d). In Figure 12.6(c), we see a weak positive relationship, i.e. Y generally increases as X increases, and in Figure 12.6(d) we see a weak negative relationship, i.e. Y generally decreases as X increases. Unfortunately, since the linear relationship is so weak, this tendency can be hard to spot.

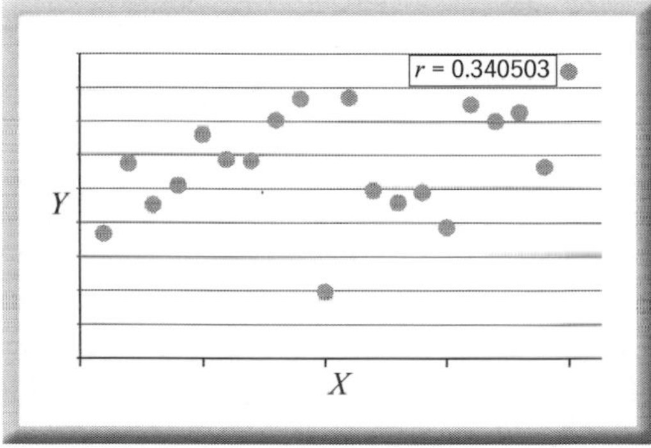

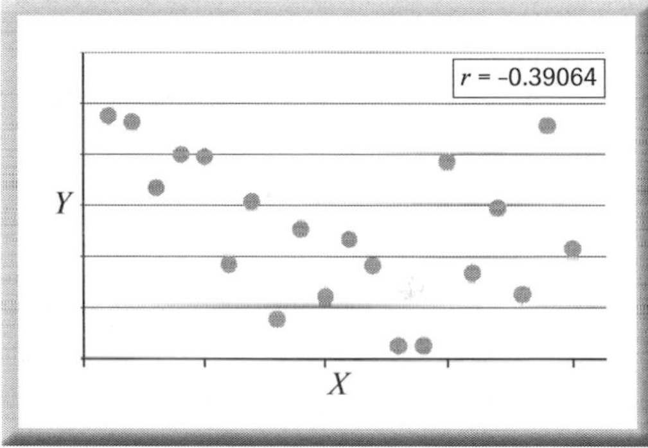

Figure 12.6(c) and (d): Example of correlation values near ±0.4, $r \approx \pm 0.4$; weak positive and weak negative correlation

- *r larger than* +0.5 *or smaller than* –0.5: Values for r larger than +0.5 or smaller than -0.5 are indications of *strong* linear relationships between the variables X and Y. In Figures 12.6(e) and (f), we see scatter plots of positive and negative correlations in the region of +0.6 and -0.6, respectively. Comparing this to plots in Figures 12.6(c) and (d), we can see that the linear trend is now much more distinct. Taking it a step further, Figures 12.6(g) and (h) show the scatter plots for correlations in the region of ±0.9; the linear trend is now very clear in these graphs.

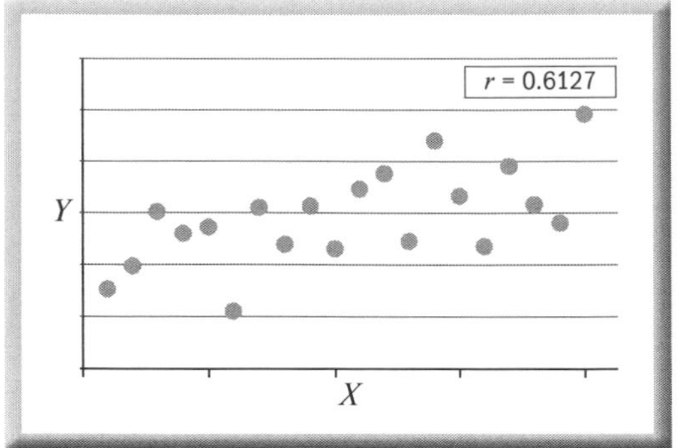

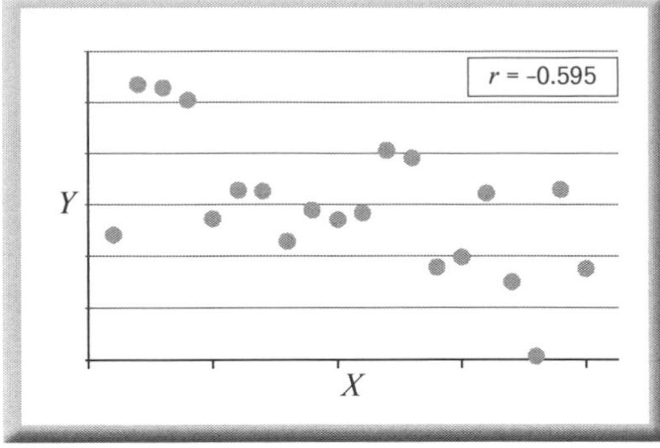

Figure 12.6(e) and (f): Example of correlation values near ±0.6, $r \approx \pm 0.6$; strong positive and negative correlation

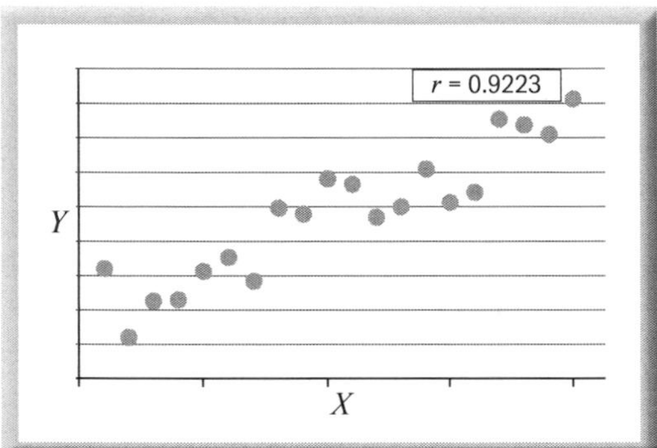

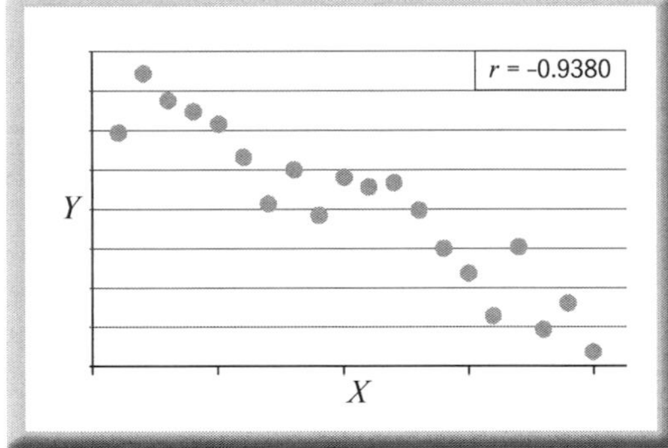

Figure 12.6(g) and (h): Example of correlation values near ±0.9, $r \approx \pm 0.9$; strong positive and negative correlation

- r-*values equal to* +1 *or* −1: If the correlation is equal to +1 or −1 then, as shown in Figures 12.6(i) and (j), there is a perfect linear relationship between *X* and *Y*. This relationship is not usually found anywhere outside of a textbook, as it is unlikely that we would find *perfect* linear relationships between data variables in practice.

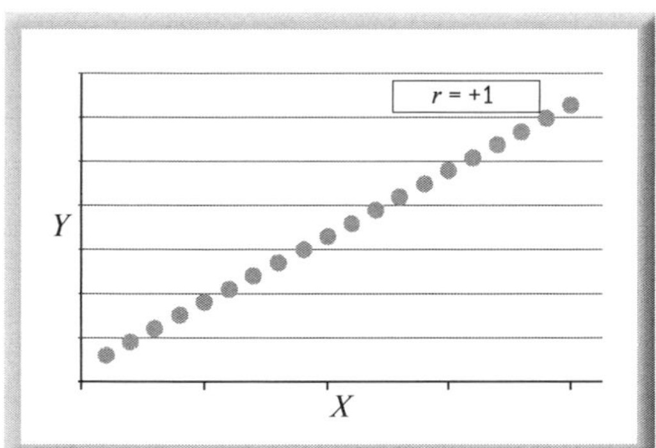

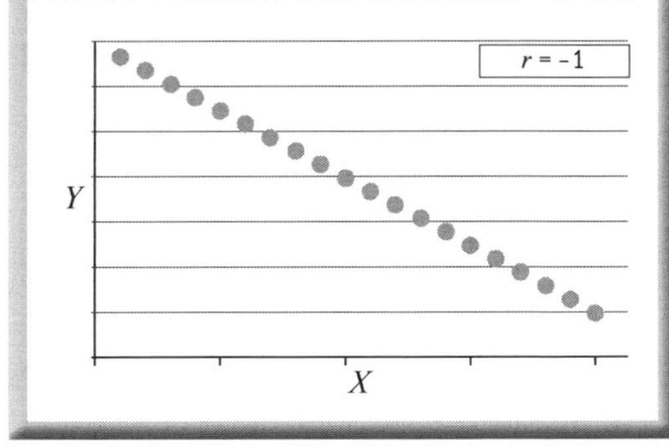

Figure 12.6(i) and (j): Example of correlation values equal to ±1, $r = \pm 1$; perfect positive and negative correlation

PROPERTIES OF r

- r always lies between -1 and 1: $-1 \le r \le 1$.
- If $r > 0$, it implies a *positive linear* relationship between X and Y.
- If $r < 0$, it implies a *negative linear* relationship between X and Y.
- If r lies between $-1 \le r \le -0.5$ or $0.5 \le r \le 1$, it indicates a *strong linear* association.
- If r lies between $-0.5 < r \le -0.3$ or $0.3 \le r < 0.5$, it indicates a *medium linear* association.
- If r lies between $-0.3 < r < 0.3$, it indicates a *weak linear* association.
- It is not influenced by the units used to measure either of the two variables; changing the unit of measurement for either variable has no discernible effect on the value of r.

Causality: Use caution when interpreting the correlation coefficient

Correlation only measures the strength of the linear relationship between two variables and does not necessarily prove a cause-and-effect relationship (although it is *sometimes* a strong indicator that a cause-and-effect relationship might exist). Consider the following example. A study was conducted in which 50 towns were surveyed to determine the relationship between the total number of children born and the total alcohol sales in a calendar year. At the end of the study, it was found that the correlation between the 'number of children born' (Y) and the 'alcohol sales' (X) for these 50 towns was $r = 0.97$, leading the analysts to (incorrectly) conclude that the sale of alcohol directly causes an increase in the number of children born in a town. Why is this conclusion flawed?

It turns out that the relationship between births and alcohol sales was actually driven by a *third* variable: 'number of people in the town'. This new variable was highly correlated with both number of births and the total alcohol sales in each town, and was thus indirectly driving the supposed correlation between the original two variables. This *indirect* correlation resulted in the analysts mistakenly concluding that the births were caused by alcohol sales, when in fact both of the variables were caused by the number of people in that town.

Always take care when making a conclusion about a causal relationship between variables when interpreting the correlation coefficient.

We now consider an example in which the correlation coefficient is calculated using Excel.

WORKED EXAMPLES

EXAMPLE 12.2

Using the data given in Example 12.1, calculate the correlation coefficient and interpret its value.

We now consider more ways to obtain the value of the correlation coefficient between the 'evaluation score' variable and the '% increase in productivity' variable:

- A method where formula (12.4) is used
- A method where formula (12.1) is used
- A method where the built-in Excel functions CORREL() or PEARSON() are used to obtain the correlation coefficient

We work through all three of these solutions below, and the Excel spreadsheet containing the computer calculations is shown in Figure 12.7.

- First, in order to use formula (12.4), we need to obtain some simple statistics using Excel. The following values are calculated using basic functions such as SUM(), SUMPRODUCT() and SUMSQ():

$$n = 20,\ \sum_{i=1}^{n} X_i = 1\,064,\ \overline{X} = 53.2$$

$$n = 20,\ \sum_{i=1}^{n} Y_i = 110.8,\ \overline{Y} = 5.54,\ \sum_{i=1}^{n} X_i Y_i = 6\,237.5$$

$$\sum_{i=1}^{n} X_i^2 = 60\,352, \text{ and } \sum_{i=1}^{n} Y_i^2 = 653.44$$

  Substituting these values into formula (12.4) we get:

$$r = \frac{\sum_{i=1}^{n} X_i Y_i - \frac{1}{n}\sum_{i=1}^{n} X_i \sum_{i=1}^{n} Y_i}{\sqrt{\left[\sum_{i=1}^{n} X_i^2 - n(\overline{X})^2\right]\left[\sum_{i=1}^{n} Y_i^2 - n(\overline{Y})^2\right]}}$$

$$= \frac{6\,237.5 - \frac{1}{20}(1\,064)(110.8)}{\sqrt{[60\,352 - 20 \times (53.2)^2][653.44 - 20 \times (5.54)^2]}}$$

$$= \frac{342.94}{(61.21438)(6.293489)}$$

$$= 0.89$$

- Second, we can use formula (12.1) to calculate this correlation. The statistics that we need to calculate here are the sample standard deviations of both variables, S_X and S_Y, and the sample covariance, S_{XY}. We can obtain these values using Excel's STDEV.S() and COVARIANCE.S() functions:

  $S_X = 14.043554$, $S_Y = 1.443825$, and $S_{XY} = 18.04947$

  Substituting these values into formula (12.1) we get:

$$r = \frac{S_{XY}}{S_X S_Y} = \frac{18.04947}{14.04354 \times 1.443825} = 0.89$$

- Finally, we can use the CORREL() and PEARSON() functions in Excel to calculate the correlation immediately. As with the other two calculations, we find that the ccorrelation is $r = 0.89$.

In all these cases, the correlation is $r = 0.89$, which is a clear indication of a strong positive linear relationship between 'evaluation score' and '% increase in productivity'. However, we cannot conclude that an increase in evaluation score *causes* an increase in the percentage productivity.

Figure 12.7 provides the Excel solutions for this calculation.

	A	B	C	D	E	F	G	H	I
1	**Example 12.2: Covariance and correlation**								
2									
3		**Employee number**	**Evaluation score (X)**	**% increase in productivity (Y)**					
4		1	47	4.2		$n =$	20	=COUNT(B4:B23)	
5		2	71	8.1		$\sum_{i=1}^{n} X_i =$	1064	=SUM(C4:C23)	
6		3	64	6.8		$\bar{X} =$	53.2	=AVERAGE(C4:C23)	
7		4	35	4.3		$\sum_{i=1}^{n} X_i^2 =$	60352	=SUMSQ(C4:C23)	
8		5	43	5		S_X	14.0435413138	=STDEV.S(C4:C23)	
9		6	60	7.5		$\sum_{i=1}^{n} Y_i =$	110.8	=SUM(D4:D23)	
10		7	38	4.7		$\bar{Y} =$	5.54	=AVERAGE(D4:D23)	
11		8	59	5.9		$\sum_{i=1}^{n} Y_i^2 =$	653.44	=SUMSQ(D4:D23)	
12		9	67	6.9		S_Y	1.4438253284	=STDEV.S(D4:D23)	
13		10	56	5.7		$\sum_{i=1}^{n} X_i Y_i =$	6237.5	=SUMPRODUCT(D4:D23,E4:E23)	
14		11	67	5.7		S_{XY}	18.04947	=COVARIANCE.S(C4:C23,D4:D23)	
15		12	57	5.4					
16		13	69	7.5	1)	$r =$	0.8901706073	=(G13-G5*G9/G4)/SQRT((G7-G4*G6^2)*(G11-G4*G10^2))	
17		14	38	3.8	2)	$r =$	0.8901704256	=G14/(G8*G12)	
18		15	54	5.9	3)	$r =$	0.8901706073	=PEARSON(C4:C23,D4:D23)	
19		16	76	6.3		$r =$	0.8901706073	=CORREL(C4:C23,D4:D23)	
20		17	53	5.7					
21		18	40	4					
22		19	47	5.2					
23		20	23	2.2					
24									

Figure 12.7: Excel solutions to calculate Pearson's correlation coefficient, *r*, using three different techniques

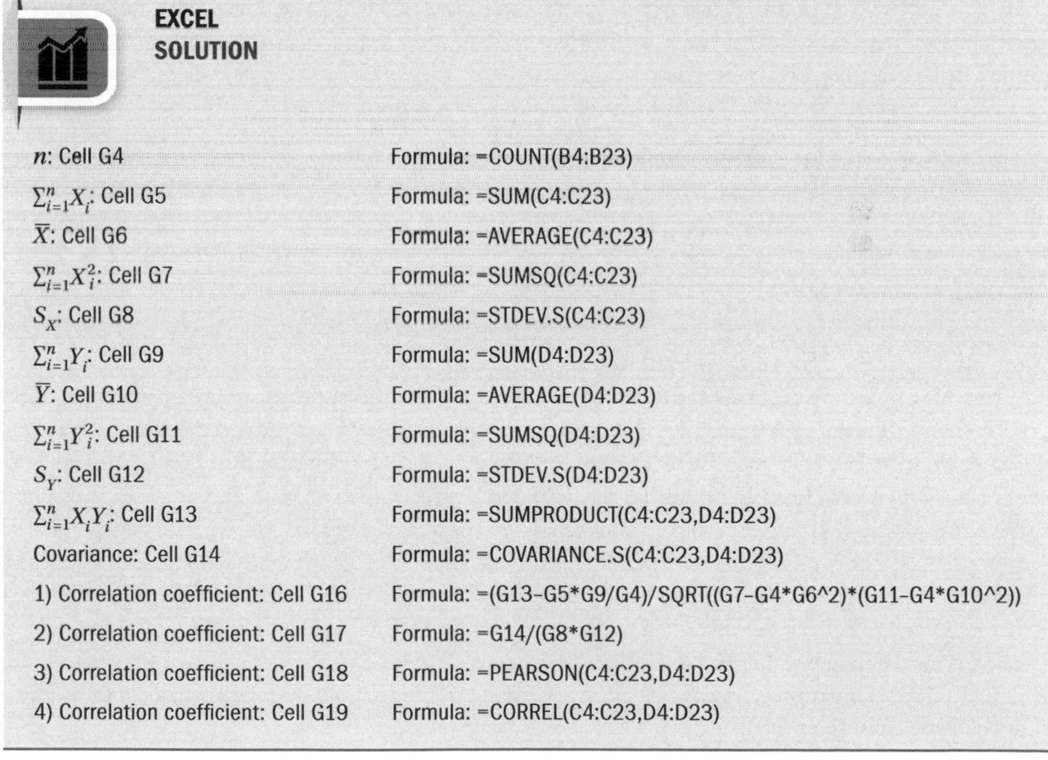

EXCEL SOLUTION

n: Cell G4	Formula: =COUNT(B4:B23)
$\sum_{i=1}^{n} X_i$: Cell G5	Formula: =SUM(C4:C23)
$\bar{X}$: Cell G6	Formula: =AVERAGE(C4:C23)
$\sum_{i=1}^{n} X_i^2$: Cell G7	Formula: =SUMSQ(C4:C23)
S_X: Cell G8	Formula: =STDEV.S(C4:C23)
$\sum_{i=1}^{n} Y_i$: Cell G9	Formula: =SUM(D4:D23)
$\bar{Y}$: Cell G10	Formula: =AVERAGE(D4:D23)
$\sum_{i=1}^{n} Y_i^2$: Cell G11	Formula: =SUMSQ(D4:D23)
S_Y: Cell G12	Formula: =STDEV.S(D4:D23)
$\sum_{i=1}^{n} X_i Y_i$: Cell G13	Formula: =SUMPRODUCT(C4:C23,D4:D23)
Covariance: Cell G14	Formula: =COVARIANCE.S(C4:C23,D4:D23)
1) Correlation coefficient: Cell G16	Formula: =(G13-G5*G9/G4)/SQRT((G7-G4*G6^2)*(G11-G4*G10^2))
2) Correlation coefficient: Cell G17	Formula: =G14/(G8*G12)
3) Correlation coefficient: Cell G18	Formula: =PEARSON(C4:C23,D4:D23)
4) Correlation coefficient: Cell G19	Formula: =CORREL(C4:C23,D4:D23)

INTERPRETATION In the above example, the value of 0.89 indicates a fairly strong positive linear association (or relationship), and this is also reflected by the scatter plot of the data.

We still have not examined how significant this linear correlation is, i.e. whether the conclusions we made about the sample data apply to the whole population. In order to do this, we need to conduct a hypothesis test. The end result will confirm if the same conclusion applies to the whole population and, more specifically, at what level of significance. The next section discusses the test for the significance of the population correlation.

12.3.2 Testing the significance of Pearson's correlation coefficient, r

In Example 12.1, we found that the correlation coefficient was 0.89, which indicates a strong correlation between the two variables. Unfortunately, the size of the sample that produced the value of 0.89 is quite small (sample size $n = 20$ from a population of 8 000 employees), and so we should check whether this provides evidence of a significant linear association between the two variables in the overall population. In other words, we want to know if this value of 0.89 is not simply due to sampling error from a population in which there is no real association. To determine this, we need to conduct an appropriate hypothesis test to check if the population value of linear association is 0.

In general, this hypothesis test assesses the possibility that the population correlation coefficient is $\rho = \rho_0$ (typically we choose $\rho_0 = 0$) versus the alternative that it is different from ρ_0, greater than ρ_0 or less than ρ_0, i.e. the null hypothesis is:

$$H_0: \rho = \rho_0$$

Versus any one of the following alternatives:

$H_1: \rho < \rho_0$	$H_1: \rho > \rho_0$	$H_1: \rho \neq \rho_0$
left-sided	right-sided	two-sided

Typically, we set ρ_0 to zero, i.e. we are interested in the hypothesis $H_0: \rho = 0$.

The only assumption that we require for this test is that the sample size needs to be large enough (in this case we can consider samples larger than 10 as being large, i.e. $n > 10$). If the sample is large, then r approximately follows a t-distribution with $df = n - 2$ degrees of freedom. The resulting test statistic that we use to test the hypothesis is then given by formula (12.5):

$$T = \frac{r - \rho_0}{\sqrt{\frac{1 - r^2}{n - 2}}} \qquad (12.5)$$

The calculated version of this test statistic is denoted by t_{cal}.

Example 12.3 illustrates how this test is conducted using the five-step hypothesis testing procedure outlined in Chapter 10.

WORKED EXAMPLES

EXAMPLE 12.3

Using the sample data given in Example 12.1, determine (using a significance level of 5%) whether the population correlation coefficient between 'evaluation score' and '% increase in productivity' is significantly different from 0.

As in previous chapters on hypothesis testing, testing of the significance is done in five steps.

Step 1: Provide the hypothesis statements H_0 and H_1

- The null hypothesis asserts that no population correlation exists: H_0: $\rho = 0$
- The alternate hypothesis simply states that the variables are correlated: H_1: $\rho \neq 0$

Step 2: Choose an appropriate test statistic

In this case, we already know that we are testing the significance of linear correlation and we use the *t*-test in formula (12.5) to test for significance. The sample is large enough, and so the assumptions are satisfied.

Step 3: Specify the significance level:

The significance level is set at $\alpha = 5\%$ (0.05).

Step 4: Calculate the relevant test statistic

Calculate the value of *r*. From Example 12.2, we know that $r = 0.89$. Use the sample data and calculate the test statistic in formula (12.5) under the assumption that H_0 is true (i.e. when $\rho = 0$). The test statistic then becomes:

$$t_{\text{cal}} = \frac{r - 0}{\sqrt{\frac{1 - r^2}{n - 2}}} = \frac{0.89}{\sqrt{\frac{1 - 0.89^2}{20 - 2}}} = 8.3$$

Step 5: Make a decision

We use both the critical value approach and the *p*-value approach to make a decision for this test.

- *Critical value approach*: In this case, the number of degrees of freedom are $df = n - 2 = 18$, and so, using Excel's T.INV function, we find that $t_{n-2,\alpha/2} = t_{18,0.025} = 2.1$. Given that t_{cal} (= 8.3) is greater than $t_{n-2,\alpha/2}$ (= 2.10), the test statistic falls in the critical region and so we **reject H_0**.
- p-*value approach*: We calculate the *p*-value as follows:

$$\begin{aligned} p\text{-value} &= 2 \times P(T > t_{\text{cal}}) \\ &= 2 \times (1 - P(T < t_{\text{cal}}) \\ &= 2 - 2 \times P(T < t_{\text{cal}}) \\ &= 2 - 2 \times P(T < 8.3) \\ &= 2 - 2 \times 0.999999927 \\ &= 0.000000146 \end{aligned}$$

$T \sim t_{18}$. This *p*-value is much smaller than $\alpha = 0.05$, and so the conclusion is also to **reject H_0**.

INTERPRETATION There is evidence to suggest that the population correlation between 'evaluation score' and '% increase in productivity', ρ, is significantly different from 0. We can thus conclude that there is a linear correlation between the two variables (at a 5% level of significance).

Figure 12.8 shows the Excel solution

	A	B	C	D	E	F	G	H
1	**Example 12.3 - Testing significance of population correlation**							
2								
3	Employee	Evaluation	% increase in		1. State	$H_0: \rho = 0$ vs. $H_1: \rho \neq 0$		
4	number	score (X)	productivity (Y)		hypothesis	Two-sided test		
5	1	47	4.2					
6	2	71	8.1					
7	3	64	6.8		2. Select test	t-test for correlation		
8	4	35	4.3					
9	5	43	5					
10	6	60	7.5		3. Set level of significance	Significance level, α =	0.05	
11	7	38	4.7					
12	8	59	5.9		4. Calculate test statistic	**Population**		
13	9	67	6.9			Correlation coefficient μ =	0	
14	10	56	5.7			**Sample**		
15	11	67	5.7			n =	20	=COUNT(A5:A24)
16	12	57	5.4			Degrees of freedom, df =	18	=G15-2
17	13	69	7.5			r =	0.8901706073	=CORREL(B5:B24,C5:C24)
18	14	38	3.8			Test statistic, t_α	8.288953608	=(G17-G13)/SQRT((1-G17^2)/G16)
19	15	54	5.9			**p-value and critical values**		
20	16	76	6.3			Upper critical value =	2.1	=T.INV(1-G10/2,G16)
21	17	53	5.7			Lower critical value =	-2.1	=T.INV(G10/2,G16)
22	18	40	4			p-value =	0.000000147	=2-2*T.DIST(G18,G16,TRUE)
23	19	47	5.2					
24	20	23	2.2		5. Decision	Test statistic compared to critical value. Test statistic lies in the rejection region. Reject H_0		
25						p-value compared to significance level, $p < \alpha$, reject H_0		
26								

Figure 12.8: Excel solution to test the if the correlation coefficient, ρ, is 0

EXCEL SOLUTION

Level of significance: Cell G10	Value
n: Cell G15	Formula: =COUNT(A5:A24)
Degrees of freedom: Cell G16	Formula: =G15-2
Pearson coefficient: Cell G17	Formula: =CORREL(B5:B24,C5:C24)
t_{cal}: Cell G18	Formula: =(G17-G13)/SQRT((1-G17^2)/G16)
Upper t-critical: Cell G20	Formula: =T.INV(1-G10/2,G16)
Lower t-critical: Cell G21	Formula: =T.INV(G10/2,G16)
p-value: Cell G22	Formula: =2-2*T.DIST(G18,G16,TRUE)

NOTE

The preceding example illustrates a two-sided test, but we can also conduct one-sided tests for questions relating to the positive or negative nature of the population correlation coefficient. For example, in Example 12.3, we could have guessed that the '% increase in productivity' and 'evaluation score' variables had a positive association (as X increases Y increases too). In this case, we would conduct the following hypothesis:

$$H_0: \rho = 0 \text{ vs } H_1: \rho > 0$$

If we then tested at α = 5%, the critical value for the decision concerning H_0 would be the right-hand side (positive) quantile, $t_{n-2,\alpha} = t_{18,0.05} = 1.73$.
In this example, the only thing that would change is the critical value, i.e. we would compare the test statistic, $t_{cal} = 8.3$ to $t_{18,0.05} = 1.73$ and thus reject H_0 (because t_{cal} lies in the rejection region).

If we reversed the test and assumed that the association was negative (i.e. as X increases, Y decreases) then the alternative hypothesis would read:

$$H_0: \rho = 0 \text{ vs } H_1: \rho < 0$$

For this hypothesis, the critical t-value would be $-t_{n-2,\alpha} = -t_{18,0.05} = -1.73$. (in this case, we would not reject H_0, because $t_{cal} = 8.3$ lies in the 'do not reject H_0' region).

12.4 Linear regression analysis

12.4.1 Introduction to linear regression analysis

In this section, we extend the concept of measuring the association between variables to include a method for fitting a straight line to the two variables (a linear model). These linear models allow us to perform the following tasks.

- We can predict the value of a dependent variable (Y) given an independent (or predictor) variable (X).
- If the line fits well, we can use it to describe the relationship between the two variables with a mathematical formula.

Analysing data that involves fitting a straight line to two data variables is called *linear regression analysis* and is one of the most widely used techniques for modelling a linear relationship between variables. It is used in a wide range of disciplines (business, economics, psychology, social sciences) to enable us to develop models that describe and predict the dependent variable.

Simple regression analysis Aims to find a linear relationship between a response variable and a possible predictor variable by the method of least squares.

12.4.2 The linear regression model

Linear regression analysis attempts to model the true population relationship between the variables X and Y in the form of a straight-line relationship:

$$Y_i = \beta_0 + \beta_1 X_i + \text{error} \tag{12.6}$$

- Y_i denotes the ith-value of the dependent variable observed at the ith given value of the independent variable (X_i).
- β_0 and β_1 are parameters representing the population y-intercept and slope, respectively.
- The parameters β_0 and β_1 are the true population values, and are thus unknown unless we can observe the whole population.

The sample relationship between these variables is given by the equation:

$$\hat{Y}_i = b_0 + b_1 X_i \tag{12.7}$$

$\hat{Y}_i$ is the ith estimated value of the dependent variable (Y_i) at the ith given value of the independent variable (X_i), and the values b_0 and b_1 are estimates of the population values of β_0 and β_1, respectively (i.e. b_0 and b_1 are the sample y-intercept and slope respectively).

A large part of the analysis of these models involves testing to see how well b_0 and b_1 estimate these true population values. This means that we ultimately use b_0 and b_1 to construct confidence intervals for β_0 and β_1, and also to create hypothesis tests for testing β_0 and β_1. However, before we get to this, we have to obtain the values of the estimators b_0 and b_1 from the observed values of X and Y. To do this, regression analysis utilises the method of **least squares** to provide the formulae for these estimators. We therefore begin our discussion of regression analysis by first looking at the method of least squares.

Least squares A criterion for fitting a specified model to observed data. It refers to finding the smallest (least) sum of squared differences between fitted and actual values.

12.4.3 Method of least squares: Estimating β_0 and β_1

Consider the scatter plot in Figure 12.9. In this graph, we see a scatter plot of observations for the variables X and Y, with three potential straight lines through the data. Note that each line passes through the × symbol in the middle of the plot. This point corresponds to the point ($\overline{X}$, $\overline{Y}$), i.e. the mean of the Xs and the mean of the Ys.

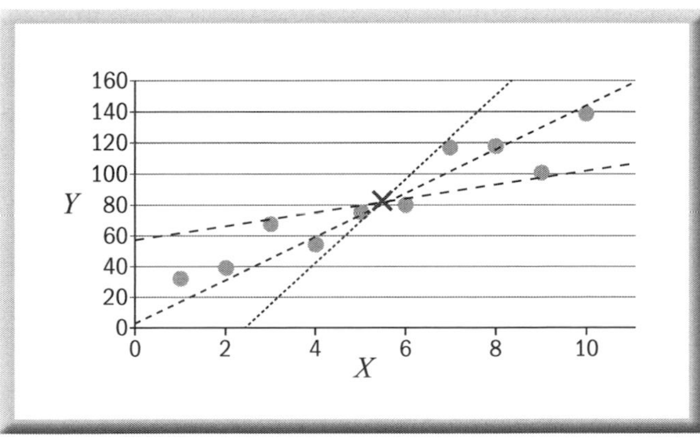

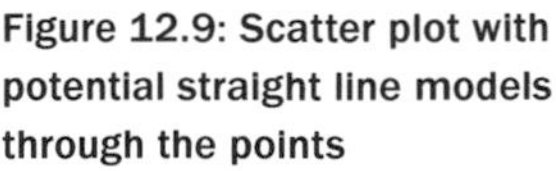
Figure 12.9: Scatter plot with potential straight line models through the points

Each of the straight lines in Figure 12.9 are possible models for the relationship between X and Y, but which one is the best?

One method to determine which line is the best is to look at the *squared vertical distances* between the Y observation (denoted Y_i) and the fitted Y-value (denoted $\hat{Y}_i$), i.e. the squared vertical distance is $(Y_i - \hat{Y}_i)^2$.

Consider the two lines in Figure 12.10. Which line fits the data better? If we had to calculate the sum of the squared vertical distances for each graph, which one would have the smaller sum?

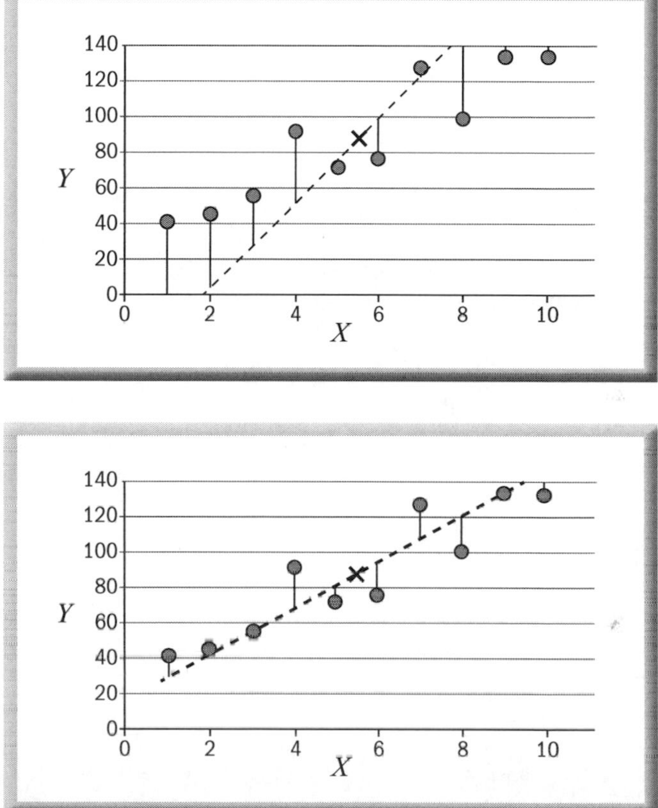

Figure 12.10: Scatter plots with two potential fitted lines, vertical distances between the line and points indicated

It appears as though the fitted line in the lower plot of Figure 12.10 would have a smaller sum of squared vertical distances (because the vertical lines connecting the dashed line and the points are generally shorter than the vertical lines in the upper plot).

Intuitively, it makes sense that the fitted line with the smaller sum of squared vertical distances will be better, because if the points are closer to the line, the vertical distances will be smaller. The method of least squares employs this idea to obtain the best straight line that passes through the point $(\overline{X}, \overline{Y})$. The best least squares line is then the one that satisfies the following criteria:

- The sum of the vertical squared distance between the data points and the line is a *minimum*.
- The sum of the vertical distances of the data points above the line equals the sum of the vertical distances of data points below the line.

Defining $\widehat{Y}_i$ as the values corresponding to the best fit straight line as shown in formula (12.7), we can express the above criteria algebraically as:

$$\sum_{i=1}^{n}(Y_i - \widehat{Y}_i)^2 = \text{minimum and } \sum_{i=1}^{n}(Y_i - \widehat{Y}_i) = 0$$

Note that the line given in formula (12.7) is completely described by the values b_0 and b_1, and so finding the best line, $\widehat{Y}_i$, is equivalent to finding the best values for b_0 and b_1. The algebraic expressions above lead to the following two *normal equations,* which we use to ultimately determine the values of b_0 and b_1:

$$\sum_{i=1}^{n} Y_i = nb_0 + b_1 \sum_{i=1}^{n} X_i$$

And:

$$\sum_{i=1}^{n} X_i Y_i = b_0 \sum_{i=1}^{n} X_i + b_1 \sum_{i=1}^{n} X_i^2$$

By solving the above equations simultaneously, we determine expressions for b_0 and b_1 such that the two conditions are satisfied. The final expressions obtained are as follows:

$$b_1 = \frac{\sum_{i=1}^{n} X_i Y_i - \frac{1}{n}\sum_{i=1}^{n} X_i \sum_{i=1}^{n} Y_i}{\sum_{i=1}^{n} X_i^2 - \frac{1}{n}\left(\sum_{i=1}^{n} X_i\right)^2} \quad (12.8)$$

And:

$$b_0 = \frac{1}{n}\sum_{i=1}^{n} Y_i - \frac{b_1}{n}\sum_{i=1}^{n} X_i \quad (12.9)$$

WORKED EXAMPLES

EXAMPLE 12.4

A high-school student is interested in the effects of sleep on the results of an exam. She decides to investigate this relationship by asking five of her friends how much sleep they got before an exam and then later asking them their exam marks. Table 12.3 shows the results.

Table 12.3: Data relating to the amount of sleep and the exam mark obtained by five students

AMOUNT OF SLEEP (HOURS), X	EXAM MARK, Y (%)
9	72
12	93
5	55
4	49
4.5	48

Determine the least squares regression line that best fits these data (i.e. calculate b_0 and b_1).

To obtain the least squares regression line, we need to first calculate b_0 and b_1 using formulae (12.8) and (12.9). We begin by calculating the following basic statistics:

$$n = 5 \qquad \sum_{i=1}^{n} X_i = 34.5 \qquad \sum_{i=1}^{n} Y_i = 317 \qquad \sum_{i=1}^{n} X_i Y_i = 2\,451$$

$$\sum_{i=1}^{n} X_i^2 = 286.25, \text{ and } \sum_{i=1}^{n} Y_i^2 = 21\,563$$

Note that formula (12.9) requires that we know the value of b_1, so we begin by first calculating b_1, by substituting the above basic statistics into formula (12.8):

$$b_1 = \frac{\sum_{i=1}^{n} X_i Y_i - \frac{1}{n}\sum_{i=1}^{n} X_i \sum_{i=1}^{n} Y_i}{\sum_{i=1}^{n} X_i^2 - \frac{1}{n}\left(\sum_{i=1}^{n} X_i\right)^2}$$

$$= \frac{2\,451 - \frac{1}{5}(34.5)(317)}{286.25 - \frac{1}{5}(34.5)^2}$$

$$= 5.471$$

Now, since $b_1 = 5.471$, we can substitute this value (along with the other basic statistics) into formula (12.9) to calculate the value of b_0:

$$b_0 = \frac{1}{n}\sum_{i=1}^{n} Y_i - \frac{b_1}{n}\sum_{i=1}^{n} X_i$$

$$= \frac{1}{5}(317) - \frac{5.471}{5}(34.5)$$

$$= 25.65$$

INTERPRETATION The following equation thus describes the best least squares regression line fit to the data. It is obtained by substituting the calculated values for b_0 and b_1 Into formula (12.7):

$$\hat{Y}_i = 25.65 + 5.471X_i$$

Example 12.5 illustrates how we can calculate the values of b_0 and b_1 from the data in Example 12.1 using Excel. We also briefly show how to display the resulting fitted line on the Excel scatter plot of the data.

WORKED EXAMPLES

EXAMPLE 12.5

Consider the data set from Example 12.1. Determine the least squares regression line that fits these data and plot the resulting straight line on the scatter plot.

The calculation for b_0 and b_1 is very similar to the calculation of the correlation coefficient (indeed, most of the same basic statistics are required for this calculation). For this example, we begin by noting the following values of the basic statistics:

$n = 20$ $\quad \sum_{i=1}^{n} X_i = 1\,064$ $\quad \sum_{i=1}^{n} Y_i = 110.8$ $\quad \sum_{i=1}^{n} X_i Y_i = 6\,237.5$

$$\sum_{i=1}^{n} X_i^2 = 60\,352, \text{ and } \sum_{i=1}^{n} Y_i^2 = 653.44$$

Therefore, substituting these values into formulae (12.8) and (12.9), we get:

$$b_1 = \frac{\sum_{i=1}^{n} X_i Y_i - \frac{1}{n}\sum_{i=1}^{n} X_i \sum_{i=1}^{n} Y_i}{\sum_{i=1}^{n} X_i^2 - \frac{1}{n}\left(\sum_{i=1}^{n} X_i\right)^2}$$

$$= \frac{6\,237.5 - \frac{1}{20}(1\,064)(110.8)}{60\,352 - \frac{1}{20}(1\,064)^2}$$

$$= 0.091519$$

And:

$$b_0 = \frac{1}{n}\sum_{i=1}^{n} Y_i - \frac{b_1}{n}\sum_{i=1}^{n} X_i$$

$$= \frac{1}{20}(110.8) - \frac{0.091519}{20}(1\,064)$$

$$= 0.6712$$

The regression line is thus:

$$\hat{Y}_i = 0.6712 + 0.091519 X_i$$

We can use Excel in a number of different ways to conduct regression analysis and calculate the required coefficients b_0 and b_1:

- By using basic Excel functions, such as SUM(), SQRT() and SUMSQ(), to manually calculate these values.
- By using the Excel functions INTERCEPT() and SLOPE().
- Using the 'Trendline' option in the scatter plot. This prints the estimated regression line on the scatter plot along with the fitted line. (This is shown in Figures 12.11 and 12.12.)
- By using the 'Regression' option in the Excel ToolPak. This method (discussed in Section 12.4.11) not only provides the fitted regression line, but also a number of other analyses that will be discussed later in the chapter.

Slope Gradient of the fitted regression line.

Intercept Value of the regression equation (Y) when the X value is equal to 0.

The Excel function to calculate the **slope**, b_1, and **intercept**, b_0, is as described below.

	A	B	C	D	E	F	G	H
1	Example 12.5 – Estimating the regression equation							
2								
3		Employee number	Evaluation score, X	% increase in productivity, Y				
4		1	47	4.2		$n =$	20	=COUNT(B4:B23)
5		2	71	8.1		$\sum_{i=1}^{n} X_i =$	1064	=SUM(C4:C23)
6		3	64	6.8		$\overline{X} =$	53.2	=AVERAGE(C4:C23)
7		4	35	4.3		$\sum_{i=1}^{n} X_i^2 =$	60352	=SUMSQ(C4:C23)
8		5	43	5				
9		6	60	7.5		$\sum_{i=1}^{n} Y_i =$	110.8	=SUM(D4:D23)
10		7	38	4.7		$\overline{Y} =$	5.54	=AVERAGE(D4:D23)
11		8	59	5.9		$\sum_{i=1}^{n} Y_i^2 =$	653.44	=SUMSQ(D4:D23)
12		9	67	6.9		$\sum_{i=1}^{n} X_i Y_i =$	6237.5	=SUMPRODUCT(D4:D23,E4:E23)
13		10	56	5.7				
14		11	67	5.7	1)	$b_1 =$	0.091519	=(G12-G5*G9/G4)/(G7-(G5^2)/G4)
15		12	57	5.4		$b_0 =$	0.6712	=G9/G4-G14*G5/G4
16		13	69	7.5				
17		14	38	3.8	2)	$b_1 =$	0.091519	=SLOPE(D4:D23,C4:C23)
18		15	54	5.9		$b_0 =$	0.6712	=INTERCEPT(D4:D23,C4:C23)
19		16	76	6.3				
20		17	53	5.7				
21		18	40	4				
22		19	47	5.2				
23		20	23	2.2				

Figure 12.11: The least squares estimates of the regression parameters obtained using Excel

EXCEL SOLUTION

n: Cell G4	Formula: =COUNT(B4:B23)
$\sum_{i=1}^{n} X_i$: Cell G5	Formula: =SUM(C4:C23)
$\overline{X}$: Cell G6	Formula: =AVERAGE(C4:C23)
$\sum_{i=1}^{n} X_i^2$: Cell G7	Formula: =SUMSQ(C4:C23)
$\sum_{i=1}^{n} Y_i$: Cell G9	Formula: =SUM(D4:D23)
$\overline{Y}$: Cell G10	Formula: =AVERAGE(D4:D23)
$\sum_{i=1}^{n} Y_i^2$: Cell G11	Formula: =SUMSQ(D4:D23)
$\sum_{i=1}^{n} X_i Y_i$: Cell G12	Formula: =SUMPRODUCT(C4:C23,D4:D23)
b_0: Cell G15	Formula: =(G12-G5*G9/G4)/(G7-(G5^2)/G4)
b_1: Cell G14	Formula: =G9/G4-G14*G5/G4
b_0: Cell G18	Formula: =SLOPE(D4:D23,C4:C23)
b_1: Cell G17	Formula: =INTERCEPT(D4:D23,C4:C23)

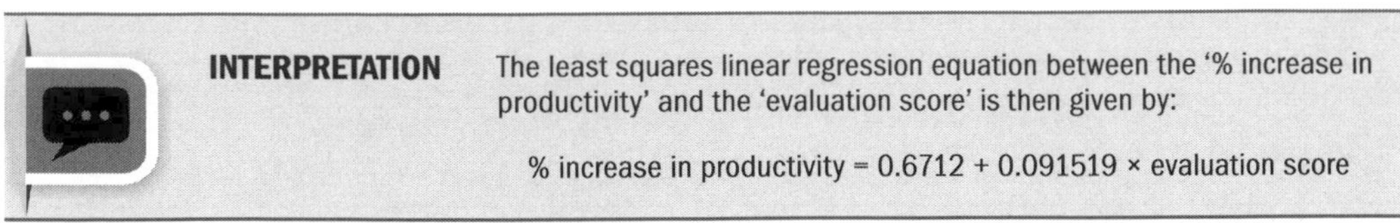

INTERPRETATION The least squares linear regression equation between the '% increase in productivity' and the 'evaluation score' is then given by:

% increase in productivity = 0.6712 + 0.091519 × evaluation score

We can also visualise this regression equation by placing a trendline on the scatter plot created in Example 12.1 (see Figure 12.3). The procedure to create this trend line is as follows:

- Create the scatter plot of the data as shown in Example 12.1 and Figure 12.3.
- Select the plot that was created and click on the 'Layout' tab in the 'Chart Tools' section that appears (shown in Figure 12.11).
- Click on the 'Trendline' button and then select 'More Trendline Options' (shown in Figure 12.11).
- The window shown in Figure 12.12 should appear. In this window, click on the 'Linear' option and check the 'Display Equation on chart' box.

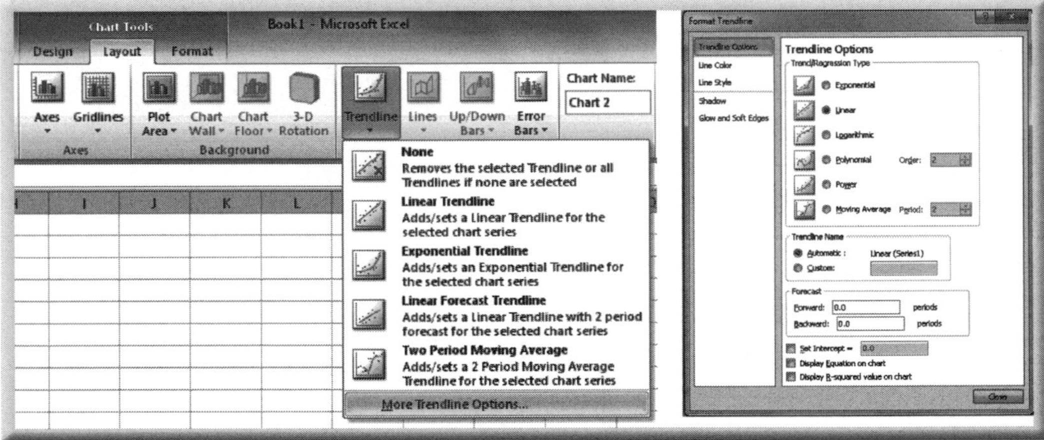

Figure 12.12: Excel: 'Trendline' options and formatting the trendline

The resulting scatter plot with overlaid regression line and regression equation is shown in Figure 12.13.

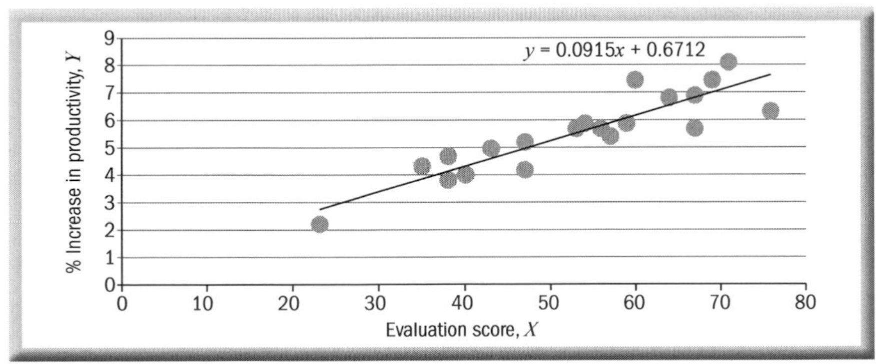

Figure 12.13: The scatter plot with regression line and regression equation

12.4.4 Fitted values and residuals

Once we have estimated our regression line we can estimate the dependent variable, Y, by evaluating the regression line in each value of the independent variable, X. This results in a list of new Y-values that correspond to each of the original observations. However, when we calculate these values, we will encounter a discrepancy between observed values of Y and those estimated by the line $\hat{Y}$. These differences are called the **residuals** (e_i) and are given by the formula:

$$i^{\text{th}} \text{ residual} = e_i = Y_i - \hat{Y}_i \qquad (12.10)$$

Y_i is the ith actual observation and $\hat{Y}_i$ is the estimated value obtained by evaluating the regression equation in X_i. Note that the vertical distances shown in Figure 12.10 are the residuals.

Residual Represents the unexplained variation (or error) after fitting a regression model.

WORKED EXAMPLES

EXAMPLE 12.6

Use the fitted model and data from Example (12.4) to determine the fitted values, $\hat{Y}_i$ and residuals, e_i. Note that the fitted regression line for these data was $\hat{Y}_i = 25.65 + 5.471\, X_i$.

To obtain the fitted values for this model, we need to evaluate the estimated regression equation in each of the observed X-values. The values are then:

$$\begin{aligned}
X_1 &= 9: & \hat{Y}_1 &= 25.65 + 5.47 \times 9 = 74.88 \\
X_2 &= 12: & \hat{Y}_2 &= 25.65 + 5.47 \times 12 = 91.29 \\
X_3 &= 5: & \hat{Y}_3 &= 25.65 + 5.47 \times 5 = 53 \\
X_4 &= 4: & \hat{Y}_4 &= 25.65 + 5.47 \times 4 = 47.53 \\
X_5 &= 4.5: & \hat{Y}_5 &= 25.65 + 5.47 \times 4.5 = 50.265
\end{aligned}$$

The corresponding residuals for these data are:

$$\begin{aligned}
X_1 &= 9 \text{ and } Y_1 = 72: & \hat{Y}_1 &= 74.88 & \Rightarrow\ e_1 &= 72 - 74.88 = -2.88 \\
X_2 &= 12 \text{ and } Y_2 = 93: & \hat{Y}_2 &= 91.29 & \Rightarrow\ e_2 &= 93 - 91.29 = 1.71 \\
X_3 &= 5 \text{ and } Y_3 = 55: & \hat{Y}_3 &= 53 & \Rightarrow\ e_3 &= 55 - 53 = 2 \\
X_4 &= 4 \text{ and } Y_4 = 49: & \hat{Y}_4 &= 47.53 & \Rightarrow\ e_4 &= 49 - 47.53 = 1.47 \\
X_5 &= 4.5 \text{ and } Y_5 = 48: & \hat{Y}_5 &= 50.265 & \Rightarrow\ e_5 &= 48 - 50.265 = -2.265
\end{aligned}$$

Note that the sum of the residuals is equal to 0. This is not surprising, because the least squares line was obtained so that the criterion $\sum_{i=1}^{n}(Y_i - \hat{Y}_i) = 0$ would be satisfied.

We can also obtain the fitted values from Excel using the TREND() function (the residuals can then also easily be obtained). Example 12.7 illustrates how we can calculate the fitted values and residuals for Example 12.1.

WORKED EXAMPLES

EXAMPLE 12.7

Use the fitted model and data from Examples 12.1 and 12.5 to determine the fitted values, $\widehat{Y}_i$ and residuals, e_i. Note that the fitted regression line for these data was $\widehat{Y}_i = 0.6712 + 0.091519\,X_i$.

In this example, we determine the fitted values, $\widehat{Y}$, using both:

- the estimated regression equation
- Excel's TREND() function.

These two approaches are shown in Figures 12.14 and 12.15 respectively. Once these fitted values are calculated, we can then obtain the residuals by simply applying the formula $e = Y - \widehat{Y}$.

Excel spreadsheet solution

	A	B	C	D	E	F	G	H	I
1	**Example 12.7 - The fitted values and residuals (a)**								
2									
3		**Employee number**	**Evaluation score, *X***	**% Increase in Productivity, *Y***		**Fitted value**		**Residual**	
4		1	47	4.2		4.973	=$F$26+$F$25*C4	-0.773	=D4-F4
5		2	71	8.1		7.169	=$F$26+$F$25*C5	0.931	=D5-F5
6		3	64	6.8		6.528	=$F$26+$F$25*C6	0.272	=D6-F6
7		4	35	4.3		3.874	=$F$26+$F$25*C7	0.426	=D7-F7
8		5	43	5		4.607	=$F$26+$F$25*C8	0.393	=D8-F8
9		6	60	7.5		6.162	=$F$26+$F$25*C9	1.338	=D9-F9
10		7	38	4.7		4.149	=$F$26+$F$25*C10	0.551	=D10-F10
11		8	59	5.9		6.071	=$F$26+$F$25*C11	-0.171	=D11-F11
12		9	67	6.9		6.803	=$F$26+$F$25*C12	0.097	=D12-F12
13		10	56	5.7		5.796	=$F$26+$F$25*C13	-0.096	=D13-F13
14		11	67	5.7		6.803	=$F$26+$F$25*C14	-1.103	=D14-F14
15		12	57	5.4		5.888	=$F$26+$F$25*C15	-0.488	=D15-F15
16		13	69	7.5		6.986	=$F$26+$F$25*C16	0.514	=D16-F16
17		14	38	3.8		4.149	=$F$26+$F$25*C17	-0.349	=D17-F17
18		15	54	5.9		5.613	=$F$26+$F$25*C18	0.287	=D18-F18
19		16	76	6.3		7.627	=$F$26+$F$25*C19	-1.327	=D19-F19
20		17	53	5.7		5.522	=$F$26+$F$25*C20	0.178	=D20-F20
21		18	40	4		4.332	=$F$26+$F$25*C21	-0.332	=D21-F21
22		19	47	5.2		4.973	=$F$26+$F$25*C22	0.227	=D22-F22
23		20	23	2.2		2.776	=$F$26+$F$25*C23	-0.576	=D23-F23
24									
25					b_1 =	0.091519	=SLOPE(C12:C31,B12:B31)		
26					b_0 =	0.6712	=INTERCEPT(C12:C31,B12:B31)		

Figure 12.14: Excel solution for determining the fitted values and residuals using the estimated regression equation

EXCEL SOLUTION (A)

b_0: Cell F25	Formula: =SLOPE(D4:D23,C4:C23)
b_1: Cell F26	Formula: =INTERCEPT(D4:D23,C4:C23)
Fitted values: Cells F4:F23	Formula: =$F$26+$F$25*C4 (Copy formula F5:F23)
Residual: Cells H4:H23	Formula: =D4-F4 (Copy formula H5:H23)

	A	B	C	D	E	F	G	H	I
1	Example 12.7 - The fitted values and residuals (b)								
2									
3		Employee number	Evaluation score, X	% Increase in Productivity, Y		Fitted value		Residual	
4		1	47	4.2		4.973	=TREND($D$4:$D$23,$C$4,$C$23,C4)	-0.773	=D4-F4
5		2	71	8.1		7.169	=TREND($D$4:$D$23,$C$4,$C$23,C5)	0.931	=D5-F5
6		3	64	6.8		6.528	=TREND($D$4:$D$23,$C$4,$C$23,C6)	0.272	=D6-F6
7		4	35	4.3		3.874	=TREND($D$4:$D$23,$C$4,$C$23,C7)	0.426	=D7-F7
8		5	43	5		4.607	=TREND($D$4:$D$23,$C$4,$C$23,C8)	0.393	=D8-F8
9		6	60	7.5		6.162	=TREND($D$4:$D$23,$C$4,$C$23,C9)	1.338	=D9-F9
10		7	38	4.7		4.149	=TREND($D$4:$D$23,$C$4,$C$23,C10)	0.551	=D10-F10
11		8	59	5.9		6.071	=TREND($D$4:$D$23,$C$4,$C$23,C11)	-0.171	=D11-F11
12		9	67	6.9		6.803	=TREND($D$4:$D$23,$C$4,$C$23,C12)	0.097	=D12-F12
13		10	56	5.7		5.796	=TREND($D$4:$D$23,$C$4,$C$23,C13)	-0.096	=D13-F13
14		11	67	5.7		6.803	=TREND($D$4:$D$23,$C$4,$C$23,C14)	-1.103	=D14-F14
15		12	57	5.4		5.888	=TREND($D$4:$D$23,$C$4,$C$23,C15)	-0.488	=D15-F15
16		13	69	7.5		6.986	=TREND($D$4:$D$23,$C$4,$C$23,C16)	0.514	=D16-F16
17		14	38	3.8		4.149	=TREND($D$4:$D$23,$C$4,$C$23,C17)	-0.349	=D17-F17
18		15	54	5.9		5.613	=TREND($D$4:$D$23,$C$4,$C$23,C18)	0.287	=D18-F18
19		16	76	6.3		7.627	=TREND($D$4:$D$23,$C$4,$C$23,C19)	-1.327	=D19-F19
20		17	53	5.7		5.522	=TREND($D$4:$D$23,$C$4,$C$23,C20)	0.178	=D20-F20
21		18	40	4		4.332	=TREND($D$4:$D$23,$C$4,$C$23,C21)	-0.332	=D21-F21
22		19	47	5.2		4.973	=TREND($D$4:$D$23,$C$4,$C$23,C22)	0.227	=D22-F22
23		20	23	2.2		2.776	=TREND($D$4:$D$23,$C$4,$C$23,C23)	-0.576	=D23-F23

Figure 12.15: Excel solution for determining the fitted values and residuals using the TREND() function

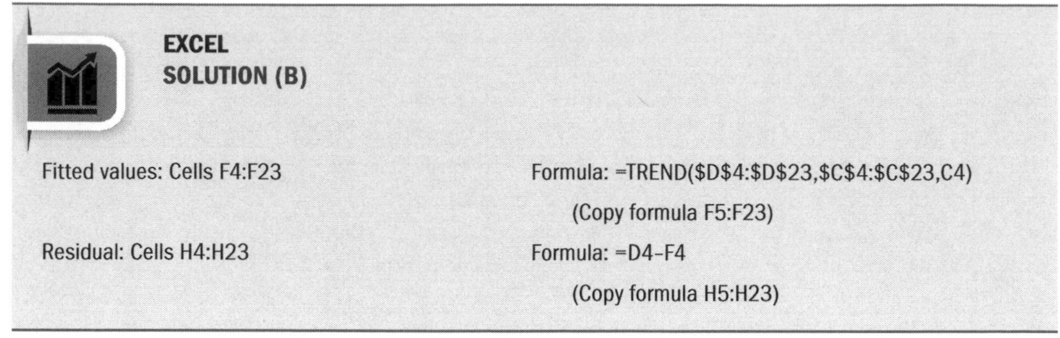

EXCEL SOLUTION (B)

Fitted values: Cells F4:F23 — Formula: =TREND($D$4:$D$23,$C$4:$C$23,C4) (Copy formula F5:F23)

Residual: Cells H4:H23 — Formula: =D4-F4 (Copy formula H5:H23)

These residuals, as we discover shortly, are a very important part of regression analysis.

12.4.5 Sums of squares

When conducting regression analysis, it is essential to be able to identify three important measures of variation: regression sum of squares (*SSR*), error sum of squares (*SSE*), and total sum of squares (*SST*).

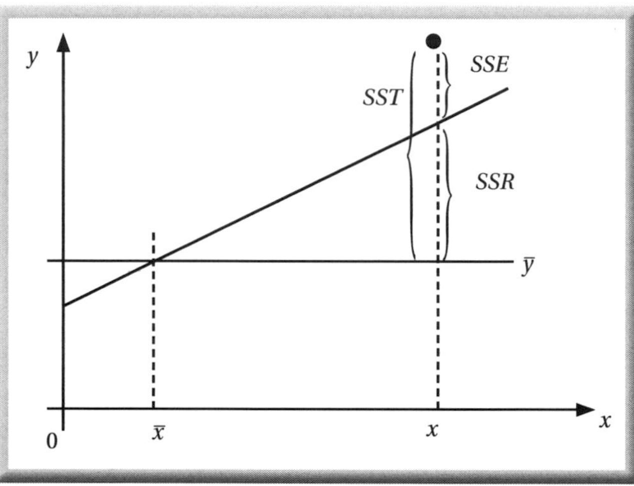

Figure 12.16: Understanding the relationship between *SST*, *SSR* and *SSE*

Figure 12.16 illustrates the relationship between these different measures, which shows that the total variation can be split into two parts: explained and unexplained variation.

- Regression sum of squares (*SSR*) – sometimes called *explained variation*:

$$SSR = \sum_{i=1}^{n}(\hat{Y}_i - \bar{Y})^2 \tag{12.11}$$

The *SSR* indicates the amount of difference between (or variation around) the fitted line and the horizontal mean line, $\bar{Y}$. Small values of *SSR* imply that the fitted line is quite horizontal (the slope is nearly zero). If the fitted line has a steep slope, the fitted line is very different from the horizontal mean line and the *SSR* will be large.

- Error sum of squares (*SSE*) – sometimes called *unexplained variation*:

$$SSE = \sum_{i=1}^{n}(Y_i - \hat{Y})^2 \tag{12.12}$$

The *SSE* is a measure of how well the data and fitted line fit together, because it is essentially just the sum of squared residuals (large values indicate poor fit; small values indicate good fit).

For the least squares fitted line, this value is a minimum as this was the criteria used to obtain the least squares regression line (see Section 12.4.3).

Note that another important quantity related to *SSE* is the 'mean error sum of squares', denoted *MSE*, and defined as:

$$MSE = \frac{SSE}{n-2} \tag{12.13}$$

- Total sum of squares (*SST*) – sometimes called the *total variation*:

$$SST = \sum_{i=1}^{n}(Y_i - \overline{Y})^2 \tag{12.14}$$

The *SST* is simply a measure of the total variation in the observed *Y*-values. Compare this value to the sample variance discussed in Chapter 3.

These sums of squares are related to one another by the expression:

$$SST = SSR + SSE \tag{12.15}$$

12.4.6 Test model reliability: Coefficient of determination (R^2)

The regression line can only partially describe the relationship between *X* and *Y*, since the variability of the observed values is not clearly described by the line (we saw this when examining the residuals). In fact, as has already been explained, the total variability of *Y* can be split into two components:

- Variability explained or accounted for by the regression line
- Unexplained variability as indicated by the residuals

Coefficient of determination (R^2) The proportion of the variance in the dependent variable that is predicted from the independent variable.

The **coefficient of determination (R^2)** is defined as the proportion of the total variation in *Y* that is explained by the variation in the independent variable *X* and so provides a way to evaluate the goodness-of-fit of the line to the data. This definition is represented by formulae (12.16) and (12.17) below:

$$R^2 = \frac{SSR}{SST} = \frac{\sum_{i=1}^{n}(\hat{Y}_i - \overline{Y})^2}{\sum_{i=1}^{n}(Y_i - \overline{Y})^2} \tag{12.16}$$

Alternatively, using formula (12.15), we can write formula (12.16) as:

$$R^2 = \frac{SST - SSE}{SST} = 1 - \frac{SSE}{SST} = 1 - \frac{\sum_{i=1}^{n}(Y_i - \hat{Y}_i)^2}{\sum_{i=1}^{n}(Y_i - \overline{Y}_i)^2} \tag{12.17}$$

By further manipulating the above equations, we can show that when using least squares estimation for straight-line models, the coefficient of determination (R^2) is simply the squared correlation coefficient:

$$R^2 = (\text{correlation coefficient})^2 = r^2 \qquad (12.18)$$

Note that the relationship in formula (12.18) *only* holds for the least squares fit for *straight-line* models involving *two* variables X and Y.

Interpretation of R^2

- The value of R^2 always lies between 0 and 1: $0 \le R^2 \le 1$.
- Values of R^2 close to 1 imply that the model is appropriate for the given data.
- Values of R^2 close to 0 imply that the model is not appropriate for the given data.

Example 12.8 illustrates the calculation of the R^2 statistic for the data in Example 12.1.

WORKED EXAMPLES

EXAMPLE 12.8

In Examples 12.1 and 12.5, the fitted model for the data was found to be $\hat{Y}_i = 0.6712 + 0.091519\,X_i$.

This line was fit to the observed data and shown in Figure 12.13. We would now like to quantify the ability of the model to describe the variation in the data, i.e. how well does the line fit the data?

To do this, we need to calculate and interpret the value of the coefficient of determination.

Using Excel, we can calculate the value of the *SSR*, *SSE* and *SST*:

$$SSE = \sum_{i=1}^{n}(Y_i - \hat{Y}_i)^2 = 8.22474$$

$$SSR = \sum_{i=1}^{n}(\hat{Y}_i - \overline{Y})^2 = 31.38553$$

$$SST = \sum_{i=1}^{n}(Y_i - \overline{Y})^2 = 39.608$$

We can then obtain the value for R^2 by substituting these values into either formula (12.16) or (12.17):

$$R^2 = \frac{SSR}{SST} = \frac{31.38553}{39.608} = 0.792404 \qquad \text{Or:} \qquad R^2 = 1 - \frac{SSE}{SST} = 1 - \frac{8.2225}{39.608} = 0.792404$$

Alternatively, we can calculate it by squaring the value of the correlation coefficient obtained in Example 12.2:

$$R^2 = r^2 = 0.89^2 = 0.792$$

Figure 12.17 illustrates the Excel solution to calculate the coefficient of determination and standard error of the estimate.

	A	B	C	D	E	F	G	H	I	J	K	L	M	N	O	P
1	Example 12.7: The fitted values and residuals (b)															
2																
3		Employee number	Evaluation score, (X)	% increase in performance (Y)		Fitted value, $\hat{Y}$		Residual, $e = Y - \hat{Y}$		$\hat{Y} - \overline{Y}$		$Y - \overline{Y}$				
4		1	47	4.2		4.973	=TREND($D$4:$D$23,$C$4:$C$23,C4)	-0.773	=D4-F4	-0.567	=F4-$F$25	-1.34	=D4-$F$25			
5		2	71	8.1		7.169	=TREND($D$4:$D$23,$C$4:$C$23,C5)	0.931	=D5-F5	1.629	=F5-$F$25	2.56	=D5-$F$25	SSE =	8.2225	=SUMSQ(H4:H23)
6		3	64	6.8		6.528	=TREND($D$4:$D$23,$C$4:$C$23,C6)	0.272	=D6-F6	0.988	=F6-$F$25	1.26	=D6-$F$25	SSR =	31.3855	=SUMSQ(J4:J23)
7		4	35	4.3		3.874	=TREND($D$4:$D$23,$C$4:$C$23,C7)	0.426	=D7-F7	-1.666	=F7-$F$25	-1.24	=D7-$F$25	SST =	39.6080	=SUMSQ(L4:L23)
8		5	43	5		4.607	=TREND($D$4:$D$23,$C$4:$C$23,C8)	0.393	=D8-F8	-0.933	=F8-$F$25	-0.54	=D8-$F$25			
9		6	60	7.5		6.162	=TREND($D$4:$D$23,$C$4:$C$23,C9)	1.338	=D9-F9	0.622	=F9-$F$25	1.96	=D9-$F$25	R^2 =	0.7924	=O6/O7
10		7	38	4.7		4.149	=TREND($D$4:$D$23,$C$4:$C$23,C10)	0.551	=D10-F10	-1.391	=F10-$F$25	-0.84	=D10-$F$25			
11		8	59	5.9		6.071	=TREND($D$4:$D$23,$C$4:$C$23,C11)	-0.171	=D11-F11	0.531	=F11-$F$25	0.36	=D11-$F$25			
12		9	67	6.9		6.803	=TREND($D$4:$D$23,$C$4:$C$23,C12)	0.097	=D12-F12	1.263	=F12-$F$25	1.36	=D12-$F$25			
13		10	56	5.7		5.796	=TREND($D$4:$D$23,$C$4:$C$23,C13)	-0.096	=D13-F13	0.256	=F13-$F$25	0.16	=D13-$F$25			
14		11	67	5.7		6.803	=TREND($D$4:$D$23,$C$4:$C$23,C14)	-1.103	=D14-F14	1.263	=F14-$F$25	0.16	=D14-$F$25			
15		12	57	5.4		5.888	=TREND($D$4:$D$23,$C$4:$C$23,C15)	-0.488	=D15-F15	0.348	=F15-$F$25	-0.14	=D15-$F$25			
16		13	69	7.5		6.986	=TREND($D$4:$D$23,$C$4:$C$23,C16)	0.514	=D16-F16	1.446	=F16-$F$25	1.96	=D16-$F$25			
17		14	38	3.8		4.149	=TREND($D$4:$D$23,$C$4:$C$23,C17)	-0.349	=D17-F17	-1.391	=F17-$F$25	-1.74	=D17-$F$25			
18		15	54	5.9		5.613	=TREND($D$4:$D$23,$C$4:$C$23,C18)	0.287	=D18-F18	0.073	=F18-$F$25	0.36	=D18-$F$25			
19		16	76	6.3		7.627	=TREND($D$4:$D$23,$C$4:$C$23,C19)	-1.327	=D19-F19	2.087	=F19-$F$25	0.76	=D19-$F$25			
20		17	53	5.7		5.522	=TREND($D$4:$D$23,$C$4:$C$23,C20)	0.178	=D20-F20	-0.018	=F20-$F$25	0.16	=D20-$F$25			
21		18	40	4		4.332	=TREND($D$4:$D$23,$C$4:$C$23,C21)	-0.332	=D21-F21	-1.208	=F21-$F$25	-1.54	=D21-$F$25			
22		19	47	5.2		4.973	=TREND($D$4:$D$23,$C$4:$C$23,C22)	0.227	=D22-F22	-0.567	=F22-$F$25	-0.34	=D22-$F$25			
23		20	23	2.2		2.776	=TREND($D$4:$D$23,$C$4:$C$23,C23)	-0.576	=D23-F23	-2.764	=F23-$F$25	-3.34	=D23-$F$25			
24																
25					$\overline{Y}$ =	5.54	=AVERAGE(D4:D23)									
26																
27																

Figure 12.17: Excel solution for Example 12.8

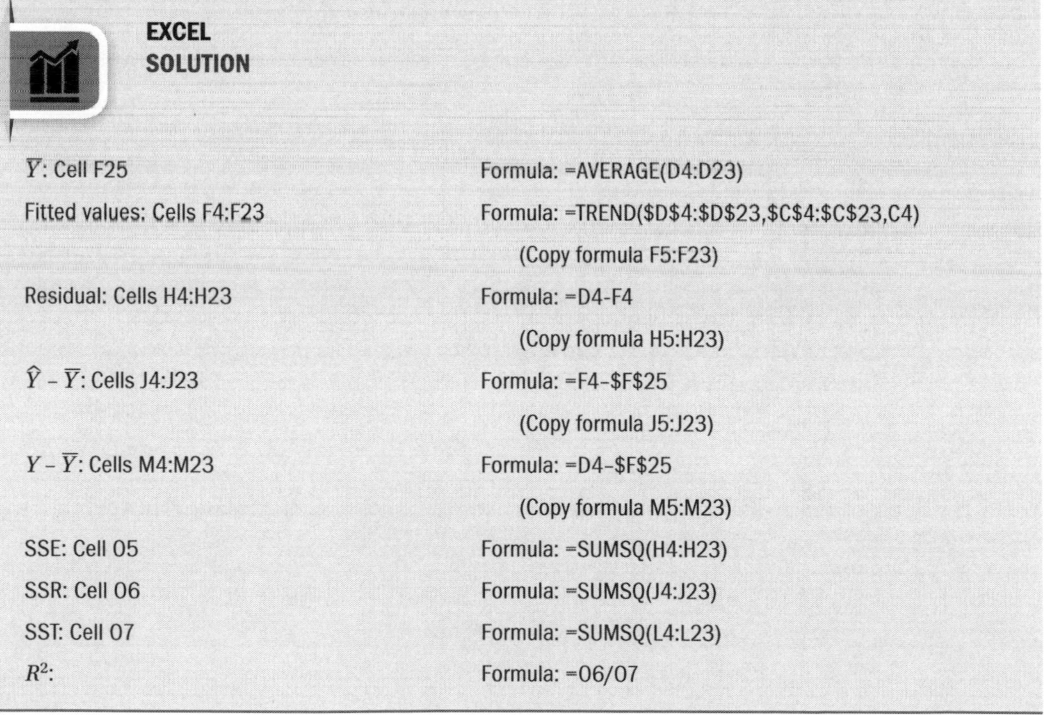

EXCEL SOLUTION

$\overline{Y}$: Cell F25 Formula: =AVERAGE(D4:D23)

Fitted values: Cells F4:F23 Formula: =TREND($D$4:$D$23,$C$4:$C$23,C4)

(Copy formula F5:F23)

Residual: Cells H4:H23 Formula: =D4-F4

(Copy formula H5:H23)

$\hat{Y} - \overline{Y}$: Cells J4:J23 Formula: =F4-$F$25

(Copy formula J5:J23)

$Y - \overline{Y}$: Cells M4:M23 Formula: =D4-$F$25

(Copy formula M5:M23)

SSE: Cell O5 Formula: =SUMSQ(H4:H23)

SSR: Cell O6 Formula: =SUMSQ(J4:J23)

SST: Cell O7 Formula: =SUMSQ(L4:L23)

R^2: Formula: =O6/O7

INTERPRETATION From Excel, the coefficient of determination is 0.79 or 79%. This value tells us that 79% of the variation in the dependent variable ('% increase in productivity') is explained by the variation in the independent variable ('evaluation score').

Conversely, this also implies that 21% (100 - 79) of the sample variability in the dependent variable is due to factors other than 'evaluation score' and is thus not explained by the regression line.

12.4.7 *t*-test for the parameter β_1

In the preceding sections, we looked at estimating the true regression line parameters, β_0 and β_1, by using the method of least squares. The result was the fitted regression line:

$$\hat{Y} = b_0 + b_1 X$$

This estimated the true relationship between X and Y:

$$Y = \beta_0 + \beta_1 X + \text{error}$$

The next step in analysing the linear relationship between X and Y is to determine whether the regression parameters are significantly different from 0. We are specifically interested in determining if β_1 is non-zero, because if this parameter is 0, it would imply that there is no meaningful linear relationship between X and Y.

The procedure that we follow to determine the significance of this parameter involves the same hypothesis testing steps that we first discussed in Chapter 10.

To determine the existence of a significant relationship between X and Y, we need to apply a t-test to check whether β_1 is equal to 0. This is essentially a test to determine if we can use the regression model. If the slope is significantly different from 0, we can use the regression equation to predict the dependent variable for any value of the independent variable. If the slope is 0, the independent variable has no value as a predictor, since for every value of the independent variable, the predicted value of the dependent variable would be equal to the sample mean, $\overline{Y}$. Therefore, if $\beta_1 = 0$ we would not be able to use the model to make useful predictions.

The specific null hypothesis that we consider for this situation is one that states there is no linear relationship between X and Y:

$$H_0: \beta_1 = 0$$

The two-sided alternative hypothesis then states that some form of linear relationship exists:

$$H_1: \beta_1 \neq 0$$

The test statistic used to test this hypothesis is given by:

$$T = \frac{b_1}{S_{b_1}} \tag{12.19}$$

Where:

$$S_{b1} = \sqrt{\frac{MSE}{\sum_{i=1}^{n} X_i^2 - \frac{1}{n}\left(\sum_{i=1}^{n} X_i\right)^2}} \qquad (12.20)$$

Note that the calculated value of the test statistic is denoted by t_{cal}.

This test statistic follows a t-distribution with $df = n - 2$ degrees of freedom if certain model assumptions hold. We discuss the assumptions, and the tests required to assess these assumptions, later in this chapter.

Example 12.9 continues the analysis of the data in Example 12.1 by testing the significance of the parameter β_1.

WORKED EXAMPLES

EXAMPLE 12.9

Using the information obtained in Examples 12.1, 12.5 and 12.8, determine if there is a significant relationship between the dependent variable, '% increase in productivity', and the dependent variable, 'evaluation score'. Conduct a hypothesis test at a 5% level of significance.

The five-step approach to conduct hypothesis tests is once again applied here.

Step 1: Provide the hypothesis statements H_0 and H_1

- $H_0: \beta_1 = 0$, i.e. there is no linear relationship between X and Y.
- $H_1: \beta_1 \neq 0$, i.e. a linear relationship exists (two-sided test).

Step 2: Choose an appropriate test statistic

We know that this is the t-test for testing whether the predictor variable is a significant contributor. We forego checking the assumptions required for this test; we discuss the assumptions later.

Step 3: Specify the significance level

The significance level is specified as 5% ($\alpha = 0.05$)

Step 4: Calculate the relevant test statistic

We can obtain the calculated value of the test statistic by applying formulae (12.19) and (12.20). The test statistic, t_{cal}, is then:

$$t_{cal} = \frac{b_1}{S_{b_1}} = \frac{0.091519}{0.011041} = 8.289$$

Where:

$$S_{b1} = \sqrt{\frac{MSE}{\sum_{i=1}^{n} X_i^2 - \frac{1}{n}\left(\sum_{i=1}^{n} X_i\right)^2}} = \sqrt{\frac{0.4568}{3\,747.2}} = 0.011041$$

The test statistic t follows a t-distribution with $n - 2$ degrees of freedom. From Excel, we also find that $t_{cal} = 8.3$.

Step 5: Make a decision

We can now test to see if this sample t-value would result in rejecting H_0. From Excel, we see that the two-sided $\alpha = 0.05$ critical t-value is $t_{n-2,\alpha/2} = t_{18,0.025} = 2.1$ and $-t_{18,0.025} = -2.1$. Since $t_{cal} > t_{n-2,\alpha/2}$ (i.e. $8.3 > 2.1$), the test statistic lies in the rejection region for H_0, i.e. **we reject H_0**. Alternatively, using the p-value approach, we find that p-value $< \alpha$ (i.e. $0.000001 < 0.05$) and so **we reject H_0**.

Figure 12.18 illustrates the Excel solution to calculate the regression equation.

	A	B	C	D	E	F	G	H
1	**Example 12.7: The fitted values and residuals (*b*)**							
2								
3	**Employee number**	**Evaluation score (*X*)**	**% increase in productivity (*Y*)**			$H_0: \beta_1 = 0$ vs. $H_1: \beta_1 \neq 0$		
4					**1. State hypothesis**	Two-sided test		
5	1	47	4.2					
6	2	71	8.1					
7	3	64	6.8		**2. Select test**	t-test for the regression parameter		
8	4	35	4.3					
9	5	43	5					
10	6	60	7.5		**3. Set level of significance**	Significance level, α =	0.05	
11	7	38	4.7					
12	8	59	5.9			**Population**		
13	9	67	6.9			Slope parameter, β_1 =	0	
14	10	56	5.7			**Sample**		
15	11	67	5.7			n =	20	=COUNT(A5:A24)
16	12	57	5.4			Degrees of freedom, df =	18	=G15-2
17	13	69	7.5			b_1 =	0.09152	=SLOPE(C5:C24,B5:B24)
18	14	38	3.8		**4. Calculate test statistic**	SSE =	8.22247	see Example 12.8
19	15	54	5.9			MSE =	0.4568	=G18/G16
20	16	76	6.3			$\sum_{i=1}^{n} X_i^2 - 1/n(\sum_{i=1}^{n} X_i)^2$ =	3747.2	=SUMSQ(B5:B24)-(SUM(B5:B24)^2/G15)
21	17	53	5.7			Test statistic, t_{cal}	8.28895	=G17/SQRT(G19/G20)
22	18	40	4			**p-value and critical values**		
23	19	47	5.2			Upper critical t-value =	2.1	=T.INV(1-G10/2,G16)
24	20	23	2.2			Lower critical t-value =	-2.1	=T.INV(G10/2,G16)
25						p-value	0.000000147	=2-2*T.DIST(G21,G16,TRUE)
26								
27					**5. Decision**	Test statistic compared to critical value. Test statistic lies in the rejection region. Reject H_0		
28						p-value compared to significance level, $p < \alpha$, reject H_0		

Figure 12.18: Excel solution for Example 12.9

EXCEL SOLUTION

Level of significance: Cell G10	Value
n: Cell G15	Formula: =COUNT(A5:A24)
Degrees of freedom: Cell G16	Formula: =G15-2
b_1: Cell G17	Formula: =SLOPE(C5:C24,B5:B24)
SSE: Cell G18	Value
MSE: Cell G19	Formula: =G18/G16
$\sum_{i=1}^{n} X_i^2 - \frac{1}{n}\left(\sum_{i=1}^{n} X_i\right)^2$: Cell G20	Formula: =SUMSQ(B5:B24)-(SUM(B5:B24)^2)/G15

t_{cal}: Cell G21	Formula: =G17/SQRT(G19/G20)
Upper t-critical: Cell G23	Formula: =T.INV(1-G10/2,G16)
Lower t-critical: Cell G24	Formula: =T.INV(G10/2,G16)
p-value: Cell G25	Formula: =2-2*T.DIST(G21,G16,TRUE)

INTERPRETATION The sample data provides evidence that a significant relationship may exist between the two variables ('% increase in productivity' and 'evaluation score') at a 5% significance level.

NOTE We can use a similar procedure to test the hypothesis on the intercept β_0. The test statistic is $T = \frac{b_0}{S_{b_0}}$, where b_0 is the least squares estimate of β_0 and S_{b_0} is its standard error:

$$S_{b_0} = \sqrt{MSE\left[\frac{1}{n} + \frac{\overline{X}^2}{\sum_{i=1}^{n} X_i^2 - \frac{1}{n}\left(\sum_{i=1}^{n} X_i\right)^2}\right]}$$

12.4.8 Prediction interval for an estimate of Y

The estimated regression equation ($\widehat{Y} = b_0 + b_1X$) provides a relationship that we can use to predict an unobserved Y-value that corresponds with a new value of X (we denote the new value of X by X_p). For example, using the information provided in Example 12.1, we may want to know what the percentage increase in productivity would be if an employee obtained an evaluation score of 30. We can easily obtain the *point* estimator for the unobserved Y-value by substituting $X_p = 30$ into the estimated equation. In this case it would be:

$$\widehat{Y}_p = 0.6712 + 0.091519 \times 30 = 3.41677\%$$

$\widehat{Y}_p$ is used to denote the estimator for the unobserved value, Y_p, that would have been observed had we observed an evaluation score $X_p = 30$ in the data.

This estimated predicted value also has a degree of uncertainty coupled to it, so we now introduce a method to express our confidence in the prediction by constructing confidence intervals for this predicted value. These confidence intervals for predicted values are called *prediction intervals.*

The prediction interval for Y_p, i.e. the Y-value that corresponds to the new X_p-value, is given by the following equation:

$$\widehat{Y}_p - \Delta < Y_p < \widehat{Y}_p + \Delta \qquad (12.21)$$

The Δ term is calculated using the equation below:

$$\Delta = t_{n-2,\alpha/2} \times \sqrt{MSE\left[1 + \frac{1}{n} + \frac{(X_p - \overline{X})^2}{\sum_{i=1}^{n} X_i^2 - \frac{1}{n}\left(\sum_{i=1}^{n} X_i\right)^2}\right]} \qquad (12.22)$$

The true, unobserved value Y_p will lie in this interval with probability $1 - \alpha$.

Example 12.10 illustrates how to construct a prediction interval for a predicted Y-value.

WORKED EXAMPLES

EXAMPLE 12.10

Use the information provided in Examples 12.1, 12.5 and 12.8.

If an employee receives a score of $X_p = 30$ in his/her evaluation, what is the predicted percentage increase in productivity for that employee?

In the preceding discussion, we saw that we could obtain a point estimator for this by calculating the fitted value at the new point, X_p. The new fitted value, denoted $\widehat{Y}_p$, is given by:

$$\widehat{Y}_p = 0.6712 + 0.091519 \times 30 = 3.41677\%$$

In other words, we could expect their productivity to increase by 3.41677% if they received a score of 30. However, since people differ, this single value is only an indication of what we could expect, on average.

Construct a 95% prediction interval for this prediction to get a better idea of the range of values we might expect from a person that scored 30.

The solution to this problem is to use formulae (12.21) and (12.22). The Excel solution follows.

From the previous Excel example, we have the following information:

$X_p = 30$, $n = 20$, significance level = 5%, $t_{n-2,\alpha/2} = 2.10092$, $MSE = 0.456804102$, $\overline{X} = 53.2$, $\sum_{i=1}^{n} X_i = 1\,064$ and $\sum_{i=1}^{n} X_i^2 = 60352$.

Substituting these values into formula (12.22) we get:

$$\Delta = t_{n-2,\alpha/2} \times \sqrt{MSE\left[1 + \frac{1}{n} + \frac{(X_p - \overline{X})^2}{\sum_{i=1}^{n} X_i^2 - \frac{1}{n}\left(\sum_{i=1}^{n} X_i\right)^2}\right]}$$

$$= 2.10092 \times \sqrt{0.456804102\left[1 + \frac{1}{20} + \frac{(30 - 53.2)^2}{(60\,352) - \frac{1}{20}(1\,064)^2}\right]}$$

$$= 1.551353666$$

Note that the point estimator for the dependent variable at the point $X_p = 30$ is:

$$\hat{Y}_p = 0.6712 + 0.091519 \times 30 = 3.41677\%$$

So, using formula (12.21) we then get the 95% prediction interval from $\hat{Y}_p$ evaluated at $X_p = 30$:

$$\hat{Y}_p - \Delta < Y_p < \hat{Y}_p + \Delta$$
$$3.41677 - 1.551353666 < Y_p < 3.41677 + 1.551353666$$
$$1.87 < Y_p < 4.97$$

Let us examine an Excel solution to calculate the prediction interval for $X_p = 30$. Figure 12.19 illustrates the Excel solution to calculate the predictor interval.

	A	B	C	D	E	F
1	**Example 12.10 - Prediction interval**					
2						
3	**Employee number**	**Evaluation score, X**	**Y% increase in productivity, Y**			
4				n =	20	=COUNT(A5:A24)
5	1	47	4.2	df =	18	=E4-2
6	2	71	8.1	X_p =	30	
7	3	64	6.8	$\bar{X}$ =	53.2	=AVERAGE(B5:B24)
8	4	35	4.3	$\hat{Y}_p$ =	3.4167591802	=TREND(C5:C24,B5:B24,E6)
9	5	43	5			
10	6	60	7.5	$(X_p - \bar{X})^2$ =	538.24	=(E6-E7)^2
11	7	38	4.7			
12	8	59	5.9	MSE =	0.4568	from Example 12.9
13	9	67	6.9			
14	10	56	5.7	$\sum_{i=1}^{n} X_i^2$ =	60352	=SUMSQ(B5:B24)
15	11	67	5.7			
16	12	57	5.4	$\sum_{i=1}^{n} X_i$ =	1064	=SUM(B5:B24)
17	13	69	7.5			
18	14	38	3.8	α =	0.05	Value
19	15	54	5.9	$t_{n-2a/2}$ =	-1.734063607	T.INV(E18,E5)
20	16	76	6.3			
21	17	53	5.7	Δ =	-1.2804551591	=E19*SQRT(E12*(1+1/E4+E10/(E14-(E16^2)/E4)))
22	18	40	4			
23	19	47	5.2	Lower pred. Int. =	4.6972143393	=E8-E21
24	20	23	2.2	Upper pred. Int. =	2.1363040211	=E8+E21
25						

Figure 12.19 Excel solution for Example 12.10

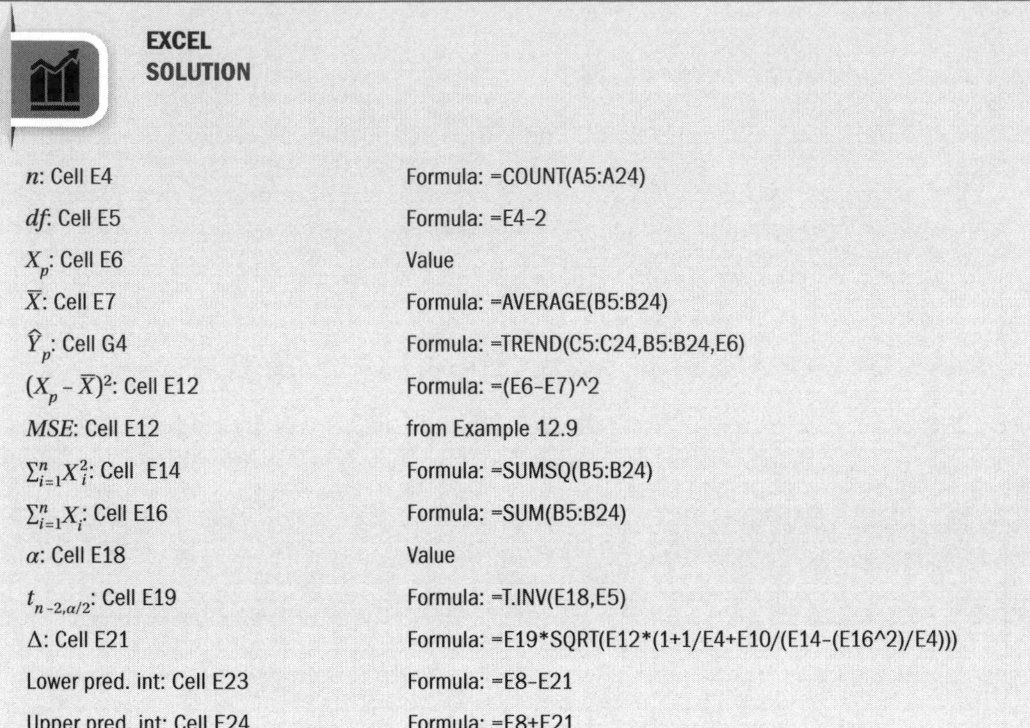

EXCEL SOLUTION

n: Cell E4	Formula: =COUNT(A5:A24)
df: Cell E5	Formula: =E4-2
X_p: Cell E6	Value
$\overline{X}$: Cell E7	Formula: =AVERAGE(B5:B24)
$\hat{Y}_p$: Cell G4	Formula: =TREND(C5:C24,B5:B24,E6)
$(X_p - \overline{X})^2$: Cell E12	Formula: =(E6-E7)^2
MSE: Cell E12	from Example 12.9
$\Sigma_{i=1}^{n} X_i^2$: Cell E14	Formula: =SUMSQ(B5:B24)
$\Sigma_{i=1}^{n} X_i$: Cell E16	Formula: =SUM(B5:B24)
α: Cell E18	Value
$t_{n-2,\alpha/2}$: Cell E19	Formula: =T.INV(E18,E5)
Δ: Cell E21	Formula: =E19*SQRT(E12*(1+1/E4+E10/(E14-(E16^2)/E4)))
Lower pred. int: Cell E23	Formula: =E8-E21
Upper pred. int: Cell E24	Formula: =E8+E21

INTERPRETATION The predicted value of the percentage increase in productivity (Y) for employees that score $X_p = 30$ in the evaluation lies somewhere between 1.87% and 4.97% (with probability 0.95). Note that this means that there is still a 5% probability that the actual value will be greater than 4.97% or smaller than 1.87%. This shows that the actual value can vary from the predicted value of 3.4%.

12.4.9 Regression assumptions

The inference (the hypothesis tests and confidence intervals) conducted in the preceding sections all rely on certain assumptions regarding the linear regression model and the data to which it is fit. These assumptions are:

- linearity
- independence of errors
- normality of errors
- constant variance.

We now discuss the detail behind each of these assumptions, along with methods for determining if they are valid assumptions or not. The discussion will use the data provided in Example 12.1 to illustrate some of the concepts.

Linearity

The assumption of *linearity* assumes that the relationship between the two variables is linear. To assess linearity, the residuals, *e*, are plotted against the independent variable, *X*. Excel ToolPak Regression will automatically create this plot if requested (see Section 12.4.11). If the data exhibit linearity, then we should observe that the residuals and *X* form no apparent pattern (tending to neither decrease, increase or have any other conspicuous shape). The points should be evenly scattered about the horizontal line corresponding to a residual value of zero.

The residual plot for the data in Example 12.1 is shown in Figure 12.20 below. We can conclude that since the points are reasonably uniformly spread around the horizontal zero line (and that no patterns are clearly evident) the assumption of linearity holds.

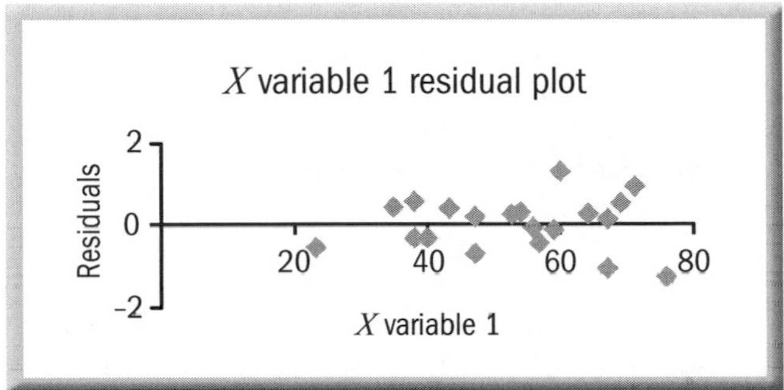

Figure 12.20: Residuals versus *X* for the data from Example 12.1

Independence of errors

The *independence of errors* assumption is a problem that occurs when data are collected over periods of time, and a data value is not independent of the previous data value measured. This effect is called *serial correlation* and can be measured using the *Durbin-Watson statistic* (not discussed in this textbook). Another expression for serial correlation, though usually used in a different context, is *autocorrelation*. The data considered in this chapter was all collected at the same time period and so we do not need to consider serial correlation (independence of errors) as a problem. This topic is beyond the scope of this textbook.

Normality of errors

The *normality assumption* requires that the measured residuals come from a normal distribution for each value of the independent variable, *X*. If this assumption is violated, the inference concerning the parameters of the regression model may not be reliable.

We can evaluate this assumption using two graphical methods:

- Construct a histogram of the residuals and check whether the shape looks roughly bell-shaped or normal.
- Create a normal probability plot of the residuals (available from the Excel ToolPak Regression solution). Data are normal if the normal probability plot depicts a straight line formed by the observations.

Figure 12.21 illustrates a normal probability plot based on the Example 12.1 data set. We observe that the relationship is fairly linear and so conclude that the normal assumption is not violated.

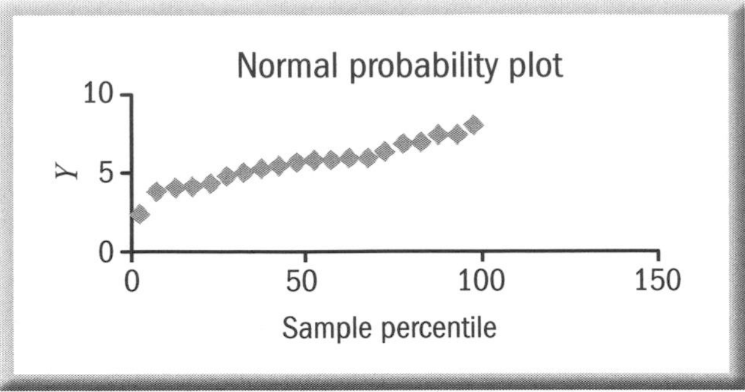

Figure 12.21: Normal probability plot for the residuals obtained from the linear model fit using the data from Example 12.1

The problem of non-normality can occur if the dependent variable is not normally distributed or the linearity assumption is violated. Like the *t*-test discussed in Chapter 10, hypothesis tests based in regression analysis are also robust against departures from this assumption. As long as the distribution of error against X is not very different from a normal distribution, then the inferences on β_0 and β_1 will not be seriously affected.

Constant variance

The final assumption of *equal variance* (or *homoscedasticity*) requires that the variability of the errors is constant for all values of X. This implies that the variance of Y-values is the same for all values of X. This assumption is important when making inferences about β_0 and β_1. If there are violations of this assumption, we can attempt to transform the dependent variable to improve model accuracy.

To test this assumption, we can construct the same plot as was used for the test for linearity (the independent variable X versus the residuals). If the errors are indeed homoscedastic (exhibit constant variance for each X), the graph should display an even scatter around the horizontal zero line (as shown in Figure 12.22). Deviations from homoscedasticity (called *heteroscedasticity*) present as megaphone shapes in the plot. Figure 12.23 shows some of the basic forms of the plot we could expect with a non-constant variance.

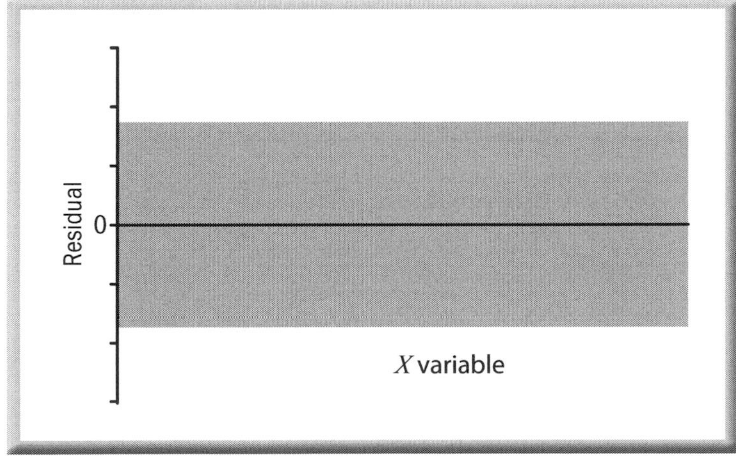

Figure 12.22: Constant variance: The typical shape of the plot of residuals versus X we could expect in the presence of constant variance

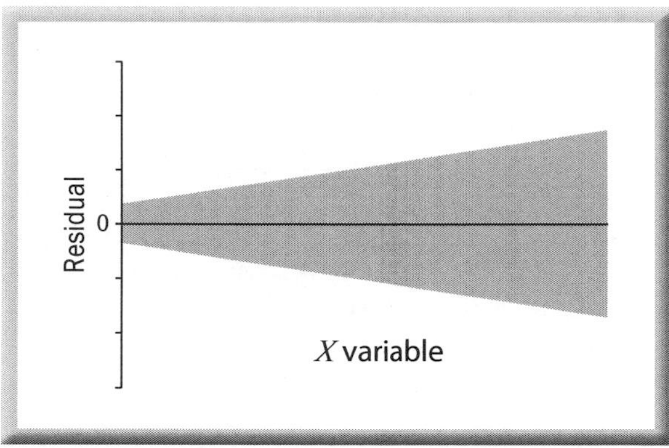

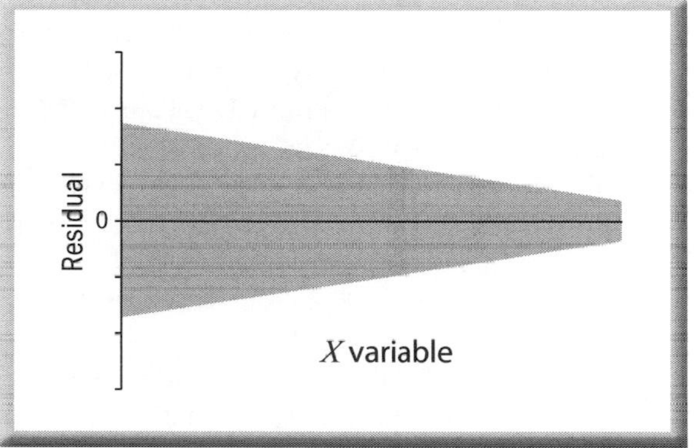

Figure 12.23: Non-constant variance: The typical shape of the plot of residuals versus X we could expect in the presence of non-constant variance

The graph in Figure 12.22 illustrates the Excel solution to check the variance assumption. We can see that the error does not grow in size as the value of X changes. This plot provides evidence that the variance assumption is not violated. If the variation in the residuals changes *greatly* as the value of X changes, we would assume that the variance assumption is violated.

If any of the four assumptions are violated, we can only conclude that linear regression is not the best method for fitting the data set and we need to find an alternative method or model.

12.4.10 Procedure for regression analysis

Now that we have discussed all of the different aspects of the regression analysis, we can look at a general approach for conducting the regression analysis. The steps that should be followed for this analysis are then as follows:

- Construct a scatter plot to identify the model (to determine if a linear relationship between the variables is appropriate).
- Fit the model to the sample data using the method of least squares.
- Assess the reliability of the model by calculating and interpreting the coefficient of determination.
- Check the model assumptions. If the model assumptions hold, then we can continue with inference on the regression parameters.

- Test whether the predictor variables are significant contributors to the regression by testing the hypothesis H_0: $\beta_2 = 0$ using a t-test.
- Construct prediction intervals for the values predicted from the linear model (optional).

12.4.11 Excel ToolPak Regression solution

We can do most of the previous calculations (though not all of them) automatically in Excel by using the Excel ToolPak. The ToolPak Regression solution provides a complete set of solutions, including:

- calculation of the equation of line
- calculation of measures of reliability
- tests for the significance of the predictor variables (t-tests).

We use Example 12.1 to illustrate the Regression ToolPak functionality in Excel. Follow these instructions to create the necessary output:

- First, type the dependent and independent variables into two columns of an Excel sheet.
- Select the 'Data' tab (see Figure 12.24).
- Click the 'Data Analysis' button (see Figure 12.24).
- Select 'Regression' from the list and click 'OK' (see Figure 12.24).
- In the 'Regression' window that appears, specify the range of Excel cells that contain the dependent variable's values (the Y-data) and the range of cells that contain the independent variable's values (the X-data) (see Figure 12.25).
- To generate the residual plots shown in Figure 12.20, check the 'Residual plots' box (see Figure 12.25) (optional).
- To generate the normal probability plots shown in Figure 12.19, check the 'Normal probability plots' box (see Figure 12.25) (optional).

	A	B	C
1	**Illustration of RegressionToolPak**		
2			
3–4	Employee number	Evaluation score (X)	% increase in productivity (Y)
5	1	47	4.2
6	2	71	8.1
7	3	64	6.8
8	4	35	4.3
9	5	43	5
10	6	60	7.5
11	7	38	4.7
12	8	59	5.9
13	9	67	6.9
14	10	56	5.7
15	11	67	5.7
16	12	57	5.4
17	13	69	7.5
18	14	38	3.8
19	15	54	5.9
20	16	76	6.3
21	17	53	5.7
22	18	40	4
23	19	47	5.2
24	20	23	2.2
25			

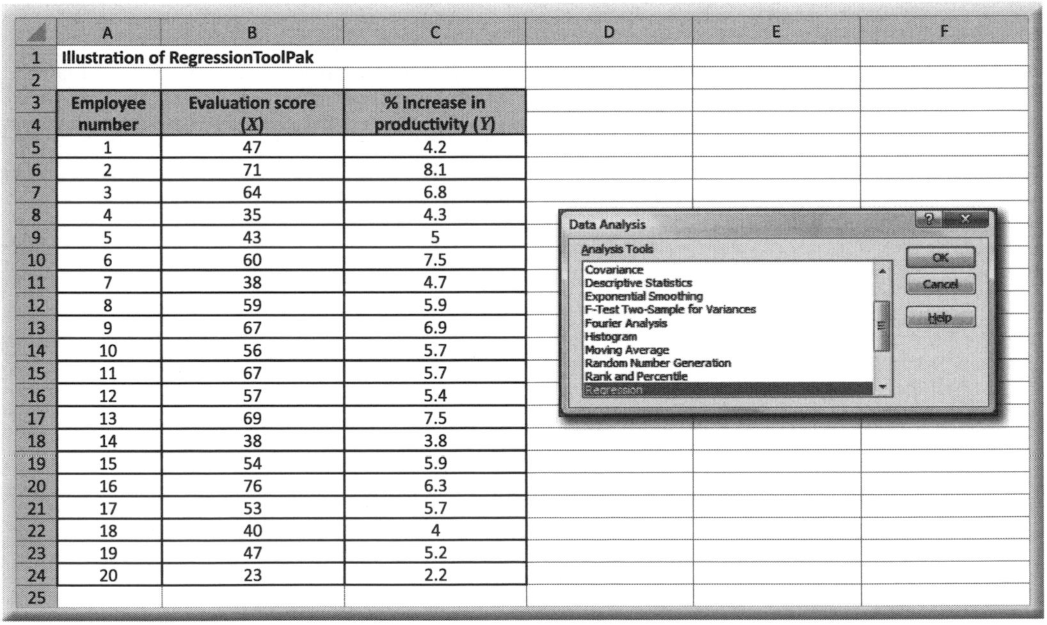

Figure 12.24: Data analysis: Regression ToolPak (a)

Regression

Input

Input Y Range: $C$5:$C$24

Input X Range: $B$5:$B$24

Labels

Constant is Zero

Confidence Level: 95 %

Output options

Output Range:

New Worksheet Ply:

New Workbook

Residuals

Residuals

Residual Plots

Standardized Residuals

Line Fit Plots

Normal Probability

Normal Probability Plots

OK

Cancel

Help

Figure 12.25: Data analysis: Regression ToolPak (b)

Figures 12.26 and 12.27 show the output for the regression analysis of the data in Example 12.1. We can find most of the analyses and calculations that were discussed in this chapter in this output.

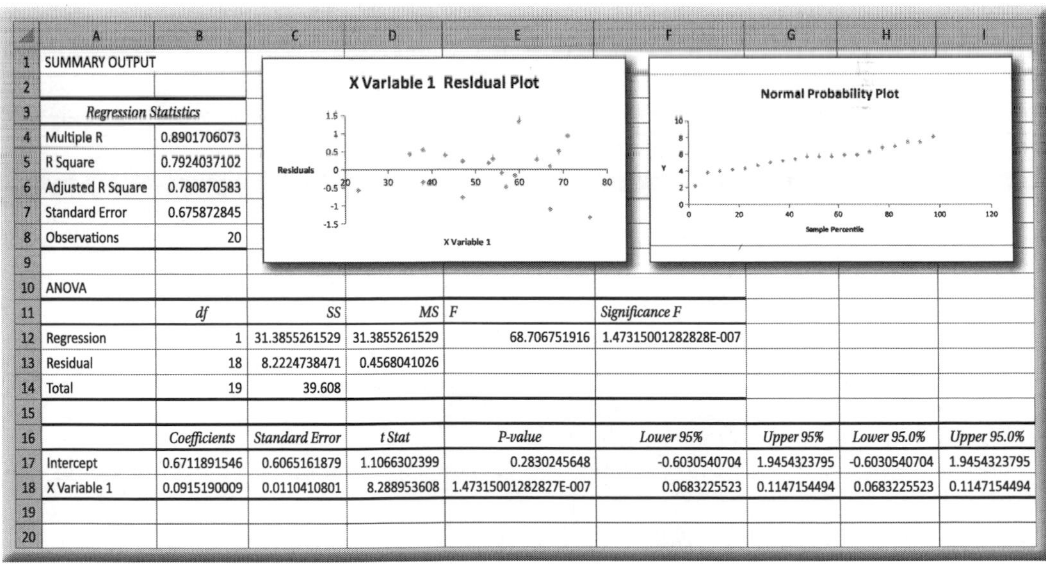

	A	B	C	D	E	F	G	H	I
1	SUMMARY OUTPUT								
2									
3	*Regression Statistics*								
4	Multiple R	0.8901706073							
5	R Square	0.7924037102							
6	Adjusted R Square	0.780870583							
7	Standard Error	0.675872845							
8	Observations	20							
9									
10	ANOVA								
11		*df*	*SS*	*MS*	F	*Significance F*			
12	Regression	1	31.3855261529	31.3855261529	68.706751916	1.47315001282828E-007			
13	Residual	18	8.2224738471	0.4568041026					
14	Total	19	39.608						
15									
16		*Coefficients*	*Standard Error*	*t Stat*	*P-value*	*Lower 95%*	*Upper 95%*	*Lower 95.0%*	*Upper 95.0%*
17	Intercept	0.6711891546	0.6065161879	1.1066302399	0.2830245648	-0.6030540704	1.9454323795	-0.6030540704	1.9454323795
18	X Variable 1	0.0915190009	0.0110410801	8.288953608	1.47315001282827E-007	0.0683225523	0.1147154494	0.0683225523	0.1147154494
19									
20									

Figure 12.26: Data analysis: Regression ToolPak (c)

22	RESIDUAL OUTPUT		
23			
24	*Observation*	*Predicted Y*	*Residuals*
25	1	4.972582195	-0.772582195
26	2	7.169038215	0.930961785
27	3	6.528405209	0.271594791
28	4	3.874354184	0.425645816
29	5	4.606506191	0.393493809
30	6	6.162329206	1.337670794
31	7	4.148911187	0.551088813
32	8	6.070810205	-0.170810205
33	9	6.802962212	0.097037788
34	10	5.796253202	-0.096253202
35	11	6.802962212	-1.102962212
36	12	5.887772203	-0.487772203
37	13	6.986000213	0.513999787
38	14	4.148911187	-0.348911187
39	15	5.613215201	0.286784799
40	16	7.626633219	-1.326633219
41	17	5.5216962	0.1783038
42	18	4.331949189	-0.331949189
43	19	4.972582195	0.227417805
44	20	2.776126174	-0.576126174

Figure 12.27: Data analysis: Regression ToolPak (d)

SUMMARY

In this chapter, we explored techniques that you can use to explore possible relationships between two variables using scatter plots and calculating a measure of correlation.

If the initial data exploration shows that we have a possible relationship between Y and X, we can attempt to fit an appropriate model to the data set using least squares regression.

Excel allows us to calculate the required statistics via its built-in statistical functions or by using the Data Analysis ToolPak tool, which includes the necessary statistics and appropriate assumption checking charts. The solution process consists of the following steps:

- Construct a scatter plot to visually assess the nature of a possible relationship between the variables.
- Fit a line to the data set using the identified relationship.
- Calculate the reliability statistics (R^2).
- Conduct appropriate t-tests to check whether the predictor variable is a significant contributor to the value of Y.
- Assess assumption violation checks.

KEY TERMS

Autocorrelation
Coefficient of determination (R^2)
Confidence interval
Covariance
Dependent variable
Equal variance
Explained variation
Homoscedasticity
Independence of errors
Independent variable
Intercept
Least squares
Linear relationship
Normality
Outliers
Pearson's correlation coefficient, r
Prediction interval for individual value
Regression analysis
Regression line
Residual
Scatter plot
Simple regression analysis
Slope
Sum of squares for error (SSE)
Sum of squares for regression (SSR)
Total sum of squares (SST)
Total variation
Unexplained variation

FORMULA SUMMARY

$$r = \frac{S_{XY}}{S_X S_Y} \tag{12.1}$$

$$S_X = \sqrt{\frac{1}{n-1}\left[\sum_{i=1}^{n} X_i^2 - n(\overline{X})^2\right]} \quad \text{and} \quad S_Y = \sqrt{\frac{1}{n-1}\left[\sum_{i=1}^{n} Y_i^2 - n(\overline{Y})^2\right]} \tag{12.2}$$

$$S_{XY} = \frac{1}{n-1}\left[\sum_{i=1}^{n} X_i Y_i - \frac{1}{n}\sum_{i=1}^{n} X_i \sum_{i=1}^{n} Y_i\right] \tag{12.3}$$

$$r = \frac{\sum_{i=1}^{n} X_i Y_i - \frac{1}{n}\sum_{i=1}^{n} X_i \sum_{i=1}^{n} Y_i}{\sqrt{\left[\sum_{i=1}^{n} X_i^2 - n(\overline{X})^2\right]\left[\sum_{i=1}^{n} Y_i^2 - n(\overline{Y})^2\right]}} \tag{12.4}$$

$$T = \frac{r - \rho_0}{\sqrt{\frac{1-r^2}{n-2}}} \tag{12.5}$$

$$Y_i = \beta_0 + \beta_1 X_i + \text{error} \tag{12.6}$$

$$\hat{Y}_i = b_0 + b_1 X_i \tag{12.7}$$

$$b_1 = \frac{\sum_{i=1}^{n} X_i Y_i - \frac{1}{n}\sum_{i=1}^{n} X_i \sum_{i=1}^{n} Y_i}{\sum_{i=1}^{n} X_i^2 - \frac{1}{n}\left(\sum_{i=1}^{n} X_i\right)^2} \tag{12.8}$$

$$b_0 = \frac{1}{n}\sum_{i=1}^{n} Y_i - \frac{b_1}{n}\sum_{i=1}^{n} X_i \tag{12.9}$$

$$i^{\text{th}} \text{ residual} = e_i = Y_i - \hat{Y}_i \tag{12.10}$$

$$SSR = \sum_{i=1}^{n}(\hat{Y}_i - \overline{Y})^2 \tag{12.11}$$

$$SSE = \sum_{i=1}^{n}(Y_i - \hat{Y})^2 \tag{12.12}$$

$$MSE = \frac{SSE}{n-2} \tag{12.13}$$

$$SST = \sum_{i=1}^{n}(Y_i - \overline{Y})^2 \tag{12.14}$$

$$SST = SSR + SSE \tag{12.15}$$

$$R^2 = \frac{SSR}{SST} = \frac{\sum_{i=1}^{n}\left(\hat{Y}_i - \overline{Y}\right)^2}{\sum_{i=1}^{n}\left(Y_i - \overline{Y}\right)^2} \tag{12.16}$$

$$R^2 = \frac{SST - SSE}{SST} = 1 - \frac{SSE}{SST} = 1 - \frac{\sum_{i=1}^{n}\left(Y_i - \hat{Y}_i\right)^2}{\sum_{i=1}^{n}\left(Y_i - \overline{Y}_i\right)^2} \tag{12.17}$$

$$R^2 = (\text{correlation coefficient})^2 = r^2 \tag{12.18}$$

$$T = \frac{b_1}{S_{b_1}} \overset{H_0}{\sim} t_{n-2} \tag{12.19}$$

$$S_{b_1} = \sqrt{\frac{MSE}{\sum_{i=1}^{n} X_i^2 - \frac{1}{n}\left(\sum_{i=1}^{n} X_i\right)^2}} \tag{12.20}$$

$$\hat{Y}_p - \Delta < Y_p < \hat{Y}_p + \Delta \tag{12.21}$$

$$\Delta = t_{n-2,\alpha/2} \times \sqrt{MSE\left[1 + \frac{1}{n} + \frac{(X_p - \overline{X})^2}{\sum_{i=1}^{n} X_i^2 - \frac{1}{n}\left(\sum_{i=1}^{n} X_i\right)^2}\right]} \tag{12.22}$$

EXERCISES

12.1 Construct a scatter plot for the following data and calculate Pearson's correlation coefficient, r. Comment of the strength of the correlation between X and Y.

Table 12.4: Data for 12.1

X	40	41	40	42	40	40	42	41	41	42
Y	32	43	28	45	31	34	48	42	36	38

12.2 Display the following data in an appropriate form and state how the variables are correlated.

Table 12.5: Data for 12.2

X	0	15	30	45	60	75	90	105	120
Y	806	630	643	625	575	592	408	469	376

12.3 Table 12.6 shows the number of vehicles and number of road deaths in 10 countries.

Table 12.6: Data for 12.3

COUNTRIES	VEHICLES PER 100 POPULATION	ROAD DEATHS PER 100 000 POPULATION
Great Britain	31	14
Belgium	32	30
Denmark	30	23
France	46	32
Germany	30	26
Ireland	19	20
Italy	35	21
Netherlands	40	23
Canada	46	30
USA	57	35

a) Construct a scatter plot and comment on the possible relationship between the two variables.
b) Calculate the product moment correlation coefficient between vehicle numbers and road deaths.
c) Use your answers to (a) and (b) to comment on your results.

12.4 The Mathematics and Statistics examination marks for a group of 10 students are shown in Table 12.7.

Table 12.7: Data for 12.4

MATHEMATICS	89	73	57	53	51	49	47	44	42	38
STATISTICS	51	53	49	50	48	21	46	19	43	43

a) Construct the scatter plot for these data.
b) Find the product moment correlation coefficient for the two sets of marks.
c) Using your answers to (a) and (b), comment on the relationship between these two variables.

12.5 In the regression equation for $\hat{y} = b_0 + b_1x$, which equation gives the value of b_0?

A $b_0 = \dfrac{\Sigma Y - b_1^2 \Sigma X}{n}$

B $b_0 = \dfrac{\Sigma Y - b_1 \Sigma X}{2n}$

C $b_0 = \dfrac{\Sigma Y - b_1 \Sigma X}{n}$

D $b_0 = \dfrac{\Sigma Y - n \Sigma X}{n}$

12.6 In the regression equation for $\hat{y} = b_0 + b_1x$, which equation gives the value of b_1?

A $b_1 = \dfrac{n\Sigma XY^2 - \Sigma X \Sigma Y}{n\Sigma X - (\Sigma X)^2}$

B $b_1 = \dfrac{n\Sigma XY - \Sigma X \Sigma Y}{n\Sigma X^2 - (\Sigma X)^2}$

C $b_1 = \dfrac{n\Sigma XY - \Sigma X \Sigma Y}{n\Sigma X - (\Sigma X)^2}$

D $b_1 = \dfrac{n\Sigma XY - \Sigma X \Sigma Y}{n\Sigma X^2 - (\Sigma X)^2}$

Use the ANOVA table to answer Questions 12.7 and 12.8.

Table 12.8: ANOVA table for 12.7 and 12.8

ANOVA	*df*	*SS*	*MS*	*F*	SIGNIFICANCE (*F*)
REGRESSION	1	37612	37612	164	<0.00001
RESIDUAL	41	9403	229.34		
TOTAL	42	47015			

12.7 Which of the following is the coefficient of determination, R^2?
A 0.78
B 1.80
C 0.80
D 1.80

12.8 What is the value of Pearson's correlation coefficient, r?
A 0.99
B 1.89
C 0.11
D 0.89

12.9 In 2007, a local market research company ascertained the amount spent on advertising and the corresponding sales revenue by seven marketing clients. The results are shown in Table 12.9.

Table 12.9: Sales and advertising data

ADVERTISING (R1 000S), X	SALES (R1 000S), Y
2	60
5	100
4	70
6	90
3	80
7	105
8	115

a) Plot a scatter plot and comment on a possible relationship between the advertising and sales amounts.
b) Use Excel regression functions to do the following tasks.
   i) Fit a simple linear regression model.
   ii) Check the model reliability (r and R^2).
   iii) Conduct appropriate inference tests (t- and F-tests).
   iv) Check model assumptions (residual and normality checks).
   v) Provide a 95% confidence interval for the predicted sales when the advertising expense is R6 500.

12.10 Fit an appropriate equation to the data set to predict the examination mark when given the assignment mark for 14 undergraduate students.

Table 12.10: Students' marks data for 12.10

ASSIGNMENT	69	42	43	40	100	80	100	90	77	47	68	50	45	41
EXAMINATION	77	66	65	65	80	71	78	75	70	60	67	61	59	58

a) Plot a scatter plot and comment on a possible relationship between the examination and assignment marks.
b) Use Excel regression functions to do the following tasks.
   i) Fit a simple linear regression model.
   ii) Check the model reliability (r and R^2).
   iii) Conduct appropriate inference tests (t- and F-tests).
   iv) Check the model assumptions (residual and normality checks).
   v) Provide a 95% confidence interval for the predicted examination mark when the assignment mark is 75.

TECHNIQUES IN PRACTICE

12.11 Bakers Ltd is concerned about the possible relationship between the amount of fat (grams) and the number of calories in a popular pie.

Table 12.11: Data for 12.11

PIE ID	AMOUNT OF FAT (g)	CALORIES	PIE ID	AMOUNT OF FAT (g)	CALORIES
1	19	410	16	33	597
2	31	580	17	31	583
3	34	590	18	37	589
4	35	570	19	39	640
5	39	640	20	23	456
6	39	680	21	43	660
7	43	660	22	22	448
8	22	465	23	30	577
9	28	567	24	34	594
10	38	610	25	35	590
11	35	576	26	41	638
12	22	434	27	34	560
13	40	690	28	43	660
14	43	660	29	45	680
15	21	435	30	29	587

a) Plot a scatter plot and comment on a possible relationship between calories and the amount of fat in the pies.

b) Use Excel Analysis ToolPak to undertake the following tasks.
   i) State the least squares regression model equation.
   ii) Comment on model reliability (r and R^2).
   iii) Is the independent variable significant (t- or F-test)?
   iv) Check the model assumptions (residual and normality checks).

12.12 Home-Made Beers Ltd employs a local transport company to deliver beers to local supermarkets. To develop better work schedules, the managers want to estimate the total daily travel time for their drivers' journeys. Initially, the managers believed that the total daily travel time would be closely related to the number of kilometres travelled in making the daily deliveries.

Table 12.12: Data for 12.12

JOURNEY	DISTANCE TRAVELLED (km), X	TRAVEL TIME (HOURS), y
1	100	9.3
2	50	4.8
3	100	8.9
4	100	6.5
5	50	4.2
6	80	6.2
7	75	7.4
8	65	6
9	90	7.6
10	90	6.1

JOURNEY	DISTANCE TRAVELLED (km), X	TRAVEL TIME (HOURS), y
11	85	7.4
12	62	6.4
13	98	8.4
14	58	4.9
15	73	6.8
16	81	7.8
17	66	6.2
18	72	7.3
19	53	4.4
20	56	4.6

a) Plot a scatter plot and comment on a possible relationship between travel time and distance travelled.

b) Use Excel Analysis ToolPak to do the following tasks.
   i) State the least squares regression model equation.
   ii) Comment on the model reliability (r and R^2).
   iii) Is the independent variable significant (F- or t- test)?
   iv) Check the model assumptions (residual and normality checks).

CHAPTER 13

TIME SERIES DATA AND ANALYSIS

CHAPTER CONTENTS

OVERVIEW

The aim of this chapter is to provide you with a set of tools that you can use to analyse data that has been collected over a period of time (time series analysis). One of the major uses of this type of analysis is to *attempt* to extrapolate the values into the future (forecast future values) by using these analyses and various other techniques.

This chapter allows you to apply a range of time series tools to tackle a number of problems related to this type of data (which occurs regularly in the fields of business, economics, social sciences, and so on).

The tools and concepts that will be discussed include:

- the graphical representations of time series data
- the identification of various components within time series data
- fitting simple models to the time series data
- extrapolating (forecasting) these models into the future
- interpreting these forecasts and their forecast errors
- calculating smoothed versions of the series
- measures to assess forecasting errors.

LEARNING OBJECTIVES

On completing this chapter, you will be able to:

- understand the time series fundamentals
- inspect and prepare data for forecasting
- graph the data and visually identify patterns
- fit an appropriate (simple) time series model
- understand the concept of smoothing
- handle seasonal time series
- use the identified model to provide an extrapolation (i.e. forecast)
- calculate a measure of error for the model fit to the data set
- solve time series related problems using Microsoft Excel.

13.1 Time series data and graphical representation

13.1.1 The definition of time series data

Time series data are somewhat different from the majority of data sets we have covered so far. In fact, the only data that we have encountered so far that is in any way similar to time series data are the data sets that contained two variables (the chapter on linear regression). Those data sets contained two variables, and we were interested in analysing the relationships between them. Time series data are similar, in the sense that we also have two variables to consider: the date/time of an observation and the observation's value. These two types of data are so similar that some of the analyses we apply to linear regression data are also used on time series data (to a limited extent).

A good example of time series data is the price of gold (or any price of commodity or stock). We can record the price of gold once every day, or determine the average price once a month, or even once a year. Each of these three methods results in a time series data set. In other words, it does not matter what units of time we use, as long as the observations are:

- *equally* and *consistently spaced in time* i.e. the time between each observation should remain the same for all observations, for example, we should not have a situation in which most observations are measured daily and some are measured every three days
- *sequential* i.e. we cannot shuffle the order of data points, skip observations or have empty values for particular moments in time.

Time series A variable measured and represented per units of time.

Forecasting A method of predicting the future values of a variable, usually represented as the time series values.

If these conditions hold then we have time series data.

Time series data A time series data set is one that contains a variable that is measured and recorded *consistently* at *sequential, equally spaced* units of time.

As noted above, time series data are collected over equally spaced periods of time. This includes, but is not limited to, collecting data:

- hourly
- daily
- weekly
- fortnightly (i.e. every second week)
- monthly
- quarterly (i.e. every three months)
- seasonally (which is very similar to collecting quarterly, but the beginning and ending dates are fixed according to the seasons)
- annually
- every decade.

The regularity of measurement will have an impact on the type of analyses that we can conduct on the data. For example, data collected annually or every decade will skip the seasonal fluctuations that occur *within* a year, and so attempting to analyse the seasonal behaviour of the observations in these types of data would be fruitless.

WHAT IS THE PURPOSE OF TIME SERIES ANALYSIS?

The primary functions of the majority of time series analysis methods are to:

- *predict* the future movements of the series
- *describe* the behaviour of the variable in the time series data set.

These two methods are interlinked, in the sense that we cannot produce a decent forecast of the series if the model that we are using does not accurately describe the data. Throughout this chapter, we will see various models that can be used to describe the behaviour of the data and, if the model is found to be accurate, we can then extend them to forecast the future behaviour of the series.

The methods for modelling the data and producing **forecasts** that we discuss in this chapter include:

- using a graph to visually forecast values (the eyeballing method)
- using a **classical approach to time series analysis** to forecast values
- using a **moving average** approach to forecast values
- using an **exponential smoothing** approach to forecast values.

The methods for forecasting, while quite different from one another, all fall within the broader category of time series analysis methods, and we describe them in greater detail in the next few sections.

13.1.2 Representing time series graphically

The first step in most time series analyses is to visualise the time series data so that we can use the appropriate analysis. Graphical representations of time series are very similar to the scatter plots discussed in Chapter 12, except that the points in the scatter plot are now connected with straight lines to signify their sequential nature.

Time series plot A time series plot is a scatter plot of the time series data observation's values against the time at which they occurred. The points are connected by straight lines to indicate that they follow one another (they are sequential).

By visualising a data set graphically, we can classify the series according to certain aspects of the time series, such as whether it is *stationary* or whether it is *seasonal* in nature.

- *Stationarity*: When a time series is **stationary**, the distribution of the observations remains the same for all time units. This means that the expected value (mean) and variance do not change as time progresses. Typical stationary time series plots appear to fluctuate evenly around an overall mean value as shown in Figure 13.1(a).
- *Non-stationarity*: When a time series is **non-stationary**, the mean and variance may change over time. This change can manifest in a number of different ways, one of which is shown in Figure 13.1(b) (here we see that just the mean increases over time).
- *Seasonality*: If time series data are said to be **seasonal**, it implies that the general behaviour of the series within a specific period or interval repeats regularly. We can usually identify when there are seasonal trends in a data set by identifying regularly repeating patterns in the graphs. Figure 13.1(c) illustrates a 12-period seasonal pattern (note that the variance also seems to be increasing over time in this figure – this would indicate that it is both seasonal *and* non-stationary).

Non-stationary time series A time series that does not have a constant mean and/or variance, and oscillates around this moving mean.

Stationary time series A time series that has a constant mean and variance, and oscillates around this mean.

Seasonal time series A time series, represented in the units of time smaller than one year, that shows a regular pattern in repeating itself over a number of these units of time.

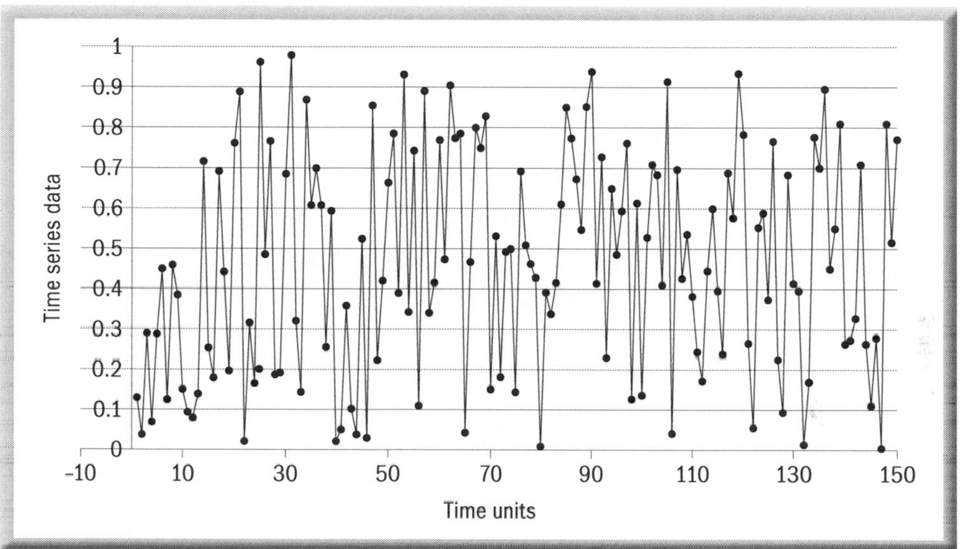

Figure 13.1(a): An illustration of a stationary time series

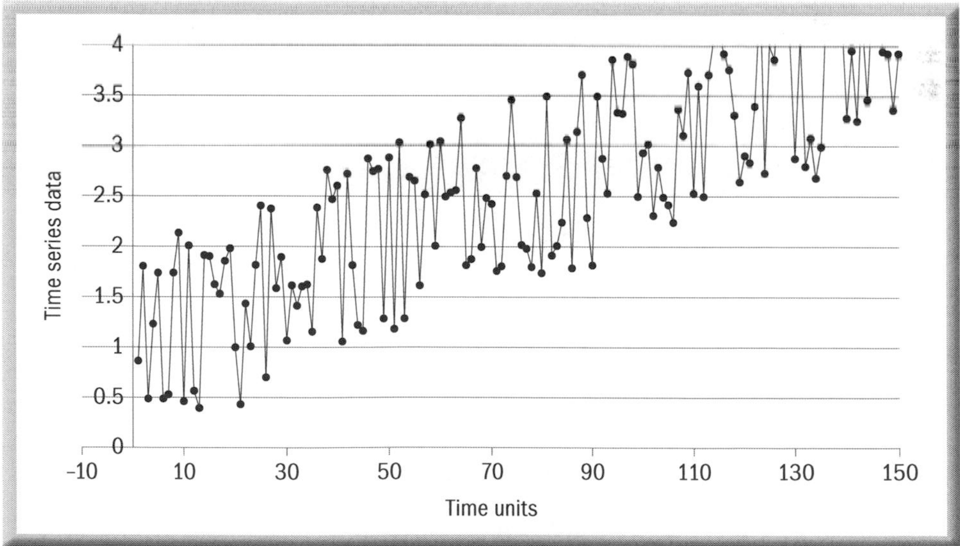

Figure 13.1(b): An illustration of a time series that is non-stationary in the mean

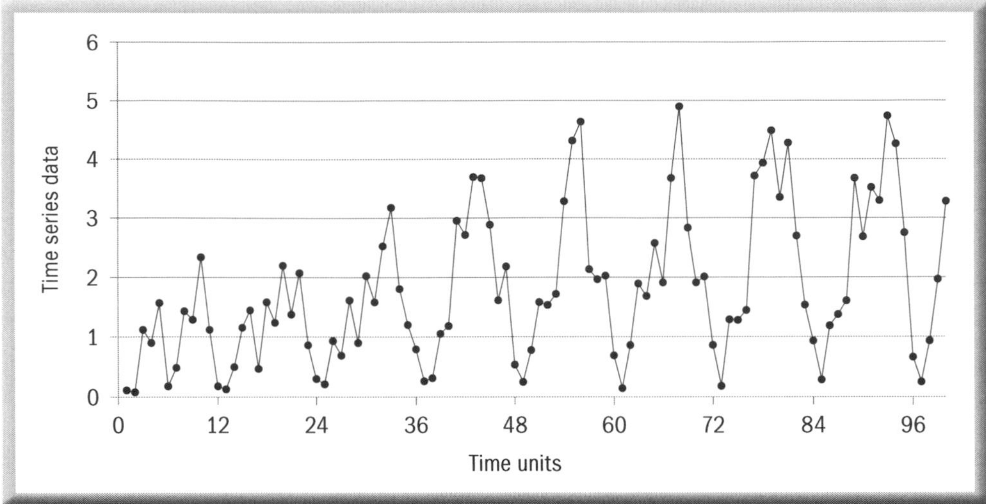

Figure 13.1(c): An illustration of a seasonal time series

Classifying a time series data set as being stationary, non-stationary, seasonal or non-seasonal will help to identify the type of analysis that we can potentially conduct on the data. For example, certain analyses are only suitable for stationary, seasonal data, but are not applicable when applied to non-stationary, seasonal data.

NOTE

Visualising and charting a time series is not an optional extra, but one of the most essential steps in time series analysis. We can learn a lot about a variable by just looking at the time series graph.

FORECASTING BY EYEBALLING

We can also use time series plots to intuitively forecast values into the future. For example, if we look at Figure 13.1(b), it is fairly clear where the series is headed in the future (we can see that since it is increasing, it is likely that future values will continue with the same trend).

Using these graphs, we can produce good *guesses* as to where the series will head in the future by simply eyeballing the series and extrapolating the future behaviour in our heads. This is an excellent informal, intuitive, quick and easy method of forecasting, but it is also *extremely* subjective and highly unscientific.

We should rather forecast with the models that we will discuss later in this chapter, in all but the most informal situations.

13.1.3 Creating a time series plot in Excel

To create a time series plot in Excel, we simply need to use Excel's 'scatter' functionality. Example 13.1 illustrates how this is done.

WORKED EXAMPLES

EXAMPLE 13.1

The following data represents the weekly profits of a businessman running a small fruit stand next to a busy road over the course of 15 weeks.

Table 13.1: Profits over a 15-week period

WEEK	PROFIT (R)	WEEK	PROFIT (R)	WEEK	PROFIT (R)
1	1 504.80	6	1 975.70	11	1 839.00
2	2 334.20	7	2 403.90	12	2 739.90
3	3 292.90	8	2 310.80	13	1 120.30
4	2 292.70	9	2 108.40	14	2 983.70
5	1 911.40	10	3 082.50	15	4 008.00

Construct the time series plot for this time series data in Excel.

In order to create the time series plot, we need to type the data into the Excel spreadsheet. In Figure 13.2, the data has been typed into columns A and B. The time units (week) appear in cells A2:A16 and the observed values (profit) appear in cells B2:B16. The steps to create a time series plot are then as follows:

- Click on the 'Insert' ribbon.
- Press the 'Scatter' button in the 'Charts' group. This will bring down some choices for the type of scatter plots we may want to create (as shown in Figure 13.2).
- For the purposes of a time series plot, we choose the 'Scatter with Straight Lines and Markers' option.

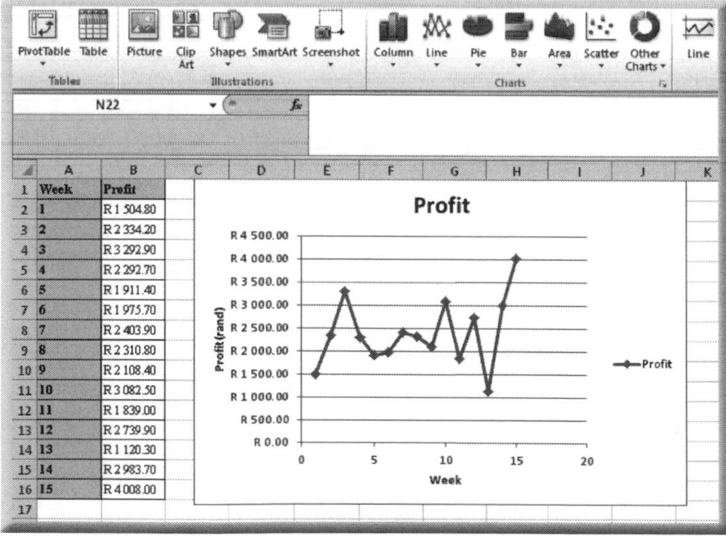

Figure 13.2: Creating a time series plot in Excel

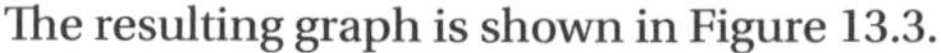

The resulting graph is shown in Figure 13.3.

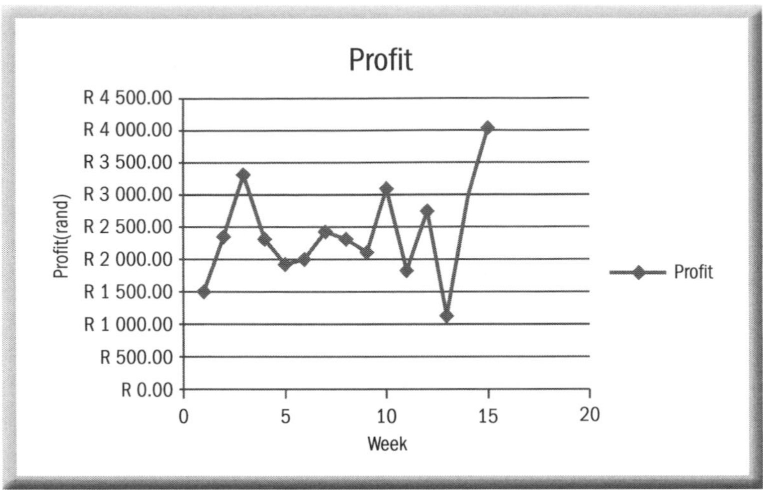

Figure 13.3: The time series plot of the time series data in Example 13.1

13.1.4 Pitfalls associated with representing time series data

We have already emphasised that when dealing with time series, it is very important to chart the data and visually inspect the data set. However, Figure 13.4 provides an example of how it is possible to graphically represent the time series data, but come to faulty conclusions.

In Figure 13.4(a), the data are plotted with a vertical axis that varies from 150 to 400 and, in this case, it appears as if the data tends to remain fairly constant around a mean that appears to be trending downwards ever so slightly. It seems reasonable to model this time series with a straight line (as shown).

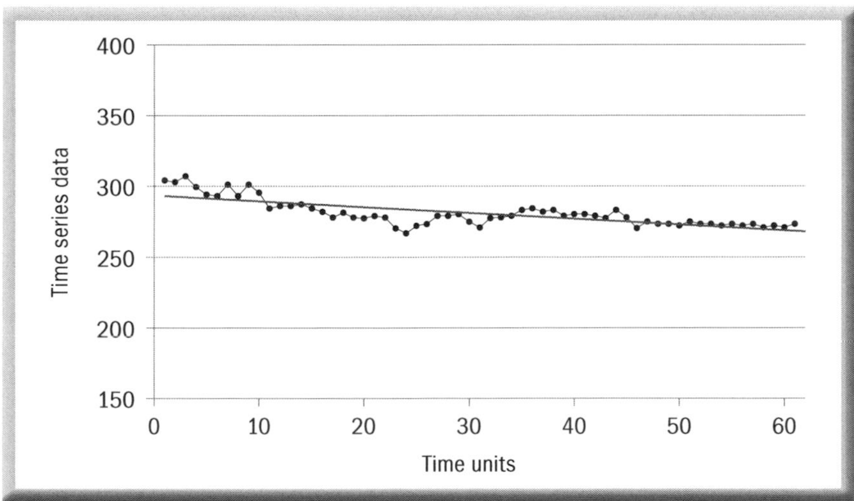

Figure 13.4(a): The time series plotted on a wide vertical axis scale (with a linear trend indicated)

In Figure 13.4(b), the same data are plotted, but now the vertical axis varies from 265 to 310. Here, the time series appears to show a much more drastic dip downwards and the mild nature of the variation around the mean seems to be much more erratic than first suspected. In these data, the straight-line model suddenly seems less reasonable and a power curve type model might work better (the linear model is shown with a solid line and the power curve model is shown with a dotted line in the figure).

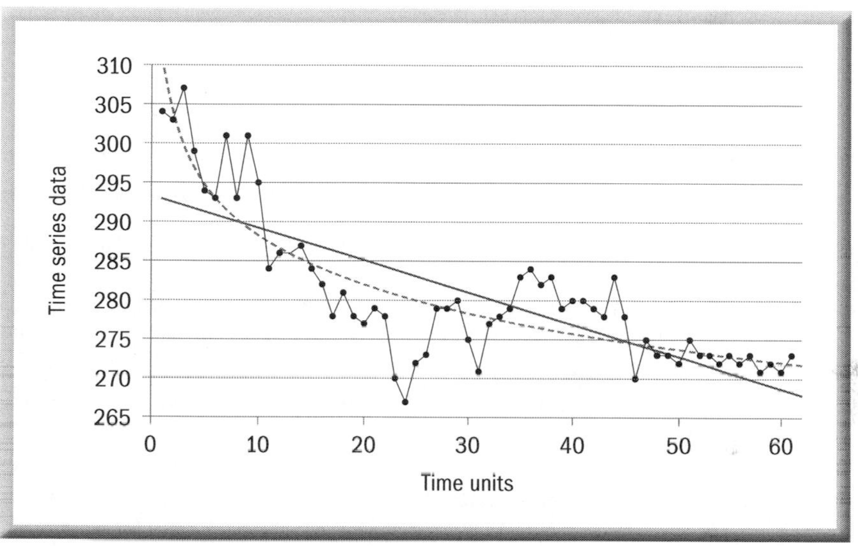

Figure 13.4(b): The same time series represented on a more focused vertical scale (a linear and power trend is shown on the plot

The above two time series are the same time series; we have simply changed the scale of the vertical axis. Clearly, depending on the *scale*, we can see almost two different time series.

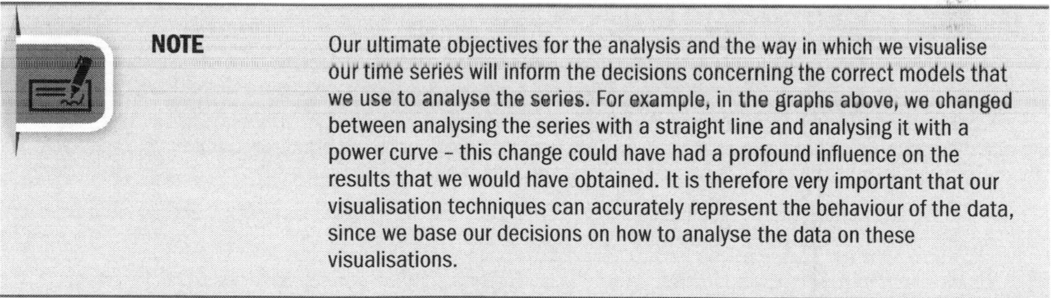

NOTE

Our ultimate objectives for the analysis and the way in which we visualise our time series will inform the decisions concerning the correct models that we use to analyse the series. For example, in the graphs above, we changed between analysing the series with a straight line and analysing it with a power curve – this change could have had a profound influence on the results that we would have obtained. It is therefore very important that our visualisation techniques can accurately represent the behaviour of the data, since we base our decisions on how to analyse the data on these visualisations.

The next instance is also very illustrative. We use the daily closing value of one of the companies quoted on the New York Exchange. The company is Emerson Electric (ticker EMR) and the daily closing values go from 5 Jan 1982 to 3 July 2008. The time series is 6 700 observations long.

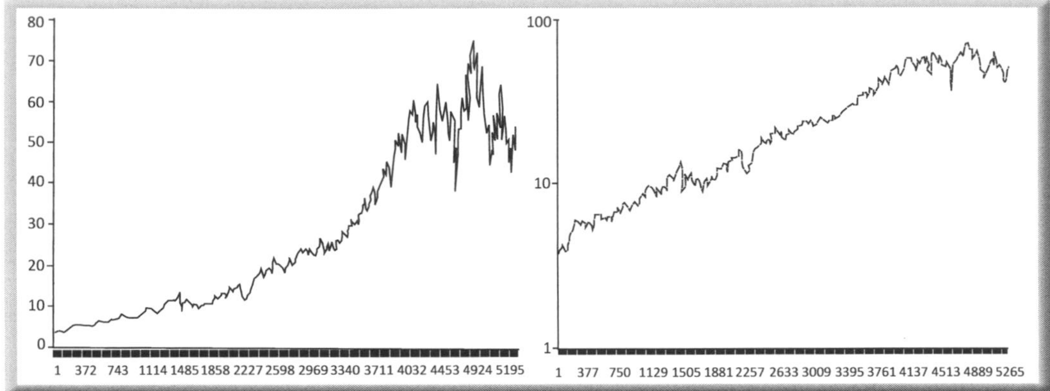

Figure 13.5: The same time series, one with original scale(left) and the other with a log scale (right)

Again, two different charts display the same data set. The first one (on the left) is a normal time series plot, indicating that the closing daily stock values have grown almost exponentially with the exception of one part when the growth slowed down. The second graph shows the same data on a logarithmic scale, indicating a linear, steady growth of the closing stock values. The slowdown now looks less dramatic.

As we can see, visualisation is very important, as is the transformation of the data, if necessary. **Transformations** can take various forms, such as taking the *log* of the values, calculating differences from the mean value of the series, simple differencing, and so on. Unfortunately, most of these techniques are not described in this textbook. It is enough to know that transformations help us to bring the data in shape so that we can then apply a particular forecasting method.

Transformations A method of changing the time series, usually to make it stationary. The most common method for transforming a time series is differencing or sometimes taking differences of every observation from the mean value.

A WORD ABOUT DIFFERENCING

Certain analyses that we discuss only apply to *stationary* time series data. However, what happens if we want to apply these techniques when the series is stubbornly *non-stationary?*

One possible solution to this problem is to transform the series so that it is becomes stationary – in particular we can use a method called **differencing**.

The principle of differencing is to subtract the previous value of a series from the current value: If Y_t represents the original (non-stationary) time series value at time t, then the differenced value at time t (denoted by d_t) is:

$$d_t = Y_t - Y_{t-1}$$

The result is that the series d_t might be stationary. If the first differences do not convert the original non-stationary series into a stationary one (because the original time series is too dynamic), then the second differences are calculated. Second differences are differences of the differences. Table 13.2 displays a brief example of a time series differenced twice.

Table 13.2: The calculations of difference of a data set

Y_1	Y_{t-1}	FIRST DIFFERENCE $d_t = Y_t - Y_{t-1}$	SECOND DIFFERENCE $d_t - d_{t-1}$
2	–	–	–
3	2	3 – 2 = 1	–
7	3	7 – 3 = 4	4 – 1 = 3
6	7	6 – 7 = –1	–1 – 4 = –5
9	6	9 – 6 = 3	3 – (–1) = 4

Differencing A method of transforming a time series, usually to achieve stationarity. Differencing involves subtracting the previous value from the current value.

13.2 The components of classical time series analysis

Earlier, we classified time series data into various types (such as stationary, non-stationary, seasonal, and so on), but we also mentioned that we can use various methods to deal with time series data and that these methods are only appropriate for certain types of data. In this chapter, we describe a few (very) basic time series analysis methods that we can employ to enable us to forecast future values. As mentioned earlier, the methods we discuss include classical time series analysis (multiplicative models) and time series smoothing and forecasting, using both moving averages and exponential smoothing. In this section, we discuss the basics of the classical time series analysis method.

Classical time series analysis starts by assuming that every time series can be decomposed into four elementary components:

- Underlying **trend** (T)
- **Cyclical** variations (C)
- **Seasonal** variations (S)
- **Irregular** variations (I)

Depending on the model, we can put these components together in different ways to represent the time series. The model that we discuss is the **multiplicative model**. It states that any time series, Y, consists of the product of the four components listed above:

$$Y = T \times C \times S \times I \tag{13.1}$$

Classical time series analysis An approach to forecasting that decomposes a time series into certain constituent components (trend, cyclical, season and random component), makes estimates of each component, and then recomposes the time series and extrapolates into the future.

Trend component A component in the classical time series analysis approach to forecasting that covers underlying directional movements of the time series.

Cyclic variation A source of variation in the classical time series approach that is characterised by long-term variations around the trend that happen irregularly and over long periods of time.

Seasonal variation A component in the classical time series analysis approach that describes the fluctuation in a time series data set that occurs regularly, predictably and over short periods of time (typically a full season will occur within one year)

Irregular component A component in the classical time series analysis approach to forecasting that is uncovered by other components. It has to be random in shape.

Classical time series multiplicative model One of the models in classical time series analysis that assumes that components (trend, cyclical, seasonal and random components) need to be multiplied to compose the time series.

Classical time series mixed model One of the models in classical time series analysis that assumes that components (trend, cyclical, seasonal and random components) need to be added and/or multiplied to compose the time series.

NOTE

In addition to a multiplicative model, we can also use an *additive model*. Sometimes the most appropriate model is a *mixed* one. Here are two examples of these models.

Additive model: $Y = T + C + S + I$

Mixed model: $Y = (T \times C \times S) + I$

The choice of which model to use is beyond the scope of this text and so we only use the multiplicative model.

Each one of the four elementary components of the multiplicative model in formula (13.1) represents a different aspect of the time series that can be extracted from the original data and analysed separately. We will see in later sections that these extracted components will also be helpful in forecasting values.

We now discuss each component separately and we show (via various illustrative graphs) how the components build up on one another to form the complete time series. To facilitate this discussion, we use the time series data given in Example 13.2.

WORKED EXAMPLES

EXAMPLE 13.2

The quarterly sales figures (recorded in R1 000 units and denoted Y) of a second-hand car dealership, recorded from the first quarter of 2001 to the first quarter of 2013 are shown in Table 13.3.

Table 13.3: Quarterly sales figures

TIME	Y	TIME	Y	TIME	Y	TIME	Y
Q1-2001	250.0396	Q3-2004	486.5222	Q1-2008	311.1388	Q3-2011	393.655
Q2-2001	311.0691	Q4-2004	341.2939	Q2-2008	471.4277	Q4-2011	437.5348
Q3-2001	381.4152	Q1-2005	323.5638	Q3-2008	527.6679	Q1-2012	301.8806
Q4-2001	387.5756	Q2-2005	418.8316	Q4-2008	427.5005	Q2-2012	403.3041
Q1-2002	337.1123	Q3-2005	351.6573	Q1-2009	286.9777	Q3-2012	384.6918
Q2-2002	369.1351	Q4-2005	461.8356	Q2-2009	329.9153	Q4-2012	425.4169
Q3-2002	420.6131	Q1-2006	262.731	Q3-2009	427.8808	Q1-2013	412.514
Q4-2002	538.6186	Q2-2006	340.2487	Q4-2009	533.7004		
Q1-2003	418.3629	Q3-2006	495.8597	Q1-2010	269.4391		
Q2-2003	412.9883	Q4-2006	510.625	Q2-2010	317.6561		
Q3-2003	546.9666	Q1-2007	389.8658	Q3-2010	448.3406		
Q4-2003	485.5747	Q2-2007	315.5394	Q4-2010	399.9968		
Q1-2004	415.3639	Q3-2007	379.2257	Q1-2011	285.5975		
Q2-2004	298.4588	Q4-2007	480.2029	Q2-2011	378.2659		

We will show how this series is decomposed into the four movement components of the classical time series model.

The resulting time series plot of the data in Example 13.2 is given in Figure 13.6.

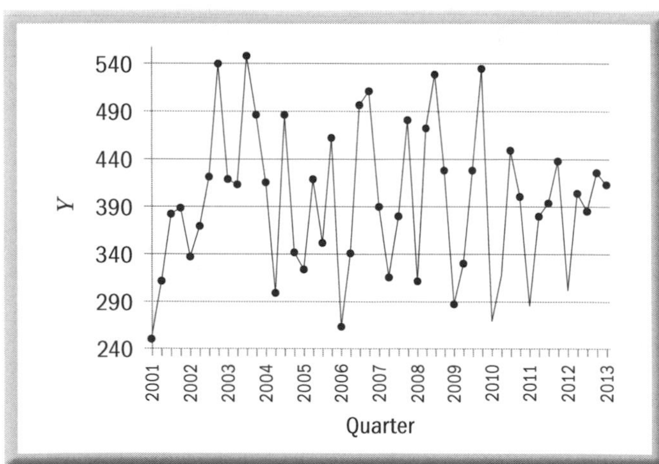

Figure 13.6: The time series plot of the time series data in Example 13.2

We now decompose these data into the trend, cyclic, seasonal and irregular variation components; each of which we will display graphically.

The trend component (T)

We have already mentioned that we can divide time series models into stationary and non-stationary time series data sets, and that non-stationarity implies that the distribution of the time series changes over time. One of the more common manifestations of this is when the series tends to move upwards or downwards over time. This overall movement, or trend, is the most basic component of a time series and is usually described by a simple straight line or curve. The trend is thus the most basic component of the time series and we use it to describe the overall movement of the series.

Figure 13.7 displays the trend (T) of the data in Example 13.2. We see here that the general long-term behaviour of the time series observations is to gradually increase over time.

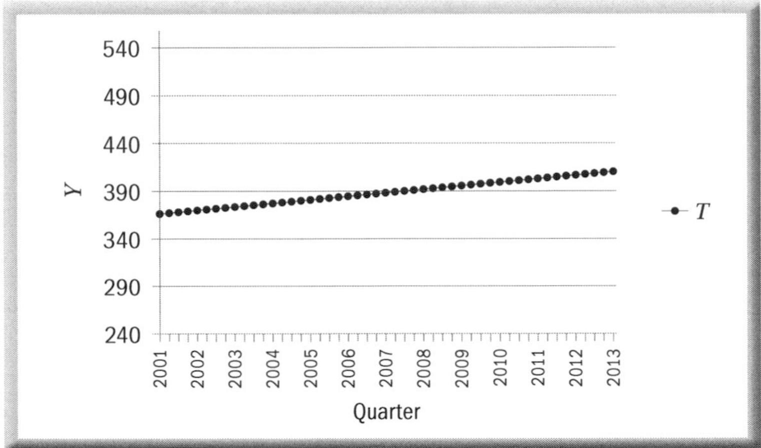

Figure 13.7: The trend or long-term behaviour (T) extracted from the time series data in Example 13.2

Section 13.3 contains a discussion on how we can extract this long-term trend from the data using the least squares method described in Chapter 12.

The cyclic variation (C)

The **cyclical component** is characterised by long-term variations around the trend that happen irregularly over fairly long periods of time (we contrast this with the seasonal component shortly). In fact, if the time series has not been recorded for a sufficient number of time units, it is possible to mistake this component for the trend.

In general, we say that a full cycle completes when the series goes up, then down and finally returns to its original position. In this long-term context, a cycle can take a number of years or even decades to complete, but the length of time taken to complete any single cycle is not fixed; typically varying in length for each full cycle (for example, the first full cycle can take seven years to complete, the second one can take two years, the next one can take 15 years, and so on).

Figure 13.8 displays the extracted cyclic component present in the data from Example 13.2, expressed as percentage deviations from the long term trend. The percentages are interpreted as indices, i.e. at the beginning of 2001, we see that the cycle starts at roughly 86% of the overall trend value, and by 2002, the cycle lies at roughly 100% of the overall trend. In Figure 13.9, these cyclical indices are combined with the overall trend to form *TC* (the trend, *T*, and cyclic, *C*, components are multiplied), and we see how the cyclic component oscillates *around* the overall trend.

This type of cycle is common in many types of business data and represents periods of *recession, depression, recovery* and *prosperity*. In this example, there are roughly three full cycles, and the amount of time it takes for one full cycle to complete is not fixed – it changes from one cycle to the next (the period of the cycle is not necessarily fixed). These cycles can take many years to complete.

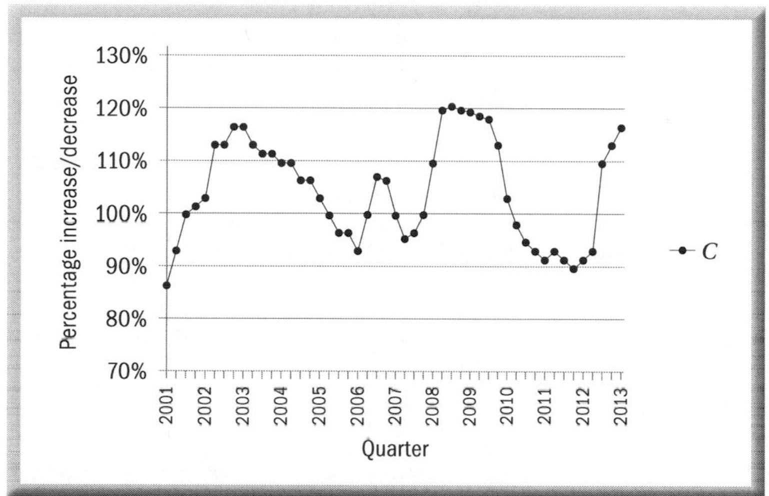

Figure 13.8: The cyclic variation (*C*) extracted from the time series data in Example 13.2 represented as percentage deviations from the trend component; roughly three full cycles have occurred in this graph

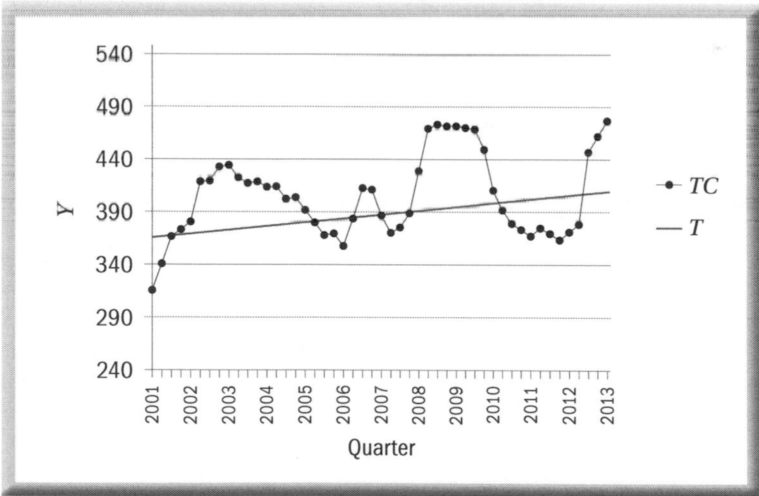

Figure 13.9: The cyclic variation (*C*) combined with the trend (*T*) to form *TC*; the result is that *TC* oscillates around *T*

We will not discuss a method for extracting only the *C* component.

The seasonal variation (S)

The seasonal component, like the cyclic component, is also a measure of fluctuation in a time series data set. However, unlike the cyclic component, the seasonal component occurs:

- regularly (the duration of a full cycle is fixed)
- predictably (the magnitude of the increase or decrease is also reasonably fixed)
- over much shorter periods of time (typically a full season will occur within one year).

The seasonal component, S, shown in Figure 13.10, is an expression of the seasonal movement in its purest form, i.e. as an index representing an increase or decrease relative to the trend and cyclic components. From Figure 13.10, we can see that the car sales figures are at their lowest in the first quarter of each year and peak in the third quarter.

Figure 13.11 shows how the seasonal component fluctuates around the cyclic component (which in turn fluctuates around the overall trend). The series TCS, shown in Figure 13.11, is simply obtained by multiplying the series TC with the S indices.

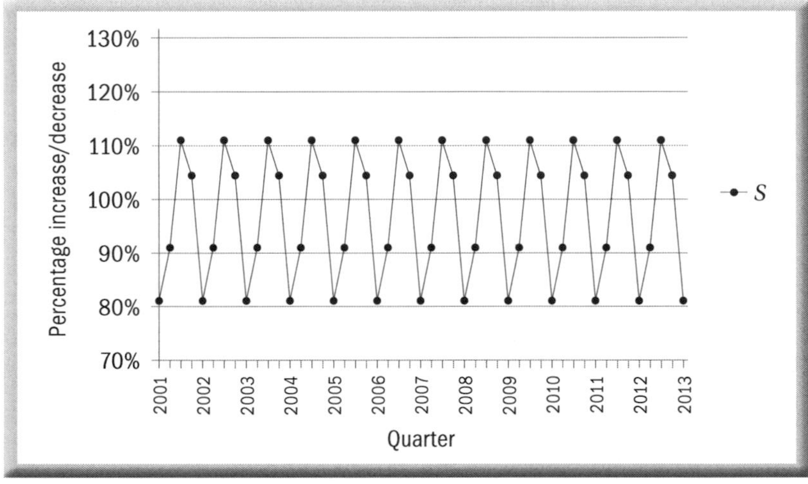

Figure 13.10: The seasonal variation (S) extracted from the time series data in Example 13.2 represented as percentage deviations from the trend and cyclic components

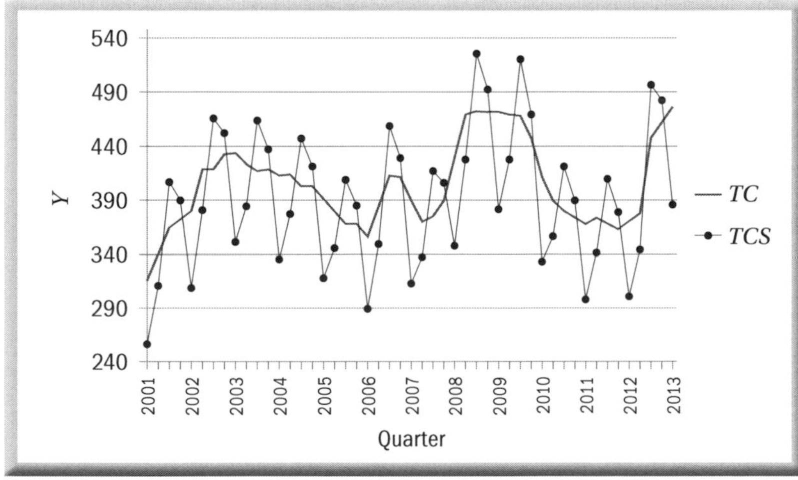

Figure 13.11: The seasonal variation (S) combined with the trend and cyclic variations (TC) to form TCS; the result is that TCS oscillates around TC

Note that if the time series consists of annual data, there is no need to worry about the seasonal component, since the seasonal (or within year) information is ignored. At the same time, if we have monthly or quarterly data, and our time series is several years long, then it will (potentially) consist of the seasonal as well as the cyclical component.

The irregular variation (I)

Finally, the irregular component represents everything else that does not fit into any of the previous three components: it is essentially noise in the data that cannot be ascribed to seasonal, cyclical or long-term fluctuations. We can attribute this noise to a myriad potential factors that could possibly affect the time series. There could be hundreds of these factors, many of which are completely unpredictable, and some of which cannot even be observed. In Example 13.2, potential factors that could have caused these unpredictable variations in the car sales over time include unobserved variables that are related to car prices (such as the price of petrol, the demand for motor vehicles and inflation), news stories reported in the media that affect the economy, and even freak weather events, among others.

Figure 13.12 shows the irregular variation expressed as an index (as a percentage deviation from the other three components) and Figure 13.13 shows how this final component combines with the *TCS* product to form the completed *TCSI* series. Figure 13.13 shows how the irregular component fluctuates around the seasonal component, which itself fluctuates around the cyclic component, which in turn fluctuates around the trend.

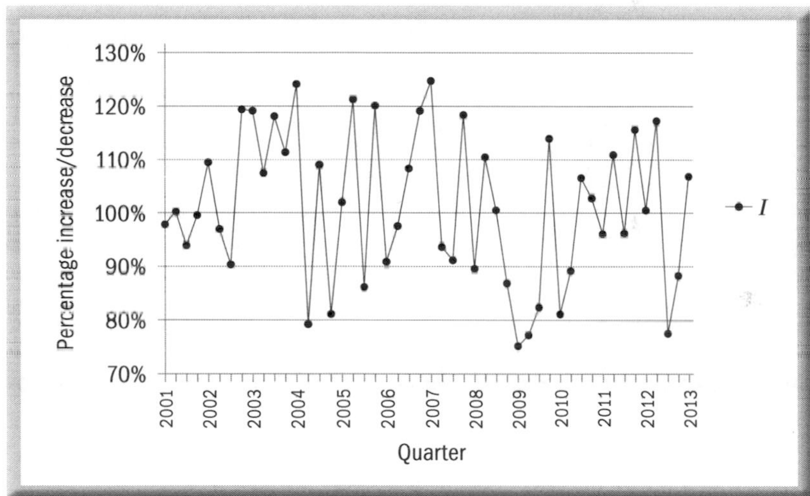

Figure 13.12: The irregular variation (I) extracted from the time series data in Example 13.2 represented as percentage deviations from the trend, cyclic and seasonal components

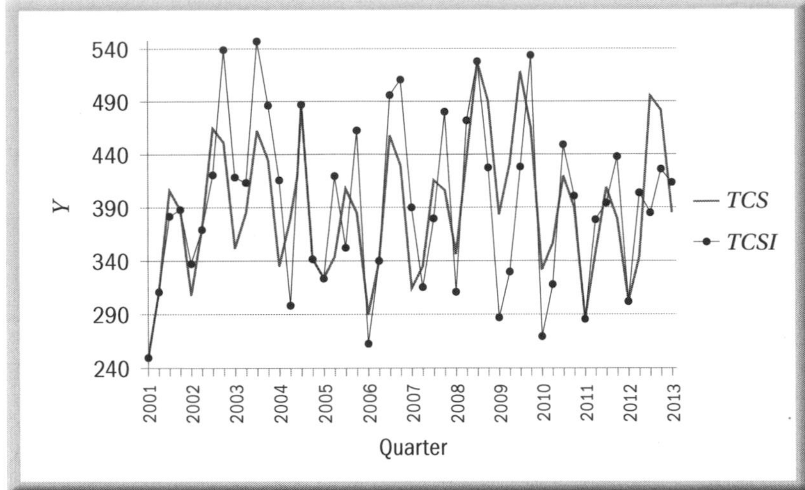

Figure 13.13: The irregular variation (I) combined with the TCS component to form the final $Y = TCSI$ time series data

In the next section, we discuss methods for extracting these components from the time series data so that we can employ them to perform basic forecasting.

13.3 Extracting classical time series components and forecasting

As we indicated in the previous section, we can extract the components of the classical multiplicative time series model from the original data set and analyse them separately.

NOTE

One method of isolating different components in a time series, or decomposing the time series, is called the *classical time series decomposition* method. This is one of the oldest approaches to forecasting.

The whole area of classical time series analysis is concerned with the theory and practice of how to decompose a time series into these components, estimate them and then recompose them to produce forecasts. For example, suppose that we are able to extract the trend and cyclic components from a series (i.e. suppose we can extract TC from $Y = TCSI$), we could then use this information to extract the SI components from the series by simply dividing $Y = TCSI$ by TC:

$$\frac{Y}{TC} = \frac{TCSI}{TC} = SI$$

In this example, we extracted SI, which is not very helpful overall, but it does illustrate how we can use the knowledge of one component to obtain the others.

In the next few sections, we see how the following components can be extracted and how they can be used to either produce forecasts or describe the series.

- We extract T from $Y = TCSI$ using least squares methods. This involves using regression equations from which forecasting will be relatively simple.

- We extract TC from $Y = TCSI$ using central moving average methods. This method (which simply smooths the data set) provides the combination of trend and cyclic components described earlier, but is not used for forecasting; it is only used to describe the long-term trend and cyclic variation and to help calculate S below. Note that we use a slightly different method of moving averages (called simple moving averages) for forecasting in Section 13.4.
- We extract S from $Y = TCSI$ using central moving average methods. By using a moving average method, we can extract the S component, which we can use to de-seasonalise the data (remove the seasonal component from the data). We can then use this de-seasonalised data to produce a forecast using least squares and then reintroduce the seasonal component back into the forecast.

13.3.1 Extracting the trend component (T) using least squares techniques

To approximate the overall (or long-term) trend of the time series, we simply use the method of least squares regression (Chapter 12) to fit a straight line between the observed time series data and the times of the observation.

We use the exact same formulae from Chapter 12, except that now the predictor variable, X, is always the equally spaced, sequential time units used in the time series data. The estimated trend at time t (i.e. $\hat{T}_t$) is given by the following straight-line equation:

$$\hat{T}_t = b_0 + b_1 t \tag{13.2}$$

t denotes the time of the observation, and b_0 and b_1 are the estimated regression coefficients. Note that since the times are always assumed to be equally spaced and sequential, the actual values of the time variable in this regression are unimportant and we can safely replace these with any sequence of equally spaced sequential numbers. Some examples are as follows:

- The time units 1 May 2001, 2 May 2001, 3 May 2001, and so on, can simply be replaced with $t = 1, 2, 3, \ldots$ or
- The time units January 2011, February 2011, March 2011, and so on can also just be replaced with $t = 1, 2, 3, \ldots$

If we use the values $t = 1, 2, 3, \ldots, n$ as the predictor/time variable, then the least squares method estimators for the regression coefficients, b_0 and b_1, (discussed in Chapter 12) are:

$$b_1 = \frac{\sum_{t=1}^{n} t\,Y_t - \frac{1}{n}\sum_{t=1}^{n} t \sum_{t=1}^{n} Y_t}{\sum_{t=1}^{n} t^2 - \frac{1}{n}\left(\sum_{t=1}^{n} t\right)^2} \tag{13.3}$$

And:

$$b_0 = \frac{1}{n}\sum_{t=1}^{n} Y_t - \frac{b_1}{n}\sum_{t=1}^{n} t \tag{13.4}$$

Y_t is the value of the time series recorded at time t. Note that formulae (13.3) and (13.4) are similar to formulae (12.8) and (12.9), and were obtained by simply replacing X_i with t.

The Excel procedures to obtain these estimates are identical to the ones used in Chapter 12 and so we will not spend too much time explaining them again. The examples that follow provide further demonstrations on how to implement these calculations in Excel.

We can use the regression formula (13.2) to produce estimated forecasts for the long-term trend, T, at any given future time value, t. The following example illustrates how we can obtain this regression equation from observed data and then use the equation to forecast future values.

NOTE

Fitting a trend to a time series and extrapolating it into the future is the most elementary form of forecasting.

WORKED EXAMPLES

EXAMPLE 13.3

The number of tickets sold for a newly opened roller-coaster ride at an amusement park over the course of 30 weeks is recorded in Table 13.4.

Table 13.4: Number of tickets sold over a 30-week period

WEEK	TICKETS	WEEK	TICKETS
1	8	16	38
2	25	17	43
3	15	18	55
4	22	19	54
5	15	20	56
6	30	21	49
7	27	22	46
8	20	23	58
9	27	24	60
10	32	25	59
11	30	26	62
12	35	27	65
13	39	28	60
14	35	29	58
15	55	30	62

Use the method of least squares to obtain an estimated forecast for the next five weeks of the long-term trend of ticket sales.

To analyse this time series data, we first create a time series plot of the data (as discussed in Section 13.1).

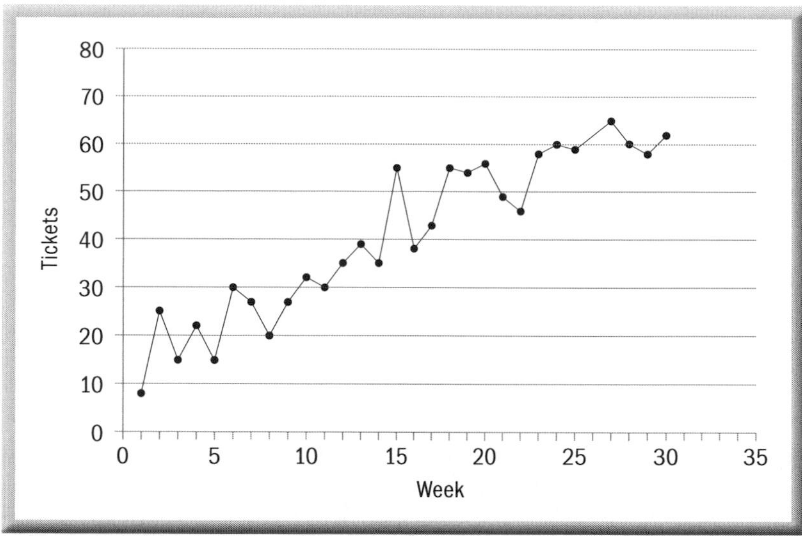

Figure 13.14: The time series plot of the ticket sales data in Example 13.3

It is clear that this time series data are non-stationary and that it appears as though the ticket sales increase with time. To obtain the least squares estimate of the linear trend for this series, $\widehat{T}_t$ we can use various methods in Excel to:

- calculate b_0 and b_1 by hand (using formulae (13.3) and (13.4)
- use formulae (13.3) and (13.4) in Excel to obtain b_0 and b_1
- use the INTERCEPT() and SLOPE() functions in the Excel spreadsheet to determine the values of the estimated coefficients, b_0 and b_1 (and thus obtain the estimated regression line)
- use the 'Add trend line' option on the plot to add the line to the plot and to display the fitted equation.

We now demonstrate all four methods above to obtain the regression line. First, to calculate these estimates by hand, we note that $n = 30$ and that we need to perform a number of interim calculations:

$$\sum_{t=1}^{30} Y_t = 1\,240 \qquad \sum_{t=1}^{30} t = 465 \qquad \sum_{t=1}^{30} tY_t = 23\,284 \qquad \sum_{t=1}^{30} t^2 = 9\,455$$

NOTE

A relatively quick way to calculate $\sum_{t=1}^{n} t$ and $\sum_{t=1}^{n} t^2$ is to use the following formulae:

$$\sum_{t=1}^{n} t = \frac{n(n+1)}{2}$$

And:

$$\sum_{t=1}^{n} t^2 = \frac{n(n+1)(2n+1)}{6}$$

Substituting these values into formula (13.3):

$$b_1 = \frac{\sum_{t=1}^{n} tY_t - \frac{1}{n}\sum_{t=1}^{n} t \sum_{t=1}^{n} Y_t}{\sum_{t=1}^{n} t^2 - \frac{1}{n}\left(\sum_{t=1}^{n} t\right)^2}$$

$$= \frac{23\,284 - \frac{1}{30}(465)(1\,240)}{9\,455 - \frac{1}{30}(465)^2}$$

$$= 1.8008231$$

And:

$$b_0 = \frac{1}{n}\sum_{t=1}^{n} Y_t - \frac{b_1}{n}\sum_{t=1}^{n} t$$

$$= \frac{1}{30}(1\,240) - \frac{1.808231}{30}(465)$$

$$= 13.30575$$

Now that we have estimated the regression parameters, we can provide the expression for the estimated long term trend:

$$\hat{T}_t = 13.30575 + 1.808231t$$

The two Excel solutions to obtain these same estimates are shown in Figure 13.15.

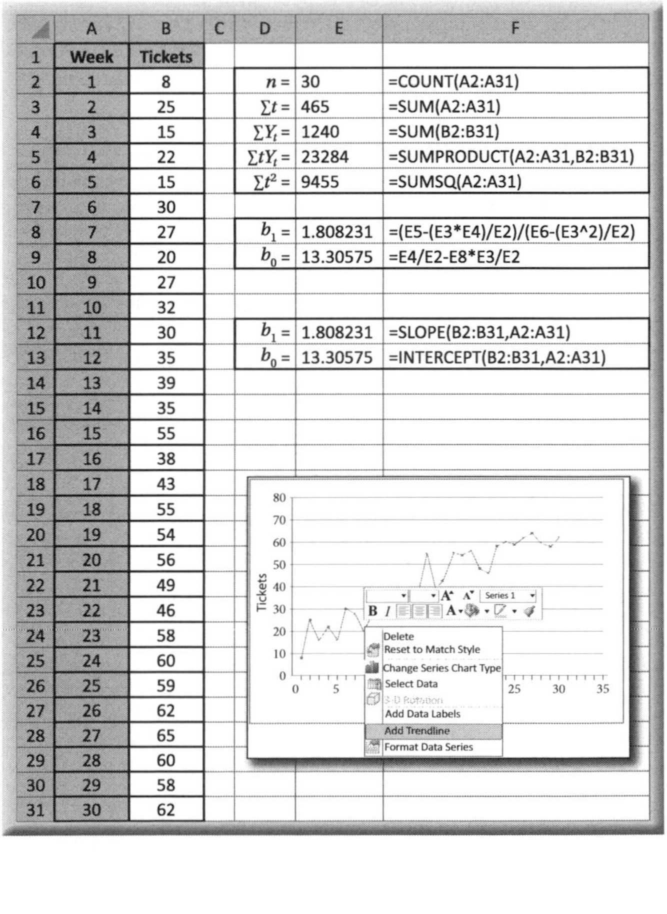

	A	B	C	D	E	F
1	Week	Tickets				
2	1	8		$n =$	30	=COUNT(A2:A31)
3	2	25		$\sum t =$	465	=SUM(A2:A31)
4	3	15		$\sum Y_t =$	1240	=SUM(B2:B31)
5	4	22		$\sum tY_t =$	23284	=SUMPRODUCT(A2:A31,B2:B31)
6	5	15		$\sum t^2 =$	9455	=SUMSQ(A2:A31)
7	6	30				
8	7	27		$b_1 =$	1.808231	=(E5-(E3*E4)/E2)/(E6-(E3^2)/E2)
9	8	20		$b_0 =$	13.30575	=E4/E2-E8*E3/E2
10	9	27				
11	10	32				
12	11	30		$b_1 =$	1.808231	=SLOPE(B2:B31,A2:A31)
13	12	35		$b_0 =$	13.30575	=INTERCEPT(B2:B31,A2:A31)
14	13	39				
15	14	35				
16	15	55				
17	16	38				
18	17	43				
19	18	55				
20	19	54				
21	20	56				
22	21	49				
23	22	46				
24	23	58				
25	24	60				
26	25	59				
27	26	62				
28	27	65				
29	28	60				
30	29	58				
31	30	62				

Figure 13.15: The Excel solution to obtain the estimated regression coefficients of the ticket sales data in Example 13.3

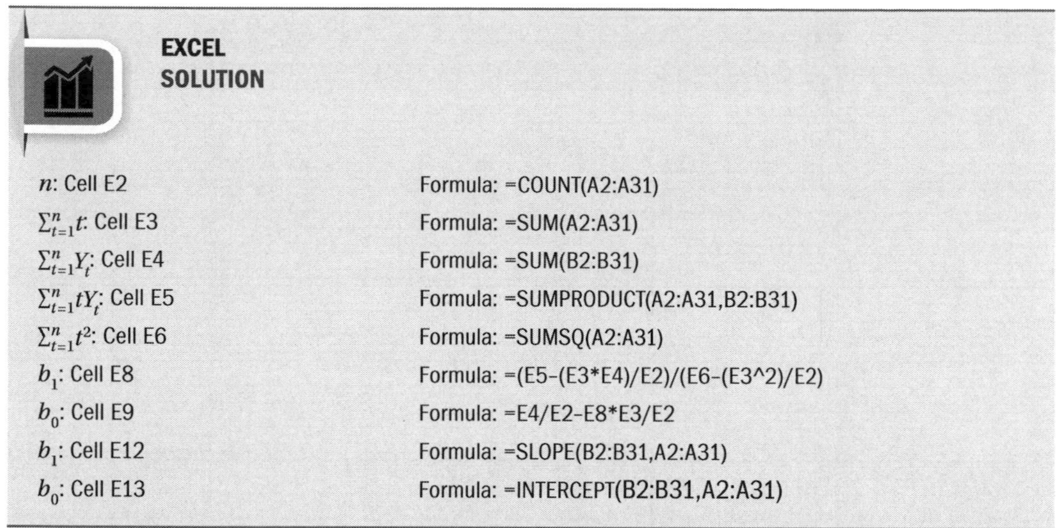

EXCEL SOLUTION

n: Cell E2	Formula: =COUNT(A2:A31)
$\sum_{t=1}^{n} t$: Cell E3	Formula: =SUM(A2:A31)
$\sum_{t=1}^{n} Y_t$: Cell E4	Formula: =SUM(B2:B31)
$\sum_{t=1}^{n} tY_t$: Cell E5	Formula: =SUMPRODUCT(A2:A31,B2:B31)
$\sum_{t=1}^{n} t^2$: Cell E6	Formula: =SUMSQ(A2:A31)
b_1: Cell E8	Formula: =(E5-(E3*E4)/E2)/(E6-(E3^2)/E2)
b_0: Cell E9	Formula: =E4/E2-E8*E3/E2
b_1: Cell E12	Formula: =SLOPE(B2:B31,A2:A31)
b_0: Cell E13	Formula: =INTERCEPT(B2:B31,A2:A31)

The fourth and final method that we use to obtain the estimated trend equation is to request it from the Excel plot. To do this, perform the following actions on the Excel graph.

- Right click on any of the nodes of the displayed time series plot and select 'Add trendline' (as shown in Figure 13.16).
- A window should appear that allows you to select various options for the trendline. Select the 'Linear' regression option and check the 'Display equation on chart' option (as shown in Figure 13.17). You can also check the 'Display R-squared on chart' option.

The result of this operation is shown in Figure 13.16. We can see that the regression equation/trendline equation agrees with the formulae calculated earlier.

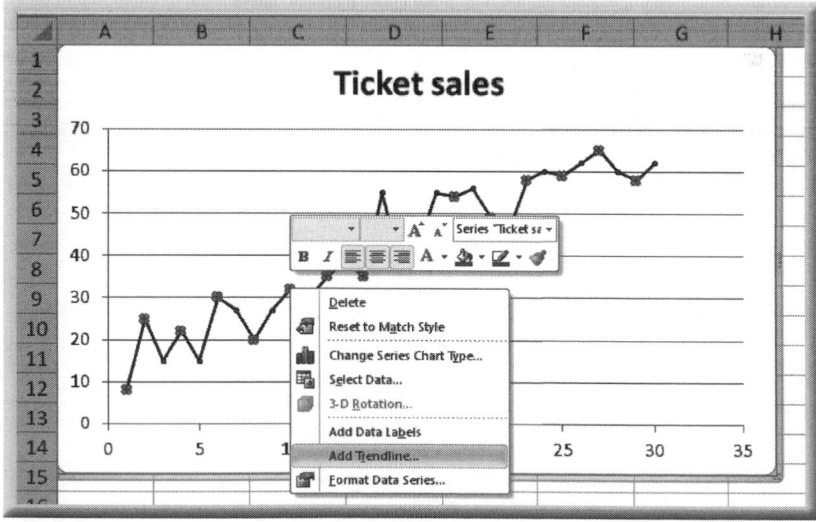

Figure 13.16: Adding a trendline to an Excel plot

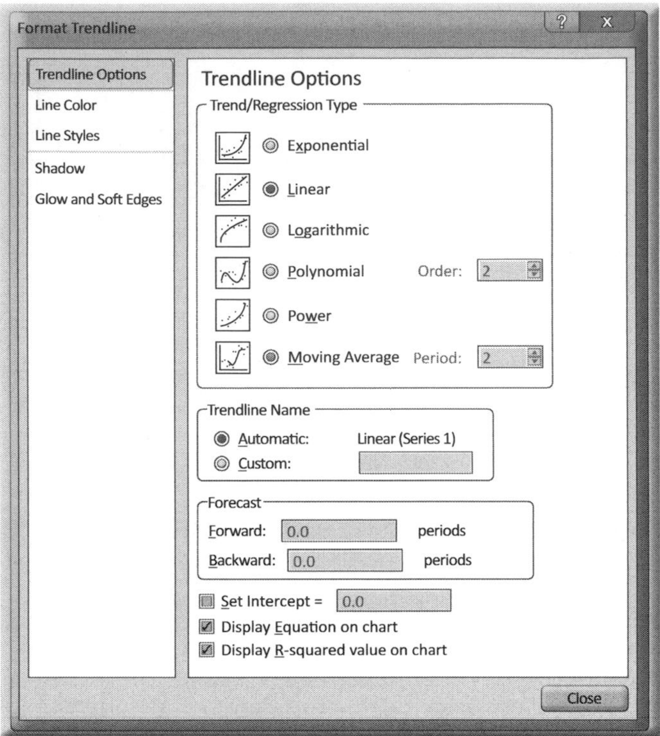

Figure 13.17: Trendline options in Excel

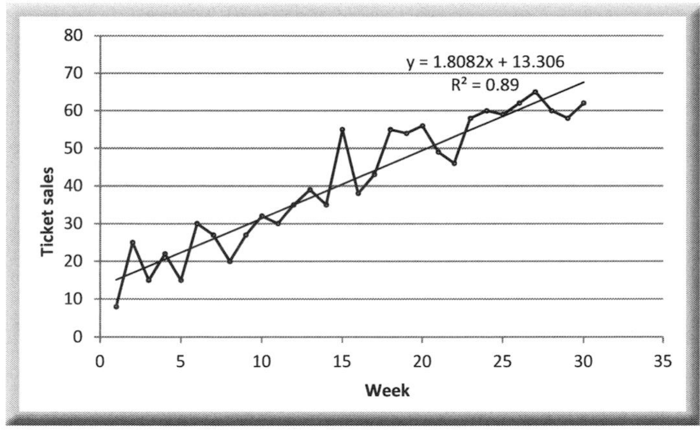

Figure 13.18: The time series plot of the ticket sales data in Example 13.3 with added trendline and equation

Now that we have an expression for $\widehat{T}_t$, we can use it to forecast future values for the next five weeks. We can do this by simply substituting the time values for these five future observations into the estimated equation:

$$\widehat{T}_t = 13.30575 + 1.808231t$$

We need to determine the value of $\widehat{T}_t$ when $t = 31$, $t = 32$, $t = 33$, $t = 34$ and $t = 35$.

NOTE The future values of t should always be a sequential continuation of the period numbers used in the past. In this case, the last observation is for period 30, which means that the future values of t are 31, 32, 33, 34 and 35.

The forecasted values of ticket sales for the next five weeks are:

$$\hat{T}_{31} = 13.30575 + 1.808231 \times (31) = 69.361$$
$$\hat{T}_{32} = 13.30575 + 1.808231 \times (32) = 71.169$$
$$\hat{T}_{33} = 13.30575 + 1.808231 \times (33) = 72.977$$
$$\hat{T}_{34} = 13.30575 + 1.808231 \times (34) = 74.786$$
$$\hat{T}_{35} = 13.30575 + 1.808231 \times (35) = 76.594$$

We can also obtain these values in Excel by applying the above equations or by using the TREND() function. These calculations are demonstrated in Figure 13.19.

	A	B	C	D	E	F
1	Week	Tickets				
2	1	8		$n =$	30	=COUNT(A2:A31)
3	2	25		$\sum_{t=1}^{n} t =$	465	=SUM(A2:A31)
4	3	15		$\sum_{t=1}^{n} Y_i =$	1240	=SUM(B2:B31)
5	4	22		$\sum_{t=1}^{n} tY_t =$	23284	=SUMPRODUCT(A2:A31,B2:B31)
6	5	15		$\sum_{t=1}^{n} t^2 =$	9455	=SUMSQ(A2:A31)
7	6	30				
8	7	27		$b_1 =$	1.808231	=(E5-(E3*E4)/E2)/(E6-(E3^2)/E2)
9	8	20		$b_0 =$	13.30575	=E4/E2-E8*E3/E2
10	9	27				
11	10	32				
12	11	30		$b_1 =$	1.808231	=SLOPE(B2:B31,A2:A31)
13	12	35		$b_0 =$	13.30575	=INTERCEPT(B2:B31,A2:A31)
14	13	39				
15	14	35				
16	15	55				
17	16	38				
18	17	43				
19	18	55				
20	19	54				
21	20	56				
22	21	49				
23	22	46				
24	23	58				
25	24	60				
26	25	59				
27	26	62				
28	27	65				
29	28	60				
30	29	58				
31	30	62				
32	31	69	=$E$13+$E$12*A32		=TREND($B$2:$B$31,$A$2:$A$31,A32)	
33	32	71	=$E$13+$E$12*A33		=TREND($B$2:$B$31,$A$2:$A$31,A33)	
34	33	73	=$E$13+$E$12*A34		=TREND($B$2:$B$31,$A$2:$A$31,A34)	
35	34	75	=$E$13+$E$12*A35		=TREND($B$2:$B$31,$A$2:$A$31,A35)	
36	35	77	=$E$13+$E$12*A36		=TREND($B$2:$B$31,$A$2:$A$31,A36)	

Figure 13.19: Forecasting the trend five weeks into the future in Example 13.3 using Excel

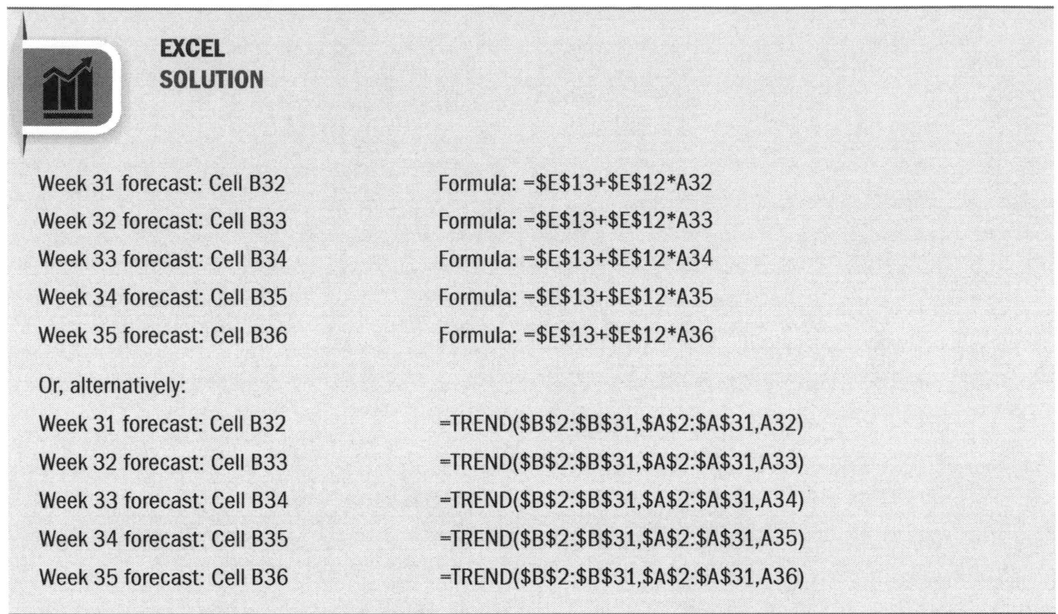

EXCEL SOLUTION

Week 31 forecast: Cell B32	Formula: =$E$13+$E$12*A32
Week 32 forecast: Cell B33	Formula: =$E$13+$E$12*A33
Week 33 forecast: Cell B34	Formula: =$E$13+$E$12*A34
Week 34 forecast: Cell B35	Formula: =$E$13+$E$12*A35
Week 35 forecast: Cell B36	Formula: =$E$13+$E$12*A36

Or, alternatively:

Week 31 forecast: Cell B32	=TREND($B$2:$B$31,$A$2:$A$31,A32)
Week 32 forecast: Cell B33	=TREND($B$2:$B$31,$A$2:$A$31,A33)
Week 33 forecast: Cell B34	=TREND($B$2:$B$31,$A$2:$A$31,A34)
Week 34 forecast: Cell B35	=TREND($B$2:$B$31,$A$2:$A$31,A35)
Week 35 forecast: Cell B36	=TREND($B$2:$B$31,$A$2:$A$31,A36)

We can obtain the graphical representation of this forecast by extrapolating the fitted regression line in Figure 13.18 to the five weeks of the forecast. This is done as follows:

- Right click on the fitted trendline and select 'Format Trendline' (shown in Figure 13.20).
- Figure 13.21 shows the window that will appear. In this window, specify the number of time units that you want to forecast forward, by typing it into the field labelled 'Forward' in the 'Forecast' block. In this case, type '5' (shown in Figure 13.21).

The resulting graph with the extrapolated trendline is shown in Figure 13.22. Note that these forecasted values agree with the values that were calculated above.

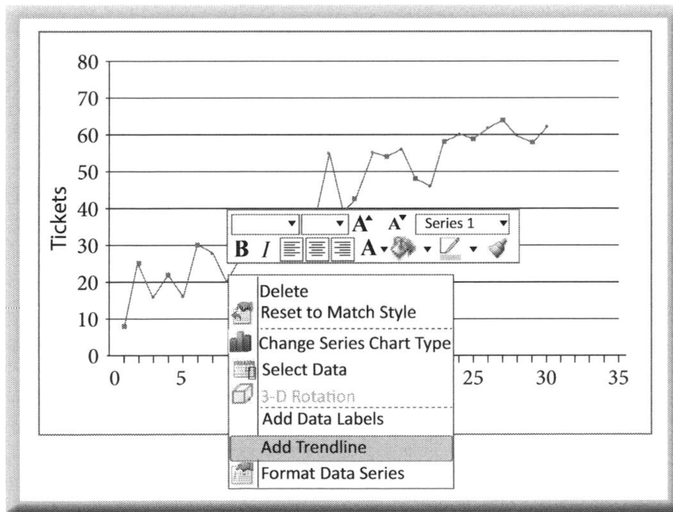

Figure 13.20: Producing graphical forecasts for the trend in Excel

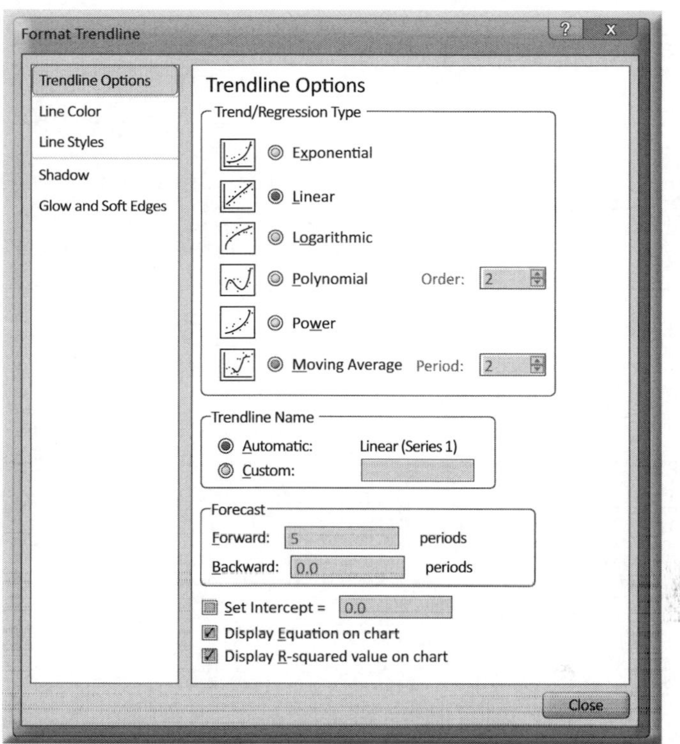

Figure 13.21: Producing graphical forecasts for the trend in Excel

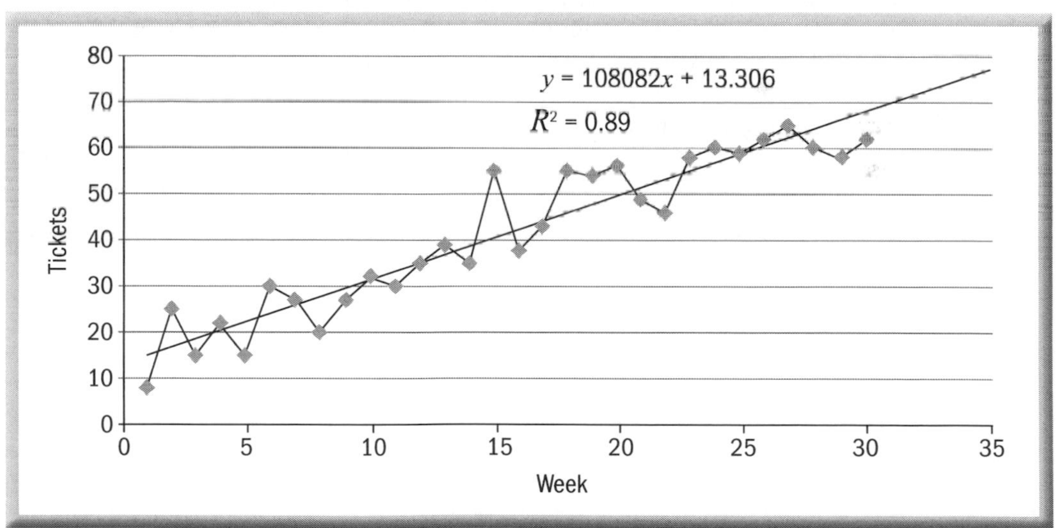

Figure 13.22: The time series plot of the ticket sales data in Example 13.4 with added trendline and five-week forecast

INTERPRETATION We found for this time series data that the estimated trend of ticket sales was given by

$$\hat{T}_t = 13.30575 + 1.808231t,$$

where t represented the week that the ticket sales were recorded.

Using this equation, we could produce an estimated forecast of the general trend of the ticket sales five weeks into the future. The values are shown in Table 13.5.

Table 13.5: Forecast sales for five weeks into the future

WEEK	FORECASTED TICKETS
31	69.361
32	71.169
33	72.977
34	74.786
35	76.594

For example, the forecasted long-term trend for ticket sales in the fifth week is 76.594. This number should be interpreted as the expected number of ticket sales that one would obtain after five weeks (or the value we would get, on average, after five weeks).

The method of least squares in the above example shows how we can extract the trend (T) from the original time series data, Y, and how we can use this trend to forecast values into the future. However, if other sources of variation (such as the seasonal component) are prevalent in a time series, they can have adverse effects on our estimation of this trend and, consequently, adverse effects on the forecasts made from the estimated trend. In the sections that follow, we briefly discuss how to remove the seasonal component so that we can obtain slightly improved forecasts in the presence of seasonality.

13.3.2 Extracting the trend and cyclic components (*TC*) using moving averages

To extract the *TC* component of a time series, we use a method called **central moving averages**. This method calculates the averages of short, overlapping sequences of observations within a time series, with the aim to smooth out various sources of fluctuation. Note that the length of the sequence used in a moving average calculation is called the **window**, and the size of this window is denoted W. The name **moving average** comes from the fact that this window is placed over the data and the *average* of the observations within the window is calculated. The window is then *moved* one time unit and the average of the new items in the window are calculated, and so on.

Central moving averages Averages of the observations in an interval (or window) around the current time period. This window is moved, the average is calculated for the items that fall within the window, and the resulting value falls in the period that appears at the centre of the window. The resulting series of averages is a central moving average series.

The averages obtained from this method form a new time series data set and, depending on the size of the window, we can use the resulting time series to describe various components contained within the original time series. We use this method to extract the *TC* component from the $Y = TCSI$ series.

To illustrate how we obtain these moving averages, consider a time series that consists of the daily values in Table 13.6.

Table 13.6: Daily observations

DAY	OBSERVATION
1	12
2	23
3	34
4	27
5	20
6	24

The moving average calculation using a window size of $W = 3$ involves simply calculating the average of a run of three consecutive observations. These calculations are shown in Figure 13.23 along with a plot of the resulting moving average time series overlaid on the original series.

DAY	OBSERVATION	MOVING AVERAGE, $W = 3$
1	12	.
2	23	$\frac{(12 + 23 + 34)}{3} = 23$
3	34	$\frac{(23 + 34 + 27)}{3} = 28$
4	27	$\frac{(34 + 27 + 20)}{3} = 27$
5	20	$\frac{(27 + 20 + 25)}{3} = 24$
6	25	.

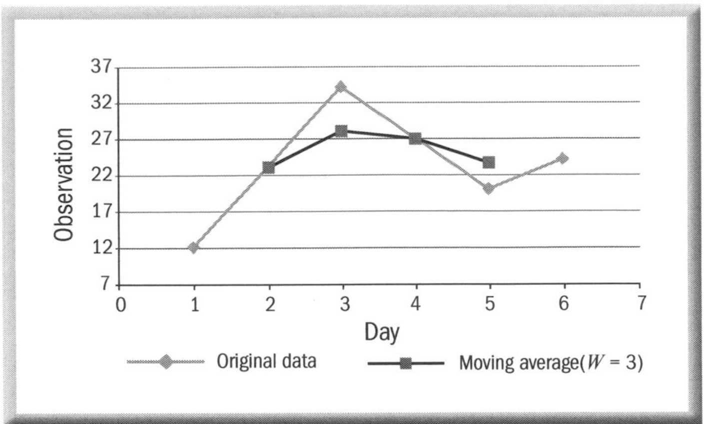

Figure 13.23: A graphical representation of the moving average calculation

There are a number of interesting things that we can note about moving averages (in general) by investigating the series calculated above.

- *Lost values*: When we calculate the moving average using this method, we lose observations at the beginning and end of the series (the moving average in the example cannot have an observation on day 1 or day 6). This is a characteristic of all moving averages and is influenced by the window size, W. As the window size increases, more observations are lost at the beginning and end of the series.
- *Moving averages series are smoother than the original series*: Note that the moving average series is not as erratic as the original set of observations (specifically, the sharp spike on day 3 is not as prominent in the moving average series). Moving average series are essentially smoothed out versions of the original series. The smoothing is caused by the fact that the values of neighbouring days are included in each moving average value, thus dampening the effect of sharp spikes in the data depending on the magnitude of the neighbouring values.
- *Observations should be centred on time units*: The value obtained from a central moving average calculation corresponds to the middle of the window that was used to calculate it. Since the window size in the above example was chosen to be an odd number, the central moving average values correspond to individual days, i.e. the moving average value of 23 is centred on day 2 because the midpoint of the window used to calculate that value is situated on day 2. Unfortunately, when W is an *even* number, the moving average values lie halfway between the time units (because the midpoint of the window will lie halfway between time units). To rectify this, we need to perform an additional moving average calculation with window size $W = 2$ on the first moving average series obtained (this is called **centring** the central moving average series).

The next example illustrates how the values of a $W = 4$ central moving average are not centred on the days of observation, but performing an additional $W = 2$ moving average on the resulting series will centre it.

In Figure 13.24, we apply a moving average with window size $W = 4$ and then apply a $W = 2$ moving average on the result.

DAY	OBSERVATION	MOVING AVERAGE, $W = 4$	CENTRED MOVING AVERAGE
1	12	.	.
2	23		.
		$\frac{(12 + 23 + 34 + 27)}{4} = 24$	
3	34		$\frac{(24 + 26)}{2} = 25$
		$\frac{(23 + 34 + 27 + 20)}{4} = 26$	
4	27		$\frac{(26 + 26.5)}{2} = 26.25$
		$\frac{(34 + 27 + 20 + 25)}{4} = 26.5$	
5	20		.
6	25		.

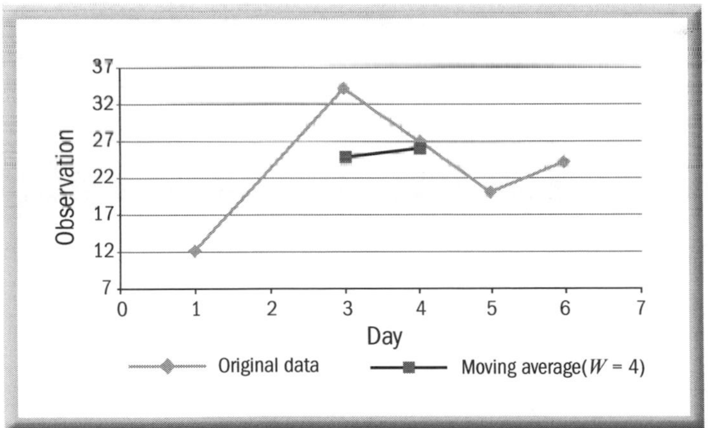

Figure 13.24: A graphical representation of a centred moving average calculation

In this example, we clearly see that the first set of moving average values are not centred on days in the original series (they lie halfway between the days). To rectify this, a second ($W = 2$) moving average is applied. The result of this centred moving average is that we can directly associate the observations with a specific day. Note also that we have lost even more values at the beginning and end of the series because the window size is larger.

When dealing with data collected over large periods of time, we can choose the window size, W, so that the moving average will smooth-out various sources of variation.

For example, suppose that we have a data set that contains data collected every month over a number of years, and that the data exhibits some seasonal and cyclic fluctuation. If a window size of 12 months is chosen to create a moving average series of these data, it is likely that the resulting moving average series will not display any seasonal or irregular fluctuations (but will still potentially display the trend and cyclic fluctuations). These spiky seasonal fluctuations are thus smoothed-out by using a moving average window of sufficient length.

NOTE

For time series with seasonal tendencies, it may be possible to remove the seasonal and irregular variation by constructing a moving average series with a window size greater than the period of the seasonal fluctuation. For example:

- If the data are collected *daily*, then a window size of 365 days or more may be appropriate to remove the seasonal and irregular fluctuations.
- A window size of 12 months would help to remove the seasonal and irregular fluctuations from data collected *monthly*.
- If the data are collected *quarterly*, then a window size of four quarters should be used.

If the window size is large enough, we assume that the moving average series is nearly identical to the original series $Y = TCSI$, except that the seasonal (S) and irregular (I) components have been smoothed out, and so we represent the moving average series by TC.

NOTE

It is a general principle that the larger the window size of the moving average, the smoother, or less dynamic, the time series of moving averages will be.

Example 13.4 looks at how to extract the TC components from a time series that exhibits all four time series components.

WORKED EXAMPLES

EXAMPLE 13.4

The quarterly milk production (measured in thousands of litres) of a small dairy is shown in Table 13.7 below. (Note that the variable t is used to enumerate the annual quarters observed in the study).

Table 13.7: Quarterly milk production (1 000s litres)

YEAR	QUARTER	t	MILK PRODUCED $Y = TCSI$
2008	1	1	2.95
	2	2	3.18
	3	3	3.30
	4	4	3.23
2009	1	5	3.18
	2	6	3.45
	3	7	3.51
	4	8	3.46
2010	1	9	3.36
	2	10	3.57
	3	11	3.76
	4	12	3.65
2011	1	13	3.55
	2	14	3.77
	3	15	3.86
	4	16	3.87
2012	1	17	3.80
	2	18	4.01
	3	19	4.13
	4	20	4.02

The time-series plot of these data, shown in Figure 13.25, shows that there is some evidence of a seasonal fluctuation in the data.

Extract only the trend and cyclic components of this series by smoothing out the seasonality and irregular variation.

We can extract the T and C components by calculating a moving average with a window size equal to the length of a year, $W = 4$. (Note that a window size of four observations constitutes a year because the observations are measured quarterly.)

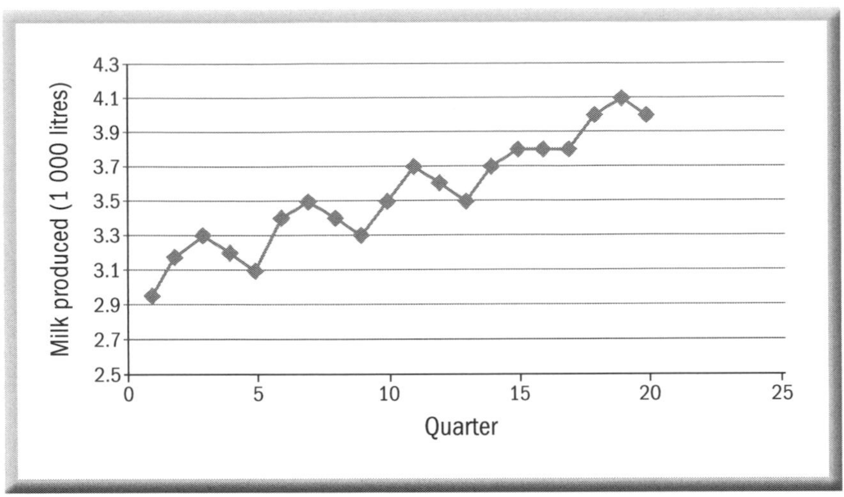

Figure 13.25: The time series plot of the quarterly milk production of a small dairy

The centred moving averages of length $W = 4$ is calculated by first calculating a moving average of length $W = 4$ from the original data. Unfortunately, these moving average values are not associated with any specific quarter. Some of the $W = 4$ moving average calculations are shown below.

YEAR AND QUARTER	MILK PRODUCED, $Y = TCSI$	MOVING AVERAGE, $W = 4$
2008: 1	2.95	·
2008: 2	3.18	
		$\frac{(2.95 + 3.18 + 3.3 + 3.23)}{4} = 3.165$
2008: 3	3.3	
		$\frac{(3.18 + 3.3 + 3.23 + 3.18)}{4} = 3.2225$
2008: 4	3.23	
		$\frac{(3.3 + 3.23 + 3.18 + 3.45)}{4} = 3.29$
2009: 1	3.18	
2009: 2	3.45	⋮
⋮	⋮	⋮

To centre these values on quarters we perform a second moving average calculation with $W = 2$ on the above moving average so that the values can be centred on a specific quarter.

YEAR AND QUARTER	MILK PRODUCED, $Y = TCSI$	MOVING AVERAGE, $W = 4$	CENTRED MOVING AVERAGE, $W = 2$
2008: 1	2.95	.	.
2008: 2	3.18		.
		3.165	
2008: 3	3.3		$\frac{(3.165 + 3.2225)}{2} = 3.19375$
		3.2225	
2008: 4	3.23		$\frac{(3.2225 + 3.29)}{2} = 3.25625$
		3.29	
2009: 1	3.18		$\frac{(3.29 + 3.3425)}{2} = 3.31625$
		3.3425	
2009: 2	3.45	⋮	⋮
⋮	⋮	⋮	⋮

It is easier to use Excel to calculate all of these moving average values. These calculations are shown in .

	A	B	C	D	E	F	G	H	P
1	Year	Quarter	t	$Y = TCSI$	$W = 4$ Uncentred		$W = 2$ Centred		
2	2008	1	1	2.95					
3		2	2	3.18	3.165	=AVERAGE(D2:D5)			
4		3	3	3.30	3.2225	=AVERAGE(D3:D6)	3.19375	=AVERAGE(E3:E4)	
5		4	4	3.23	3.29	=AVERAGE(D4:D7)	3.25625	=AVERAGE(E4:E5)	
6	2009	1	5	3.18	3.3425	=AVERAGE(D5:D8)	3.31625	=AVERAGE(E5:E6)	
7		2	6	3.45	3.4	=AVERAGE(D6:D9)	3.37125	=AVERAGE(E6:E7)	
8		3	7	3.51	3.445	=AVERAGE(D7:D10)	3.4225	=AVERAGE(E7:E8)	
9		4	8	3.46	3.475	=AVERAGE(D8:D11)	3.46	=AVERAGE(E8:E9)	
10	2010	1	9	3.36	3.5375	=AVERAGE(D9:D12)	3.50625	=AVERAGE(E9:E10)	
11		2	10	3.57	3.585	=AVERAGE(D10:D13)	3.56125	=AVERAGE(E10:E11)	
12		3	11	3.76	3.6325	=AVERAGE(D11:D14)	3.60875	=AVERAGE(E11:E12)	
13		4	12	3.65	3.6825	=AVERAGE(D12:D15)	3.6575	=AVERAGE(E12:E13)	
14	2011	1	13	3.55	3.7075	=AVERAGE(D13:D16)	3.695	=AVERAGE(E13:E14)	
15		2	14	3.77	3.7625	=AVERAGE(D14:D17)	3.735	=AVERAGE(E14:E15)	
16		3	15	3.86	3.825	=AVERAGE(D15:D18)	3.79375	=AVERAGE(E15:E16)	
17		4	16	3.87	3.885	=AVERAGE(D16:D19)	3.855	=AVERAGE(E16:E17)	
18	2012	1	17	3.80	3.9525	=AVERAGE(D17:D20)	3.91875	=AVERAGE(E17:E18)	
19		2	18	4.01	3.99	=AVERAGE(D18:D21)	3.97125	=AVERAGE(E18:E19)	
20		3	19	4.13					
21		4	20	4.02					

Figure 13.26: The calculation of the centred central moving averages in Excel

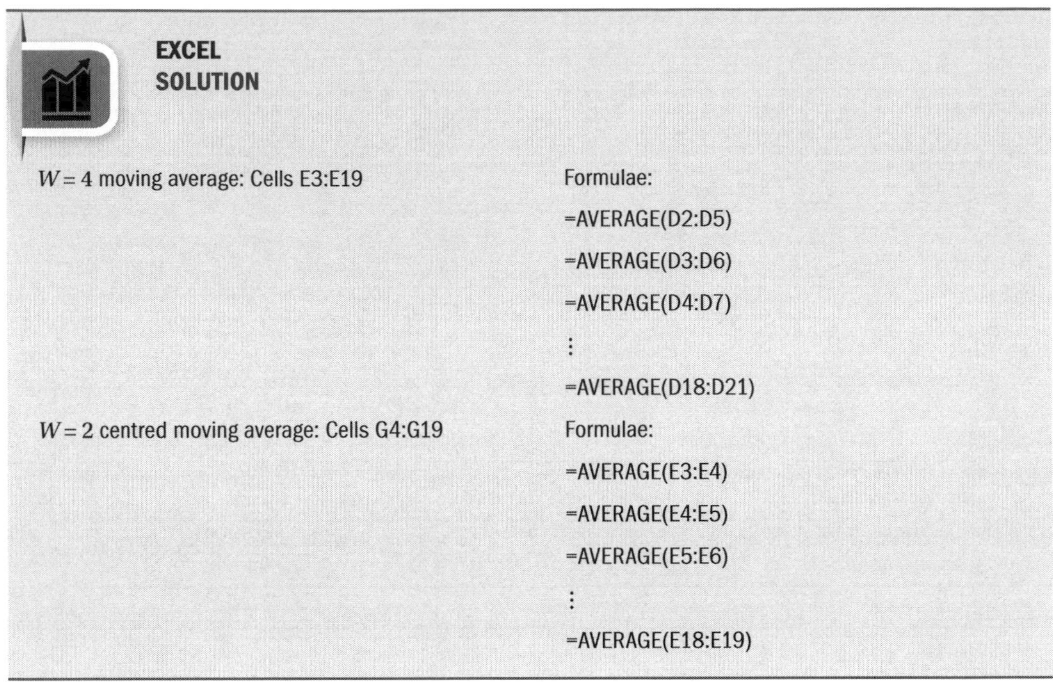

EXCEL SOLUTION

$W = 4$ moving average: Cells E3:E19

Formulae:

=AVERAGE(D2:D5)

=AVERAGE(D3:D6)

=AVERAGE(D4:D7)

⋮

=AVERAGE(D18:D21)

$W = 2$ centred moving average: Cells G4:G19

Formulae:

=AVERAGE(E3:E4)

=AVERAGE(E4:E5)

=AVERAGE(E5:E6)

⋮

=AVERAGE(E18:E19)

Note that the values calculated for the $W = 4$ moving average in Figure 13.26 appear to be centred on the quarters, but that is only because it is not possible to have the values appear in-between cells. The centring is still absolutely necessary in this case.

Once we have calculated this four-quarter moving average, we can plot the series and compare it to the original series. These plots are shown in Figure 13.27.

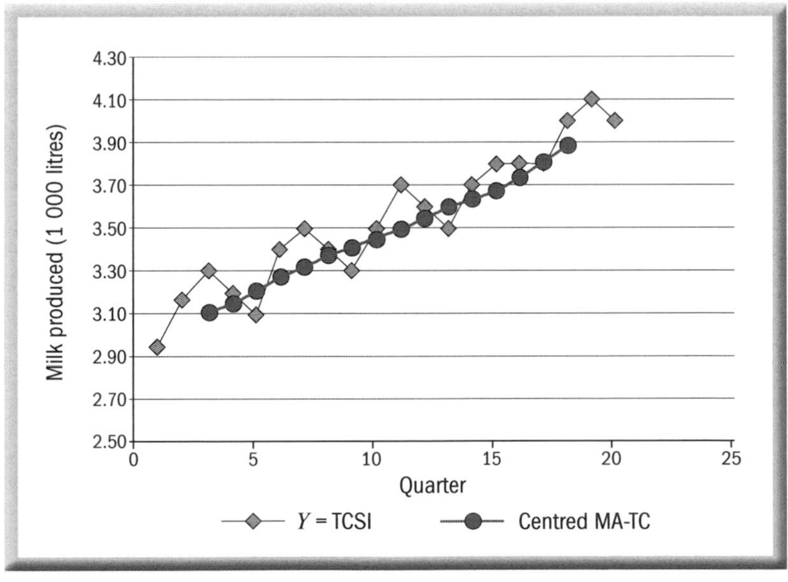

Figure 13.27: The time series plot of the centred $W = 4$ moving average series when compared to the original series

The centred moving average series shown in Figure 13.27 is clearly smoother than the original series. This new series is an approximation of the *TC* component of the original $Y = TCSI$ series, since the *SI* component has been removed using moving average calculations. We can conclude, based on Figure 13.27, that the general trend of the milk production of the dairy farm is increasing over time and that there does not appear to be much evidence of a cyclic component (although this might be because we have not observed the series for a long enough period of time).

13.3.3 Extracting the seasonal component (*S*) using moving averages, de-seasonalising the time series and forecasting

In this section, we will discuss how we can extract the seasonal component, *S*, from the data series.

The reasons for extracting the seasonal component from the series are the following:

- Extracting the seasonal component from the data enables us to analyse it separately. It provides information concerning the general seasonal behaviour of the time series.
- We can remove the seasonal component entirely from the series ('de-seasonalising' the data) thereby allowing more accurate approximation of the long-term trend of the series using methods such as least squares.
- If we can forecast using the trend, we can add additional information to the forecast by also incorporating the general seasonal component into the forecast. This will increase the precision of the forecast if there is seasonality in the data.

We begin by looking at how to extract this component and then discuss how we could use this component to improve forecasts.

Extracting the seasonal component, *S*

The procedure that we follow to extract the seasonal component is based on the following four steps.

Step 1: Extract the *TC* component from $Y = TCSI$ using the central moving average method. We discussed this in the previous section (Section 13.3.2).

Step 2: Isolate the *SI* component of the series by dividing each of the original $Y = TCSI$ series values by their corresponding *TC* series value:

$$SI = \frac{Y}{TC} = \frac{TCSI}{TC}$$

Step 3: Once we have obtained the *SI* component (these are called the specific seasonal indices) we remove the *I* component by taking modified averages over the common time units (the modification involves removing the largest and smallest value from the calculation of the average). For example, if the data are recorded quarterly, then we would obtain the modified average of the *SI*-values for each quarter, resulting in four averages, one for each quarter. If the data are recorded monthly, we have to calculate the modified average of *SI* for each month, resulting in 12 separate averages.

Step 4: Finally, these average values are scaled so that, when we add them together, they add up to the number of units that make up a year. The result, called general seasonal indices, is denoted by *S*. For example, if the series is recorded quarterly, the sum of the four scaled *S*-values must add up to 4. If the series is recorded monthly, the 12 scaled *S*-values must add up to 12. We do this so that these quantities can be interpreted as indices. Note that this procedure averages out the irregular component, I.

Example 13.5 illustrates these steps using the information from Example 13.4.

WORKED EXAMPLES

EXAMPLE 13.5

Continuing Example 13.4: We are now interested in extracting the seasonal component from the quarterly milk production (measured in 1 000s of litres) of the small dairy.

The *centred* moving average calculations used to extract TC are now also included in the data set. Note that the calculations required to obtain the values in this table are shown in Figure 13.26 of Example 13.4.

Table 13.8: Milk production, including the moving average calculations

YEAR	QUARTER	MILK PRODUCED, $Y = TCIS$	CENTRED MOVING AVERAGE, $W = 4\ TC$
2008	1	2.95	
	2	3.18	
	3	3.30	3.19375
	4	3.23	3.25625
2009	1	3.18	3.31625
	2	3.45	3.37125
	3	3.51	3.4225
	4	3.46	3.46
2010	1	3.36	3.50625
	2	3.57	3.56125
	3	3.76	3.60875
	4	3.65	3.6575
2011	1	3.55	3.695
	2	3.77	3.735
	3	3.86	3.79375
	4	3.87	3.855
2012	1	3.80	3.91875
	2	4.01	3.97125
	3	4.13	
	4	4.02	

We now use the four steps described above to extract *S*, the seasonal component from the series.

Step 1: In this case, the calculations required to extract the *TC* component were discussed in Example 13.4. The *TC* component is shown in the given data set.

Step 2: To isolate the *SI* component, we simply need to divide the original *Y*-values by the *TC*-values calculated in step 1. Table 13.9 illustrates some of the calculations required to do this (not all calculations are shown).

Table 13.9: Calculations required to divide the original *Y* values by the *TC* values

YEAR	QUARTER	MILK PRODUCED $Y = TCIS$	CENTRED MOVING AVERAGE, $W = 4$ TC	$\frac{TCSI}{TC} = SI$
2008	1	2.95		
	2	3.18		
	3	3.30	3.19375	$\frac{3.30}{3.19375} = 1.033$
	4	3.23	3.25625	$\frac{3.23}{3.25625} = 0.992$
⋮	⋮	⋮	⋮	⋮
2012	1	3.80	3.91875	$\frac{3.8}{3.91875} = 0.970$
	2	4.01	3.97125	$\frac{4.01}{3.97125} = 1.010$
	3	4.13		
	4	4.02		

Step 3: The *SI* component values calculated for each quarter in step 2 are summarised in Table 13.10. (Note that the values have been rounded off to three decimal places.)

Table 13.10: Summary of *SI* component values

QUARTER	2008	2009	2010	2011	2012
1		0.959	0.958	0.961	0.970
2		1.023	1.002	1.009	1.010
3	1.033	1.026	1.042	1.017	
4	0.992	1.000	0.998	1.004	

To remove the *I* component from *SI*, we calculate the modified average for each quarter (across the years), i.e. we first remove the largest and smallest value for each quarter and calculate the average of the remaining values. These calculations are shown in the following table.

Table 13.11: Calculations to remove the *I* component from *SI*

QUARTER	2008	2009	2010	2011	2012	MODIFIED AVERAGE
1		0.959	~~0.958~~	0.961	0.970	$\frac{0.959 + 0.961}{2} = 0.960$
2		~~1.023~~	~~1.002~~	1.009	1.010	$\frac{1.009 + 1.010}{2} = 1.0095$
3	1.033	1.026	~~1.042~~	~~1.017~~		$\frac{1.033 + 1.026}{2} = 1.0295$
4	~~0.992~~	1.000	0.998	~~1.004~~		$\frac{1.000 + 0.998}{2} = 0.999$

Step 4: We need to multiply the modified averages obtained in step 3 with a scaling factor, so that they add up to 4. Currently, the modified averages add up to 0.96 + 1.0095 + 1.0295 + 0.999 = 3.998 Therefore, the scaling factor that we can apply to the modified averages to ensure that they sum to 4 is:

$$\frac{4}{3.998} = 1.000500025$$

The scaled values, i.e. the general seasonal indices, denoted by *S*, are shown in Table 13.12.

Table 13.12: General seasonal indices

QUARTER	MODIFIED AVERAGE	SCALING FACTOR	*S*
1	$\frac{0.959 + 0.961}{2} = 0.960$	× 1.00050025 =	0.96048024
2	$\frac{1.009 + 1.010}{2} = 1.0095$	× 1.00050025 =	1.010005003
3	$\frac{1.033 + 1.026}{2} = 1.0295$	× 1.00050025 =	1.030015008
4	$\frac{1.000 + 0.998}{2} = 0.999$	× 1.00050025 =	0.999499749
		Sum:	4

Note that the sum of these *S*-values is equal to 4.

As usual, we can conduct all of these calculations in Excel. The Excel solution is shown in Figure 13.28.

	A	B	C	D	E	F
1	Year	Quarter	$Y = TCSI$	Moving average, $W=4$ TC	SI	
2	2008	1	2.95			
3		2	3.18			
4		3	3.30	3.19375	1.0332681018	=C4/D4
5		4	3.23	3.25625	0.9919385797	=C5/D5
6	2009	1	3.18	3.31625	0.9589144365	=C6/D6
7		2	3.45	3.37125	1.0233592881	=D7/D7
8		3	3.51	3.4225	1.0255661066	=C8/D8
9		4	3.46	3.46	1	=C9/D9
10	2010	1	3.36	3.50625	0.9582887701	=C10/D10
11		2	3.57	3.56125	1.0024570025	=C11/D11
12		3	3.76	3.60875	1.0419120194	=C12/D12
13		4	3.65	3.6575	0.997949419	=C13/D13
14	2011	13	3.55	3.695	0.9607577808	=C14/D14
15		14	3.77	3.735	1.0093708166	=C15/D15
16		15	3.86	3.79375	1.0174629325	=C16/D16
17		16	3.87	3.855	1.0038910506	=C17/D17
18	2012	17	3.80	3.91875	0.9696969697	=C18/D18
19		18	4.01	3.97125	1.009757633	=C19/D19
20		19	4.13			
21		20	4.02			
22						

	H	I	J	K	L	M	N	O
2							Modified averages	
3	Quarter	2008	2009	2010	2011	2012		
4	1		0.9589144365	0.9582887701	0.9607577808	0.9696969697	0.9598361086	=(SUM(I4:M4)-MIN(I4:M4)-MAX(I4:M4))/2
5	2		1.0233592881	1.0024570025	1.0093708166	1.009757633	1.0095642248	=(SUM(I5:M5)-MIN(I5:M5)-MAX(I5:M5))/2
6	3	1.0332681018	1.0255661066	1.0419120194	1.0174629325		1.0294171042	=(SUM(I6:M6)-MIN(I6:M6)-MAX(I6:M6))/2
7	4	0.9919385797	1	0.997949419	1.0038910506		0.9989747095	=(SUM(I7:M7)-MIN(I7:M7)-MAX(I7:M7))/2
8							3.9977921471	=SUM(N4:N7)
10					Scaling		S	
11					1.000552268	=4/N8	0.9603661955	=N4*$L$11
12							1.0101217749	=N5*$L$11
13							1.0299856184	=N6*$L$11
14							0.9995264113	=N7*$L$11

Figure 13.28: The Excel solution for Example 13.5

EXCEL SOLUTION

SI: Cells E4:E19

Formulae:

=C4/D4

=C5/D5

=C6/D6

⋮

=C19/D19

Copy and paste the Cells E4–E19 into Cells I6–M5 as follows:

	Cell J4 = E6	Cell K4 = E10	Cell L4 = E14	Cell M4 = E18
	Cell J5 = E7	Cell K5 = E11	Cell L5 = E15	Cell M5 = E19
Cell I6 = E4	Cell J6 = E8	Cell K6 = E12	Cell L6 = E16	
Cell I7 = E5	Cell J7 = E9	Cell K7 = E13	Cell L7 = E17	

Modified averages: Cells N4:N7

Forlmula:

=(SUM(J4:M4)-MIN(J4:M4)-MAX(J4:M4))/2

=(SUM(J5:M5)-MIN(J5:M5)-MAX(J5:M5))/2

=(SUM(I6:L6)-MIN(I6:L6)-MAX(I6:L6))/2

=(SUM(I7:L7)-MIN(I7:L7)-MAX(I7:L7))/2

Sum of modified averages: Cell N8	Formula: =SUM(N4:N7)
Scaling factor: Cell L11	Formula :=4/N8
Seasonal Indices, *S*: Cells N11:N14	Formulae: =N4*$L$11 =N5*$L$11 =N6*$L$11 =N7*$L$11

INTERPRETATION

The general seasonal indices, *S*, for this series are thus:

- For the first quarter: 0.96048024
- For the second quarter: 1.010005003
- For the third quarter: 1.030015008
- For the fourth quarter: 0.999499749

We can interpret these values as indices that indicate how much higher or lower the general values of the series are within a particular quarter. For instance, we could say the following:

- In the first quarter, the values of the milk production are roughly 4% lower than the general trend of the data.
- In the second quarter, the values are roughly 1% higher.
- The values are roughly 3% higher in the third quarter.
- The values are about 0.05% lower in the fourth quarter

Producing seasonally adjusted forecasts

As stated earlier, the purpose of extracting the seasonal component is to:

- enable us to describe the general seasonal fluctuation in the data
- remove the seasonal fluctuation from the time series so that we can analyse the data without having to worry about the seasonal aspect (de-seasonalise the data)
- improve the least squares forecasts of the trend by introducing the seasonal component into the forecast.

In the previous example, we addressed the first point, i.e. extract the seasonal component so that we can analyse the general seasonal fluctuation in the data. In the next example, we attempt to forecast values of the series by basing the least squares line estimator on the de-seasonalised data. The forecasts produced from this analysis will then have the seasonal component reintroduced so that the forecasts exhibit the same seasonal fluctuation as the rest of the data.

The steps that we follow to produce these seasonally adjusted forecasts are the following.

Step 1: Obtain the seasonal indices, S, by following the procedure described in the previous section.

Step 2: De-seasonalise the data by dividing the original time series data by the seasonal component corresponding to the relevant time unit. For example, if the series was collected quarterly, we would divide each of the observations that appear in the first quarter by the seasonal index value associated with the first quarter. The result is a series that contains only the trend, cyclic and irregular components of the series:

$$\frac{Y}{S} = \frac{TCSI}{S} = TCI$$

Step 3: Fit the least squares model to this de-seasonalised series and forecast values using this model.

Step 4: Reintroduce the seasonal component into the forecast by multiplying the forecasted values with the appropriate seasonal index. For example, if we collected quarterly data and produced a forecast for the second quarter using a least squares method, we would multiply this forecasted value by the seasonal index associated with the second quarter.

The forecasted values obtained using this procedure display the same general seasonal fluctuations that appeared in the original data series, thus making them slightly more accurate when forecasting.

We illustrate these four steps using the data from Examples 13.4 and 13.5. In Example 13.6, we attempt to forecast values one year into the future by incorporating the seasonal component extracted in Example 13.5.

WORKED EXAMPLES

EXAMPLE 13.6

Continuing Examples 13.4 and 13.5: The dairy farmer in Example 13.5 now wants to predict the milk production for the next year (the year 2013).

Use the steps described above to produce a forecast for all four quarters of 2013.

Table 13.13: Milk produced (1 000s litres) per quarter

YEAR	QUARTER	t	MILK PRODUCED $Y = TCIS$
2008	1	1	2.95
	2	2	3.18
	3	3	3.30
	4	4	3.23

YEAR	QUARTER	t	MILK PRODUCED $Y = TCIS$
2009	1	5	3.18
	2	6	3.45
	3	7	3.51
	4	8	3.46
2010	1	9	3.36
	2	10	3.57
	3	11	3.76
	4	12	3.65
2011	1	13	3.55
	2	14	3.77
	3	15	3.86
	4	16	3.87
2012	1	17	3.80
	2	18	4.01
	3	19	4.13
	4	20	4.02

We now follow the four steps described to produce the seasonally adjusted forecast for the four quarters of 2013.

Step 1: The seasonal indices obtained in Example 13.4 are shown in Table 13.14.

Table 13.14: Seasonal indices by quarter

QUARTER 1	QUARTER 2	QUARTER 3	QUARTER 4
0.96048024	1.010005003	1.030015008	0.999499749

Step 2: Dividing the original quarterly data series by the corresponding quarterly seasonal indices, we get Table 13.15.

Table 13.15: Dividing the original quarterly data series by the corresponding seasonal indices

YEAR	QUARTER	t	MILK PRODUCED $Y = TCIS$	S	DE-SEASONALISED DATA $TCI = \frac{TCIS}{S}$
2008	1	1	2.95	0.96037	$\frac{2.95}{0.96037} = 3.0717$
	2	2	3.18	1.01012	$\frac{3.18}{1.01012} = 3.1481$
	3	3	3.30	1.02999	$\frac{3.30}{1.02999} = 3.2039$
	4	4	3.23	0.99953	$\frac{3.23}{0.99953} = 3.2315$
2009	1	5	3.18	0.96037	$\frac{3.18}{0.96037} = 3.3112$
	2	6	3.45	1.01012	$\frac{3.45}{1.01012} = 3.4154$
	3	7	3.51	1.02999	$\frac{3.51}{1.02999} = 3.4078$
	4	8	3.46	0.99953	$\frac{3.46}{0.99953} = 3.4616$
⋮	⋮		⋮	⋮	⋮
2012	1	17	3.80	0.96037	$\frac{3.80}{0.96037} = 3.9568$
	2	18	4.01	1.01012	$\frac{4.01}{1.01012} = 3.9698$
	3	19	4.13	1.02999	$\frac{4.13}{1.02999} = 4.0097$
	4	20	4.02	0.99953	$\frac{4.02}{0.99953} = 4.0219$

Step 3: We use Excel to fit the least squares straight-line model to this de-seasonalised series. The resulting least squares estimate of the straight line equation for the *TCI* (de-seasonalised) component is then (using the SLOPE() and INTERCEPT() functions in Excel):

$$(\widehat{TCI})_t = 3.0523 + 0.0502t$$

We can use this formula to forecast the *TCI*-values for the four quarters of 2013 by simply noting that the time values, t, for the four quarters of 2013 are $t = 21$, $t = 22$, $t = 23$ and $t = 24$. The forecasted values from this model are then:

$$\begin{aligned}
&2013 - \text{Quarter 1: } (\widehat{TCI})_{21} = 3.0523 + 0.0502 \times 21 = 4.107\\
&2013 - \text{Quarter 2: } (\widehat{TCI})_{22} = 3.0523 + 0.0502 \times 22 = 4.157\\
&2013 - \text{Quarter 3: } (\widehat{TCI})_{23} = 3.0523 + 0.0502 \times 23 = 4.207\\
&2013 - \text{Quarter 4:: } (\widehat{TCI})_{24} = 3.0523 + 0.0502 \times 24 = 4.257
\end{aligned}$$

These forecasts do not contain any information about the seasonal fluctuations in the quarters. In the final step, we reintroduce this seasonal information.

Step 4: We now multiply the forecasts obtained in step 3 by the seasonal indices obtained in step 1. Each forecasted quarter is multiplied by the seasonal index of the corresponding quarter, e.g., the forecast of the first quarter of 2013 is multiplied by the seasonal index of the first quarter. Finally, the seasonally adjusted forecasts are given in Table 13.16.

Table 13.16: Seasonally adjusted forecasts

YEAR	QUARTER	t	FORECASTS, $\widehat{(TCI)}_t = 3.0523 + 0.0502t$	S	SEASONALLY ADJUSTED FORECASTS, $\widehat{(TCI)}_t \times S$
2013	1	21	4.107	0.96037	4.107 × 0.96037 = 3.944
	2	22	4.157	1.01012	4.157 × 1.01012 = 4.199
	3	23	4.207	1.02999	4.207 × 1.02999 = 4.333
	4	24	4.257	0.99953	4.257 × 0.99953 = 4.255

The Excel solution is shown in Figure 13.29.

	A	B	C	D	E	F	G	H	I	J	K	L	M	N	O
1	Year	Quarter	t	$Y = TCSI$	Deseasonalised data, TCI			$(TCI)t = 3.0523 + 0.0502t$			Trend with seasonality reintroduced			S	
2	2008	1	1	2.95	3.0717449385	=D2/$N$2		3.1025493203	=$N$8+C2*$N$10		2.9795834869	=H2*$N$2		0.9603661955	
3		2	2	3.18	3.1481352834	=D3/$N$3		3.152771069	=$N$8+C3*$N$10		3.184682708	=H3*$N$3		1.0101217749	
4		3	3	3.30	3.2039282308	=D4/$N$4		3.2029928178	=$N$8+C4*$N$10		3.2990365381	=H4*$N$4		1.0299856184	
5		4	4	3.23	3.2315304162	=D5/$N$5		3.2532145665	=$N$8+C5*$N$10		3.2516738809	=H5*$N$5		0.9995264113	
6	2009	1	5	3.18	3.3112369168	=D6/$N$2		3.3034363152	=$N$8+C6*$N$10		3.172508566	=H6*$N$2			
7		2	6	3.45	3.4154297886	=D7/$N$3		3.353658064	=$N$8+C7*$N$10		3.3876030358	=H7*$N$3		Intercept	
8		3	7	3.51	3.4078145727	=D8/$N$4		3.4038798127	=$N$8+C8*$N$10		3.5059472538	=H8*$N$4		3.0523275715	=INTERCEPT(E2:E21,C2:C21)
9		4	8	3.46	3.4616393933	=D9/$N$5		3.4541015614	=$N$8+C9*$N$10		3.452465738	=H9*$N$5		Slope	
10	2010	1	9	3.36	3.4986654215	=D10/$N$2		3.5043233102	=$N$8+C10*$N$10		3.365433645	=H10*$N$2		0.0502217487	=SLOPE(E2:E21,C2:C21)
11		2	10	3.57	3.5342273465	=D11/$N$3		3.5545450589	=$N$8+C11*$N$10		3.5905233637	=H11*$N$3			
12		3	11	3.76	3.6505364084	=D12/$N$4		3.6047668076	=$N$8+C12*$N$10		3.7128579695	=H12*$N$4			
13		4	12	3.65	3.6517294177	=D13/$N$5		3.6549885564	=$N$8+C13*$N$10		3.6532575951	=H13*$N$5			
14	2011	1	13	3.55	3.6965066209	=D14/$N$2		3.7052103051	=$N$8+C14*$N$10		3.5583587241	=H14*$N$2			
15		2	14	3.77	3.7322232763	=D15/$N$3		3.7554320538	=$N$8+C15*$N$10		3.7934436916	=H15*$N$3			
16		3	15	3.86	3.7476251426	=D16/$N$4		3.8056538026	=$N$8+C16*$N$10		3.9197686852	=H16*$N$4			
17		4	16	3.87	3.8718336566	=D17/$N$5		3.8558755513	=$N$8+C17*$N$10		3.8540494523	=H17*$N$5			
18	2012	1	17	3.80	3.9568239886	=D18/$N$2		3.9060973	=$N$8+C18*$N$10		3.7512838031	=H18*$N$2			
19		2	18	4.01	3.969818392	=D19/$N$3		3.9563190488	=$N$8+C19*$N$10		3.9963640195	=H19*$N$3			
20		3	19	4.13	4.0097647252	=D20/$N$4		4.0065407975	=$N$8+C20*$N$10		4.1266794009	=H20*$N$4			
21		4	20	4.02	4.0219047286	=D21/$N$5		4.0567625463	=$N$8+C21*$N$10		4.0548413094	=H21*$N$5			
22	2013	1	21					4.106984295	=$N$8+C22*$N$10		3.9442088821	=H22*$N$2			
23		2	22					4.1572060437	=$N$8+C23*$N$10		4.1992843473	=H23*$N$3			
24		3	23					4.2074277925	=$N$8+C24*$N$10		4.3335901166	=H24*$N$4			
25		4	24					4.2576495412	=$N$8+C25*$N$10		4.2556331665	=H25*$N$5			
26															

Figure 13.29: The Excel solution for Example 13.7

EXCEL SOLUTION

De-seasonalised data: Cells E2:E21	Formulae:
	=D2/$N$2
	=D3/$N$3
	=D4/$N$4
	=D5/$N$5
	=D6/$N$2
	=D7/$N$3
	=D8/$N$4
	=D9/$N$5
	⋮
	=D21/$N$5
Intercept: Cell N8	Formula: =INTERCEPT(E2:E21,C2:C21)
Slope: Cell N10	Formula: =SLOPE(E2:E21,C2:C21)
Least squares fitted values: Cells H2:H21	Formulae:
	=$N$8+C2*$N$10
	=$N$8+C3*$N$10
	=$N$8+C4*$N$10
	⋮
	=$N$8+C21*$N$10
Forecasted values: Cells H22:H25	Formulae:
	=$N$8+C22*$N$10
	=$N$8+C23*$N$10
	=$N$8+C24*$N$10
	=$N$8+C25*$N$10
Least squares fitted values with seasonality reintroduced: Cells K2:K21	Formulae:
	=H2*$N$2
	=H3*$N$3
	=H4*$N$4
	=H5*$N$5
	=H6*$N$2

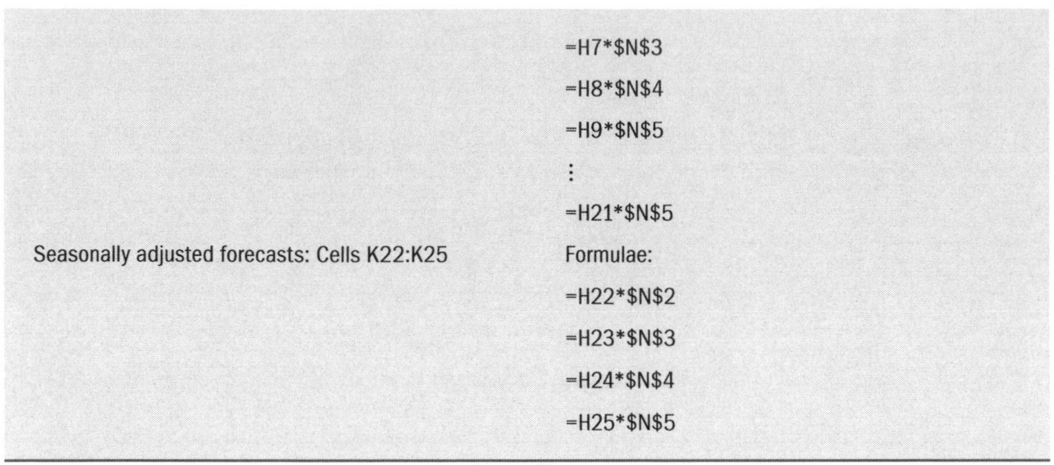

	=H7*$N$3
	=H8*$N$4
	=H9*$N$5
	⋮
	=H21*$N$5
Seasonally adjusted forecasts: Cells K22:K25	Formulae:
	=H22*$N$2
	=H23*$N$3
	=H24*$N$4
	=H25*$N$5

The seasonally adjusted forecasts are shown in Figure 13.30 (they are represented by the points to the right of the vertical line.

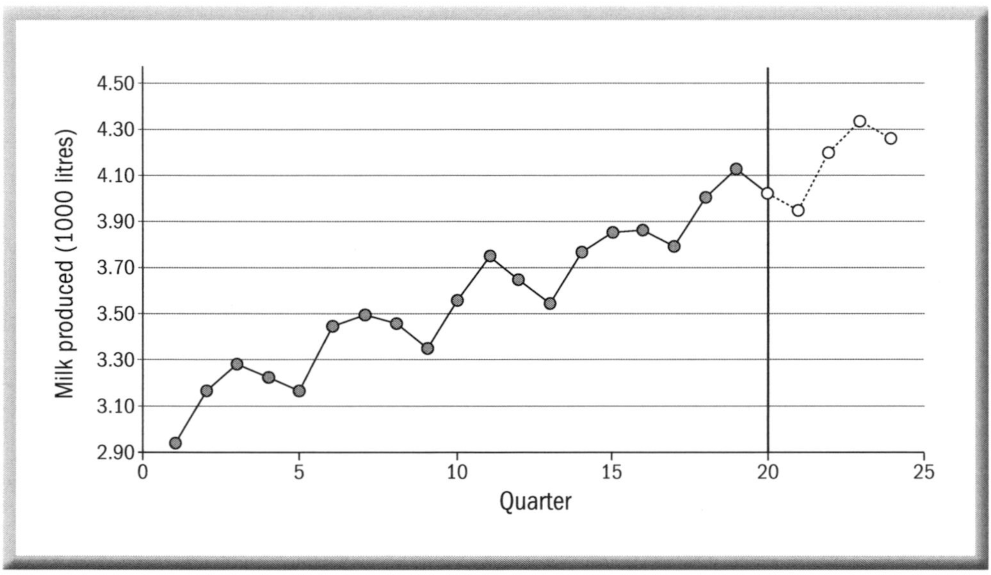

Figure 13.30: The plot of the forecasted milk production values for the 2013 period

In Figure 13.30, we see that the forecast follows the same trend and seasonal structure of the original series, thus making it preferable to the straight-line forecast we would have obtained without the seasonal adjustment.

13.4 Time series smoothing and forecasting

In this section, we explore the use of time series smoothing techniques and how they can be used to produce forecasts. The smoothing techniques that we employ include a method based on moving averages (slightly different from the technique discussed in the previous section) and a method called **exponential smoothing**.

13.4.1 Simple moving averages and forecasting

The moving average calculations discussed in the previous section are called central moving averages, because the window used to calculate the averages is centred on a particular time unit with observations on either side of that central point. This central method of moving average calculation is not suitable for forecasting, because it loses observations on either side of the series (there will always be missing values at the beginning of the series *and* at the end of the series).

We discuss another, more appropriate, method of moving averages in this section. This method involves using a window that is not centred on a time unit, but rather determines the current moving average by calculating the average of the current time series value and the previous ($W - 1$)-values. The calculation is fundamentally the same as the central moving average, except that the moving average value is placed at the end of the window used for the calculation, rather than in the middle. We refer to this type of moving average as a **simple moving average.**

Simple moving averages Averages of the observations in an interval (or window) that include and precede the current time period. This window is moved, the average is calculated for the items that fall within the window, and the resulting value falls on the period that appears at the end of the window. The resulting series of averages is a simple moving average series.

Simple moving averages

In general, the simple moving average value, M_t, of time series values, Y_i, at some time t using a window size of W is given by:

$$M_t = \frac{1}{W} \sum_{i=t-W+1}^{t} Y_i \text{ for } W \leq t \leq n \tag{13.5}$$

t is the current time period, W is the window length used in the moving average calculation, Y_t is the original time series value at time t, and n is the total number of observations in the time series.

This form of moving average is typically only useful for producing forecasts in the following situations:

- If the time series data set is reasonably stationary in the mean (it does not exhibit any obvious trends upwards or downwards).
- If the time series data does not exhibit seasonality effects.
- If we are only interested in forecasting one time period into the future.

If these conditions are not met, the forecasting methods discussed earlier might be more appropriate.

We can now look at how we can calculate these moving average values using a simple time series data set. Consider the following data set consisting of five observations in a time series.

Table 13.17: Five time series observations

PERIOD (t)	TIME SERIES VALUES (Y_t)
1	220
2	250
3	150
4	220
5	200

The simple moving average with window size equal to 3, i.e. $W = 3$ at a specific time period $t = 5$ is calculated as:

$$\begin{aligned} M_5 &= \frac{1}{W}\sum_{i=5-W+1}^{5} Y_i \\ &= \frac{1}{3}\sum_{i=3}^{5} Y_i \\ &= \frac{1}{3}(Y_3 + Y_4 + Y_5) \\ &= \frac{1}{3}(150 + 220 + 200) \\ &= 190 \end{aligned}$$

Therefore, the simple moving average value at time $t = 5$ is $M_5 = 190$. The remaining simple moving average values ($t = 3$ and $t = 4$) are calculated and shown in Table 13.18. Note that we cannot calculate the simple moving average for $t = 1$ or $t = 2$ because there are not enough previous observations for the calculations in these periods.

Table 13.18: Simple moving average values for the observations in Table 13.17

PERIOD (t)	TIME SERIES VALUES (Y_t)	MOVING AVERAGE VALUES, $W = 3$ (M_t)
1	220	–
2	250	–
3	150	$\frac{(150 + 250 + 220)}{3} = 206.67$
4	220	$\frac{(220 + 150 + 250)}{3} = 206.67$
5	200	$\frac{(200 + 220 + 150)}{3} = 190$

This type of moving average *only* loses values at the beginning of the series and not at the end (unlike the central moving averages described earlier, which lose values on both ends).

Forecasting with simple moving averages

We can use these simple moving averages to forecast exactly one period into the future by simply shifting the moving average down one period, i.e. the forecast for time $t + 1$ is simply the moving average value at time t, M_t.

For example, the one-period-into-the-future forecast for Table 13.18 will then simply be generated by shifting the M_t values down one time unit (Table 13.19).

Table 13.19: One-period-into-the-future forecast for Table 13.18

PERIOD (t)	TIME SERIES VALUES (Y_t)	FORECASTED VALUES, $W = 3$
1	220	–
2	250	–
3	150	–
4	220	$\frac{(150 + 250 + 220)}{3} = 206.67$
5	200	$\frac{(220 + 150 + 250)}{3} = 206.67$
6	–	$\frac{(200 + 220 + 150)}{3} = 190$

Therefore, the forecast for the future time period $t = 6$ is just $M_5 = 190$.

The choice of the window length in this form of forecasting will have a large influence on the results, since larger window sizes result in smoother moving average series, while smaller window sizes result in more dynamic' series.

- *Smoother series (large window sizes)*: The benefit of 'smooth' moving average series' is that the forecasts reflect the overall mean of the data more accurately and thus can be used to make general forecasts where the mean of the series will be one period into the future (the larger the window length, the more general the forecast).
- *Rougher series (small window sizes)*: If we choose a smaller window length, the forecast is slightly more in tune with the underlying series. Forecasts made from moving average series with shorter window lengths (while still reasonably smooth) are more dynamic and tend to capture short-term fluctuations better. They are appropriate if we want to make forecasts that give more weight to the effect that the short term fluctuation of the series has on the forecast.

Please note that we should *avoid* using the simple moving average forecasting technique for forecasting *non-stationary* data (data with a regularly increasing or decreasing trend) or for data with a *seasonal* component.

The next example employs the same idea to forecast a single month into the future using a moving average approach.

WORKED EXAMPLES

EXAMPLE 13.7

The total amount of money that a particular household spends on telecommunication devices (cellular phone contract payments, air-time, internet data bundles, and so on) is recorded monthly for a period of two years. This series is given in Table 13.20.

Table 13.20: Total amount of money spent by a household on telecommunication devices

YEAR	MONTH	t	MONEY SPENT (RAND), Y
2011	Jan	1	3 310
	Feb	2	3 215
	Mar	3	2 992
	Apr	4	2 842
	May	5	2 715
	Jun	6	2 859
	Jul	7	3 105
	Aug	8	3 250
	Sep	9	3 510
	Oct	10	3 210
	Nov	11	3 097
	Dec	12	2 465
2012	Jan	13	2 805
	Feb	14	2 959
	Mar	15	3 155
	Apr	16	3 542
	May	17	3 088
	Jun	18	3 394
	Jul	19	3 784
	Aug	20	3 521
	Sep	21	3 464
	Oct	22	3 012
	Nov	23	2 989
	Dec	24	3 246

The household in the study would like to use these data to produce forecasts for the upcoming months so that they can budget for other expenses.

Use a moving average approach (with window size of 4, i.e. $W = 4$) to forecast the amount of money spent in January 2013.

We begin by plotting the time series (see Figure 13.31) and note that this data set does not exhibit a linear trend, nor does it appear to contain any seasonal fluctuations. We can thus use simple moving averages to forecast one month into the future.

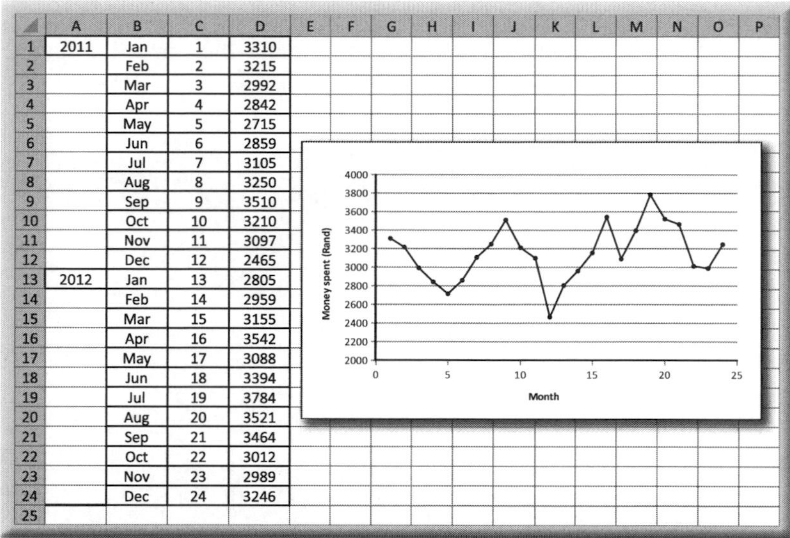

	A	B	C	D
1	2011	Jan	1	3310
2		Feb	2	3215
3		Mar	3	2992
4		Apr	4	2842
5		May	5	2715
6		Jun	6	2859
7		Jul	7	3105
8		Aug	8	3250
9		Sep	9	3510
10		Oct	10	3210
11		Nov	11	3097
12		Dec	12	2465
13	2012	Jan	13	2805
14		Feb	14	2959
15		Mar	15	3155
16		Apr	16	3542
17		May	17	3088
18		Jun	18	3394
19		Jul	19	3784
20		Aug	20	3521
21		Sep	21	3464
22		Oct	22	3012
23		Nov	23	2989
24		Dec	24	3246
25				

Figure 13.31: The time series plot of the 'money spent on telecommunications' data in Example 13.7

The simple moving average with window length $W = 4$ is calculated using formula (13.5). These calculations are given in Table 13.21.

Table 13.21: Simple moving average of the 'money spent on telecommunications' data in Example 13.8

t	MONEY SPENT (RAND), Y_t	SIMPLE MOVING AVERAGE, $W = 4$, (M_t)
1	3 310	
2	3 215	
3	2 992	
4	2 842	$\frac{3\,310 + 3\,215 + 2\,992 + 2\,842}{4} = 3\,089.75$
5	2 715	$\frac{3\,215 + 2\,992 + 2\,842 + 2\,715}{4} = 2\,941$
6	2 859	$\frac{2\,992 + 2\,842 + 2\,715 + 2\,859}{4} = 2\,852$
⋮	⋮	⋮
21	3 464	$\frac{3\,394 + 3\,784 + 3\,521 + 3\,464}{4} = 3\,540.75$
22	3 012	$\frac{3\,784 + 3\,521 + 3\,464 + 3\,012}{4} = 3\,445.25$
23	2 989	$\frac{3\,521 + 3\,464 + 3\,012 + 2\,989}{4} = 3\,246.5$
24	3 246	$\frac{3\,464 + 3\,012 + 2\,989 + 3\,246}{4} = 3\,177.75$

Once we have the M_t-values, we can easily obtain the forecast for January 2013 ($t = 25$) by simply shifting the moving average series down one month. The forecasted values are given in Table 13.21.

Table 13.22: Forecasted values for January 2013

t	MONEY SPENT (RAND), Y_t	FORECAST
1	2 369	
2	2 490	
3	2 610	
4	2 621	
5	2 715	$\frac{3\,310 + 3\,215 + 2\,992 + 2\,842}{4} = 3\,089.75$
6	2 859	$\frac{3\,215 + 2\,992 + 2\,842 + 2\,715}{4} = 2\,941$
⋮	⋮	⋮
21	3 464	$\frac{3\,088 + 3\,394 + 3\,784 + 3\,521}{4} = 3\,812$
22	3 012	$\frac{3\,394 + 3\,784 + 3\,521 + 3\,464}{4} = 3\,540.75$
23	2 989	$\frac{3\,784 + 3\,521 + 3\,464 + 3\,012}{4} = 3\,445.25$
24	3 246	$\frac{3\,521 + 3\,464 + 3\,012 + 2\,989}{4} = 3\,246.5$
25		$\frac{3\,464 + 3\,012 + 2\,989 + 3\,246}{4} = 3\,177.75$

Therefore, the forecasted amount of money that the family will spend in January 2013 is R3 177.75 using a simple moving average approach with window size $W = 4$.

We can also easily obtain these moving average and forecasted values using Excel. The solution for this particular problem is shown in Figure 13.32.

	A	B	C	D	E	F	G
1	*t*	Money spent (Rand)	Moving average ($W = 4$)		Forecast		
2							
3	1	3310					
4	2	3215					
5	3	2992					
6	4	2842	3089.75	=AVERAGE(B3:B6)			
7	5	2715	2941.00	=AVERAGE(B4:B7)	3089.75	=AVERAGE(B3:B6)	
8	6	2859	2852.00	=AVERAGE(B5:B8)	2941.00	=AVERAGE(B4:B7)	
9	7	3105	2880.25	=AVERAGE(B6:B9)	2852.00	=AVERAGE(B5:B8)	
10	8	3250	2982.25	=AVERAGE(B7:B10)	2880.25	=AVERAGE(B6:B9)	
11	9	3510	3181.00	=AVERAGE(B8:B11)	2982.25	=AVERAGE(B7:B10)	
12	10	3210	3268.75	=AVERAGE(B9:B12)	3181.00	=AVERAGE(B8:B11)	
13	11	3097	3266.75	=AVERAGE(B10:B13)	3268.75	=AVERAGE(B9:B12)	
14	12	2465	3070.50	=AVERAGE(B11:B14)	3266.75	=AVERAGE(B10:B13)	
15	13	2805	2894.25	=AVERAGE(B12:B15)	3070.50	=AVERAGE(B11:B14)	
16	14	2959	2831.50	=AVERAGE(B13:B16)	2894.25	=AVERAGE(B12:B15)	
17	15	3155	2846.00	=AVERAGE(B14:B17)	2831.50	=AVERAGE(B13:B16)	
18	16	3542	3115.25	=AVERAGE(B15:B18)	2846.00	=AVERAGE(B14:B17)	
19	17	3088	3186.00	=AVERAGE(B16:B19)	3115.25	=AVERAGE(B15:B18)	
20	18	3394	3294.75	=AVERAGE(B17:B20)	3186.00	=AVERAGE(B16:B19)	
21	19	3784	3452.00	=AVERAGE(B18:B21)	3294.75	=AVERAGE(B17:B20)	
22	20	3521	3446.75	=AVERAGE(B19:B22)	3452.00	=AVERAGE(B18:B21)	
23	21	3464	3540.75	=AVERAGE(B20:B23)	3446.75	=AVERAGE(B19:B22)	
24	22	3012	3445.25	=AVERAGE(B21:B24)	3540.75	=AVERAGE(B20:B23)	
25	23	2989	3246.50	=AVERAGE(B22:B25)	3445.25	=AVERAGE(B21:B24)	
26	24	3246	3177.75	=AVERAGE(B23:B26)	3246.50	=AVERAGE(B22:B25)	
27	25				3177.75	=AVERAGE(B23:B26)	

Figure 13.32: The Excel solution to Example 13.7

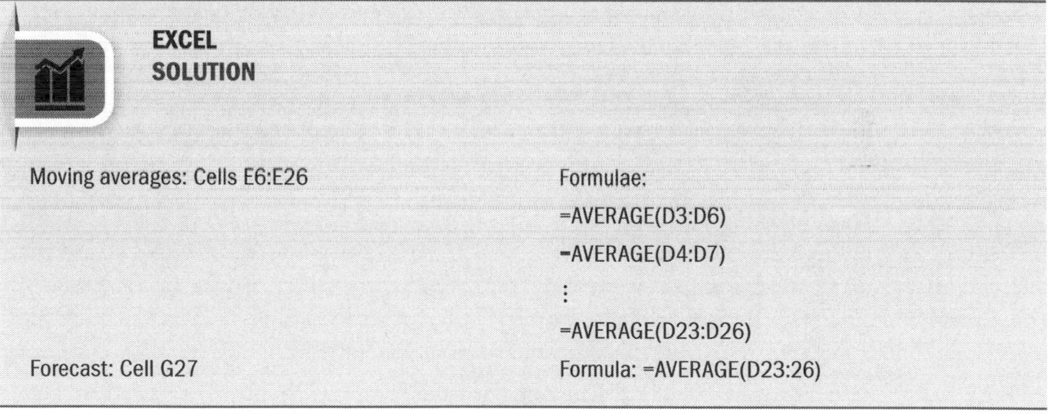

EXCEL SOLUTION

Moving averages: Cells E6:E26	Formulae: =AVERAGE(D3:D6) =AVERAGE(D4:D7) ⋮ =AVERAGE(D23:D26)
Forecast: Cell G27	Formula: =AVERAGE(D23:26)

By plotting all three of these series (the original series, the moving average series and the forecasted series) on the same set of axes, we can clearly see how the moving average is a smoother version of the original series and also how the forecast behaves (see Figure 13.33). Note that the forecast series in Figure 13.33 is identical to the moving average series, except that it has shifted over by one time unit (this should also be clear from the way it was calculated in the Excel sheet of Figure 13.32). We can also see the forecast for the time unit $t = 25$ (i.e. January 2013) in the plot, which appears to the right of the vertical line.

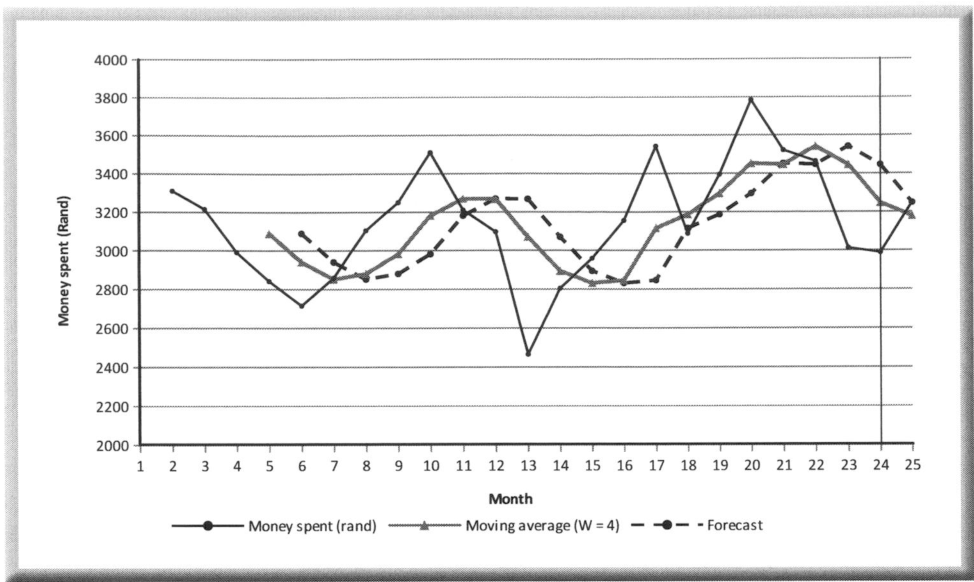

Figure 13.33: Plot of the original time series data for Example 13.7, the simple moving average and the forecasted values

NOTE

To easily add the moving average series to an existing time series plot in Excel, use the following steps:

- In an existing time series, right-click on any point on the plotted line to bring up the pop-up menu containing the options for that series (as shown in Figure 13.34 below).

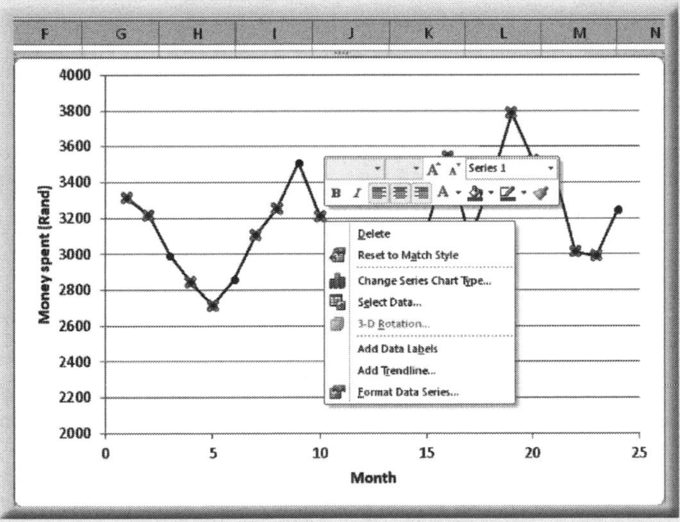

Figure 13.34: The pop-up menu for the options for the plotted series

- Select the 'Add Trendline' option to bring up the 'Format Trendline' window shown in Figure 13.35.

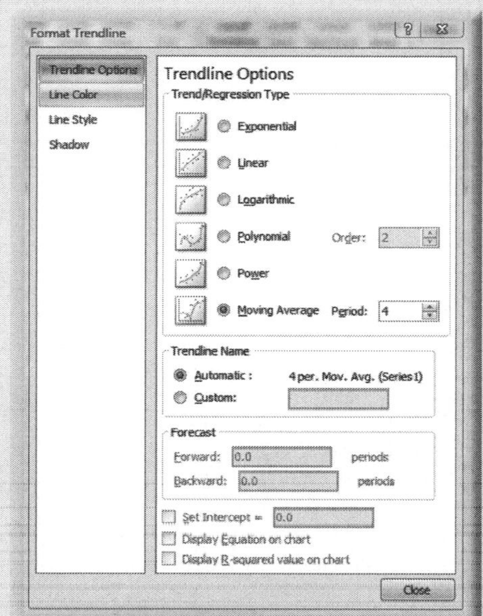

Figure 13.35: The 'Format Trendline' window for plotting the simple moving average on a time series plot

- In this window, select the 'Moving Average' in the 'Trendline Options', and specify the window length by changing the 'Period' option (in Figure 13.35, the window length is chosen to be $W = 4$).
- Once done, click on 'Close' and the moving average trendline should appear on your time series plot (as in Figure 13.33).

NOTE The simple moving average discussed in this section has the following properties:

- The larger the window size, W, the smoother the resulting moving average.
- It only loses values at the beginning of the series and not at the end (unlike the central moving averages described earlier, which lose values at both ends).
- Moving averages are an acceptable forecasting technique, provided we are interested in forecasting *only one future period for stationary* and *non-seasonal* data.
- If the window size is equal to the length of the series, there will only be one moving average value and it will be equal to the sample mean of the time series data set.
- If the time series is *stationary in the mean* (it doesn't trend upwards or downwards), then the larger the value of W, the better the estimator of the true underlying mean. In general, the sample mean of the whole time series is the best estimator for the overall underlying mean of the series.

- The smooth simple moving average values lag behind the original values. The length of this lag is directly related to the window length, W (i.e. the larger the value of W, the greater the lag). For example, in Figure 13.36, we have a series and a simple moving average with window length $W = 3$. Clearly the behaviour of the moving average is similar to the original series, but is delayed by a few time units (i.e. peaks and dips that appear in the original series only register in the moving average series a few time units later).

	A	B	C	D
1	t	Time series, Y	Moving average ($W = 3$)	
2	1	60.192		
3	2	120.368		
4	3	131.716		
5	4	91.708	104.092	=AVERAGE(B2:B4)
6	5	76.456	114.597	=AVERAGE(B3:B5)
7	6	60.028	99.960	=AVERAGE(B4:B6)
8	7	50.156	76.064	=AVERAGE(B5:B7)
9	8	52.432	62.213	=AVERAGE(B6:B8)
10	9	84.336	54.205	=AVERAGE(B7:B9)
11	10	123.300	62.308	=AVERAGE(B8:B10)
12	11	133.560	86.689	=AVERAGE(B9:B11)
13	12	109.596	113.732	=AVERAGE(B10:B12)
14	13	88.978	121.578	=AVERAGE(B12:B13)
15	14	109.348	99.287	=AVERAGE(B13:B14)
16	15	160.320	119.549	=AVERAGE(B14:B16)
17				

Figure 13.36: Illustration of the lag that appears in moving averages

13.4.2 Exponential smoothing and forecasting

Exponential smoothing One of the methods of forecasting that uses a constant (or several constants) to predict future values by smoothing the past values in the series. The effect of this constant decreases exponentially as the older observations are taken into calculation.

The concept of **exponential smoothing** assumes that a predictor for the time series at some time t is equal to one of the previous predicted value plus some fraction, α, of the error made when predicting the previous value. Essentially, we are saying that the current predicted value is the same as the previous one, but that, if we made a mistake when predicting the previous value, we should adjust the current value by an amount that is proportional to the error made previously. Formula (13.6) expresses the concept of exponential smoothing mathematically:

$$F_1 = Y_1$$

And:

$$F_t = F_{t-1} + \alpha(Y_{t-1} - F_{t-1}) \qquad t = 2, 3, 4, \ldots \qquad (13.6)$$

- F_t is the exponential smoothing predicted value at time t.
- Y_{t-1} is the value of the series at time $t - 1$.
- α is the dampening or smoothing constant (this value lies between 0 and 1, i.e. $0 \leq \alpha \leq 1$, although it is almost always chosen to be between 0 and 0.5).
- $Y_{t-1} - F_{t-1}$ is the error or difference that occurs at time $t - 1$ when attempting to estimate Y_{t-1} by using F_{t-1}.

Note that the initial predicted value is the same as the initial value of the series, i.e. $F_1 = Y_1$, but that in general, F_t (for $t \geq 2$) is given by formula (13.6).

By rearranging formula (13.6), we get a slightly different form of the exponential smoothing values:

$$F_t = \alpha Y_{t-1} + (1 - \alpha)F_{t-1} \tag{13.7}$$

This form of exponential smoothing is the one that is more commonly used. It shows that the exponential smoothing values are simply a weighted average between the previous time series value, Y_{t-1}, and the previous exponential smoothing value, F_{t-1}. However, if we take F_{t-1} and apply formula (13.7) again we get:

$$F_{t-1} = \alpha Y_{t-2} + (1 - \alpha)F_{t-2}$$

The F_{t-1}-value depends on Y_{t-2} and F_{t-2}. Applying this rule iteratively, we will also find that F_{t-2} depends on Y_{t-3} and F_{t-3} (and, in turn, F_{t-3} depends on Y_{t-4} and F_{t-4}, and so on). Following this chain of dependencies means that the F_t-value in formula (13.7) depends not only on Y_{t-1}, but also on all of the values Y_{t-2}, Y_{t-3}, ... , Y_2 and Y_1. We can express this relationship mathematically (using some basic algebra) as:

$$F_t = \alpha Y_t + \alpha(1 - \alpha)Y_{t-1} + \alpha(1 - \alpha)^2 Y_{t-2} + \ldots$$

Note how the effect of each Y is determined by the α-value. Specifically, the effect of Y decreases exponentially as we move further into the past (hence the name *exponential* smoothing).

This dependence on past values of exponential smoothing is in contrast with the simple moving average method of forecasting, which only uses the previous ($W - 1$)-values.

We can also use formula (13.7) to see how the α constant affects the smoothness of the series.

- If we choose α so that it is close to 0 (for example, 0.1 or 0.2), then the value of F_t will put less importance on the Y_{t-1}-value and greater importance on the F_{t-1}-value. This means that sharp jumps in the underlying series will not greatly affect the predicted values. The series instead gives more importance to the previous exponential smoothed values, F_{t-1}, F_{t-2}, ... The result is that we obtain a very smooth series for small α-values.
- If we choose α so that it is close to 1 (for example, 0.9 or 0.8), then the value of F_t will put greater importance on the values of Y_{t-1} and less importance on F_{t-1}. This means that sharp jumps in the underlying series will greatly affect the predicted values. The series will then be much more prone to movement when there is movement in the underlying series. The result is that we obtain a very rough series for large α-values.

NOTE

Why do we multiply the error by the fraction α? If every current predicted value depends on the previous one, which in turn depends on the one before that, and so on, then all the previous errors are in fact embedded in every current observation or forecast. By taking a fraction of error, we are in fact dampening (or reducing) the influence that every previous observation and its associated error has on the current predicted value.

As with the moving average method, the exponential smoothing method also requires that the time series data does not contain a linear increasing or decreasing trend nor a seasonal component. Also, we can only use forecasting for exponential smoothing to forecast one time period into the future.

Example 13.8 shows how we can construct the exponentially smoothed series and how we can use it to forecast one time unit into the future. In the example, we also consider different values for α and note how they influence the exponentially smoothed series.

WORKED EXAMPLES

EXAMPLE 13.8

Using the same data in Example 13.7, forecast the amount of money spent in January 2013 using exponential smoothing.

We use two different values of the smoothing constant α to construct the exponential smoothing series. We begin by calculating the exponential smoothed values using $\alpha = 0.1$. Some of the calculations are given in the table below (note that we use formula (13.7) to calculate these exponential smoothed values).

Table 13.23: Exponential smoothing, α = 0.1

t	MONEY SPENT (RAND) Y_t	EXPONENTIAL SMOOTHING, $\alpha = 0.1$
1	$Y_1 = 3\ 310$	$F_1 = Y_1 = 3\ 310$
2	$Y_2 = 3\ 215$	$F_2 = \alpha Y_1 + (1 - \alpha)F_1 = 0.1 \times 3\ 310 + 0.9 \times 3\ 310 = 3\ 310$
3	$Y_3 = 2\ 992$	$F_3 = \alpha Y_2 + (1 - \alpha)F_2 = 0.1 \times 3\ 215 + 0.9 \times 3\ 310 = 3\ 300.5$
4	$Y_4 = 2\ 842$	$F_4 = \alpha Y_3 + (1 - \alpha)F_3 = 0.1 \times 2\ 992 + 0.9 \times 3\ 300.5 = 3\ 269.65$
5	$Y_5 = 2\ 715$	$F_5 = \alpha Y_4 + (1 - \alpha)F_4 = 0.1 \times 2\ 842 + 0.9 \times 3\ 269.65 = 3\ 226.885$
6	$Y_6 = 2\ 859$	$F_6 = \alpha Y_5 + (1 - \alpha)F_5 = 0.1 \times 2\ 715 + 0.9 \times 3\ 226.885 = 3\ 175.6965$
⋮	⋮	⋮
21	$Y_{21} = 3\ 464$	$F_{21} = \alpha Y_{20} + (1 - \alpha)F_{20} = 0.1 \times 3\ 521 + 0.9 \times 3\ 209.8108 = 3\ 240.9297$
22	$Y_{22} = 3\ 012$	$F_{22} = \alpha Y_{21} + (1 - \alpha)F_{21} = 0.1 \times 3\ 464 + 0.9 \times 3\ 240.9297 = 3\ 263.2367$

t	MONEY SPENT (RAND) Y_t	EXPONENTIAL SMOOTHING, $\alpha = 0.1$
23	Y_{23} = 2 989	$F_{23} = \alpha Y_{22} + (1 - \alpha)F_{22} = 0.1 \times 3\ 012 + 0.9 \times 3\ 263.2367 = 3\ 238.1131$
24	Y_{24} = 3 246	$F_{24} = \alpha Y_{23} + (1 - \alpha)F_{23} = 0.1 \times 2\ 989 + 0.9 \times 3\ 238.1131 = 3\ 213.2018$
25		$F_{25} = \alpha Y_{24} + (1 - \alpha)F_{24} = 0.1 \times 3\ 246 + 0.9 \times 3\ 213.2018 = 3\ 216.4816$

The forecasted value for January 2013 ($t = 25$) is R3 216.48 using an exponential smoother with $\alpha = 0.1$.

Next, we consider the same forecast, but we now use $\alpha = 0.9$. Most of the calculations, using formula (13.7), are given in Table 13.24.

Table 13.24: Exponential smoothing, α = 0.9

t	MONEY SPENT (RAND) Y_t	EXPONENTIAL SMOOTHING, $\alpha = 0.9$
1	Y_1 = 3 310	$F_1 = Y_1 = 3\ 310$
2	Y_2 = 3 215	$F_2 = \alpha Y_1 + (1 - \alpha)F_1 = 0.9 \times 3\ 310 + 0.1 \times 3\ 310 = 3\ 310$
3	Y_3 = 2 992	$F_3 = \alpha Y_2 + (1 - \alpha)F_2 = 09 \times 3\ 215 + 0.1 \times 3\ 310 = 3\ 224.5$
4	Y_4 = 2 842	$F_4 = \alpha Y_3 + (1 - \alpha)F_3 = 0.9 \times 2\ 992 + 0.1 \times 3\ 224.5 = 3\ 015.25$
5	Y_5 = 2 715	$F_5 = \alpha Y_4 + (1 - \alpha)F_4 = 0.9 \times 2\ 842 + 0.1 \times 3\ 015.25 = 2\ 859.325$
6	Y_6 = 2 859	$F_6 = \alpha Y_5 + (1 - \alpha)F_5 = 0.9 \times 2\ 715 + 0.1 \times 2\ 859.325 = 2\ 729.4325$
⋮	⋮	⋮
21	Y_{21} = 3 464	$F_{21} = \alpha Y_{20} + (1 - \alpha)F_{20} = 0.9 \times 3\ 521 + 0.1 \times 3\ 742.3532 = 3\ 543.1353$
22	Y_{22} = 3 012	$F_{22} = \alpha Y_{21} + (1 - \alpha)F_{21} = 0.9 \times 3\ 464 + 0.1 \times 3\ 543.1353 = 3\ 471.9135$
23	Y_{23} = 2 989	$F_{23} = \alpha Y_{22} + (1 - \alpha)F_{22} = 0.9 \times 3\ 012 + 0.1 \times 3\ 471.9135 = 3\ 057.9914$
24	Y_{24} = 3 246	$F_{24} = \alpha Y_{23} + (1 - \alpha)F_{23} = 0.9 \times 2\ 989 + 0.1 \times 3\ 057.9914 = 2\ 995.8991$
25		$F_{25} = \alpha Y_{24} + (1 - \alpha)F_{24} = 0.9 \times 3\ 246 + 0.1 \times 2\ 995.8991 = 3\ 220.9899$

For this choice of $\alpha = 0.9$, our forecasted value for January 2013 is R3 220.99, which is very similar to the previous estimate based on $\alpha = 0.1$.

Naturally, we can calculate the same quantities in Excel. We can also use the plot function to create time series plots to graphically represent these exponentially smoothed series.

The Excel calculations are given in Figure 13.37 and the time series plots are shown in Figure 13.38.

	A	B	C	D	E	F	G	H	I	J	K
1 2			t	Money spent (rand) Y	Exponential smoothing, $\alpha = 0.1$		Exponential smoothing, $\alpha = 0.9$				
3	2011	Jan	1	3310	3310	=D3	3310	=D3			$\alpha = 0.1$
4		Feb	2	3215	3310	=$K$3*D3+(1-$K$3)*E3	3310	=$K$5*D3+(1-$K$5)*G3			
5		Mar	3	2992	3300.5	=$K$3*D4+(1-$K$3)*E4	3224.5	=$K$5*D4+(1-$K$5)*G4			$\alpha = 0.9$
6		Apr	4	2842	3269.65	=$K$3*D5+(1-$K$3)*E5	3015.25	=$K$5*D5+(1-$K$5)*G5			
7		May	5	2715	3226.885	=$K$3*D6+(1-$K$3)*E6	2859.325	=$K$5*D6+(1-$K$5)*G6			
8		Jun	6	2859	3175.6965	=$K$3*D7+(1-$K$3)*E7	2729.4325	=$K$5*D7+(1-$K$5)*G7			
9		Jul	7	3 105	3144.02685	=$K$3*D8+(1-$K$3)*E8	2846.04325	=$K$5*D8+(1-$K$5)*G8			
10		Aug	8	3 250	3140.124165	=$K$3*D9+(1-$K$3)*E9	3079.104325	=$K$5*D9+(1-$K$5)*G9			
11		Sep	9	3 510	3151.1117485	=$K$3*D10+(1-$K$3)*E10	3232.9104325	=$K$5*D10+(1-$K$5)*G10			
12		Oct	10	3 210	3187.00057365	=$K$3*D11+(1-$K$3)*E11	3482.29104325	=$K$5*D11+(1-$K$5)*G11			
13		Nov	11	3 097	3189.300516285	=$K$3*D12+(1-$K$3)*E12	3237.229104325	=$K$5*D12+(1-$K$5)*G12			
14		Dec	12	2 465	3180.070464657	=$K$3*D13+(1-$K$3)*E13	3111.022910433	=$K$5*D13+(1-$K$5)*G13			
15	2012	Jan	13	2 805	3108.563418191	=$K$3*D14+(1-$K$3)*E14	2529.602291043	=$K$5*D14+(1-$K$5)*G14			
16		Feb	14	2 959	3078.207076372	=$K$3*D15+(1-$K$3)*E15	2777.460229104	=$K$5*D15+(1-$K$5)*G15			
17		Mar	15	3 155	3066.286368735	=$K$3*D16+(1-$K$3)*E16	2940.846022910	=$K$5*D16+(1-$K$5)*G16			
18		Apr	16	3 542	3075.157731861	=$K$3*D17+(1-$K$3)*E17	3133.584602291	=$K$5*D17+(1-$K$5)*G17			
19		May	17	3 088	3121.841958675	=$K$3*D18+(1-$K$3)*E18	3501.158460229	=$K$5*D18+(1-$K$5)*G18			
20		Jun	18	3 394	3118.457762808	=$K$3*D19+(1-$K$3)*E19	3129.315846023	=$K$5*D19+(1-$K$5)*G19			
21		Jul	19	3 784	3146.011986527	=$K$3*D20+(1-$K$3)*E20	3367.531584602	=$K$5*D20+(1-$K$5)*G20			
22		Aug	20	3 521	3209.810787874	=$K$3*D21+(1-$K$3)*E21	3742.353158460	=$K$5*D21+(1-$K$5)*G21			
23		Sep	21	3464	3240.929709087	=$K$3*D22+(1-$K$3)*E22	3543.135315846	=$K$5*D22+(1-$K$5)*G22			
24		Oct	22	3012	3263.236738178	=$K$3*D23+(1-$K$3)*E23	3471.913531585	=$K$5*D23+(1-$K$5)*G23			
25		Nov	23	2989	3238.113064360	=$K$3*D24+(1-$K$3)*E24	3057.991353158	=$K$5*D24+(1-$K$5)*G24			
26		Dec	24	3246	3213.201757924	=$K$3*D25+(1-$K$3)*E25	2995.899135316	=$K$5*D25+(1-$K$5)*G25			
27	2013	Jan	25		3216.481582132	=$K$3*D26+(1-$K$3)*E26	3220.989913532	=$K$5*D26+(1-$K$5)*G26			

Figure 13.37: The Excel solution for the simple exponential smoothing for Example 13.8

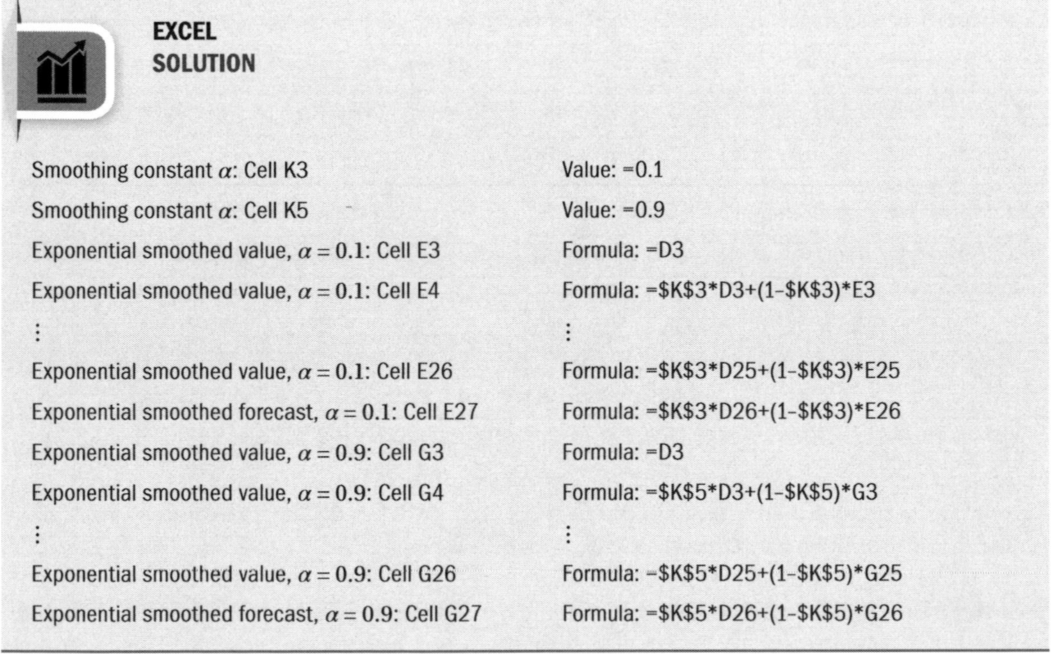

EXCEL SOLUTION

Smoothing constant α: Cell K3	Value: =0.1
Smoothing constant α: Cell K5	Value: =0.9
Exponential smoothed value, $\alpha = 0.1$: Cell E3	Formula: =D3
Exponential smoothed value, $\alpha = 0.1$: Cell E4	Formula: =$K$3*D3+(1-$K$3)*E3
⋮	⋮
Exponential smoothed value, $\alpha = 0.1$: Cell E26	Formula: =$K$3*D25+(1-$K$3)*E25
Exponential smoothed forecast, $\alpha = 0.1$: Cell E27	Formula: =$K$3*D26+(1-$K$3)*E26
Exponential smoothed value, $\alpha = 0.9$: Cell G3	Formula: =D3
Exponential smoothed value, $\alpha = 0.9$: Cell G4	Formula: =$K$5*D3+(1-$K$5)*G3
⋮	⋮
Exponential smoothed value, $\alpha = 0.9$: Cell G26	Formula: =$K$5*D25+(1-$K$5)*G25
Exponential smoothed forecast, $\alpha = 0.9$: Cell G27	Formula: =$K$5*D26+(1-$K$5)*G26

We can see from the plot in Figure 13.38 that the smaller value of α results in a smoother series, while the series with the larger value of α is more closely linked to the fluctuations in the original time series. Another interesting point to note in this plot is that the exponentially smoothed series lags behind the underlying time series, i.e. peaks and dips in the exponentially smoothed series appear a few periods after they appear in the original series.

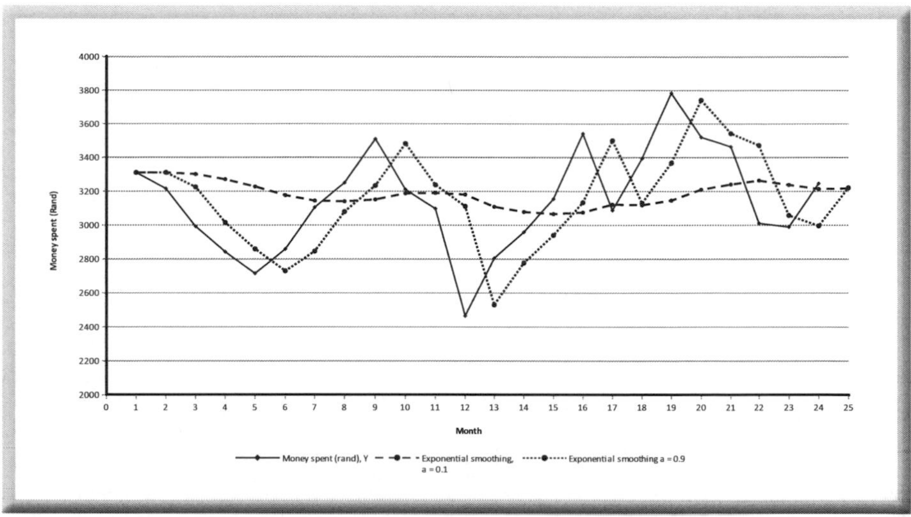

Figure 13.38: Time series plots for the exponential smoothed series in Example 13.8

NOTE Simple exponential smoothing, just like the moving averages method, is an acceptable forecasting technique, providing that the time series is reasonably stationary, exhibits no seasonality and we are interested in forecasting only one future period.

As an alternative to using the formulae to find the exponential smoothed series, Excel gives us an option to use the exponential smoothing method from the data analysis add-in pack. To apply it, follow these steps:

- Open the 'Data' ribbon and then the 'Data Analysis' button in the 'Analysis' group.
- In the dialogue box that appears, select 'Exponential Smoothing', as illustrated in Figure 13.39.

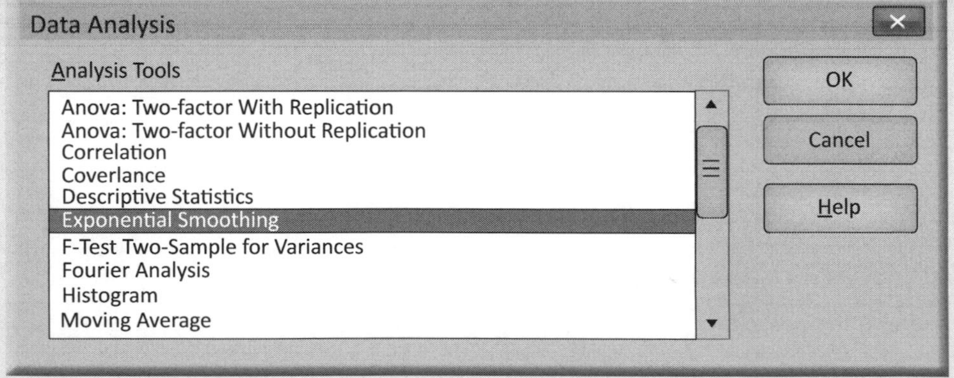

Figure 13.39: Activating the data analysis add-in pack

- Selecting the 'Exponential smoothing' option and pressing OK will trigger another dialogue box, in which we need to define some of the parameters. Figure 13.40 shows an example of selecting a data range B2:B16 and selecting an output range of C2:C16.

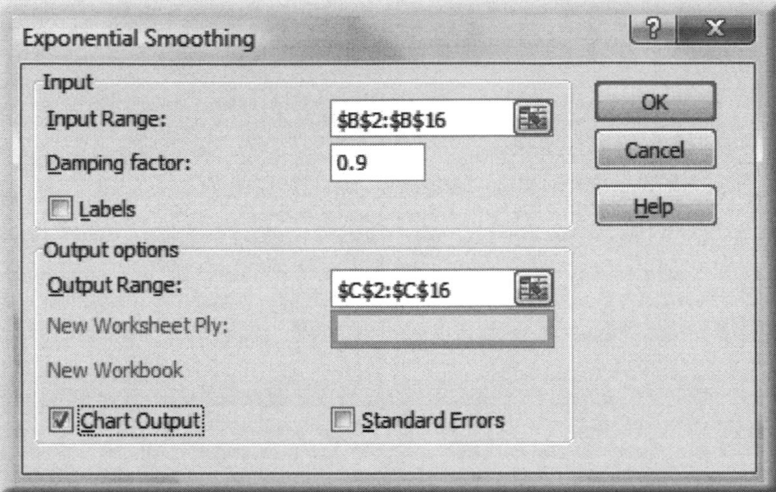

Figure 13.40: Selecting a data set for exponential smoothing from the 'Data Analysis' add-in

- In Figure 13.40, we see that a damping factor of 0.9 is chosen. The damping factor is equal to $1 - \alpha$, so in this example, we specify $1 - \alpha = 0.9$ or $\alpha = 0.1$.
- We can also choose to display the chart output. This charted output (along with the Excel spreadsheet's cells) is shown in Figure 13.41.

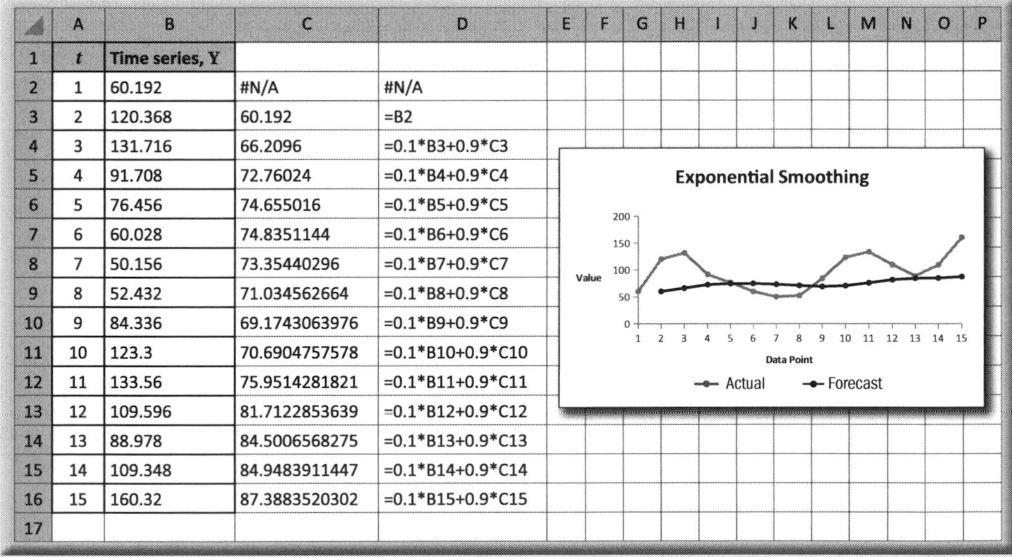

	A	B	C	D
1	*t*	Time series, Y		
2	1	60.192	#N/A	#N/A
3	2	120.368	60.192	=B2
4	3	131.716	66.2096	=0.1*B3+0.9*C3
5	4	91.708	72.76024	=0.1*B4+0.9*C4
6	5	76.456	74.655016	=0.1*B5+0.9*C5
7	6	60.028	74.8351144	=0.1*B6+0.9*C6
8	7	50.156	73.35440296	=0.1*B7+0.9*C7
9	8	52.432	71.034562664	=0.1*B8+0.9*C8
10	9	84.336	69.1743063976	=0.1*B9+0.9*C9
11	10	123.3	70.6904757578	=0.1*B10+0.9*C10
12	11	133.56	75.9514281821	=0.1*B11+0.9*C11
13	12	109.596	81.7122853639	=0.1*B12+0.9*C12
14	13	88.978	84.5006568275	=0.1*B13+0.9*C13
15	14	109.348	84.9483911447	=0.1*B14+0.9*C14
16	15	160.32	87.3883520302	=0.1*B15+0.9*C15
17				

Figure 13.41: Data analysis chart output for exponential smoothing option

NOTE Excel uses the expression 'Damping factor' rather than smoothing constant, or α. Damping factor is defined as $(1 - \alpha)$. In other words, if you want α to be 0.1, you must specify in Excel the value of the damping factor as 0.9.

13.5 Forecasting errors

13.5.1 Error measurement

One of the primary reasons for using forecasting as a tool is to try to reduce uncertainty. The better the forecasts, the lower the uncertainty that surrounds the variable we forecast. We can never eliminate uncertainty, but good forecasts can reduce it to an acceptable level. What would we consider to be a good forecast? An intuitive answer is that it has to be the forecast with the smallest error when compared with an actual event. The problem with this statement is that we cannot measure the error until the event has happened, by which time it is too late to say that our forecast was, or was not, good. In a way, we would like to measure the error before the future unfolds. How do we do this? As we demonstrated in this chapter, when forecasting, we always used the model to back-fit the existing time series. This is sometimes called back-casting, or more appropriately, ex-post forecasting. Once we have produced **ex-post forecasts**, it is easy to measure deviations from the actual data. These deviations are **forecasting errors** and they will tell us how good our method or model is.

Ex-post forecasts Values produced from a forecasting model that are fitted to historical data.

Forecasting errors A difference between the actual and the forecasted value in the time series.

INTERPRETATION The main assumption we make here is that whichever model shows the smallest error in the past, will probably make the smallest errors when extrapolated in the future. In other words, the model with the smallest historical errors will reduce the uncertainty that the future brings. This is the key assumption.

Calculating errors, or engaging in **error management**, is an easy task. We can define an error as the difference between what actually happened and what we thought would happen. In the context of forecasting time series and models, error is the difference between the actual data and the data produced by a model or ex-post forecasts. We can express this with an equation:

$$e_t = Y_t - \hat{Y}_t \tag{13.8}$$

- e_t is an error for a period t.
- Y_t is the actual value in a period t.

- $\hat{Y}_t$ is the forecasted value for the same period (note that we have used different symbols to denote this forecasted value depending on which method we were discussing, for example, for exponential smoothing, the forecasted value was denoted F_t and for the moving averages method, we denoted it M_t).

Error management A method of validating the quality of forecasts. It involves calculating the mean error, the mean squared error, the percentage error, and so on.

Figure 13.42 shows an example of how to calculate forecasting errors using formula (13.8).

	A	B	C	D	E
1	Period	Observed, Y	Forecast, $\hat{Y}$	Error, e	
2	1	100	130	-30	=B2-C2
3	2	250	150	100	=B3-C3
4	3	150	210	-60	=B4-C4
5	4	220	250	-30	=B5-C5
6	5	320	320	0	=B6-C6
7	SUM	1040	1060	-20	
8		=SUM(B2:B6)	=SUM(C2:C6)	=SUM(D2:D6)	

Figure 13.42: Excel spreadsheet of the calculation of errors from a forecast

In the above example, by using some simple method, we produced back-forecasts that clearly deviate from the actual historical values. Figure 13.43 shows the results in a graphical way.

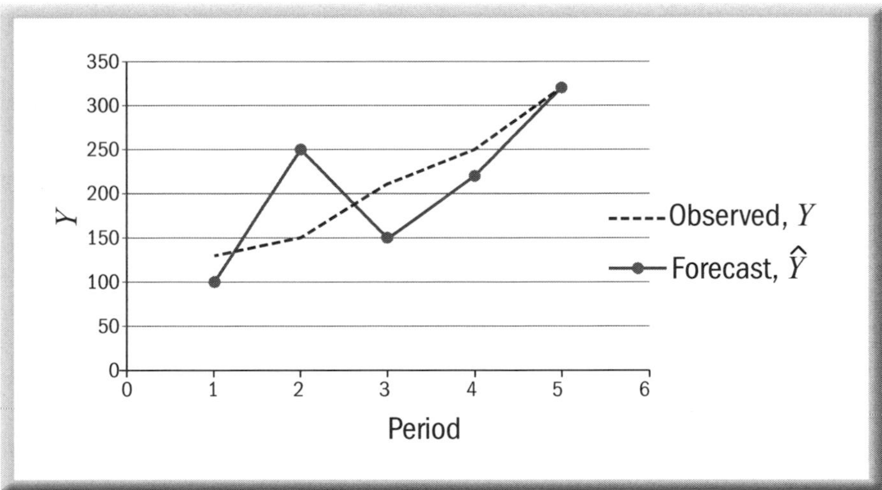

Figure 13.43: A chart showing actual and forecasted values

For period 1 ($t = 1$), our method exceeded actual values, which is presented as –30, because errors are calculated as observed minus forecasted. For period $t = 2$, our method underscored by 100. For period 6 ($t = 6$), for example, our method was perfect and it had not generated any errors. What can we conclude from this? If these were the first five weeks of our new business venture, and if we add all these numbers together, then our cumulative forecast for these five weeks would have been 1 060. In reality, the business generated 1 040. This implies that the method we used made a cumulative error of –20, or given the above formula, it overestimates the reality by 20 units. If we divide this cumulative value by the number of weeks to which it applies, i.e. 5, we get the average value of our error:

$$\bar{e} = \frac{1}{n}\sum_{t=1}^{n} e_t = \frac{1}{n}\sum_{t=1}^{n}\left(Y_t - \hat{Y}_t\right) = -\frac{20}{5} = -4$$

INTERPRETATION The average error that our method generates per period is -4, and because errors are defined as differences between the actual and forecast values, this means that, on average, the actual values are 4 units *lower* than our forecasts. Given earlier assumptions that the method will probably continue to perform in the future as in the past (assuming there are no dramatic or step changes), our method will probably generate similar errors in the future.

Assuming that we decided to experiment with some other method, and assuming that the average error that this other method generated was 2, which method would you rather use to forecast your business venture? The answer, hopefully, is very straightforward. The second method is somewhat pessimistic (the actual values are 2 units per period *above* the forecast values), but in absolute terms 2 is less than 4. Therefore, we would recommend the second method as a much better model for forecasting this particular business venture. In the above example, not only have we decided which forecasting method reduces uncertainty more, but we have also learnt how to use two different methods of measuring this uncertainty. Using errors as measures of uncertainty, we learnt how to calculate an average, or mean error, and we implied that an absolute average error also makes sense to be estimated. In practice, we also use other error measurements.

13.5.2 Types of errors

In fact, we use many error measurements to assess how good the forecasts are. The four more commonly used error measurements are the **mean error (*ME*)**, the mean absolute error (sometimes called the **mean absolute deviation** and abbreviated as ***MAD***), the **mean square error (*MSE*)** and the **mean percentage error (*MPE*)**. These errors are calculated as follows:

$$ME = \frac{1}{n}\sum_{t=1}^{n} e_t = \frac{1}{n}\sum_{t=1}^{n}\left(Y_t - \hat{Y}_t\right) \tag{13.9}$$

$$MAD = \frac{1}{n}\sum_{t=1}^{n} |e_t| = \frac{1}{n}\sum_{t=1}^{n} |Y_t - \hat{Y}_t| \tag{13.10}$$

$$MSE = \frac{1}{n}\sum_{t=1}^{n} e_t^2 = \frac{1}{n}\sum_{t=1}^{n}\left(Y_t - \hat{Y}_t\right)^2 \tag{13.11}$$

$$MPE = \frac{1}{n}\sum_{t=1}^{n}\frac{e_t}{Y_t} = \frac{1}{n}\sum_{t=1}^{n}\frac{\left(Y_t - \hat{Y}_t\right)}{Y_t} \tag{13.12}$$

Mean error (*ME*) The mean value of all the differences between the actual and forecasted values in the time series.

Mean absolute deviation (*MAD*) The mean value of all the differences between the actual and forecasted values in the time series. The differences between these values are represented as absolute values, i.e. the effects of the sign are ignored.

Mean square error (*MSE*) The mean value of all the differences between the actual and forecasted values in the time series. The differences between these values are squared to avoid positive and negative differences cancelling each other.

Mean percentage error (*MPE*) The mean value of all the differences between the actual and forecasted values in the time series. The differences between these values are represented as percentage values.

Mean absolute percentage error (*MAPE*) The mean value of all the differences between the actual and forecasted values in the time series. The differences between these values are represented as absolute percentage values, i.e. the effects of the sign are ignored.

Sometimes, *MPE* causes problems in Excel (due to negative values), in which case it is better to estimate the **mean absolute percentage error (*MAPE*)**:

$$MAPE = \frac{1}{n}\sum_{t=1}^{n}\frac{|e_t|}{Y_t} = \frac{1}{n}\sum_{t=1}^{n}\frac{|Y_t - \hat{Y}_t|}{Y_t} \tag{13.13}$$

In Excel, it is very easy to calculate these errors. Using our previous short example, these errors are calculated as shown in Figure 13.44.

	A	B	C	D	E	F	G	H	I	J	K	L	M
1	Period	Observed, Y	Forecast, $\hat{Y}$	Error, e		Absolute error, $[e]$		Squared errors, e^2		Percentage error, e/Y		Absolute percentage error, $\|e\|/Y$	
2	1	100	130	-30	=B2-C2	30	=ABS(D2)	900	=D2^2	-30	=100*D2/B2	30	=100*F2/B2
3	2	250	150	100	=B3-C3	100	=ABS(D3)	10000	=D3^2	40	=100*D3/B3	40	=100*F3/B3
4	3	150	210	-60	=B4-C4	60	=ABS(D4)	3600	=D4^2	-40	=100*D4/B4	40	=100*F4/B4
5	4	220	250	-30	=B5-C5	30	=ABS(D5)	900	=D5^2	-13.63636364	=100*D5/B5	13.63636364	=100*F5/B5
6	5	320	320	0	=B6-C6	0	=ABS(D6)	0	=D6^2	0	=100*D6/B6	0	=100*F6/B6
7													
8	*ME* =	-4	=AVERAGE(D2:D6)										
9	*MAD* =	44	=AVERAGE(F2:F6)										
10	*MSE* =	3080	=AVERAGE(H2:H6)										
11	*MPE* =	-8.727272727	=AVERAGE(J2:J6)										
12	*MAPE* =	24.72727273	=AVERAGE(L2:L6)										

Figure 13.44: Calculating various errors

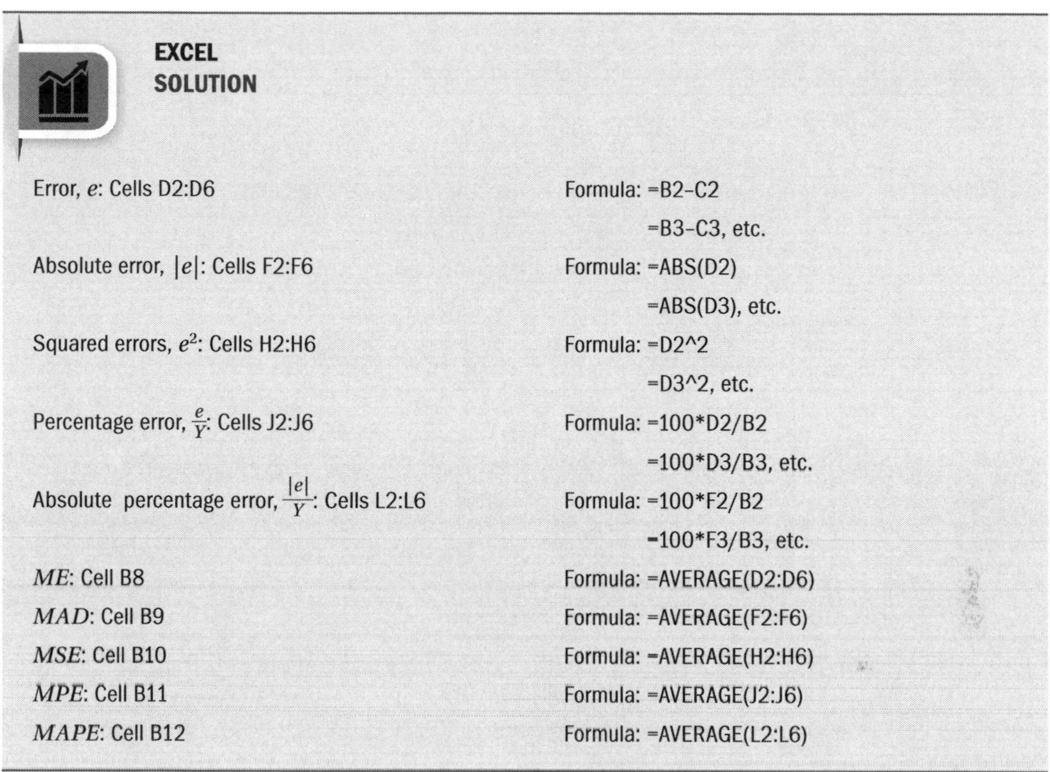

EXCEL SOLUTION

Error, *e*: Cells D2:D6	Formula: =B2-C2
	=B3-C3, etc.
Absolute error, $\lvert e \rvert$: Cells F2:F6	Formula: =ABS(D2)
	=ABS(D3), etc.
Squared errors, e^2: Cells H2:H6	Formula: =D2^2
	=D3^2, etc.
Percentage error, $\frac{e}{Y}$: Cells J2:J6	Formula: =100*D2/B2
	=100*D3/B3, etc.
Absolute percentage error, $\frac{\lvert e \rvert}{Y}$: Cells L2:L6	Formula: =100*F2/B2
	=100*F3/B3, etc.
ME: Cell B8	Formula: =AVERAGE(D2:D6)
MAD: Cell B9	Formula: =AVERAGE(F2:F6)
MSE: Cell B10	Formula: =AVERAGE(H2:H6)
MPE: Cell B11	Formula: =AVERAGE(J2:J6)
MAPE: Cell B12	Formula: =AVERAGE(L2:L6)

Column H in Figure 13.45 is identical to column G. The only difference is that we used Excel percentage formatting to present the numbers as percentages rather than as decimal values. Instead of calculating individual errors (as in columns D–I) and adding all the individual error values (as in row 7) or calculating the average (as in row 8), we could have calculated all these errors with a single formula line for each type of error. Using some of the built-in Excel functions, these errors can be calculated as shown in Figure 13.45.

	A	B	C	D	E	F	G	H	I
1	Period	Observed, *Y*	Forecast, $\hat{Y}$	Error, *e*					
2	1	100	130	-30	=B2-C2		*ME* =	-4	=(SUM(B2:B6)-SUM(C2:C6))/COUNT(B2:B6)
3	2	250	150	100	=B3-C3		*MAD* =	44	=SUM(ABS(D2:D6))/COUNT(D2:D6)
4	3	150	210	-60	=B4-C4		*MSE* =	3080	=SUMXMY2(B2:B6,C2:C6)/COUNT(B2:B6)
5	4	220	250	-30	=B5-C5		*MPE* =	-8.727272727	=100*SUM(((B2:B6)-(C2:C6))/(B2:B6))/COUNT(B2:B6)
6	5	320	320	0	=B6-C6		*MAPE* =	24.72727273	=100*SUM(ABS((B2:B6)-(C2:C6))/(B2:B6))/COUNT(B2:B6)

Figure 13.45: Single-cell formulae for calculating the *ME*, *MAD*, *MSE*, *MPE* and *MAPE*

EXCEL SOLUTION (ALTERNATIVE)

ME: Cell H2	Formula: =(SUM(B2:B6)-SUM(C2:C6))/COUNT(B2:B6)
MAD: Cell H3	Formula: {=SUM(ABS(D2:D6))/COUNT(D2:D6)}
MSE: Cell H4	Formula: =SUMXMY2(B2:B6,C2:C6)/COUNT(B2: B6)
MPE: Cell H5	Formula: {=100*SUM(((B2:B6)-(C2:C6))/(B2:B6))/COUNT(B2:B6)}
MAPE: Cell H6	Formula: {=SUM(ABS((B2:B6)-(C2:C6))/(B2:B6))/COUNT(B2:B6)}

NOTE

Note that the *MAD*, *MPE* and *MAPE* formulae have curly brackets on both sides. Do not enter these brackets manually. Excel enters the brackets automatically if, after you type in the formula, you do not just press the Enter button, but CTRL+SHIFT+ENTER buttons (i.e. all three at the same time). This means that the range is treated as an *array*.

For the sake of clarity, Figure 13.45 reproduces the spreadsheet as it should look if we had used the single-cell formulae for the error calculations. Again, note that the curly brackets for *MAD, MPE* and *MAPE* are not visible by observing formulae in cells I3, I5 and I6. However, they are visible in the formula bar.

13.5.3 Interpreting errors

How do we interpret the above five different error measurements?

- *ME (mean error)*: We have already stated that *ME* indicates that the actual data are, on average, 4 units per period above the forecasted values. This is a good indication, but the problem is that positive and negative deviations eliminate each other, so we may end up with a forecast that jumps up and down around the actual values, never providing exact forecasts, and yet the *ME* could be 0.
- *MAD (mean absolute deviations)*: To eliminate the above problem with *ME*, we can calculate *MAD*. *MAD* indicates that if we eliminate overestimates and underestimates in our forecasts, a typical bias that our method shows (regardless of whether it is positive or negative) is 44 units per period. This is a typical error, regardless of the direction in which our forecasts went when estimating the actual values.
- *MSE (mean squared error)*: The meaning of the *MSE* is more difficult to interpret, for the simple reason that we have taken the square values of our errors. What is a square value of something? The rationale is that if there are some big deviations in our forecast from the actual values, then in order to magnify these deviations, we need to square them. Let's take an example of two hypothetical errors for a period. Let one error reading show 2 and the other one 10. The second error is 5 times larger than the first one. However, when we square these two numbers, 100 (10 × 10) is 25 times larger than 4 (2 × 2). This is what we mean by magnifying large errors. So, the higher the *MSE*, the more extreme are the deviations of our forecast from the actual values.

This is particularly useful when comparing two forecasts. If the *MSE* obtained from the first forecast is larger than the *MSE* from the second, then the first forecast contains more extreme deviations than the second.

- *MPE (mean percentage error)*: The interpretation of the *MPE* is very intuitive. It tells us that, on average, an error constitutes x% of the actual value or, as in our case, *MPE* = –8.73%. This means that, on average, our forecasting errors overshot the actual values by 8.73% (remember that a negative error means that a forecasts overshooting the actual values and a positive error undershoots). However, this implies that, just as with the *ME*, we could have a series of overshoots and undershoots (as in our example), and yet gain an average value of almost 0.
- *MAPE (mean absolute percentage error)*: The mean absolute percentage error (*MAPE*) addresses the above problem. It shows us the value of 0.2473. In other words, if we disregard positive and negative variations of our forecasts from the actual values, we make, on average, an absolute error of 24.73%.

SUMMARY

In this chapter, we focused on univariate time series analysis as a primary tool for extrapolating time series and forecasting. We described what the prerequisites are before we start selecting a forecasting method, namely, ensuring that all the observations are recorded in the same units of time, that no observations are missing, that there are no unexpected outliers and that the time series is transformed, if necessary, and that we produce the time series graph before proceeding.

We introduced various trend models as well as how to fit them to time series, producing the ex-post forecasts. We also addressed forecasting in the presence of seasonality, by using the classical time series analysis approach. Other alternative methods to forecasting were introduced, such as the moving average method and exponentials smoothing. The relevance of the smoothing constant α was explained. Once we mastered various forecasting methods and techniques, we focused on forecasting errors and how to measure them. The relevance of various error indicators (*ME*, *MSE*, *MAD*, and so on) was introduced, as well as how to interpret them to select the best forecast.

KEY TERMS

Central moving averages
Classical time series analysis
Classical time series decomposition
Classical time series mixed model
Classical time series multiplicative method
Cyclic variation
Differencing
Error management
Error measurements
Exponential smoothing
Ex-post forecasts
Forecasting
Forecasting errors
Irregular component
Linear trend model
Mean absolute deviation (*MAD*)
Mean absolute percentage error (*MAPE*)
Mean error (*ME*)
Mean percentage error (*MPE*)
Mean square error (*MSE*)
Non-stationary time series
Seasonality
Seasonal variation
seasonal time series

Simple moving average
Stationary time series
Time period
Time series
Time series data
Time series forecasting
Time series plot
Time series smoothing
Transformations
Trend component

FORMULA SUMMARY

$$Y = T \times C \times S \times I \tag{13.1}$$

$$\hat{T}_t = b_0 + b_1 t \tag{13.2}$$

$$b_1 = \frac{\sum_{t=1}^{n} t\,Y_t - \frac{1}{n}\sum_{t=1}^{n} t \sum_{t=1}^{n} Y_t}{\sum_{t=1}^{n} t^2 - \frac{1}{n}\left(\sum_{t=1}^{n} t\right)^2} \tag{13.3}$$

$$b_0 = \frac{1}{n}\sum_{t=1}^{n} Y_t - \frac{b_1}{n}\sum_{t=1}^{n} t \tag{13.4}$$

$$M_t = \frac{1}{W}\sum_{i=t-W+1}^{t} Y_i \quad \text{for } W \le t \le n \tag{13.5}$$

$$F_t = F_{t-1} + \alpha(Y_{t-1} - F_{t-1}) \quad t = 2, 3, 4, \ldots \tag{13.6}$$

$$F_t = \alpha Y_{t-1} + (1 - \alpha)F_{t-1} \tag{13.7}$$

$$e_t = Y_t - \hat{Y}_t \tag{13.8}$$

$$ME = \frac{1}{n}\sum_{t=1}^{n} e_t = \frac{1}{n}\sum_{t=1}^{n}\left(Y_t - \hat{Y}_t\right) \tag{13.9}$$

$$MAD = \frac{1}{n}\sum_{t=1}^{n} |e_t| = \frac{1}{n}\sum_{t=1}^{n} |Y_t - \hat{Y}_t| \tag{13.10}$$

$$MSE = \frac{1}{n}\sum_{t=1}^{n} e_t^2 = \frac{1}{n}\sum_{t=1}^{n}\left(Y_t - \hat{Y}_t\right)^2 \quad (13.11)$$

$$MPE = \frac{1}{n}\sum_{t=1}^{n}\frac{e_t}{Y_t} = \frac{1}{n}\sum_{t=1}^{n}\frac{\left(Y_t - \hat{Y}_t\right)}{Y_t} \quad (13.12)$$

$$MAPE = \frac{1}{n}\sum_{t=1}^{n}\frac{|e_t|}{Y_t} = \frac{1}{n}\sum_{t=1}^{n}\frac{|Y_t - \hat{Y}_t|}{Y_t} \quad (13.13)$$

EXERCISES

13.1 Chart the following time series and decide if it is stationary and/or seasonal.

x	1	2	3	4	5	6	7	8	9	10
y	2	5	6	6	4	5	7	5	8	9

13.2 Chart the following time series and decide if it is stationary and/or seasonal. Extract the movement components T, S and C from this time series using the methods discussed and attempt to forecast 4 units into the future.

x	1	2	3	4	5	6	7	8	9	10	11	12	13	14	15
y	1	3	5	3	1	3	5	7	5	3	5	7	9	7	5

13.3 Is it possible to have a time series that is non-seasonal and non-stationary? If so, what would you call it and can you draw a graph showing what such a series would look like?

13.4 Difference the time series from 13.1. Would you say that the differenced time series from 13.1 is stationary? If not, what would you do to make it stationary?

13.5 If the time series components were extracted as in the example below, how would you reconstruct the time series ($\hat{Y}$) using: a) an additive model and b) a mixed model?

T	90	95	100	105	110	115	120	125	130
C	2	4	6	4	2	4	6	4	2
I	5	3	4	6	5	6	4	5	4
$\hat{Y}$									

13.6 If a time series can be best fitted with the long-term trend whose equation is $y = a + bx + cx^2$, would you say that this is a linear model?

13.7 Extrapolate the time series below, three time periods in the future. Use Excel's TREND function. Why do you think it would not make sense to extrapolate this time series 10 time periods in the future?

X	1	2	3	4	5	6	7	8	9	10	11	12
Y	230	300	290	320	350	400	350	400	420			

13.8 By including more observations in a moving average interval, would you say that it will smooth the time series more than moving averages calculated on the basis of the fewer observations included in the moving average interval?

13.9 Can you extrapolate a time series five time periods in the future using the moving average forecasting method? Explain your answer.

13.10 Produce two forecasts for the time series below using exponential smoothing. Use $\alpha = 0.1$ for the first set of forecasts and $\alpha = 0.9$ for the second set of forecasts. What can you conclude?

X	1	2	3	4	5	6	7	8	9
Y	230	300	290	320	350	400	350	400	420

13.11 If the damping factor in the Excel data analysis add-in is defined as 0.65, what is the equivalent value of the smoothing constant (α)?

13.12 Explain the difference between accuracy and precision. What are the consequences if your forecasts are precise but not accurate? Can you have accurate forecasts that are not precise?

13.13 Why is the *MAD* type of error measurement preferred over the *ME* type of error?

13.14 Two forecasts were produced, as shown below. The *ME* for the second forecast is seven times larger than the *ME* for the first forecast. However, the *MSE* is 20 times larger. Can you explain why?

X	Y	$\widehat{Y}_1$	$\widehat{Y}_2$	e_1	e_2
1	230	230	230	0	0
2	300	305	305	–5	–5
3	290	295	295	–5	–5
4	320	320	320	0	0
5	350	345	345	5	5

X	Y	$\widehat{Y}_1$	$\widehat{Y}_2$	e_1	e_2
6	400	402	350	–2	50
7	350	355	355	–5	–5
8	400	395	395	5	5
9	420	420	420	0	0
	$ME =$	–0.78	5.78		
	$MSE =$	14.33	291.67		

13.15 Is it acceptable to see some regularity in pattern when examining the series of residuals or forecasting errors?

13.16 The closer the actual observations are to the diagonal line when compared with forecasted values on a scatter plot, the better the forecasts. Is this correct?

TECHNIQUES IN PRACTICE

13.17 AfriSoft is considering diversifying and entering the South African housing market. It is only interested in a short-term investment. To help it with the decision and to assess the market, its analysts have extracted a time series that covers South African supply of houses for sale at current sales rate. The time series is not adjusted for seasonality and the data set reflects true market movements. The table below covers data from January 2004 to June 2008 (Year Y, Month M, Value V).

Table 13.25: data from January 2004 to June 2008

Y	M	V	Y	M	V	Y	M	V	Y	M	V	Y	M	V
2004	01	4.2	2005	01	4.8	2006	01	5.9	2007	01	8.2	2008	01	11
2004	02	3.6	2005	02	4	2006	02	6.1	2007	02	8	2008	02	10
2004	03	3	2005	03	3.5	2006	03	5.1	2007	03	6.8	2008	03	10
2004	04	3.5	2005	04	3.8	2006	04	5.6	2007	04	6.5	2008	04	9
2004	05	3.3	2005	05	3.7	2006	05	5.5	2007	05	6.9	2008	05	9
2004	06	3.7	2005	06	4	2006	06	5.8	2007	06	7.5	2008	06	9
2004	07	4.2	2005	07	3.9	2006	07	6.9	2007	07	8	2008	07	
2004	08	4	2005	08	4.3	2006	08	6.5	2007	08	8.9	2008	08	
2004	09	4.4	2005	09	5	2006	09	7	2007	09	9.9	2008	09	
2004	10	4.1	2005	10	4.7	2006	10	7.5	2007	10	9	2008	10	
2004	11	5	2005	11	5.9	2006	11	7.8	2007	11	11	2008	11	
2004	12	5.2	2005	12	5.9	2006	12	7.6	2007	12	11	2008	12	

Analyse the data and produce a forecast. Pay specific attention to the following.

a) Graph the time series.
b) Decide on the type of time series.
c) Use the best suited method and produce forecasts until the end of 2008 (six time periods in the future).
d) Measure the quality of your forecast.
e) Decide what would be your recommendations, from the data analysis point of view, to AfriSoft.

13.18 Bakers Ltd is concerned about the influence of petrol prices on their profit margins. The owner of the company looked at weekly petrol prices (cents per litre) for Gauteng and compiled a time series. The series is from 14 November 2000 to 4 August 2003. The data in cents per litre are shown below in columns.

Table 13.26: Cents per litre for Gauteng from 14 November 2000 to 4 August 2003

250.1	238.6	291.5	269.1	249.7	296.2	296.1	330.9	334.2	423.8
241.6	244.3	287.9	261.5	245	302.6	293.2	331	335.7	423.5
235.8	245.6	283.7	255.9	240.2	304.4	290.7	328.9	341.1	424.7
232.2	261.6	290.5	251.7	237.6	307.1	288.6	328.5	338.5	424.8
234.3	261.7	295.8	247.4	236.2	313.5	287.3	327.8	340.1	424.2
236.8	273.7	299.3	243	236.2	315.1	287.5	327.6	342.9	421.9
238.1	279.7	302	239.9	239.6	313.1	288.9	329.4	349.8	412.7
244.2	292	305.2	239.1	246.6	313.5	293.8	334	362.6	405.1
254	306.4	307.6	238.5	268	310.4	293.2	332.4	375.3	
254.8	304.9	309.1	242.8	271.3	307.6	292.7	329.1	376.9	
257.7	303.6	305.3	248.9	273.4	307.5	292.5	328.7	385.9	
255.6	301.6	300	247.6	275.9	306.6	298.6	326	393.1	
253.1	298.9	294.4	252.2	281.4	307	304	326.1	408.3	
248.8	296.4	287.5	253.9	287.3	303.6	319.6	327.4	412.1	
242.4	292.5	279.3	253.5	295.7	300.4	328.6	333.2	418.3	

The owner is not familiar with forecasting, but knows how to use the trending function. Put yourself in his shoes and do the following.

a) Chart the time series.
b) Pick the most suitable curve to fit to the data set.
c) Extrapolate the data another 20 time periods in the future.
d) What do you think you need to do to preserve your profit margins?

13.19 Home-Made Beers Ltd is considering investing in technology stocks. As a test case, it looked at the stock price of AfriSoft adjusted monthly closing values of stocks between 1 March 2001 and 1 August 2008. The time series is given in columns below.

Table 13.27: Stock price of AfriSoft adjusted monthly closing values of stocks between 1 March 2001 and 1 August 2008

26.21	30.25	26.02	25.57	22.5	21.52
25.72	29.42	27.17	23.93	22.4	22.09
27.51	27.38	25.24	23.66	21.75	25.5
28.32	27.68	26.72	23.36	20.88	24.67
28.42	30.22	24.73	24.3	21.69	26.94
28.28	29.24	24.76	24.36	20.54	28.01
27.1	28.75	26.35	22.38	20.1	27.15
32.35	28.02	24.57	22.29	20.07	24.59
35.33	26.69	23.83	21.27	21.86	21.63
33.35	25.08	24.76	22.63	24.39	24.12
36.41	23.39	24.2	23.59	22.61	27.98
29.14	22.65	23.12	23.35	18.49	30.86
28.42	22.02	24.07	21.93	20.75	29.25
28.58	23.39	25.06	22.3	20.29	28.64
29.05	26.35	25.48	23.58	23.13	23.12

Use the exponential smoothing method and experiment with various levels of constant α. What impact does this have on your forecasts and how does it change the forecasting errors? Recommend which forecasting Home-Made Beers Ltd should use and why.

CHAPTER 14

CHI-SQUARED AND NON-PARAMETRIC HYPOTHESIS TESTING

CHAPTER CONTENTS

OVERVIEW

In Chapters 10 and 11, we explored a series of parametric tests to assess whether the differences between means (or variances) are statistically significant. With those parametric tests, we were interested in testing the values of the unknown population parameters such as the population mean (μ), variance (σ^2) or proportion (π), but these techniques required some fairly strict assumptions:

- The observations are measured on an interval or a ratio scale.
- The underlying population is normally distributed.
- The population variances are equal.

Unfortunately, we often encounter data that do not satisfy these parametric assumptions and so the techniques discussed in the previous chapters would not be appropriate.

In this chapter, we discuss how to perform certain tests when these assumptions are not valid. We begin by looking at a test for measuring the association between variables that are not measured on an interval or ratio scale (i.e. when the first assumption is violated and we have categorical variables measured on an ordinal or nominal scale). The closest parametric equivalent to this test would be the correlation test discussed in Chapter 12 (although strictly speaking, the correlation test only tests for *linear* association and not *general* association as will be discussed here).

Next, we look at non-parametric methods that we can use to replace the parametric tests for *location* discussed in Chapters 10 and 11. These methods will all be based on ranks. Essentially, the idea underlying these tests is to replace the data values (ordinal, interval or ratio-scaled data values) with the ranks, or ordering values, of the data. The benefit of doing this is that the above assumptions are not required for these tests, since a whole other theory governs rank data (as opposed to the traditional normal theory for the tests discussed in Chapters 10 and 11, which required these assumptions for the tests to work).

This chapter provides an overview to the chi-squared test for the association between categorical variables and non-parametric rank-based tests that we can use when parametric methods are not appropriate.

LEARNING OBJECTIVES

On completing this chapter, you should be able to:

- apply the chi-squared test to test for association between categorical variables
- apply the chi-squared test to measure the difference between two proportions from two samples
- apply the sign test to one sample
- apply the Wilcoxon signed-rank t-test to two paired samples
- apply the Mann-Whitney test to two independent samples
- solve problems using Microsoft Excel.

Test of association Allows the comparison of two attributes in a sample of data to determine if there is any relationship between them.

Sign test Designed to test a hypothesis about the location of a population distribution.

Wilcoxon signed-rank *t*-test Designed to test a hypothesis about the location of the population median (one or two matched pairs).

Mann-Whitney test Used to test the null hypothesis that two populations have identical distribution functions against the alternative hypothesis that the two distribution functions differ only with respect to location (median), if at all.

Contingency table A table of frequencies classified according to the values of the variables in question.

14.1 Chi-squared tests

The **chi-squared test** is a versatile and widely used test that applies when dealing with data that are categorical (or nominal or qualitative) in nature, i.e. data that are not naturally represented using a number. Examples include variables related to questions such as 'Do you agree?', which takes on the values 'Yes' or 'No', or the variable 'Colour of your eyes', which can potentially take on values 'Blue', 'Green' or 'Brown'. Note that these data can appear in the form of the single variable frequency tables that were discussed in Chapter 2, but also as two variable frequency tables (called **contingency tables**), which we discuss later in this section. The chi-squared test then operates by comparing the *observed* values in a frequency table to the values that we would *expect* if a given hypothesis is true.

Chi-squared test Apply to test if the observed values from sample data match the values we expect under the null hypothesis. We can thus use this test to test for independence or goodness of it.

Consider the following simple example: Suppose that a study is conducted where $n = 100$ students were randomly selected from a university and are interviewed. Each one is asked the question 'What is the colour of your eyes?' and they were given the response choices 'Blue', 'Green' or 'Brown'. The following frequency table of these observed responses is obtained.

Table 14.1: Frequency table of observed responses

	BLUE EYES	GREEN EYES	BROWN EYES
OBSERVED FREQUENCY	30	20	50

The analyst in charge of the study had hypothesised that the distribution of eye colours in the population would be evenly distributed, i.e. the probability that you have green eyes, blue eyes or brown eyes is the same. Formally, we can express this hypothesis as:

$$H_0: \pi_{\text{blue}} = \pi_{\text{green}} = \pi_{\text{brown}} = \frac{1}{3}$$

π_{blue}, π_{green} and π_{brown} represent the population probabilities of having blue, green or brown eyes, respectively. The alternative hypothesis would simply be that the probabilities are not all equal. Under this null hypothesis, we can construct a table of **expected frequencies** by simply multiplying the hypothesised probabilities by the sample size n.

Table 14.2: Table of expected values

	BLUE EYES	GREEN EYES	BROWN EYES
EXPECTED FREQUENCY	$\pi_{\text{blue}} \times n = \frac{1}{3} \times 100 = 33\frac{1}{3}$	$\pi_{\text{green}} \times n = \frac{1}{3} \times 100 = 33\frac{1}{3}$	$\pi_{\text{brown}} \times n = \frac{1}{3} \times 100 = 33\frac{1}{3}$

By inspecting the two tables, we can clearly see that they differ, but by how much? How would we measure this difference? Is the difference statistically significant?

The statistic that we use to measure the difference between these two tables is called the **chi-squared statistic** and it is defined as:

$$X^2 = \sum_{i=1}^{N} \frac{(O_i - E_i)^2}{E_i} \overset{H_0}{\sim} \chi^2_{N-1} \qquad (14.1)$$

N denotes the total number of cells in the table, O_i is the frequency observed in the ith cell and E_i is the frequency expected in the ith cell. This statistic follows a chi-squared distribution with $N - 1$ degrees of freedom under the assumption of the null hypothesis. The value of the resulting statistic is intuitively simple to interpret the following:

- If χ^2_{cal} is close to 0, then the frequencies in the observed table are nearly identical to the frequencies in the expected table i.e. the frequencies expected under the null hypothesis match the **observed frequencies**. If this happens, then the observed data support the statement made in the null hypothesis.
- If χ^2_{cal} is larger than 0, then there are differences between the observed table and the expected table. The larger the value, the larger the difference between the two tables. If the value is very large, it serves as evidence that the statement made in the null hypothesis is not true.

Observed frequency The frequencies actually obtained in each cell of the table from our random sample.

Expected frequency The frequencies that you would expect to see in each cell of the table if the null hypothesis were true.

The calculation of the chi-squared test statistic in the example above is then:

$$\begin{aligned}
\chi^2_{\text{cal}} &= \frac{(O_{\text{blue}} - E_{\text{blue}})^2}{E_{\text{blue}}} + \frac{(O_{\text{green}} - E_{\text{green}})^2}{E_{\text{green}}} + \frac{(O_{\text{brown}} - E_{\text{brown}})^2}{E_{\text{brown}}} \\
&= \frac{\left(30 - 33\frac{1}{3}\right)^2}{33\frac{1}{3}} + \frac{\left(20 - 33\frac{1}{3}\right)^2}{33\frac{1}{3}} + \frac{\left(50 - 33\frac{1}{3}\right)^2}{33\frac{1}{3}} \\
&= \frac{1}{3} + 5\frac{1}{3} + 8\frac{1}{3} \\
&= 14
\end{aligned}$$

The value of the chi-squared test statistic is clearly larger than 0, but is it significantly different from 0? We can determine this by specifying a significance level (for example, $\alpha = 0.05$) and using the quantiles of the chi-squared distribution with $N - 1 = 3 - 1 = 2$ degrees of freedom. The resulting critical value is written as $\chi^2_{2,1-\alpha} = \chi^2_{2,0.95} = 5.991465$ (we can obtain this value using Excel's CHISQ.INV function). If the observed value of the test statistic is larger than the critical value, it suggests that H_0 should be rejected. In this case, we see that $\chi^2_{\text{cal}} = 14$ is much larger than $\chi^2_{2,0.95} = 5.991465$, so we would *reject* the hypothesis that people's eye colours are equally distributed.

This example illustrates how we can use the chi-squared test to test any hypothesis made on the true probabilities of the levels of a categorical variable. In this example, we specified a simple structure for the probabilities (all equal to one another), but any structure can be tested with this test. As noted, the hypotheses in chi-squared tests typically describe some probability aspect of the variable(s) of interest. The chi-squared test essentially just compares the probabilities *estimated* in the data to the probabilities *stated* in the hypothesis.

These tests are considered to be non-parametric because they do not require any strict assumptions on the distribution of the populations from which the data are obtained; the data only need to be categorical in nature.

In this section, we consider two particular applications of the chi-square test:

- Comparing two or more sample proportions where we have categorical data.
- Undertaking a chi-squared test of association between two categorical variables, i.e. can we say that the two variables are independent or do they exhibit some sort of association?

These two tests require the use of two-dimensional frequency tables, which are called contingency tables. We need to briefly discuss these tables before we can continue the discussion on the chi-squared tests.

14.1.1 Contingency tables

A contingency table is basically the two variable version of the frequency tables for categorical variables mentioned in Chapter 2. The two variables that are used in these tables are both categorical, nominal-scaled variables and are denoted X and 'Y in the following discussion. The number of unique levels of variable X is r, and the number of unique levels of the Y variable is c (the reason for the letters r and c is that X's levels will form the *rows* of the table, and Y's levels will form the *columns*). We use the symbol O_{ij} to denote the observed number of items in the sample that fall within the ith level of the X-variable and the jth level of the Y-variable. The total frequency of all observations is n:

$$\sum_{i=1}^{r}\sum_{j=1}^{c} O_{ij} = n$$

Table 14.3 shows the basic form of a contingency table based on n observations on two categorical variables, X and Y, with r and c levels, respectively.

Table 14.3: The general form of the contingency table

O_{ij} represents the number (frequency) of items in the sample that fall in the ith level of X and the jth level of Y. For example, O_{12} denotes the number of items in the first level of X and second level of Y.

The row totals are the frequencies of each level of X, for example, R_2 is the total number of items in the second level of X.

		Y				
		Column $j=1$	Column $j=2$	...	Column $j=c$	Row totals
X	Row $i=1$	O_{11}	O_{12}	...	O_{1c}	$\sum_{j=1}^{c} O_{1j} = R_1$
	Row $i=2$	O_{21}	O_{21}	...	O_{2c}	$\sum_{j=1}^{c} O_{2j} = R_2$
	$\vdots$	$\vdots$	$\vdots$	$\ddots$	$\vdots$	$\vdots$
	Row $i=r$	O_{r1}	O_{r2}	...	O_{rc}	$\sum_{j=1}^{c} O_{rj} = R_r$
Column totals		$\sum_{i=1}^{r} O_{i1} = C_1$	$\sum_{i=1}^{r} O_{i2} = C_2$	...	$\sum_{i=1}^{r} O_{ic} = C_c$	$\sum_{i=1}^{r}\sum_{j=1}^{c} O_{ij} = n$

The column totals are the frequencies of each level of Y, for example, C_2 is the total number of items in the second level of Y.

n is the total number of observations in the data set.

We refer to contingency tables with r rows and c columns as $(c \times r)$ contingency tables.

Example 14.1 illustrates how raw data can be converted into a contingency table.

WORKED EXAMPLES

EXAMPLE 14.1

A small study involving $n = 10$ randomly sampled students is conducted to determine their thoughts on a new proposal to only serve healthy food in the campus's cafeteria. The students were asked the question 'Do you think that the cafeteria should only serve healthy food?' and were given the response options 'Agree', 'Undecided' and 'Disagree'. The smoking status of each student sampled was also recorded (i.e. the question 'Do you smoke?' was asked with options of 'Yes' and 'No').

The data in Table 14.4 were obtained.

Table 14.4: Results of healthy food opinion and smoking status questionnaire

	X HEALTHY FOOD OPINION	*Y* SMOKING STATUS		*X* HEALTHY FOOD OPINION	*Y* SMOKING STATUS
1	Agree	No	6	Agree	No
2	Undecided	No	7	Undecided	No
3	Agree	Yes	8	Undecided	Yes
4	Disagree	Yes	9	Disagree	Yes
5	Disagree	No	10	Undecided	Yes

Construct the (3 × 2) contingency table from these data.

The two categorical variables in the data set are thus 'Healthy food opinion' (X) with $r = 3$ levels and 'Smoking status' (Y) with $c = 2$ levels. The total sample size is $n = 10$. To construct the contingency table, we simply need to count how many times each combination of levels occurs and then tabulate the frequency in the form shown in Table 14.5.

Table 14.5: The (3 × 2) contingency table constructed from the data in Example 14.1

		Y SMOKING STATUS		Row totals
		(1) Yes	(2) No	
X HEALTHY FOOD OPINION	(1) Agree	$O_{11} = 1$	$O_{12} = 2$	$R_1 = 3$
	(2) Undecided	$O_{21} = 2$	$O_{22} = 2$	$R_2 = 4$
	(3) Disagree	$O_{31} = 2$	$O_{32} = 1$	$R_3 = 3$
Column totals		$C_1 = 5$	$C_2 = 5$	$n = 10$

The values in the contingency tables can be used to *estimate* the probabilities of the occurrences of the same events in the population (compare these observed tables to the probability tables discussed in Chapter 4, Section 4.4.2). The following few calculations illustrate how probabilities relating to the population of students can be *estimated* from the sample information provided in the contingency table.

- The probability that a student agrees with the health food proposal (i.e. $P(X = \text{Agree})$), can be *estimated* by $\frac{R_1}{n} = \frac{3}{10} = 0.3$
- The probability that a student is not a smoker ($P(Y = \text{No})$), can be estimated by $\frac{C_2}{n} = \frac{5}{10} = 0.5$
- The joint probability that a person is both undecided on the issue of healthy food in the cafeteria *and* is a smoker ($P(X = \text{Undecided} \cap Y = \text{Yes})$), can be *estimated* by $\frac{O_{21}}{n} = \frac{2}{10} = 0.2$
- The conditional probability that a person disagrees with the healthy food proposal, given that they smoke $\left(P(Y = \text{Disagree} \mid X = \text{Yes}) = \frac{P(Y = \text{Disagree} \cap X = \text{Yes})}{P(X = \text{Yes})}\right)$ is estimated by $\frac{O_{31}}{C_1} = \frac{2}{5} = 0.4$

Now that we have established what a contingency table is and what it is capable of, we can continue with the discussion of the chi-squared test.

14.1.2 Tests of independence

The chi-squared test of independence is a hypothesis test used to determine whether two categorical variables (the data from which we can arrange in a contingency table) are significantly independent of one another.

The null hypothesis for this test states that the row and column variables are not associated or independent, and can be written informally as:

H_0: Variable X is independent of variable Y
H_1: They are associated somehow

However, a more formal version of this hypothesis can be obtained by first recalling from Chapter 4 that independence between two events, A and B, is defined as:

$$P(A \cap B) = P(A)P(B)$$

This probability can be defined in terms of the probabilities estimated in the contingency table:

$$P(X = i \cap Y = j) = P(X = i)P(Y = j)$$

This means that the hypothesis of independence can now be written as:

H_0: $P(X = i \cap Y = j) = P(X = i) \times P(Y = j)$
H_1: $P(X = i \cap Y = j) \neq P(X = i) \times P(Y = j)$
$i = 1, 2, \ldots, r$ and $j = 1, 2, \ldots, c$

The chi-squared test that can be used to test this hypothesis is calculated as:

$$X^2 = \sum_{i=1}^{r}\sum_{j=1}^{c}\frac{(O_{ij} - E_{ij})^2}{E_{ij}} \overset{H_0}{\sim} \chi^2_{df} \tag{14.2}$$

O_{ij} are the observed frequencies in the contingency table and E_{ij} are the frequencies that we would expect if the variables were independent. This test statistic follows a chi-squared distribution with df degrees of freedom defined as:

$$df = (r - 1)(c - 1) \tag{14.3}$$

r denotes the number of rows (levels of x) and c denotes the number of columns (levels of Y).

Recall that the expected frequencies are those frequencies that would have been obtained if the null hypothesis was true and, since the null hypothesis states that $P(X = i \cap Y = j) = P(X = i)P(Y = j)$, the expected frequency in the ith row and j^{th} column should just be $E_{ij} = nP(X = i)P(Y = j)$.

Unfortunately, since we do not know the values of $P(X = i)$ or $P(Y = j)$, we need to estimate them from the data:

$P(X = i)$ is estimated by $\frac{R_i}{n}$ and $P(Y = j)$ is estimated by $\frac{C_j}{n}$

Therefore, if the null hypothesis is true, then the *estimated* expected frequencies E_{ij} can be calculated using the following equation:

$$E_{ij} = n\frac{R_i}{n}\frac{C_j}{n} = \frac{R_i C_j}{n} \tag{14.4}$$

R_i and C_j are the ith row total and i^{th} column total of the observed contingency table, as defined in Table 14.3.

The test statistic in formula (14.2) has the same interpretation as the statistic in formula (14.1); if the values in the expected table and observed table are close to one another, then the test statistic's value will be close to 0, which indicates that X and Y are indeed independent. Conversely, if we find large differences between the observed and expected frequencies, we have evidence to suggest some dependence does exist between the two categorical variables. Statistical hypothesis testing allows us to confirm whether the difference is statistically significant.

The region of rejection is identified using either the p-value method or by calculating the critical value, as in all previous tests.

WORKED EXAMPLES

EXAMPLE 14.2

A university samples $n = 485$ of its students to determine whether males and females differ in their preference for five courses offered. The main goal of the study is to determine whether there is some association between the courses chosen and the student's gender.

In this study, the two categorical variables being investigated are 'Gender' (with levels 'Male' and 'Female') and 'Course' (with levels 'A101', 'D102', 'M101', 'S101' and 'T101'). The resulting table is called a (5×2) contingency table, because it consists of 5 rows and 2 columns. To determine whether gender and course preference are associated, conduct a chi-squared test of independence at a $\alpha = 0.05$ level of significance.

Table 14.6: The (5×2) contingency table of observed frequencies for Example 14.2

Observed frequencies		***Y* Gender**		Row totals
		(1) Male	(2) Female	
Course	(1) A101	$O_{11} = 45$	$O_{12} = 86$	$R_1 = 131$
	(2) D102	$O_{21} = 52$	$O_{22} = 67$	$R_2 = 119$
	(3) M101	$O_{31} = 50$	$O_{32} = 19$	$R_3 = 69$
	(4) S101	$O_{41} = 50$	$O_{42} = 32$	$R_4 = 82$
	(5) T101	$O_{51} = 69$	$O_{52} = 15$	$R_5 = 84$
Column totals		$C_1 = 266$	$C_2 = 219$	$n = 485$

In order to conduct the chi-squared test for independence between 'Course' and 'Gender', we first need to construct the *expected frequencies* table using formula (14.4). Table 14.7 below shows how this table is constructed.

Table 14.7: The (5×2) contingency table of expected frequencies for Example 14.2

Observed frequencies		*Y* **Gender**		Row totals
		(1) Male	(2) Female	
Course	(1) A101	$E_{11} = \frac{R_1C_1}{n} = \frac{(131)(266)}{485} = 71.8474$	$E_{12} = \frac{R_1C_2}{n} = \frac{(131)(219)}{485} = 59.1526$	$R_1 = 131$
	(2) D102	$E_{21} = \frac{R_2C_1}{n} = \frac{(119)(266)}{485} = 65.266$	$E_{22} = \frac{R_2C_2}{n} = \frac{(119)(219)}{485} = 53.7340$	$R_2 = 119$
	(3) M101	$E_{31} = \frac{R_3C_1}{n} = \frac{(69)(266)}{485} = 37.8433$	$E_{32} = \frac{R_3C_2}{n} = \frac{(69)(219)}{485} = 31.1567$	$R_3 = 69$
	(4) S101	$E_{41} = \frac{R_4C_1}{n} = \frac{(82)(266)}{485} = 44.9732$	$E_{42} = \frac{R_4C_2}{n} = \frac{(82)(219)}{485} = 37.0268$	$R_4 = 82$
	(5) T101	$E_{51} = \frac{R_5C_1}{n} = \frac{(84)(266)}{485} = 46.0701$	$E_{52} = \frac{R_5C_2}{n} = \frac{(84)(219)}{485} = 37.9299$	$R_5 = 84$
Column totals		$C_1 = 266$	$C_2 = 219$	$n = 485$

Now that we have all of the necessary elements, we can begin testing the hypothesis. We use the same five-step procedure for hypothesis testing outlined in Chapter 10 to conduct this hypothesis test.

Step 1: Provide the hypothesis statements H_0 and H_1

- H_0: Gender and course preference are not associated (they are independent).
- H_1: There is an association between gender and course preference (they are dependent).

Step 2: Choose an appropriate test statistic

In this problem we have:

- *two categorical* data variables (gender and course)

- a sample of size $n = 485$ drawn from the population of students and each student provides information regarding these two variables; the frequency counts are then summarised within a contingency table.

The question of interest is whether these two variables are *independent* of one another.

This information leads us to conclude that a chi-squared test of independence would be suitable for this problem.

Step 3: Specify the significance level
A significance level of $\alpha = 0.05$ is specified.

Step 4: Calculate the relevant test statistic
The test statistic in formula (14.2) must now be calculated to test this hypothesis. To calculate this statistic, we first need the observed frequencies (O_{ij}) and the expected frequencies under H_0 (E_{ij}), both of which are provided in Tables 14.6 and 14.7. Recall that the expected frequencies are those frequencies calculated under the assumption that H_0 is true (it is what we would expect the table to look like if 'Course' and 'Gender' were independent). The calculated value of the test statistic is then:

$$\chi^2_{\text{cal}} = \sum_{i=1}^{r}\sum_{j=1}^{c}\frac{(O_{ij} - E_{ij})^2}{E_{ij}}$$

$$= \frac{(45 - 71.8474)^2}{71.8474} + \frac{(86 - 59.1526)^2}{59.1526} + \frac{(52 - 65.266)^2}{65.266} + \frac{(67 - 53.734)^2}{53.734} + \frac{(50 - 37.8433)^2}{37.8433} + \frac{(19 - 31.1567)^2}{31.1567}$$

$$+ \frac{(50 - 44.9732)^2}{44.9732} + \frac{(32 - 37.0268)^2}{37.0268} + \frac{(69 - 46.0701)^2}{46.0701} + \frac{(15 - 37.9299)^2}{37.9299}$$

$$= 10.0321 + 12.1851 + 2.6964 + 3.2751 + 3.9052 + 4.7433 + 0.5619 + 0.6824 + 11.4126 + 13.8619$$

$$= 63.356$$

The test statistic's value is thus 63.356.

Using formula (14.3), we can calculate the degrees of freedom for the test:

$$df = (r - 1)(c - 1) = (5 - 1)(2 - 1) = 4$$

Step 5: Make a decision
We use both the critical value approach and the p-value approach to make a decision for this test.

- *Using critical values*: The critical value approach requires that we first calculate the chi-squared critical value, $\chi^2_{df,1-\alpha}$. No tables are provided for this critical value calculation, but fortunately we can use the Excel function CHISQ.INV for this. The chi-squared critical value with $df = (r - 1)(c - 1) = 4$ degrees of freedom and significance level $\alpha = 0.05$ is $\chi^2_{4,0.95} = 9.49$. We note that the observed value of the test statistic, $\chi^2_{\text{cal}} = 63.356$, is greater than $\chi^2_{4,0.95} = 9.49$, and so we **reject H_0** and conclude that the variables 'Gender' and 'Course' exhibit some form of dependence.
- *Using the p-value approach*: The p-value is calculated as:

$$p = P(X^2 > \chi^2_{\text{cal}}) = 1 - P(X^2 > \chi^2_{\text{cal}})$$

X^2 is a chi-squared random variable with *df* degrees of freedom. We can calculate this value using Excel's CHISQ.DIST function. From Excel, we find that the *p*-value is 5.7×10^{-13}. Comparing this value to the selected significance level, $\alpha = 0.05$, we must conclude that **H_0 should be rejected** (because $p < \alpha$).

The Excel solution and spreadsheet is shown in Figure 14.1.

	A	B	C	D	E	F	G	H	I	J	K	L
1	Chi-squared test for independence											
2				Gender								
3				Males	Females	Column totals			Hypothesis test			
4		Course	A101	45	86	131	=SUM(D4:E4)	Step 1:	H_0: Gender and course are independent			
5			D102	52	67	119	=SUM(D5:E5)		H_1: Gender and course are dependent			
6			M101	50	19	69	=SUM(D6:E6)					
7			S101	50	32	82	=SUM(D7:E7)		Choose the appropriate test			
8			T101	69	15	84	=SUM(D8:E8)	Step 2:	Chi-square test for independence			
9			Row totals	266	219	485	=SUM(D9:E9)		Categorical data variables (gender and course)			
10				=SUM(D4:D8)	=SUM(E4:E8)							
11								Step 3:	Select level of significance			
12	Expected frequencies and test statistic									Signficance level, α =	0.05	
13												
14	Gender	Course	O_{ij}	E_{ij}		$(O_{ij}-E_{ij})^2/E_{ij}$			Calculate test statistic			
15	Male	A101	45	71.8474	=F4*$D$9/$F$9	10.0321	=(C15-D15)^2/D15			χ^2_{cal} =	63.3562	=SUM(F15:F24)
16	Male	D102	52	65.2660	=F5*$D$9/$F$9	2.6964	=(C16-D16)^2/D16					
17	Male	M101	50	37.8433	=F6*$D$9/$F$9	3.9052	=(C17-D17)^2/D17			Critical value		
18	Male	S101	50	44.9732	=F7*$D$9/$F$9	0.5619	=(C18-D18)^2/D18	Step 4:		r =	5	=COUNT(D4:D8)
19	Male	T101	69	46.0701	=F8*$D$9/$F$9	11.4126	=(C19-D19)^2/D19			c =	2	=COUNT(D4:E4)
20	Female	A101	86	59.1526	=F4*$E$9/$F$9	12.1852	=(C20-D20)^2/D20			df =	4	=(K18-1)*(K19-1)
21	Female	D102	67	53.7340	=F5*$E$9/$F$9	3.2751	=(C21-D21)^2/D21		Critical value	$\chi^2_{df,\alpha}$ =	9.487729037	=CHISQ.INV(1-K12,K20)
22	Female	M101	19	31.1567	=F6*$E$9/$F$9	4.7433	=(C22-D22)^2/D22			p-value =	5.70990E-13	=1-CHISQ.DIST(K15,K20,TRUE)
23	Female	S101	32	37.0268	=F7*$E$9/$F$9	0.6824	=(C23-D23)^2/D23					
24	Female	T101	15	37.9299	=F8*$E$9/$F$9	13.8619	=(C24-D24)^2/D24		Make a decision			
25								Step 5:	Since $\chi^2_{cal} > \chi^2_{df,\alpha}$ (63.36 > 9.48), reject H_0			
26									The gender and course variables exhibit statistical dependence.			

Figure 14.1: The Excel solution to Example 14.2

EXCEL SOLUTIONS

Observed frequencies: Cells D4:E8	Values
Total number of males: Cell D9	Formula: =SUM(D4:D8)
Total number of females: Cell E9	Formula: =SUM(E4:E8)
Total number of students taking the A101 course: Cell F4	Formula: =SUM(D4:E4)
Total number of students taking the D102 course: Cell F5	Formula: =SUM(D5:E5)
Total number of students taking the M101 course: Cell F6	Formula: =SUM(D6:E6)
Total number of students taking the S101 course: Cell F7	Formula: =SUM(D7:E7)
Total number of students taking the T101 course: Cell F8	Formula: =SUM(D8:E8)
Grand total: Cell F9	Formula: =SUM(D9:E9)
Rearranged table:	
O: Cells C15:C24	Values

E: Cell D15	Formula: =F4*$D$9/$F$9
Cell D16	Formula: =F5*$D$9/$F$9
Cell D19	Formula: =F8*$D$9/$F$9
Cell D20	Formula: =F4*$E$9/$F$9
Cell D21	Formula: =F5*$E$9/$F$9
Cell D24	Formula: =F8*$E$9/$F$9
(O–E)2/E: Cell F15	Formula: =(C15-D15)^2/D15
	Copy formula F15:F24
Significance level: Cell K12	Value
χ^2_{cal}: Cell K15	Formula: =SUM(F15:F24)
r: Cell K18	Formula: =COUNT(D5:D9)
c: Cell K19	Formula: =COUNT(D5:E5)
df: Cell K20	Formula: =(K18-1)*(K19-1)
Critical value $\chi^2_{df,\alpha}$: Cell K21	Formula: =CHISQ.INV(1-K12,K20)
p-value: Cell K22	Formula: =1-CHISQ.DIST(K15,K20,TRUE)

NOTE The p-value is given by the Excel function: =1−CHISQ.DIST(test statistic,df,TRUE).

The critical value, $\chi^2_{df,\alpha}$, is given by the Excel function: =CHISQ.INV(1−α,df).

We can also use the function CHISQ.TEST to conduct this hypothesis test. This function accepts two tables as its arguments. The first table is the observed frequency table and the second table is the frequency table expected under the null hypothesis. The Excel spreadsheet in Figure 14.2 uses the calculations obtained in Figure 14.1 to illustrate this function.

	A	B	C	D	E	F	G	H	I	J	K	L
1	Chi-squared test for Independence											
2				Gender								
3			O_{ij}	Males	Females	Column totals			Hypothesis test			
4		Course	A101	45	86	131	=SUM(D4:E4)	Step 1:	H_0: Gender and course are independent			
5			D102	52	67	119	=SUM(D5:E5)		H_1: Gender and course are dependent			
6			M101	50	19	69	=SUM(D6:E6)					
7			S101	50	32	82	=SUM(D7:E7)		Choose the appropriate test			
8			T101	69	15	84	=SUM(D8:E8)	Step 2:	Chi-square test for independence			
9			Row totals	266	219	485	=SUM(D4:E8)		Categorical data variables (gender and course)			
10				=SUM(D4:D8)	=SUM(E4:E8)							
11								Step 3:	Select level of significance			
12				Gender					Signficance level, α =		0.05	
13			E_{ij}	Males	Females	Column totals						
14		Course	A101	71.8474	59.1526	131		Step 4:	Calculate test statistic			
15			D102	65.266	53.734	119				p-value =	5.7099E-13	=CHISQ.TEST(D4:E8,D14:E18)
16			M101	37.8433	31.1567	69						
17			S101	44.9732	37.0268	82			Make a decision			
18			T101	46.0701	37.9299	84		Step 5:	Since $p < \alpha$, reject H_0			
19			Row totals	266	219	485			The gender and course variables exhibit statistical dependence.			

Figure 14.2: The alternate Excel solution to Example 14.2

EXCEL SOLUTIONS

Observed frequencies: Cells D4:E8	Values
Expected frequencies: Cells D14:E18	Values (obtained in Figure 14.1 or Table 14.6)
p-value: Cell K15	Formula: =CHISQ.TEST(D4:E8,D14:E18)

INTERPRETATION There is a significant relationship or association between the category variables 'Gender' and 'Course': they are not independent.

We can identify which cells in the observed table exhibit the greatest deviation from the frequencies expected under independence by looking at the calculation of the quantity $\frac{(O_{ij} - E_{ij})^2}{E_{ij}}$ in Figure 14.1.

Here we see that this quantity is very large for cells associated with courses A101 and T101 (for example, note that this value is equal to 13.8619 for females taking course T101 and is 11.4126 for males taking the course T101). This indicates that the frequencies of males and females taking courses A101 and T101 differ substantially from the frequencies we would have expected if 'Course' and 'Gender' were independent.

The course S101, on the other hand, appears to produce very small values for the quantity $\frac{(O_{ij} - E_{ij})^2}{E_{ij}}$, which would suggest that the frequencies of males and females in this course conform to what we would have expected if the two variables were independent.

The implication of the Chi-squared test is that the males and females seem to have preferences for subjects, i.e. it does not appear as though the distribution of males and females is the same for each course. Rather, we find that the distribution of males and females is highly *dependent* on which course is chosen. We see that courses such as M101 and T101 have a higher concentration of male students, while courses such as A101 and D102 have higher concentrations of female students.

NOTE

Figure 14.3 illustrates the relationship between the *p*-value and the test statistic in Example 14.2.

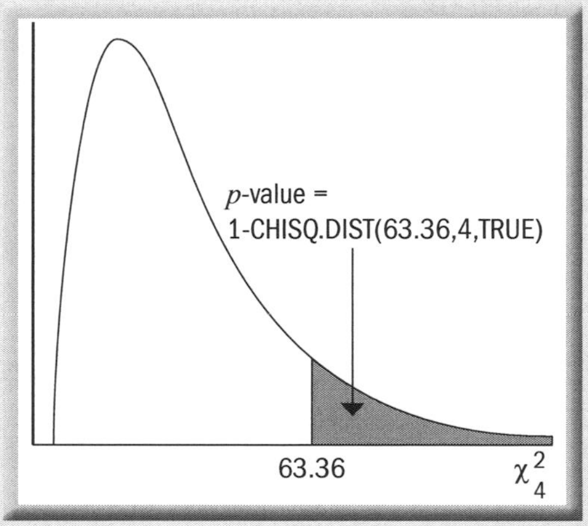

Figure 14.3: The relationship between the calculated value of the test statistic and the *p*-value in Example 14.2

NOTE

For the chi-squared test to give meaningful results, the *expected frequency* for each cell is required to be at least 5. Cochran (a statistician that worked on this problem in the 1950s) suggested that if the degrees of freedom are greater than 1, then tolerable accuracy can be obtained, provided 80% of expected frequencies are greater than or equal to 5 and no cell has an expected frequency less than 1. If this criterion cannot be met, then you need try to increase the sample size and/or combine classes to eliminate frequencies that are too small.

In the example, you may have noticed that the frequency counts are discrete variables that are mapped onto the continuous χ^2-distribution. In cases where we have an expected frequency for each cell that is less than or equal to 5, we need to apply the statistic incorporating Yates' correction for continuity, given by:

$$X^2 = \sum_{i=1}^{N} \frac{(|O_i - E_i| - 0.5)^2}{E_i} \quad (14.5)$$

14.1.3 Test differences in proportions for two samples

In Chapter 11 (Section 11.6), we explored the application of the Z-test to solve problems involving two proportions. If we are concerned that the parametric assumptions are not valid, then we can use the chi-squared test to test two independent proportions or apply the McNemar χ^2- or Z-test, which uses a normal approximation for two paired (or dependent) samples.

Chi-squared test for samples drawn from two independent populations

In this situation, we have two samples (samples A and B) drawn from two independent populations (populations A and B). Each sample consists of observations made on a variable, X, that can only take on two values, for example, 'Success' or 'Failure'. The total number of observations in sample A will be denoted by n_A and the number of 'Success' observations will be denoted by x_A. Similarly, n_B and x_B will denote the total number of items and number of successes in sample B, respectively.

In this problem, we are interested in testing the equality of the population probability of 'success' in populations A (denoted π_A) and B (denoted π_B), i.e. we are interested in testing the hypothesis:

$$H_0: \pi_A = \pi_B$$

Versus the alternative hypothesis:

$$H_1: \pi_A \neq \pi_B$$

Note that we will only consider the two-sided alternative in the test that follows.

This hypothesis must now be tested using the frequencies provided in the two samples, which can be summarised as two separate simple frequency tables.

Table 14.8: The two frequency tables summarising the hypothesis test

		SAMPLE A
X	SUCCESSES	x_A
	FAILURES	$n_A - x_A$
Total		n_A

		SAMPLE B
X	SUCCESSES	x_B
	FAILURES	$n_B - x_B$
Total		n_B

Of course, we could also easily represent these two tables in a single (2 × 2) contingency table, as shown in Table 14.9.

Table 14.9: General form of the contingency tables of observed frequencies used for comparing two population proportions

OBSERVED FREQUENCIES		SAMPLE A	SAMPLE B	Row total
X	SUCCESS	$O_{11} = x_A$	$O_{12} = x_B$	$R_1 = x_A + x_B$
	FAILURE	$O_{12} = n_A - x_A$	$O_{22} = n_B - x_B$	$R_2 = n - x_A - x_B$
Column total		$c_1 = n_A$	$c_2 = n_B$	$n = n_A + n_B$

This table represents the contingency table of observed values in the sample. Now, to test the hypothesis of equal probabilities using the chi-squared test statistic in formula (14.2), we first need to establish the table of values expected under H_0. Under H_0, both samples produce the same probabilities, and so we could ignore the distinction between the two groups when estimating the probability of success, i.e. the estimated population probability of success (under H_0) would simply be:

$$\hat{\pi}_0 = \frac{R_1}{n} = \frac{x_A + x_B}{n_A + n_B}$$

The expected table must now reflect the null hypothesis, but the column total must be the same as the observed table. To do this, we can calculate the estimated expected frequencies of 'Success' in both samples by multiplying the estimated combined probability of 'Success' ($\hat{\pi}_0$) by the number of items in a particular sample. Similarly, for the frequency of 'Failure', we multiply the estimated combined probability of 'Failure' ($1 - \hat{\pi}_0$) by the number of items in a particular sample. These calculations are shown in formula (14.6):

$$E_{1j} = C_j\hat{\pi}_0 = \frac{R_1C_j}{n} \quad \text{and} \quad E_{2j} = C_j(1 - \hat{\pi}_0) = \frac{R_2C_j}{n} \quad j = 1, 2 \qquad (14.6)$$

The general form of the expected table is then given in Table 14.10.

Table 14.10: General form of the contingency tables of observed frequencies used for comparing two population proportions

EXPECTED FREQUENCIES		SAMPLE A	SAMPLE B	Row total
X	SUCCESS	$E_{11} = \frac{R_1C_1}{n} = \frac{(x_A + x_B)n_A}{n_A + n_B}$	$E_{12} = \frac{R_1C_2}{n} = \frac{(x_A + x_B)n_B}{n_A + n_B}$	$R_1 = x_A + x_B$
	FAILURE	$E_{12} = \frac{R_2C_1}{n} = \frac{(n - x_A - x_B)n_A}{n_A + n_B}$	$E_{22} = \frac{R_2C_2}{n} = \frac{(n - x_A - x_B)n_B}{n_A + n_B}$	$R_2 = n - x_A - x_B$
Column total		$C_1 = n_A$	$C_2 = n_B$	$n = n_A + n_B$

As before, we can now test the hypothesis by simply calculating the value of the chi-squared test statistic in formula (14.2) using the observed and expected frequencies:

$$X^2 = \sum_{i=1}^{2}\sum_{j=1}^{2}\frac{(O_{ij} - E_{ij})^2}{E_{ij}} \overset{H_0}{\sim} \chi_1^2 \quad (14.7)$$

We also calculate the degrees of freedom using the formula given in (14.3), but since these contingency tables are always (2 × 2), we have that $r = 2$ and $c = 2$, so the degrees of freedom are just equal to 1:

$$df = (r - 1)(c - 1) = (2 - 1)(2 - 1) = 1$$

Example 14.3 illustrates how we apply this test using actual data. The Excel solution is also provided.

WORKED EXAMPLES

EXAMPLE 14.3

A mine safety officer is concerned about the work conditions in one of the mine shafts (Shaft A) of a particular mine. In particular, he has been told that the mine shaft's ventilation is faulty, causing some of the miners to suffer from respiratory related illnesses. The safety officer collects data to determine how many of the miners that have reported illnesses or injuries suffered from respiratory related problems (the sample is collected over the course of a year). He then collects similar data from another shaft (Shaft B) where the ventilation system is known to work.

In Shaft A, 89 of the 153 miners that reported injuries or illnesses reported respiratory related issues. In Shaft B, 164 people reported illnesses or injuries, and 76 of these were respiratory system related.

The following 2 × 2 contingency table (see Table 14.11) is constructed to summarise these data.

Table 14.11: Observed frequencies for injuries/illnesses reported at the two shafts

OBSERVED FREQUENCIES	SHAFT A (VENTILATION PROBLEMS)	SHAFT B (NO VENTILATION PROBLEMS)	Row total
REPORTED RESPIRATORY RELATED PROBLEMS	89	76	165
REPORTED SOME OTHER INJURY/ILLNESS	64	88	152
Column total	153	164	317

Test the hypothesis that the probability that a person that suffers a respiratory related problem is the same in both shafts (given that the person suffered some form of injury or illness). Test at a significance level of $\alpha = 0.05$.

To test this hypothesis, we begin by constructing the expected frequencies table using formula (14.6) and Table 14.11.

Table 14.12: Expected frequencies for injuries/illnesses reported at the two shafts

EXPECTED FREQUENCIES	SHAFT A (VENTILATION PROBLEMS)	SHAFT B (NO VENTILATION PROBLEMS)	Row total
REPORTED RESPIRATORY RELATED PROBLEMS	$E_{11} = \frac{R_1C_1}{n}$ $= \frac{(165)(153)}{317}$ $= 79.637$	$E_{12} = \frac{R_1C_2}{n}$ $= \frac{(165)(164)}{317}$ $= 85.363$	165
REPORTED SOME OTHER INJURY/ILLNESS	$E_{12} = \frac{R_2C_1}{n}$ $= \frac{(152)(153)}{317}$ $= 73.363$	$E_{22} = \frac{R_2C_2}{n}$ $= \frac{(152)(164)}{317}$ $= 78.637$	152
Column total	153	164	317

The five-step procedure described in Chapter 10 can now be followed to test the hypothesis.

Step 1: Provide the hypothesis statements H_0 and H_1

The population probabilities that a miner suffers respiratory problems (given that some injury or illness was reported) is denoted π_A for Shaft A and π_B for Shaft B. The null and alternative hypotheses are as follows:

- H_0: $\pi_A = \pi_B$ (i.e. probabilities in both shafts are the same)
- H_1: $\pi_A \neq \pi_B$ (i.e.probabilities differ)

Step 2: Choose an appropriate test statistic

In this scenario we have the following:

- Two samples drawn from two independent populations. The first population consists of the miners from Shaft A that reported injuries/illnesses and the second population consists of miners from Shaft B that reported injuries/illnesses. The samples are collected over a single year.
- The variable of interest is categorical ('Suffered injury/illness' is the variable with two levels: 'Respiratory problem' and 'Some other problem').
- The data are frequencies that can be arranged in a 2×2 contingency table.
- The hypothesis concerns comparing the probabilities in the two populations.

These considerations lead us to use the chi-squared test for the difference between two independent populations' probabilities.

Step 3: Specify the significance level

The specified significance level is $\alpha = 0.05$

Step 4: Calculate the relevant test statistic

The chi-squared test requires that we use the observed frequencies in Table 14.11 and the expected frequencies calculated in Table 14.12. The calculated value of the test statistic in formula (14.7) is then:

$$\begin{aligned}\chi^2_{\text{cal}} &= \sum_{i=1}^{2}\sum_{j=1}^{2}\frac{(O_{ij} - E_{ij})^2}{E_{ij}} \\ &= \frac{(89 - 79.637)^2}{79.637} + \frac{(76 - 85.363)^2}{85.363} + \frac{(64 - 73.363)^2}{73.363} + \frac{(88 - 78.637)^2}{78.637} \\ &= 1.1008 + 1.0270 + 1.1950 + 1.1148 \\ &= 4.4376\end{aligned}$$

Step 5: Make a decision

We use both the critical value approach and the p-value approach to make a decision for this test.

- *Using critical values*: The critical value approach requires that we first calculate the chi-squared critical value, $\chi^2_{df,\alpha}$, using Excel's CHISQ.INV function. In this case, we have $\alpha = 0.05$ and $df = 1$, so the critical value is $\chi^2_{1,0.05} = 3.841459$. When we compare the observed value of the test statistic to this critical value, we find that $4.4376 = \chi^2_{\text{cal}} > \chi^2_{1,0.05} = 3.841459$ and so we **reject H_0**, and conclude that the variables of the two probabilities are not equal.
- *Using the p-value approach*: We can calculate the p-value using Excel's CHISQ.DIST function. From Excel, we find that the p-value is 0.035161, which is smaller than the specified significance level, $\alpha = 0.05$, so we **reject H_0**.

	A	B	C	D	E	F	G	H	I	J	K	L
1	**Chi-squared test for probabilities from two independent populations**											
2												
3		**Observed frequencies**										
4												
5			**Shaft A**	**Shaft B**					**Hypothesis test**			
6	**Reported illness or injury**	**Respiratory**	89	76	**165**	=SUM(C6:D6)		**Step 1:**	$H_0: \pi_A = \pi_B$			
7		**Other**	64	88	**152**	=SUM(C7:D7)			$H_1: \pi_A \neq \pi_B$			
8			**153**	**164**	**317**	=SUM(E6:E7)						
9			=SUM(C6:C7)	=SUM(D6:D7)	=SUM(C8:D8)				**Choose the appropriate test**			
10								**Step 2:**	Chi-square test for two independent populations' probabilities			
11		O_{ij}		E_{ij}		$(O_{ij}-E_{ij})^2/E_{ij}$			Categorical data variables (Shaft and reported illness/injury)			
12		89	=C6	79.6372	=E6*C8/E8	1.1008	=(B12-D12)^2/D12					
13		76	=D6	85.3628	=E6*D8/E8	1.0269	=(B13-D13)^2/D13	**Step 3:**	**Select level of significance**			
14		64	=C7	73.3628	=E7*C8/E8	1.1949	=(B14-D14)^2/D14		Signficance level, α =		0.05	
15		88	=D7	78.6372	=E7*D8/E8	1.1148	=(B15-D15)^2/D15					
16									**Calculate test statistic**			
17										χ^2_{cal} =	4.4374	=SUM(F12:F15)
18												
19										Critical value		
20								**Step 4:**		r =	2	=COUNTA(E6:E7)
21										c =	2	=COUNTA(C8:D8)
22										df =	1	=(K20-1)*(K21-1)
23									Critical value	$\chi^2_{df,\alpha}$ =	3.8415	=CHISQ.INV(1-K14,K22)
24										p-value =	0.0352	=1-CHISQ.DIST(K17,K22,TRUE)
25												
26									**Make a decision**			
27								**Step 5:**	Since $\chi^2_{cal} > \chi^2_{df,\alpha}$ (4.4374 > 3.8415), reject H_0			
28									The two population probabilities are not equal.			

Figure 14.4: The Excel solution to Example 14.3

EXCEL SOLUTIONS

Data series: Cells C6:D7

Sum row 1: Cell E6	Formula: =SUM(C6:D6)
Sum row 2: Cell E7	Formula: =SUM(C7:D7)
Sum column 1: Cell C8	Formula: =SUM(C6:C7)
Sum column 2: Cell D8	Formula: =SUM(D6:D7)
Grand total: Cell E8	Formula: =SUM(E6:E7)
O: Cell B12	Formula: =C6
O: Cell B13	Formula: =D6
O: Cell B14	Formula: =C7
O: Cell B15	Formula: =D7
E: Cell D12	Formula: =E6*C8/E8
E: Cell D13	Formula: =E6*D8/E8
E: Cell D14	Formula: =E7*C8/E8
E: Cell D15	Formula: =E7*D8/E8
(O - E)^2/E: Cell F12	Formula: =(B12-D12)^2/D12
(O - E)^2/E: Cell F13	Formula: =(B13-D13)^2/D13
(O - E)^2/E: Cell F14	Formula: =(B14-D14)^2/D14

(O - E)^2/E: Cell F15	Formula: =(B15-D15)^2/D15
Significance Level, α: Cell K14	Value
χ^2_{cal}: Cell K17	Formula: =SUM(F12:F15)
r: Cell K20	Formula: =COUNTA(E6:E7)
c: Cell K21	Formula: =COUNTA(C8:D8)
df: Cell K22	Formula: =(K20-1)*(K21-1)
$\chi^2_{df,\alpha}$: Cell K23	Formula: =CHISQ.INV(1-K14,K22)
p-value: Cell K24	Formula: =1-CHISQ.DIST(K17:K22,TRUE)

INTERPRETATION There is a significant difference in the proportions of the probability of respiratory problems between Shaft A and Shaft B.

NOTE If you decided that the significance level was 1% ($\alpha = 0.01$), then we would have the opposite decision, given that the two-sided p-value > α (0.035161 > 0.01). In this case, we would not reject H_0 and conclude that there is no significant difference between the two probabilities. This is an example of modifying your decision based on how confident you would like to be with your overall decision.

NOTE For the chi-squared test to give meaningful results, the expected frequency for each cell in the 2 × 2 contingency table is required to be at least 5. If this is not the case, then the χ^2-distribution is not a good approximation to the sum of the ratios $\sum\frac{(O-E)^2}{E}$. Exact tests (not discussed in this text) would be more appropriate in these situations.

In Example 14.3, the probability distribution of the frequency of 'Success' (which is a *discrete* binomial random variable) is approximated by the *continuous* χ^2-distribution. In these cases, we can apply the Yates' correction for continuity given by formula (14.5).

In Section 11.6, we compared two sample proportions using a normal approximation. When we have 1 degree of freedom, we can show that the following simple relationship exists between the value of χ^2_{cal} and the corresponding value of Z: $\chi^2_{\text{cal}} = (z_{\text{cal}})^2$.

If we are interested in testing for direction in the alternative hypothesis (for example, H_1: $\pi_1 > \pi_2$ or H_1: $\pi_1 < \pi_2$), we cannot use a χ^2-test but instead have to undertake a normal distribution Z-test to test for direction.

The two proportion solution can be extended to more than two proportions, but this is beyond the scope of this textbook.

McNemar's chi-squared test (and Z-test) for samples drawn from two dependent populations (McNemar's test for matched pairs)

McNemar's test for matched pairs A non-parametric method used on nominal data to determine whether the row and column marginal frequencies are equal.

The previous test explored the application of the chi-squared test to compare two proportions taken from random independent samples. However, if the populations are dependent (or paired), then we need to use **McNemar's chi-squared** test (or Z-test) to compare the two proportions.

The type of situation to which we would apply this test typically involves measurements made on a variable before and after some sort of intervention (which can be some activity/treatment/event that occurs). Once again, the variable of interest is a nominal-scaled binary variable (i.e. it can only take on two unordered values, like 'Success' and 'Failure', or 'Yes' and 'No', and so on). Examples of this include the following:

- At the beginning of a political campaign, a sample of people is surveyed to determine the proportion of people that 'Like' and 'Dislike' a particular candidate. During the course of the campaign, some scandal emerges that could affect public opinion regarding the candidate. After the scandal, the same individuals used in the original survey are surveyed again to determine if they 'Like' or 'Dislike' the candidate. The variable of interest here is 'Opinion' with two levels: 'Like' and 'Dislike'. The same individuals are used in both surveys, so the two samples are dependent. The research question here would be: Is the distribution of 'Like' and 'Dislike' the same before and after the scandal?
- In a study to determine the effect of a new course on students' literacy, a sample of 100 students is randomly selected. Before running the course, the students take a simple reading test, which they can either 'Pass' or 'Fail'. After running the course, the students are asked to take another reading test. The variable of interest is 'Reading test result', which can take on the values 'Pass' or 'Fail'. The samples are dependent because the same students are used in both tests. The research question is: Does the course affect the ability of students to pass the reading test?

The McNemar test is interested in determining if the distribution of 'Success' and 'Failure' responses before and after the intervention is the same. The informal hypothesis is then:

- H_0: The distribution before is the same as the distribution after.
- H_1: The distributions before and after differ.

More formally, we will denote the before probability of 'Success' by π_{before} and the probability of before 'Failure' by $1 - \pi_{\text{before}}$. Similarly, the probability of after 'Success' and 'Failure' is denoted by π_{after} and $1 - \pi_{\text{after}}$, respectively. Determining if the before and after distributions are equivalent simply boils down to testing if π_{before} is equal to π_{after}. The hypothesis is then:

- $H_0: \pi_{\text{before}} = \pi_{\text{after}}$
- $H_1: \pi_{\text{before}} \neq \pi_{\text{after}}$

Naturally, when data are collected, we will only observe the number of times (or frequency) of successes and failures before and after some intervention. These frequencies can be summarised, in general, in a 2×2 contingency table like the one shown in Table 14.13.

Table 14.13: A general 2 × 2 contingency table for before and after measurements on a binary variable

		AFTER		
		SUCCESS	**FAILURE**	Row (before) total
BEFORE	**SUCCESS**	a	b	$a+b$
	FAILURE	c	d	$c+d$
Column (after) total		$a+c$	$b+d$	$n=a+b+c+d$

The frequencies in the contingency table, Table 14.13, are now denoted by *a*, *b*, *c* and *d*. This notation is used to simplify some of the statistics that will be calculated.

NOTE

Note that the frequency b denotes the number of items that changed from 'Success' before the intervention to 'Failure' after the intervention (similarly, c denotes the number of items switching from 'Failure' before to 'Success' after the intervention).

The frequencies b and c are thus very important in indicating how the distribution of 'Success' and 'Failure' changes after the intervention (if they are small then it indicates no changes after the intervention; if they are large it indicates large changes after the intervention).

Using Table 14.13, we can estimate the probabilities π_{before} and π_{after}:

$$\hat{\pi}_{\text{before}} = p_{\text{before}} = \frac{a+b}{n} \tag{14.8}$$

$$\hat{\pi}_{\text{after}} = p_{\text{after}} = \frac{a+c}{n} \tag{14.9}$$

The hypothesis – to determine the difference between the two proportions – can be tested using either a *Z*- or chi-squared test. It is important to note that the chi-squared test cannot be used for left- or right-sided tests. In that situation, you would have to use a *Z*-test.

The test statistics that will be used for these tests are the following.

- *McNemar Z-test*: To test the null hypothesis, we can use the McNemar *Z*-test statistic defined by formula (14.10), which follows an approximate standard normal distribution under H_0:

$$Z = \frac{b-c}{\sqrt{b+c}} \overset{H_0}{\sim} N(0, 1) \tag{14.10}$$

- *McNemar χ^2-test*: To test the null hypothesis, we can also use the McNemar χ^2-test statistic defined by formula (14.11):

$$X^2 = (Z)^2 = \frac{(b-c)^2}{b+c} \overset{H_0}{\sim} \chi_1^2 \tag{14.11}$$

Note the relationship between X^2 and Z.

Example 14.4 will help to illustrate this test.

WORKED EXAMPLES

EXAMPLE 14.4

The manufacturers of the J-phone cellular phone have created a new marketing campaign that aims to target children between the ages of 10 and 15. The marketing department wants to determine the effectiveness of their campaign by surveying 621 randomly chosen children in this age group before the marketing campaign is rolled out and then surveying the same children again one month after the launch of the marketing campaign.

In the study, the question 'Do you favour the J-phone over another brand?' with choices 'I favour the J-phone' and 'I favour another brand' is put to the children. The frequencies of these responses are recorded before and after the launch of the campaign, and summarised in Table 14.14.

Table 14.14: Summary of responses before and after the J-phone campaign

BEFORE THE LAUNCH OF THE MARKETING CAMPAIGN	AFTER THE LAUNCH OF THE MARKETING CAMPAIGN	
	FAVOURS THE J-PHONE	FAVOURS ANOTHER BRAND
FAVOURS THE J-PHONE	287	89
FAVOURS ANOTHER BRAND	45	200

Does the marketing campaign change their preference towards the J-phone? Test these hypotheses at $\alpha = 0.05$.

In this case, we have two groups who are surveyed before and after an event, and so we are dealing with paired samples. To answer the research question, we can use McNemar's test for two sets of nominal data that are randomly selected.

The five-step procedure for hypothesis testing discussed in Chapter 10 will once again be used to test this hypothesis.

Step 1: Provide the hypothesis statements H_0 and H_1

The population proportions of favouring the J-phone before and after the campaign are π_{before} and π_{after}, respectively. The null and alternative hypothesis to determine if there are differences between the proportions is follows:

- H_0: $\pi_{\text{before}} = \pi_{\text{after}}$
- H_1: $\pi_{\text{before}} \neq \pi_{\text{after}}$

Step 2: Choose an appropriate test statistic

In this scenario we have the following:

- A sample of children recorded before and after a marketing campaign (i.e. dependent values).
- The variable of interest is nominal categorical (i.e. the variable is 'Do you favour the J-phone over another brand?' with levels 'I favour the J-phone' and 'I favour another brand').
- The data are frequencies that can be arranged in a 2×2 contingency table.
- The hypothesis concerns comparing the distribution of the children's preferences before and after the campaign.

These considerations lead us to use the McNemar chi-squared test or Z-test for the difference between two independent populations' probabilities.

Step 3: Specify the significance level

The specified level of significance is $\alpha = 0.05$

Step 4: Calculate the relevant test statistic

Calculate the statistics in formulae (14.10) and (14.11):

$$z_{\text{cal}} = \frac{b - c}{\sqrt{b + c}} = \frac{89 - 45}{\sqrt{89 + 45}} = 3.801021$$

And:

$$\chi^2_{\text{cal}} = (z_{\text{cal}})^2 = \frac{(b - c)^2}{b + c} = \frac{(89 - 45)^2}{89 + 45} = 14.447761$$

Step 5: Make a decision

We will use both the p-value approach and the critical value approach to test this hypothesis.

- *Critical value approach*: The calculated value of the test statistics (calculated above) are $z_{\text{cal}} = 3.801021$ and $\chi^2_{\text{cal}} = 14.447761$.
- We can find the critical value for the Z-test using the Excel function NORM.INV. In this case, the critical values are $z_{\alpha/2} = z_{0.025} = 1.96$ and $-z_{\alpha/2} = -z_{0.025} = -1.96$. We can see that the test statistic lies in the 'reject H_0' region, because $z_{\text{cal}} = 3.801021 > z_{0.025} = 1.96$; we therefore **reject H_0**.
- Similarly for the χ^2-test, we can obtain the critical value using the Excel function CHISQ.INV. The critical value is $\chi^2_{1,\alpha} = \chi^2_{1,0.05} = 3.8415$. The test statistic is much larger than the critical value, i.e. $\chi^2_{\text{cal}} = 14.447761 > \chi^2_{1,0.05} = 3.8415$, and so we come to the same conclusion as before: **reject H_0**. We conclude that there is indeed a significant difference between the distribution of preference for the J-phone before and after the campaign.
- p-*value approach*: We can find the p-value for the Z-statistic from Excel by using the NORM.S.DIST function (note that the same p-value is obtained from the χ^2 statistic using the CHISQ.DIST function). From Excel (see Table 14.13), we find that the two-sided p-value is 0.00014, which is much smaller than the specified significance level, $\alpha = 0.05$, so we **reject H_0**. We conclude that there is indeed a significant difference between the distribution of preference for the J-phone before and after the campaign.

Figure 14.5 illustrates the Excel solution for the McNemar Z-and χ^2-tests.

	A	B	C	D	E	F	G	H	I	J	K	L
1	**McNemar test for probabilities from two dependent populations (matched pair test)**											
2												
3												
4			After									
5			J-phone	Other				Step 1:	**Hypothesis test**			
6	Before	J-phone	287	89	376	=SUM(C6:D6)			H_0: $\pi_{before} = \pi_{after}$			
7		Other	45	200	245	=SUM(C7:D7)			H_1: $\pi_{before} \neq \pi_{after}$			
8			332	289	621	=SUM(E6:E7)						
9			=SUM(C6:C7)	=SUM(D6:D7)	=SUM(E6:E7)			Step 2:	**Choose the appropriate test**			
10									McNemar Z- or chi-square test for two dependent populations' probabilities			
11									Nominal categorical data variables (favour J-phone or not)			
12												
13								Step 3:	**Select level of significance**			
14									Signficance level, α =		0.05	
15												
16								Step 4:	**Calculate test statistic**			
17										z_{cal} =	3.801021073	=(D6-C7)/SQRT(D6+C7)
18										χ^2_{cal} =	14.44776119	=K17^2
19									Critical value			
20									Lower critical value $-z_{\alpha/2}$ =		-1.96	=NORM.S.INV(K14/2)
21									Upper cirtical value $z_{\alpha/2}$ =		1.96	=NORM.S.INV(1-K14/2)
22									Critical value	$\chi^2_{df,\alpha}$ =	3.8415	=CHISQ.INV(1-K14,1)
23									(Z-test) p-value =		0.000144	=2*(1-NORM.S.DIST(ABS(K17),TRUE))
24									(Chi-squared test) p-value =		0.000144	=1-CHISQ.DIST(K18,1,TRUE)
25												
26								Step 5:	Make a decision			
27									Since $p < \alpha$ (0.00014 < 0.05), reject H_0			
28									The probability distribution before and after the campaign differs.			

Figure 14.5: The Excel solution to Example 14.4

EXCEL SOLUTIONS

Data series: Cells C6:D7	
Sum row 1: Cell E6	Formula: =SUM(C6:D6)
Sum row 2: Cell E7	Formula: =SUM(C7:D7)
Sum column 1: Cell C8	Formula: =SUM(C6:C7)
Sum column 2: Cell D8	Formula: =SUM(D6:D7)
Grand total: Cell E8	Formula: =SUM(E6:E7)=SUM(C8:D8)
Level: Cell K14	Value
z_{cal} = Cell K17	Formula: =(D6–C7)/SQRT(D6+E7)
χ^2_{cal}: Cell K18	Formula: =K17^2
Lower $-z_{\alpha/2}$: Cell K20	Formula: =NORM.S.INV(K14/2)
Upper $z_{\alpha/2}$: Cell K21	Formula: =NORM.S.INV(1–K14/2)
χ^2_{α} = Cell K22	Formula: =CHISQ.INV(1–K14,1)
Z two-sided p-value: Cell K23	Formula: =2*(1-NORM.S.DIST(ABS(K17),TRUE))
χ^2 p-value: Cell K24	Formula: =1-CHISQ.DIST(K18,1,TRUE)

INTERPRETATION There is a significant difference in the preferences of the J-phone before and after the marketing campaign. This may seem like a positive thing for the marketing campaign for the J-phone until you realise that the proportion of children that favour the phone after the campaign is actually lower than it was before the campaign (and we have just shown that this proportion is *significantly* lower).

This would seem to suggest that the marketing campaign had the reverse effect on the children: it drove them to favouring other phone brands.

14.2 Non-parametric (or distribution-free) tests

Many statistical tests require that your data follow a normal distribution. Unfortunately, this is not always the case. In some instances, it is possible to transform the data to make them follow a normal distribution; in others this is not possible or the sample size might be so small that it is difficult to ascertain whether the data are normally distributed. In such cases, it is necessary to use a statistical test that does not require the data to follow a particular distribution. In this section, we explore three non-parametric tests for testing the location of the data:

- the sign test
- the Wilcoxon signed-rank test
- the Mann-Whitney U-test

Table 14.15 compares the non-parametric tests with the parametric tests for one and two samples as discussed in Chapters 10 and 11.

Table 14.15: A summary of the non-parametric tests and the hypotheses to which they can be applied

TEST	PARAMETRIC TEST	NON-PARAMETRIC TEST
One sample	One sample Z-test or one sample t-test	Sign test or Wilcoxon signed-rank test
Paired samples	Two paired sample t-test	Sign test Wilcoxon signed-rank test
Independent samples	Two independent sample t-test	Mann-Whitney test (Wilcoxon rank sum test)

In order to calculate the Wilcoxon signed-rank test statistic and the Mann-Whitney U-test statistic, we need to use the ranks of the data instead of the original data points.

For this reason, we begin the discussion of non-parametric statistics by first looking at how we can obtain the ranks of data.

14.2.1 Calculating ranks of data

The ranks of data are, essentially, the ordering numbers of observations in a data set. For example, if we have three observations $x_1 = 99$, $x_2 = 23$ and $x_3 = 74$, then the rank of x_1 is 3 (it is third in the ordered set), the rank of x_2 is 1 (it is first in the ordered set) and the rank of x_3 is 2 (it is second in the ordered set). We use the notation R_i to represent the rank of the ith observation in a data set. Table 14.16 illustrates how the observation values are linked to their corresponding rank values.

Table 14.16: How observed values are linked to rank values

OBSERVATION NUMBER	DATA	RANK
1	$x_1 = 99$	$R_1 = 3$
2	$x_2 = 23$	$R_2 = 1$
3	$x_3 = 74$	$R_3 = 2$

We can interpret R_i (the rank of x_i) to mean that x_i is the R_i^{th} *smallest* value in the data set. For example, in Table 14.16, we see that for data point $x_3 = 74$, the rank is $R_3 = 2$, i.e. x_3 is the second smallest value in the data set.

Many non-parametric statistics (such as the Wilcoxon signed-rank test and the Mann-Whitney U-test) use the ranks of data rather than the actual original data values. This is done because the distribution of the rank values does not strictly depend on the distribution of the underlying values, and so tests based on these rank values (rather than the original values) do not require certain strict assumptions (like those found in parametric tests) in order for them to work.

A simple way to obtain the ranks of a data set of size n is to first sort the data and then simply number the sorted values from 1 to n. This method works well when there are no repeated values in the data set, but will fail when there are repeated data values (this will be explored shortly).

Consider obtaining the ranks of the data values (ages of $n = 7$ individuals) given in Table 14.17.

Table 14.17: Ages of $n = 7$ individuals

AGES						
$x_1 = 25$	$x_2 = 44$	$x_3 = 65$	$x_4 = 23$	$x_5 = 41$	$x_6 = 19$	$x_7 = 38$

If we sort these data and then number the values from 1 to 7, we get the ranks of the 'Age' variable's values (shown in Table 14.18).

Table 14.18: Sorted ages of $n = 7$ individuals and their ranks

(SORTED) AGES						
$x_6 = 19$	$x_4 = 23$	$x_1 = 25$	$x_7 = 38$	$x_5 = 41$	$x_2 = 44$	$x_3 = 65$
RANKS, R						
$R_6 = 1$	$R_4 = 2$	$R_1 = 3$	$R_7 = 4$	$R_5 = 5$	$R_2 = 6$	$R_3 = 7$

Rearranging the data back into its original ordering, the data and ranks can be expressed as shown in Table 14.19.

Table 14.19: Ages of $n = 7$ individuals and their ranks

OBSERVATION NUMBER	DATA, x_i	RANK, R_i
1	25	3
2	44	6
3	65	7
4	23	2
5	41	5
6	19	1
7	38	4

Dealing with tied ranks

The above procedure is, unfortunately, not very useful when there are **tied** values in the original data set. For example, if we were to replace observation number 4 (i.e. $x_4 = 23$) in Table 14.18 with $x_4 = 25$, then there would be a problem, because there is already a person aged 25 in the data set, and their rank is 3. Will the rank of the new observation, x_4, remain with a rank value of 2, or will it change to 3? The age 25 cannot be both the 2nd AND 3rd smallest value in the data set. Fortunately, this problem can easily be resolved simply by using the average of the ranks for tied observations – in this case both observations with value 25 would get the rank value of $\frac{(2+3)}{2} = 2.5$.

Tied ranks Two or more data values share a rank value.

In Table 14.20, we have data collected by recording the weights of $n = 9$ guinea pigs (in grams).

Table 14.20: Weights of $n = 9$ guinea pigs

WEIGHTS OF GUINEA PIGS (g)								
$x_1 = 750$	$x_2 = 690$	$x_3 = 660$	$x_4 = 690$	$x_5 = 750$	$x_6 = 760$	$x_7 = 680$	$x_8 = 690$	$x_9 = 690$

We see here that the value 690 appears four times and the value 750 appears twice. In an attempt to rank the data, we will first sort these data and naively assign numbers 1 to 9 to each observation. This is illustrated in Table 14.21.

Table 14.21: Sorted weights of $n = 9$ guinea pigs and their (incorrect) ranks

(SORTED) WEIGHTS OF GUINEA PIGS (g)								
$x_3 = 660$	$x_7 = 680$	$x_2 = 690$	$x_4 = 90$	$x_8 = 690$	$x_9 = 690$	$x_1 = 750$	$x_5 = 750$	$x_6 = 760$
(INCORRECT) RANK, R?								
$R_3 = 1$	$R_7 = 2$	$R_2 = 3$	$R_4 = 4$	$R_8 = 5$	$R_9 = 6$	$R_1 = 7$	$R_5 = 8$	$R_6 = 9$

Unfortunately, this system of ranking suggests that the value 690 is the 3rd, 4th, 5th and 6th smallest value in the data set. It cannot be all four. The system we use to deal with ties involves calculating the average of these naïve ordering values for items that have the same value, and then assigning this average ordering value as the rank of the item. In this example, the value 690 has ordering value 3, 4, 5 and 6, and the average of these values is $\frac{(3+4+5+6)}{4} = \frac{18}{4} = 4.5$. Therefore, the rank of 690 is 4.5. Similarly, the value 750 also appears to be tied at the ordered 7th and 8th positions. The rank for 750 is then the average $\frac{(7+8)}{2} = 7.5$. The ranks of the remaining untied values are then just the corresponding ordering values. The ranked data are shown in Table 14.22 below.

Table 14.22: Sorted weights of $n = 9$ guinea pigs and their (correct) ranks

(SORTED) WEIGHTS OF GUINEA PIGS (g)								
$x_3 = 660$	$x_7 = 680$	$x_2 = 690$	$x_4 = 690$	$x_8 = 690$	$x_9 = 690$	$x_1 = 750$	$x_5 = 750$	$x_6 = 760$
(CORRECT) RANK, R								
$R_3 = 1$	$R_7 = 2$	$R_2 = 4.5$	$R_4 = 4.5$	$R_8 = 4.5$	$R_9 = 4.5$	$R_1 = 7.5$	$R_5 = 7.5$	$R_6 = 9$

Rearranging the data back into the original ordering, the data and ranks can be expressed as shown in Table 14.23.

Table 14.23: Weights of $n = 9$ guinea pigs and their (correct) ranks

OBSERVATION NUMBER	DATA, x_i	RANK, R_i
1	750	7.5
2	690	4.5
3	660	1
4	690	4.5
5	750	7.5
6	760	9
7	680	2
8	690	4.5
9	690	4.5

Fortunately, we do not have to do these calculations by hand. Excel's RANK.AVG function allows us to calculate the ranks for data values (using average ranks for tied values, as discussed above). The function RANK.AVG accepts three arguments:

RANK.AVG(DataValue,RangeOfVaues,1)

- The first argument, *DataValue,* is the value in a data set whose rank you would like to calculate.
- The second argument, *RangeOfValues,* is the range of data values from which ranks are calculated.
- The third argument is used to indicate whether the ranks should reflect ascending or descending ranking. The value 1 indicates that ascending ranks should be reported.

Figure 14.6 illustrates how to obtain the ranks for the data given in Table 14.19.

	A	B	C	D	E	F	G	H	I	J
1	**Ranks of data**									
2										
3	**Observation number**	**Weights of guinea pigs (g)**	**Rank**							
4										
5	1	750	7.5	=RANK.AVG(B5,$B$5:$B$13,1)						
6	2	690	4.5	=RANK.AVG(B6,$B$5:$B$13,1)						
7	3	660	1	=RANK.AVG(B7,$B$5:$B$13,1)						
8	4	690	4.5	=RANK.AVG(B8,$B$5:$B$13,1)						
9	5	750	7.5	=RANK.AVG(B9,$B$5:$B$13,1)						
10	6	760	9	=RANK.AVG(B10,$B$5:$B$13,1)						
11	7	680	2	=RANK.AVG(B11,$B$5:$B$13,1)						
12	8	690	4.5	=RANK.AVG(B12,$B$5:$B$13,1)						
13	9	690	4.5	=RANK.AVG(B13,$B$5:$B$13,1)						
14										

Figure 14.6: The Excel calculation of ranks for the data in Table 14.23

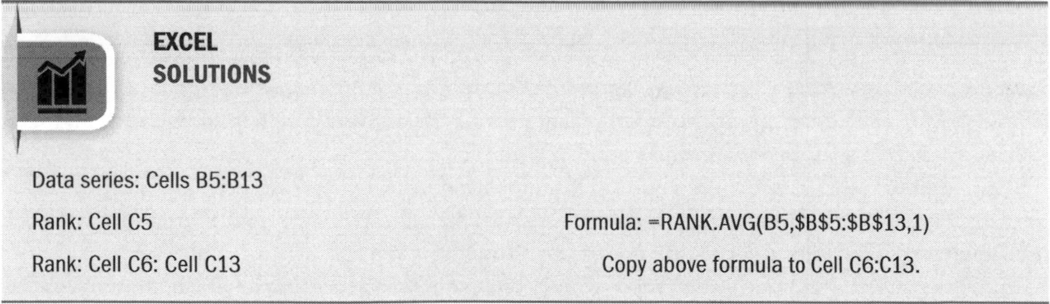

EXCEL SOLUTIONS

Data series: Cells B5:B13

Rank: Cell C5 — Formula: =RANK.AVG(B5,$B$5:$B$13,1)

Rank: Cell C6: Cell C13 — Copy above formula to Cell C6:C13.

Now that we have looked at how ranks can be calculated, we can discuss the non-parametric tests themselves. We start by discussing the sign test (which does not employ ranks in its calculation) and then move on to the Wilcoxon signed-rank test and the Mann-Whitney U-test (both of which employ ranks).

14.2.2 The sign test

The sign test is a non-parametric test that we can use to test simple hypotheses concerning the location parameter of a single population or two dependent populations, i.e. we can use this non-parametric test instead of the parametric tests for location for a single population (discussed in Sections 10.2 and 10.3) and the two dependent population t-test (discussed in Section 11.5). Hence, we can use the sign test to assess the validity of the following types of hypotheses:

- To determine whether the population median value, ν, is equal to some specified population value, ν_0, versus the alternative that it is larger, smaller or unequal to this value, i.e. the null and alternative hypotheses are:

$$H_0: \nu = \nu_0$$

vs

$H_1: \nu < \nu_0$	$H_1: \nu > \nu_0$	$H_1: \nu \neq \nu_0$
left-sided	right-sided	two-sided

- To determine if the population location parameter of two dependent (paired) populations (population A and B) are equivalent or not: If we create a new population of values by taking the differences between observations from the dependent populations (which we denote by $x_{i,A}$ and $x_{i,B}$), we can call the ith observation from this new population $x_{\text{diff}} = x_{i,A} - x_{i,B}$. We can now base the test for the difference in population locations on simply testing if the median of this new differenced population (denoted by ν_{diff}) is equal to some specified value ν_0. (Usually we choose $\nu_0 = 0$, which indicates that the medians of both populations are the same.) The null and alternative hypotheses are:

$$H_0: \nu_{\text{diff}} = \nu_0$$

vs

$H_1: \nu_{\text{diff}} < \nu_0$	$H_1: \nu_{\text{diff}} > \nu_0$	$H_1: \nu_{\text{diff}} \neq \nu_0$
left-sided	right-sided	two-sided

This test is very similar to the one-population test mentioned above. The only difference is that, in this problem, we begin with two populations, but artificially create a single population from these two. In the end, it is just a one-population problem.

Note that the tests for location based on the sign test differ slightly from the parametric tests for location in that the parametric tests for location are all based on the population mean, μ, whereas the sign tests for location typically deal with the population median, ν.

The basic mechanics of the sign test involves checking *how many* of the n observations in the sample data exceed the null hypothesised value of the median, ν_0. If ν_0 is indeed the true median we would expect that each value in the sample will be larger than this value with a probability of 0.5. This means that the total number of items in the sample that exceed ν_0 should be a binomial random variable, denoted T, with parameters n and 0.5 (see Chapter 6 for more detail on the binomial distribution). The sign test simply tests if this is the case, i.e. it checks if the distribution of the number of items that exceed ν_0, T, is indeed binomially distributed with parameters n and 0.5.

The test statistic and p-value for the sign test, used to test the hypothesis that the median from a single population is equal to the specified value ν_0, are calculated using the following simple algorithm.

ALGORITHM FOR CALCULATING THE SIGN TEST STATISTIC AND p-VALUE

- We are given n data values: $X_1, X_2, \ldots, X_n$. Subtract the value υ_0 from each of these values and call the result $D_1, D_2, \ldots, D_n$:
- $D_i = X_1 - \upsilon_0, \qquad i = 1, 2, \ldots, n$
- Count the number of D_i-values that are positive (i.e. determine the sign of the D_i-values and count how many are positive). Call the total number of positive values S_+.
- Similarly, count how many D_i-values are equal to 0 and call this total S_0.
- Determine the p-value by calculating the probability:
  - (for a left-sided test: H_1: $\nu < \nu_0$) $p = P(T \leq S_+)$
  - (for a right-sided test: H_1: $\nu > \nu_0$) $p = P(T \geq S_+) = 1 - P(T \leq S_+ - 1)$
  - (for two-sided tests: H_1: $\nu \neq \nu_0$) $p = 2\min(P(T \geq S_+), P(T \leq S_+))$
- T is a binomial random variable with parameters $n - S_0$ and 0.5. (Note that we use $n - S_0$ and not just n because we need to correct for the number of items exactly equal to 0.)

As always, if the p-value is smaller than α, we will reject H_0.

Note: These probability calculations can be accomplished quite easily using Excel's BINOM.DIST function.

As with all tests (even non-parametric ones), there are some assumptions that need to be satisfied before the test can be performed. Fortunately, in this case, they are not very restrictive. The only assumptions of the sign test are that:

- the samples used are randomly drawn from the population
- the population has a continuous distribution.

Examples 14.5 and 14.6 illustrate how we can use the sign test to test hypotheses made concerning the population median.

WORKED EXAMPLES

EXAMPLE 14.5

A biological researcher is interested in determining if the population location measure (mean or median) of the weights of guinea pigs is equal to 700 g. Unfortunately, he suspects that the population of guinea pig weights is not normally distributed and so he must rely on non-parametric tests to test this hypothesis.

The data collected in Table 14.24 is obtained from a random sample of $n = 9$ guinea pigs.

Table 14.24: Weights of guinea pigs (g)

WEIGHTS OF GUINEA PIGS (g), X_i
750
690
660
690
750
760
680
690
690

Use the sign test and test the hypothesis that the population median weight of guinea pigs is equal to 700 g (versus the alternative that it is not equal to 700 g) at a 5% level of significance.

The five-step procedure discussed in Chapter 10 will be used to test this hypothesis.

Step 1: Provide the hypothesis statements H_0 and H_1

The null hypothesis is: H_0: $\nu = 700$

The population median weight of guinea pigs is hypothesised to be equal to 700 g. The alternative hypothesis is then: H_1: $\nu \neq 700$

Step 2: Choose an appropriate test statistic

The considerations for this test include the following:

- *The number of populations in the study*: A sample from one population is being considered.
- *The research question*: The hypothesis concerns the population median.
- *Assumptions underlying the test:* The sign test only has two assumptions that need to be considered, i.e. the data must be a random sample from the population and the population must at least be continuously distributed. Both of these assumptions hold.

We will use the sign test for a single population to test this hypothesis.

Step 3: Specify the significance level

The significance level is specified as $\alpha = 0.05$ (or 5%).

Step 4: Calculate the relevant test statistic and p-value

The algorithm for the sign test proceeds as follows:

- Begin by calculating the differences (note that $\nu_0 = 700$ in this example):

$$D_i = X_i - 700,\ i = 1, 2, \ldots, n$$

This gives the new data in Table 14.25.

Table 14.25: New data of guinea pig weights

WEIGHTS OF GUINEA PIGS (g), X_i	D_i
750	750 – 700 = 50
690	690 – 700 = –10
660	660 – 700 = –40
690	690 – 700 = –10
750	750 – 700 = 50
760	760 – 700 = 60
680	680 – 700 = –20
690	690 – 700 = –10
690	690 – 700 = –10

- The number of positive values of D_i in this data set are $S_+ = 3$.
- The number of times D_i exactly equal to 0 is $S_0 = 0$.
- Calculate the following probability for the two-sided test:

$$\begin{aligned} p &= 2\min(P(T \geq S_+), P(T \leq S_+)) \\ &= 2\min(P(T \geq 3), P(T \leq 3)) \\ &= 2\min(0.2539, 0.9102) \\ &= 2(0.2539) \\ &= 0.5078 \end{aligned}$$

T is a binomial random variable with parameters $n - S_0 = 9 - 0 = 9$ and 0.5.

Step 5: Make a decision

Since the p-value is 0.5078, which is much larger than the specified significance level of $\alpha = 0.05$, we will **not reject the null hypothesis**, i.e. the median weight is not significantly different from 700 g.

The Excel solution for this example is given in Figure 14.7.

	A	B	C	D	E	F	G	H	I	J
1	**Sign test for a single population median**									
2							**Hypothesis test**			
3		**Weights of guinea pigs (g)**	D_i			**Step 1:**	$H_0: \nu = 700$	$\nu_0 =$	700	
4							$H_1: \nu \neq 700$			
5		750	50	=B5-$I$3						
6		690	-10	=B6-$I$3			**Choose the appropriate test**			
7		660	-40	=B7-$I$3		**Step 2:**	Test for the median			
8		690	-10	=B8-$I$3			Data randomly drawn from a continuous distribution			
9		750	50	=B9-$I$3						
10		760	60	=B10-$I$3		**Step 3:**	**Select level of significance**			
11		680	-20	=B11-$I$3				Signficance level, $\alpha =$	0.05	
12		690	-10	=B12-$I$3						
13		690	-10	=B13-$I$3			**Calculate test statistic**			
14								$S_+ =$	3	=COUNTIF(C5:C13,">0")
15								$S_0 =$	0	=COUNTIF(C5:C13,"=0")
16								$n =$	9	=COUNT(C5:C13)
17						**Step 4:**		$n - S_0 =$	9	=I16-I15
18							$P(T \geq S_+) = 1 - P(T \leq S_+ - 1) =$		0.91015625	=1-BINOM.DIST(I14-I,I17,0.5,TRUE)
19								$P(T \leq S_+) =$	0.25390625	=BINOM.DIST(I14,I17,0.5,TRUE)
20								p-value =	0.5078125	=2*MIN(I18,I19)
21										
22							**Make a decision**			
23						**Step 5:**	Since $p > \alpha$, therefore do not reject H_0			
24							The median weight is not significantly different from 700 grams			

Figure 14.7: The Excel solution for Example 14.5

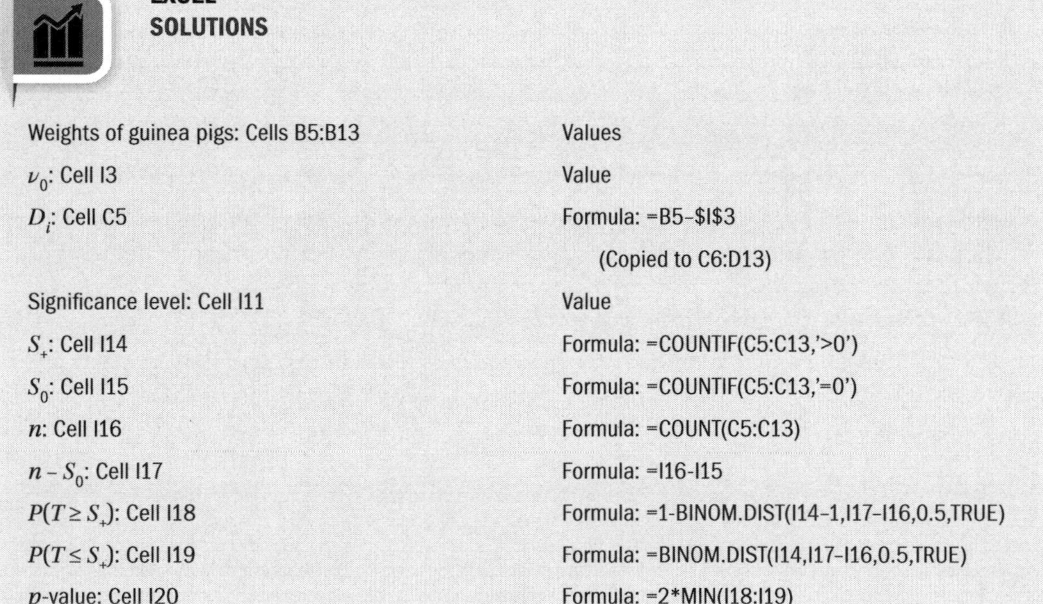

EXCEL SOLUTIONS

Weights of guinea pigs: Cells B5:B13	Values
ν_0: Cell I3	Value
D_i: Cell C5	Formula: =B5-$I$3
	(Copied to C6:D13)
Significance level: Cell I11	Value
S_+: Cell I14	Formula: =COUNTIF(C5:C13,'>0')
S_0: Cell I15	Formula: =COUNTIF(C5:C13,'=0')
n: Cell I16	Formula: =COUNT(C5:C13)
$n - S_0$: Cell I17	Formula: =I16-I15
$P(T \geq S_+)$: Cell I18	Formula: =1-BINOM.DIST(I14–1,I17–I16,0.5,TRUE)
$P(T \leq S_+)$: Cell I19	Formula: =BINOM.DIST(I14,I17–I16,0.5,TRUE)
p-value: Cell I20	Formula: =2*MIN(I18:I19)

INTERPRETATION There is not enough evidence to suggest that the population median weight of guinea pigs is statistically different from 700 g.

In Example 14.6, we consider a two-dependent population problem.

WORKED EXAMPLES

EXAMPLE 14.6

The record low Mathematics marks of students in the Gauteng area are of some concern to the Department of Education. Specifically, they are concerned that the students leaving matric are unable to deal with the Mathematics that they will face in tertiary institutions like universities and colleges. To rectify the problem, a Mathematics bridging course is planned. To test the effectiveness of the bridging course, a sample of 16 students is randomly chosen to participate in a small study.

A Mathematics proficiency test is given to each of the students before they take part in the bridging course and then, after they have completed the course, they are given a similar test again. The main question of interest is whether the bridging course has any effect on the Mathematics proficiency of students.

To test this, they would like to know if the population median marks for the before and after groups are similar.

The data collected are given in Table 14.26.

Table 14.26: Before and after marks

BEFORE MARK, X_i	AFTER MARK, Y_i
56	61
66	67
67	60
54	61
43	35
79	76
56	68
67	70

BEFORE MARK, X_i	AFTER MARK, Y_i
89	88
50	57
63	63
69	76
61	59
73	78
77	85
57	69

Test whether the population median of marks increases after the students take the bridging course, i.e. test if the population median of the population of differences $Y_i - X_i$ is greater than 0. Use the sign test and test at a significance level of 5%.

The five-step hypothesis testing procedure for testing this hypothesis is given below.

Step 1: Provide the hypothesis statements H_0 and H_1

The null hypothesis is: $H_0: \nu_{\text{diff}} = 0$

ν_{diff} is the population median of the population of differences of after and before marks. The alternative hypothesis is then: $H_1: \nu_{\text{diff}} > 0$

Step 2: Choose an appropriate test statistic

The considerations for this test include the following.

- *The number of populations in the study*: Samples are drawn from two dependent populations.
- *The research question*: The hypothesis concerns the population median of the differenced population.
- *Assumptions underlying the test*: The sign test only has two assumptions that need to be considered: the data must be a random sample from the population and the population must at least be continuously distributed. Both of these assumptions hold.

We will use the sign test for two dependent populations to test this hypothesis (which is essentially the same as the one-population test, because we work with the differenced population only).

Step 3: Specify the significance level

The significance level is specified as $\alpha = 0.05$ (or 5%)

Step 4: Calculate the relevant test statistic and p-value

The algorithm for the sign test proceeds as follows:

- Begin by calculating the differences between the before and after test scores, and then subtracting the hypothesised median from this differenced data. (Note that $\nu_0 = 0$ in this example.)

$$D_i = Y_i - X_i - 0, \quad i = 1, 2, \ldots, n$$

The data are then shown in Table 14.27.

Table 14.27: The difference between the before and after marks

BEFORE MARK, X_i	AFTER MARK, Y_i	D_i
56	61	5
66	67	1
67	60	–7
54	61	7
43	35	–8
79	76	–3
56	68	12
67	70	3

BEFORE MARK, X_i	AFTER MARK, Y_i	D_i
89	88	–1
50	57	7
63	63	0
69	76	7
61	59	–2
73	78	5
77	85	8
57	69	12

- The number of positive values of D_i in this data set is $S_+ = 10$.
- The number of times D_i is exactly equal to 0 is $S_0 = 1$.
- Calculate the following probability for the right-sided test:

$$p = P(T \geq S_+) = 1 - P(T \leq S_+ - 1) = 1 - 0.849 = 0.1509$$

- T is a binomial random variable with parameters $n - S_0 = 16 - 1 = 15$ and 0.5.

Step 5: Make a decision

Since the p-value is 0.1509, which is much larger than the specified significance level of $\alpha = 0.05$, we will **not reject the null hypothesis**, i.e. the population median of the differenced population is not significantly different from 0.

Excel solution

The Excel solution is shown in Figure 14.8.

	A	B	C	D	E	F	G	H	I	J	K	L	M
1	Sign test for two dependent populations (matched pairs)												
2										Hypothesis test			
3		Before Mark, X_i	After Mark, Y_i	Diffi = $Y_i - X_i$		D_i			Step 1:	H_0: $\nu_{diff} = 0$	ν_0 =	0	
4										H_1: $\nu_{diff} \neq 0$			
5		56	61	5	=C5-B5	5	=D5-$L$3						
6		66	67	1	=C6-B6	1	=D6-$L$3			Choose the appropriate test			
7		67	60	-7	=C7-B7	-7	=D7-$L$3		Step 2:	Test for the median of the difference of two dependent populations			
8		54	61	7	=C8-B8	7	=D8-$L$3			Data randomly drawn from a continuous distribution			
9		43	35	-8	=C9-B9	-8	=D9-$L$3						
10		79	76	-3	=C10-B10	-3	=D10-$L$3		Step 3:	Select level of significance			
11		56	68	12	=C11-B11	12	=D11-$L$3				Signficance level, α =	0.05	
12		67	70	3	=C12-B12	3	=D12-$L$3						
13		89	88	-1	=C13-B13	-1	=D13-$L$3			Calculate test statistic			
14		50	57	7	=C14-B14	7	=D14-$L$3				S_+ =	10	=COUNTIF(F5:F20,">0")
15		63	63	0	=C15-B15	0	=D15-$L$3				S_0 =	1	=COUNTIF(F5:F20,"=0")
16		69	76	7	=C16-B16	7	=D16-$L$3				n =	16	=COUNT(F5:F20)
17		61	59	-2	=C17-B17	-2	=D17-$L$3		Step 4:		$n - S_0$ =	15	=L16-L15
18		73	78	5	=C18-B18	5	=D18-$L$3				$P(T \geq S_+) = 1 - P(T \leq S_+ - 1)$ =	0.1509	=1-BINOM.DIST(I14-I,I17,0.5,TRUE)
19		77	85	8	=C19-B19	8	=D19-$L$3						
20		57	69	12	=C20-B20	12	=D20-$L$3				p-value =	0.1509	=L18
21													
22										Make a decision			
23									Step 5:	Since $p > \alpha$, therefore do not reject H_0			
24										The median of the differenced population is not significantly different from 0			

Figure 14.8: The Excel solution for Example 14.6

EXCEL SOLUTIONS

Before X_i marks: Cells B5:B20	Values
After Y_i marks: Cells C5:C20	Values
$\text{diff}_i = Y_i - X_i$: Cells D5:D20	Formula: =C5-B5 (Copied to D6:D20)
ν_0: Cell L3	Value
D_i: Cell F5	Formula: =F5-$L$3 (Copied to F6:F20)
Significance level α: Cell L11	Value
S_+: Cell L14	Formula: =COUNTIF(F5:F20,">0")
S_0: Cell L15	Formula: =COUNTIF(F5:F20,"=0")
n: Cell L16	Formula: =COUNT(F5:F20)
$n - S_0$: Cell L17	Formula: =L16-L15
$P(T \geq S_+)$: Cell L18	Formula: =1-BINOM.DIST(L14-1,L17,0.5,TRUE)
p-value: Cell L20	Formula: =L18

INTERPRETATION From the sample data, we have sufficient statistical evidence that the marks after the bridging course are not significantly higher.

14.2.3 Wilcoxon signed-rank test

Like the sign test, the Wilcoxon signed-rank test is used to test the null hypothesis that the median of a distribution is equal to some specified value, ν_0. It can be used in exactly the same situations as the sign test (so the null and alternative hypotheses for one population test for location and two dependent population tests for location, which were stated in 14.2.2, are also valid here). The primary differences between the Wilcoxon signed-rank test and the sign test are the following:

- The Wilcoxon signed-rank test uses the ranks of the data.
- The Wilcoxon signed-rank test requires an additional assumption that the data be symmetrically distributed.
- The Wilcoxon signed-rank test requires the use of specific tables to obtain p-values and critical values for testing the hypothesis.
- If the assumption of symmetry holds, then the Wilcoxon can reject the null hypothesis more accurately than the sign test, i.e. it is more powerful.

The algorithm for calculating the Wilcoxon signed-rank test is given below.

ALGORITHM FOR CALCULATING THE WILCOXON SIGNED-RANK TEST STATISTIC

- We are given n data values: $X_1, X_2, ..., X_n$. Subtract the value ν_0 from each of these values, calculate the absolute value of these values and denote them $D_1, D_2, ..., D_n$.

$$D_i = |X_i - \nu_0|, \qquad i = 1, 2, ..., n$$

- Obtain the ranks of the D_i-values and denote them $R_1, R_2, ..., R_n$.
- Count how many D_i-values are equal to 0 and call this total S_0.
- Calculate the sum of the ranks that correspond to positive values of the quantity $X_i - \nu_0$. Formally stated, we must calculate:

$$T_+ = \sum_{\{i: x_i - \nu_0 > 0\}} R_i$$

That is, sum the R_i-values for those values of $_i$ where $X_i - \nu_0 > 0$.

- (Only perform this last step if $n > 20$.) Calculate the normal statistic:

$$z_{cal} = \frac{T_+ - \mu_+}{\sigma_+} \overset{H_0}{\sim} N(0, 1) \tag{14.12}$$

Where:

$$\mu_+ = \frac{n'(n'+1)}{4} \tag{14.13}$$

$$\sigma_+ = \sqrt{\frac{n'(n'+1)(2n'+1)}{24}} \tag{14.14}$$

And:

$$n' = n - S_0 \tag{14.15}$$

When the number of observations is small ($n \leq 20$), we need to consult tables in Appendix D to get critical values for the test, but where the number of observations is large ($n > 20$), we can use the Z-test and obtain critical values from Excel's NORM.S.INV function. In both cases, if the test statistic lies in the rejection region defined by the critical values, we reject H_0. The critical values for the normal approach are obtained using the same procedures described for the tests in Chapters 10 and 11, but the critical values obtained from the tables in Appendix D (i.e. for smaller samples) can be a bit trickier. Below is a short description of how to use the tables with some simple demonstrations.

HOW TO GET CRITICAL VALUES USING APPENDIX D

To illustrate how to use the tables in Appendix D to obtain the critical values for the Wilcoxon signed-rank test for small samples, we will consider a number of simple situations and, in each case, define the appropriate critical values using the tables.

We can obtain the lower critical values, denoted $\tau_{n,\alpha}$, in Appendix D by simply finding the value in the table that corresponds to the given n (row) and α (column) values. Unfortunately, since the table only reports the lower critical values (i.e. the left-sided test's critical value), we need to manipulate it for the right-sided and two-sided tests. These modifications are summarised in Table 14.28.

Table 14.28: Modifications necessary for Appendix D tables for right-sided and two-sided tests

HYPOTHESIS STATEMENT	REJECT H_0 IF:
Left-sided test: $H_0: \nu = \nu_0$ vs $H_1: \nu < \nu_0$	$T_+ \leq \tau_{n,\alpha}$
Right-sided test: $H_0: \nu = \nu_0$ vs $H_1: \nu > \nu_0$	$T_+ \geq \frac{n(n+1)}{2} - \tau_{n,\alpha}$
Two-sided test: $H_0: \nu = \nu_0$ vs $H_1: \nu \neq \nu_0$	$T_+ \leq \tau_{n,\alpha/2}$ or $T_+ \geq \frac{n(n+1)}{2} - \tau_{n,\alpha/2}$

Some examples of these hypotheses and associated critical values are shown below.

- Scenario I: We have a sample of size $n = 15$ and want to test the following left-sided hypothesis (at a significance level of $\alpha = 5\%$):

$$H_0: \nu = 2 \text{ vs } H_1: \nu < 2$$

  The lower critical value is obtained from the table in Appendix D by looking in the column labelled $\alpha = 0.05$ and the row labelled $n = 15$. The critical value is thus $\tau_{15,0.05} = 30$. We reject H_0 if T_+ is *smaller* than 30.

- Scenario II: We have a sample of size $n = 6$ and want to test the following right-sided hypothesis (at a significance level of $\alpha = 10\%$):

$$H_0: \nu = 100 \text{ vs } H_1: \nu > 100$$

  Looking in the column labelled $\alpha = 0.1$ and the row labelled $n = 6$ in the table in Appendix D, we find that $\tau_{6,0.1} = 3$. We reject H_0 if T_+ is *greater* than $\frac{n(n+1)}{2} - \tau_{6,0.1} = \frac{(6 \times 7)}{2} - 3 = 18$.

- Scenario III: A sample of size $n = 10$ is used in the following two-sided test (at a significance level of $\alpha = 5\%$):

$$H_0: \nu = 0 \text{ vs } H_1: \nu \neq 0$$

  The lower critical value for $\frac{\alpha}{2} = \frac{0.05}{2} = 0.025$ and $n = 10$ is found to be $\tau_{10,0.025} = 8$. Therefore, we reject H_0 if T_+ is smaller than 8 or if T_+ is greater than $\frac{n(n+1)}{2} - \tau_{10,0.025} = \frac{(10 \times 11)}{2} - 8 = 47$

We now consider some complete examples of this test and see how the test statistic, T_+, is calculated using data values.

WORKED EXAMPLES

EXAMPLE 14.7

The marketing department of the J-phone cellular phone wants to target specific age groups in their marketing campaigns. The CEO of the company has claimed that the median age of the users is at least 30 years old (i.e. 30 years old or older).

To test this claim, a (very) small sample of $n = 7$ randomly chosen customers is obtained (the data are shown in Table 14.29).

Table 14.29: Data sampling the median age of J-phone users

Ages, X_i	25	44	65	23	41	19	38

Assuming that the distribution of ages is roughly symmetrical, but not necessarily normally distributed, test the hypothesis that the median age is more than 30 using the Wilcoxon signed-rank test at a significance level of $\alpha = 0.05$.

Step 1: Provide the hypothesis statements: H_0 and H_1
The null and alternative hypotheses are: H_0: $\nu = 30$ and H_1: $\nu > 30$

Step 2: Choose an appropriate test statistic
The considerations for this test include the following.

- *The number of populations in the study*: Samples are drawn from a single population.
- *The research question*: The hypothesis concerns the population median of the ages of users.
- *Assumptions underlying the test*: It is assumed that the underlying data are roughly symmetrical and the data are known to be randomly sampled from the population.

These conditions indicate that the Wilcoxon signed-rank test would be an appropriate test for this scenario.

Step 3: Specify the significance level
The significance level is specified as $\alpha = 0.05$ (or 5%)

Step 4: Calculate the relevant test statistic
The algorithm for the sign test proceeds as follows.

- Calculate the absolute difference between the data values and the hypothesised value of the median.

Table 14.30: Calculating the difference between the data values and the hypothesised value of the median

CASE NUMBER, i	AGES, X_i	$X_i - 30$	$D_i = \lvert X_i - 30\rvert$
1	25	–5	5
2	44	14	14
3	65	35	35

CASE NUMBER, i	AGES, X_i	$X_i - 30$	$D_i = \|X_i - 30\|$
4	23	–7	7
5	41	11	11
6	19	–11	11
7	38	8	8

- Obtain the ranks of the D_i-values.

Table 14.31: Obtaining the D_i-values

CASE NUMBER, i	AGES, X_i	$X_i - 30$	$D_i = \|X_i - 30\|$	R_i
1	25	–5	5	1
2	44	14	14	6
3	65	35	35	7
4	23	–7	7	2
5	41	11	11	4.5
6	19	–11	11	4.5
7	38	8	8	3

- The number of D_i-values that are equal to 0 is $S_0 = 0$.
- The sum of the ranks that correspond to positive values of the quantity $X_i - \nu_0$ is:

$$\begin{aligned} T_+ &= \sum_{\{i: X_i - \nu_0 > 0\}} R_i \\ &= R_2 + R_3 + R_5 + R_7 \\ &= 6 + 7 + 4.5 + 3 \\ &= 20.5 \end{aligned}$$

Step 5: Make a decision

For this test, we need to determine the right-sided critical values using the tables in Appendix D. The left-sided critical value reported in Appendix D that corresponds to the sample size $n = 7$ and $\alpha = 0.05$ is $\tau_{7,0.05} = 3$. Therefore the right-sided critical value is $\frac{n(n+1)}{2} - \tau_{6,0.1} = \frac{(7 \times 8)}{2} - 3 = 25$. That is, we reject H_0 if T_+ is greater than 25. In this example, $T_+ = 20.5$ (which is *less than* 25), so we conclude that we **do not reject** the null hypothesis, i.e. the population median of the ages is not significantly greater than 30.

Excel solution

The Excel solution is shown in Figure 14.9.

	A	B	C	D	E	F	G	H	I	J	K	L	M	N
1			Wilcoxon signed-rank test for a single population median											
2											Hypothesis test			
3		Ages, X	X_i - 30		$D_i = \|X_i - 30\|$		R_i			Step 1:	H_0: ν = 30	ν_0 =	30	
4											H_1: $\nu \neq$ 30			
5		25	-5	=B5-$M$3	5	=ABS(B5-$M$3)	1	=RANK.AVG(E5,$E$5:$E$11,1)						
6		44	14	=B6-$M$3	14	=ABS(B6-$M$3)	6	=RANK.AVG(E6,$E$5:$E$11,1)			Choose the appropriate test			
7		65	35	=B7-$M$3	35	=ABS(B7-$M$3)	7	=RANK.AVG(E7,$E$5:$E$11,1)		Step 2:	Test for the median			
8		23	-7	=B8-$M$3	7	=ABS(B8-$M$3)	2	=RANK.AVG(E8,$E$5:$E$11,1)			Data randomly drawn from a continuous symmetric distribution			
9		41	11	=B9-$M$3	11	=ABS(B9-$M$3)	4.5	=RANK.AVG(E9,$E$5:$E$11,1)						
10		19	-11	=B10-$M$3	11	=ABS(B10-$M$3)	4.5	=RANK.AVG(E10,$E$5:$E$11,1)		Step 3:	Select level of significance			
11		38	8	=B11-$M$3	8	=ABS(B11-$M$3)	3	=RANK.AVG(E11,$E$5:$E$11,1)			Signficance level, α =		0.05	
12														
13											Calculate test statistic			
14												T_+ =	20.5	=SUMIF(C5:C11,">0",G5:G11)
15												S_0 =	0	=COUNTIF(E5:E11,"=0")
16										Step 4:		n =	7	=COUNT(E5:E11)
17												$n - S_0$ =	7	=M16-M15
18														
19											Lower critical value	$\tau_{n,\alpha}$ =	3	
20												$n(n+1)/2 - \tau_{n,\alpha}$	25	=M17*(M17+1)/2-M19
21														
22											Make a decision			
23										Step 5:	Since $T+ < n(n+1)/2 - \tau_{n,\alpha}$ therefore do not reject H_0			
24											The median age is not greater than 30 years			

Figure 14.9: The Excel solution for Example 14.7

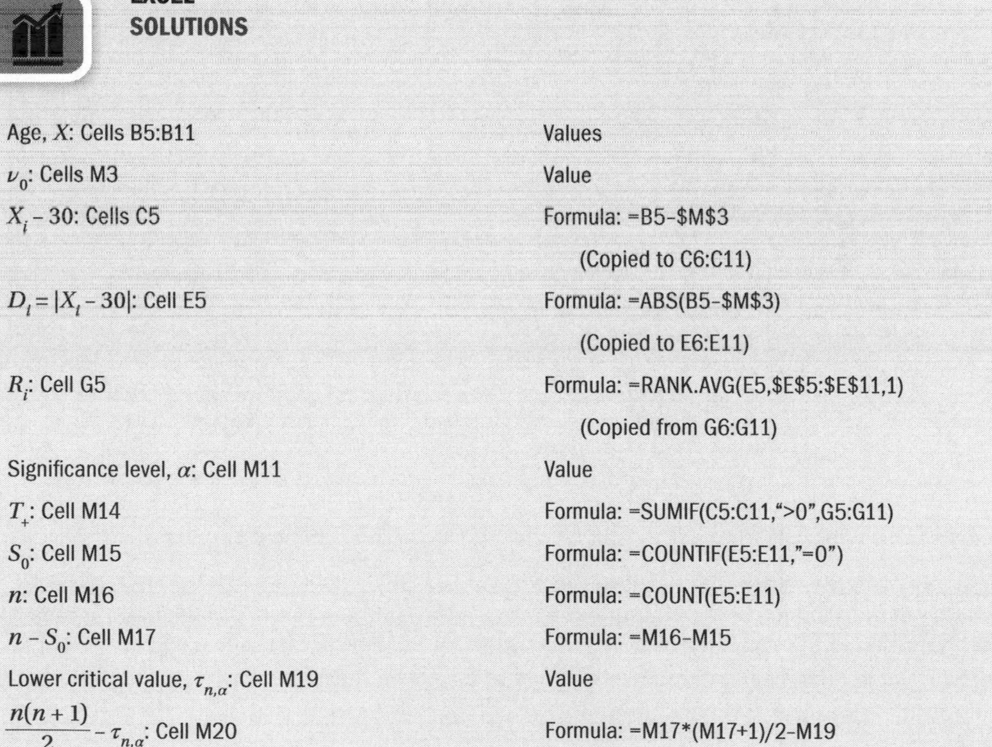

EXCEL SOLUTIONS

Age, X: Cells B5:B11	Values
ν_0: Cells M3	Value
X_i – 30: Cells C5	Formula: =B5-$M$3
	(Copied to C6:C11)
$D_i = \|X_i - 30\|$: Cell E5	Formula: =ABS(B5-$M$3)
	(Copied to E6:E11)
R_i: Cell G5	Formula: =RANK.AVG(E5,$E$5:$E$11,1)
	(Copied from G6:G11)
Significance level, α: Cell M11	Value
T_+: Cell M14	Formula: =SUMIF(C5:C11,">0",G5:G11)
S_0: Cell M15	Formula: =COUNTIF(E5:E11,"=0")
n: Cell M16	Formula: =COUNT(E5:E11)
$n - S_0$: Cell M17	Formula: =M16-M15
Lower critical value, $\tau_{n,\alpha}$: Cell M19	Value
$\frac{n(n+1)}{2} - \tau_{n,\alpha}$: Cell M20	Formula: =M17*(M17+1)/2-M19

INTERPRETATION From the sample data, we do not have sufficient statistical evidence to conclude that the ages of customers are greater than 30 years.

Example 14.8 illustrates a situation where the Wilcoxon test is applied to two dependent populations. In this example, we also need to use the large sample normal approximation, because sample sizes greater than 20 are not listed in the tables of Appendix D.

WORKED EXAMPLES

EXAMPLE 14.8

Suppose that Slim-Gym, a locally run health and fitness club, is offering a weight-loss programme that claims to result in a 7kg weight loss in the first 30 days. Twenty-four subjects were selected for a study, and their weights before and after the weight-loss programme were recorded. The results are presented in Table 14.32.

Table 14.32: Weight-loss programme survey results

	WEIGHT BEFORE (kg)	WEIGHT AFTER (kg)		WEIGHT BEFORE (kg)	WEIGHT AFTER (kg)		WEIGHT BEFORE (kg)	WEIGHT AFTER (kg)
1	60	56.1	9	62.8	57.1	17	69.7	64.1
2	55.2	50.8	10	66	56.2	18	83.2	72
3	70.9	64	11	73	69	19	62.1	55.7
4	76.2	68.7	12	68.4	62.6	20	69.4	62.8
5	64.3	56.5	13	60	55.2	21	62.8	56.5
6	83.2	74.3	14	55.2	51.2	22	66	58.6
7	62.1	57.2	15	70.9	60.2	23	73.5	70.8
8	69.4	65.8	16	77.5	70.7	24	69.6	62.6

Assuming that the distribution of the weight loss (calculated as after minus before) variable is symmetrical, test the claim that the population median amount of weight lost is equal to 7 kg versus the alternative that the weight loss is less than 7 kg. Test the hypothesis at a significance level of 5%.

The five-step hypothesis testing procedure for testing this hypothesis is given below.

Step 1: Provide the hypothesis statements H_0 and H_1

The null hypothesis must reflect that the difference between the weight after the treatment is 7 kg lower than the before measurement. This means that, under the null hypothesis, the population median of weight loss values should be equal to –7 kg. (Note that the calculation after and before should result in a negative value if there was weight loss.) The null hypothesis is then:

$$H_0: \nu_{\text{diff}} = -7$$

ν_{diff} is the population median of weight loss values. The alternative hypothesis will then indicate that the population median is greater than –7 kg (i.e. the individuals lost less than 7 kg):

$$H_1: \nu_{diff} > -7$$

Step 2: Choose an appropriate test statistic

The considerations for this test include the following.

- *The number of populations in the study*: Samples are drawn from two dependent populations.
- *The research question*: The hypothesis concerns the population median of the differenced population.
- *Assumptions underlying the test*: It is assumed that the underlying data are roughly symmetrical and the data are known to be randomly sampled from the population.

We will use the Wilcoxon signed-rank test for two dependent populations to test this hypothesis.

Step 3: Specify the significance level

The significance level is specified as $\alpha = 0.05$ (or 5%)

Step 4: Calculate the relevant test statistic and *p*-value

The algorithm for the sign test proceeds as follows:

- Calculate the absolute difference between the weight-loss values and the hypothesised value of the median, $H_0 = -7$:

$$\begin{aligned} D_i &= |\text{weight loss} - \nu_0| \\ &= |(\text{after} - \text{before}) + 7| \end{aligned}$$

Table 14.33: Calculating the weight difference

	WEIGHT BEFORE (kg)	WEIGHT AFTER (kg)	D_i		WEIGHT BEFORE (kg)	WEIGHT AFTER (kg)	D_i		WEIGHT BEFORE (kg)	WEIGHT AFTER (kg)	D_i
1	60	56.1	3.1	9	62.8	57.1	1.3	17	69.7	64.1	1.4
2	55.2	50.8	2.6	10	66	56.2	2.8	18	83.2	72	4.2
3	70.9	64	0.1	11	73	69	3	19	62.1	55.7	0.6
4	76.2	68.7	0.5	12	68.4	62.6	1.2	20	69.4	62.8	0.4
5	64.3	56.5	0.8	13	60	55.2	2.2	21	62.8	56.5	0.7
6	83.2	74.3	1.9	14	55.2	51.2	3	22	66	58.6	0.4
7	62.1	57.2	2.1	15	70.9	60.2	3.7	23	73.5	70.8	4.3
8	69.4	65.8	3.4	16	77.5	70.7	0.2	24	69.6	62.6	0

- Obtain the ranks of the D_1-values.

Table 14.34: Obtaining the ranks of the D_1-values.

	WEIGHT LOSS, v_i	D_i	R_i
1	3.1	3.1	20
2	2.6	2.6	16
3	0.1	0.1	2
4	–0.5	0.5	6
5	–0.8	0.8	9
6	–1.9	1.9	13
7	2.1	2.1	14
8	3.4	3.4	21
9	1.3	1.3	11
10	–2.8	2.8	17
11	3	3	18.5
12	1.2	1.2	10
13	2.2	2.2	15
14	3	3	18.5
15	–3.7	3.7	22
16	0.2	0.2	3
17	1.4	1.4	12
18	–4.2	4.2	23
19	0.6	0.6	7
20	0.4	0.4	4.5
21	0.7	0.7	8
22	–0.4	0.4	4.5
23	4.3	4.3	24
24	0	0	1

- The number of D_1-values that are equal to 0 is $S_0 = 1$.
- The sum of the ranks that correspond to positive values of the quantity *weight loss* – v_0 is:

$$T_+ = \sum_{\{i\ Weight\ loss - v_0 > 0\}} R_i$$
$$= 20 + 16 + 2 + 14 + 21 + 11 + 18.5 + 10 + 15 + 18.5 + 3 + 12 + 7 + 4.5 + 8 + 24$$
$$= 204.5$$

- The Z statistic is calculated using the T_+-value given above. However, before we calculate this statistic, we first need to calculate n', μ_+ and σ_+:

$$n' = n - S_0 = 24 - 1 = 23$$

$$\mu_+ = \frac{n'(n'+1)}{4} = \frac{23(24)}{4} = 138$$

$$\sigma_+ = \sqrt{\frac{n'(n'+1)(2n'+1)}{24}} = \sqrt{\frac{23(24)(47)}{24}} = 32.879$$

The test statistic is then:

$$z_{\text{cal}} = \frac{T_+ - \mu_+}{\sigma_+}$$
$$= \frac{204.5 - 138}{32.879}$$
$$= 2.023$$

Step 5: Make a decision

We will use both the critical value approach and the p-value approach to make a decision for this test.

- *Critical value approach*: For this example, the test statistic follows a $N(0, 1)$ distribution and the $\alpha = 0.05$ right-sided critical value is thus $z_{0.05} = 1.645$ (obtained from the NORM.S.INV function in Excel). The test statistic's calculated value is $z_{cal} = 2.023$, which is larger than the critical value. Therefore we **reject H_0**.
- *p-value approach*: We can calculate the right-sided test's p-value using the Excel function NORM.S.DIST or by using formula (10.2) from Chapter 10:

$$\begin{aligned} p\text{-value} &= P(Z > z_{cal}) \\ &= P(Z > 2.023) \\ &= 1 - P(Z < 2.023) \\ &= 1 - 0.9785 \\ &= 0.0215 \end{aligned}$$

This p-value is clearly much smaller than the prescribed significance level of $\alpha = 0.05$. Therefore, since p-value $= 0.0215 < \alpha = 0.05$, **we reject H_0** at a 5% level of significance.

INTERPRETATION From the sample data, we have sufficient statistical evidence to conclude that the median weight loss value is greater than -7 kg, i.e. the individuals using this procedure for weight loss will lose less than 7 kg.

The Excel solution is shown in Figure 14.10.

	A	B	C	D	E	F	G	H	I	J	K	L	M	N
1	**Wilcoxon test paired procedure for two dependent populations (n > 20)**													
2	X_i	Y_i	$Y_i - X_i - \nu_0$								**Hypothesis test**			
3	Before	After			D_i		R_i			Step 1:	H_0: ν_{diff} = -7	ν_0 =	-7	
4	60	56.1	3.1	=B4-A4-$M$3	3.1	=ABS(C4)	20	=RANK.AVG(E4,$E$4:$E$27,1)			H_1: ν_{diff} > -7			
5	55.2	50.8	2.6	=B5-A5-$M$3	2.6	=ABS(C5)	16	=RANK.AVG(E5,$E$4:$E$27,1)						
6	70.9	64	0.1	=B6-A6-$M$3	0.1	=ABS(C6)	2	=RANK.AVG(E6,$E$4:$E$27,1)			**Choose the appropriate test**			
7	76.2	68.7	-0.5	=B7-A7-$M$3	0.5	=ABS(C7)	6	=RANK.AVG(E7,$E$4:$E$27,1)		Step 2:	Test for the median of the difference of the 'differenced' population			
8	64.3	56.5	-0.8	=B8-A8-$M$3	0.8	=ABS(C8)	9	=RANK.AVG(E8,$E$4:$E$27,1)			Data randomly drawn from paired, continuous, symmetric distributions			
9	83.2	74.3	-1.9	=B9-A9-$M$3	1.9	=ABS(C9)	13	=RANK.AVG(E9,$E$4:$E$27,1)						
10	62.1	57.2	2.1	=B10-A10-$M$3	2.1	=ABS(C10)	14	=RANK.AVG(E10,$E$4:$E$27,1)		Step 3:	**Select level of significance**			
11	69.4	65.8	3.4	=B11-A11-$M$3	3.4	=ABS(C11)	21	=RANK.AVG(E11,$E$4:$E$27,1)			Signficance level, α =		0.05	
12	62.8	57.1	1.3	=B12-A12-$M$3	1.3	=ABS(C12)	11	=RANK.AVG(E12,$E$4:$E$27,1)						
13	66	56.2	-2.8	=B13-A13-$M$3	2.8	=ABS(C13)	17	=RANK.AVG(E13,$E$4:$E$27,1)			**Calculate test statistic**			
14	73	69	3	=B14-A14-$M$3	3	=ABS(C14)	18.5	=RANK.AVG(E14,$E$4:$E$27,1)				T_+ =	204.5	=SUMIF(C4:C27,">0",G4:G27)
15	68.4	62.6	1.2	=B15-A15-$M$3	1.2	=ABS(C15)	10	=RANK.AVG(E15,$E$4:$E$27,1)				S_0 =	1	=COUNTIF(E4:E27,"=0")
16	60	55.2	2.2	=B16-A16-$M$3	2.2	=ABS(C16)	15	=RANK.AVG(E16,$E$4:$E$27,1)				n =	24	=COUNT(E4:E27)
17	55.2	51.2	3	=B17-A17-$M$3	3	=ABS(C17)	18.5	=RANK.AVG(E17,$E$4:$E$27,1)			$n' = n - S_0$ =		23	=M16-M15
18	70.9	60.2	-3.7	=B18-A18-$M$3	3.7	=ABS(C18)	22	=RANK.AVG(E18,$E$4:$E$27,1)		Step 4:				
19	77.5	70.7	0.2	=B19-A19-$M$3	0.2	=ABS(C19)	3	=RANK.AVG(E19,$E$4:$E$27,1)				μ_+ =	138	=M17*(M17+1)/4
20	69.7	64.1	1.4	=B20-A20-$M$3	1.4	=ABS(C20)	12	=RANK.AVG(E20,$E$4:$E$27,1)				σ_+ =	32.879	=SQRT(M17*(M17+1)*(M17*2+1)/24)
21	83.2	72	-4.2	=B21-A21-$M$3	4.2	=ABS(C21)	23	=RANK.AVG(E21,$E$4:$E$27,1)			$Z = (T_+ - \mu_+)/\sigma_+$ =		2.023	=(M14-M19)/M20
22	62.1	55.7	0.6	=B22-A22-$M$3	0.6	=ABS(C22)	7	=RANK.AVG(E22,$E$4:$E$27,1)			Critical value z_α =		1.645	=NORM.S.INV(1-M11)
23	69.4	62.8	0.4	=B23-A23-$M$3	0.4	=ABS(C23)	4.5	=RANK.AVG(E23,$E$4:$E$27,1)				p-value =	0.0215	=1-NORM.S.DIST(M21,TRUE)
24	62.8	56.5	0.7	=B24-A24-$M$3	0.7	=ABS(C24)	8	=RANK.AVG(E24,$E$4:$E$27,1)						
25	66	58.6	-0.4	=B25-A25-$M$3	0.4	=ABS(C25)	4.5	=RANK.AVG(E25,$E$4:$E$27,1)			**Make a decision**			
26	73.5	70.8	4.3	=B26-A26-$M$3	4.3	=ABS(C26)	24	=RANK.AVG(E26,$E$4:$E$27,1)		Step 5:	Since $p > \alpha$, therefore do not reject H_0			
27	69.6	62.6	0	=B27-A27-$M$3	0.0	=ABS(C27)	1	=RANK.AVG(E27,$E$4:$E$27,1)			The median weight loss value is greater than -7 kg (i.e. Individuals lose less than 7 kg)			

Figure 14.10: The Excel solution for Example 14.8

EXCEL SOLUTIONS

Before weight, X_i: Cells A4:A27	Values
After weight, Y_i: Cells B4:B27	Values
ν_0: Cells M3	Value
$Y_i - X_i - \nu_0$: Cells C4	Formula: =B4-A4-$M$3 (Copied to C5:C27)
$D_i = \lvert Y_i - X_i - \nu_0 \rvert$: Cell E4	Formula: =ABS(C4) (Copied to E5:E27)
R_i: Cell G4	Formula: =RANK.AVG(E4,$E$4:$E$27,1) (Copied from G5:G27)
Significance level, α: Cell M11	Value
T_+: Cell M14	Formula: =SUMIF(C4:C27,">0",G4:G27)
S_0: Cell M15	Formula: =COUNTIF(E4:E27,"=0")
n: Cell M16	Formula: =COUNT(E4:E27)
$n' = n - S_0$: Cell M17	Formula: =M16-M15
μ_+: Cell M19	Formula: =M17*(M17+1)/4
σ_+: Cell M20	Formula: =SQRT(M17*(M17+1)*(M17*2+1)/24)
$z_{\text{cal}} = \frac{T_+ - \mu_+}{\sigma_+}$: Cell M21	Formula: =(M14-M19)/M20
Critical value, z_α: Cell 22	Formula: =NORM.S.INV(1-M11)
p-value: Cell M23	Formula: =1-NORM.S.DIST(M21,TRUE)

14.2.4 Mann-Whitney *U*-test for two independent samples

The Mann-Whitney U-test is a non-parametric test that we can use in place of the t-tests for two independent populations (discussed in Sections 11.3 and 11.4). It is used to test the null hypothesis that two samples come from the populations with the same location measure (i.e. have the same median) or alternatively, whether observations in one sample tend to be larger than observations in the other. Although it is a non-parametric test, it does assume that the two distributions are similar in shape. Where the samples are small, we need to use tables of critical values to find out whether to reject the null hypothesis. However, where the sample is large, we can use a test based on the normal distribution.

The basic premise of the test is that once all the values in the two samples are put into a single ordered list, if they come from the same parent population, then the rank at which values from sample A and sample B appear will be by chance. If the two samples come from different populations, then the rank at which the sample values appear will not be random and there will be a tendency for values from one of the samples to have lower ranks than values from the other sample. We are thus testing for different locations of the two samples.

For this test, we will focus only on situations where both samples sizes are greater than 10, i.e. $n_A > 10$ and $n_B > 10$, and so we can use large sample normal approximation for the distribution of the Mann-Whitney U-statistic. For smaller sample sizes, we would need to use tables that provide the critical values for these sample sizes (but these tables will not be used or discussed in this text).

If we define ν_A and ν_B as the population medians for populations A and B, respectively, then the hypothesis statements for the Mann-Whitney test are:

$$H_0: \nu_A = \nu_B$$

Versus the alternatives:

$H_1: \nu_A < \nu_B$	$H_1: \nu_A > \nu_B$	$H_1: \nu_A \neq \nu_B$
left-sided	right-sided	two-sided

The algorithm used to obtain the test statistic is described below.

ALGORITHM FOR CALCULATING THE MANN-WHITNEY U-TEST STATISTIC

- We are given n_A data values from sample A: $X_1, X_2, ..., X_{n_A}$, and n_B data values from sample B: $Y_1, Y_2, ..., Y_{n_B}$. Pool all of these observations into a single data set:

$$X_1, X_2, ..., X_{n_A}, Y_1, Y_2, ..., Y_{n_B}$$

- (Note that the first n_A observations are from sample A and the next n_B observations are from sample B.)
- Determine the ranks of this entire pooled set of observations. Denote these ranks $R_1, R_2, ..., R_{n_A+n_B}$. (Note that the first n_A ranks are associated with observations from sample A and the next n_B ranks are associated with the observations from sample B.)
- Calculate the sum of ranks associated with sample A: $T_A = \sum_A R_i$, and calculate the sum of ranks associated with sample B: $T_B = \sum_B R_i$. (Note that in terms of the way the data were arranged in the first point, the sum T_A is simply the sum of the first n_A ranks and U_B is the sum of the last n_B ranks.)
- Calculate the quantities U_A and U_B as follows:

$$U_A = n_A n_B + \frac{n_A(n_A+1)}{2} - T_A \tag{14.16}$$

$$U_B = n_A n_B + \frac{n_B(n_B+1)}{2} - T_B \tag{14.17}$$

- Calculate the Mann-Whitney U-test statistic by determining the minimum between U_A and U_B:

$$U = \min(U_A, U_B) \tag{14.18}$$

- Finally, calculate the normal statistic:

$$Z = \frac{U - \mu_U}{\sigma_U} \overset{H_0}{\sim} N(0, 1) \tag{14.19}$$

μ_U is defined as:

$$\mu_U = \frac{n_A n_B}{2} \tag{14.20}$$

σ_U is given by:

$$\sigma_U = \sqrt{\frac{n_A n_B (n_A + n_B + 1)}{12}} \tag{14.21}$$

The test is thus conducted by calculating the test statistic and then comparing the result to the standard normal quantiles or by calculating p-values from the standard normal distribution (which is very similar to the way in which the tests in Chapters 10 and 11 were conducted).

The assumptions under which the Mann-Whitney test is conducted are as follows:

- Independent random samples are obtained from each population.
- The sample sizes are both larger than 10 (so that we can apply the normal approximation).
- The two populations are continuous and have the same shape.

If these assumptions are not satisfied, then it is possible that the resulting conclusions will be faulty.

In Example 14.9, we look at how we can conduct this non-parametric test using some sample data.

WORKED EXAMPLES

EXAMPLE 14.9

A local training firm has developed an innovative programme to improve the performance of students on the courses it offers. To assess whether a new training programme improves students' performance, the firm collects a random sample of 11 students from a population of students that studied via the traditional method (population A) and a sample of 11 students from the population of students that studied using the new programme (population B).

The firm has analysed previous data, and the outcome of the results provides evidence that the distributions are not normally distributed but are skewed to the left. This information provides concerns at the suitability of using a two sample independent t-test to undertake the analysis, and they instead decide to use the non-parametric Mann-Whitney U-test for two independent populations.

The data obtained in this study are given in Table 14.35.

Table 14.35: Data obtained in the study of the innovative programme to improve students' performance

	MARKS OF STUDENTS	
	TRADITIONAL METHOD (A)	NEW PROGRAMME (B)
1	68	81
2	61	83
3	63	78

	MARKS OF STUDENTS	
	TRADITIONAL METHOD (A)	NEW PROGRAMME (B)
4	63	82
5	65	87
6	69	84
7	85	83
8	68	80
9	70	79
10	59	74
11	68	87

Test the hypothesis that the median mark of students using the new programme is greater than the median mark of students using the traditional method. Test at a 5% level of significance.

The five-step procedure for testing this hypothesis is given below.

Step 1: Provide the hypothesis statements H_0 and H_1

The hypothesis to be tested is whether the population median marks of students using the new programme (population B) is greater than the population median of the students using the traditional method. The null hypothesis is used to state the situation where these medians are equal, whereas the alternative hypothesis states the situation in which population B's median is greater:

$$H_0: \nu_A = \nu_B$$

vs

$$H_1: \nu_A < \nu_B$$

Step 2: Choose an appropriate test statistic

The following considerations lead us to use the Mann-Whitey U-test statistic to perform this test.

- *The number of populations in the study*: A random sample from each of two independent populations is being used in this situation.
- *The research question*: The primary question of interest is whether the two population medians are equal or whether one is greater than the other (a left-sided test in this case).
- *Assumptions underlying the test*: The sample sizes are both greater than 10 and the distributions of both populations are assumed to be similar and continuous.

Step 3: Specify the significance level

The significance level is specified as $\alpha = 0.05$ (or 5%).

Step 4: Calculate the relevant test statistic

The algorithm for calculating the Mann-Whitney U-test statistic for this test is given below:

- The observations from both groups are pooled together.
- The ranks of the pooled data set are obtained (Table 14.36).

Table 14.36: Ranks of the pooled data set

GROUPING	MARKS	RANKS, R_i
A	68	7
A	61	2
A	63	3.5
A	63	3.5
A	65	5
A	69	9
A	85	20
A	68	7
A	70	10
A	59	1
A	68	7
B	81	15
B	83	17.5
B	78	12
B	82	16
B	87	21.5
B	84	19
B	83	17.5
B	80	14
B	79	13
B	74	11
B	87	21.5

- The sum of the ranks associated with sample A is:

$$\begin{aligned} T_A &= \sum_A R_i \\ &= 7 + 2 + 3.5 + 3.5 + 5 + 9 + 20 + 7 + 10 + 1 \\ &= 75 \end{aligned}$$

- The sum of the ranks associated with sample B is:

$$\begin{aligned} T_B &= \sum_B R_i \\ &= 15 + 17.5 + 12 + 16 + 21.5 + 19 + 17.5 + 14 + 13 + 11 + 21.5 \\ &= 178 \end{aligned}$$

- Calculate the quantities U_A and U_B using formulae (14.16) and (14.17):

$$\begin{aligned} U_A &= n_A n_B + \frac{n_A(n_A+1)}{2} - T_A \\ &= (11)(11) + \frac{11(11+1)}{2} - 75 \\ &= 121 + 66 - 75 \\ &= 112 \end{aligned}$$

$$\begin{aligned} U_B &= n_A n_B + \frac{n_B(n_B+1)}{2} - T_B \\ &= (11)(11) + \frac{11(11+1)}{2} - 178 \\ &= 121 + 66 - 178 \\ &= 9 \end{aligned}$$

- The Mann-Whitney U-test statistic is then the minimum of U_A and U_B:

$$U = \min(U_A, U_B) = \min(112, 9) = 9$$

- The Z-statistic is obtained by first calculating μ_U and σ_U using formulae (14.20) and (14.21):

$$\mu_U = \frac{n_A n_B}{2} = \frac{(11)(11)}{2} = 60.5$$

And:

$$\sigma_U = \sqrt{\frac{n_A n_B (n_A + n_B + 1)}{12}} = \sqrt{\frac{(11)(11)(11+11+1)}{12}} = 15.2288$$

Using formula (14.19), we then calculate the Z-statistic (which is denoted z_{cal}):

$$\begin{aligned} z_{\text{cal}} &= \frac{U - \mu_U}{\sigma_U} \\ &= \frac{9 - 60.5}{15.2288} \\ &= -3.382 \end{aligned}$$

Step 5: Make a decision

We can reach a decision concerning this hypothesis by using both a critical value approach and a *p*-value approach.

- *Critical value approach*: We will use the quantiles of the normal distribution to define the rejection region of this test and, because it is a left-sided test based on a normally distributed test statistic, we will use the lower normal quantile: $-z_{\alpha} = -z_{0.05} = -1.645$. The test statistic's value is compared to this critical value and, if the test statistic lies in the rejection region (which is the region to the left of the critical value), then we reject H_0. The test statistic's value is –3.382, which does indeed lie in the rejection region and so we **reject H_0**.
- p-*value approach*: The *p*-value for this test is calculated as:

$$\begin{aligned} p\text{-value} &= P(Z < z_{\text{cal}}) \\ &= 0.00036 \end{aligned}$$

(We obtained this probability using the Excel function NORM.S.DIST.) In this example, the *p*-value is smaller than the specified significance level $\alpha = 0.05$, therefore, we **reject H_0**.

Figure 14.11 illustrates the Excel Mann-Whitney *U*-test solution.

	A	B	C	D	E	F	G	H	I	J
1	Mann-Whitney test for two independent populations (sample sizes > 10)									
2	Group	Marks of students	Ranks				Hypothesis test			
3						Step 1:	H_0: $\nu_A = \nu_B$			
4	A	68	7	=RANK.AVG(B4,$B$4:$B$25,1)			H_1: $\nu_A < \nu_B$			
5	A	61	2	=RANK.AVG(B5,$B$4:$B$25,1)						
6	A	63	3.5	=RANK.AVG(B6,$B$4:$B$25,1)			Choose the appropriate test			
7	A	63	3.5	=RANK.AVG(B7,$B$4:$B$25,1)		Step 2:	Test for the medians of two independent populations.			
8	A	65	5	=RANK.AVG(B8,$B$4:$B$25,1)			Data randomly drawn from two continuous, similarly shaped distributions			
9	A	69	9	=RANK.AVG(B9,$B$4:$B$25,1)						
10	A	85	20	=RANK.AVG(B10,$B$4:$B$25,1)		Step 3:	Select level of significance			
11	A	68	7	=RANK.AVG(B11,$B$4:$B$25,1)				Signficance level, α =	0.05	
12	A	70	10	=RANK.AVG(B12,$B$4:$B$25,1)						
13	A	59	1	=RANK.AVG(B13,$B$4:$B$25,1)			Calculate test statistic			
14	A	68	7	=RANK.AVG(B14,$B$4:$B$25,1)				n_A =	11	=COUNTIF(A4:A25,"=A")
15	B	81	15	=RANK.AVG(B15,$B$4:$B$25,1)				n_B =	11	=COUNTIF(A4:A25,"=B")
16	B	83	17.5	=RANK.AVG(B16,$B$4:$B$25,1)				T_A =	75	=SUMIF(A4:A25,"=A",C4:C25)
17	B	78	12	=RANK.AVG(B17,$B$4:$B$25,1)				T_B =	178	=SUMIF(A4:A25,"=B",C4:C25)
18	B	82	16	=RANK.AVG(B18,$B$4:$B$25,1)				U_A =	112	=I14*I15+II4*(I14+1)/2-I16
19	B	87	21.5	=RANK.AVG(B19,$B$4:$B$25,1)		Step 4:		U_B =	9	=I14*I15+II4*(I14+1)/2-i17
20	B	84	19	=RANK.AVG(B20,$B$4:$B$25,1)				U =	9	=MIN(I19,I18)
21	B	83	17.5	=RANK.AVG(B21,$B$4:$B$25,1)				μ_U =	60.5	=I14*I15/2
22	B	80	14	=RANK.AVG(B22,$B$4:$B$25,1)				σ_U =	15.229	=SQRT(I14*I15*(I14+I15+1)/12)
23	B	79	13	=RANK.AVG(B23,$B$4:$B$25,1)				$Z = (U - \mu_U)/\sigma_U$ =	-3.382	=(I20-I21)/I22
24	B	74	11	=RANK.AVG(B24,$B$4:$B$25,1)				Critical value $-z_{\alpha}$ =	-1.645	=NORM.S.INV(I11)
25	B	87	21.5	=RANK.AVG(B25,$B$4:$B$25,1)				*p*-value =	0.00036	=NORM.S.DIST(I23,TRUE)
26										
27							Make a decision			
28						Step 5:	Since $p < \alpha$, therefore do not reject H_0			
29							The median of Group A is significantly lower than Group B			

Figure 14.11: The Excel solution for Example 14.9

EXCEL SOLUTIONS

Groups: Cells A4:A25	Values
Marks: Cells B4:B25	Values
Rank: Cell C4	Formula: =RANK.AVG(B4,$B$4:$B$25,1) (Copied from C4:C25)
Significance level: Cell I11	Value
n_A: Cell I14	Formula: =COUNTIF(A4:A25,"=A")
n_B: Cell I15	Formula: =COUNTIF(A4:A25,"=B")
T_A: Cell I16	Formula: =SUMIF(A4:A25,"=A",C4:C25)
T_B: Cell I17	Formula: =SUMIF(A4:A25,"=B",C4:C25)
U_A: Cell I18	Formula: =I14*I15+I14*(I14+1)/2-I16
U_B: Cell I19	Formula: =I14*I15+I15*(I15+1)/2-I17
U: Cell I20	Formula: =MIN(I19,I18)
μ_U: Cell I21	Formula: =I14*I15/2
σ_U: Cell I22	Formula: =SQRT(I14*I15*(I14+I15+1)/12)
$Z = (U - \mu_U)/\sigma_U$: Cell I23	Formula: =(I20-I21)/I22
Critical value $-z_\alpha$: Cell I24	Formula: =NORM.S.INV(I11)
p-value: Cell H29	Formula: =NORM.S.DIST(I23,TRUE)

INTERPRETATION Based on the data, there is sufficient evidence to indicate (at a 5% significance level) that the performance of the students using the new programme has improved compared to the students using the traditional method.

SUMMARY

In this chapter, we have explored the concept of hypothesis testing for data involving categorical data using the chi-squared distribution, and extended the parametric tests to the case of non-parametric tests (or so-called distribution-free tests), which do not require the assumption of the population (or sample) distributions being normal.

In the case of the chi-squared test, we looked at a range of applications, including testing for differences in proportions and testing for association. In the case of non-parametric tests, we looked at a range of tests, including the sign test for one sample, two-paired sample Wilcoxon signed-rank test, and two independent samples Mann-Whitney test.

KEY TERMS

Chi-squared distribution
Chi-squared statistic
Chi-squared test
Contingency table
Degrees of freedom
Expected frequency
Mann-Whitney *U*-test
McNemar's test for matched pairs
Observed frequency
Ranks
Sign test
Test of association
Tests of dependence
Tests of independence
Tied ranks
Wilcoxon signed-rank *t*-test

FORMULA SUMMARY

$$X^2 = \sum_{i=1}^{N} \frac{(O_i - E_i)^2}{E_i} \overset{H_0}{\sim} \chi^2_{N-1} \quad (14.1)$$

$$X^2 = \sum_{i=1}^{r}\sum_{j=1}^{c} \frac{\left(O_{ij} - E_{ij}\right)^2}{E_{ij}} \overset{H_0}{\sim} \chi^2_{df} \quad (14.2)$$

$$df = (r-1)(c-1) \quad (14.3)$$

$$E_{ij} = n\frac{R_i}{n}\frac{C_j}{n} = \frac{R_i C_j}{n} \quad (14.4)$$

$$X^2 = \sum_{i=1}^{N} \frac{\left(|O_i - E_i| - 0.5\right)^2}{E_i} \quad (14.5)$$

$$E_{1j} = C_j\hat{\pi}_0 = \frac{R_1 C_j}{n} \quad \text{and} \quad E_{2j} = C_j(1 - \hat{\pi}_0) = \frac{R_2 C_j}{n} \quad (14.6)$$

$$X^2 = \sum_{i=1}^{2}\sum_{j=1}^{2} \frac{\left(O_{ij} - E_{ij}\right)^2}{E_{ij}} \overset{H_0}{\sim} \chi^2_1 \quad (14.7)$$

$$\hat{\pi}_{\text{before}} = p_{\text{before}} = \frac{a+b}{n} \quad (14.8)$$

$$\hat{\pi}_{\text{after}} = p_{\text{after}} = \frac{a+c}{n} \quad (14.9)$$

$$Z = \frac{b - c}{\sqrt{b + c}} \overset{H_0}{\sim} N(0, 1) \quad (14.10)$$

$$X^2 = (Z)^2 = \frac{(b - c)^2}{b + c} \overset{H_0}{\sim} \chi_1^2 \quad (14.11)$$

$$Z = \frac{T_+ - \mu_+}{\sigma_+} \overset{H_0}{\sim} N(0, 1) \quad (14.12)$$

$$\mu_+ = \frac{n'(n' + 1)}{4} \quad (14.13)$$

$$\sigma_+ = \sqrt{\frac{n'(n' + 1)(2n' + 1)}{24}} \quad (14.14)$$

$$n' = n - S_0 \quad (14.15)$$

$$U_A = n_A n_B + \frac{n_A(n_A + 1)}{2} - T_A \quad (14.16)$$

$$U_B = n_A n_B + \frac{n_B(n_B + 1)}{2} - T_B \quad (14.17)$$

$$U = \min(U_A, U_B) \quad (14.18)$$

$$Z = \frac{U - \mu_U}{\sigma_U} \overset{H_0}{\sim} N(0, 1) \quad (14.19)$$

$$\mu_U = \frac{n_A n_B}{2} \quad (14.20)$$

$$\sigma_U = \sqrt{\frac{n_A n_B (n_A + n_B + 1)}{12}} \quad (14.21)$$

EXERCISES

14.1 A business consultant requests that you perform some preliminary calculations before analysing a data set using Excel.

a) Calculate the number of degrees of freedom for a contingency table with 3 rows and 4 columns.
b) Find the critical χ^2-value with a significance level of 5% and 1%. What Excel function would you use to find this value?
c) Describe how you would use Excel to calculate the test's p-value. What is the value of the p-value if the calculated chi-squared test statistic equals 14.92? What would your conclusion be in this case?

14.2 A trainee risk manager for an investment bank has been told that the level of risk is directly related to the industry type (manufacturing, retail, financial). For the data presented in the contingency table below, analyse whether the perceived risk depends on the type of industry identified (assess at 5%).

Table 14.37: Contingency table for the level of perceived risk

		INDUSTRIAL CLASS		
		MANUFACTURING	RETAIL	FINANCIAL
LEVEL OF RISK	LOW	81	38	16
	MODERATE	46	42	33
	HIGH	22	26	29

14.3 A manufacturing company is concerned by the number of defects produced in the manufacture of office furniture. The firm operates three shifts and has classified the number of defects as low, moderate, high or very high. Is there any evidence to suggest a relationship between types of defect and shifts (assess at 5%)?

Table 14.38: Number of defects during each of the three shifts

SHIFT	DEFECT TYPE			
	LOW	MODERATE	HIGH	VERY HIGH
1	29	40	91	25
2	54	65	63	8
3	70	33	96	38

14.4 A local trade association is concerned at the level of business activity within the local region. As part of a research project, a random sample of business owners was surveyed on how optimistic they were for the coming year. Based on the contingency table below, do we have any evidence to suggest different levels of optimism for business activity (assess at 5%)?

Table 14.39: Levels of optimism for business activity within the local region

OPTIMISM LEVEL	TYPE OF BUSINESS			
	BANKERS	MANUFACTURERS	RETAILERS	FARMERS
HIGH	38	61	59	96
NO CHANGE	16	32	27	29
LOW	11	26	35	41

14.5 A group of students at a school volunteered to sit a test to assess the effectiveness of a new method to teach Afrikaans to English-speaking students. To assess the effectiveness, students sit two different tests with one test in English and the other test in Afrikaans. Is there any evidence to suggest that the student test performances in English are replicated by their test performances in Afrikaans (assess at 5%)?

Table 14.40: Test results of the two exams

AFRIKAANS	ENGLISH		
	≥ 60%	40% – 59%	< 40%
≥ 60%	90	81	8
40% – 59%	61	90	8
< 40%	29	39	6

14.6 The petrol prices during the summer of 2013 have raised concerns among new car sellers that potential customers are taking prices into account when choosing a new car. To provide evidence to test this possibility, a group of five local car showrooms agree to ask fleet managers and individual customers during August 2013 whether they are influenced by petrol prices. The results are shown in Table 14.41.

Table 14.41: Data on whether potential new customers are influenced by petrol prices

ARE PETROL PRICES INFLUENCING YOU IN PURCHASING?	FLEET CUSTOMERS	INDIVIDUAL CUSTOMERS
YES	56	66
NO	23	36

At a 5% level of significance, is there any evidence for the concerns raised by the car showroom owners? Answer this question using both the critical test statistic and *p*-value.

14.7 A business analyst has been asked to confirm the effectiveness of a marketing campaign on people's attitudes to global warming. To confirm that the campaign was effective, a group of 500 people were randomly selected from the population and asked the simple question about whether they agree that national governments should be concerned, with an answer of 'Yes' or 'No'. The results are shown in Table 14.42.

Table 14.42: Data on the effectiveness of a marketing campaign on global warming

BEFORE CAMPAIGN	AFTER CAMPAIGN	
	YES	NO
YES	202	115
NO	89	75

At a 5% level of significance, is there any evidence that the campaign has increased the number of people requesting that national governments should be concerned that global warming is an issue? Answer this question using both the critical test statistic and *p*-value.

14.8 A researcher has undertaken a sign test with the following results: sum of positive and negative signs are 15 and 4 respectively with 3 ties. Assess whether there is evidence that the median value is greater than 0.5 (assess at 5%).

14.9 A teacher of 40 university students studying the application of Excel within a business context is concerned that students are not taking a group work assignment seriously. This is deemed to be important given that the group work element contributes to the development of personal development skills. To assess whether this is a problem, the module tutor devised a simple experiment that judged the individual level of cooperation by each individual student within their own group. In the experiment, a rating scale was employed to measure the level of cooperation: 1 = limited cooperation, 5 = moderate cooperation and 10 = complete cooperation. The form of the testing consisted of an initial observation, a two-hour lecture on working in groups and a final observation. Given the raw data below, conduct a relevant test to assess whether we can observe that cooperation has significantly changed (assess at 5%).

5 , 8	4 , 6	3 , 3	6 , 5	8 , 9	10 , 9	8 , 8	4 , 8	5 , 5	8 , 9
3 , 5	5 , 4	6 , 5	4 , 4	7 , 8	7 , 9	9 , 9	8 , 7	5 , 8	5 , 6
8 , 7	8 , 8	3 , 4	5 , 6	6 , 7	4 , 8	7 , 8	9 , 10	10 , 10	8 , 9
8 , 8	4 , 6	4 , 5	7 , 8	5 , 7	7 , 9	8 , 10	3 , 6	5 , 6	7 , 8

14.10 A leading university advertises in its promotional material that its class sizes at one of its campuses are no greater than 25. Recently, the university has received a number of complaints from disgruntled students who have complained that class sizes are greater than 25 for the majority of its courses at the campus. To assess this claim, the company randomly selects 15 classes and measures the class sizes as follows: 32, 19, 26, 25, 28, 21, 29, 22, 27, 28, 26, 23, 26, 28 and 29. Undertake an appropriate non-parametric test to assess whether there is any justification to the complaints (assess at 5%). What would your decision be if you assessed at 1%?

14.11 A company is planning to introduce new packaging for a product that has used the same packaging for over 20 years. Before it makes a decision about the new packaging, it decides to ask a panel of 20 participants to rate the current and proposed packaging (using a rating scale of 'do not change' = 0 to 'change' = 100). Using an appropriate non-parametric test, determine if there is any evidence that the new packaging is more favourably received compared to the old packaging (assess at 5%).

Table 14.43: Ratings of whether a company should change its packaging

PARTICIPANT	BEFORE	AFTER	PARTICIPANT	BEFORE	AFTER
1	80	9	11	37	40
2	75	82	12	55	68
3	84	96	13	80	88
4	65	68	14	85	95
5	40	45	15	17	21
6	72	79	16	12	18
7	41	30	17	15	21
8	10	22	18	23	25
9	16	12	19	34	45
10	17	24	20	61	80

14.12 A local manufacturer is concerned at the number of errors made by machinists in the production of kites for a multinational retail company. To reduce the number of errors being made, the company decides to retrain all staff in a new set of procedures to minimise the problem. To assess whether the training worked, a random sample of 10 machinists were selected and the number of errors made before and after the training is given in Table 14.44.

Table 14.44: Data regarding whether training helped to reduce machinist errors

	MACHINIST									
	1	**2**	**3**	**4**	**5**	**6**	**7**	**8**	**9**	**10**
BEFORE	49	34	30	46	37	28	48	40	42	45
AFTER	22	23	32	24	23	21	24	29	27	27
	11	**12**	**13**	**14**	**15**	**16**	**17**	**18**	**19**	**20**
BEFORE	29	45	32	44	49	28	44	39	47	41
AFTER	23	29	37	22	33	27	35	32	35	24
	21	**22**	**23**	**24**	**25**	**26**	**27**	**28**	**29**	**30**
BEFORE	33	38	35	35	47	47	48	35	41	35
AFTER	37	37	24	23	23	37	38	30	29	31

Is there any evidence that the training reduced the number of errors (assess at 5%)?

14.13 Two groups of randomly selected students are tested on a regular basis as part of professional appraisals that are conducted on a two-year cycle by a leading financial services company based in Gauteng. The first group has eight students with their sum of the ranks equal to 65 and the second group has nine students. Is there sufficient evidence to suggest that the performance of the second group is higher than the performance of the first group (assess at 5%)?

14.14 The sale of new homes is closely tied to the level of confidence in the financial markets. A developer builds new homes in two different countries (Namibia and Botswana) and is concerned that there is a direct relationship between the country and the interest rates available to build properties. To find answers, the developer decides to undertake market research to see what interest rates would be available if he decided to borrow R300 000 over 20 years from five financial institutions in Namibia and eight financial institutions in Botswana. Based on the data in Table 14.45, is there any evidence to suggest that the interest rates are significantly different?

Table 14.45: Interest rates available in Namibia and Botswana to build properties

NAMIBIA	10.20	10.97	10.63	10.70	10.50	10.30	10.65
	10.25	10.75	11.00				
BOTSWANA	10.60	10.80	11.40	10.90	11.10	11.20	10.89
	10.78	11.05	11.15	10.85	11.16	11.18	

TECHNIQUES IN PRACTICE

14.15 AfriSoft is concerned about the time taken to react to customer complaints and has implemented a new set of procedures for its support centre staff. The customer service director has instructed that a suitable test is applied to a new sample to assess whether the new target mean time for responding to customer complaints is 28 days.

Table 14.46: The time taken to respond to complaints (in days)

20	33	33	29	24	30
40	33	20	39	32	37
32	50	36	31	38	29
15	33	27	29	43	33
31	35	19	39	22	21
28	22	26	42	30	17
32	34	39	39	32	38

a) Conduct an appropriate non-parametric required test to assess whether evidence exists that the mean time to respond to complaints is greater than 28 days.
b) What would happen to your results if the population mean time to react to customer complaints changes to 30 days?

14.16 Bakers Ltd is currently undertaking a review of the delivery vans used to deliver products to customers. The company runs two types of delivery van (type A – recently purchased – and type B – at least three years old), which are supposed to be capable of achieving 20 km per litre of petrol. A new sample has now been collected as shown in Table 14.47.

Table 14.47: Fuel consumption figures (km/ℓ) for the two van types; 15 for van type A and 21 for B

VAN TYPE A	VAN TYPE B
17.68	15.8
18.72	39.1
29.49	9.3
29.64	12.3
9.31	15.5
22.38	40.1
20.23	20.4

VAN TYPE A	VAN TYPE B
29.42	34.8
25.22	19.8
13.52	15.0
14.01	28.9
	33.9
	27.1
	19.8

VAN TYPE A	VAN TYPE B	VAN TYPE A	VAN TYPE B
28.80	3.7		23.6
17.57	13.6		29.7
9.13	35.1		28.2
20.98	33.3		

a) Assuming that the population distance travelled does *not* vary as a normal distribution, is there any evidence to suggest that the two types of delivery vans differ in their mean distance travelled?

b) Based on your analysis, is there any evidence to suggest that the new delivery vans meet the mean average of 20 km per litre?

14.17 Home-Made Beers Ltd is developing a low-calorie lager with a mean designed calorie count of 43 calories per 100 ml. The new product development team are having problems with the production process and have collected two independent random samples to assess whether the target calorie count is being met (assume the population of calorie count values is normally distributed).

Table 14.48: Calorie counts of two samples (A and B) of beer bottles; each sample consists of 22 bottles

SAMPLE A	SAMPLE B	SAMPLE A	SAMPLE B
49.7	39.4	45.2	34.5
45.9	49.5	40.5	43.5
37.7	39.2	31.9	37.8
40.6	49.7	41.9	39.7
34.8	39.5	39.8	41.1
51.4	45.4	54.0	33.6
34.3	38.2	47.8	35.8
63.1	44.1	29.3	44.6
41.2	58.7	31.7	38.4
41.4	47.1	45.1	29.1
41.1	59.7	47.9	30.7

a) Are both production processes (each sample is taken from the different production processes) achieving similar median number of calories?

b) Is it likely that the target average number of calories is being achieved?

CHAPTER 15

ANALYSIS OF VARIANCE

CHAPTER CONTENTS

OVERVIEW

In Chapters 10, 11 and 14, we dealt with hypothesis tests (using both parametric and non-parametric tests) concerning the parameters of only one or two populations. In this chapter, we extend these testing concepts to tests concerning multiple populations. In particular, we consider the analysis of variance (ANOVA) F-test for population means from multiple populations and the Kruskal-Wallis test, which is a non-parametric test for population medians from multiple populations.

LEARNING OBJECTIVES

On completing this chapter, you should be able to:

- identify an appropriate statistical test for data sets with more than two groups
- test hypotheses concerning the population means of multiple populations using a parametric analysis of variance (ANOVA) approach
- test hypotheses concerning the population medians of multiple populations using a non-parametric Kruskal-Wallis test
- test hypotheses using Microsoft Excel.

15.1 Introduction

In Chapters 11 and 14, we explored techniques to test whether two population means are equal. In those two chapters, we were interested in questions of the form, for example, 'Do people spend equal amounts at two supermarkets on average?' In this question, we could test the hypothesis that the two population means are equal using a suitable two sample Z- or t-test (or we could even use a non-parametric test). However, what would happen if the question was extended to more than two supermarkets or populations? What would happen if the question of interest was 'Do people spend equal amounts at *three* supermarkets on average?' One possible solution would be to conduct a series of paired comparisons between each of the means of the populations, for example, if we had supermarkets A, B and C, with population means denoted μ_A, μ_B and μ_C, respectively, we would consider tests to compare all the pairs of means, i.e. we would test $\mu_A = \mu_B$, $\mu_A = \mu_C$ and $\mu_B = \mu_C$.

Unfortunately, using this pairwise approach can be unwieldy if the number of populations is large. We end up doing a large number of tests even for a small number of populations. Consider the situation where we have five populations: if we want to compare each pair of means, we would have to test a total of 10 separate pairs of hypotheses. This approach is tedious and, occasionally, difficult to interpret.

Thankfully, we do not always need to rely on this pairwise approach, as there is a test called the *ANalysis Of VAriance* (ANOVA) *F-test,* which we can use to determine the equality of more than two population means using a single test.

Analysis of variance is based on the following simple idea. If we consider the values of the sample means of several different groups (for example, we have three groups with means $\overline{X}_A$, $\overline{X}_B$ and $\overline{X}_C$), then the variance of these mean values will be 0 if the sample mean values are equal to one another. However, if these mean values differ, then the variance of the sample mean values will be larger than 0. In other words we can *analyse the variance* of the means to determine the equality of the means.

Consider the following simple example. The sample mean amount of money that people spend at three supermarkets is:

$\overline{X}_A = \text{R}350.00 \qquad \overline{X}_B = \text{R}350.00 \qquad \overline{X}_C = \text{R}350.00$

The average of these three values is R350.00 and the sample variance is equal to 0. In this example, the means are equal and so the variance is 0. Suppose now that the means are given by:

$\overline{X}_A = \text{R}350.00 \qquad \overline{X}_B = \text{R}350.00 \qquad \overline{X}_C = \text{R}400.00$

The mean spending in Supermarket C is slightly greater compared to in the other two. The average of these three values is R366.67 and the sample variance is R833.33. Note that if even one of the means is different from the others, it changes the variances of the mean values. The variance of the mean values is therefore a good indicator of whether the mean values are the same (which would produce a value equal to 0) or whether they differ (which would produce values greater than 0).

The conclusion in the above example is slightly over-simplified. This is because it is based only on sample data, and so we could not conclude that the population means are different simply because the variance of the sample means is large. We cannot make conclusions regarding population means based only on the fact that the sample means differ. One reason for this is that we do not know how large this variance should be before we can conclude that there is a significant difference between the population means. To overcome this issue, we need to standardise this value by incorporating the variation from each of the groups and applying the hypothesis testing techniques that were discussed in the previous chapters. The resulting test is called the analysis of variance (ANOVA) *F*-test for equality of population means.

As with the other parametric tests discussed in Chapters 10 and 11, the analysis of variance test is also subject to a number of assumptions that affect the successful application of the test. (The assumptions include normality of populations, independence of values and equal population variances.) If these assumptions cannot be satisfied, then we should apply a non-parametric test for multiple population means (similar to the methods discussed in Chapter 13). The non-parametric test that we can use as an alternative to the parametric ANOVA *F*-test, is the Kruskal-Wallis test. This test is based on the ranks of the data, rather than the observed values of the data.

In the next few sections, we discuss both the ANOVA *F*-test for comparing the means of multiple populations and the non-parametric alternative: the Kruskal-Wallis test.

15.2 ANOVA test for the means of multiple populations

We now consider the various aspects of the ANOVA test (also called the *one-way ANOVA test* or *single factor ANOVA test*), including formulating the hypothesis statement, the assumptions underlying the test, testing these assumptions, calculating the test statistic and the follow-up tests that should be conducted.

In this section, we discuss the test in the following order:

- The main ANOVA hypothesis statement and the assumptions of the test
- Calculating the *F*-test statistic when all the assumptions are satisfied
- The follow-up (or post-hoc) tests that must be conducted if we reject the main ANOVA hypothesis

- The procedures used to test whether the assumptions underlying the main ANOVA test actually hold (in practice this is done before conducting the main test)

15.2.1 The hypothesis statement and assumptions of the ANOVA test

The null hypothesis in an ANOVA is that the population means of k separate populations are equal versus the alternative that at least one population mean is different from the rest. Formally stated, these hypotheses become:

$$H_0: \mu_1 = \mu_2 = \mu_3 = \ldots = \mu_k$$

H_1: At least one population mean is different from the rest

μ_i represents the population mean of population i. Note that we sometimes also formulate the alternate hypothesis as 'H_1: not all population means are equal'. We can state the alternative hypothesis in either way.

One-way analysis of variance shares many of the same assumptions required by the t-test for two populations (discussed in Chapter 11). These assumptions include the following:

1. The test can only be applied to data that are at least on the interval scale of measurement.
2. The samples for each group should be *random* samples selected from their respective populations.
3. The populations are assumed to be independent.
4. The population standard deviations (i.e. variances) in each group are equal (the so-called **homogeneity of variances** assumption).
5. The populations are normally distributed.

Homogeneity of variance Population variances are equal.

Assumptions 1, 2 and 3 are considerations that will come up during the design of the experiment. (With proper planning and consideration, these conditions will be met.) Assumptions 4 and 5 are inherent to the population. They are unknown at the start of the experiment and must be tested before being accepted. If the data do not satisfy these assumptions (for example, if there is marked difference in variance, or the data are highly skewed and non-normal), we should consider using non-parametric tests, which require neither assumption.

15.2.2 Calculating the ANOVA F-test statistic

In this subsection, we look at how to calculate the ANOVA F-test statistic for testing the hypothesis of equal population means. For now, we assume that the assumptions are satisfied but, in later sections, we investigate procedures for testing the validity of the assumptions.

Before we move on to calculating the test statistic, we first need to introduce some basic notation that is required in order to understand both the data and statistics:

- k denotes the number of populations being investigated in the study.
- n_j denotes the size of the sample drawn from the jth population (i.e. it is the jth sample's size).
- n denotes the total sample size of all k samples, i.e. $n = n_1 + n_2 + \ldots + n_k$.

- The data values of the n_j items sampled from population j are represented by $X_{j,1}, X_{j,2}, \ldots, X_{j,nj}$, i.e. $X_{j,i}$ is the ith value from sample j.
- $\overline{X}_j$ denotes the sample mean of the data values in sample j:

$$\overline{X}_j = \frac{1}{n_j}\sum_{i=1}^{n_j} X_{j,i} \qquad (15.1)$$

- $\overline{X}$ denotes the mean of the k mean values (the overall mean):

$$\overline{X} = \frac{1}{n}\sum_{j=1}^{k}\sum_{i=1}^{n_j} X_{j,i} = \frac{1}{n}\sum_{j=1}^{k} n_j \overline{X}_j \qquad (15.2)$$

Example 15.1 shows how we can identify these quantities in a simple data set.

WORKED EXAMPLES

EXAMPLE 15.1

A study is conducted to determine the effect that three different dog food brands have on the mean lifetime of dogs. The study is conducted with 15 dogs (all of the same breed and gender) who are made to eat one of three brands of dog food their entire lives. Each of the dog food types is randomly assigned to 5 dogs in the study.

The study began in 1991 and ended in 2001 (when the final dog died). Table 15.1 shows the data of the lifetimes of the dogs (in months).

Table 15.1: Dog food data set

DOG FOOD TYPE 1	DOG FOOD TYPE 2	DOG FOOD TYPE 3
$X_{1,1} = 100$	$X_{2,1} = 56$	$X_{3,1} = 106$
$X_{1,2} = 88$	$X_{2,2} = 43$	$X_{3,2} = 113$
$X_{1,3} = 76$	$X_{2,3} = 24$	$X_{3,3} = 130$
$X_{1,4} = 115$	$X_{2,4} = 96$	$X_{3,4} = 125$
$X_{1,5} = 45$	$X_{2,4} = 59$	$X_{3,5} = 63$

There are $k = 3$ populations (each sample of 5 dogs assigned to each dog food type represents a sample from the population of dogs that eat a particular dog food type).

The sample sizes for each group are $n_1 = n_2 = n_3 = 5$ and the total sample size is $n = 15$.

The sample means from each dog food type are:

$$\overline{X}_1 = \frac{1}{5}(100 + 88 + 76 + 115 + 45) = 84.8 \text{ months}$$

$$\overline{X}_2 = \frac{1}{5}(56 + 43 + 24 + 96 + 59) = 55.6 \text{ months}$$

$$\overline{X}_3 = \frac{1}{5}(106 + 113 + 130 + 125 + 63) = 107.4 \text{ months}$$

The overall mean value of all 15 observations is $\overline{X} = 82.6$ months.

The purpose of the study is to determine if the population mean lifetimes of dogs differs in each of the different dog food groups. To test this hypothesis, we need to conduct the ANOVA F-test.

As described in the introduction, we use the ANOVA test statistic to test the hypothesis that the population means are all equal by considering the variation of the values of the sample means (the *between-groups* variation) relative to the variation of the data within each of these groups (the *within-group* variation). We calculate these sources of variation using the sums of squares and their associated degrees of freedom. The sums of squares represent the main variation that can be converted into a statistic that describes the variance (similar to the sample variance) by dividing by the associated degrees of freedom. The main idea behind analysis of variance involves the fact that the total sums of squares of the data (which represent the total variation in the data) can be partitioned into the following two other sums of squares:

- The sums of squares describing the variation *between* the group means (the *between group sums of squares*):

$$SSBetween = \sum_{j=1}^{k} n_j \left(\overline{X}_j - \overline{\overline{X}}\right)^2 \tag{15.3}$$

- The sums of squares describing the remaining variation, which is the variation *within* the groups (the *within group sums of squares*):

$$SSWithin = \sum_{j=1}^{k} \sum_{i=1}^{n_j} n_j \left(X_{ij} - \overline{X}_j\right)^2 \tag{15.4}$$

The total variation in the data, calculated using the *total sums of squares* is:

$$SSTotal = \sum_{j=1}^{k} \sum_{i=1}^{n_j} n_j \left(X_{ij} - \overline{\overline{X}}\right)^2 \tag{15.5}$$

This can be split:

$$SSTotal = SSBetween + SSWithin$$

The degrees of freedom associated with *SSTotal*, *SSBetween* and *SSWithin* are:

$$df_{\text{Total}} = n - 1 \tag{15.6}$$

$$df_{\text{Between}} = k - 1 \tag{15.7}$$

$$df_{\text{Within}} = n - k \tag{15.8}$$

The estimated variance associated with each of these sums of squares is then equal to the sums of squares divided by their respective degrees of freedom. The resulting variances, called the *mean sums of squares*, are denoted by:

$$\text{Mean total sums of squares} = MSTotal = \frac{SSTotal}{df_{\text{Total}}} = \frac{SSTotal}{n - 1} \tag{15.9}$$

$$\text{Mean between sums of squares} = MSBetween = \frac{SSBetween}{df_{\text{Between}}} = \frac{SSBetween}{k - 1} \tag{15.10}$$

$$\text{Mean within sums of squares} = MSWithin = \frac{SSWithin}{df_{\text{Within}}} = \frac{SSWithin}{n-k} \quad (15.11)$$

We can calculate the ANOVA F-statistic using the following formula:

$$F = \frac{\text{variance between groups}}{\text{variance within groups}} = \frac{MSBetween}{MSWithin} \overset{H_0}{\sim} F_{df_{\text{Between}}, df_{\text{Within}}} \quad (15.12)$$

The calculated value of this test statistic is denoted by F_{cal}.

If there are large variations between the values of the treatment group means, the numerator of F_{cal} (and therefore F_{cal} itself) will be large and the null hypothesis is likely to be rejected. However, if the group means are equal (or relatively similar), the numerator should have a value close to 0, producing an F-statistic close to, or equal to, 0.

Large values of F_{cal} are therefore evidence against the null hypothesis of equality of population means. We use the critical value of the F-distribution with $df_{Between}$ and df_{Within} degrees of freedom to determine how large the value of the F-statistic should be to reject the null hypothesis, i.e. the critical value is $F_{\alpha, df_{Between}, df_{Within}}$, where α is the specified level of significance. The rule for rejecting H_0 is then:

$$\text{Reject } H_0 \text{ if } F_{\text{cal}} > F_{\alpha, df_{\text{Between}}, df_{\text{Within}}}$$

The p-value for the test is calculated as:

$$p\text{-value} = P(F > F_{\text{cal}}) = 1 - P(F < F_{\text{cal}})$$

F is an F-distributed random variable with df_{Between} and df_{Within} degrees of freedom.

The relationship between the p-values, critical values and test statistic is shown in Figure 15.1.

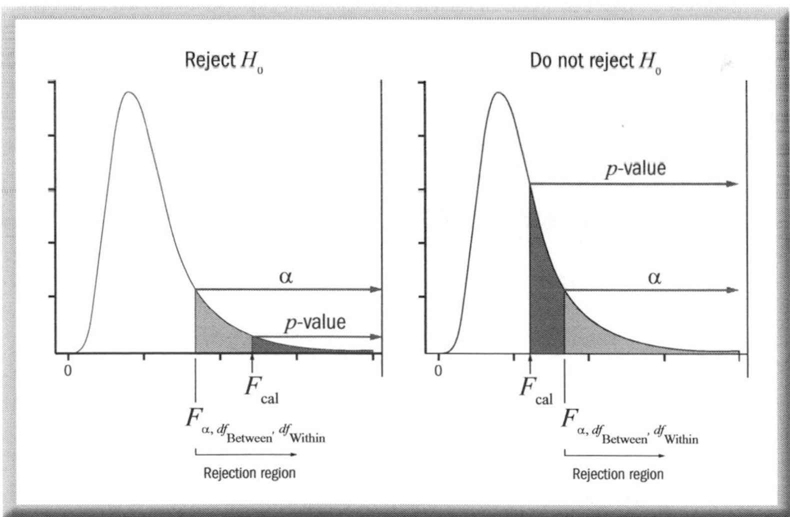

Figure 15.1: The rejection regions for the ANOVA F-test

The F-statistic, and all the associated sums of squares, mean sums of squares and degrees of freedom, are usually summarised in an ANOVA table. Table 15.2 shows the general form of this table.

Table 15.2: The ANOVA table

SOURCE OF VARIATION	SUM OF SQUARES	DEGREES OF FREEDOM, df	MEAN SQUARE (VARIANCE)	F
BETWEEN GROUPS	$SSBetween$	df_{Between}	$MSBetween$	F
WITHIN GROUPS	$SSWithin$	df_{Within}	$MSWithin$	
TOTAL	$SSTotal$	df_{Total}	$MSTotal$	

NOTE

You can obtain the contents of Table 15.2, along with a corresponding p-value and a critical F-value based on a chosen significance level using Excel's built-in Data Analysis ToolPak.

Note that this built-in ANOVA test procedure only works when there is an equal number of values in each group.

Example 15.2 illustrates how to conduct this ANOVA test.

WORKED EXAMPLES

EXAMPLE 15.2

Use the data in Table 15.1 of Example 15.1 to test the hypothesis that the population mean lifetimes of dogs that eat the three different types of dog food are the same, i.e. test the hypothesis:

$$H_0: \mu_1 = \mu_2 = \mu_3$$

vs

$$H_1: \text{Not all equal}$$

μ_1, μ_2 and μ_3 denote the population mean lifetimes of dogs that eat dog food types 1, 2 and 3, respectively.

Assume that all assumptions regarding normality, independence and homogeneity of variances are satisfied. Test the hypothesis using a significance level of $\alpha = 0.05$.

The five-step procedure for hypothesis testing will once again be used to test this hypothesis.

Step 1: Provide the hypothesis statements H_0 and H_1

- *Null hypothesis*: H_0: $\mu_1 = \mu_2 = \mu_3$, i.e. the population mean lifetimes are all equal.
- *Alternative hypothesis*: H_1: Not all equal, i.e. at least one population mean is different.

Step 2: Choose an appropriate test statistic

The following information is provided.

- *The number of populations in the study*: A sample from each of the three populations is being considered.
- *The research question*: The primary question is whether the population means of the three populations are all the same. If all the population means are the same, we can conclude that the dog food type does not have an effect on the mean lifetimes of the dogs. If they differ, we can conclude that the dog food type has some effect on the mean lifetimes of the dogs.
- *Assumptions underlying the test*: As stated, we accept that the assumptions of the ANOVA *F*-test are satisfied in this scenario. This means that we have equal variances in each population, the populations are all normally distributed and the observations are all independent. This information leads us to the conclusion that the ANOVA *F*-test is the most appropriate test in this scenario.

Step 3: Specify the significance level

The significance level is specified as $\alpha = 0.05$ (or 5%)

Step 4: Calculate the relevant test statistic

To calculate the test statistic, we first need to calculate $\overline{X}_1$, $\overline{X}_2$ and $\overline{X}_3$ using formula (15.1):

$$\begin{aligned}\overline{X}_1 &= \frac{1}{5}\sum_{i=1}^{n_1} X_{1,i}\\ &= \frac{1}{5}(100 + 88 + 76 + 115 + 45) = 84.8\\ \overline{X}_2 &= \frac{1}{5}\sum_{i=1}^{n_2} X_{2,i}\\ &= \frac{1}{5}(56 + 43 + 24 + 96 + 59) = 55.6\\ \overline{X}_3 &= \frac{1}{5}\sum_{i=1}^{n_3} X_{3,i}\\ &= \frac{1}{5}(106 + 113 + 130 + 125 + 63) = 107.4\end{aligned}$$

The overall mean, using formula (15.2), is:

$$\begin{aligned}\overline{\overline{X}} &= \frac{1}{15}\sum_{j=1}^{3} 5 \times \overline{X}_j\\ &= \frac{1}{15}(5 \times 84.8 + 5 \times 55.6 + 5 \times 107.4)\\ &= 82.6\end{aligned}$$

Next, we need to calculate the values of *SSBetween* and *SSWithin* using formulae (15.3) and (15.4), respectively:

$$\begin{aligned}SSBetween &= \sum_{j=1}^{3} 5 \times \left(\overline{X}_j - \overline{\overline{X}}\right)^2\\ &= 5 \times [(84.8 - 82.6)^2 + (55.6 - 82.6)^2 + (107.4 - 82.6)^2]\\ &= 5 \times [4.84 + 729 + 615.04]\\ &= 5 \times 1\,348.88\\ &= 6\,744.4\end{aligned}$$

$$
\begin{aligned}
SSWithin &= \sum_{j=1}^{3}\sum_{i=1}^{5}\left(X_{j,i} - \overline{X}_j\right)^2 \\
&= (100 - 84.8)^2 + (88 - 84.8)^2 + (76 - 84.8)^2 + (115 - 84.8)^2 + (45 - 84.8)^2 \\
&\quad + (56 - 55.6)^2 + (43 - 55.6)^2 + (24 - 55.6)^2 + (96 - 55.6)^2 + (59 - 55.6)^2 \\
&\quad + (106 - 107.4)^2 + (113 - 107.4)^2 + (130 - 107.4)^2 + (125 - 107.4)^2 + (62 - 107.4)^2 \\
&= 231.04 + 10.24 + 77.44 + 912.04 + 1\,584.04 + 0.16 + 158.76 + 998.56 + 1\,632.16 \\
&\quad + 11.56 + 196 + 31.36 + 510.76 + 309.76 + 1\,971.36 \\
&= 8\,441.2
\end{aligned}
$$

The mean sums of squares can then be obtained using formulae (15.10) and (15.11):

$$MSBetween = \frac{SSBetween}{3 - 1} = \frac{6\,744.4}{2} = 3\,372.2$$

$$MSWithin = \frac{SSWithin}{15 - 3} = \frac{8\,441.2}{12} = 703.4333$$

Finally, the calculated value of the F-test in formula (15.12) is:

$$F_{\text{cal}} = \frac{MSBetween}{MSWithin} = \frac{3\,372.2}{703.4333} = 4.794$$

Step 5: Make a decision

We will use both the critical value approach and the p-value approach to make a decision for this test.

- *Critical value approach*: The significance level was chosen to be $\alpha = 0.05$ and the degrees of freedom of the test statistic are $df_{\text{Between}} = k - 1 = 3 - 1 = 2$ and $df_{\text{Within}} = n - k = 15 - 3 = 12$, and so the critical value for this test is:

  $$F_{0.05,2,12} = 3.8853$$

  Note: We obtained this critical value using Excel's F.INV function as discussed in Section 7.5 of Chapter 7. Since $F_{\text{cal}} = 4.794 > 3.8853$, we **reject H_0**. The rejection region is shown in Figure 15.2.
- p-*value approach*: We calculate the p-value for this test using Excel's F.DIST function. Formally, we need to calculate the following quantity:

  $$
  \begin{aligned}
  p\text{-value} &= P(F > F_{\text{cal}}) \\
  &= P(F > 4.794) \\
  &= 1 - P(F < 4.794) \\
  &= 1 - 0.9705006 \\
  &= 0.0294994
  \end{aligned}
  $$

The p-value is smaller than the specified significance level, $\alpha = 0.05$, so we **reject H_0**. Figure 15.2 graphically displays the value of the p-values relative to the significance level.

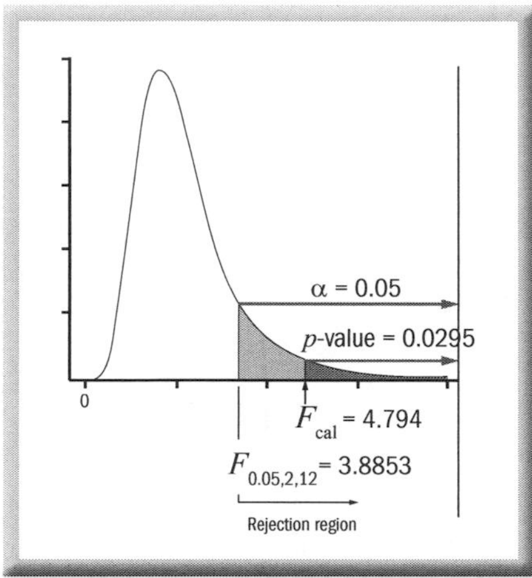

Figure 15.2: Graphical representation of the critical values, test statistic value and p-value of the test in Example 15.2

Excel solution

The Excel solution for this test is shown in Figure 15.3. Note that in this solution, the data values are arranged into a single column (cells B4 to B18) and the second column is used to indicate which group the data values belong to (i.e. the cells C4 to C18 show which dog food type was used).

	A	B	C	D	E	F	G	H	I	J	K	L	M
1	**Example 15.2: ANOVA F-test**												
2										**Hypothesis test**			
3	**Dog food**	**Lifetimes**							**Step 1:**	H_0: $\mu_1 = \mu_2 = \mu_3$			
4		100	231.04	=(B4-$F$4)^2	$\bar{X}_1$ =	84.8	=AVERAGE(B4:B8)			H_1: not all equal			
5		88	10.24	=(B5-$F$4)^2	n_1 =	5	=COUNT(B4:B8)						
6	**Type 1**	76	77.44	=(B6-$F$4)^2						**Choose the appropriate test**			
7		115	912.04	=(B7-$F$4)^2					**Step 2:**	The test involves testing multiple population means, use the F-test.			
8		45	1584.04	=(B8-$F$4)^2						Assumptions of normality and homogeneity hold.			
9		56	0.16	=(B9-$F$9)^2	$\bar{X}_2$ =	55.6	=AVERAGE(B9:B13)						
10		43	158.76	=(B10-$F$9)^2	n_2 =	5	=COUNT(B9:B13)		**Step 3:**	**Select level of significance**			
11	**Type 2**	24	998.56	=(B11-$F$9)^2							Signficance level, α =	0.05	
12		96	1632.16	=(B12-$F$9)^2									
13		59	11.56	=(B13-$F$9)^2						**Calculate test statistic**			
14		106	1.96	=(B14-$F$14)^2	$\bar{X}_3$ =	107.4	=AVERAGE(B14:B18)				k =	3	
15		113	31.36	=(B15-$F$14)^2	n_3 =	5	=COUNT(B14:B18)				n =	15	=COUNT(C4:C18)
16	**Type 3**	130	510.76	=(B16-$F$14)^2							*SSBetween* =	6744.4	=F5(F4-F19)^2+F10*(F9-F19)^2+F15*(F14-F19)^2
17		125	309.76	=(B17-$F$14)^2					**Step 4:**		*SSWithin* =	8441.2	=SUM(C4:C18)
18		63	1971.36	=(B18-$F$14)^2							*MSBetween* =	3372.2	=L16/(L14-1)
19					$\bar{X}$ =	82.6	=AVERAGE(B4:B18)				*MSWithin* =	703.4333333	=L17/(L15-L14)
20					n =	15	=COUNT(C4:C18)				F_{cal} =	4.793915557	=L18/L19
21											Critical value $F_{\alpha,2,12}$ =	3.8853	=F.INV(1-L11,L14-1,L15-L14)
22											p-value =	0.0295	=1-F.DIST(L20,L14-1,L15-L14,TRUE)
23													
24										**Make a decision**			
25									**Step 5:**	Since $p < \alpha$, therefore reject H_0			
26										The population means are not all equal			

Figure 15.3: Excel solution to the ANOVA F-test in Example 15.2

EXCEL SOLUTIONS

Dog lifetimes: Cells B4:B18	Values
$\bar{X}_1$: Cell F4	Formula: =AVERAGE(B4:B8)
$\bar{X}_2$: Cell F9	Formula: =AVERAGE(B9:B13)
$\bar{X}_3$: Cell F14	Formula: =AVERAGE(B14:B18)
$\bar{X}$: Cell F19	Formula: =AVERAGE(B4:B18)
n_1: Cell F5	Formula: =COUNT(B4:B8)
n_2: Cell F10	Formula: =COUNT(B9:B13)
n_3: Cell F15	Formula: =COUNT(B14:B18)
n: Cell F19	Formula: =COUNT(B4:B18)
$(X_{1,i} - \bar{X}_1)^2$: Cells C4:C8	Formula: =(B4-$F$4)^2
	(Copy to cells C4 to C8)
$(X_{2,i} - \bar{X}_2)^2$: Cells C9:C13	Formula: =(B9-$F$9)^2
	(Copy to cells C9 to C14)
$(X_{3,i} - \bar{X}_3)^2$: Cells C14:C18	Formula: =(B14-$F$14)^2
	(Copy to cells C14 to C18)
Significance α: Cell L11	Value
k: Cell L14	Value
n: Cell L15	Formula: =COUNT(C4:C18)
SSBetween: Cell L16	Formula: =F5*(F4-F19)^2+F10*(F9-F19)^2+F15*(F14-F19)^2
SSWithin: Cell L17	Formula: =SUM(C4:C18)
MSBetween: Cell L18	Formula: =L16/(L14-1)
MSWithin: Cell L19	Formula: =L17/(L15-L14)
Critical value, $F_{\alpha,2,12}$: Cell L21	Formula: =F.INV(1-L11,L14-1,L15-L14)
p-value: Cell L22	Formula: =1-F.DIST(L20,L14-1,L15-L14,TRUE)

A different Excel solution involves using the 'ANOVA single factor' option in Excel's Data Analysis ToolPak. To use this method, first arrange the data into columns as shown in Figure 15.4.

	A	B	C
1	**Example 15.2: ANOVA *F*-test**		
2	**Dog food**		
3	**Type 1**	**Type 2**	**Type 3**
4	100	56	106
5	88	43	113
6	76	24	130
7	115	96	125
8	45	59	63

Figure 15.4: Arrange the data from Example 15.2 into columns to use the Data Analysis ToolPak solution

Next, click on the 'Data' tab and press the 'Data Analysis' button to bring up the 'Data Analysis' window as shown in Figure 15.5. (Note that the 'Data Analysis Add-in' must be activated for this button to appear.)

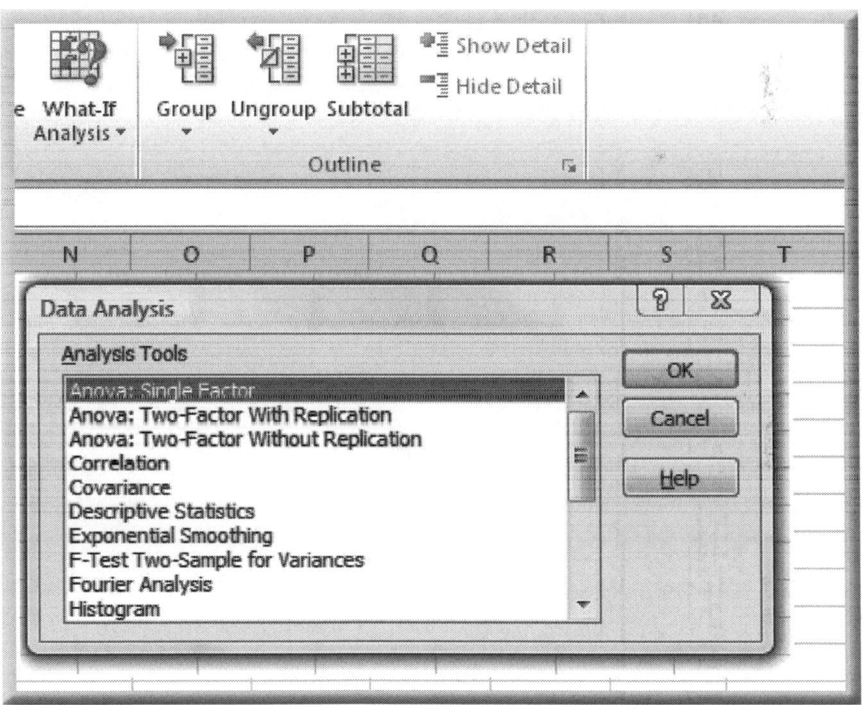

Figure 15.5: Click on the 'Data Analysis' button in the 'Data' ribbon to open the 'Data Analysis' window

In the 'Data Analysis' window, select 'ANOVA: Single Factor' to open the single factor ANOVA window (as shown in Figure 15.6). In this window, select the data range ('Input Range') and indicate whether the grouping is in columns or rows. In Figure 15.6, we have selected the range A3:C8. Now, because this range includes the group headings 'Type 1', 'Type 2' and 'Type 3', we also have to check the box marked 'Labels in first row'. Finally, specify the significance level, α, by typing the value in the field labelled 'Alpha'. Press 'OK' to produce the output.

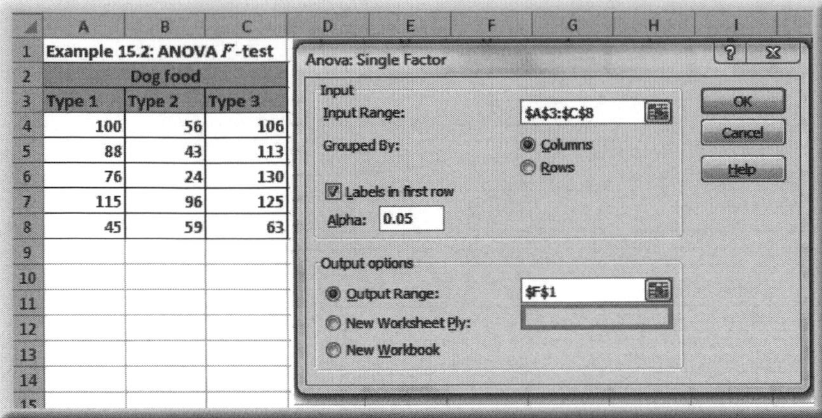

Figure 15.6: The single-factor ANOVA window settings

The output from this procedure is shown in Figure 15.7. Note that the basic statistics for each group is calculated (the size, sum, mean and variance of the data in each group), as well as the ANOVA table containing the *F*-statistic, critical value and *p*-value for this test. The results are identical to the calculations conducted previously.

	A	B	C	D	E	F	G	H	I	J	K	L
1	Example 15.2: ANOVA *F*-test					Anova: Single Factor						
2	Dog food											
3	Type 1	Type 2	Type 3			SUMMARY						
4	100	56	106			*Groups*	*Count*	*Sum*	*Average*	*Variance*		
5	88	43	113			Type 1	5	424	84.8	703.7		
6	76	24	130			Type 2	5	278	55.6	700.3		
7	115	96	125			Type 3	5	537	107.4	706.3		
8	45	59	63									
9												
10						ANOVA						
11						*Source of Variation*	*SS*	*df*	*MS*	*F*	*P-value*	*F crit*
12						Between Groups	6744.4	2	3372.2	4.793915557	0.0295007736	3.8852938347
13						Within Groups	8441.2	12	703.4333333333			
14												
15						Total	15185.6	14				
16												

Figure 15.7: The output for the Data Analysis ToolPak's ANOVA test for Example 15.2

INTERPRETATION

Using either method of calculation we find that we reject the null hypothesis (at an $\alpha = 0.05$ level of significance) that the population mean lifetimes of dogs using the three different dog foods are the same. We conclude that at least one of these population means differ.

Another way to interpret this result is to say that dog food type is a significant factor when it comes to determining lifetimes of dogs because, depending on which dog food type they eat, the dogs' mean lifetimes differ.

If we conclude from an ANOVA F-test that the population means are all equal (i.e. if we do not reject the null hypothesis), then we can end our analysis; we have reached a satisfactory conclusion. However, if we conclude that the population means are not all equal (i.e. if we reject the null hypothesis as in Example 15.2), then we are led directly into a new question: 'If the population means are not all equal, which ones differ and which ones are the same?'

The next section on post-hoc tests will answer this new question.

15.2.3 The Bonferroni post-hoc tests of individual pairs of means

If we conclude that the null hypothesis of equal population means is not valid, we need to determine which pairs of population means are the same and which ones differ. An analysis like this that occurs *after* the main hypothesis test is called *a posteriori* or *post-hoc* analysis. There are a number of different types of tests that can determine which pairs of means differ, but we only consider the simplest of these: the *Bonferroni t-test.*

If there are k populations, we can use the Bonferroni t-test to test all possible pairs of population means. For example, if $k = 4$, we can use the Bonferroni to test the following $g = \frac{k(k-1)}{2} = \frac{4(4-1)}{2} = 6$ hypotheses:

$$
\begin{array}{lll}
H_0: \mu_1 = \mu_2 & \text{vs} & H_1: \mu_1 \neq \mu_2 \\
H_0: \mu_1 = \mu_3 & \text{vs} & H_1: \mu_1 \neq \mu_3 \\
H_0: \mu_1 = \mu_4 & \text{vs} & H_1: \mu_1 \neq \mu_4 \\
H_0: \mu_2 = \mu_3 & \text{vs} & H_1: \mu_2 \neq \mu_3 \\
H_0: \mu_2 = \mu_4 & \text{vs} & H_1: \mu_2 \neq \mu_4 \\
H_0: \mu_3 = \mu_4 & \text{vs} & H_1: \mu_3 \neq \mu_4
\end{array}
$$

In many ways, the Bonferroni test is similar to the two population tests for population means discussed in Section 11.4 of Chapter 11, except that the critical regions for these tests have been adapted to compensate for the fact that there are multiple pairs of population means being tested simultaneously. Unfortunately, when we have k groups, we wind up testing a total of $g = \frac{k(k-1)}{2}$ hypotheses, each with significance level of α (i.e. the probability of a type 1 error – the error of incorrectly rejecting the null hypothesis), which means that the overall probability of a type 1 error (for all tests considered simultaneously) is considerably higher than α. The Bonferroni test attempts to control the overall probability of a type 1 error by ensuring that it is no greater than the original specified level of significance.

In general, the hypotheses that we test are given by:

$$H_0: \mu_i = \mu_j \quad \text{vs} \quad H_1: \mu_i \neq \mu_j \qquad i, j = 1, 2, \ldots, k$$

Bonferroni t-test A statistical procedure that adjusts the alpha level to allow multiple t-tests to be used following the ANOVA.

Multiple comparisons Occur when one considers a set or family of statistical inferences simultaneously.

We can use the **Bonferroni multiple comparison *t*-test**, defined in formula (15.13), to address this problem of testing g pairs of means simultaneously:

$$T_{i,j} = \frac{X_i - X_j}{\sqrt{MSWithin\left(\frac{1}{n_i} + \frac{1}{n_j}\right)}} \overset{H_0}{\sim} t_{n-k} \quad (15.13)$$

n is the total sample size of all k groups in the original ANOVA test, n_i and n_j are the sample sizes of groups i and j, $\overline{X}_i$ and $\overline{X}_i$ are the sample means of groups i and j, and *MSWithin* is the mean within sum of squares calculated from the original ANOVA test. The calculated version of this test statistic is denoted $t_{i,j,\text{cal}}$.

The test statistic follows a t_{n-k}-distribution under H_0 when the assumptions specified in the ANOVA test are satisfied. However, in order to determine the correct decision rules for rejecting H_0 based on the critical values and *p*-values for this test, we need to introduce the Bonferroni correction. The decision rules for the Bonferroni *t*-test then are defined as follows:

- *Critical value approach*: The critical values that are used for all $g = \frac{k(k-1)}{2}$ tests for the pairs of population means are $-t_{\alpha/(2g),\, n-k}$ and $t_{\alpha/(2g),\, n-k}$. Note that the Bonferroni correction involves simply dividing α by g. We reject the null hypothesis H_0: $\mu_i = \mu_j$ if $t_{i,j,\text{cal}} < -t_{\alpha/(2g),\, n-k}$ or if $t_{i,j,\text{cal}} > t_{\alpha/(2g),\, n-k}$. We can use the Excel function T.INV to obtain these critical values.
- p-*value approach*: We calculate the *p*-value as usual, i.e. if $t_{i,j,\text{cal}} > 0$:

$$p\text{-value} = 2 - 2P\left(T < t_{i,j,\text{cal}}\right) \quad (15.14)$$

And if $t_{i,j,\text{cal}} > 0$ then:

$$p\text{-value} = 2P\left(T < t_{i,j,\text{cal}}\right) \quad (15.15)$$

T is a random variable that follows a t-distribution with $n - k$ degrees of freedom. We reject H_0: $\mu_i = \mu_j$ if *p*-value $< \frac{\alpha}{g}$ (note once again that dividing α by g is the Bonferroni correction). We can obtain these probabilities using Excel's T.DIST function.

Example 15.3 illustrates calculating the critical values and *p*-values of the tests for the different pairs of means.

WORKED EXAMPLES

EXAMPLE 15.3

In Example 15.2, we concluded that the population mean lifetimes of dogs for each of the three different dog food types differed.

We now want to determine which pairs of dog food types produce similar mean lifetimes and which pairs produce significantly different lifetimes.

Once again, assume that all assumptions are satisfied and test these hypotheses with an overall significance level of $\alpha = 0.05$.

The Bonferroni post-hoc tests for the ANOVA test in Example 15.2 are conducted using the five-step hypothesis testing procedure.

Step 1: Provide the hypothesis statements H_0 and H_1

The $g = \frac{k(k-1)}{2} = \frac{3(3-1)}{2} = 3$ tests in this procedure have the following null and alternative hypothesis statements:

$$H_0: \mu_1 = \mu_2 \quad \text{vs} \quad H_1: \mu_1 \neq \mu_2$$
$$H_0: \mu_1 = \mu_3 \quad \text{vs} \quad H_1: \mu_1 \neq \mu_3$$
$$H_0: \mu_2 = \mu_3 \quad \text{vs} \quad H_1: \mu_2 \neq \mu_3$$

We need to test all g = 3 of these hypotheses simultaneously.

Step 2: Choose an appropriate test statistic

Since the null hypothesis was rejected in the main ANOVA *F*-test, we need to conduct this series of post-hoc tests to determine which means differ. There are multiple tests conducted simultaneously on the pairs of means of three populations, therefore we conclude that the Bonferroni multiple comparison *t*-test is the appropriate test in this scenario.

Step 3: Specify the significance level

The overall significance level for all the tests is specified as $\alpha = 0.05$ (or 5%)

Step 4: Calculate the relevant test statistic

We need to calculate a test statistic for each of the $g = 3$ hypothesis statements given above using the test statistic stated in formula (15.13). Fortunately, all of the necessary basic statistics required to calculate these statistics are provided in Example 15.2:

$$MSWithin = 703.4333$$
$$n_1 = n_2 = n_3 = 5$$
$$\overline{X}_1 = 84.8 \qquad \overline{X}_2 = 55.6 \qquad \overline{X}_3 = 107.4$$

The test statistics are:

- For the hypothesis $H_0: \mu_1 = \mu_2$:

$$t_{1,2,\text{cal}} = \frac{\overline{X}_1 - \overline{X}_2}{\sqrt{MSWithin\left(\frac{1}{n_1} + \frac{1}{n_2}\right)}}$$

$$= \frac{84.8 - 55.6}{\sqrt{703.4333\left(\frac{1}{5} + \frac{1}{5}\right)}}$$

$$= 1.7408$$

- For the hypothesis $H_0: \mu_1 = \mu_3$:

$$t_{1,3,\text{cal}} = \frac{\overline{X}_1 - \overline{X}_3}{\sqrt{MSWithin\left(\frac{1}{n_1} + \frac{1}{n_3}\right)}}$$

$$= \frac{84.8 - 107.4}{\sqrt{703.4333\left(\frac{1}{5} + \frac{1}{5}\right)}}$$

$$= -1.3473$$

- For the hypothesis $H_0: \mu_2 = \mu_3$:

$$t_{2,3,\text{cal}} = \frac{\overline{X}_2 - \overline{X}_3}{\sqrt{MSWithin\left(\frac{1}{n_2} + \frac{1}{n_3}\right)}}$$

$$= \frac{55.6 - 107.4}{\sqrt{703.4333\left(\frac{1}{5} + \frac{1}{5}\right)}}$$

$$= -3.0881$$

Step 5: Make a decision

The decision rules for these tests are as follows.

- *Critical value approach*: The Bonferroni corrected critical values for this test are defined as $\pm t_{\frac{\alpha}{2g}, n-k} = \pm t_{\frac{0.05}{2\times 3}, 15-3} = \pm t_{0.0083,12} = \pm 2.78$. Therefore, if the test statistic is greater than 2.78 or less than -2.78, we reject the corresponding null hypothesis.
  - For the hypothesis $H_0: \mu_1 = \mu_2$ $t_{1,2,\text{cal}} = 1.7408$: This value lies between $-t_{0.0083,12} = -2.78$ and $t_{0.0083,12} = 2.78$. We will **not reject H_0** and conclude that μ_1 and μ_2 are not significantly different.
  - For the hypothesis $H_0: \mu_1 = \mu_3$ $t_{1,3,\text{cal}} = -1.3473$: This value lies between $-t_{0.0083,12} = -2.78$ and $t_{0.0083,12} = 2.78$. We will **not reject H_0** and conclude that μ_1 and μ_3 are not significantly different.
  - For the hypothesis $H_0: \mu_2 = \mu_3$ $t_{2,3,\text{cal}} = -3.0081$: This value lies outside the range of $-t_{0.0083,12} = -2.78$ and $t_{0.0083,12} = 2.78$. We **reject H_0** and conclude that μ_2 and μ_3 are significantly different.
- p-*value approach*: The *p*-value for each hypothesis is calculated using either formula (15.14) or formula (15.15), depending on the sign of the test statistic. Each *p*-value is then compared to $\frac{\alpha}{g} = \frac{0.05}{3} = 0.0167$ to determine whether the corresponding null hypothesis should be rejected. We use Excel's T.DIST function to evaluate these probabilities.
  - For the hypothesis $H_0: \mu_1 = \mu_2$: We have a positive test statistic, so we use formula (15.14) to calculate the *p*-value.

$$\begin{aligned} p\text{-value} &= 2 - 2P(T < t_{1,2,\text{cal}}) \\ &= 2 - 2P(T < 1.7408) \\ &= 2 - 2 \times 0.9464 \\ &= 0.1073 \end{aligned}$$

This p-value is larger than $\frac{\alpha}{g} = 0.0167$ and so we **do not reject H_0**, and conclude that μ_1 is not significantly different from μ_2.

- For the hypothesis H_0: $\mu_1 = \mu_3$: We have a negative test statistic, so we use formula (15.15) to calculate the p-value.

$$\begin{aligned} p\text{-value} &= 2P(T < t_{1,3,\text{cal}}) \\ &= 2P(T < -1.3473) \\ &= 2 \times 0.10139 \\ &= 0.2028 \end{aligned}$$

This p-value is larger than $\frac{\alpha}{g} = 0.0167$ and so we **do not reject H_0**, and conclude that μ_1 is not significantly different from μ_3.

- For the hypothesis H_0: $\mu_2 = \mu_3$: We have a negative test statistic, so we use formula (15.15) to calculate the p-value.

$$\begin{aligned} p\text{-value} &= 2P(T < t_{2,3,\text{cal}}) \\ &= 2P(T < -3.0881) \\ &= 2 \times 0.0047 \\ &= 0.0094 \end{aligned}$$

This p-value is smaller than $\frac{\alpha}{g} = 0.0167$ and so we **reject H_0**, and conclude that μ_2 is significantly different from μ_3

Table 15.3 summarises the results from the $g = 3$ tests that were conducted.

Table 15.3: A summary of the Bonferroni corrected tests for all pairs of means

	SIGNIFICANCE	CRITICAL VALUES	$t_{i,j,\text{cal}}$	p-VALUE	DECISION
GROUPS 1 AND 2	$\frac{\alpha}{g} = \frac{0.05}{3} = 0.0167$	±2.78	1.7408	0.1073	Do not reject H_0
GROUPS 1 AND 3			−1.3473	0.2028	Do not reject H_0
GROUPS 2 AND 3			−3.088	0.0094	Reject H_0

Excel solution

The Excel solution for these Bonferroni hypothesis tests is given in Figure 15.8.

	A	B	C	D	E	F
1						
2		Step 1:	**Hypothesis test**			
3			$H_0: \mu_1 = \mu_2$ vs $H_1: \mu_1 \neq \mu_2$			
4			$H_0: \mu_1 = \mu_3$ vs $H_1: \mu_1 \neq \mu_3$			
5			$H_0: \mu_2 = \mu_3$ vs $H_1: \mu_2 \neq \mu_3$			
6						
7		Step 2:	**Choose the appropriate test**			
8			The test involves testing multiple comparisons of pairs of means after the main ANOVA F-test. The			
9			Bonferroni multiple comparison test can be used.			
10						
11		Step 3:	**Select level of significance**			
12				Overall signficance level, α =	0.05	
13				Significance level =	0.016666667	=E12/E17
14						
15		Step 4:	**Calculate test statistic**			
16				k =	3	
17				g =	3	=E16*(E16-1)/2
18				n =	15	
19				$n_1 = n_2 = n_3$ =	5	
20				$\bar{X}_1$ =	84.8	
21				$\bar{X}_2$ =	55.6	
22				$\bar{X}_3$ =	107.4	
23				$MSWithin$ =	704.4333	
24			**Compare**			
25			1 to 2:	$t_{1,2,cal}$ =	1.7408	=(E20-E21)/SQRT($E$23*(1/$E$19+1/$E$19))
26			1 to 3:	$t_{1,3,cal}$ =	-1.3473	=(E20-E22)/SQRT($E$23*(1/$E$19+1/$E$19))
27			2 to 3:	$t_{2,3,cal}$ =	-3.0881	=(E21-E22)/SQRT($E$23*(1/$E$19+1/$E$19))
28						
29			1 to 2:	p-value =	0.1073	=2-2*T.DIST(E25,E18-E16,TRUE)
30			1 to 3:	p-value =	0.2028	=2*T.DIST(E26,E18-E16,TRUE)
31			2 to 3:	p-value =	0.0094	=2*T.DIST(E27,E18-E16,TRUE)
32				Critical value, $t_{\alpha/2,\alpha,12}$ =	2.7794623	=T.INV(1-E13/2,E18-E16)
33						
34						
35		Step 5:	**Make a decision**			
36			We only reject H_0 when comparing group 2 to group 3.			
37			We conclude that only group 2 and 3 are significantly different.			

Figure 15.8: Excel solution to the ANOVA F-test in Example 15.3

EXCEL SOLUTIONS

k: Cell E16	Value
g: Cell E17	Formula: =E16*(E16-1)/2
n: Cell E18	Value
$n_1 = n_2 = n_3$: Cell E19	Value
$\overline{X}_1$: Cell E20	Value
$\overline{X}_2$: Cell E21	Value
$\overline{X}_3$: Cell E22	Value
$MSWithin$: Cell E23	Value
$t_{1,2,\text{cal}}$: Cell E25	Formula: =(E20-E21)/SQRT($E$23*(1/$E$19+1/$E$19))
$t_{1,3,\text{cal}}$: Cell E26	Formula: =(E20-E22)/SQRT($E$23*(1/$E$19+1/$E$19))
$t_{2,3,\text{cal}}$: Cell E27	Formula: =(E21-E22)/SQRT($E$23*(1/$E$19+1/$E$19))
(1-2) p-value: Cell E29	Formula: =2-2*T.DIST(E25,E18-E16,TRUE)
(1-3) p-value: Cell E30	Formula: =2*T.DIST(E26,E18-E16,TRUE)
(2-3) p-value: Cell E31	Formula: =2*T.DIST(E27,E18-E16,TRUE)
Critical value, $t_{\alpha/g,12}$: Cell E32	Formula: =T.INV(1-E13/2,E18-E16)

INTERPRETATION

From the analysis, we can conclude that there is no significant difference between the population mean lifetimes of dogs that eat dog food types 1 and 2, nor is there a significant difference between the population mean lifetimes of dogs that eat dog food types 1 and 3 (i.e. we could not reject the hypotheses H_0: $\mu_1 = \mu_2$ or H_0: $\mu_1 = \mu_3$).

However, it would appear that there is a significant difference between the population mean lifetimes of dogs that eat dog food types 2 and 3 (we rejected the hypothesis H_0: $\mu_2 = \mu_3$).

This result allows us to more precisely follow-up the conclusion made by the ANOVA F-test in Example 15.2, in which we concluded that not all mean lifetimes were equal. We can now conclude that the only pair of mean lifetimes that were not equal was groups 2 and 3; the remaining pairs were not significantly different.

15.2.4 Checking assumptions

In the preceding sections, we conducted the ANOVA F-test and the follow-up Bonferroni multiple comparison post-hoc t-tests. Unfortunately, all these tests are based on the assumptions that the data are drawn from normally distributed populations with equal variances. In this section, we consider some informal methods for testing whether these assumptions are valid or not. Please note that we would typically check these assumptions before actually conducting any of the aforementioned tests, since the correctness of the p-values and critical values relies on these assumptions being satisfied.

Checking for equal variances

There are a number of sophisticated methods for determining if the variances are equal, but we will only consider the following simple rule of thumb that we can use to indicate whether differing variances will actually cause serious problems with the ANOVA F-test.

If the largest sample variance is more than four times greater than the smallest sample variance, this is evidence that the differences in variances will cause problems in the ANOVA F-test.

We define the sample variance within the jth group by:

$$S_j^2 = \frac{1}{n_j - 1}\sum_{i=1}^{n_j}(X_{j,i} - \overline{X}_j)^2 \qquad j = 1, 2, \ldots, k$$

n_j is the sample size of the jth group, $X_{j,i}$ is the ith observation in the jth group, and $\overline{X}_j$ is the sample mean in the jth group.

The largest of these sample variances is denoted:

$$S^2_{\text{max}} = \max(S_1^2, S_2^2, \ldots, S_k^2)$$

The smallest sample variance is denoted:

$$S^2_{\text{min}} = \min(S_1^2, S_2^2, \ldots, S_k^2)$$

RULE OF THUMB FOR DETERMINING THE SEVERITY OF DEVIATIONS FROM THE ASSUMPTION OF HOMOGENOUS VARIANCES

If the ratio of the largest and smallest sample variance is greater than 4, then the concerns associated with non-homogeneous variances are problematic, i.e. there are problems with unequal variances if:

$$\frac{S^2_{\text{max}}}{S^2_{\text{min}}} > 4 \qquad (15.16)$$

Checking for normality

To check for normality, we again use the normal QQ-plot. The steps required to construct the normal QQ-plot are given below.

STEPS FOR CONSTRUCTING A NORMAL QQ-PLOT

- Given data $X_1, X_2, \ldots, X_n$ calculate the ranks of the data denoted $R_1, R_2, \ldots, R_n$ (use Excel's RANK.AVG function to do this)
- Use Excel to calculate the standard normal quantiles associated with the estimated probability $\frac{R_i}{(n+1)}$, i.e. use NORM.S.INV evaluated in the point probability $\frac{R_i}{(n+1)}$. Call the results $Q_1, Q_2, \ldots, Q_n$
- Create a plot of X_i-values against Q_i

However, when constructing this plot to check the assumptions of the ANOVA F-test, we first need to subtract the individual group means from the observations. In other words, instead of using the original data values $X_{j,i}$, we use the following centred observations:

$$e_{j,i} = X_{j,i} - \overline{X}_j \tag{15.17}$$

We then construct the QQ-plot using these new $e_{j,i}$ values. As usual, if the plot forms a straight line, it indicates that the assumption of normality holds.

NOTE

The deviation from normality has to be extremely severe before it has a noticeable impact on the reliability of the p-values and critical values of the ANOVA F-test. Small deviations are permissible.

Example 15.4 uses the data from Examples 15.1, 15.2 and 15.3, and assesses the assumptions of constant variance and normality using these simple checks.

WORKED EXAMPLES

EXAMPLE 15.4

In Examples 15.2 and 15.3, we assumed that the lifetimes of dogs that ate the different dog food types were normally distributed and that the variances in each group were equal. However, this assumption is not automatically true; we need to check these assumptions before starting the analysis.

Check these assumptions to determine if the p-values and critical values calculated in the previous examples are reliable.

We begin by checking if the differing variances will cause a problem in the analysis. The sample variances for each group can be calculated as follows:

$$S_1^2 = \frac{1}{5-1}\sum_{i=1}^{5}(X_{1,i} - \overline{X}_1)^2 = 703.7$$

$$S_2^2 = \frac{1}{5-1}\sum_{i=1}^{5}(X_{2,i} - \overline{X}_2)^2 = 700.3$$

$$S_3^2 = \frac{1}{5-1}\sum_{i=1}^{5}(X_{3,i} - \overline{X}_3)^2 = 706.3$$

The largest and smallest variances are denoted $S^2_{max} = 706.3$ and $S^2_{min} = 700.3$, and the ratio in formula (15.16) is:

$$\frac{S^2_{max}}{S^2_{min}} = \frac{706.3}{700.3} = 1.008568 < 4$$

This indicates that the differing variances are too small to be of any concern.

The QQ-plot, constructed in Excel, requires that we first centre the observations. We can centre the observations in Table 15.1 by using formula (15.17). The means of each group were calculated as $\overline{X}_1 = 84.8$, $\overline{X}_2 = 55.6$ and $\overline{X}_3 = 107.4$, and the centred observations are shown in Table 15.4 below.

Table 15.4: Centred observations for Examples 15.1, 15.2, 15.3 and 15.4

DOG FOOD TYPE 1	DOG FOOD TYPE 2	DOG FOOD TYPE 3
$X_{1,1} - 84.8 = 15.2$	$X_{2,1} - 55.6 = 0.4$	$X_{3,1} - 107.4 = -1.4$
$X_{1,2} - 84.8 = 3.2$	$X_{2,2} - 55.6 = -12.6$	$X_{3,2} - 107.4 = 5.6$
$X_{1,3} - 84.8 = -8.8$	$X_{2,3} - 55.6 = -31.6$	$X_{3,3} - 107.4 = 22.6$
$X_{1,4} - 84.8 = 30.2$	$X_{2,4} - 55.6 = 40.4$	$X_{3,4} - 107.4 = 17.6$
$X_{1,5} - 84.8 = 39.8$	$X_{2,5} - 55.6 = 3.4$	$X_{3,5} - 107.4 = -44.4$

The normal QQ-plot based on these values is shown in Figure 15.9 below.

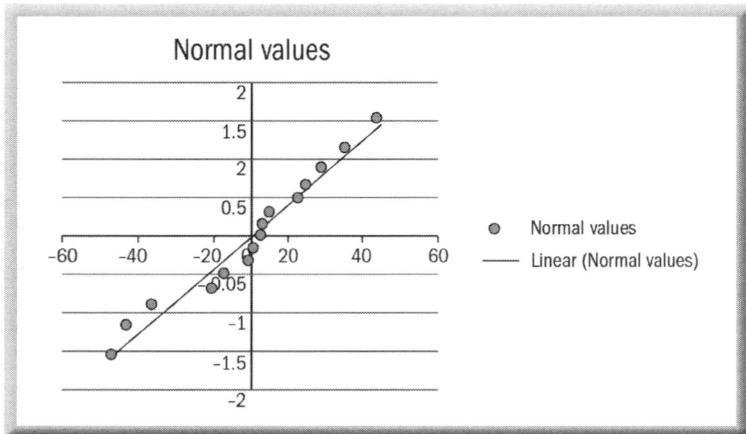

Figure 15.9: QQ-plot of the centred values

The dots in the QQ-plot show a fair amount of deviation from the straight line, from which we could conclude that the data are not from a normal distribution. However, the deviations do not seem so severe that they will have an excessive impact on the inference.

In situations like this where there is doubt concerning the normality of the data, it is usually safest to also apply a non-parametric version of the test to see if the same result is obtained (i.e. we should apply both the ANOVA *F*-test and the Kruskal-Wallis test – to be discussed in the next section – to determine if the population means differ).

Figure 15.10 illustrates the Excel solution.

	A	B	C	D	E	F	G	H
1	**Example 15.4: Checking model assumptions**							
2								
3	Dog food	Lifetime	Centred values		Ranks		Normal values	
4	Type 1	100	15.2	=B4-$C$22	11	=RANK.AVG(C4,$C$4:$C$18,1)	0.4888	=NORM.S.INV(E4/($C$20+1))
5		88	3.2	=B5-$C$22	8	=RANK.AVG(C5,$C$4:$C$18,1)	0	=NORM.S.INV(E5/($C$20+1))
6		76	-8.8	=B6-$C$22	5	=RANK.AVG(C6,$C$4:$C$18,1)	-0.4888	=NORM.S.INV(E6/($C$20+1))
7		115	30.2	=B7-$C$22	14	=RANK.AVG(C7,$C$4:$C$18,1)	1.1503	=NORM.S.INV(E7/($C$20+1))
8		45	-39.8	=B8-$C$22	2	=RANK.AVG(C8,$C$4:$C$18,1)	-1.1503	=NORM.S.INV(E8/($C$20+1))
9	Type 2	56	0.4	=B9-$C$23	7	=RANK.AVG(C9,$C$4:$C$18,1)	-0.1573	=NORM.S.INV(E9/($C$20+1))
10		43	-12.6	=B10-$C$23	4	=RANK.AVG(C10,$C$4:$C$18,1)	-0.6745	=NORM.S.INV(E10/($C$20+1))
11		24	-31.6	=B11-$C$23	3	=RANK.AVG(C11,$C$4:$C$18,1)	-0.8871	=NORM.S.INV(E11/($C$20+1))
12		96	40.4	=B12-$C$23	15	=RANK.AVG(C12,$C$4:$C$18,1)	1.5341	=NORM.S.INV(E12/($C$20+1))
13		59	3.4	=B13-$C$23	9	=RANK.AVG(C13,$C$4:$C$18,1)	0.1573	=NORM.S.INV(E13/($C$20+1))
14	Type 3	106	-1.4	=B14-$C$24	6	=RANK.AVG(C14,$C$4:$C$18,1)	-0.3186	=NORM.S.INV(E14/($C$20+1))
15		113	5.6	=B15-$C$24	10	=RANK.AVG(C15,$C$4:$C$18,1)	0.3186	=NORM.S.INV(E15/($C$20+1))
16		130	22.6	=B16-$C$24	13	=RANK.AVG(C16,$C$4:$C$18,1)	0.8871	=NORM.S.INV(E16/($C$20+1))
17		125	17.6	=B17-$C$24	12	=RANK.AVG(C17,$C$4:$C$18,1)	0.6745	=NORM.S.INV(E17/($C$20+1))
18		63	-44.4	=B18-$C$24	1	=RANK.AVG(C18,$C$4:$C$18,1)	-1.5341	=NORM.S.INV(E18/($C$20+1))
19								
20		$n =$	15	=COUNT(B4:B18)				
21								
22		$\bar{X}_1 =$	84.8	=AVERAGE(B4:B8)				
23		$\bar{X}_2 =$	55.6	=AVERAGE(B9:B13)				
24		$\bar{X}_3 =$	107.4	=AVERAGE(B14:B18)				
25								
26		$S_1^2 =$	703.7	=VAR.S(B4:B8)				
27		$S_2^2 =$	700.3	=VAR.S(B9:B13)				
28		$S_3^2 =$	706.3	=VAR.S(B14:B18)				
29								
30		$S^2_{max} =$	706.3	=MAX(C26:C28)				
31		$S^2_{min} =$	700.3	=MIN(C26:C28)				
32								
33		$S^2_{max}/S^2_{min} =$	1.00857	=C30/C31				
34								

Normal values

-50 -40 -30 -20 -10 0 10 20 30 40 50

2 1.5 1 0.5 0 -0.5 -1 -1.5 -2

Normal values
Linear (Normal values)

Figure 15.10: Excel solution for Example 15.4

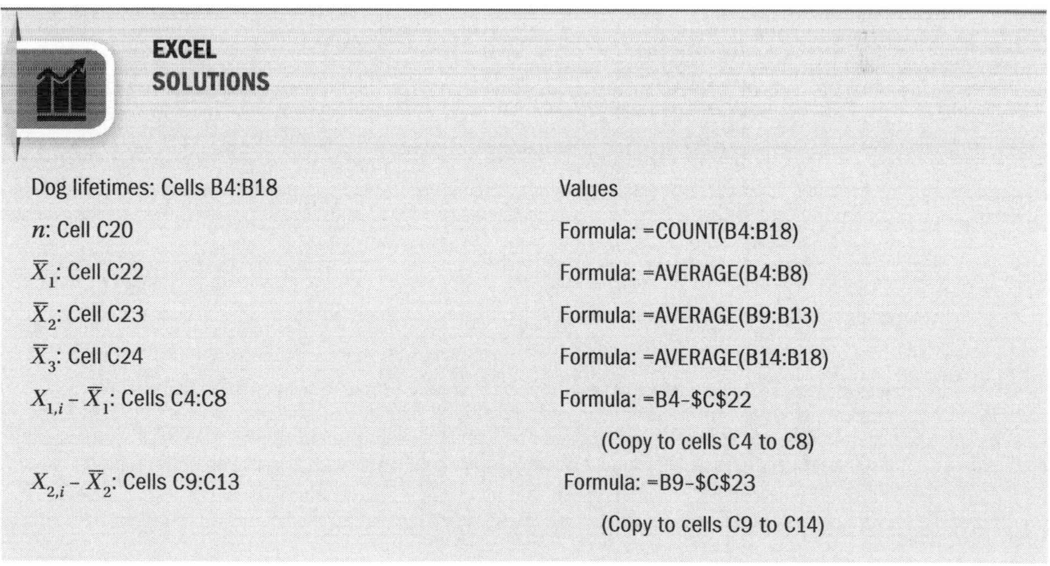

EXCEL SOLUTIONS

Dog lifetimes: Cells B4:B18	Values
n: Cell C20	Formula: =COUNT(B4:B18)
$\bar{X}_1$: Cell C22	Formula: =AVERAGE(B4:B8)
$\bar{X}_2$: Cell C23	Formula: =AVERAGE(B9:B13)
$\bar{X}_3$: Cell C24	Formula: =AVERAGE(B14:B18)
$X_{1,i} - \bar{X}_1$: Cells C4:C8	Formula: =B4-$C$22 (Copy to cells C4 to C8)
$X_{2,i} - \bar{X}_2$: Cells C9:C13	Formula: =B9-$C$23 (Copy to cells C9 to C14)

$X_{3,i} - \overline{X}_3$: Cells C14:C18	Formula: =B14-$C$24 (Copy to cells C14 to C18)
S_1^2: Cell C26	Formula: =VAR.S(B4:B8)
S_2^2: Cell C27	Formula: = VAR.S(B9:B13)
S_3^2: Cell C28	Formula: = VAR.S(B14:B18)
S_{max}^2: Cell C30	Formula: = MAX(C26:C28)
S_{min}^2: Cell C31	Formula: = MIN(C26:C28)
$\frac{S_{max}^2}{S_{min}^2}$: Cell C33	Formula: = C30/C31
Ranks: Cells E4:E18	Formula: =RANK.AVG(C4,$C$4:$C$18,1) (Copy to cells E4 to E18)
Normal values: Cells G4:G18	Formula: =NORM.S.INV(E4/($C$20+1)) (Copy to cells G4 to G18)

INTERPRETATION It appears as though the assumption of constant variance is satisfied, but the assumption of normality is in doubt. This means that the inference in Examples 15.2 and 15.3 (i.e. the p-values and critical values that were calculated) is questionable.

To overcome this problem, we discuss a non-parametric method in the next section that we can use to test equality of multiple population means when model assumptions are not satisfied: the Kruskal-Wallis test.

15.2.5 Steps in testing multiple means using the ANOVA

To summarise, the one-factor ANOVA solution procedure consists of the steps outlined in Table 15.5.

Table 15.5: Steps in testing multiple means using the ANOVA approach

STEP 1	Check the assumption that the variances are the same. Use the rule of thumb given in formula (15.16).
STEP 2	Check the normality assumption. Use a QQ-plot of the centred observations (using formula (15.17) to centre them).
STEP 3	If the assumptions hold, perform a one-way ANOVA. Use the ANOVA table in Table 15.2 and formula (15.12) to test the hypothesis that all k population means are equal, i.e. H_0: $\mu_1 = \mu_2 = \ldots = \mu_k$.
STEP 4	If we reject H_0 in Step 3, conduct a Bonferroni post-hoc test to determine which pairs of means differ. Use formula (15.13) to test all $g = \frac{k(k-1)}{2}$ possible pairs of population means, i.e. hypotheses of the form H_0: $\mu_i = \mu_j$, where $i, j = 1, 2, \ldots, k$.

If the assumptions in Steps 1 and 2 do not hold, then we cannot continue with the traditional ANOVA tests for equal population means. In these cases, a non-parametric alternative to the ANOVA F-test called the Kruskal-Wallis test should be used instead.

15.3 The non-parametric Kruskal-Wallis test

If the data are unsuitable for an ANOVA (i.e. when there is marked heterogeneity of variance, the data are not normally distributed or if the data are measured on an ordinal scale), we should use a non-parametric (distribution-free) test, which requires neither homogeneity of variance nor normality. The **Kruskal-Wallis test** is the non-parametric alternative to the ANOVA test. This test uses the group ranks to assess whether the group median values from k different populations are equal. Formally stated, the null and alternative hypotheses are:

$H_0: \upsilon_1 = \upsilon_2 = \ldots = \upsilon_k$

H_1: not all equal

ν_j denotes the population median from population j.

Kruskal-Wallis test for two medians A non-parametric, rank-based test that compares the medians of three or more independent groups.

To test this hypothesis, we use the ranks of the data rather than the actual data, i.e. instead of using the data $X_{j,i}$ as in the ANOVA test, we use the ranks $R_{j,i}$. We obtain these rank values by pooling all n of the $X_{j,i}$ data values and then ranking them. The value $R_{j,i}$ then represents the rank of the ith observation in the jth group.

The mean rank value in each of the k groups is denoted $\overline{R}_j$ and is calculated as:

$$\overline{R}_j = \frac{1}{n_j}\sum_{i=1}^{n_j} R_{j,i} \tag{15.18}$$

The overall mean rank is denoted $\overline{\overline{R}}$, defined as:

$$\overline{\overline{R}} = \frac{1}{n}\sum_{j=1}^{k}\sum_{i=1}^{n_j} R_{j,i} = \frac{n+1}{2} \tag{15.19}$$

Now, similar to the ANOVA F-test, we calculate the *between sums of squares* and the *total sums of squares* for these rank values to produce the test statistic for comparing the population medians. The *between sums of squares* for the ranks is defined as:

$$SSBetweenRanks = \sum_{j=1}^{k} n_j\left(\overline{R}_j - \overline{\overline{R}}\right)^2 \tag{15.20}$$

The total sums of squares for the ranks is defined as:

$$SSTotalRanks = \sum_{j=1}^{k}\sum_{i=1}^{n_j}\left(R_{j,i} - \overline{\overline{R}}\right)^2 \tag{15.21}$$

The Kruskal-Wallis test statistic is then:

$$H = \frac{(n-1)SSBetweenRanks}{SSTotalRanks} \overset{H_0}{\sim} \chi^2_{k-1} \tag{15.22}$$

Fortunately, when there are no tied ranks in the data set, formula (15.22) simplifies to:

$$H = \frac{12}{n(n+1)}\sum_{j=1}^{k} n_j \overline{R}^2_j - 3(n+1) \overset{H_0}{\sim} \chi^2_{k-1} \tag{15.23}$$

The Kruskal-Wallis test follows a χ^2-distribution with $k - 1$ degrees of freedom. We denote the calculated value of the test statistic H_{cal} and we reject the null hypothesis if $H_{cal} > \chi^2_{\alpha,k-1}$. Alternatively, reject H_0 if the p-value is smaller than α:

$$p\text{-value} = P(X > H_{cal})$$

X is a χ^2 distributed random variable with $k - 1$ degrees of freedom.

Note that even though this Kruskal-Wallis test is considered to be non-parametric or distribution free, there are still some minor assumptions underlying the test:

- The groups are drawn at random from the population.
- The groups are independent of each other.
- The groups have a similar distribution shape and variability.
- The measured variable should be a continuous variable.

If we reject H_0, then it is possible to conduct a post-hoc test on the population medians to determine which medians differ and which are the same. The multiple comparison procedure is very similar to the procedure given for the ANOVA test. It involves simple $g = \frac{k(k+1)}{2}$ pairs of two-population tests conducted using the Mann-Whitney U-test, but with a Bonferroni adjusted significance level α (i.e. we simply divide the α-value by g).

NOTE

Each group size should have at least five data values, although each group can have a different number of data values.

For two samples, the Kruskal-Wallis test is the same as the Mann-Whitney U-test (see Section 8.2.3).

It is tempting to *always* use the Kruskal-Wallis test to compare multiple population location parameters, but if the ANOVA F-test assumptions hold, it is advisable to use the F-test rather than the Kruskal-Wallis test because the F-test provides a more accurate test in that case.

Example 15.5 illustrates how we conduct this test using the same data in Examples 15.1 to 15.4.

WORKED EXAMPLES

EXAMPLE 15.5

In Example 15.4, we were uncertain about the normality of the data, and so we needed to consider the fact that the ANOVA test might not be adequate. We can use the Kruskal-Wallis non-parametric procedure to assess whether the median dog lifetimes are equivalent.

The Kruskal-Wallis test is based on the ranks of the data, which we have calculated and shown in Table 15.6.

Table 15.6: Dog lifetime and rank data for Example 15.5

DOG FOOD TYPE	DOG LIFETIMES	RANKS
1	$X_{1,1} = 100$	$R_{1,1} = 10$
1	$X_{1,2} = 88$	$R_{1,2} = 8$
1	$X_{1,3} = 76$	$R_{1,3} = 7$
1	$X_{1,4} = 115$	$R_{1,4} = 13$
1	$X_{1,5} = 45$	$R_{1,5} = 3$
2	$X_{2,1} = 56$	$R_{2,1} = 4$
2	$X_{2,2} = 43$	$R_{2,2} = 2$
2	$X_{2,3} = 24$	$R_{2,3} = 1$
2	$X_{2,4} = 96$	$R_{2,4} = 9$
2	$X_{2,5} = 59$	$R_{2,5} = 5$
3	$X_{3,1} = 106$	$R_{3,1} = 11$
3	$X_{3,2} = 113$	$R_{3,2} = 12$
3	$X_{3,3} = 130$	$R_{3,3} = 15$
3	$X_{3,4} = 125$	$R_{3,4} = 14$
3	$X_{3,5} = 63$	$R_{3,5} = 6$

Step 1: Provide the hypothesis statements H_0 and H_1

- H_0: $\nu_1 = \nu_2 = \nu_3$, i.e. the population median lifetimes are all equal to one another.
- H_1: Not all equal, i.e. at least one population median is different from the rest.

Step 2: Choose an appropriate test statistic

The following information is provided.

- *The number of populations in the study*: A sample from each of three populations is being considered here.
- *The research question*: The primary question of interest is whether the population median lifetimes of the dogs in the three populations are the same.

- *Assumptions underlying the test*: The data used in this example are continuous. The Kruskal-Wallis test also requires that the data are randomly drawn and that the groups are independent of one another. This appears to have been satisfied by the way in which the data were collected. We also saw in Example 15.4, that the variances in each group are reasonably similar. The assumptions for the Kruskal-Wallis test seem to be satisfied in this case.

Step 3: Specify the significance level

The significance level is specified as $\alpha = 0.05$ (or 5%)

Step 4: Calculate the relevant test statistic

The ranks of the data are provided in Table 15.6, so we only need to calculate the mean rank in each group using formula (15.18): $\overline{R}_1$, $\overline{R}_2$ and $\overline{R}_3$:

$$\begin{aligned}\overline{R}_1 &= \frac{1}{5}\sum_{i=1}^{n_1} R_{1,i} \\ &= \frac{1}{5}(10 + 8 + 7 + 13 + 3) = 8.2 \\ \overline{R}_2 &= \frac{1}{5}\sum_{i=1}^{n_2} R_{2,i} \\ &= \frac{1}{5}(4 + 2 + 1 + 9 + 5) = 4.2\end{aligned}$$

And:

$$\begin{aligned}\overline{R}_3 &= \frac{1}{5}\sum_{i=1}^{n_3} R_{3,i} \\ &= \frac{1}{5}(11 + 12 + 15 + 14 + 6) = 11.6\end{aligned}$$

The overall mean of the ranks is, using formula (15.19):

$$\overline{\overline{R}} = \frac{n+1}{2} = \frac{16}{2} = 8$$

Next, the values of *SSBetweenRanks* and *SSTotalRanks* need to be calculated:

$$\begin{aligned}SSBetweenRanks &= \sum_{j=1}^{3} 5 \times \left(\overline{R}_j - \overline{\overline{R}}\right)^2 \\ &= 5 \times [(8.2 - 8)^2 + (4.2 - 8)^2 + (11.6 - 8)^2] \\ &= 137.2\end{aligned}$$

And:

$$\begin{aligned}SSTotalRanks &= \sum_{j=1}^{3}\sum_{i=1}^{5}\left(\overline{R}_j - \overline{\overline{R}}\right)^2 \\ &= (10 - 8)^2 + (8 - 8)^2 + (7 - 8)^2 + (13 - 8)^2 + (3 - 8)^2 \\ &\quad + (4 - 8)^2 + (2 - 8)^2 + (1 - 8)^2 + (9 - 8)^2 + (5 - 8)^2 \\ &\quad + (11 - 8)^2 + (12 - 8)^2 + (15 - 8)^2 + (14 - 8)^2 + (6 - 8)^2 \\ &= 4 + 0 + 1 + 25 + 25 + 16 + 36 + 49 + 1 + 9 + 9 + 16 + 49 + 36 + 4 \\ &= 280\end{aligned}$$

The calculated value of the Kruskal-Wallis test statistic in formula (15.22) is:

$$H_{cal} = \frac{(n-1)SSBetweenRanks}{SSTotalRanks} = \frac{(15-1)137.2}{280} = 6.86$$

Step 5: Make a decision

We will use both the critical value approach and the p-value approach to make a decision for this test.

- *Critical value approach*: The significance level was chosen to be $\alpha = 0.05$ and the associated critical value is calculated from a χ^2-distribution with $k - 1 = 3 - 1 = 2$ degrees of freedom. The critical value is then:

$$\chi^2_{\alpha,2} = 5.9914645$$

We can obtain these critical values using the CHISQ.INV function in Excel. The test statistic is smaller than the critical value, i.e. $H_{cal} = 6.86 > 5.9914645$, and so **we reject H_0.**

- p-*value approach*: We can use the CHISQ.DIST function in Excel to calculate the p-value. The p-value is:

$$\begin{aligned} p\text{-value} &= P(X > H_{cal}) \\ &= P(X > 6.86) \\ &= 1 - P(X < 6.86) \\ &= 1 - 0.9676 \\ &= 0.0324 \end{aligned}$$

The p-value is smaller than the specified significance level, $\alpha = 0.05$, so **we reject H_0.**

The Excel solution is shown in Figure 15.11.

	A	B	C	D	E	F	G	H
1	Example 15.5: Kruskal-Wallis test							
2								
3	Dog food	Lifetimes	Ranks		$(R_{j,i} - \bar{\bar{R}})^2$			
4	Type 1	100	10	=RANK.AVG(B4,$B$4:$B$18,1)	4	=(C4-$C$23)^2		
5		88	8	=RANK.AVG(B5,$B$4:$B$18,1)	0	=(C5-$C$23)^2		
6		76	7	=RANK.AVG(B6,$B$4:$B$18,1)	1	=(C6-$C$23)^2		
7		115	13	=RANK.AVG(B7,$B$4:$B$18,1)	25	=(C7-$C$23)^2		
8		45	3	=RANK.AVG(B8,$B$4:$B$18,1)	25	=(C8-$C$23)^2		
9	Type 2	56	4	=RANK.AVG(B9,$B$4:$B$18,1)	16	=(C9-$C$23)^2		
10		43	2	=RANK.AVG(B10,$B$4:$B$18,1)	36	=(C10-$C$23)^2		
11		24	1	=RANK.AVG(B11,$B$4:$B$18,1)	49	=(C11-$C$23)^2		
12		96	9	=RANK.AVG(B12,$B$4:$B$18,1)	1	=(C12-$C$23)^2		
13		59	5	=RANK.AVG(B13,$B$4:$B$18,1)	9	=(C13-$C$23)^2		
14	Type 3	106	11	=RANK.AVG(B14,$B$4:$B$18,1)	9	=(C14-$C$23)^2		
15		113	12	=RANK.AVG(B15,$B$4:$B$18,1)	16	=(C15-$C$23)^2		
16		130	15	=RANK.AVG(B16,$B$4:$B$18,1)	49	=(C16-$C$23)^2		
17		125	14	=RANK.AVG(B17,$B$4:$B$18,1)	36	=(C17-$C$23)^2		
18		63	6	=RANK.AVG(B18,$B$4:$B$18,1)	4	=(C18-$C$23)^2		
19								
20		$\bar{R}_1 =$	8.2	=AVERAGE(C4:C8)				
21		$\bar{R}_2 =$	4.2	=AVERAGE(C9:C13)				
22		$\bar{R}_3 =$	11.6	=AVERAGE(C13:C18)				
23		$\bar{\bar{R}}_3 =$	8	=AVERAGE(C4:C18)	=(C24+1)/2			
24		$n =$	15	=COUNT(C4:C18)				
25		$n_1 = n_2 = n_3 =$	5	=COUNT(B4:B8)				
26								

	I	J	K	L	M
1					
2		Hypothesis test			
3	Step 1:	$H_0: \upsilon_1 = \upsilon_2 = \upsilon_3$			
4		H_1: not all equal			
5					
6		Choose the appropriate test			
7	Step 2:	The test involves testing multiple population medians; use the Kruskal-Wallis. The data are continuous, randomly drawn, and appear to have similar variability.			
8					
9					
10	Step 3:	Select level of significance			
11			Signficance level, $\alpha =$	0.05	
12					
13		Calculate test statistic			
14			$k =$	3	
15			$n =$	15	=COUNT(C4:C18)
16			$SSBetweenRanks =$	137.2	=C25*(C20-C23)^2+C25*(C21-C23)^2+C25(C22-C23)^2
17			$SSTotalRanks =$	280	=SUM(E4:E18)
18	Step 4:				
19					
20			$H_{cal} =$	6.86	=(L15-1)*L16/L17
21			Critical value, $\chi^2_{,\alpha,2} =$	5.991645	=CHISQ.INV(1-L11,L14-1)
22			p-value =	0.0323869	=1-CHISQ.DIST(L20,L14-1,TRUE)
23					
24		Make a decision			
25	Step 5:	Since $p < \alpha$ we therefore reject H_0			
26		The population medians are not all equal.			

Figure 15.11: Excel solution for Example 15.5

EXCEL SOLUTIONS

Dog lifetimes: Cells B4:B18	Values
Ranks: Cells C4:C18	Formula: =RANK.AVG(B4,$B$4:$B$18,1)
	(Copy this formula to C4 to C18)
$(R_{j,i} = \bar{\bar{R}})^2$: Cells E4:E18	Formula: =(C4-$C$23)^2
	(Copy this formula to E4 to E18)
R_1: Cell C20	Formula: =AVERAGE(C4:C8)
$\bar{R}_2$: Cell C21	Formula: =AVERAGE(C9:C13)
$\bar{R}_3$: Cell C22	Formula: =AVERAGE(C14:C18)
$\bar{\bar{R}}$: Cell C23	Formula: =AVERAGE(C4:C18)
n: Cell C24	Formula: =COUNT(C4:C18)
$n_1 = n_2 = n_3$: Cell C25	Formula: =COUNT(C4:C8)
Significance level: Cell L11	Value
k: Cell L14	Value
n: Cell L15	Formula: =COUNT(C4:C18)
SSBetweenRanks: Cell L16	Formula: =C25*(C20-C23)^2+C25*(C21-C23)^2+C25*(C22-C23)^2
SSTotalRanks: Cell L17	Formula: =SUM(E4:E18)
H_{cal}: Cell L20	Formula: =(L15-1)*L16/L17
Critical value: Cell L22	Formula: =CHISQ.INV(1-L11,L14-1)
p-value: Cell L23	Formula: =1-CHISQ.DIST(L20,L14-1,TRUE)

INTERPRETATION The conclusion from the Kruskal-Wallis test is that the population median lifetimes of the dogs are not all equal. This agrees with the conclusion from the plain ANOVA F-test.

SUMMARY

In this chapter, we looked at the ANOVA or analysis of variance test, which is a test based on the analysis of the variation between the sample means in the data and the variation of the data within each group. We can use this test to reach conclusions about the equality of population means from multiple independent populations. However, this test relies on a number of restrictive assumptions, which are not always satisfied, and so we also discussed the Kruskal-Wallis test, which is a non-parametric alternative to the ANOVA F-test.

KEY TERMS

Analysis of variance (ANOVA)
Between group degrees of freedom
Between group sums of squares
Bonferroni *t*-test
Degrees of freedom
F-distribution
F-statistic (F_{cal})
Homogeneity of variance
Kruskal-Wallis test for two medians
Mean square
Model assumption
Multiple comparisons
Normality
One-factor ANOVA
Overall mean
QQ plot
Sample mean
Sample size
Tied ranks
Total degrees of freedom
Total sum of squares
Treatment
Within (error) groups sum of squares

FORMULA SUMMARY

$$\bar{X}_j = \frac{1}{n_j}\sum_{i=1}^{n_j} X_{j,i} \quad (15.1)$$

$$\bar{\bar{X}} = \frac{1}{n}\sum_{j=1}^{k}\sum_{i=1}^{n_j} X_{j,i} = \frac{1}{n}\sum_{j=1}^{k} n_j \bar{X}_j \quad (15.2)$$

$$SSBetween = \sum_{j=1}^{k} n_j\left(\bar{X}_j - \bar{\bar{X}}\right)^2 \quad (15.3)$$

$$SSWithin = \sum_{j=1}^{k}\sum_{i=1}^{n_j}\left(X_{ij} - \bar{X}_j\right)^2 \quad (15.4)$$

$$SSTotal = \sum_{j=1}^{k}\sum_{i=1}^{n_j} n_j\left(X_{ij} - \bar{\bar{X}}\right)^2 \quad (15.5)$$

$$df_{\text{Total}} = n - 1 \quad (15.6)$$

$$df_{\text{Between}} = k - 1 \quad (15.7)$$

$$df_{\text{Within}} = n - k \tag{15.8}$$

$$\text{Mean total sums of squares} = MSTotal = \frac{SSTotal}{df_{\text{Total}}} = \frac{SSTotal}{n-1} \tag{15.9}$$

$$\text{Mean between sums of squares} = MSBetween = \frac{SSBetween}{df_{\text{Between}}} = \frac{SSBetween}{k-1} \tag{15.10}$$

$$\text{Mean within sums of squares} = MSWithin = \frac{SSWithin}{df_{\text{Within}}} = \frac{SSWithin}{n-k} \tag{15.11}$$

$$F = \frac{\text{variance between groups}}{\text{variance within groups}} = \frac{MSBetween}{MSWithin} \overset{H_0}{\sim} F_{df_{\text{Between}}, df_{\text{Within}}} \tag{15.12}$$

$$T_{i,j} = \frac{\overline{X}_i - \overline{X}_j}{\sqrt{MSWithin\left(\frac{1}{n_i} + \frac{1}{n_j}\right)}} \overset{H_0}{\sim} t_{n-k} \tag{15.13}$$

$$p\text{-value} = 2 - 2P\left(T < t_{i,j,\text{cal}}\right) \tag{15.14}$$

$$p\text{-value} = 2P\left(T < t_{i,j,\text{cal}}\right) \tag{15.15}$$

$$\frac{S^2_{\max}}{S^2_{\min}} > 4 \tag{15.16}$$

$$e_{j,i} = X_{j,i} - \overline{X}_j \tag{15.17}$$

$$\overline{R}_j = \frac{1}{n_j}\sum_{i=1}^{n_j} R_{j,i} \tag{15.18}$$

$$\overline{\overline{R}} = \frac{1}{n}\sum_{j=1}^{k}\sum_{i=1}^{n_j} R_{j,i} = \frac{n+1}{2} \tag{15.19}$$

$$SSBetweenRanks = \sum_{j=1}^{k} n_j \left(\bar{R}_j - \bar{\bar{R}}\right)^2 \quad (15.20)$$

$$SSTotalRanks = \sum_{j=1}^{k} \sum_{i=1}^{n_j} \left(R_{j,i} - \bar{\bar{R}}\right)^2 \quad (15.21)$$

$$H = \frac{(n-1)SSBetweenRanks}{SSTotalRanks} \overset{H_0}{\sim} \chi^2_{k-1} \quad (15.22)$$

$$H = \frac{12}{n(n+1)} \sum_{j=1}^{k} n_j \bar{R}^2_j - 3(n+1) \overset{H_0}{\sim} \chi^2_{k-1} \quad (15.23)$$

EXERCISES

15.1 A manufacturing firm conducts a quality assurance test on five machines that are used to manufacture pins with a design pin diameter of 0.125 + 0.005 cm. Five randomly selected pins from each machine are measured and the results are displayed in Table 15.7.

Table 15.7: Pin diameters from five machines

MANUFACTURING MACHINE				
A	**B**	**C**	**D**	**E**
0.125	0.118	0.123	0.126	0.118
0.127	0.122	0.125	0.128	0.129
0.125	0.120	0.125	0.126	0.127
0.126	0.124	0.124	0.127	0.120
0.128	0.119	0.126	0.129	0.121

a) Describe the one-way analysis of variance and list the model assumptions.
b) Check that the model assumptions are not violated.
c) Based on the sample data collected, can we assume that the machines are producing pins with the same diameter?
d) If the test results suggest a difference, can we say where the difference between pairs is significant?

15.2 A university department is reviewing the delivery methods it uses to teach and assess a range of subject modules. The university department decides to undertake a series of controlled tests to assess the suitability of a particular method of delivery before implementing the new method across all subject modules. To test the hypothesis that the proposed method improves performance, the department randomly placed four students into three different groups, in which each student will experience one method of delivery only, and all sessions are taught by the same lecturer to reduce lecturer bias. The data are shown in Table 15.8.

Table 15.8: Marks of four students under different delivery methods of subject modules

STUDENT	LECTURE + SEMINAR	WORKSHOP	WORKSHOP AND VIRTUAL LEARNING ENVIRONMENT
1	16	19	24
2	21	20	21
3	18	21	22
4	13	20	25

a) Describe the one-way analysis of variance and list the model assumptions.
b) Check that the model assumptions are not violated.
c) Based on the sample data collected, can we assume that the three methods have the same average mark?
d) If the test results suggest a difference, can we say where the difference between pairs is significant?

15.3 A car magazine decides to test whether the average distance travelled per litre between three four-wheel-drive cars are the same

Table 15.9: Average distance travelled per litre of three different four-wheel drive cars

CAR A	CAR B	CAR C
15.2	14.8	15.1
15.4	14.4	14.3
14.8	14.3	14.6
14.4	14.1	13.9
14.7	14.4	14.6

a) Describe the one-way analysis of variance and list the model assumptions.
b) Check that the model assumptions are not violated.
c) Based on the sample data collected, can we assume that the cars have the same average miles per gallon?
d) If the test results suggest a difference, can we say where the difference between pairs is significant?

15.4 In Question 15.1, you used a one-factor analysis of variance to test the null hypothesis that the machines produce pins with the same pin diameter. Describe the analysis of variance assumptions that list the assumptions that we could test statistically. If the assumptions are violated, which non-parametric test could we use to confirm that the pin diameters are the same? Conduct the appropriate non-parametric test to test this null hypothesis.

15.5 A local airport authority is concerned at the service provided to customers by one of the airlines that uses the airport. The airport authority decides to randomly select nine individuals to assess the three airlines who currently use the airport. The individuals rate only one airline.

Table 15.10: Ranks of the three airlines that use the airport

AIRLINE A	4	3	3	3	4	4	3	4	3
AIRLINE B	2	3	3	3	4	4	3	4	3
AIRLINE C	2	3	3	3	3	1	3	2	2

a) Describe why the one-way analysis of variance is not appropriate to this data set.
b) List the model assumptions.
c) Based on the sample data collected, can we assume that the airlines are rated the same?

15.6 In Question 15.3, we assumed that the one-factor assumptions were not violated. Describe and conduct an appropriate non-parametric test to test whether the cars have the same average miles per gallon.

15.7 A car manufacturing company has three factories and each factory makes a range of car models. Car mileage varies from factory to factory due to a number of differences in the production methods. The company has decided to test this hypothesis by asking six test drivers to drive the same model car produced by the three factories. The mileage data are shown in Table 15.11. Is there a difference in the mean car mileage?

Table 15.11: Car mileage of the same car model produced at three different factories

	FACTORY		
DRIVER	**A**	**B**	**C**
1	33.3	34.5	37.4
2	33.4	34.8	36.8
3	32.9	33.8	37.6
4	32.6	33.4	36.6
5	32.5	33.7	37.0
6	33.0	33.9	36.7

15.8 A regional bus company is expanding the number of routes from the city district to the financial centre of a major city in the Western Cape. The bus company has conducted several time tests to determine which route to use from four possible routes to the city centre. To eliminate the effect of the driver, each driver was timed on how long it took to drive each route. Is there a difference in the mean travel time?

Table 15.12: Route travel time of four different routes by five different drivers

	ROUTE TRAVEL TIME (MINUTES)			
DRIVER	**1**	**2**	**3**	**4**
1	18	17	21	22
2	16	23	23	22
3	21	21	26	22
4	23	22	29	25
5	25	24	28	25

TECHNIQUES IN PRACTICE

15.9 AfriSoft is concerned about the time taken to react to customer complaints and has implemented a new set of procedures for its support centre staff. The customer service director has received a series of reports that directly links the complaints to one particular member of the support centre. To be fair, the customer service director has requested that all support staff (A, B, C, D, E and F) are monitored and the time to respond for the first seven customer complaints is recorded in Table 15.13.

Table 15.13: Time taken to respond to the first seven customer complaints (days)

TIME TO RESPOND TO CUSTOMER COMPLAINTS (DAYS)					
A	**B**	**C**	**D**	**E**	**F**
20	33	33	29	24	30
40	33	20	39	32	37
32	50	36	31	38	29
15	33	27	29	43	33
31	35	19	39	22	21
28	22	26	42	30	17
32	34	39	39	32	38

a) Is the homogeneity of variance violated?
b) Is the mean time to respond the same?

c) If the result is significant, describe a suitable multiple comparison test.
d) Describe the non-parametric test you would apply if the assumptions were violated. Conduct the non-parametric test and comment on the results.

15.10 Bakers Ltd is currently reviewing the delivery vans used to deliver products to customers. The company decides to review three possible new routes to a new superstore situated on the outskirts of the city. To remove driver variability, each driver tests the same delivery van on each route and the time to complete the route is recorded in Table 15.14.

Table 15.14: Time taken to drive three possible new routes

	TIME (MINUTES)		
DRIVER	**A**	**B**	**C**
1	17.7	15.8	115.5
2	18.7	20.1	22.4
3	26.5	24.5	24.5
4	26.6	28.0	215.3
5	115.6	25.5	23.4
6	22.4	28.1	26.6
7	20.3	22.4	23.1

a) Is the homogeneity of variance violated?
b) Is the mean route tlme the same?
c) If the result is significant, describe a suitable multiple comparison test.
d) Describe the non-parametric test you would apply if the assumptions were violated. Conduct the non-parametric test and comment on the results.

APPENDIX A:

MATHEMATICAL REVISION

The aim of this chapter is to provide you with a set of tools which can be used to study the topics in this book and will be useful to you throughout your studies.

A.1 Basic mathematical operators and functions

A.1.1 A number raised to a power

When we say that a "number is raised to the power k" then what we mean is that the number is multiplied by itself k times. The notation for "powers" is to put the number of times it is to be multiplied by itself as a superscript to the number, for example, "the number x to the power k" would be written as x^k. The interpretation is

$$x^k = \underbrace{x \times x \times \ldots \times x}_{k\text{ times}}.$$

NOTE

In the expression x^k

- The term x is called the "base" and
- The term k is called the "exponent" or "power".

The simplest method to calculate numbers raised to a power is to multiply the base of the expression with itself as many times as is indicated in the exponent. The following example illustrates how these calculations are performed.

WORKED EXAMPLES

EXAMPLE A.1

a) For example, the number 3^2 is said 'three to the power two' or 'three squared' and means

$$3^2 = 3 \times 3 = 9$$

b) The number 2^3 is said 'two to the power three' or 'two cubed' and means

$$2^3 = 2 \times 2 \times 2 = 8$$

c) The number 16^4 is said 'sixteen to the power four' and means

$$16^4 = 16 \times 16 \times 16 \times 16 = 65\ 536$$

We could use the method described earlier to calculate 2^3 (i.e. multiplying out the power by hand) or we could use the Excel operator "^"or the Excel function POWER to undertake the calculation.

WORKED EXAMPLES

EXAMPLE A.2

We will use the Excel operator "^" and the Excel function POWER to calculate all three powers mentioned in Example A.1. These calculations are shown in Figure A.1.

	A	B	C
1	**"Three to the power two" 3²**		
2	Value =	3	
3	3² =	9	=B2^2
4	3² =	9	=POWER(B2,2)
5	**"Two to the power three" 2³**		
6	Value =	2	
7	2³ =	8	=B6^3
8	2³ =	8	=POWER(B6,3)
9	**"Sixteen to the power four" 16⁴**		
10	Value =	16	
11	16⁴ =	65536	=B10^4
12	16⁴ =	65536	=POWER(B10,4)

Figure A.1: Excel calculation of powers

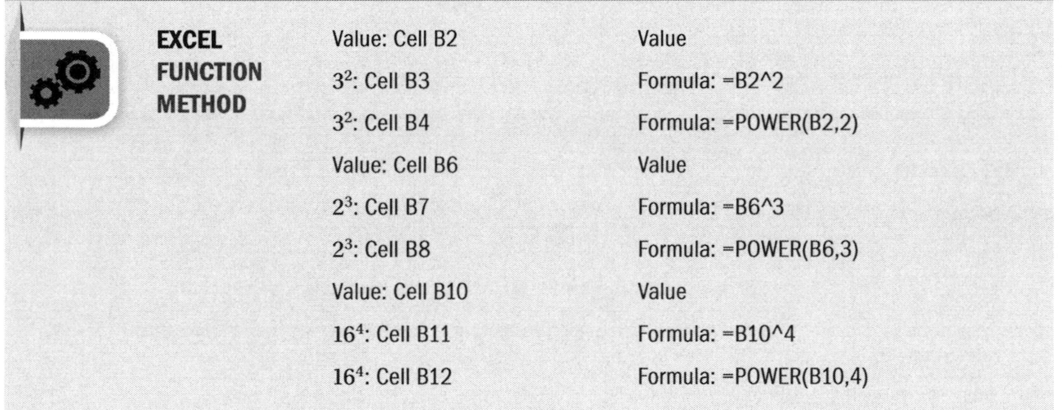

EXCEL FUNCTION METHOD

Value: Cell B2	Value
3^2: Cell B3	Formula: =B2^2
3^2: Cell B4	Formula: =POWER(B2,2)
Value: Cell B6	Value
2^3: Cell B7	Formula: =B6^3
2^3: Cell B8	Formula: =POWER(B6,3)
Value: Cell B10	Value
16^4: Cell B11	Formula: =B10^4
16^4: Cell B12	Formula: =POWER(B10,4)

A.1.2 Square roots

The sign $\sqrt{\ }$ means 'the square root of,' and you must find a number which when multiplied by itself gives the answer in the sign.

NOTE

Raising a number to the power $\frac{1}{2}$ is equivalent of calculating the square root of a number, i.e.

$$\sqrt{x} = x^{\frac{1}{2}}$$

WORKED EXAMPLES

EXAMPLE A.3

The square root of the number 16 is that number, when multiplied by itself, will result in 16. In this case, the square root of 16 is 4 because

$$4^2 = 4 \times 4 = 16$$

and so:

$$\sqrt{16} = \sqrt{4 \times 4} = 4$$

We can also write the square root in terms of a number raised to the power $\frac{1}{2}$:

$$\sqrt{16} = 16^{\frac{1}{2}} = 4$$

The square root of the number 0.25 is equal to the square root of the number $\frac{25}{100}$ which in turn is equal to the square root of the number 25 divided by the square root of the number 100. We can determine the square roots of 25 and 100 as follows:

$$\sqrt{25} = \sqrt{5 \times 5} = 5$$

and a

$$\sqrt{100} = \sqrt{10 \times 10} = 10$$

The result is that the square root of 0.25 is:

$$\sqrt{0.25} = \sqrt{\frac{25}{100}} = \frac{\sqrt{25}}{\sqrt{100}} = \frac{5}{10} = 0.5$$

Expressed as a power we have:

$$\sqrt{0.25} = 0.25^{\frac{1}{2}} = 0.5$$

The Excel function SQRT can be used to calculate the square root of a number.

WORKED EXAMPLES

EXAMPLE A.4

We can use Excel to calculate the square roots of 16 and 0.25 as was shown in Example 2.3. The results are shown in Figure A.2.

	A	B	C
1	**"Square root of 16" $\sqrt{16}$**		
2	Value =	16	
3	$\sqrt{16}$ =	4	=SQRT(B2)
4	$\sqrt{16}$ =	4	=B2^(1/2)
5	**"Square root of 25" $\sqrt{25}$**		
6	Value =	25	
7	$\sqrt{25}$ =	5	=SQRT(B6)
8	$\sqrt{25}$ =	5	=B6^(1/2)
9	**"Square root of 100" $\sqrt{100}$**		
10	Value =	100	
11	$\sqrt{100}$ =	10	=SQRT(B10)
12	$\sqrt{100}$ =	10	=B10^(1/2)
13	**"Square root of 0.25" $\sqrt{0.25}$**		
14	Value =	0.25	
15	$\sqrt{0.25}$ =	0.5	=SQRT(B14)
16	$\sqrt{0.25}$ =	0.5	=B14^(1/2)
17	$\sqrt{0.25}$ =	0.5	=B7/B11

Figure A.2: Excel calculation of square roots

EXCEL FUNCTION METHOD

Value: Cell B2	Value
$\sqrt{16}$: Cell B3	Formula: =SQRT(B2)
$\sqrt{16}$: Cell B4	Formula: =B2^(1/2)
Value: Cell B6	Value
$\sqrt{25}$: Cell B7	Formula: =SQRT(B6)
$\sqrt{25}$: Cell B8	Formula: =B6^(1/2)
Value: Cell B10	Value
$\sqrt{100}$: Cell B11	Formula: =SQRT(B10)
$\sqrt{100}$: Cell B12	Formula: =B10^(1/2)
Value: Cell B14	Value
$\sqrt{0.25}$: Cell B15	Formula: =SQRT(B15)
$\sqrt{0.25}$: Cell B16	Formula: =B15^(1/2)
$\sqrt{0.25}$: Cell B17	Formula: =B7/B11

A.1.3 Mathematical constants (π and e)

The mathematical constant π is defined to be (roughly)

$$\pi \approx 3.14159265358979$$

The number is considered to be an irrational number because it cannot be written using a finite number of decimals or by using a repeating sequence of decimals.

The definition of π is simply the number of times that the diameter of a circle fits into the circumference of the circle.

The value of π can be obtained using the Excel function PI.

The mathematical constant, called "Euler's number", is defined to be (roughly)

$$e \approx 2.71828182845905$$

Like π, e is also an irrational number. This number appears in many mathematical, statistical and financial calculations. It also forms the base of the natural logarithm (see Section A.1.4)

The Excel function EXP is used to obtain this number. This function accepts a single argument (the power to which to raise the number e). For example, we would type EXP(2) to calculate e^2 or EXP(4) To calculate e^4.

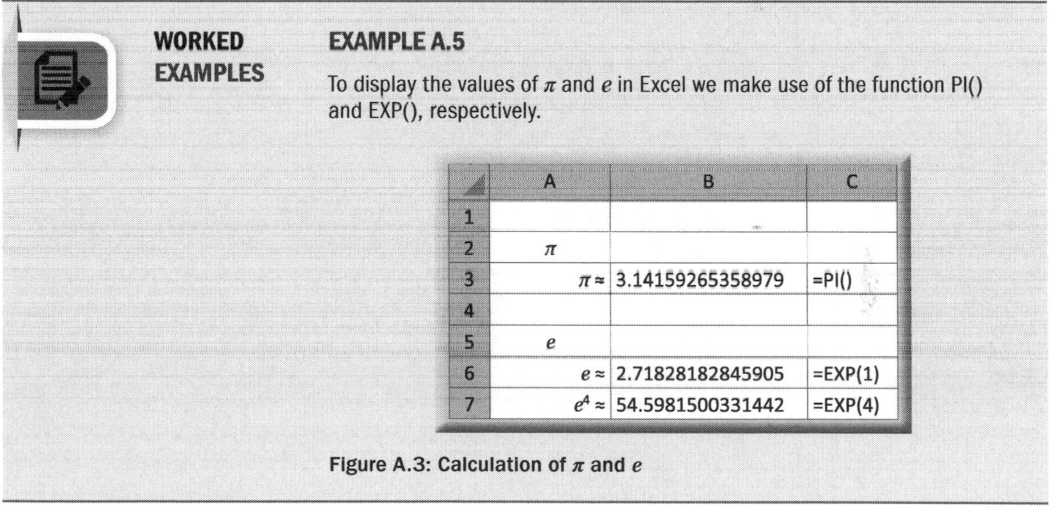

WORKED EXAMPLES

EXAMPLE A.5

To display the values of π and e in Excel we make use of the function PI() and EXP(), respectively.

	A	B	C
1			
2	π		
3	$\pi \approx$	3.14159265358979	=PI()
4			
5	e		
6	$e \approx$	2.71828182845905	=EXP(1)
7	$e^4 \approx$	54.5981500331442	=EXP(4)

Figure A.3: Calculation of π and e

EXCEL FUNCTION METHOD

π: Cell B3	Formula: =PI()
e: Cell B6	Formula: =EXP(1)
e^4: Cell B7	Formula: =EXP(4)

A.1.4 Logarithms and natural logarithms

Logarithms are functions that can answer questions like:

If $10^x = 1\ 000$, *what is the value of* x?

In this question, the base 10 is raised to some unknown power, x, but the result is known to be 1 000. The logarithm (or log) simply takes the known quantities in this expression, places them all on one side of the equation, and places the unknown part on the other side. For this question, therefore, we have:

$$\log_{10} 1\ 000 = x$$

This expression is then the formal way to provide an answer to the question posed above. In this case, the answer is $\log_{10} 1\ 000 = 3$ because $10^3 = 1\ 000$.

The general form of a log is:

$$\log_b y = x$$

which, written as a power, would be

$$b^x = y$$

Note that the base, b, is the same in both the power and log expression. Different choices of b will naturally lead to different answers, but the most commonly used bases are:

- $b = 2$,
- $b = 10$, and
- $b = e$ (Euler's number).

When e is used as the base of the log then we call the log a natural logarithm and denote it by either ln or log (without indicating the base).

NOTE Some basic rules for using logarithms are:

- The log of 1 is always 0 (no matter what the base is):

$$\log_b(1) = 0$$

- The log of y with base x can be written as the ratio of the log of y and the log of x with a common base a:

$$\log_x(y) = \frac{\log_a(y)}{\log_b(x)}$$

- The log of $\frac{1}{x}$ is equal to negative log of x:

$$\log\left(\frac{1}{x}\right) = -\log(x)$$

- The log of a product is equal to the sum of logs of the items forming the product:

$$\log_b(x \times y) = \log_b(x) + \log_b(y)$$

- The log of a quotient is equal to the difference between the log of the numerator and the log of the denominator:

$$\log_b\left(\frac{x}{y}\right) = \log_b(x) - \log_b(y)$$

- The log of x raised to the power k is equal to the k times the log of x:

$$\log(x^k) = k \log(x).$$

The following Excel functions are used to calculate various types of logs:

- LOG: This function is used when you want to specify a particular base.
- LOG10: This function is used when the base is equal to 10.
- LN: This function is used when the base is equal to e.

The next example illustrates how these logs can be calculated using Excel's built-in functions.

WORKED EXAMPLES

EXAMPLE A.6

The calculation of logarithms. The Excel solutions are shown in Figure A.4.

a) The log with base 3 of the number 81 is the number x that satisfies $3^x = 81$,

$$\log_3(81) = 4$$

This is because $3^4 = 81$. We will use the Excel function LOG for this calculation.

b) The log (with base 10) of the number 100 is the number x that satisfies the expression $10^x = 100$. In this case we would have $x = 2$. Written as a log this expression is:

$$\log_{10}(100) = 2$$

We will use the Excel function LOG10 for this calculation.

c) The log expression $\log_8(1\ 024)$ can be written as the ratio:

$$\log_8(1\ 024) = \frac{\log_2(1\ 024)}{\log_2(8)} = \frac{10}{3} = 3.3333$$

because $\log_2(1\ 024) = 10$ and $\log_2(8) = 3$

d) The natural log (i.e. a log with base e) of the number 40 is the number x that satisfies the expression $e^x = 40$. We can then calculate it as:

$$\ln(40) = 3.688879454$$

In other words, $e^{3.688879454} = 40$. The Excel function LN will be used here.

	A	B	C
1	**a) The log (base 3) of 81.**		
2	Value =	81	
3	Base =	3	
4	$\log_2(81)$ =	4	=LOG(B2,B3)
5	**b) The log (base 10) of 100.**		
6	Value =	100	
7	Base =	10	
8	$\log_{10}(100)$ =	**2**	=LOG10(B6)
9	$\log_{10}(100)$ =	**2**	=LOG(B6,B7)
10	**c) The log (base 8) of 1024.**		
11	Value =	1024	
12	Base =	2	
13	$\log_2(1024)$ =	10	=LOG(B11,B12)
14	Value =	8	
15	Base =	2	
16	$\log_2(8)$ =	3	=LOG(B14,B15)
17	$\frac{\log_2(1024)}{\log_2(8)}$ =	3.33333333333333	=B13/B16
18			
19	Value =	1024	
20	Base =	8	
21	$\log_8(1024)$ =	3.33333333333333	=LOG(B19,B20)
22	**d) The log (base e) of 40.**		
23	Value =	40	
24	Base =	e	
25	ln(40) =	3.68887945411394	=LN(B23)

Figure A.4: Calculation of logs in Example A.6

EXCEL FUNCTION METHOD

Value: Cell B2	Value
Base: Cell B3	Value
$\log_3(81)$: Cell B4	Formula: =LOG(B2,B3)
Value: Cell B11	Value
Base: Cell B12	Value
$\log_2(1\,024)$: Cell B13	Formula: =LOG(B11,B12)
Value: Cell B14	Value
Base: Cell B15	Value
$\log_2(8)$: Cell B16	Formula: =LOG(B14,B15)
$\frac{\log_2(1\,024)}{\log_2(8)}$: Cell B17	Formula: =B13/B16
Value: Cell B19	Value
Base: Cell B20	Value
log8(1 024): Cell B21	Formula: =LOG(B19,B20)
Value: Cell B23	Value
Base: Cell B24	Value
ln(40): Cell B25	Formula: =LN(B23)

A.1.5 Sum notation

The sum of the n numbers $x_1 + x_2 + x_3 + \ldots + x_n$ can be expressed using "sum" notation as follows:

$$\sum_{i=1}^{n} x_i$$

This notation makes use of the symbol Σ which is simply the Greek symbol for an uppercase S; it stands for "Sum".

In the expression above, an index i is used as a placeholder for the numbers 1, 2, ..., n. The starting value of this index is always displayed below the Σ and the ending value above the Σ. The index value in the expression on the right of the Σ is then replaced with all of these possible index values and then added together.

Note: The index symbol is typically chosen to be a lowercase letter like i, j or k.

Consider the following examples:

1) The sum 8 + 9 + 10 + 11 + 12 = 50 can be written, using sum notation as

$$\sum_{j=8}^{12} j$$

In this example the index j starts at 8 (written below the Σ as $j = 8$) and ends at 12 (written above the Σ). The j-values then take on the integer values between 8 and 12, i.e. $j = 8, 9, 10, 11, 12$. The index values to the right of the Σ are then replaced with the numbers 8, 9, 10, 11, and 12, and then the terms are added together. In this case the expression to the right of Σ is just j so we simply sum the index values:

$$\sum_{j=8}^{12} j = \underbrace{8}_{j=8} + \underbrace{9}_{j=9} + \underbrace{10}_{j=10} + \underbrace{11}_{j=11} + \underbrace{12}_{j=12} = 50$$

2) Consider the following sum:

$$\sum_{k=1}^{4} 5^k + k$$

This sum can be calculated by first noting that the index k ranges from 1 up to 4, i.e. $k = 1, 2, 3, 4$. If we replace the k index that appears in the expression to the right of Σ with each of these possible index values, we get:

$k = 1$:	$5^1 + 1 = 6$
$k = 2$:	$5^2 + 2 = 27$
$k = 3$:	$5^3 + 3 = 128$
$k = 4$:	$5^4 + 4 = 629$

Finally, adding them up, the result is:

$$\sum_{k=1}^{4} 5^k + k = \underbrace{6}_{k=1} + \underbrace{27}_{k=2} + \underbrace{128}_{k=3} + \underbrace{629}_{k=4} = 790$$

3) Suppose now that we define the variables y_1, y_2, y_3, y_4, and y_5 as follows:

$y_1 = 157$
$y_2 = 201$
$y_3 = 759$
$y_4 = 254$
$y_5 = 110$

If we want to use the sum notation to sum these values together we only need to define an index, say i, that runs from 1 to 5, ($i = 1, 2, 3, 4, 5$) and then sum the general expression y_i over all possible values of i. The notation then becomes:

$$\sum_{i=1}^{5} y_i = \underbrace{y_1}_{i=1} + \underbrace{y_2}_{i=2} + \underbrace{y_3}_{i=3} + \underbrace{y_4}_{i=4} + \underbrace{y_5}_{i=5}$$
$$= \underbrace{157}_{i=1} + \underbrace{201}_{i=2} + \underbrace{759}_{i=3} + \underbrace{254}_{i=4} + \underbrace{110}_{i=5}$$
$$= 1\,481$$

The Excel function SUM can be used to calculate the sums of values in an Excel sheet. This corresponds to the third example given above. The next example illustrates how the SUM function can be used.

WORKED EXAMPLES

EXAMPLE A.7

Suppose we want to use Excel to calculate the sum of the values:

$y_1 = 157$
$y_2 = 201$
$y_3 = 75$
$y_4 = 254$
$y_5 = 110$

To do this we simply type these values into an Excel sheet and then apply the SUM function to those specific cells. Figure A.5 illustrates this calculation.

	A	B	C
1	$y_1 =$	157	
2	$y_2 =$	201	
3	$y_3 =$	759	
4	$y_4 =$	254	
5	$y_5 =$	110	
6	$\sum_{i=1}^{5} y_1 =$	1481	=SUM(B1:B5)

Figure A.5: Excel calculation of the sum of the values in Example A.7

EXCEL FUNCTION METHOD

y_1: Cell B1	Value
y_2: Cell B2	Value
y_3: Cell B3	Value
y_4: Cell B4	Value
y_5: Cell B5	Value
$\sum_{i=1}^{5} y_i$	Formula: =SUM(B1:B5)

A.1.6 Factorial notation

We denote the factorial of n as $n!$ (which is read "n factorial") and we define it as

$$n! = n \times (n - 1) \times \ldots \times 2 \times 1$$

For example,

$$5! = 5 \times 4 \times 3 \times 2 \times 1 = 120$$
$$3! = 3 \times 2 \times 1 = 6$$

and

$$2! = 2 \times 1 = 2$$

Note that $1! = 1$ and $0! = 1$

The Excel function FACT can be used to calculate factorials of numbers. The next example illustrates these calculations.

WORKED EXAMPLES

EXAMPLE A.8

Using Excel we can calculate the factorial of numbers using the function FACT. In this example we will illustrate the calculation of 5!, 3! and 2!

	A	B	C
1	Value =	5	
2	5! =	120	=FACT(B1)
3			
4	Value =	3	
5	3! =	6	=FACT(B4)
6			
7	Value =	2	
8	2! =	2	=FACT(B7)

Figure A.6: Excel calculation of the factorials in Example A.8

EXCEL FUNCTION METHOD		
	Value: Cell B1	Value
	5!: Cell B2	Formula: =FACT(B1)
	Value: Cell B4	Value
	3!: Cell B5	Formula: =FACT(B4)
	Value: Cell B7	Value
	2!: Cell B8	Formula: =FACT(B7)

A.1.7 Combination notation

The term $\binom{n}{r}$, which is read "*n* combination *r*", is used to determine the number of possible combinations (or ways) one can choose '*r*' items from a group of '*n*' items (if we assume that the order in which the items are chosen is not important). We define $\binom{n}{r}$ as follows

$$\binom{n}{r} = \frac{n!}{r!\,(n-r)!}$$

For example, to count the number of ways one can obtain 2 successes if one makes 5 attempts we calculate

$$\binom{5}{2} = \frac{5!}{2!\,(5-2)!} = \frac{5!}{2!\,(3)!}$$

but

$$5! = 5 \times 4 \times 3 \times 2 \times 1 = 120$$
$$3! = 3 \times 2 \times 1 = 6$$

and

$$2! = 2 \times 1 = 2$$

therefore

$$\binom{5}{2} = \frac{5!}{2!\,(3)!} = \frac{120}{6 \times 2} = \frac{120}{12} = 10$$

That is, there are 10 possible ways of obtaining 2 successes from 5 attempts.

The Excel function COMBIN is used to perform these calculations more easily. Example A.9 illustrates the calculation of $\binom{5}{2}$.

WORKED EXAMPLES

EXAMPLE A.9

We can calculate the combination $\binom{5}{2}$ in Excel using either the function COMBIN or by using the function FACT in conjunction with the definition of the combination.

	A	B	C	D	E	F	G
1	Choose	2	values from	5	choices		
2							
3					$\binom{5}{2}=$	10	=COMBIN(D1,B1)
4					$\frac{5!}{2!\,(3)!}=$	10	=FACT(D1)/(FACT(B1)*FACT(D1-B1))

Figure A.7: Excel calculation of the combinations in Example A.9

EXCEL FUNCTION METHOD

Choose: Cell B1	Value
From: Cell D1	Value
$\binom{5}{2}$: Cell F3	Formula: =COMBIN(D1,B1)
$\frac{5!}{2!\,(3!)}$: Cell F4	Formula: =FACT(D1)/(FACT(B1)*FACT(D1-B1))

A.2 Excel functions

Excel contains a range of statistical functions that are useful in solving business related problems. As many of these functions are subject of this book, we will just list them here and return to them through the remaining chapters of the book.

Table A.1: List of Excel functions for mathematical and statistical calculations

Excel function	Description
AVEDEV(number 1,number 2,...)	Returns the average of the absolute deviations of data points from their mean.
AVERAGE(number 1,number 2,...)	Returns the average of its arguments.
BINOM.DIST(number_s,trials,probability_s, cumulative)	Returns the individual term binomial distribution.
BINOM.INV(trials,probability_s,alpha)	Returns the smallest integer value for which the cumulative binomial distribution is less than or equal to a criterion value.

Excel function	Description
CHISQ.DIST(x,degrees_freedom)	Returns the one-tailed probability of the chi-square (χ^2) distribution.
CHISQ.INV(probability,degrees_freedom)	Returns the inverse of the chi-square (χ^2) distribution.
CHISQ.TEST(actual_range,expected_range)	Returns the test for independence.
COMBIN(number,number_chosen)	Returns the number of combinations for a given number of objects.
CONFIDENCE.NORM(alpha,standard_dev,size)	Returns a confidence interval for a normal distributed population.
CONFIDENCE.T(alpha,standard_dev,size)	Returns a confidence interval for a t-distributed population.
CORREL(array1,array2)	Returns the correlation coefficient between two data sets.
COUNT(value1,value2,...)	Counts how many numbers are in the list of arguments.
COUNTA(value1,value2,...)	Counts how many non-blank values in the list of arguments.
COVARIANCE.P(array1,array2)	Returns the population covariance, the average of the products of paired deviations.
COVARIANCE.S(array1,array2)	Returns the sample covariance, the average of the products of paired deviations.
DEVSQ(number1,number2,...)	Returns the sum of squares of deviations.
FACT(number)	Returns the factorial of a number.
F.DIST(x,degrees_freedom1,degrees_freedom2)	Returns the F probability distribution.
F.INV(probability,degrees_freedom1, degrees_freedom2)	Returns the inverse of the F probability distribution.
FORECAST(x,known_y's,known_x's)	Returns a value along a linear trend.
FREQUENCY(data_array,bins_array)	Returns a frequency distribution as a vertical array.
F.TEST(array1,array2)	Returns the result of an F-test.
GEOMEAN(number1,number2,...)	Returns the geometric mean.
GROWTH(known_ys,known_xs,new_xs,const)	Returns value along an exponential trend.
HARMEAN(number1,number2,...)	Returns the geometric mean.
HYPGEOM.DIST(sample_s,number_sample, population_s,number_population)	Returns the hypergeometric distribution (used in sampling without replacement from a finite population).
INT(number)	Returns a number down to the nearest integer.
INTERCEPT(known_y's,known_x's)	Returns the intercept of the linear regression line.

Excel function	Description
KURT(number1,number2,...)	Returns the kurtosis of a data set.
LARGE(array,k)	Returns the kth largest value in a data set.
LINEST(known_ys,known_xs,const,stats)	Returns the parameters of a linear trend.
LN(number)	Returns the natural logarithm of a number.
LOG(number,base)	Returns the logarithm of a number with a specified base.
LOG10(number)	Returns the logarithm of a number with base equal to 10.
MAX(number1,number2,...)	Returns the maximum value in a list of arguments.
MEDIAN(number1,number2,...)	Returns the median of the given numbers.
MIN(number1,number2,...)	Returns the minimum value in a list of arguments.
MODE.MULT(number1,number2,...)	Returns a vertical array of the most common value in a data set.
MODE.SNGL(number1,number2,...)	Returns the most common value in a data set.
NORM.DIST(x,mean,standard_dev,cumulative)	Returns the normal cumulative distribution.
NORM.INV(probability,mean,standard_dev)	Returns the inverse of the normal cumulative distribution.
NORM.S.DIST(Z)	Returns the standard normal cumulative distribution.
NORM.S.INV(probability)	Returns the inverse of the standard normal cumulative distribution.
PEARSON(array1,array2)	Returns the Pearson product moment correlation coefficient.
PERCENTILE.EXC(array,k)	Returns the kth percentile of values in a range; exclusive.
PERCENTILE.INC(array,k)	Returns the kth percentile of values in a range; inclusive.
PERCENTRANK.EXC(array,x,significance)	Returns the percentage rank of a value in a data set; exclusive.
PERCENTRANK.INC(array,x,significance)	Returns the percentage rank of a value in a data set; inclusive.
PERMUT(number,number_chosen)	Returns the number of permutations for a given number of objects.
PI()	Returns the value of π.
POISSON.DIST(x,mean,cumulative)	Returns the Poisson probability distribution.
POWER(number,power)	Returns the number raised to a power.

Excel function	Description
PROB(x_range,prob_range,lower_limit,upper_limit)	Returns the probability that values in a range are between two limits.
QUARTILE.EXC(array,quart)	Returns the quartile of a data set; exclusive.
QUARTILE.INC(array,quart)	Returns the quartile of a data set; inclusive.
RANK.AVG(number,ref,order)	Returns the rank of a number in a list of numbers. Ties are averaged.
RSQ(known_ys,known_xs)	Returns the coefficient of determination, R^2, value of the linear regression line.
SKEW(number1,number2,...)	Returns the skewness of a distribution.
SLOPE(known_ys,known_xs)	Returns the slope of the linear regression line.
SMALL(array,k)	Returns the kth smallest value in a data set.
SQRT(number)	Returns the square root of a number.
STANDARDISE(x,mean,standard_dev)	Returns a normalised value.
STDEV.P(number1,number2,...)	Calculates standard deviation based on the entire population.
STDEV.S(number1,number2,...)	Estimates standard deviation based on a sample.
STEYX(known_ys,known_xs)	Returns the standard error of the predicted y-value for each x in the regression.
SUM(number1,number2,...)	Returns the sum of the numbers within a specified range.
SUMPRODUCT(array1,array2,...)	Returns the sum of the products of corresponding items in each range of values.
SUMSQ(number1,number2,...)	Returns the sum of the squared numbers within a specified range.
T.DIST(x,degrees_freedom,tails)	Returns the Student's t-distribution.
T.INV(probability,degrees_freedom)	Returns the inverse of the Student's t-distribution for the specified degrees of freedom.
TREND(known_ys,known_xs,new_xs,const)	Returns values along a linear trend.
TRIMMEAN(array,percent)	Returns the mean of the interior of a data set.
T.TEST(array1,array2,tails,type)	Returns the probability associated with a Student's t-test.
VAR.P(number1,number2,...)	Calculates variance based on the entire population.
VAR.S(number1,number2,...)	Calculates variance based on a sample.
Z.TEST(array,x,sigma)	Returns the two-tailed p-value of a Z-test.

APPENDIX B:

MICROSOFT EXCEL 2010

Microsoft Excel provides a series of tools that can be used to undertake the analysis of data sets as well as a presentation tool for reporting your results. This chapter describes Excel 2010, which is part of the *Office 2010* suite of programs. It is assumed that you are familiar with *Microsoft Windows* and know how to perform tasks such as accessing commands from the menus on the menu bar, selecting items, and entering information into a dialog box. This chapter will describe the Excel skills required to enable the Excel user to undertake the statistical tests described within each chapter of this textbook.

OVERVIEW

A *spreadsheet* is a table of cells arranged in *rows* and *columns*. The data values in each cell can take many forms, such as text, dates, times, and numbers (including currency and percentages).

The relationships between cells are called formulae. If you change the value in a cell, the contents of any cells that depend on that value will change automatically. This enables you to study what-if scenarios.

Excel can create and manipulate spreadsheets (which are called *worksheets*). It can also produce *graphs* (known as *charts*) and can link one worksheet to another.

Furthermore, Excel can be used to solve a variety of mathematical, statistical, and financial problems. This textbook is concerned with the application of the Excel spreadsheet to solve business statistics focused problems.

LEARNING OBJECTIVES

On completing this chapter, you should be able to:

- create a new Excel workbook and worksheets
- save and close workbooks
- format cells
- select a cell or a range of cells
- enter data into a cell or a range of cells, e.g. numbers, text
- create and modify cell formulae
- create and apply names to a cell range
- print worksheets and workbooks and apply preview before printing worksheets
- understand that Excel can create a table and chart
- apply Excel functions to solve statistical problems
- load Excel Analysis ToolPak add-in to solve a range of statistical problems
- insert an Excel worksheet and chart into Microsoft Word.

B.1 Introduction to Microsoft Excel 2010

A spreadsheet is basically a document which has been divided into rows and columns. Excel is designed to ease the management of numbers and calculations. Various menu commands and buttons make it easy to arrange and format columns of numbers and to calculate totals, averages, percentages, financial, statistical, and scientific formulae. The look of a spreadsheet application derives from the account ledgers that have been used to keep records for centuries. Ledger pages are lined off into rows and columns to record such things as items in inventory, income and expenses, debits and credits. The biggest advantage of a spreadsheet over these paper-based ledgers is the ability to update calculations automatically as new data are added to the worksheet.

B.1.1 Components of an Excel spreadsheet

The following list provides the definition of some of the terminology that will be used in this section. It is recommended that you familiarise yourself with these terms before continuing.

(a) Worksheets

A worksheet is a single sheet containing rows and columns into which formulae, values, charts, and tables can be entered. Worksheets will be used to store, manipulate, calculate, analyse data and create tables and charts.

(b) Workbooks

These are a collection of sheets stored in the same file on the disk. By keeping related worksheets in the same workbook, it is easy to make simultaneous changes and edits to all workbook sheets at one time, or to consolidate related sheets or to do calculations involving multiple sheets. The maximum number of sheets in Excel 2010 is limited only by your machine's memory (this will typically mean that more than 255 sheets can be created).

(c) A row

A row is a line of horizontal cells within a spreadsheet; each row is identified by a unique number, e.g. A1, A2, A3, A4, A5, etc. Within each worksheet there are 1 048 576 rows.

(d) A column

A column is a line of vertical cells within a spreadsheet; each column is identified by a unique letter or combination of letters, e.g. A1, B1, C1, D1, E1, etc. Within each worksheet there are 16 384 columns (ranging from A to XFD).

(e) A cell

A cell is the intersection of a row and a column, which has a unique address or reference. For example where column C and row 8 intersect is cell C8. You use cell references when you write formulae or refer to cells.

(f) Absolute cells

A reference such as $A$2 tells Excel how to find a cell based on the exact location of that cell in the worksheet. An absolute reference is designated by adding a dollar sign ($) before the column letter and the row number.

(g) A range

A selection of multiple cells is referred to as a range. A single cell in some circumstances may represent a range.

(h) Charts

Excel can create charts quickly to visually represent a data set stored in a worksheet. A range of chart types can be created, including: *pie charts, bar charts, line graphs* and *scatter plots.*

(i) Macros

Excel can be used to develop and store macros that can be used to undertake frequently applied tasks.

(j) Presentations

Excel has a range of drawings and formatting tools that can be used to create high-quality presentations. These presentations can then be printed or copied to a word processing or presentation software package.

B.1.2 Loading Excel

Depending on your version of Windows, Excel can be opened in a number of ways. If you are using Windows XP or Windows 7, then select Start to display the Start menu > Select All Programs > Select Office > Select Excel. Excel opens and displays an empty workbook as illustrated in Figure B.1:

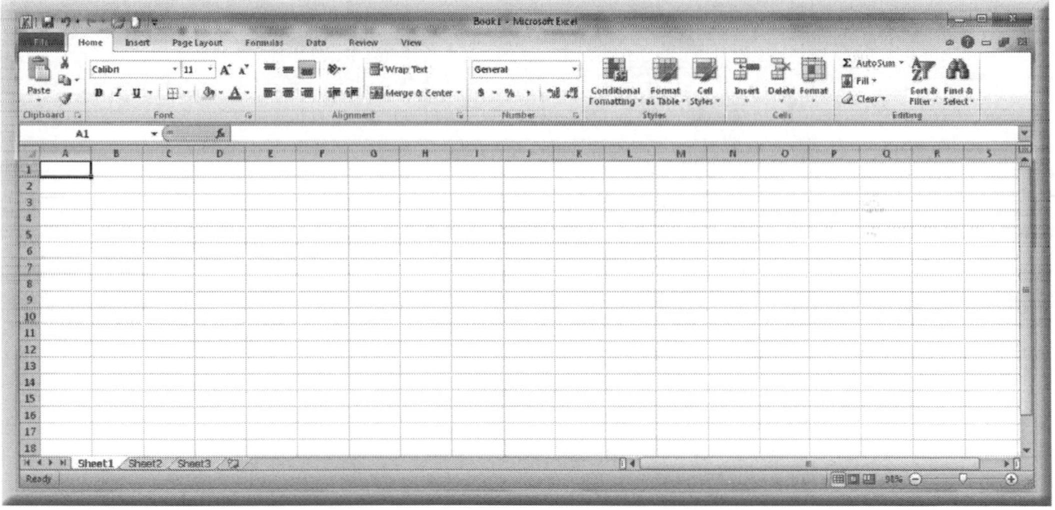

Figure B.1: An empty Excel workbook

In Excel, the normal file type is referred to as a workbook. The first blank workbook displayed by Excel is called Book1 (see the top of Figure B.1). Each workbook contains sheets that are referred to as worksheets if they contain a spreadsheet and as chart sheets if they contain just a graph. A new worksheet usually has three worksheets but more can be added if required. The screen display is made up of the worksheet which is divided into rows (with headings 1, 2, 3 ...) and columns (with headings A, B, C ...). Although you cannot see them there are 16 384 columns and 1 048 576 rows. This means that there are more than 17 billion individual cells in one worksheet. At the top of the Excel workspace is the title bar displaying Microsoft Excel followed by the name of the current workbook (Book1 in this case). Below that is the menu bar and toolbars. Then, just above the row of column headings, are the Name box containing the address of the active cell (A1 at the moment) and the Formula Bar displaying the contents of the active cell (blank at the moment).

B.1.3 Navigating around the worksheet

Some basic navigation of the cells in the Excel worksheet is described below:
Selecting a cell
To select a cell:

a) Position the cursor over the cell.
b) Click the left mouse button once.
c) The cell will then become highlighted with a dark border, with the cell reference number appearing in the upper left portion of the screen.

Selecting a range of cells
If you wish to select more than one cell in a worksheet:

a) Click on the first cell in the range.
b) Holding the left mouse button down, drag the cursor to the last cell in the range and release the mouse button. The area of the range will be highlighted.

Select an entire row
Click the cursor in the row heading, i.e. the numbers running down the left-hand side of the worksheet.

Select an entire column
Click the cursor in the column heading, i.e. the alphabetic letters on the top of the worksheet.

B.1.4 Help

Excel has a comprehensive, easy-to-use help system. The Help menu can be brought up by clicking on the symbol at the top right corner of the Excel window. The help window is displayed in Figure B.2. If you need help on any topic in Excel, simply type the name of the topic in the field marked "Search" and then click on the magnifying glass. Various articles will then appear to help answer the questions you may have on the topic of interest.

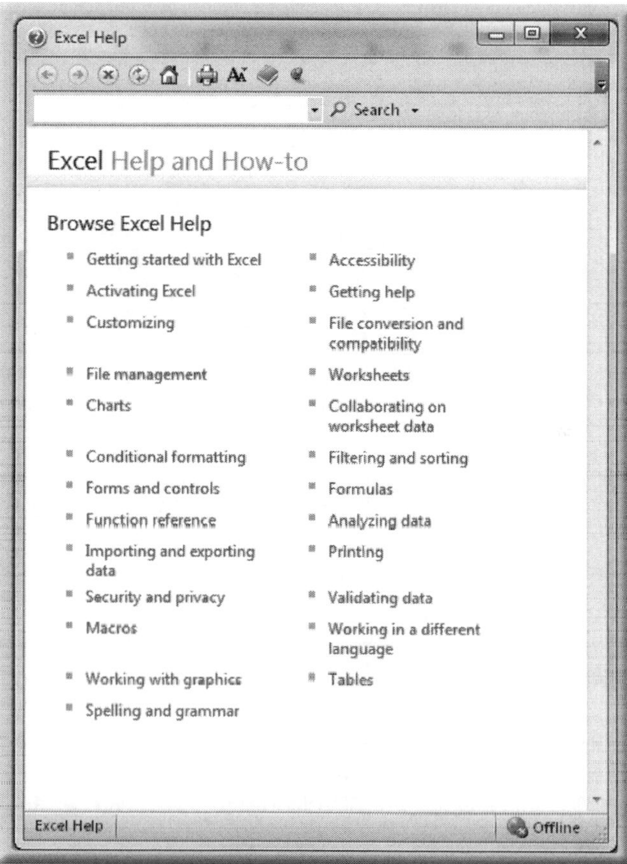

Figure B.2: Excel "Help" window

B.1.5 Saving a workbook

Your workbook can be saved to a local hard disk or stored on an external storage device, e.g. USB memory stick. To save a workbook on a particular drive, follow these steps:

a) Click on tab labelled "File" and then select either "Save" or "Save as".
b) A "Save As" box will appear. In the "File name" field, type a file name and save to an appropriate location on the storage drive. It is very important to save any work created at regular time intervals.

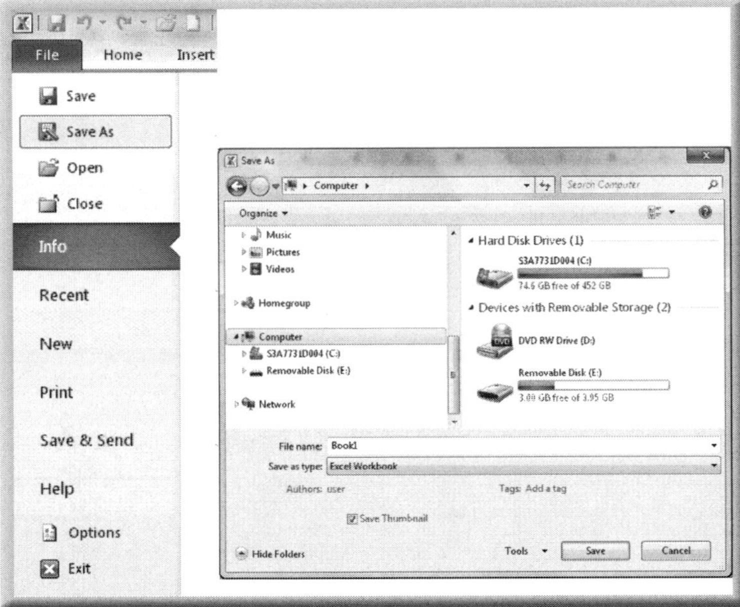

Figure B.3: Excel's "Save As" screen

c) The default name of the workbook will be something like "Book1.xlsx" (as shown in Figure B.3). Delete this name by pressing the Backspace or Delete key on your keyboard.
d) Enter the name of your workbook (e.g. Appendix B.xlsx). Excel will automatically give it a file extension (.xlsx). The file extension (.xlsx) denotes the file to be an Excel 2010 spreadsheet.
e) On the left side of the screen, navigate to the desired drive and folder. In Figure B.4 we have selected the "Work" folder on the "U:" drive.
(f) Click on the button marked "Save". The name of the document is displayed at the top of the screen.

B.1.6 Opening an existing workbook

To open an existing Excel file, make use of the following steps:

a) Click on tab marked "File" and click on the "Open" button (shown on the left side of Figure B.5). The "Open" screen shown in Figure B.5 will appear.
b) Select the drive you require (e.g. C:\) by navigating through the directory structure on the left side of the "Open" window.

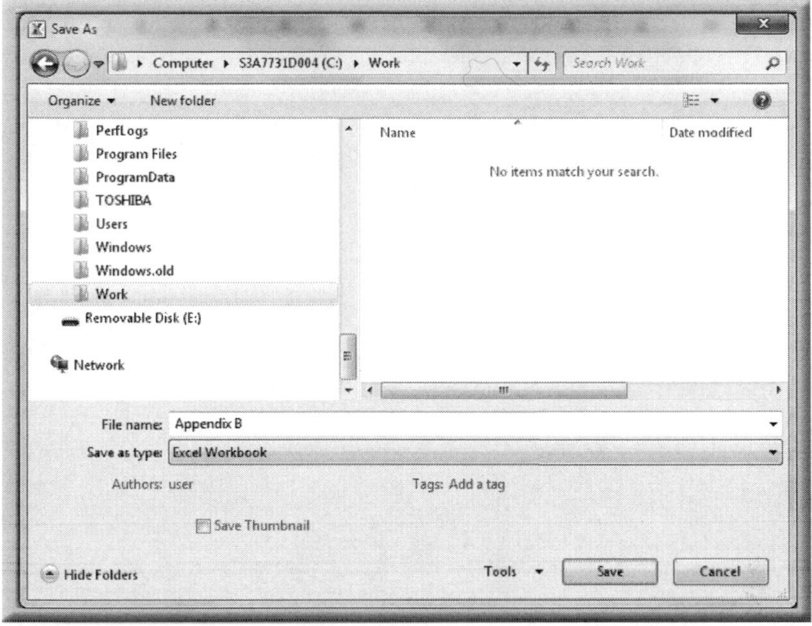

Figure B.4: Saving the files as "Appendix B.xlsx" in the folder "Work" on the "U:" drive

c) Click on the directory the file is in (if any).
d) Click on the file you wish to open.
e) Click on the "Open" button.

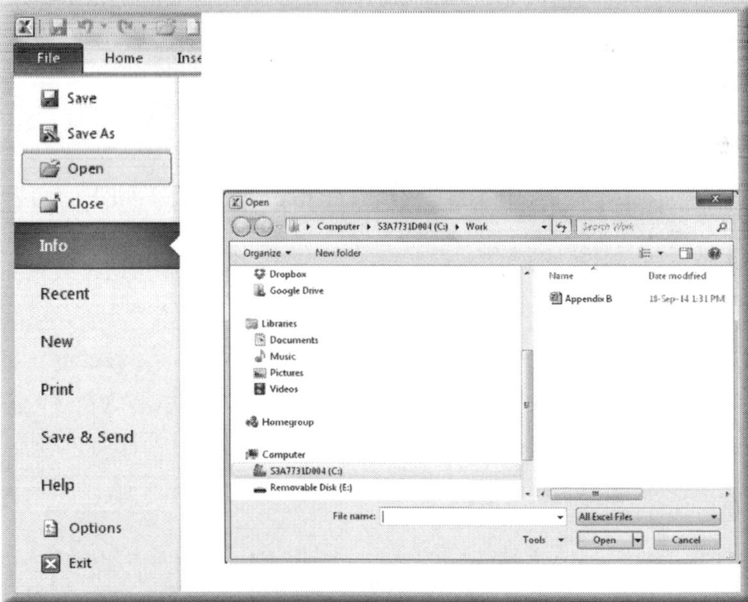

Figure B.5: Opening an Excel document

B.1.7 Closing a workbook

You can close a workbook at any time. From the File tab, select "Close" (as in Figure B.6). If you have made any changes to the workbook since it was last saved, you will be asked whether you wish to save those changes. Click "Save" to keep the changes or "Don't save" to discard them. You can rename the file if you wish to keep the changes made but save it to a different Excel file.

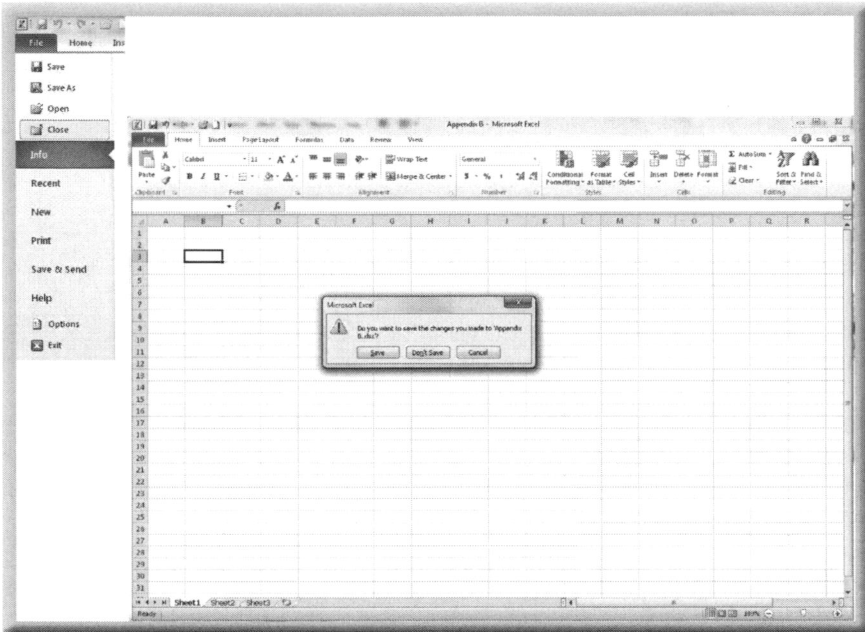

Figure B.6: Closing an Excel document

B.1.8 Switch to a new worksheet

Click on the tab at the bottom of the screen to select the next sheet. Since you have multiple worksheets, it is advisable to use them in sequential order to avoid confusion. Worksheets (sheet 1, sheet 2, ...) can be moved by dragging the worksheet tab to the left or right to reorder the worksheets.

Figure B.7: The worksheet tabs at the bottom of the Excel window - switch between sheets in a workbook by clicking on the appropriate tab

B.1.9 Creating a new worksheet

To create a new worksheet in your workbook click on the tab (shown in Figure B.7) marked with the "new worksheet" symbol. This symbol will always appear on the furthest right side of the tabs at the bottom of the screen.

B.1.10 Creating a new workbook

Click on File tab and select "New". A frame containing possible templates for your Excel document will appear (shown in Figure B.8). To keep things simple, simply double-click on the "Blank workbook" template (default) and a brand new workbook will appear. Note: the original workbook also remains open behind the new one until you close it.

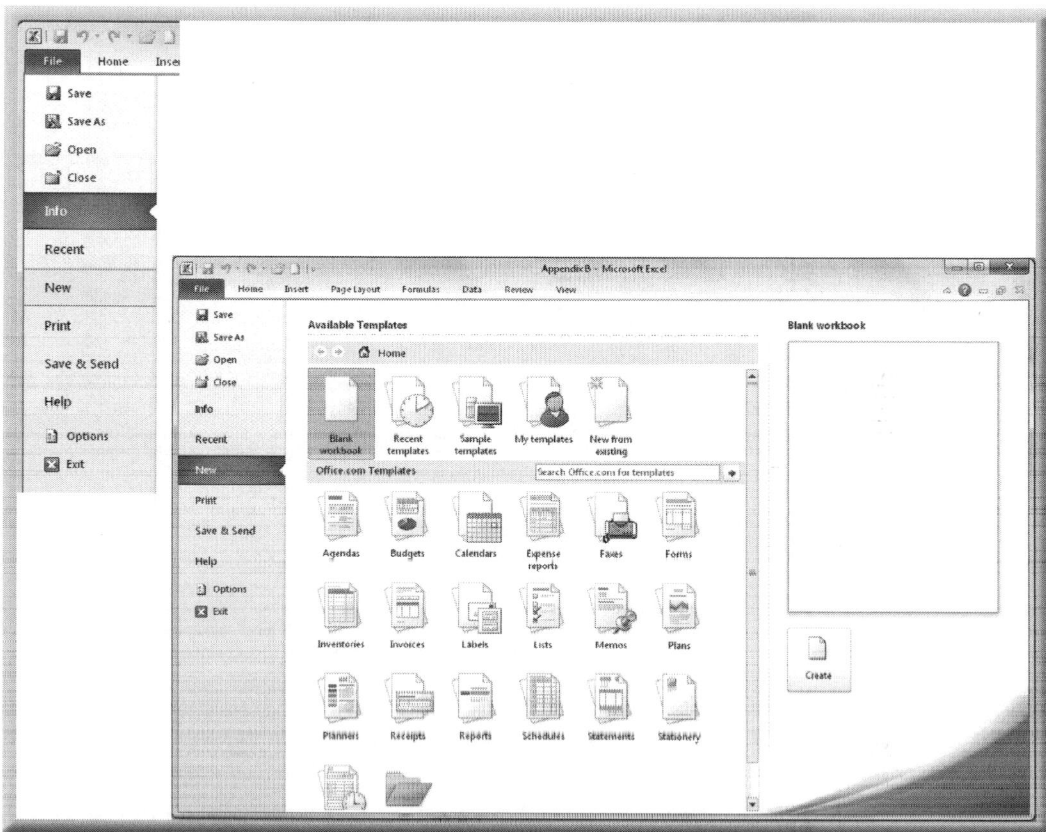

Figure B.8: Creating a new, blank workbook in Excel

B.1.11 Printing and print review

To print the contents of an Excel worksheet, click on the File tab and select "Print". The print functionality in Excel automatically displays a "preview" of the work to be printed as shown on the right side of Figure B.9. One can browse through the contents of the printed document using the arrows at the bottom of the page and various other printing options are made available on the left.

The options made available to you under "Setting" allow you to:

- select the printer to print to,
- indicate what part of the worksheet to print (see Table B.1 for some options), and
- how the document will be printed (one-sided/two-sided, collated, landscape/portrait, page size, margin size, and scaling).

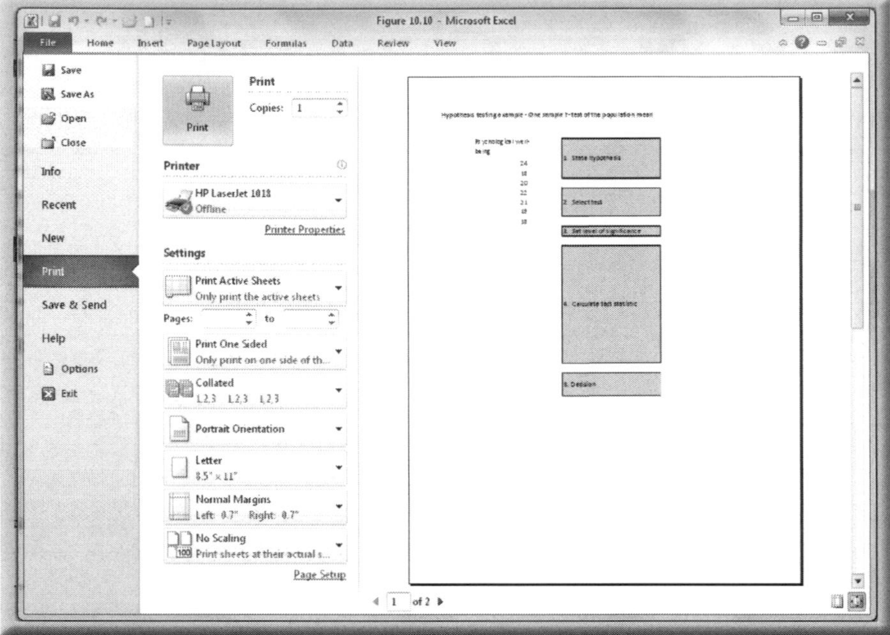

Figure B.9: Printing an Excel worksheet

Table B.1: Some options for printing the Excel file (under settings)

Option	Description
Print Active Sheet(s)	Prints a current or selected worksheet(s), this is also a default setting.
Print Entire Workbook	Prints all sheets in the workbook.
Selection	Prints a selected range of cells.

Once you are satisfied will all the settings (the default ones should be adequate for most applications) you can begin printing by clicking on the large "Print" button.

B.1.12 What to do if you encounter a damaged Excel file

If an Excel file is corrupted due to a computer crash (or other problem) then Excel will automatically attempt to save a file. The *Document Recovery* task pane shows the files that were open at the time of the computer crash. It identifies the original version of the file and the recovered version of the file. After you open the recovered version, you can then save its changes by first selecting the file you want to keep and then saving the file (as described earlier). The *AutoRecover* feature is set to automatically save changes to your workbook (provided that the file has already been saved) every ten minutes. You can modify this time by choosing clicking on the File tab and selecting "Options". The "Excel Options" window will appear. Select "Save" from the menu on the left. The pane that opens allows you to alter a number of save settings, including the duration of the "AutoRecover" feature.

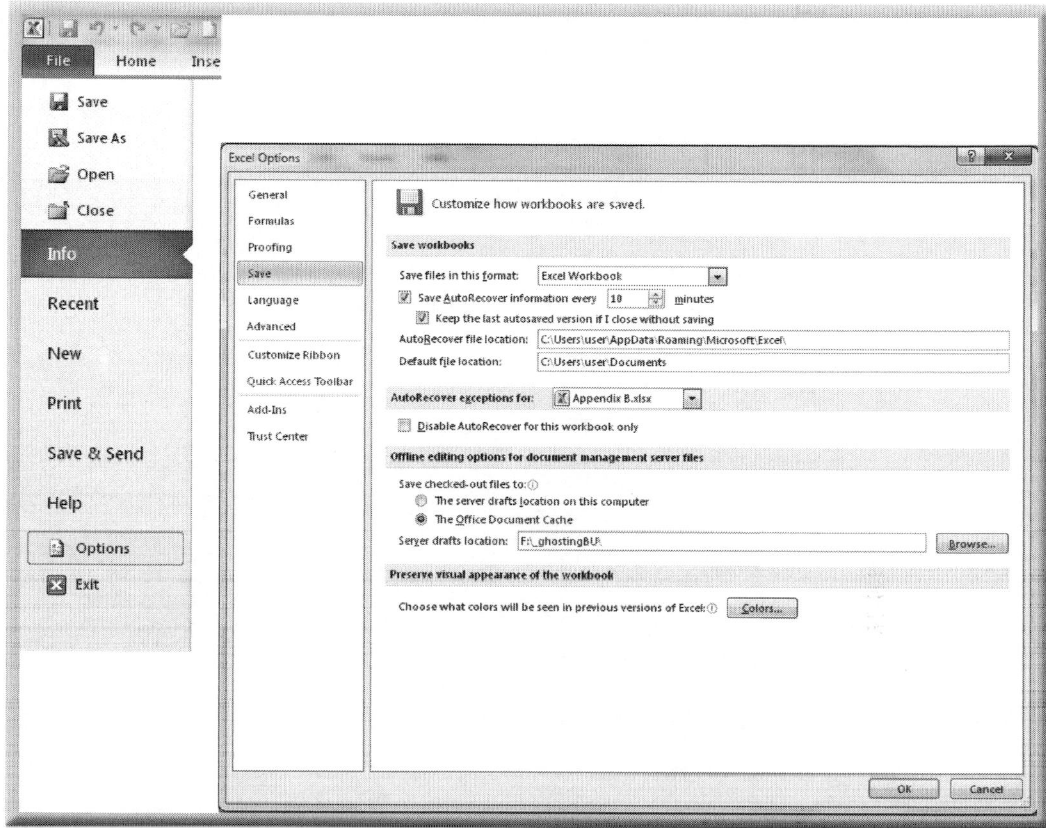

Figure B.10: Excel options: Changing the "AutoRecover" time duration

B.2 Entering data and formatting

Data are entered into the worksheet by moving the cursor to the appropriate position on the screen, clicking the left mouse button to select the cell, and then typing the information required. The characters you type will then appear in the active cell and on the formula bar. When you have finished typing data into a cell you should signal the end of that data by pressing the enter key. There are two basic types of information that can be entered into a worksheet: constants and formulae. The constants are of four basic types:

- numeric values,
- text values,
- date values, and
- time values.

Two special types of constants, called logical values and error values, are also recognised by Excel but are not discussed in this textbook. Numeric values include only the digits 0–9 and some special characters such as:

Table B.2: Some special characters recognised by Excel

+	–	E	e	(	)	.	,	£	%	/

A numeric cell entry can maintain precision up to 15 digits. If you enter a number that is too long, Excel converts it to scientific notation. For example, is you type 97867985685859300, it will be stored as 97867985685859300, and displayed as 9.78668E+16.

NOTE

The scientific notation in Excel uses an "E" to represent powers of 10. For example, the number 1000 can be expressed in "plain" scientific notation as

$$1 \times 10^3$$

but in Excel it would appear as

1.0E + 03

The following table shows a few more of these conversions:

Number	Scientific notation	Excel Scientific notation
0.00000003423	3.423×10^{-8}	3.423E–08
120 930 898 562 123	$1.20930898562123 \times 10^{14}$	1.20930898562123E+14
8 298.81	8.29881×10^3	8.29881E+03

Sometimes, although the number is stored correctly in the cell, the cell is not wide enough to display it properly. In those cases, Excel will round the number off or display a string of # signs. To solve this problem increase the width of the column. A text entry can contain up to 32 767 characters but only 1024 characters will display in the cell and all will be displayed in the formula bar. If the text you enter will not fit in the particular width of your cell, Excel lets it overlap the adjacent cell unless that cell already contains an entry, in which case the extra text can be thought of as being tucked behind the adjacent cell. By default, text is left-justified in a cell whereas numbers are right-justified.

B.2.1 Entering data in a cell

The cells in an Excel worksheet can be edited quite easily. The following steps describe how the cell C3 can be edited.

a) Select a cell in which you want to enter data. For the example displayed in Figure B.11, the cell C3 is selected.
b) Type in the entry. The entry will appear in the formula bar as it is typed. In the example in Figure B.11, the value "1" is typed.
c) To enter what you have typed press the Return key, or click on the Tick mark next to the formula bar to enter the value.

C3 | f_x 1

	A	B	C	D
1	1	2		
2	2	3		
3	3	4	1	
4	4	5		
5	5	5		

Figure B.11: Entering data into the cells in an Excel worksheet

B.2.2 Modifying data in a cell

If you are in the process of entering data in a cell and you notice that you have made a mistake, it is easy to correct it. Press the Backspace key to delete a character to the left of the cursor or the Delete key to delete a character to the right of the cursor. If you want to edit the contents of a cell then you should double-click on the cell and make the required alterations either in the cell itself or on the formula bar. If you want to clear the cell of its contents (formula and data), formats, comments, or all three, you can select that cell with a single click of the left mouse button, select the "Home" tab and then click on the "Clear" button (on the far right, shown in Figure B.12). From here you can choose

- Clear all,
- Clear Formats,
- Clear Contents,
- Clear Comments, and
- Clear Hyperlinks.

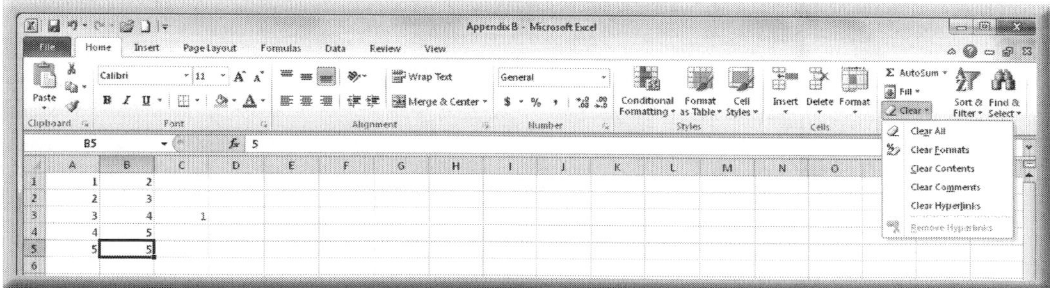

Figure B.12: Clearing data in a cell

B.2.3 Entering data into a range

In Excel, any rectangular area of cells is known as a *range*. The range is defined by the top-left and bottom-right corner cell references separated by a colon (:). So, C8:G15 represents the range of cells cornered by C8 and G15. To enter the same data into a range of cells:

a) Select the range.
b) Enter the data.
c) Hold down the CTRL key and press Return. All of the cells in the range should now contain the same data, or
   i) Select the cell containing the data.
   ii) Move the mouse pointer to the bottom right corner of the cell until the pointer changes to a cross.
d) Hold down the left mouse button and drag the cross in the direction you wish to fill, and then release the mouse button.

B.2.4 Cancelling a cell entry

To cancel a cell entry before you have pressed return, press the Escape key (Esc), or click on the Cross (see Figure B.11) to cancel the entry.

B.2.5 Undoing a cell entry

To undo a cell entry after you have pressed the return key click on the symbol at the extreme top left of the Excel window, or press CTRL + Z.

B.2.6 Entering numbers

Numbers are constant values containing only the following characters: 1 2 3 4 5 6 7 8 9 0 – + / . € e £ $ % , ( ). Once a number has been entered into a cell, it may then be formatted by using the following buttons found in the "Number" section of the "Home" tab (i.e. click on the "Home" tab and find the section in the ribbon marked "Numbers"):

Table B.3: Options for number formats in the in the "Numbers" section of the "Home" tab

Symbol	Style	Effect
	Currency Style	Applies the currently defined currency style to selected cells
%	Percent Style	Applies the currently defined percent style to selected cells
,	Comma Style	Applies the currently defined comma style to selected cells
←.0 .00	Increase Decimal place	Adds one decimal place to the number format each time you click the button
.00 →.0	Decrease Decimal place	Removes one decimal place from the number each time you click the button

B.2.7 Entering dates or times

If you type a date or time change (e.g.13/4/8 or 16:21) directly into a cell Excel should automatically recognise it as such and change the cell formatting from general to the appropriate date or time format. The program will normally align it to the right of the cell and display it in the formula bar in a standard format (e.g. 13/04/2008 or 16:21:00).

Table B.4: Date formats in Excel

If you type	Excel formatting
12/06/08	dd/mm/yy
12-June-08	dd-mmm-yy
31-Oct	dd-mmm
Oct 13 2008	Mmm dd,yyyy
24/05/08 3:21	dd/mm/yy hh:mm
3:45 PM	h:mm AM/PM
3:35:30 PM	h:mm:ss AM/PM
13:50	hh:mm
13:50:35	hh:mm:ss

The displayed formats in particular cells can be modified by right clicking on the cell, selecting "Format Cells...". You can either choose a date format from the Category box or select Custom to define your own cell format. Regardless of how the date (or time) is displayed, the actual value stored in the cell is a long numeric value, e.g. the date variable 13/04/2008 would be stored under general format as 39 752.

B.2.8 Entering text

To enter text, select a cell and type the text. A cell can hold up to 255 characters. You can format the characters within a cell individually but note that if there are more than 255 characters in the cell then the cell will show '#########'. This problem can be resolved by applying text wrapping to the cell.

B.2.9 Formatting a worksheet

You can use many formatting options in Excel to add emphasis to your data, or make the worksheet easier to read. To apply cell formats you can either use the Toolbar or the Menu bar. You can change various aspects of the format of the cells you have selected by first clicking on the "Home" tab, and then finding the "Font" section.

a) To apply or change font size
   i) Click on the down arrow to the right of the font size selection box [11 ▼].
   ii) To select the size you require use the scroll bar arrows to move up or down the list of available sizes, then click on a number.
   iii) The selected font size will appear in the font size box.

b) To apply or change font type:
   i) Click on the down arrow to the right of the font type selection box, Calibri ▼.
   ii) To select the font you require use the scroll bar arrows to scroll through the list of available fonts, then click on a font type.
   iii) The selected font type will appear in the font box.
c) To bold text
   i) Click on **B** button on the tool bar to enable **bold** type.
   ii) Enter text and click on **B** button again to return to normal.
d) To apply italic text
   i) Click on *I* button on the tool bar to enable *Italic* type.
   ii) Enter text and click on *I* button again to return to normal.
e) To apply underlined text
   i) Click on U button on the tool bar to enable Underlined text.
   ii) Enter text and click on U button again to return to normal.
f) Aligning text
   i) Highlight the cell.
   ii) Click on one of the following alignment boxes in the toolbar, to apply the desired alignment:

Table B.5: Alignment symbols in Excel

Symbol	Alignment type
≡	Left Alignment
≡	Centred
≡	Right Alignment
Merge & Center	Centre Across Columns (when a number of columns are highlighted)

B.2.10 Column widths and row heights

In a new worksheet all columns and rows are set to a standard size. Rows automatically adjust to the largest font entered into a row. You may need to adjust the column width if you are entering more than eight characters.

a) Column width
   You can format one or a number of columns in the following manner:
   i) Highlight the columns you wish to alter by clicking on the letter label for the column(s).
   ii) Right click on the column to bring up the formatting options.
   iii) Click on "Column Width" and a small "Column Width" window will appear (see Figure B.13).
   iv) Enter the column width you require.
   v) Click on OK.

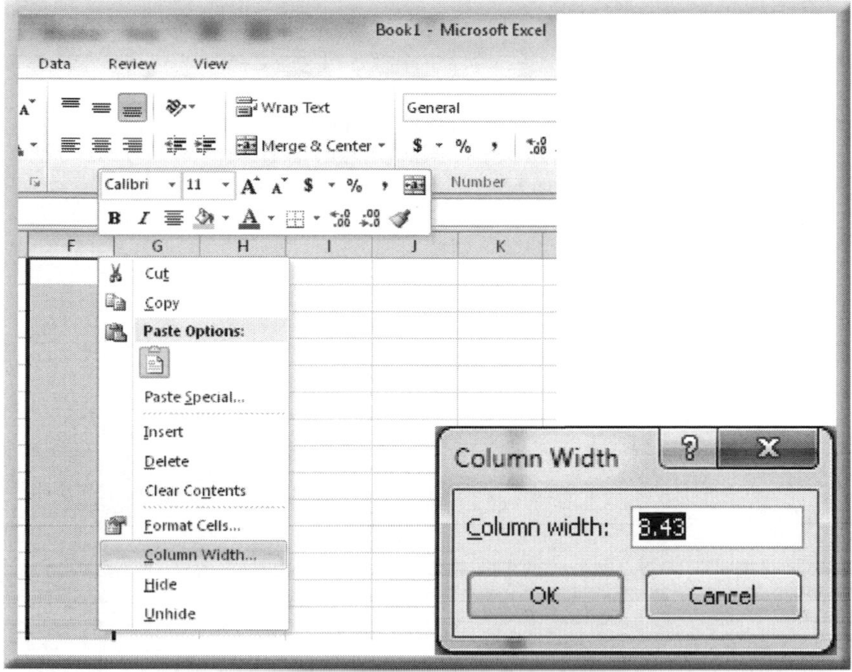

Figure B.13: Altering the column width in Excel

b) Row height

You can format one or a number of columns in the following manner:

i) Highlight the rows you wish to alter by clicking on the number label for the row(s).

ii) Right click on the row to bring up the formatting options.

iii) Click on "Row Height" and a small "Row Height" window will appear (see Figure B.14).

iv) Enter the row height you require.

v) Click on OK.

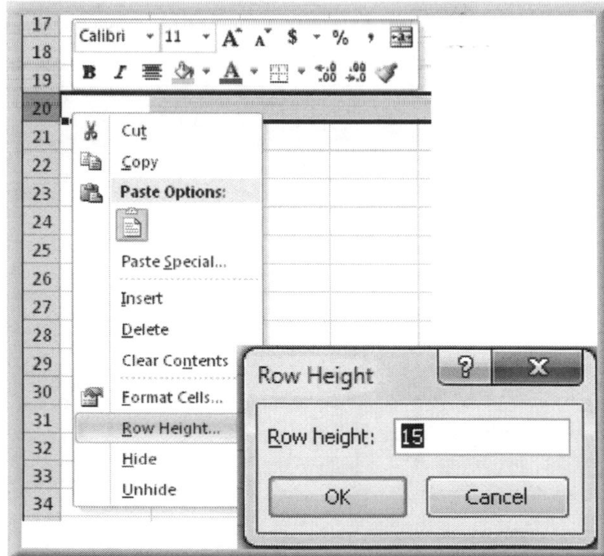

Figure B.14: Altering the row width in Excel

B.2.11 Naming a worksheet

The information on Sheet1 might refer to a particular project. It would make sense to name the sheet (or worksheet) accordingly.

a) Right-click on the tab names at the bottom of the Excel sheet..
b) Select "Rename" from the menu that appears (see Figure B.15).
c) Type your project name into the text box and press the Enter key.

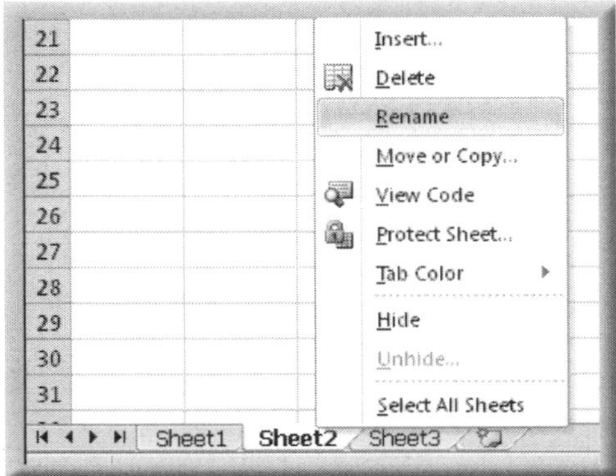

Figure B.15: Altering the name of a sheet in Excel

B.2.12 Inserting and deleting rows and columns

Extra rows and columns can be inserted whenever you wish. As an example, insert a row between rows 8 and 9.

a) Right-click on the row name 8.
b) Select "Insert" (see the left part of Figure B.16).

Now, try inserting a column between columns B and C.

a) Right-click on the column name B.
b) Select "Insert" (see the right part of Figure B.16).

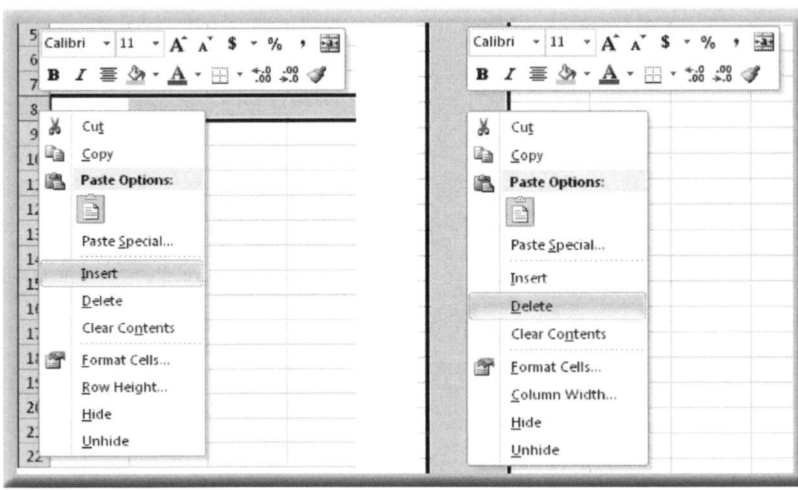

Figure B.16: Inserting rows (left) and columns (right) in an Excel sheet

To *delete* a row or column, right-click on its name and select "Delete" from the menu which appears.

B.2.13 Spell checking

Excel allows you to check the spelling of your work.

a) Select a cell with text.
b) Click on the "Review" tab and then click on the "Spelling" button. A window will appear either telling you that the spelling is correct or it will provide suggestions to correct your spelling (see Figure B.17).

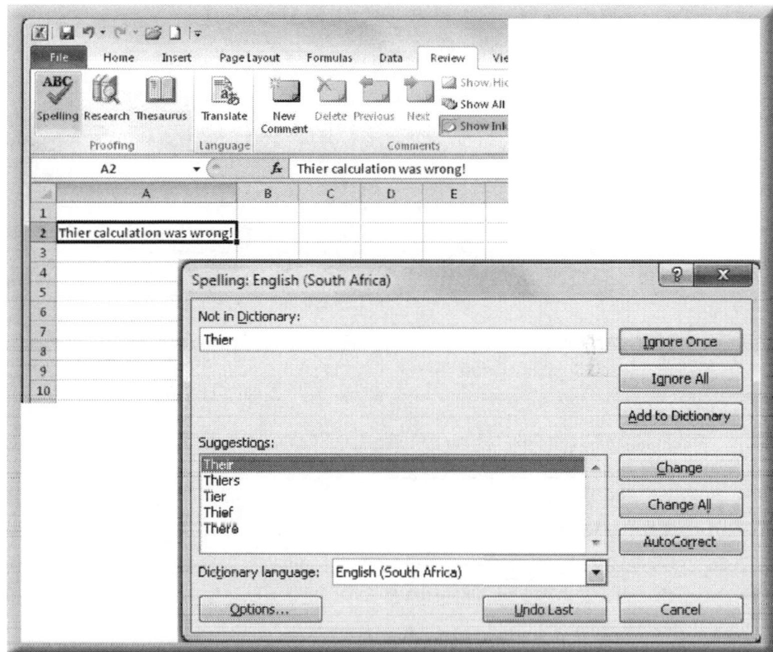

Figure B.17:
Spell checking in Excel

B.3 Performing calculations

Excel can be used to develop simple solutions to data problems. The nature of these problems can be mathematical, statistical and financial. This textbook will explore how you solve statistical problems using Excel.

B.3.1 Entering formulae

Using a formula can help you analyse data on a worksheet. With a formula you can perform operations, such as addition, multiplication, and comparison on worksheet values. Excel formulae always begin with an equals sign, e.g. =7/8, =3*5+4/7, =3*A3, and =A3*A3.

a) Select the cell in which you want to enter a formula.
b) Type an equals sign (=) to activate the formula bar. If you forget to type an equals sign the rest of the line will be treated as text.
c) Enter the formula.
d) Press Enter, or click on the Tick mark to the left of the formula bar.

B.3.2 Understanding operators

Table B.6 shows some of the mathematical operators that can be used to create formulae:

Table B.6: Operators in Excel

Symbol	Explanation
%	Percent
^	Exponentiation
* and /	Multiplication and division
+ and –	Addition and subtraction (or negation when placed before a value, i.e. –1)
&	Text joining
=	Equal
>	Greater than
<	Less than
>=	Greater than or equal to
<=	Less than or equal to
< >	Not equal to

It should be noted that the list is in order of priority starting with Percent (highest priority) and ending with Comparisons (lowest priority), e.g. =, >, …, < >. If you want to alter the order of priority, use parentheses (brackets) to group expressions, e.g. (i) $\frac{9+3}{2}$ is equal to 10.5 and not equal to 6, (ii) $\frac{(9+3)}{2}$ is equal to 6.

B.3.3 The Range operator, :

The colon (:) allows one to specify a reference to all the cells within a range of values. The general format is to type "CELL1:CELL2". In Figure B.18, we see a reference to the cells starting in cell B3 and extending in a rectangle to cell C5. This cell range is written "B3:C5".

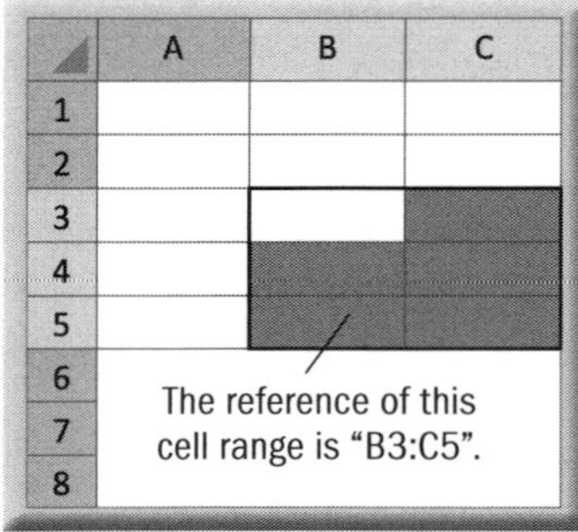

Figure B.18: Illustration of the cell Range "B3:C5"

B.3.4 Editing a formula

To edit an existing formula:

a) Click on the cell containing the formula. The formula will then appear in the formula bar.
b) Press the F2 function key. You may now edit the formula, or position the cursor in the formula bar at the point you wish to change.
c) Press the Return key.

B.3.5 Creating and applying names

Names make formulae easier to read, understand, and maintain. You can change or delete names that have been defined previously and define a constant or computed value that you intend to use later. Names appear in the reference area of the formula bar when you select a named cell or an entire named range. In the example below we will name the monthly sales data in cells C3:E3 and name this range Sales_Quarterly.

a) Select the Range you wish to name, e.g. C3:E3

	A	B	C	D	E
1					
2			January	February	March
3		Sales	R234 000.00	R456 000.00	R120 000.00
4		Expenses	R124 000 00	R30 900.00	R234 000.00
5		Profit	R110 000.00	R425 100.00	–R114 000.00

Figure B.19: Illustration of how to name a range of cell in Excel

b) Right click on the range and select "Define Name..." from the menu bar.
c) In the window that appears enter the name to be applied to the range, e.g. Sales_Quarterly.
d) Click on OK.

The name may then be used in a formula, instead of using the cell locations and is easier to interpret and remember, e.g. SUM(Sales_Quarterly) instead of SUM(C3:E3).

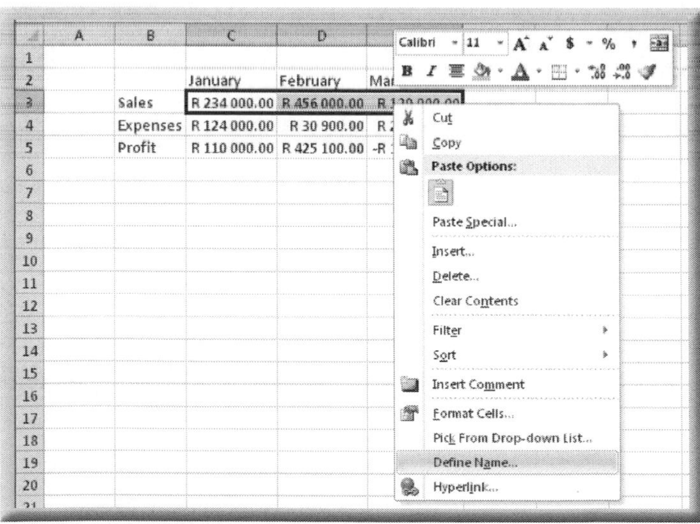

Figure B.20: Illustration of how to name a range of cell in Excel – Define the name

B.3.6 Copying formulae to adjacent cells

Rather than retyping a formula in each of the adjacent cells it is much more convenient to copy the formulae across.

a) Position the cursor over the cell containing the formula.
b) Notice the bottom right corner of the selected cell? Notice how it has a small square? Notice how the mouse cursor changes when you hover over this small square? Click and hold (with the left mouse button) on this small square and drag the formula over the cells you want to fill.

B.3.7 Using absolute and relative references

The $ sign in a cell will tell Excel how to treat your references when copying the contents of a cell. To illustrate this concept consider what happens to the following formulae in Cell C14 that are copied to D15:

- =C14 becomes =D15
- =$C14 becomes =$C15
- =C$14 becomes =D$14
- =$C$14 becomes =$C$14

This simple example illustrates the $ sign acting as an 'anchor' to fix the row number or column letter. You will find when creating a spreadsheet solution (or model) that a term in the equation can be considered to be constant. To illustrate this concept consider an example where you would like to calculate price (p) based upon demand for a product (d) where the relationship between price and demand is given by the equation $p = 2d$. We can see that no matter what the value of p, or d, the number 2 does not change. The number 2 is fixed (or constant) and in a spreadsheet this value would be fixed using the $ sign.

WORKED EXAMPLES

EXAMPLE B.1

Consider solving this problem for price when the demand undergoes a unit change from 1 to 4.

B2 fx =2*A2

	A	B	C
1	Demand	Price	
2	1	2	
3	2	4	
4	3	6	
5	4	8	

Figure B.21: Excel illustration for Example B.1

We can see from the equation in cell B2 that price =2*A2. When we copy the formula down then the price is calculated for a demand change from 1, 2, 3, and 4.

WORKED EXAMPLES

EXAMPLE B.2

This same problem can be solved by fixing the value of the number 2 in the spreadsheet (cell C3) shown. In this case the price in cell C7 is given by the formula price =C3*B7. When we copy the formula down from C7 to C10 the price value is calculated for the demand change.

C7 fx =C3*B7

	A	B	C
1			
2			
3		Constants=	2
4			
5			
6		Demand	Price
7		1	2
8		2	0
9		3	0
10		4	#VALUE!

Figure B.22: Excel illustration for Example B.2

We note from the spreadsheet solution that the price in cell C8 is zero and not the correct value of 4. Inspecting the equation in cell C8 we note that the formula is price =C4*B8. The B8 reference is correct but C4 is incorrect and should read C3, which represents the position of the number 2.

WORKED EXAMPLES

EXAMPLE B.3

To solve this problem we fix the cell position of the number 2 and we achieve this using the Excel $ sign. Therefore, in cell C7 we insert the correct price equation =$C$3*B7.

C7 fx =$C$3*B7

	A	B	C
1			
2			
3		Constants=	2
4			
5			
6		Demand	Price
7		1	2
8		2	4
9		3	6
10		4	8

Figure B.23: Excel illustration for Example B.3

The use of $C$3 is to fix the value of the number 2. If we now copy the formula down from C7 to C10 we can see that we have the correct values for price based upon changing demand.

B.3.8 IF function

The IF function is very useful in solving numerical problems and enables the user to ask questions of the type 'Is this true or false' and then undertake a particular action.

The technique can be illustrated by exploring the marks for two examination tests in which the tutor would like to find out which students obtained a higher mark for test 1 compared to test 2.

Table B.7: Student test data

Student	Test 1	Test 2
A	46	56
B	67	65
C	34	67
D	78	66

This problem can be solved by using the IF function.

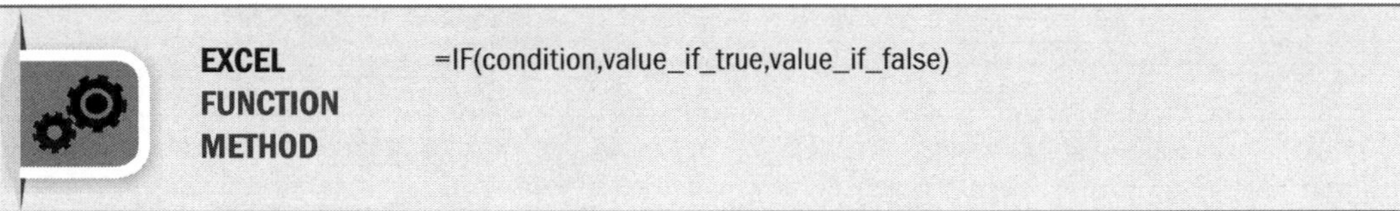

To solve this problem we insert the data into Excel (Figure B.25). Test 1 (C4:C7) and Test 2 (D4:D7). In cell E4, insert =IF(C4>D4,"Larger","Smaller"). This will place the text 'Smaller' in cell E4 (46<56).

E4 =IF(C4>D4,"Larger","Smaller")

	A	B	C	D	E
1					
2					
3		Student	Test 1	Test 2	Test1>Test2
4		A	46	56	Smaller
5		B	67	65	Larger
6		C	34	67	Smaller
7		D	78	66	Larger

Figure B.24: Excel illustration of the IF function using the student test data from Table B.7

Now complete for the other three students by copying the formula down from cell E4 to E7.

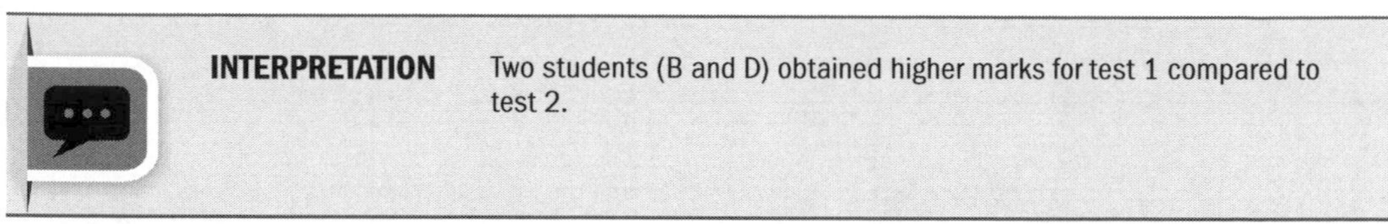

INTERPRETATION Two students (B and D) obtained higher marks for test 1 compared to test 2.

B.3.9 Insert function

Excel provides the user with a range of built in functions which will allow a range of statistical techniques to be applied to a data set. A range of functions will be employed in later chapters but for the time being we will be content with being able to call the function,

a) Click on the "Formulas" tab.
b) Select "Insert function" (see Figure B.25). You can find a detailed list of all the Excel functions in Appendix A.

Figure B.25: The options under the "Function Library" section of the "Formulas" tab in Excel

B.3.10 Copying formulae and values

To copy formulae and values use the copy [Copy] and paste [Paste] buttons on the "Home" tab's ribbon.

B.3.11 Installing the Excel ToolPak add-in

Together with individual functions, Excel provides the Data Analysis ToolPak add-in to help perform many statistical analyses.

To install this add-in, perform the following steps:

a) Click on the "File" tab and then click on "Options" (as shown in Figure B.26).
b) In the "Excel Options" window that appears, select the "Add-Ins" option from the left menu (as shown in Figure B.26).
c) Next to the "Manage" drop-down list, click on the "Go..." button.
d) This will bring up the "Add-Ins" window (shown in Figure B.27). From this window check the "Analysis ToolPak" option and then press "OK".

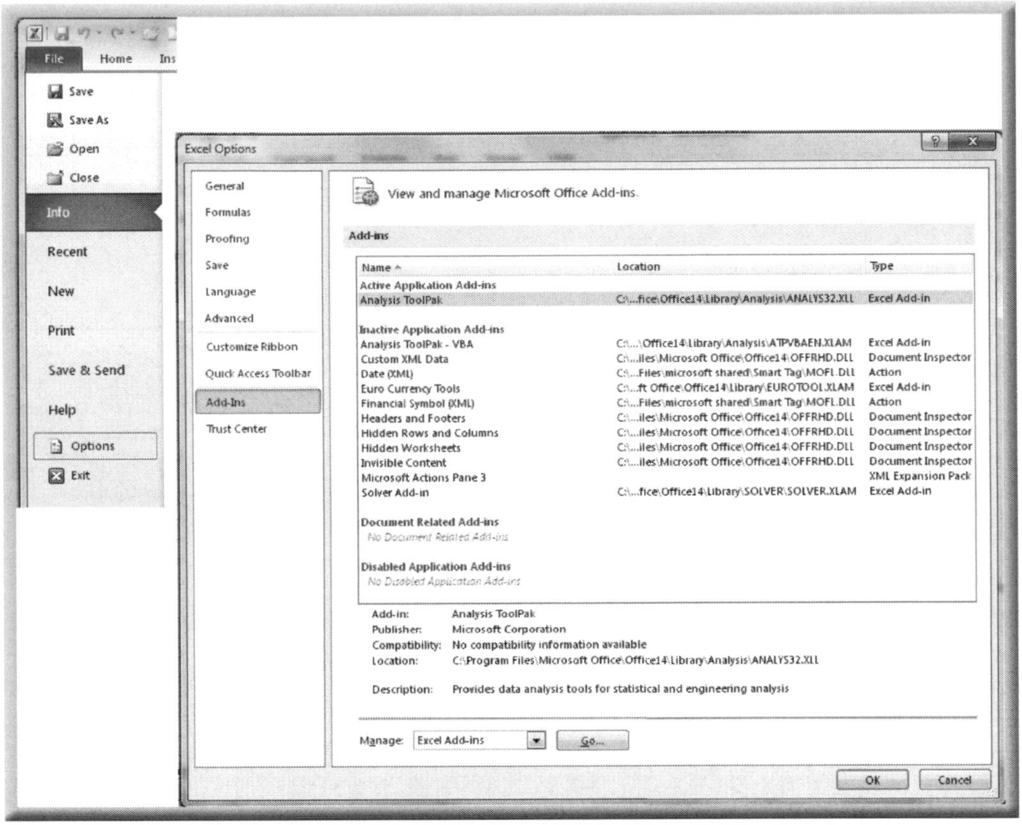

Figure B.26: Opening the "Add-Ins" options in Excel

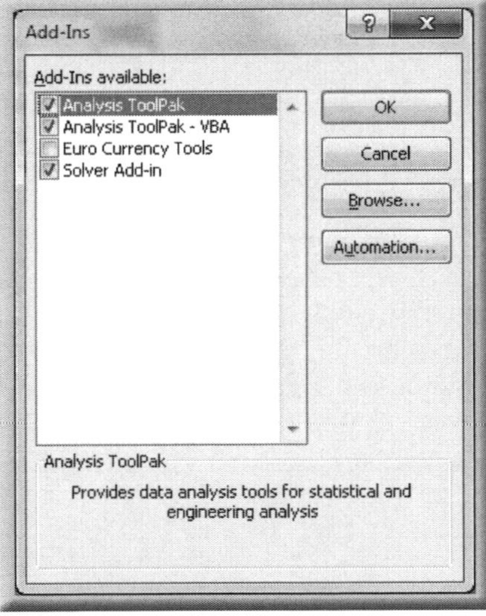

Figure B.27: Adding the "Analysis Toolpak" into Excel

When installed you will find an extra button called "Data Analysis" to the far right of the "Data" tab (shown in Figure B.28). Clicking on this button will open the Data Analysis ToolPak wherein you can perform a variety of statistical analyses on the data in an Excel sheet.

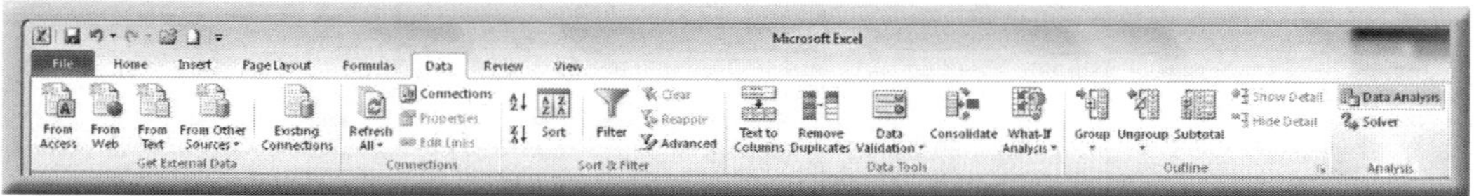

Figure B.28: The "Data Analysis" button in the far right side of the "Data" tab ribbon

APPENDIX C:

NORMAL DISTRIBUTION TABLES

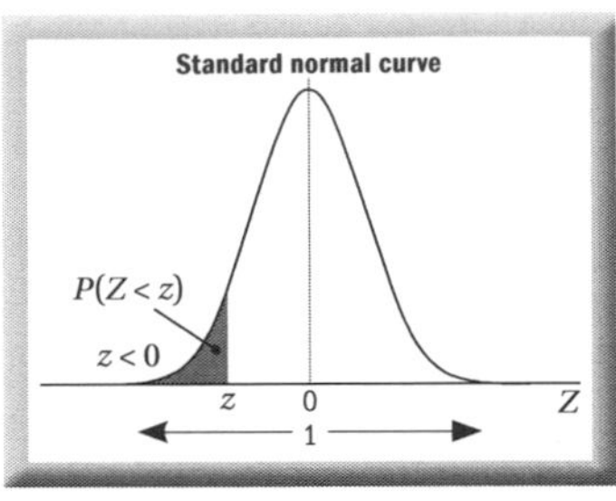

Table C.1: Standard normal table (negative z scores)

Std Norm	0.00	0.01	0.02	0.03	0.04	0.05	0.06	0.07	0.08	0.09
–3.4	0.0003	0.0003	0.0003	0.0003	0.0003	0.0003	0.0003	0.0003	0.0003	0.0002
–3.3	0.0005	0.0005	0.0005	0.0004	0.0004	0.0004	0.0004	0.0004	0.0004	0.0003
–3.2	0.0007	0.0007	0.0006	0.0006	0.0006	0.0006	0.0006	0.0005	0.0005	0.0005
–3.1	0.0010	0.0009	0.0009	0.0009	0.0008	0.0008	0.0008	0.0008	0.0007	0.0007
–3.0	0.0013	0.0013	0.0013	0.0012	0.0012	0.0011	0.0011	0.0011	0.0010	0.0010
–2.9	0.0019	0.0018	0.0018	0.0017	0.0016	0.0016	0.0015	0.0015	0.0014	0.0014
–2.8	0.0026	0.0025	0.0024	0.0023	0.0023	0.0022	0.0021	0.0021	0.0020	0.0019
–2.7	0.0035	0.0034	0.0033	0.0032	0.0031	0.0030	0.0029	0.0028	0.0027	0.0026
–2.6	0.0047	0.0045	0.0044	0.0043	0.0041	0.0040	0.0039	0.0038	0.0037	0.0036
–2.5	0.0062	0.0060	0.0059	0.0057	0.0055	0.0054	0.0052	0.0051	0.0049	0.0048
–2.4	0.0082	0.0080	0.0078	0.0075	0.0073	0.0071	0.0069	0.0068	0.0066	0.0064
–2.3	0.0107	0.0104	0.0102	0.0099	0.0096	0.0094	0.0091	0.0089	0.0087	0.0084
–2.2	0.0139	0.0136	0.0132	0.0129	0.0125	0.0122	0.0119	0.0116	0.0113	0.0110
–2.1	0.0179	0.0174	0.0170	0.0166	0.0162	0.0158	0.0154	0.0150	0.0146	0.0143
–2.0	0.0228	0.0222	0.0217	0.0212	0.0207	0.0202	0.0197	0.0192	0.0188	0.0183
–1.9	0.0287	0.0281	0.0274	0.0268	0.0262	0.0256	0.0250	0.0244	0.0239	0.0233
–1.8	0.0359	0.0351	0.0344	0.0336	0.0329	0.0322	0.0314	0.0307	0.0301	0.0294
–1.7	0.0446	0.0436	0.0427	0.0418	0.0409	0.0401	0.0392	0.0384	0.0375	0.0367
–1.6	0.0548	0.0537	0.0526	0.0516	0.0505	0.0495	0.0485	0.0475	0.0465	0.0455
–1.5	0.0668	0.0655	0.0643	0.0630	0.0618	0.0606	0.0594	0.0582	0.0571	0.0559
–1.4	0.0808	0.0793	0.0778	0.0764	0.0749	0.0735	0.0721	0.0708	0.0694	0.0681
–1.3	0.0968	0.0951	0.0934	0.0918	0.0901	0.0885	0.0869	0.0853	0.0838	0.0823
–1.2	0.1151	0.1131	0.1112	0.1093	0.1075	0.1056	0.1038	0.1020	0.1003	0.0985
–1.1	0.1357	0.1335	0.1314	0.1292	0.1271	0.1251	0.1230	0.1210	0.1190	0.1170
–1.0	0.1587	0.1562	0.1539	0.1515	0.1492	0.1469	0.1446	0.1423	0.1401	0.1379
–0.9	0.1841	0.1814	0.1788	0.1762	0.1736	0.1711	0.1685	0.1660	0.1635	0.1611
–0.8	0.2119	0.2090	0.2061	0.2033	0.2005	0.1977	0.1949	0.1922	0.1894	0.1867
–0.7	0.2420	0.2389	0.2358	0.2327	0.2297	0.2266	0.2236	0.2206	0.2177	0.2148
–0.6	0.2743	0.2709	0.2676	0.2643	0.2611	0.2578	0.2546	0.2514	0.2483	0.2451
–0.5	0.3085	0.3050	0.3015	0.2981	0.2946	0.2912	0.2877	0.2843	0.2810	0.2776
–0.4	0.3446	0.3409	0.3372	0.3336	0.3300	0.3264	0.3228	0.3192	0.3156	0.3121
–0.3	0.3821	0.3783	0.3745	0.3707	0.3669	0.3632	0.3594	0.3557	0.3520	0.3483
–0.2	0.4207	0.4168	0.4129	0.4090	0.4052	0.4013	0.3974	0.3936	0.3897	0.3859
–0.1	0.4602	0.4562	0.4522	0.4483	0.4443	0.4404	0.4364	0.4325	0.4286	0.4247
0.0	0.5000	0.4960	0.4920	0.4880	0.4840	0.4801	0.4761	0.4721	0.4681	0.4641

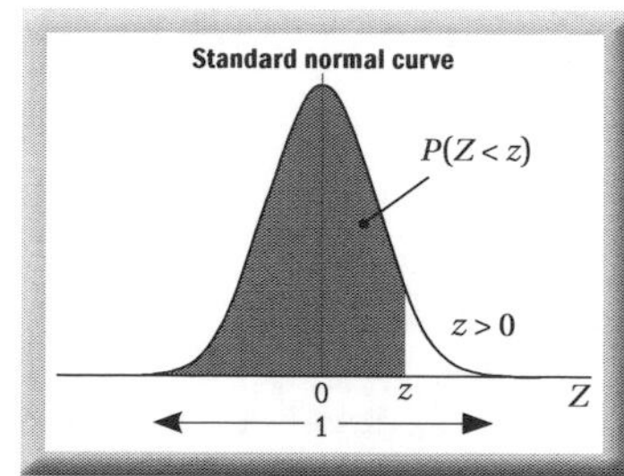

Table C.2: Standard normal table (positive z scores)

Std Norm	0.00	0.01	0.02	0.03	0.04	0.05	0.06	0.07	0.08	0.09
0.0	0.5000	0.5040	0.5080	0.5120	0.5160	0.5199	0.5239	0.5279	0.5319	0.5359
0.1	0.5398	0.5438	0.5478	0.5517	0.5557	0.5596	0.5636	0.5675	0.5714	0.5753
0.2	0.5793	0.5832	0.5871	0.5910	0.5948	0.5987	0.6026	0.6064	0.6103	0.6141
0.3	0.6179	0.6217	0.6255	0.6293	0.6331	0.6368	0.6406	0.6443	0.6480	0.6517
0.4	0.6554	0.6591	0.6628	0.6664	0.6700	0.6736	0.6772	0.6808	0.6844	0.6879
0.5	0.6915	0.6950	0.6985	0.7019	0.7054	0.7088	0.7123	0.7157	0.7190	0.7224
0.6	0.7257	0.7291	0.7324	0.7357	0.7389	0.7422	0.7454	0.7486	0.7517	0.7549
0.7	0.7580	0.7611	0.7642	0.7673	0.7704	0.7734	0.7764	0.7794	0.7823	0.7852
0.8	0.7881	0.7910	0.7939	0.7967	0.7995	0.8023	0.8051	0.8078	0.8106	0.8133
0.9	0.8159	0.8186	0.8212	0.8238	0.8264	0.8289	0.8315	0.8340	0.8365	0.8389
1.0	0.8413	0.8438	0.8461	0.8485	0.8508	0.8531	0.8554	0.8577	0.8599	0.8621
1.1	0.8643	0.8665	0.8686	0.8708	0.8729	0.8749	0.8770	0.8790	0.8810	0.8830
1.2	0.8849	0.8869	0.8888	0.8907	0.8925	0.8944	0.8962	0.8980	0.8997	0.9015
1.3	0.9032	0.9049	0.9066	0.9082	0.9099	0.9115	0.9131	0.9147	0.9162	0.9177
1.4	0.9192	0.9207	0.9222	0.9236	0.9251	0.9265	0.9279	0.9292	0.9306	0.9319
1.5	0.9332	0.9345	0.9357	0.9370	0.9382	0.9394	0.9406	0.9418	0.9429	0.9441
1.6	0.9452	0.9463	0.9474	0.9484	0.9495	0.9505	0.9515	0.9525	0.9535	0.9545
1.7	0.9554	0.9564	0.9573	0.9582	0.9591	0.9599	0.9608	0.9616	0.9625	0.9633
1.8	0.9641	0.9649	0.9656	0.9664	0.9671	0.9678	0.9686	0.9693	0.9699	0.9706
1.9	0.9713	0.9719	0.9726	0.9732	0.9738	0.9744	0.9750	0.9756	0.9761	0.9767
2.0	0.9772	0.9778	0.9783	0.9788	0.9793	0.9798	0.9803	0.9808	0.9812	0.9817
2.1	0.9821	0.9826	0.9830	0.9834	0.9838	0.9842	0.9846	0.9850	0.9854	0.9857
2.2	0.9861	0.9864	0.9868	0.9871	0.9875	0.9878	0.9881	0.9884	0.9887	0.9890
2.3	0.9893	0.9896	0.9898	0.9901	0.9904	0.9906	0.9909	0.9911	0.9913	0.9916
2.4	0.9918	0.9920	0.9922	0.9925	0.9927	0.9929	0.9931	0.9932	0.9934	0.9936
2.5	0.9938	0.9940	0.9941	0.9943	0.9945	0.9946	0.9948	0.9949	0.9951	0.9952
2.6	0.9953	0.9955	0.9956	0.9957	0.9959	0.9960	0.9961	0.9962	0.9963	0.9964
2.7	0.9965	0.9966	0.9967	0.9968	0.9969	0.9970	0.9971	0.9972	0.9973	0.9974
2.8	0.9974	0.9975	0.9976	0.9977	0.9977	0.9978	0.9979	0.9979	0.9980	0.9981
2.9	0.9981	0.9982	0.9982	0.9983	0.9984	0.9984	0.9985	0.9985	0.9986	0.9986
3.0	0.9987	0.9987	0.9987	0.9988	0.9988	0.9989	0.9989	0.9989	0.9990	0.9990
3.1	0.9990	0.9991	0.9991	0.9991	0.9992	0.9992	0.9992	0.9992	0.9993	0.9993
3.2	0.9993	0.9993	0.9994	0.9994	0.9994	0.9994	0.9994	0.9995	0.9995	0.9995
3.3	0.9995	0.9995	0.9995	0.9996	0.9996	0.9996	0.9996	0.9996	0.9996	0.9997
3.4	0.9997	0.9997	0.9997	0.9997	0.9997	0.9997	0.9997	0.9997	0.9997	0.9998

APPENDIX D:

WILCOXON SIGNED-RANK TEST TABLE

Table D.1 displays the lower critical values for the Wilcoxon signed-rank test. They are defined as:

$$P(T_+ \leq \tau_{n,\alpha}) = \alpha$$

The upper critical values are calculated as

$$\frac{n(n+1)}{2} - \tau_{n,\alpha}$$

Table D.1: Wilcoxon signed-rank test table

$\tau_{n,\alpha}$	α					
	0.25	**0.1**	**0.05**	**0.025**	**0.01**	**0.005**
3	1					
4	2	0				
5	4	2	0			
6	6	3	2	0		
7	9	5	3	2	0	
8	12	8	5	3	1	0
9	16	10	8	5	3	1
10	20	14	10	8	5	3
11	24	17	13	10	7	5
12	29	21	17	13	9	7
13	35	26	21	17	12	9
14	40	31	25	21	15	12
15	47	36	30	25	19	15
16	54	42	35	29	23	19
17	61	48	41	34	27	23
18	69	55	47	40	32	27
19	77	62	53	46	37	32
20	86	69	60	52	43	37

STUDENT EXERCISES ANSWERS

Chapter 2

2.1 The entries in the "Castings" column are confusing because the first two classes overlap, and the 3rd and 4th classes are (apparently) the same thing. The column labelled "Weight of Metal" is ambiguous because it is not clear what the values in this column represent (are these values frequencies or weight measurements? What does the total value of 290 represent?).

2.2 a)

Bin	Frequency	Class	Frequency
49.5	0		
54.5	1	[50; 55)	1
59.5	2	[55; 60)	2
64.5	13	[60; 65)	13
69.5	10	[65; 70)	10
74.5	12	[70; 75)	12
79.5	21	[75; 80)	21
84.5	5	[80; 85)	5
89.5	9	[85; 90)	9
94.5	3	[90; 95)	3
99.5	4	[95; 100)	4
More	0		

b)

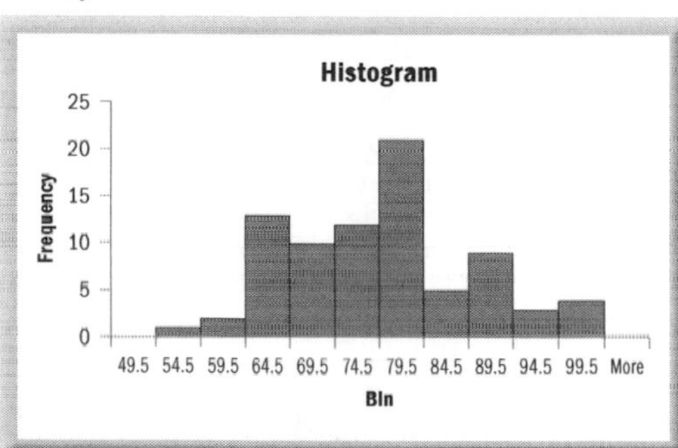

c)

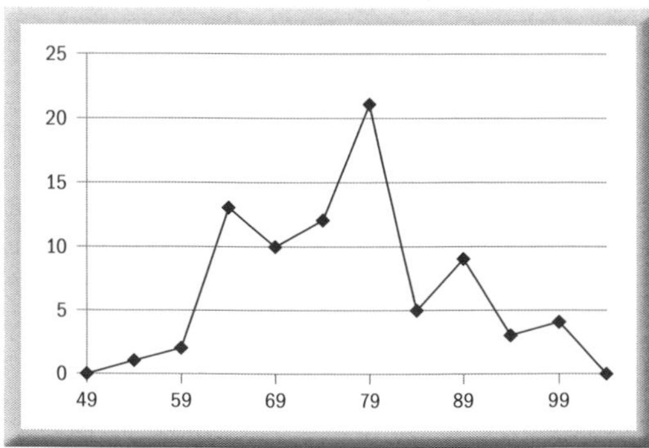

2.3

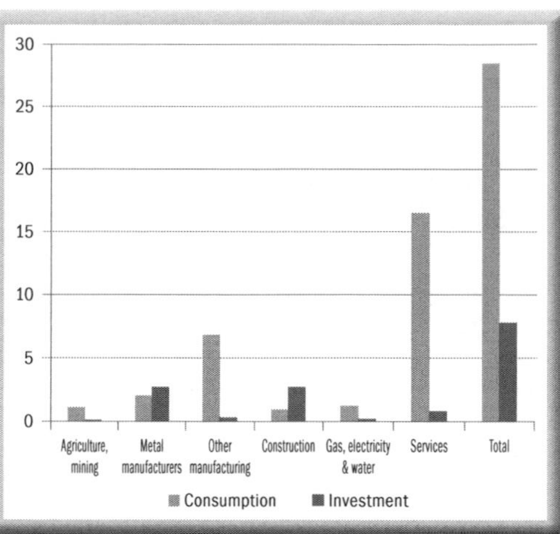

2.4 a)

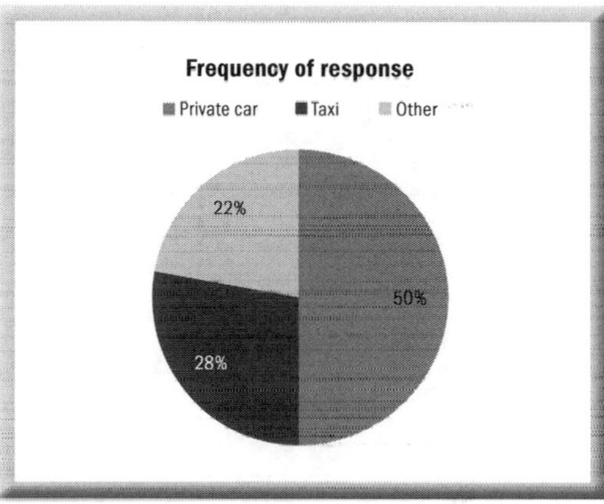

b)

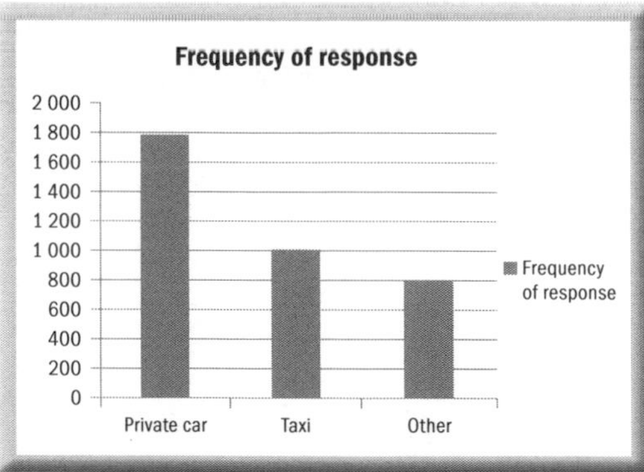

c) The majority of people use private cars. The remaining people are fairly evenly split between the other two modes of transport.

2.5 a)

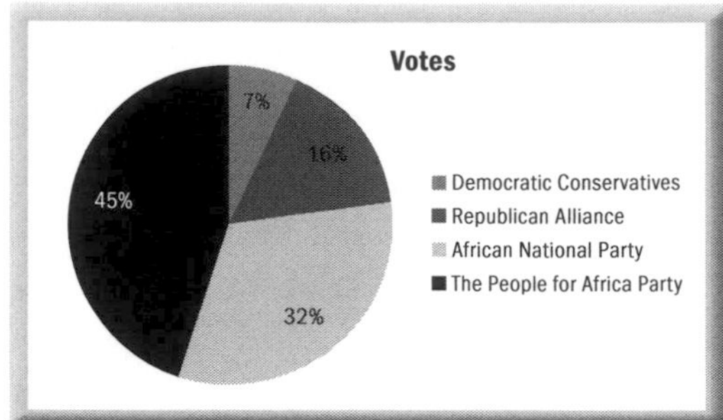

b)]

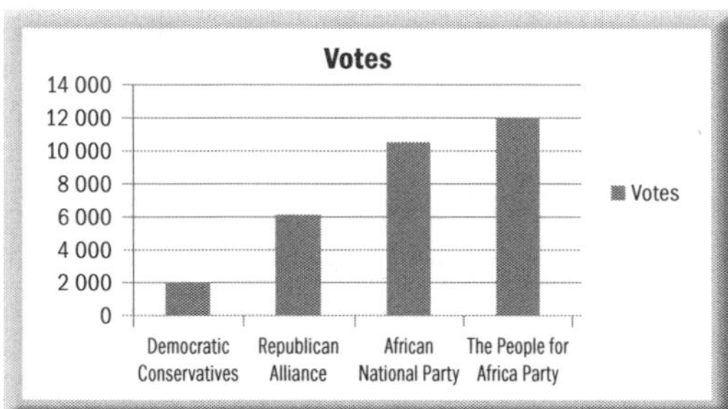

c) The majority of people voted for "The People for Africa" party. The next best party was the "African National" party. The "Democratic Conservatives" received the fewest votes, getting less than 10% of the total votes.

2.6

29.999	*Frequency*		Class	Frequency	
74.999	13		[30; 75)	13	
119.999	14		[75; 120)	14	
164.999	12		[120; 165)	12	
209.999	7		[165; 210)	7	
254.999	2		[210; 255)	2	
299.999	1		[255; 300)	1	
344.999	1		[300; 345)	1	
More	0				

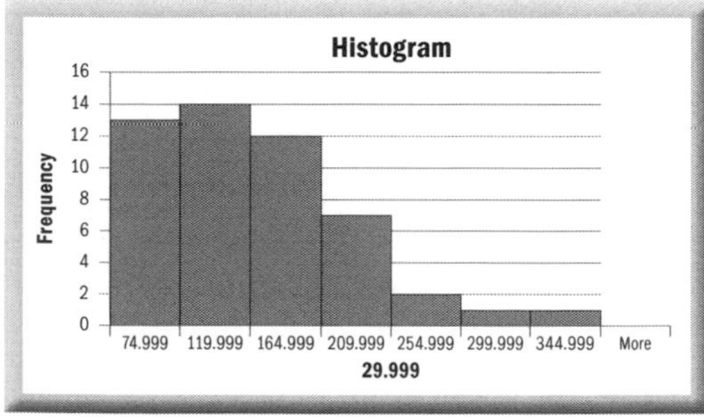

Chapter 3

3.1 a) Mean = 44 and median = 28. Note the large difference in the two values.

b) Standard deviation = 42.2 and IQR = 67.5

c) Pearson's coefficient of skewness (PCS) = 1.13 and Fisher's skewness coefficient = 1.09

d) The data are mildly skewed to the right, with points centred roughly around 30 to 40 and have a standard deviation of about 42 units (the middle half of the observations lie within a range of 67.5 units).

3.2 Mean = 100.17 and median = 99. Both measures of average support the IQ statement. Note that the sample size is small. The issue of sample size will be discussed in chapters on confidence intervals and hypothesis testing.

3.3 Mean = 46.17 and median = 49.5.
Mean – uses all data values with no extreme values identified.
Median is the 50th percentile value and can be used if extreme values are identified.
In this question the two measures of location are approximately equal and we can say that there is no evidence of extreme values in the data set.

3.4 Mean = 2.9; median = 3; and mode = 2 ; $Q_1 = 2$ and $Q_3 = 4$

3.5 Mean salary R670 000, the median is R600 000 and the standard deviation is R108 093.53.

3.6 a)

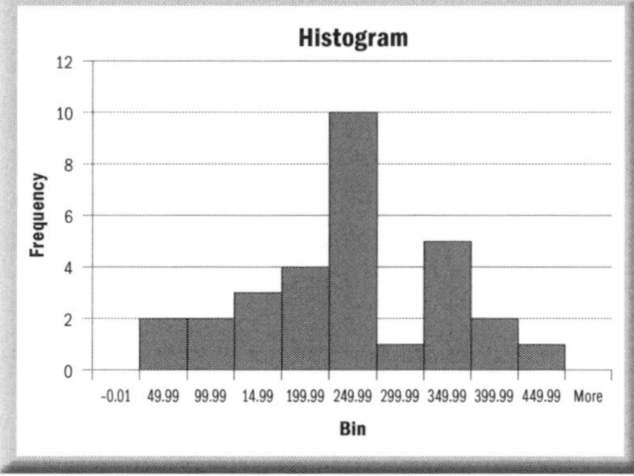

We can see from the histogram that we have a slightly skewed distribution.

b) Mean = 215.33; median = 220.

c) Range = 410; IQR = 135; standard deviation = 135.

d) In this case we would use the median rather than the mean as the measure of average.

3.7 Ungrouped mean = 27; grouped mean = 27.0513. The difference between the two is caused by the fact that we essentially "throw away" a small amount of information when grouping data.

3.8 a) Mean nail length = 5.13 mm
b)

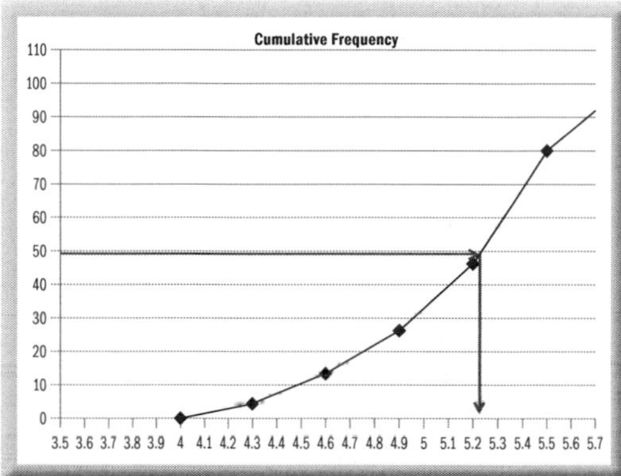

Median from Cumulative Frequency graph = 5.22 mm
c) Median from formula = 5.23 mm.

3.9 a) Mean from formula = 48.7
b)

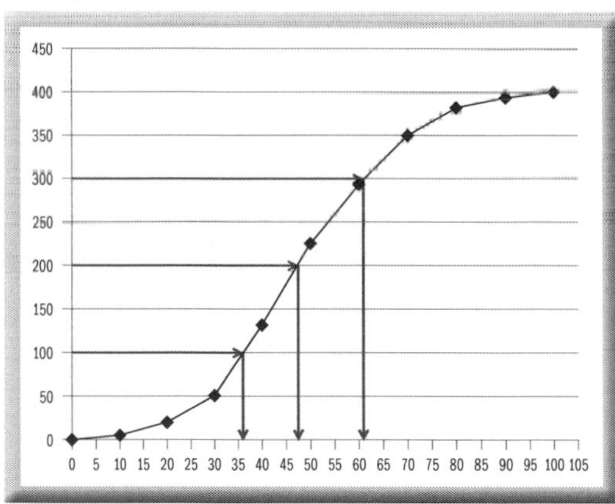

From CF graph: median = 47.2; upper quartile Q_3 = 60.8; lower quartile Q_1 = 35.7

3.10 Mean = 2.97; standard deviation = 1.85

3.11 Range = 21; mean = 67.48; standard deviation = 4.36

3.12

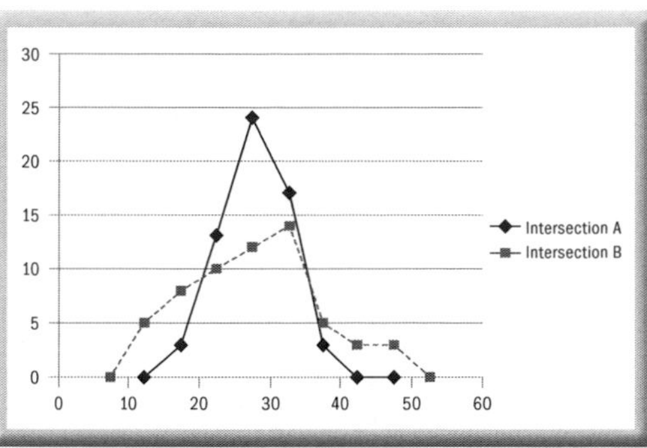

Intersection A: Mean = 27.8;
Standard deviation = 4.77;
Coefficient of variation = 17.14%;
Intersection B: Mean = 27.8;
Standard deviation = 9.11;
Coefficient of variation = 32.72%.
We can see from the frequency polygons that the distributions have the same mean average value but distribution B is slightly more dispersed than distribution A.

3.13 a)

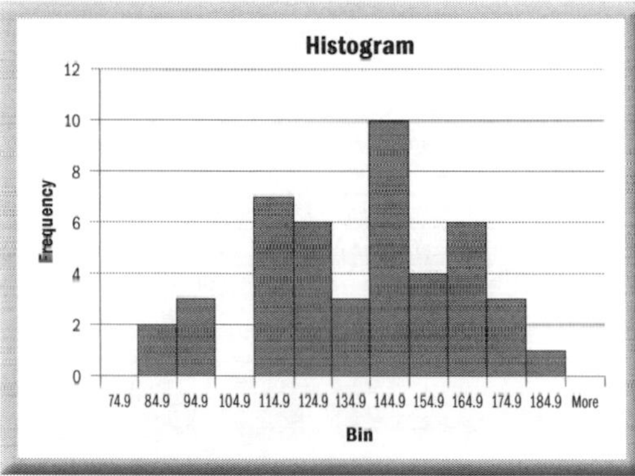

We can see from the histogram that the pattern consists of an uneven pattern in the data.
b) From Excel, mean = 132.13; median = 136; standard deviation = 24.68; semi-interquartile range = 18.
c) From the histogram we have no evidence of extreme values within the data set and we have a range of data values between the minimum and maximum values. In this case we can see that the mean and median are approximately equal and therefore we would use the mean to represent the distance travelled.

d) From Excel, skewness = –0.298 (values slightly bunched up to the higher end of the data values); and kurtosis = 0.542 (evidence of a slight flat distribution). Compare these two values with the error equations:

- for skewness the guideline is that the value must lie between $\pm 2\sqrt{\frac{6}{45}} = \pm 0{,}73$ in order for it to be "not extreme," and
- for kurtosis the guideline is that the value must lie between $\pm 2\sqrt{\frac{25}{45}} = \pm 1.46$, in order for it to be "not extreme."

We can see that we do not have a problem with either extreme skewness or extreme kurtosis within the data set.

3.14 a) Five-number summary: $Q_1 = 1.075$; minimum = 0.27; median = 1.395; maximum = 4.89; $Q_3 = 1.775$

b) Distance from Q_3 to the median (1.775 – 1.395 = 0.38) is approximately equal to distance from median to Q_1 (1.395 – 1.075 = 0.32). Distance from largest value to Q_3 (4.89 – 1.775 = 3.115) is greater than between Q_1 and minimum value (1.075 – 0.27 = 0.805) which indicates right skewness.

c)

Column 1	
Mean	1.524
Standard Error	0.121916
Median	1.395
Mode	0.76
Standard Deviation	0.771066
Sample Variance	0.594543
Kurtosis	8.79998
Skewness	2.33687
Range	4.62
Minimum	0.27
Maximum	4.89
Sum	60.96
Count	40

We can see from this screenshot that the value of skewness is 2.34. This value is greater than the error measurement of: $\pm 2\sqrt{\frac{6}{40}} = \pm 0.77$, and we conclude that the data distribution is significantly skewed to the right.

d) Given that this data set is heavily skewed we would use the median to represent the average and semi-interquartile range to represent the measure of spread.

3.15 a) Five-number summary: $Q_1 = 110\,530$; minimum = 75 558; median = 154 752; maximum = 272 487; $Q_3 = 197\,236$.

b) Distance from Q_3 to the median (= 42 484) is approximately equal to distance from median to Q_1 (= 44 222). Distance from largest value to Q_3 (= 75 251) is greater than between Q_1 and minimum value (= 34 972) which indicates right skewness.

c) We can see from this screenshot that the value of skewness is = 0.38. This value is less than the error measurement of: $\pm 2\sqrt{\frac{6}{50}} = \pm 0.69$ and we conclude that the data distribution is not significantly skewed to the right.

Column 1	
Mean	160690.9
Standard Error	7758.996
Median	154752
Mode	#N/A
Standard Deviation	54864.39
Sample Variance	3.01E+09
Kurtosis	–0.79286
Skewness	0.383286
Range	196929
Minimum	75558
Maximum	272487
Sum	8034544
Count	50

d) Given that this data set is not significantly skewed we would use the mean to represent the average and standard deviation to represent the measure of spread.

Chapter 4

4.1 a) Set of 52 playing cards:
Ω = {A♦, 2♦, 3♦, ..., K♦, A♥, 2♥, 3♥, ..., K♥, A♣, 2♣, 3♣, ..., K♣, A♠, 2♠, 3♠, ..., K♠}

b) Gender of males (M) and females (F):
Ω = {M, M, M, M, M, M, F, F, F, F, F}

c) Sample space consists of nine sample points (☆) as follows:
Ω = {WW, WD, WL, DW, DD, DL, LW, LD, LL}
where W = Win, D = Draw, and L = Lose

4.2 $A = \{5, 8\}$
$B = \{2, 3, 4\}$
$C = \{1, 2, 5, 6\}$
Only events A and B are mutually exclusive (A and C have "5" in common; B and C have "2" in common).

4.3 Use official records to correlate the number of 25-year-olds passing a driving test at the first attempt with the total number sitting the test. This would be undertaken for a particular time frame and the probability would represent the probability for this time frame only. This is likely to change if you were to repeat the calculation for a different time frame (different sample).

4.4 a) $\frac{4}{25}$ b) $\frac{7}{10}$ c) $\frac{43}{50}$ d) $\frac{5}{8}$ e) $\frac{7}{100}$

4.5 a) 0.024 b) 0.452

Chapter 5

5.1

x	$P(X = x)$
0	$\frac{4}{8} \times \frac{5}{9} \times \frac{6}{10} = \frac{1}{6}$
1	$\frac{5}{8} \times \frac{6}{9} \times \frac{4}{10} + \frac{5}{8} \times \frac{4}{9} \times \frac{6}{10} + \frac{4}{8} \times \frac{5}{9} \times \frac{6}{10} = \frac{1}{2}$
2	$\frac{6}{8} \times \frac{3}{9} \times \frac{4}{10} + \frac{3}{8} \times \frac{6}{9} \times \frac{4}{10} + \frac{3}{8} \times \frac{4}{9} \times \frac{6}{10} = \frac{3}{10}$
3	$\frac{2}{8} \times \frac{3}{9} \times \frac{4}{10} = \frac{1}{30}$

$$P(X > 1) = \frac{3}{10} + \frac{1}{30} = \frac{1}{3}$$

$$60 \times P(X > 1) = 60 \times \frac{1}{3} = 20$$

5.2 a) $E(A) = E(B) =$ R10 000
b) $Var(A) = 100\ 600\ 000$ and $Var(B) = 101\ 200\ 000$. Investment B.
c) Investment A yields a better profit profile; the variance is lower for A compared to B – reduces overall risk.

Chapter 6

6.1 a) Probability distribution: $P(X = 0) = 0.0256$; $P(X = 1) = 0.1536$; $P(X = 2) = 0.3456$; $P(X = 3) = 0.1296$
b)

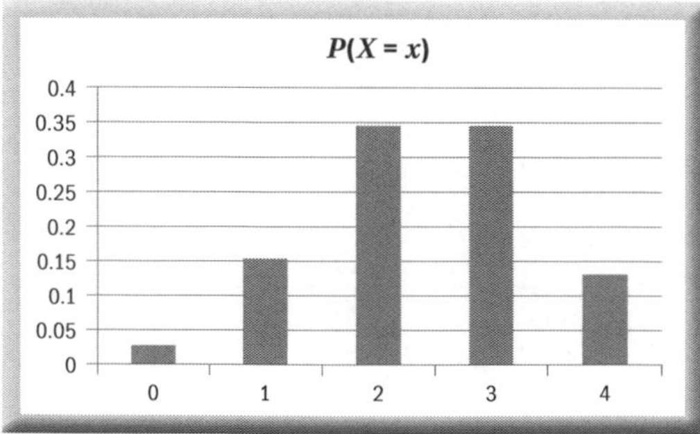

6.2 a) PAll women) = 0.004096
b) P(3 men) = 0.27648
c) P(< 3 women) = 0.54432

6.3 P(second sample taken) = 0.142525; P(production line stopped) = 0.02034

6.4 P(at least 3 voted) = 0.6768

6.5 a) P(no accidents) = 0.3164
b) P(at least two accidents) = $P(X > 2) = 0.2617$
c) Expected cost is R18 066.41
d) Reject bid based upon expected cost.

6.6 Mean =1.2; variance =1.2

6.7 a) P(one machine not working) = 0.2707
b) P(more than one machine not working) = 0.5940

6.8 P(one or more defective) = 0.3935 = 39.35%

6.9 a) P(free from faults) = 0.6703
b) Length > 0.5129 m
c) No

6.10 a) $P(X = 0) = 0.1353$; $P(X = 1) = 0.2707$; $P(X = 2) = 0.02707$; $P(X = 3) = 0.1804$; mean = 2
b) Expected daily profit = R27.07

6.11 a) P(no accidents in month) = 0.074
b) P(more than one accident per month) = 0.733

Chapter 7

7.1 a) $P(X < 95) = 0.1587$
b) $P(95 < X < 105) = 0.6827$
c) $P(105 < X < 115) = 0.1573$
d) $P(93 < X < 99) = 0.3400$

7.2 a) $P(Z < -1) = 0.1587$
b) $P(-1 < Z < 1) = 0.6827$
c) $P(1 < Z < 3) = 0.1573$
d) $P(-1.4 < Z < -0.2) = 0.3400$

7.3 a) $P(X > 11) = 0.4207$
b) $P(X < 11) = 0.5793$
c) $P(X < 5) = 0.1587$
d) $P(X > 5) = 0.8413$
e) $P(5 < X < 11) = 0.4206$

7.4 P(replaced) = 0.1819 (or 18.19%)

7.5 a) P(reject) = 0.1685
b) P(reject) = 0.0956
c) Adjust standard deviation to 2.13 ohms.

7.6 a) $P(W < 1) = 0.8247$
b) $P(-1 < W < 0.5) = 0.5085$
c) $P(X < 10) = 0.5595$
d) $P(X > 5) = 0.8912$
e) $P(4 < X < 9) = 0.4152$

f) $P(Y < 1.5) = 0.6912$
g) $P(Y > 0.2) = 0.8250$

Chapter 8

8.1 a) $\mu = 800$ and $\overline{\overline{X}} = 800$

8.2 a) $\overline{X} \sim N(10, 2)$
b) $\overline{X} \sim N(10, 1)$
c) $\overline{X} \sim N(10, 0.25)$
Increased sample size reduces the size of the error ($\sigma_{\overline{X}}$).

8.3 a) $\overline{X} \sim N(63, 2.5)$
b) $\overline{X} \sim N(63, 1.667)$
c) $\overline{X} \sim N(63, 1)$

8.4 See Example 8.8.

8.5 a) Expected number $n = 3\,413$ items
b) 34%
c) For $n = 10$; $\sigma_{\overline{X}} = 0.9487$. For $n = 40$, $\sigma_{\overline{X}} = 0.4743$.

8.6 a) $P(0.4 < \text{p} < 0.6) = 0.9545$
b) $P(0.35 < \text{p} < 0.65) = 0.9973$
c) $P(0.5 < \text{p} < 0.65) = 0.4987$

8.7 P(African National Party win) = 0.0206 or 2%

8.8 a) P(desired accuracy) = 0.6826 or 68%
b) P(desired accuracy) = 0.98758 or 99%

8.9 P(average cost exceeds R11.10) = 0.00256 or 0.26%

Chapter 9

9.1 Population estimates: mean = 7.14; standard deviation = 1.808; standard error = 0.8085

9.2 Population estimates: mean = 8.7; standard deviation = 0.2550

9.3 Unbiased population estimates: mean = 0.2538; variance = 0.011

9.4 $P(12.12 < \overline{X}_B < 12.14) = 0.4762$

9.5 Population estimates: proportion = 0.6; standard error = 0.11

9.6 Estimate number of fish in lake = 10 000

9.7 90% CI for population mean is [1.1218; 1.1382]

9.8 a) 90% CI for D is [9.5065; 10.4935]
b) Sample size = 553

9.9 95% CI for population mean is [23.09; 26.25]

9.10 Sample size = 6

Chapter 10

10.1 a) Mean quantity from sample (μ_s) ≠ mean quantity within contract (μ_c)
b) H_0: $\mu_s = \mu_c$; H_1: $\mu_s \neq \mu_c$
c) The alternate hypothesis H_1: $[\mu]_S \neq [\mu]_C$ is thus a two-sided test.

10.2

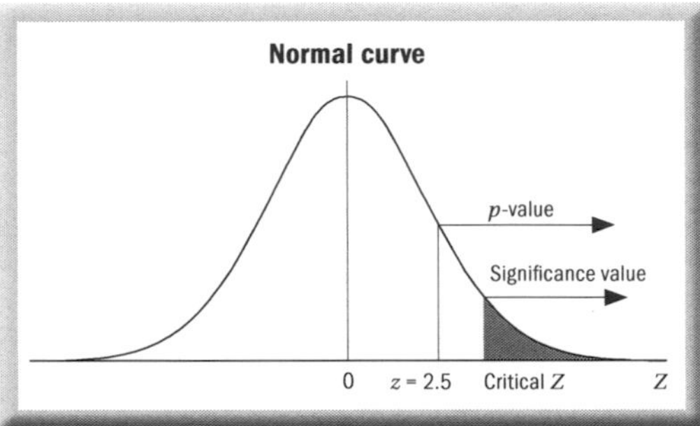

10.3 a) ±2.326
b) -2.054
c) +2.054

10.4 p-value = 0.000287. Reject the null hypothesis; there is a difference.

10.5 Do not reject H_0 ($z_{\text{cal}} = 1.77$; two tail p-value = 0.076; $z_\alpha = \pm 1.96$)

10.6 Reject H_0 ($z_{\text{cal}} = 2.83$; two tail p-value = 0.0047; $z_\alpha = \pm 1.96$)

10.7 a) ±3.055 b) -2.681 c) +2.681

10.8 a) When σ unknown; n small; population normally distributed (or approximately)
b) p-value = 0.032564

10.9 Do not reject H_0 at 5% ($t_{\text{cal}} = -2.165$; two tail p-value = 0.053; $t_{\text{cal}} = \pm 2.201$)

10.10 Reject H_0 at 5% ($z_{\text{cal}} = -2.37$; two tail p-value = 0.033; $t_\alpha = \pm 2.145$)

Chapter 11

11.1 a) H_0: $\sigma_A^2 = \sigma_B^2$ vs. H_1: $\sigma_A^2 \neq \sigma_B^2$
Do not reject H_0, the population variances are not significantly different. ($f_{\text{cal}} = 1.3002$; p-value = 0.2345; $F_\alpha = 1.8221$)
b) H_0: $\mu_A = \mu_B$ vs. H_1: $\mu_A \neq \mu_B$ (conduct the "equal variances t-test")
Reject H_0, the population means are not equal. ($t_{\text{cal}} = 2.5374$, two tail p-value = 0.0137; $t_\alpha = \pm 1.999$)

11.2 a) H_0: $\mu_A = \mu_B$ vs. H_1: $\mu_A \neq \mu_B$
Reject H_0, the population means are not equal. (t_{cal} 2.1049, two tail p-value = 0.0390; $t_\alpha = \pm 1.9955$)
b) H_0: $\mu_A = \mu_B$ vs. H_1: $\mu_A \neq \mu_B$
Reject H_0, the population means are not equal. ($t_{cal} = 2.1049$, two tail p-value = 0.0390; $t_\alpha = \pm 1.9960$)
(the conclusions obtained under both assumptions are nearly identical because the sample standard deviations are so close to one another, $S_A = 4.052$ and $S_B = 4.046$).

11.3 H_0: $\pi_A = \pi_B$ vs. H_1: $\pi_A \neq \pi_B$
Reject H_0, the population proportions are not equal. ($z_{cal} = -2.3086$, two tail p-value = 0.0210; $z_\alpha = \pm 1.96$)

11.4 H_0: $\pi_A = \pi_B$ vs. H_1: $\pi_A \neq \pi_B$
Do not reject H_0, the population proportions are not significantly different.($z_{cal} = 1.6676$, two tail p-value = 0.0954; $z_\alpha = \pm 1.96$)

11.5 H_0: $\mu_A = \mu_B$ vs. H_1: $\mu_A \neq \mu_B$ (conduct the "equal variances t-test")
Reject H_0, the population means are not equal. ($t_{cal} = -2.4427$, two tail p-value = 0.0189; $t_\alpha = \pm 2.0181$)

11.6 H_0: $\mu_A = \mu_B$ vs. H_1: $\mu_A \neq \mu_B$ (conduct the "equal variances t-test")
Reject H_0, the population means are not equal. ($t_{cal} = 5.7837$, two tail p-value = 0.00001; $t_\alpha = \pm 2.0796$)

11.7 H_0: $\mu_D = 0$ vs. H_1: $\mu_D > 0$
For $\alpha = 0.05$: Reject H_0, the population mean "after" is greater than "before". ($t_{cal} = 2.1541$, right tail p-value = 0.02457; $t_\alpha = \pm 1.7613$).
For $\alpha = 0.01$: Do not reject H_0, the population mean "after" is *not* greater than "before". ($t_{cal} = 2.1541$, right tail p-value = 0.02457; $t_\alpha = \pm 2.6245$).

11.8 H_0: $\mu_D = 0$ vs. H_1: $\mu_D \neq 0$
Do not reject H_0, the population mean "Project mark" is not greater than "Research Methods Mark". ($t_{cal} = 2.0534$, two tail p-value = 0.0592; $t_\alpha = \pm 1.7613$).

11.9 H_0: $\sigma_A^2 = \sigma_B^2$ vs. H_1: $\sigma_A^2 \neq \sigma_B^2$
Reject H_0, the population variances are significantly different. ($f_{cal} = 3.0178$; p-value = 0.0060; $F_\alpha = 2.0518$)

11.10 H_0: $\sigma_A^2 = \sigma_B^2$ vs. H_1: $\sigma_A^2 \neq \sigma_B^2$
Do not reject H_0, the population variances are not significantly different. ($f_{cal} = 0.8011$; p-value = 0.6533; $F_\alpha = 3.2590$)1%

11.11 H_0: $\mu_A = \mu_B$ vs. H_1: $\mu_A \neq \mu_B$ (conduct the "unequal variances t-test")
Reject H_0, the population means are not equal. ($t_{cal} = -2.1714$, two tail p-value = 0.0410; $t_\alpha = \pm 2.0739$)

11.12 H_0: $\mu_A = \mu_B$ vs. H_1: $\mu_A \neq \mu_B$ (conduct the "unequal variances t-test")
Reject H_0, the population means are not equal. ($t_{cal} = 5.6400$, two-tail p-value < 0.0001; $t_\alpha = \pm 2.1314$)

Chapter 12

12.1 $r = 0.84$. Scatter plot and Pearson's correlation coefficient seems to suggest a strong positive correlation but look at the scatter plot and how the data points are lined up with only three x-values (40, 41, 42).

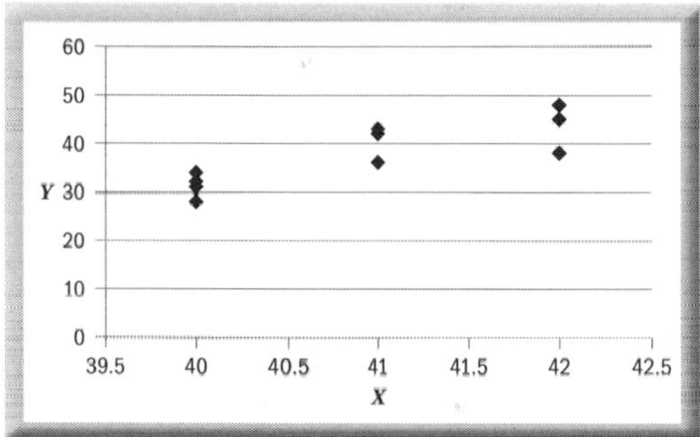

12.2 $r = -0.93$. Scatter plot and Pearson's correlation coefficient suggest a strong negative correlation.

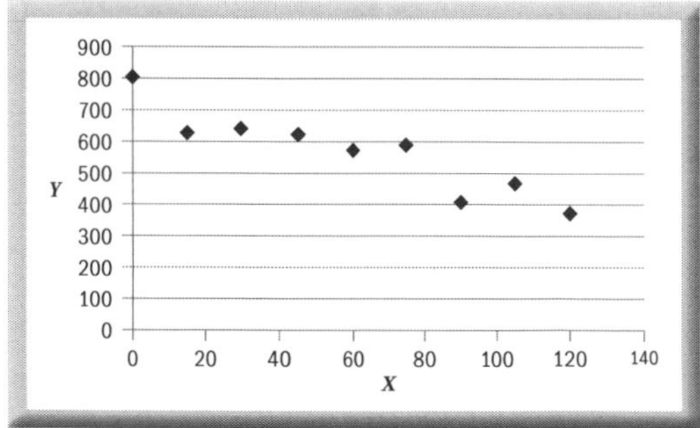

12.3 a), b) and c) $r = 0.72$. Scatter plot and Pearson's correlation coefficient suggest a strong positive correlation.

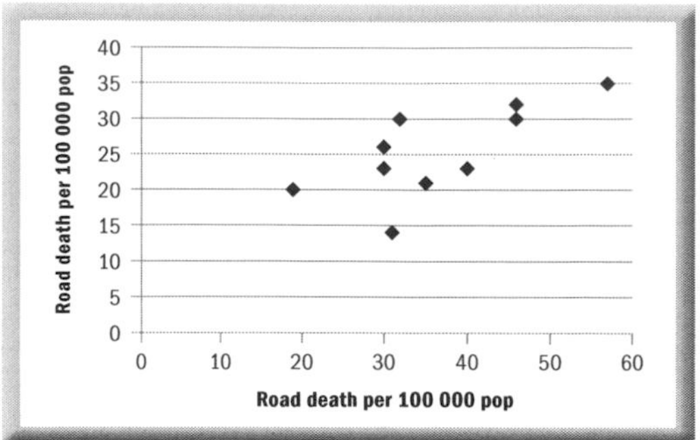

12.4 a)

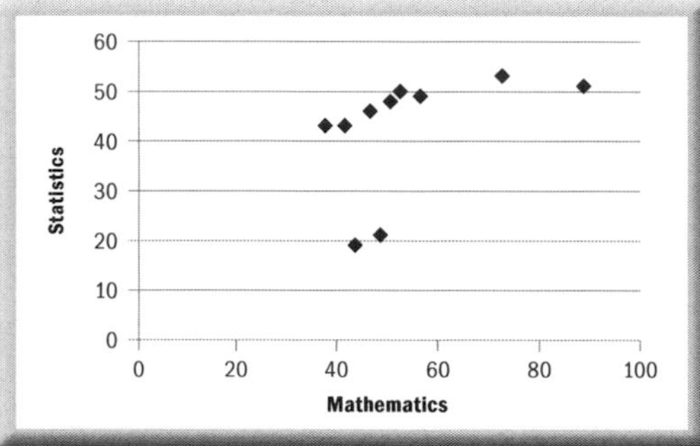

b) $r = 0.47$.

c) Scatter plot and Pearson's correlation coefficient suggest a weak to medium positive correlation.

12.5 C

12.6 B

12.7 C

12.8 D

12.9 a)

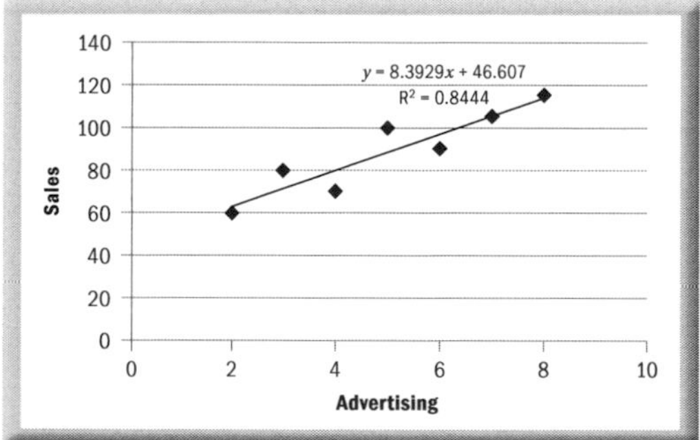

The correlation is $r = 0.92$ indicating a strong linear relationship between advertisements and sales. A linear regression model should work between these two variables.

b) To solve this problem use Analysis ToolPak – Regression to provide the following set of solutions:

i) The fitted model is: $\widehat{Y} = 46.607 + 8.393X$

ii) The model fit statistics are: $r = 0.92$, and $R^2 = 0.84$ or 84%, indicating a good fit.

iii) Testing if the true parameter β_1 is zero we have two separate tests (the F-test statistic is 27.14 and the t-test statistic is 5.21). Both produce the same p-value (0.003440115) for testing the validity of the hypothesis H_0: $\beta_1 = 0$. We therefore reject H_0 and conclude that the coefficient is significantly different from zero (and that Advertising significantly impacts Sales in a linear way).

iv) Assumption checks:

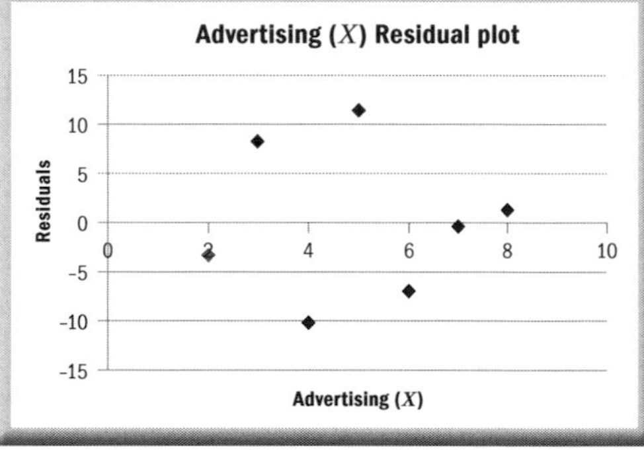

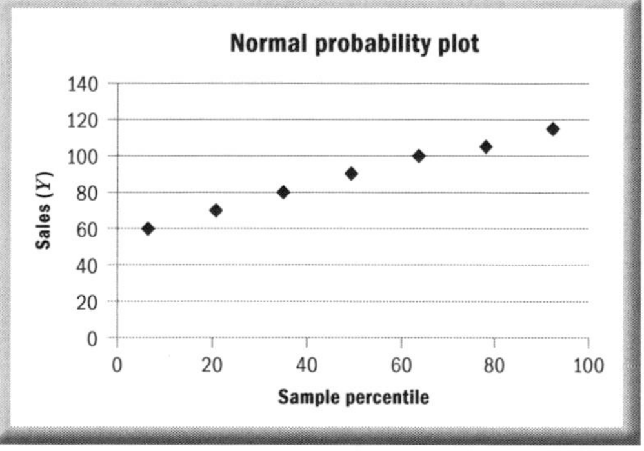

We can see from the scatter plot that we have no observed pattern within the residual plot and we can assume that the linearity assumption is not violated. Furthermore, the residual and hence the

variance are not growing in size and are bounded between a high and low point. From this we conclude that the variance assumption is not violated.
From the normal probability plot we have a fairly linear relationship and we conclude that the normal assumption is not violated.

v) The model evaluated at advertising expenditure equal to R6500 is:

$$\widehat{Y} = 46.607 + 8.393(6.5) = 101.1615.$$

The Δ-value is then calculated as given in the text. We get $\Delta = 24.2374$ and so the interval is:

$$[\widehat{Y} - \Delta;\ \widehat{Y} + \Delta]$$
$$[101.1615 - 24.2374;\ 101.1615 + 24.2374]$$
$$[76.9241;125.3989]$$

12.10 a)

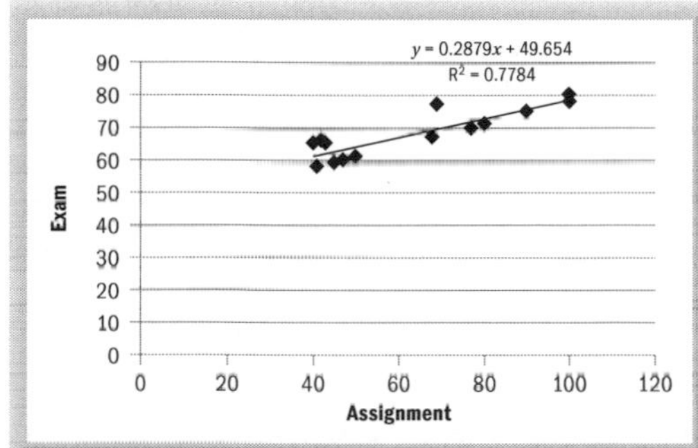

The correlation is $r = 0.88$ indicating a strong linear relationship between Assignment mark and Exam mark. A linear regression model should work between these two variables.

b) To solve this problem use Analysis ToolPak - Regression to provide the following set of solutions:
   i) The fitted model is $\widehat{Y} = 49.6537 + 0.2879X$
   ii) $r = 0.88$, and $R^2 = 0.78$ or 78%, indicating a good fit.
   iii) Testing if the true parameter β_1 is zero we have two separate tests (the F-test statistic is 42.14 and the t-test statistic is 6.4916). Both produce the same p-value (0.0000297) for testing the validity of the hypothesis H_0: $\beta_1 = 0$. We therefore reject H_0 and conclude that the coefficient is significantly different from zero (and that the Assignment mark significantly impacts the Exam mark in a linear way).
   iv) Assumption checks:

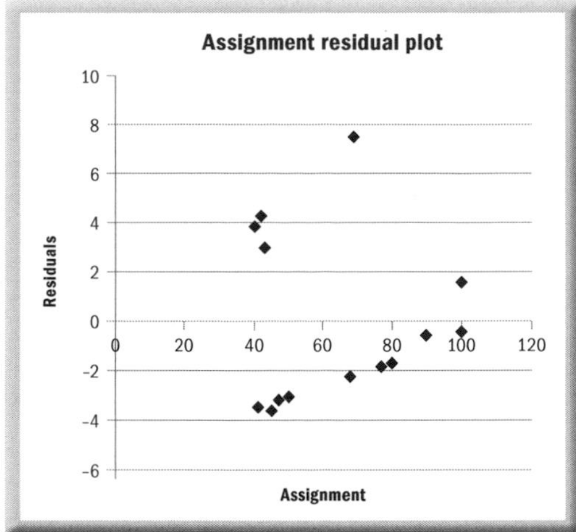

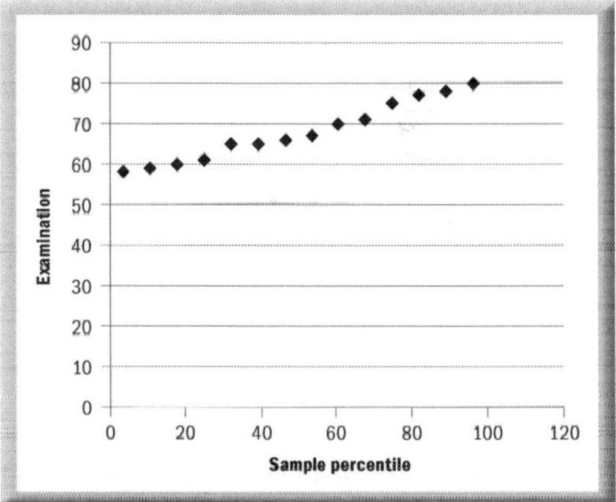

We can see from the scatter plot that we have no observed pattern within the residual plot and we can assume that the linearity assumption is not violated. Furthermore, the residual and hence the variance are not growing in size and are bounded between a high and low point. From this we conclude that the variance assumption is not violated. From the normal probability plot we have a fairly linear relationship and we conclude that the normal assumption is not violated.

v) The model evaluated at advertising expenditure equal to 75 is:

$$\widehat{Y} = 49.6537 + 0.2879(75) = 71.2497$$

The Δ-value is then calculated as given in the text. We get $\Delta = 8.2053$ and so the interval is:

$$[\widehat{Y} - \Delta;\ \widehat{Y} + \Delta]$$
$$[71.2497 - 8.2053;\ 71.2497 + 8.2053]$$
$$[63.0444;\ 79.4550]$$

Chapter 13

13.1 The time series is non-stationary, but we cannot tell if it is seasonal too. First of all, we do not clearly see the pattern, but more importantly, the time units have not been defined. If the time units are not less than annual, we cannot talk about seasonality.

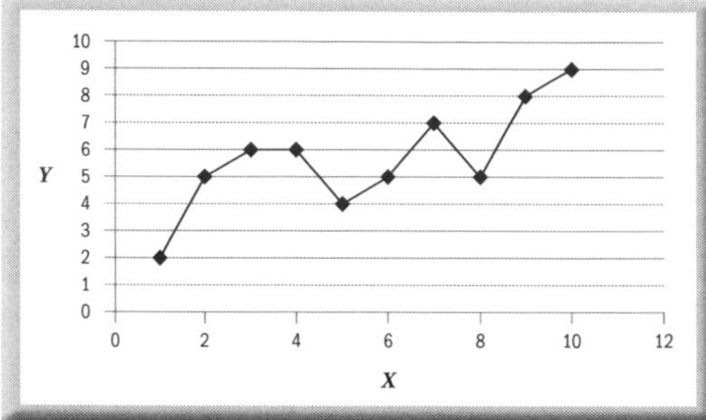

13.2 The seasonality is 5 as the pattern seems to repeat itself every five time periods.

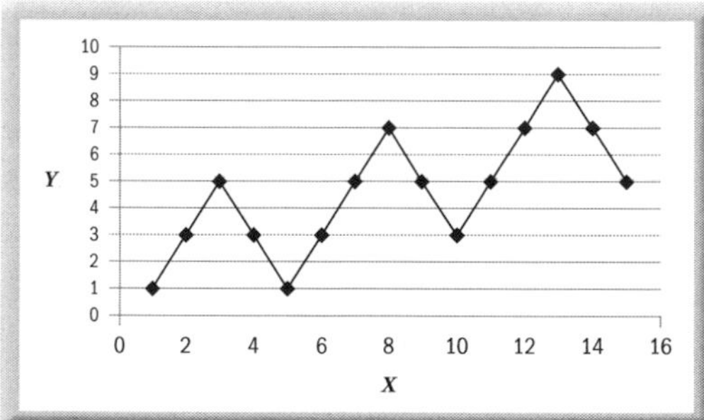

Using a 5-unit moving average we can extract the SI component. The specific season indices can then be obtained for the 5 units:

Unit 1	Unit 2	Unit 3	Unit 4	Unit 5
0.42372	0.8236	1.156705	1.598604	0.997371

The T component can be extracted using linear regression techniques and the forecasted values for the time units 16, 17, 18, and 19 are then:

16 (unit 2)	17 (unit 3)	18 (unit 4)	19 (unit 5)
7.457143	7.814286	8.171429	8.528571

Applying the seasonal index correction we get:

16 (unit 2)	7.457143 × 0.8236 = 6.1417
17 (unit 3)	7.814286 × 1.1567 = 9.0388
18 (unit 4)	8.171429 × 1.5986 = 13.0629
19 (unit 5)	8.528571 × 0.99737 = 8.5062

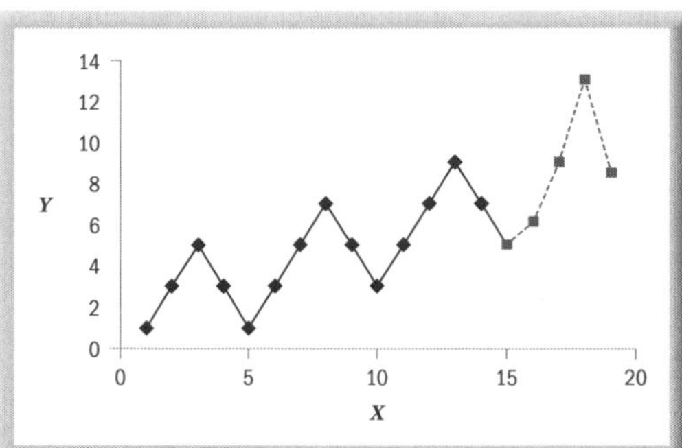

13.3 Yes, it is. A non-seasonal and non-stationary time series is a simple time series that has a mean that increases (or decreases) steadily over time (see, for example, Figure 13.1(b)).

13.4 Yes, the differenced time series appears to be stationary.

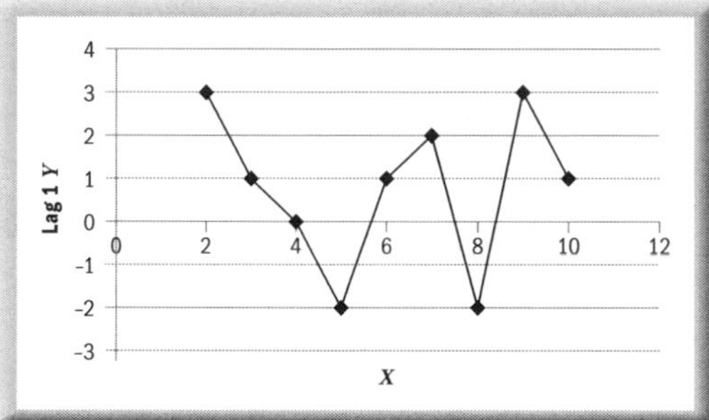

13.5

T	90	95	100	105	110	115	120	125	130
C	2	4	6	4	2	4	6	4	2
I	5	3	4	6	5	6	4	5	4
Additive	97	102	110	115	117	125	130	134	136

13.6 No, then stated formula is not a linear trend formula, but a quadratic equation formula. The corresponding trend for this equation has a parabolic shape.

13.7 The trend is calculated and extrapolated. The TREND function for the first cell, for example, is: =TREND($B$17:$J$17, $B$16:$J$16, B16), etc.

X	1	2	3	4	5	6	7	8	9	10	11	12
Y	230	300	290	30	350	400	350	400	420			
Trend	256	277	298	319	340	361	382	403	424	445	466	487

It would not make sense to extrapolate the time series much further in the future. A general rule is that we cannot go too far in the future, as it becomes meaningless, in particular if the history is not long enough. A rule of thumb says that the future extrapolation should be a maximum of one third of the historical time series. In our case, this is only up to three future observations.

13.8 Yes, the more observations we include in the moving average interval, the more 'smooth' this newly calculated time series of moving averages will be. In the extreme, if we take all the values of the time series in the moving average, we eventually get just a standard average, which is a very 'smooth' horizontal line.

13.9 It is not feasible to extrapolate a time series using simple moving average method more than one time period in the future. The whole 'forecasting' approach of using moving averages is based on a simple principle that we just shift the moving average value of the previous interval to the time period that follows the time interval. It would make no sense to extend this further in the future.

13.10 The two forecasts, each with a different value of [ ] are as follows:

X	1	2	3	4	5	6	7	8	9
Y	230	300	290	320	350	400	350	400	420
$\hat{Y}\alpha$ = **0.1**	230	230	237	242	250	260	274	282	293
$\hat{Y}\alpha$ = **0.99**	230	230	293	290	317	347	395	354	395

We observe that the small value of [ ] has a greater effect on smoothing of the time series. The conclusion is that for non-stationary and more dynamic time series a larger value of [ ] is probably more appropriate.

13.11 If Excel Damping Factor is 0,65, then the value of alpha is 0.35 ([ ] = 1 – Damping Factor).

13.12 If we take the analogy of shooting at a target, then we can say that we are accurate if all our shots are inside the target. However, if they are scattered around the target, then we are not precise. Clearly we want all the shots clustered as narrowly as possible around the middle of the target. The same applies to forecasting. Our ex-post forecasts might not be identical to actual observations, i.e. we are not accurate, but they closely follow the actual observations, which means we are precise. Conversely it is not possible, i.e. we cannot have accurate forecasts that are not precise as this makes no sense.

13.13 Mean error (*ME*) is a result of adding up all errors and dividing them by the total number of errors. If some errors are positive and some negative, when we add them up we might end up with zero sum (positives cancelling out the negatives). We do not have this problem if we use the mean absolute error (*MAD*), as all the values will be positive.

13.14 *MSE* is very sensitive to large errors. In our example only one forecasted value in the second forecast is radically different from the same value in the first forecast. However, the error that this one forecast creates is quite large. The *ME* is not so sensitive to these individual extremes and shows the *ME* for the second forecast only seven times higher. The *MSE*, on the other hand, is very sensitive to large deviations and it 'penalises' the second forecast with much larger value.

13.15 No, it is not acceptable to see any pattern in residuals. If there is any pattern, then this means that we have not used the most adequate model. Effectively, in this case our forecasting method is not adequate and we need to find another one that will represent the dynamics of the time series better.

13.16 Yes, this is correct. The diagonal line between the actual vs. ex-post forecasted values is the ideal line.

Chapter 14

14.1 a) 6
b) 12.59; 16.81
c) 0.021

14.2 $\chi^2_{cal} = 28.88$; $\chi^2_A = 9.49$; *p*-value = 8.28E-6
Association exists between industrial class and level of risk

14.3 $\chi^2_{cal} = 48.07$; $\chi^2_A = 12.59$; *p*-value = 3.14E-8
Association exists between shift and defect type

14.4 $\chi^2_{cal} = 7.35$; $\chi^2_A = 12.59$; *p*-value = 0.29
No association exists between optimism level and type of business

14.5 $\chi^2_{cal} = 6.68$; $\chi^2_A = 9.49$; *p*-value = 0.154
Association exists between performance in English and Afrikaans [borderline decision – alternative decision if 1% significance]

14.6 $\chi^2_{cal} = 0.77$; $\chi^2_A = 3.84$; p-value = 0.37. Do not reject H_0. No evidence that customers are taking into account petrol prices when buying cars.

14.7 $\chi^2_{cal} = 4.04$; $\chi^2_A = 3.84$; p-value = 0.044. Reject H_0. Evidence that campaign has altered the proportion voting yes [borderline decision]

14.8 Upper one sided p-value = 0.009605. Reject H_0. Evidence suggests that $\nu > 0.5$.

14.9 H_0: median difference > 0; X is binomial with: $n = 40 - 8 = 32$ and $p = 0.5$; $S_+ = 26$; upper one sided p-value = $P(X \geq 26) = 0.00027$. Reject H_0. Results are significantly different.

14.10 H_0: median = 25; H_1: median > 25;. X is binomial with $n = 15 - 1 = 14$; $S_+ = 10$; upper one-sided p-value = $P(X \geq 10) = 0.0898$. Do not reject H_0. Class sizes are not significantly larger.

14.11 H_0: median difference > 0;. X is binomial with: $n = 20 - 0 = 20$ and $p = 0.5$; $S_+ = 17$; upper one-sided p-value = $P(X \geq 17) = 0.0013$. Reject H_0. Results are significantly different afterwards.

14.12 H_0: median difference < 0;. X is binomial with: $n = 30 - 0 = 30$ and $p = 0.5$; $S_+ = 3$; upper one sided p-value = $P(X \leq 3) = 0.0000042$. Reject H_0. Results are significantly lower afterwards.

14.13 If we assume a normal approximation: $\mu = 36$; $\sigma = 10.39$; $z_{cal} = 0.6255$; upper one-tail $z_\alpha = 1.645$; upper one tail p-value = 0.2658. Do not reject H_0. No evidence of an improvement in performance.

14.14 Given the sample size apply a normal approximation: $\mu = 65$; $\sigma = 16.1245$; $z_{cal} = -3.0078$; two-tail $z_\alpha = +1.96$; two-tail p-value = 0.0026. Accept H_1. Evidence suggests interest rates are significantly different. (If you changed to a 1% significance level then you would reverse this decision.)

Chapter 15

15.1
a) See Section 15.2.1
b) The ratio of variances is 17.3, which is much larger than the rule-of-thumb of 4. Evidence suggests variance significantly different – use non-parametric test.
c) One-way ANOVA results: $f_{cal} = 5.2 > F_\alpha = 2.87$ (p-value = 0.005 < 0.05). Therefore, there is sufficient evidence to reject the hypothesis that the levels are all the same.
d) Bonferroni t-test significant differences: A-B, B-D.

15.2
a) See Section 15.2.1
b) The ratio of variances is 17, which is much larger than the rule-of-thumb of 4. Evidence suggests variance significantly different – use non-parametric test.
c) One-way ANOVA results: $f_{cal} = 7.04 > F_\alpha = 4.26$ (p-value = 0.01442 < 0.05). Therefore, there is sufficient evidence to reject the hypothesis that the levels are all the same.
d) Bonferroni t-test significant differences: A-C.

15.3
a) See Section 15.2.1
b) The ratio of variances is 3, which is much less than the rule-of-thumb of 4. Evidence suggests variances are not significantly different.
c) One-way ANOVA results: $f_{cal} = 2.5 > F_\alpha = 3.89$ (p-value = 0.1237 > 0.05). Therefore, there is sufficient evidence to not reject the hypothesis that the levels are all the same.
d) Bonferroni t-test not required – if you undertook the test you would find all comparisons not significant.

15.4 Kruskal-Wallis: $H = 12.152$ > critical chi-square = 9.49 (p-value = 0.016 < 0.05). Reject H_0. Therefore, there is sufficient evidence to reject the hypothesis that the levels are all the same.

15.5
a) Ranked data.
b) See Section 15.2.1 for one-way ANOVA model assumptions.
c) Kruskal-Wallis: $H = 8.47$ > critical chi-square = 5.99 (p-value = 0.014467 < 0.05). Reject H_0. Therefore, the airlines are not rated the same by the nine individuals.

15.7 Kruskal-Wallis: $H = 4.288$ < critical chi-square = 5.99 (p-value = 0.117 < 0.05). Do not reject H_0. Therefore, the average distance is the same.

15.8 Kruskal-Wallis: $H = 13.86$ > critical chi-square = 5.99 (p-value = 0.004 < 0.05). Reject H_0. Therefore, the performances are significantly different.

GLOSSARY

The ISI glossary of statistical terms provides definitions in a number of different languages: http://isi.cbs.nl/glossary/index.htm.

Adjusted R^2 Adjusted R squared measures the proportion of the variation in the dependent variable accounted for by the explanatory variables.

Alpha, α Alpha refers to the probability of type I error. Also called the *significance level*, it is the probability of rejecting the null hypothesis when it is true. Not to be confused with the symbol alpha in a time series context, i.e. exponential smoothing, where alpha is the smoothing constant.

Alternative hypothesis (H_1) The alternative hypothesis, H_1, is a contrasting statement to the null hypothesis; it indicates the possible alternative values of the population parameter, which can be contrasted against the specific statement made in the null hypothesis.

Analysis of variance (ANOVA) Analysis of variance is a method for testing the hypothesis that multiple population means are equal.

Arithmetic mean The sum of a number of measurements made on items divided by the total number of items.

Autocorrelation Autocorrelation is the correlation between members of a time series of observations and the same values shifted at a fixed time interval.

Beta, β Beta refers to the probability of a type II error. It is the probability of not rejecting the null hypothesis when it is false.

Binomial probability distribution A probability distribution that describes the probabilities of occurrence of a binomial random variable.

Binomial random variable A discrete random variable that describes the number of successful outcomes of n independent trials that can either succeed (with probability p) or fail (with probability $1 - p$).

Bonferroni t-test The Bonferroni test is a statistical procedure that adjusts the alpha level to allow multiple t-tests to be used following the ANOVA F-test.

Categorical variable A set of data is said to be categorical if the values or observations belonging to it can be sorted according to category.

Central Limit Theorem The Central Limit Theorem states that whenever a random sample is taken from any distribution, then the sample mean will be approximately normally distributed with mean μ and variance $\frac{\sigma^2}{n}$.

Central tendency Measures the location of the middle or the centre of a distribution.

Chi-square distribution The chi-square distribution is a continuous theoretical distribution. It is skewed to the right and positive. It is used directly or indirectly in many tests of significance.

Chi-square test Apply the chi-square distribution to test if the observed sample data match the values we expect under the null hypothesis. We can use it to test for independence or goodness-of-fit.

Classical additive time series model One of the models in classical time series analysis that assumes that components (trend, cyclical, seasonal, and random component) need to be added to compose the time series.

Classical time series analysis Approach to forecasting that decomposes a time series into certain constituent components (trend, cyclical, seasonal and random component), makes estimates of each component and then re-composes the time series and extrapolates into the future.

Classical time series mixed model One of the models in classical time series analysis that assumes that components (trend, cyclical, seasonal, and random component) need to be added and multiplied to compose the time series.

Classical time series multiplicative model One of the models in classical time series analysis that assumes that components (trend, cyclical, seasonal and random components) need to be multiplied to compose the time series.

Coefficient of determination (R^2) The proportion of the variance in the dependent variable that is explained by the independent variable.

Coefficient of variation The coefficient of variation measures the spread of a set of data as a proportion of its mean.

Confidence interval A confidence interval provides a range of possible values that the true parameter value can assume along with the degree of confidence ($1 - \alpha$) that the true parameter value lies within the interval.

Contingency table A contingency table is a table containing the number of elements (frequencies) classified according to the categorical levels of the two variables.

Continuous probability distribution If a random variable is a continuous variable, its probability distribution is called a continuous probability distribution.

Continuous variable A set of data is said to be continuous if the values belong to a continuous interval of real values.

Covariance Covariance is a measure that describes the manner and degree to which two variables vary with respect to one another.

Critical value The critical value for a hypothesis test is a limit where the value of the sample test statistic is judged to be such that the null hypothesis may be rejected.

Cumulative frequency distribution For continuous variables, the cumulative frequency for a value x is the total number of scores that are less than x. For discrete variables it is the total number of scores that are less than or equal to x.

Cyclical component A component in the classical time series analysis approach to forecasting that covers cyclical movements of the time series, usually taking place over a number of years.

Degrees of freedom Refers to the number of independent observations in a sample minus the number of population parameters that must be estimated from sample data.

Differencing A method of transforming a time series, usually to achieve stationarity. Differencing means that every current value in the time series is subtracted from the previous value.

Directional test Implies a direction for the implied hypothesis (left-sided or right-sided tests).

Discrete probability distribution If a random variable is a discrete variable, its probability distribution is called a discrete probability distribution.

Discrete variable A set of data is said to be discrete if the values belonging to it can be counted as 1, 2, 3, ...

Dispersion The variation between data values is called dispersion.

Error measurement A method of validating the quality of forecasts. Involves calculating the mean error, the mean squared error, the percentage error, etc.

Estimate An estimate is an indication of the value of an unknown quantity based on observed data.

Event An event is any collection of outcomes of an experiment.

Expected frequency In a contingency table the expected frequencies are the frequencies that you would predict in each cell of the table, if you knew only the row and column totals, and if you assumed that the variables under comparison were independent.

Expected value The expected value of a random data variable indicates its population average value.

Exponential smoothing One of the methods of forecasting that uses a constant (or several constants) to predict future values by 'smoothing' the past values in the series. The effect of this constant decreases exponentially as the older observations are taken into calculation.

Exponential trend An underlying time series trend that follows the movements of an exponential curve.

Ex-post forecasts Values produced from a forecasting model that are fitted to historical data.

Factor A factor of an experiment is a controlled independent variable; a variable whose levels are set by the experimenter.

Five-number summary A five-number summary is especially useful when we have so many data that it is sufficient to present a summary of the data rather than the whole data set. The five-number summary consists of the median, first and third quartile, and the minimum and maximum.

Forecasting A method of predicting the future values of a variable, usually represented as the time series values.

Forecasting errors A difference between the actual and the forecasted value in the time series.

Forecasting horizon A number of the future time units until which the forecasts will be extended.

Frequency distributions Systematic method of showing the number of occurrences of observational data in order from least to greatest.

Frequency polygon A graph made by joining the middle-top points of the columns of a frequency histogram.

***F*-test for variances** Tests whether two population variances are the same based upon sample values.

Grouped frequency distributions Data arranged in intervals to show the frequency with which the possible values of a variable occur.

Histogram A histogram is a way of summarising data that are measured on an interval scale (either discrete or continuous).

Homogeneity of variance Population variances are equ al.

Hypothesis test procedure A series of steps to determine whether to accept or reject a null hypothesis, based on sample data.

Independent events Two events are independent if the occurrence of one of the events has no influence on the occurrence of the other event.

Intercept Value of the regression equation (y) when the x-value is equal to 0.

Interquartile range The interquartile range is a measure of the spread of, or dispersion within, a data set. It is defined as the difference between the largest quartile and the smallest quartile.

Interval scale An interval scale is a scale of measurement where the distance between any two adjacent units of measurement (or intervals) is the same but the zero point is arbitrary.

Irregular component A component in the classical time series analysis approach to forecasting that Is uncovered by other components. It has to be random in shape.

Kruskal-Wallis test for multiple medians The Kruskal-Wallis test compares the medians of three or more independent groups.

Kurtosis Kurtosis is a measure of the 'peakedness' of the distribution.

Least squares The method of least squares is a criterion for fitting a specified model to observed data. It refers to finding the smallest (least) sum of square differences between fitted and actual values.

Level The unique levels of a factor or independent variable used in an experiment.

Level of confidence The confidence level is the probability value ($1 - \alpha$) associated with a confidence interval.

Linear relationship Simple linear regression aims to find a linear relationship between a response variable and a possible predictor variable by the method of least squares.

Linear trend model A model that uses the straight line equation to approximate the time series.

Mann-Whitney *U*-test The Mann-Whitney *U*-test is used to test the null hypothesis that two populations have identical distribution functions against the alternative hypothesis that the two distribution functions differ only with respect to location (median), if at all.

McNemar's test for matched pairs McNemar's test is a non-parametric method used on nominal data to determine whether the row and column marginal frequencies are equal.

Mean The mean is a measure of the average data value for a data set.

Mean absolute deviations (*MAD*) The mean value of all the differences between the actual and forecasted values in the time series. The differences between these values are represented as absolute values, i.e. the effects of the sign are ignored.

Mean absolute percentage error (*MAPE*) The mean value of all the differences between the actual and forecasted values in the time series. The differences between these values are represented as absolute percentage values, i.e. the effects of the sign are ignored.

Mean error (*ME*) The mean value of all the differences between the actual and forecasted values in the time series.

Mean percentage error (*MPE*) The mean value of all the differences between the actual and forecasted values in the time series. The differences between these values are represented as percentage values.

Mean square error (*MSE*) The mean value of all the differences between the actual and forecasted values in the time series. The differences between these values are squared to avoid positive and negative differences cancelling each other.

Median The median is the value halfway through the ordered data set. It is defined such that 50% of the data points are larger than this value and 50% of the data points are smaller than this value.

Mode The mode is the most frequently occurring value in a set of discrete data.

Moving averages Averages calculated for a limited number of periods in a time series. Every subsequent period excludes the first observation from the previous period and includes the one following the previous period. This becomes a series of moving averages.

Multiple comparisons Multiple comparisons occur when one considers a set or family of statistical inferences simultaneously.

Nominal scale A set of data is said to be nominal if the values belonging to it can be assigned a label rather than a number.

Non-parametric Non-parametric tests are often used in place of their parametric counterparts when certain assumptions about the underlying population are questionable. These tests make very few (or no) assumptions about the (parametric) distribution of the sample data used in the test.

Non-stationary time series A time series that does not have a constant mean and oscillates around this moving mean.

Normal distribution The normal distribution is a symmetrical, bell-shaped curve, centred at its expected value.

Normal probability plot Graphical technique to assess whether the data are normally distributed.

Null hypothesis (H_0) The null hypothesis H_0 represents a theory regarding the population parameters that has been put forward but has not been proved.

Observed frequency In a contingency table, the observed frequencies are the frequencies actually obtained in each cell of the table from our random sample.

Ogive (or cumulative frequency polygon) A distribution curve in which the frequencies are cumulative.

One-tail test A one-tail test is a statistical hypothesis test in which the values for which we can reject the null hypothesis, H_0, are located entirely in one tail of the probability distribution.

Ordinal variable A set of data is said to be ordinal if the values belonging to it can be ranked.

Outlier An outlier is an observation in a data set which is far removed in value from the others in the data set.

Parametric Any statistic computed by procedures that assume the data were drawn from a particular theoretical distribution (which can be described by one or more parameters).

Pearson's coefficient of correlation Pearson's correlation coefficient measures the linear association between two variables that have been measured on interval or ratio scales.

Point estimate A point estimate (or estimator) is any quantity calculated from the sample data which is used to provide information about the population.

Poisson distribution A distribution used to describe the probabilities associated with the outcomes of a Poisson random variable. It has a single parameter, λ, that denotes both the mean and variance of the distribution.

Poisson random variable A discrete random variable that typically describes the number of occurrences of a rare event over a particular interval (time, distance, area, etc.).

Population mean The population mean is the mean value of all possible values in the population.

Population standard deviation The population standard deviation is the standard deviation of all possible values in the population.

Population variance The population variance is the variance of all possible values in the population.

Practical limits The practical lower and upper limits of the class intervals of a frequency table that need to be specified in Excel to ensure that we get the same logical results as those stipulated by the theoretical *stated limits* (see *stated limits*).

Probability A probability expresses the likely occurrence of a particular event as a number between 0 and 1.

p-value The p-value is the probability of getting a value of the test statistic as extreme as or more extreme than that observed by chance alone, if the null hypothesis is true.

Qualitative variable Variables can be classified as descriptive or categorical.

Quantitative variable Variables can be classified using numbers.

Quartiles Quartiles are values that divide a sample of data into four groups containing an equal number of observations.

Random sample A random sample is a sampling technique where we select a sample from a population of values. The probability that a single element from the population will be taken up in the sample is known beforehand.

Ranks List data in order of size.

Range The range of a data set is a measure of the dispersion of the observations. It is defined as the difference between the largest and smallest value in the data set.

Ratio-scaled variable Ratio data are continuous data where both differences and ratios are interpretable and have a natural zero.

Region of rejection The range of values that leads to rejection of the null hypothesis.

Residuals Residuals are used to indicate the differences between the values we observe in the data and the values we obtain from our model. They are defined as the difference between the observed and modelled values.

Sample space The sample space is an exhaustive list of all the possible outcomes of an experiment.

Sampling distribution The sampling distribution describes how a sample statistic varies when calculated from all samples of size n drawn from a single population.

Sampling error Sampling error refers to the discrepancy (or error) between the information provided by a sample and the information contained in the entire population. It is inherent to all samples.

Scatter plot A scatter plot is a plot of one variable against another variable.

Seasonal component A component in the classical time series analysis approach to forecasting that covers seasonal movements of the time series, usually taking place inside one year's horizon.

Seasonal time series A time series, represented in the units of time smaller than a year, that shows as a regular pattern in repeating itself over a number of these units of time.

Significance level, α The significance level of a statistical hypothesis test is a fixed probability of incorrectly rejecting the null hypothesis, H_0, if it is in fact true.

Sign test The sign test is a non-parametric test designed to test a hypothesis about the location of a population distribution.

Simple regression analysis Simple linear regression aims to find a linear relationship between a response variable and a possible predictor variable by the method of least squares.

Skewness Skewness is defined as asymmetry in the distribution of the data values.

Slope Gradient of the fitted regression line.

Standard deviation Measure of the dispersion of the observations (it is the square root of the variance).

Standard error of forecast The square root of the variance of all forecasting errors.

Stated limits The theoretical lower and upper limits of the class intervals of a frequency table. Compare this to the *practical limits* of the class intervals that need to be used in Excel.

Statistic A statistic is a quantity that is calculated from a sample of data.

Statistical independence Two events are independent if the occurrence of one of the events gives us no information about whether or not the other event will occur.

Stationary time series A time series that has a constant mean and oscillates around this mean.

Student's t-distribution The t-distribution is a theoretical distribution that is symmetrical about zero and is used to describe the sampling distribution of the t-statistic.

Symmetrical A data set is symmetrical when the data values are distributed in the same way above and below the middle value.

Test of association A test for association allows the comparison of two attributes in a sample of data to determine if there is any relationship between them. The chi-square test of association is often used for ordinal-scaled data variables.

Test statistic A test statistic is a quantity calculated from our sample of data and used to determine the validity of the null hypothesis. It typically measures the 'distance' between a hypothesised parameter and a sample statistic.

Tied ranks Two or more data values share a rank value.

Time period An unit of time by which the variable is defined (an hour, day, month, year, etc.).

Time series A variable measured and represented per units of time.

Time series plot A chart of a change in variable against time.

Transformations A method of changing the time series, usually to make it stationary. Most common method for transforming the time series is differencing or sometimes taking differences of every observation from the mean value.

Trend component A component in the classical time series analysis approach to forecasting that covers underlying directional movements of the time series.

Two-tail test A two-tail test is a statistical hypothesis test in which the values for which we can reject the null hypothesis, H_0, are located in both tails of the probability distribution.

Type I error, A type I error occurs when the null hypothesis is rejected when it is in fact true.

Type II error, A type II error occurs when the null hypothesis, H_0, is not rejected when it is in fact false.

Unbiased When the mean of the sampling distribution of a statistic is equal to a population parameter, that statistic is said to be an unbiased estimator of the parameter.

Variable A variable is a symbol that can take on any of a specified set of values.

Variance Measure of the dispersion of the observations.

Wilcoxon signed-rank test The Wilcoxon signed-rank test is a non-parametric test designed to test a hypothesis about the location of the population median (one or two matched pairs).

INDEX

Page numbers in **bold** point to definitions